Rock 'n' Roll and the Cleveland Connection

D1594918

Rock 'n' Roll and the Cleveland Connection

Deanna R. Adams

The Kent State University Press Kent and London

© 2002 by The Kent State University Press, Kent, Ohio 44242

All rights reserved

Library of Congress Catalog Card Number 00-012105

ISBN 0-87338-691-4

Manufactured in the United States of America

07 06 05 04 03 02   5 4 3 2 1

Frontispiece: Joey and the Continentals, ca. early 1960s. *Courtesy of Don Evans.*

Designed by Will Underwood. Composed by Christine Brooks and Will Underwood
in Monotype Garamond & Helvetica Condensed. Printed & bound by Thomson-Shore, Inc.

Library of Congress Cataloging-in-Publication Data

Adams, Deanna R., 1954–

Rock 'n' roll and the Cleveland connection / Deanna R. Adams.

    p. cm.

Includes index.

ISBN 0-87338-691-4 (pbk. : alk. paper) ∞

1. Rock music—Ohio—Cleveland Region—History and criticism.

2. Radio broadcasting—Ohio—Cleveland Region—History. I. Title.

ML3534.A26 2001

781.66'09771'32—dc21

00-012105

British Library Cataloging-in-Publication data are available.

To my husband, Jeff,

and daughters, Danielle and Tiffany—

my own personal "roadies" who carried the burden

of living with an obsessed writer.

Contents

Foreword

I've been lucky. Most of my life I've been able to make a living doing something I truly love—making music with a group of people I loved playing with. And, with the wisdom of hindsight, I realize that it doesn't get a whole lot better than that.

I've had the chance to see most of the world and crossed this great country more times than I can remember (even if the view was somewhat skewed as we moved up the food chain of musical transportation: dad's car, Volkswagon bus, van, bigger van, motor home, touring bus, and the occasional airplane). I've seen it all. But I've never lived anywhere else but here on the North Coast. And that's been just fine with me.

These days it's hard to find someone who wasn't in some sort of band at sometime or other. But back in the mid-sixties, it was still uncharted waters for most of us who decided to make the journey. It may sound ludicrous at this point, but you can't imagine just how daunting a task it was to find someone who actually had a drum kit (let alone had any idea how to play it). And back then being a musician ranked only slightly above being a convicted felon!

For most, it was a journey that ended almost as fast as it began. The good ones made it all look so easy; in fact, it was anything but easy. Having trouble keeping your relationship together? Try it with four or five participants (especially when one of them is a lead singer). How about getting to a gig and finding out that 99 percent of those present are deeply offended by the length of your hair and feel it is their personal obligation to make you see the error of your fashion ways. The list of things to test your resolve was endless.

But, there was always that brass ring (or should I say gold record), the intoxicating sound of applause, and the look in the eye of that cute little thing in the front row that, at least for a fleeting moment, made you feel like the fifth (or sixth) Beatle. And when you actually heard songs on the radio by such local legends as the Twilighters, Bocky and the Visions, the Outsiders, or the Choir, then maybe, just maybe, there was hope for you and your motley band of dreamers.

It would be hard to remember a time when music wasn't of utmost importance in my life—either as a fan or a musician. So for me, this book has, happily, opened a floodgate of memories, and almost every one of them makes me smile!

To chronicle the musical history of a major city (and do it right!) is a task of Herculean proportions. But Deanna Adams was up for it. And although *Rock 'n' Roll and the Cleveland Connection* is certainly a trip down memory lane, it is also an insightful look at the history and changes that took place right here on the North Coast and at those musicians who provided the soundtrack that ran through the lives of all involved.

I know that writing this book was a labor of love for Deanna. And I think I'm safe in saying the same for the journey of all the musicians, deejays, club owners, promoters, journalists, and others she has talked to and written about.

As one of my favorite writers once said, "All you get to keep are the memories, and you got to make the good ones last." That's what it all comes down to—moments and memories. I hope you find as many great ones here as I did.

Michael Stanley

Acknowledg- ments

I believe no author can produce anything worthwhile without a great support system. I am fortunate to have one that extends beyond my wildest dreams. Appreciation goes to my mother, Virginia "Ginnie" Jenkins Fedorko, and late grandmother, Viola Jenkins, who in their very different ways, and through their enthusiasm and example, contributed to my determination and strong work ethic—both traits essential to the completion of this project.

I'm grateful to the many who helped me during the writing of this book. First, I give heartfelt thanks to my best friend and husband, Jeff, whose understanding, patience, and pride allow me to achieve my goals. Without his unwavering love, encouragement, and support, I could not have accomplished this sometimes overwhelming undertaking, and I am truly grateful. My daughters, Danielle (who's been a great "secretary") and Tiffany (whose laughter always lifts me higher), have learned to be great housekeepers, and they continually keep me centered. They are constant and blessed reminders to me of what is truly important in life. Thanks go also to my brother, Dennis Fedorko, whose recollections of the early coffeehouse days, clubs, and stories helped me in my research of the "good ol' days." And I very much appreciate both my mother and mother-in-law, MaryAnn Adams, for tending to my children as I ran off to do research, conduct interviews, and take the occasional "mental health" day. And kudos to my patient brother-in-law and computer expert, David Adams, who "saved" this book several times when I went "oops!" or "oh, no!" And to my longtime, treasured friends who give me encouragement and support merely by being a part of my life—special thanks go to Nina Morris Mosher and Diane Taylor, who were always there for me throughout this massive project. For all those occasions and many laughs— thanks, girlfriends.

Everyone needs a mentor, and I've been fortunate to have one of the best in Lea Leever Oldham, who has been not only invaluable with her editorial knowhow, but whose confidence in my ability, and this project, has guided me every step of the way. As a result, she's become a cherished and trusted friend. Bless you, Lea.

And of course, thanks to my "support group," the Writers of the Western Reserve—especially Charlotte Pertz, Nancy Piazza, Aileen Gilmour, Jan Thompson, Robert

T. Brown, and Bill Warnock—for their valuable assistance, encouragement, and much comic relief at our monthly meetings.

Throughout the making of this book, I was amazed at how many people made themselves available to me. Most agreed to phone interviews or welcomed me into their busy offices or homes. Each not only gave generously of their time and knowledge but also told me, "Because I feel strongly about what you are doing, I'll help you any way I can." And they did. One call led to another and another, and three hundred people later . . . ! Although each has my sincere thanks, special appreciation goes to John Awarski, Billy Bass, Brian Chalmers, Jim Clevo, Kevin Dugan, Bob Ferrell, Jimmy Fox, John Gorman, Jim Jones, Hank and Henry LoConti, Janet Macoska, Buddy Maver, Bill "Mr. Stress" Miller, Bill Peters, "Peanuts," Steve Popovich, Denny Sanders, David Spero, Danny Sheridan, Rich Spina, Michael Stanley, and Walt Tiburski. Their cooperation and enthusiasm, along with that of so many others, not only was invaluable but *made* this book. Their involvement and recollections give this book the authenticity I so much wanted it to have. Also much appreciation goes to everyone at The Kent State University Press, particularly director John Hubbell and his assistant, Sandy Clark; editors Joanna Hildebrand Craig, Erin Holman, and Perry Sundberg; and designers Will Underwood and Chris Brooks, for their assistance, steadfast encouragement, and great enthusiasm over this project.

There were, however, those who declined to participate. Every reasonable and possible attempt was made to personally interview those in this chronology. Yet there were some individuals who, although deserving, did not make it into this history simply because my resources were limited without their cooperation. Lucky for me, and for readers, those incidents were few. In cases when one did not return my calls or letters, I often found the necessary information through other reliable sources. Much gratitude also goes to the many helpful and hard-working librarians at the Cleveland, Cuyahoga County, and Euclid libraries for their indispensable aid in guiding me to the information I sought.

Finally, to everyone who rocks 'n' rolls in Cleveland—enjoy. This is your history. This is *your* book.

Preface

You have to realize that every rock band started out as a local band somewhere. Springsteen was a local act in New Jersey, the Doors in L.A., Grateful Dead in San Francisco. Personally, I'm glad for us it's here in Cleveland. And if given a choice of only one place to be big, I'd want it to be in my hometown.

—Michael Stanley, of the Michael Stanley Band

In 1966, I attended my first dance at the Euclid Rollerdrome. I was twelve, and the band playing that night was called the Mods. This group of talented young musicians—whose repertoire included music by the Yardbirds, Cream, the Left Banke, and even the Beatles and the Stones—captured our hearts because they played the music we wanted to hear—and played live, right in my hometown. Soon our weekends found us begging our parents to drive us wherever the group was playing.

Because the Mods (guitarists Wally Bryson, Dan Klawon, Dave Smalley, bassist Dave Burke, and drummer Jim Bonfanti) played an eclectic mix of songs from the most popular rock groups—and played them well—they quickly became a household word in nearly every North Coast home harboring a teenager. Although the group changed names and band members often, its musical appeal endured, and the band became internationally recognized a few years later as the Raspberries, fronted by singer/songwriter Eric Carmen.

One of my favorite Mods memories is of the time some friends and I sang the Beatles tune, "Ob-La-di, Ob-La-da (Life Goes On)" on stage with them at the now-defunct Chesterland Hullabaloo. There were several "Hullabaloo" clubs in those days, a concept taken from the national hit TV show of the same name. These clubs were fashioned exclusively for the thirteen-to-eighteen-year-old set, served nothing stronger than rootbeer, and were the hippest places for young people to go to see their favorite bands play live.

I recall seeing the James Gang perform at the Mentor Hullabaloo with a young guitarist talented beyond his years, Joe Walsh. Then a Kent State student, Walsh became the yardstick by which every aspiring local guitarist measured himself (though we must include the equally accomplished Glenn Schwartz and Phil Keaggy in this category as well). We knew we had something special in Walsh, but little did we know how "big" he would become. It's fun to listen to the accounts of local fans who witnessed firsthand that musical growth. And there are a slew of memories of other area groups as well, and we Cleveland "boomers" all have our favorites.

So, to all those extraordinary musicians whose vital sounds live on in our forever-young hearts, we are grateful for the joy you gave and continue to give us. Because of and despite the realities of Vietnam, racism, and civil unrest, we "flower children" of the postwar generation flicked on our stereos, plugged in an amp, grabbed an air guitar, clamped on a set of headphones and left our troubles behind, lost in the charismatic world of rock 'n' roll.

It was a great time to be young.

There's a lot of history there. A lot of Cleveland history, which I hope doesn't become forgotten. I mean, there's a whole generation that is totally unaware of that history.

—Anton Fier, former Pere Ubu drummer (*Scene,* 1996)

This book is not intended to be a definitive history of rock music in Cleveland, documenting every fact or thoroughly analyzing every decade. Rather, it is about those people and events responsible for making this the "Rock 'n' Roll Capital of the World." From its inception, this book was intended to highlight Cleveland's rock stories, the changing eras, and most importantly, the music.

It is my hope that this book should finally put to rest the oft-asked question from out-of-towners: Why is the Rock Hall in Cleveland? To locals, the answer is obvious. After all, those who grew up in this city are all too aware of the vast talents that have flourished here, finding success only on the North Coast. Yet despite the fact many of these groups or individuals have largely been ignored by the rest of the world, their undeniable musical talent is no less noteworthy.

We've witnessed the rise of some amazing talents who made names for themselves in this new music genre and were fortunate enough to enjoy our favorite sounds on the radio and watch the groups perform on TV. There were local programs, such as *The Gene Carroll Show* and Don Webster's *Upbeat,* as well as national shows like Dick Clark's *American Bandstand, Don Kirshner's Rock Concert, Midnight Special,* and even the conservative *Ed Sullivan Show* got into the act. Who needed MTV?!

But the greatest excitement came from watching bands from our neighborhoods, who went from playing in garages, basements, and school gyms to roller rinks and "nike-sights" (teens' dance clubs) before moving on to the big time within a surprisingly short period of time. The Outsiders, the James Gang, Damnation of Adam Blessing, and the Raspberries spring immediately to mind.

Rock 'n' Roll and the Cleveland Connection attempts to honor all those who made Cleveland proud when the city was merely an outlet for late-night jokes and when "Cleveland—You Got to Be Tough" t-shirts were popular. These people, with their various musical contributions, played a major part in keeping our city's spirit alive. It is this musical legacy that can no longer be ignored or denied.

Hundreds of great bands emerged from Northeast Ohio; to include them all would be nearly impossible. Those highlighted here are ones most often mentioned and fondly remembered by fans. Yet one group stands alone. No area band was more warmly embraced or as enduring as the Michael Stanley Band, which in one form or another has entertained us for more than two decades. Michael Stanley remains a treasured fixture in our hometown, and he continues to sell out concerts and pump out new releases. MSB's unprecedented popularity here on the North Coast is in spite of and in defiance of the question that Cleveland fans consider to be the greatest musical mystery of this generation. (For out-of-towners who haven't a clue what that question is, refer to Chapter 12.)

No book on the area's rock music scene would be complete without including a woman who literally invented her own career. The term "rock writer" began with the now-legendary Jane Scott. After attending the Beatles' first concert at Public Hall on September 15, 1964, Scott returned for their second visit two years later at Municipal Stadium as the *Plain Dealer's* new rock reporter. She considers that last Beatles concert to be one of the top cultural events in Cleveland history and one of her most exciting days as a newspaper columnist. Now in her eighties, this phenomenal journalist continues to interview everyone who's anyone in rock and roll and shows no sign of stopping. Indeed, no one knows rock like Jane Scott.

Of course, if radio disc jockeys don't play the music, the music dies. And this town has not been without its influential record spinners. Alan Freed was just the beginning. The ageless Bill Randle is himself a book-worthy subject. And did you know Casey Kasem fine-tuned his long-running broadcasting career in this town? Then came KYW's Jerry G., who was deemed "the World's Handsomest Disc Jockey" and whose popularity escalated with the Beatles' arrival in Cleveland. But, when it came to rock and roll in those electrifying early days, no radio station could shake, rattle, and roll like WMMS-FM.

Consider Kid Leo, deejay for WMMS from 1971 to 1988, who helped skyrocket many a career, including those of David Bowie, Bruce Springsteen, and Southside Johnny: today he is vice president for album promotion at Columbia Records. He and his prominent 'MMS colleagues had a major impact on the rock industry from their North Coast base. The history and character of that powerhouse station echo the music it plays: young, rebellious, controversial, and not about to roll over and die.

And finally, the fans deserve credit as well, for they faithfully followed these groups through the joys and trials of the most unstable of careers. Indeed, time does fly when you're having fun! If nothing else, we Boomers have some great stories to tell our kids . . . and grandkids.

Part 1
In the
Beginning

1 The Deejays Who Got the Rock Rolling

In the early fifties, when rock was in its embryonic stage, Cleveland was considered one of the hottest radio markets in the country. The Ohio city was sandwiched between New York and Chicago, making it an important testing ground for new records and recording artists. From then on, the North Coast became a music force to be reckoned with, through both its influence and its reputation for breaking new artists, greatly due to the foresight of enterprising deejays. Indeed, there have been hundreds of noteworthy area disc jockeys in the past five decades. We must begin, however, with those radio pioneers who burst open those stubborn doors of rock, the legends whose power dominated the airwaves.

Alan Freed

Born in the South, rock and roll quickly spread north, thanks to radio stations such as WLAC-AM in Nashville, whose powerful reach spread all the way to northern Ohio. In its elusive beginnings, there wasn't a label for this musical genre, an eclectic mix of gospel, country, bluegrass, and jazz, but mostly rhythm and blues. Yet, once a few brave disc jockeys at radio stations in cities around the country—including Atlanta,

Alan Freed poses with a puppet he used on his short-lived WXEL-TV show in 1951. *Photo by Lynn Rebman. Cleveland Press Collection, Cleveland State University.*

New Orleans, Berkeley, Washington, D.C., Buffalo, and Cleveland—began spinning these unusual sounds, the music world was never again the same. An increasing number of listeners tuned in; and whether they loved or hated this new music, they were certainly paying attention. And that's precisely what Cleveland deejay Alan Freed wanted.

As folklore has it (the story is said to have been "romantically altered" by Freed over the years), Freed, the disk jockey for station WJW-AM, was visiting Record Rendezvous, Cleveland's biggest and busiest record store, one fateful day in the spring of 1951. Intrigued by the number of white teens looking for "black music," Freed watched as they rummaged through crates containing R&B records. At store owner Leo Mintz's suggestion, Freed kicked off a late-night show a few months later that played nothing but this type of music, then referred to as "race" or "colored" music. Although not the first disc jockey to spin R&B music (there was Zena "Daddy" Sears in Atlanta, George "Hound Dog" Lorenz in Buffalo, Tom "Big Daddy" Donahue in Washington, and Phil McKernan in Berkeley), Freed was the first white radio man to do so on the North Coast.

The program, which immediately followed Freed's classical "Record Rendezvous" show, was dubbed "The Moondog Show." It opened with Todd Rhodes's blues instrumental called "Blues for the Red Boy," although Freed renamed it "Blues for the Moondog" in keeping with the theme. Freed introduced his listeners to "Moondog Sympathy," a song that featured a dog howling mournfully. While it played, the imaginative deejay would attempt to calm the moaning mutt: "Come on now, Moondog, please stop howling, you'll wake the neighbors." He would then play an R&B tune, his voice yowling in tune with the record's bluesy saxophone as his hands (protected by golf gloves) pounded out a rapid beat on a thick Cleveland telephone book.

"The Moondog Show" found a captive audience. With the station's 50,000-watt clear-channel signal, the show—which became "The Moondog Rock 'n' Roll Party"—attracted teens of all races. Call-ins and written requests came from both the inner city and predominantly white neighborhoods such as Shaker Heights. Millions of teens were tuned in as Freed began his show: "Hello, everybody, how y'all tonight? This is Alan Freed, the ol' king of the Moondoggers, and it's time for some blues and rhythm records for all the gang in Moondog kingdom from the Midwest to the East Coast."

With Freed's tremendous popularity and increased R&B record sales, it became apparent that this style of music needed its own identity. Whether Freed or Mintz was directly responsible for naming the style will forever remain a question. Nonetheless, Freed was the first to broadcast the phrase on the air, calling the beat-driven tunes "rock 'n' roll," thus forever separating it from its twin, R&B. Although not a new phrase, having been used for years as sexual innuendo, "rock 'n' roll" was the newest term for this musical genre. And the flamboyant deejay who'd had some rough career beginnings was now an integral part of rock and roll as well as a legendary presence in Cleveland's music history.

The Makings of a Legend

Aldon James Freed was born on December 21, 1921, in Windber, Pennsylvania. In 1933, when Alan was twelve, the family moved to Salem, Ohio. About this time brother Charles brought home a microphone, and Al J., as he was called, began carrying it with him wherever he went. The second of three sons born to Charles and Maude Freed, Al J. showed musical promise early and listened to the radio incessantly. Aside from working on the school newspaper and yearbook, the active teen won several roles in school dramas. But his greatest interest was music. Every day the young Freed stayed after school in the band room. He played trombone in the Salem Senior High School band, was a drum major, and fronted a band called "The Sultans of Swing," which played at school dances and assemblies.

Graduating in 1940, Freed briefly attended Ohio State University, where he majored in journalism, but left a year later to join the army. This stint was also short-lived; he was discharged in 1942 due to a severe ear infection (which led to some hearing damage, though apparently did not affect his ear for music). Returning to Salem, Freed met the first of his three wives, Betty Lou Bean of nearby Lisbon. While working at Mullins Manufacturing Company, Freed attended a Youngstown broadcasting school, and then worked at several small-town radio stations in 1945 before settling, for a time, at Akron's WAKR as a news and sports announcer. Two years later he started his own radio program, "Request Review," which allowed him to play his favorite classical music. The program produced top ratings.

According to some accounts, it was at WAKR that Freed began playing some of the R&B tunes he'd often hear on Nashville's WLAC, which he could pick up in Akron. By 1949, Freed's popularity was established, and he asked for a raise. When management turned him down, Freed walked across the street to WADC, the competing station. However, he was still under contract with WAKR, and soon a judgment banned him from broadcasting on any competing station for one year. So Freed promptly took his talents to Cleveland. He first landed a job as host of a movie show at WXEL-TV, Channel 9 (now WJW, Channel 8), becoming the first television disc jockey in the country. By 1950 he joined radio station WJW. Broadcasting from the sixth floor of the Playhouse Square Building (1375 Euclid Avenue), he would soon become a nationally known deejay and radio legend.

When his Moondog Show debuted on July 11, 1951, and was an immediate hit, Freed paved the way for his contemporaries (although others who tried emulating him often fell short). Although more deejays began playing R&B music, many did not possess whatever quality Freed had that grabbed his listeners by storm. With his love for the new sound and his unprecedented driving, energetic voice and style, Freed realized early on the potential and ran with it, ultimately becoming the creative force and organizer (along with partners Leo Mintz and promoter Lew Platt) behind what would be the world's first documented rock and roll concert.

The First-Ever Rock Concert

With high hopes, Freed, Mintz, and Platt booked the huge Cleveland Arena, a sports venue that hosted hockey games, boxing matches, and the world-renowned Harlem Globetrotters basketball team. In fear of not selling enough tickets to pay for the event, Freed heavily promoted it on his evening radio show.

The Moondog Coronation Ball took place at the late, great Arena on March 21, 1952, and became not only the first rock concert but possibly the shortest running one as well. Word of the show—which boasted popular acts such as the Dominoes, Paul

Williams and the Hucklebuckers, Tiny Grimes and the Rocking Highlanders, Danny Cobb, Varetta Dillard, and other "sensational stars"—spread and a reported mob of almost 25,000 mostly black fans showed up at the 10,000-capacity hall.

"We had so much fun at first, dancing and listening to the music," concertgoer Ruby Johnson recalled in a 1989 *Plain Dealer* article. Saxophonist Williams opened the show, but the good times were short-lived. Within an hour, fights erupted in the cramped conditions. Those standing outside in the near-freezing weather heard the music and began pushing open the doors, causing riot conditions. Photographer Peter Hastings was there that night, and his photograph is quite possibly the only known one of the historic event.

"Peter was an independent photographer and was given an assignment by a PR lady [Ann Koblitz] hired by Leo Mintz and his group [Freed and Platt]," recalls Hastings's widow, Gloria. "I believe he took two shots and then retreated because of the chaos. But he did realize rather quickly that his photo would be newsworthy, and he sold . . . the only live-action shot of the Moondog Coronation Ball to the *Cleveland Press*." According to photographer Albert Willinger, who arrived with Hastings, "By the time we got there, the glass from the broken-down doors was all over the place. There was a

The infamous Moondog Coronation Ball, March 21, 1952. *Photo by Peter Hastings. Courtesy of Gloria Hastings.*

mass of people on the floor dancing. But soon the fighting started and it was pandemonium! And when Mintz found out about the picture, he threatened to sue us because, of course, that would be bad publicity. But Ann talked him out of it."

As things escalated, concertgoer Estelene Lawrence got carried away, literally. In a December 1992 special issue of *Life* magazine called "Forty Years of Rock 'n' Roll," Lawrence told of the arena doors crashing down and of her body being carried into the building by the unruly crowd.

On vacation in Miami, Mintz came home for the concert. He arrived at the event just in time to witness the mass hysteria. Apparently he saw all he needed to see and left. The fire marshal closed the place down, leaving the Cleveland police in charge of getting the crowd to leave the premises. The place was rockin' and rollin'.

Accounts of the cause of the melee vary. Stuart Mintz, Leo's son, said that his father sold the 7,500 tickets—the number of arena seats—in one day but that the problem arose when his uncle had an additional 7,500 tickets made up but failed to print the words "second show" on them, resulting in a vast oversell. Others blamed the sponsors for willfully overselling the concert.

The next evening Freed unknowingly made rock history when he gave an emotional on-air speech apologizing to his fans for the "big fiasco" and summoning the audience to call in. "If you're with us, tell the switchboard operator, 'I'm with the Moondog Show.' If you're against us, tell the operator that, too." Not surprisingly, Freed received tremendous support. That rowdy, rebellious, and short-lived concert paralleled the music, making it the event that birthed rock and roll. And from that time on, Freed would be forever known as "the jock who started the riot." Despite the premature labor pains, Cleveland and Freed had unwittingly introduced an entertainment phenomenon, and the young fans responded.

Freed WINS New York

Even with the less-than-favorable press, that first concert did not stop the controversial deejay. Freed continued to sponsor shows. A couple more were held at the Arena— a weekend event called "The Moondog Maytime Ball" and a Sunday "Teenagers' Matinee." But for the most part, he was careful to book smaller halls with reserved seats. In August 1952, Freed hosted a show at Akron's Summit Beach Ballroom featuring two popular New York acts, the Clovers and Charles Brown. It was attended by more than 3,000 fans, with a nearly equal mix of blacks and whites. By all accounts, each concert went off without a hitch.

Freed then ventured into the business side, creating his own independent recording label, called Champagne. He turned R&B quintet the Crazy Sounds into the Moonglows. After recording on his label and performing at the popular Circle Theater, the group went to Chicago where they recorded "Sincerely" for Chance Records. (Freed was given coauthor credit, though he had nothing to do with the song's lyrics.) That recording sold 300,000 copies and successfully crossed over from the R&B to the pop charts. A few years later the more popular McGuire Sisters covered the song and made it the number-one hit of 1955.

By August 1954, Freed, having gained national attention through his flamboyant radio persona and controversial concerts, moved to New York City radio station WINS 1010 (inspired, no doubt, by an unprecedented $75,000-a-year contract). His new show was syndicated, enabling Clevelanders and others in major cities to listen. In New York his popularity grew to even greater heights. There were fan clubs, concerts, and basic Moondog mania. That same year, *Billboard* named Freed the top R&B disc jockey in the country. And while other deejays began calling themselves the "Kings of Rock 'n' Roll," *Billboard* put all doubts aside by proclaiming Freed "the undisputed king of radio programming." Then came four movies featuring Freed, all within a two-year period: *Rock Around the Clock,* with Bill Haley and the Comets; *Don't Knock the Rock,* with Little Richard and Bill Haley (1956); *Rock, Rock, Rock,* with Chuck Berry; and *Mr. Rock and Roll,* with Freed and ex-boxer Rocky Graziano (1957). The latter imitated Freed's early rock life by depicting a deejay trying to save a concert featuring Little Richard, Chuck Berry, LaVern Baker, and Clyde McPhatter, some of rock's most popular artists of the day. Another film in 1959, *Go, Johnny, Go,* credits Freed as producer as well. Unfortunately, Freed was not around to see *American Hot Wax,* the 1978 biopic that is now considered a rock film classic.

Price Tag

But like most great successes, it all came with a price. First off was the controversy over Freed's famous trademark. It seems a street musician by the name of Thomas Louis "Moondog" Hardin had recorded "Moondog Symphony," the howling song Freed used in his show. Hardin, who even had a few on-air moments at New York's WNEW in the late 1940s, claimed that he used the nickname as early as 1947. A lawsuit followed, and the court ruled in Hardin's favor, barring Freed from using the title for his radio program and from playing the song. Thereafter he called his show "Alan Freed's Rock 'n' Roll Party."

Just as the buzz from the Moondog title dispute was dying down, a new one sprang up. From the time Freed started playing black music in Ohio, he'd had his share of critics, although most remained silent. New York City was altogether different. There many people saw Freed as a white man making money off black men's labors. There were meetings, protests, and news reports decrying this insult on black Americans. In addition, rock and roll was fast becoming synonymous with juvenile delinquency, placed in the same category as the knife-wielding motorcycle maniacs depicted in the 1954 Marlon Brando movie *The Wild One.*

By 1957 an anti-rock campaign was acting in major cities in New York, Massachusetts, Alabama, and California. Among the protesters were school officials, Sunday preachers, editorial columnists, and, because of the furor, recording company execs. This prompted many deejays to put a conservative lid on their promotion of rock music. But Freed refused to kowtow; he continued to advertise rock shows on his program, determined to save the good name of rock 'n' roll (with proceeds often going to charity).

Boston proved to be Freed's worst enemy. When his 1958 "Big Beat" tour with Jerry Lee Lewis rolled into the Boston Arena on May 3, all hell broke loose. The Associated Press reported riots among the 6,000 attending the concert, with one stabbing outside the arena. Many eyewitnesses, however, would concede that the violence happened after, not during, the show and not, as the media led the public to believe, because of it. Freed's third wife, Inga, would later say that every crime that occurred within a one-hundred-mile radius of the Boston Arena that night was blamed on Freed and his racially mixed music. Freed became the fall guy, the only one arrested and indicted for inciting a riot.

In addition to fueling the nation's rock haters, this episode played a significant role in the cancellation of Freed's concert tour as well as his firing from WINS soon afterward. Though Freed, as well as his faithful fans, was upset by the station management's actions, he was quickly grabbed up by WABC in conjunction with his own ABC television show, *The Big Beat*. And then came payola.

The Establishment Speaks

"Payola" referred to record companies and distributors who would pay popular deejays to play certain records. Although this practice wasn't against the law at the time, one was expected to report such income to the IRS. It's been said that payola was just "part of the business" and a practice dating back to vaudeville days. Even Dick Clark has gone on record to say that payola was common practice in the industry. The late 1950s saw many congressional investigations, including the McCarthy hearings, the Dodd committee hearings on TV sex and violence (yes, even then!), the quiz show scandals, and the Jimmy Hoffa investigations; and in his book *Rock, Roll and Remember,* Clark said that he believed that congressmen who investigated the quiz shows got so caught up in the publicity that they went after payola in order to satisfy their newfound sense of celebrity. Perhaps even more convenient, it allowed the perfect excuse to attack rock music and its proponents.

The end result of the payola scandals left many deejays in the dust (255 disc jockeys in twenty-six states were reportedly investigated), but none were affected as greatly as Freed. Already controversial, and known for his influence on teen audiences, Freed was challenged. While he admitted that he didn't refuse any "gifts" from grateful record promoters, the formidable disc jockey staunchly denied ever playing a particular song merely for gratuities. But Freed's failure to report those "gifts" to the IRS was his big mistake. His late brother David once noted Alan's remark that he'd never play a song strictly for money because it would cause his career would go down the tubes; he merely played what he wanted and was never bribed into playing a song that he didn't believe was good.

That notwithstanding, after months of legal battles, against his lawyer's advice, Freed plea-bargained and was indicted in 1960 for accepting $30,000 in return for playing records during 1958–59. During the next two years, life as he knew it ended. First, the once-vibrant deejay was forced to resign from his WABC radio show, bidding a tearful good-bye to his beloved fans as "Shimmy, Shimmy Ko-Ko-Bop" by Little Anthony and the Imperials played in the background. Then, a few days later, he was replaced as host of *The Big Beat*. He bounced from one radio station to another in New York, Los Angeles, and Miami. Finally, with charges pending from the 1958 Boston riots, a disillusioned Freed, wanting to avoid any chance of prison time, pleaded guilty to two counts of taking bribes in 1962. He was fined $300 and given a six-month suspended jail sentence. The controversy that followed Alan Freed throughout his career had finally caught up with him.

The Beginning of the End

Alan Freed was a man of many passions. His reputation for carousing and falling in love while still married was legendary and resulted in two divorces. But it was his love affair with the bottle (he favored scotch) that proved to be his greatest downfall. (It was fitting that Freed's sponsors were often beer companies, such as Erin Brew Beer in Cleveland and Greisedick in New York City.) Sad evidence of his destructive habit came in the form of a car accident in the spring of 1953 in Shaker Heights, when, intoxicated, he smashed his car into a tree. The incident landed him in a Cleveland hospital with a ruptured spleen and liver, a punctured lung, collapsed veins, a mutilated face (requiring extensive plastic surgery), and smashed kneecaps. Doctors warned the thirty-two year old that continued drinking would guarantee irreparable damage to his liver, but Freed seemed determined to live up to his favorite motto: "Live fast, die young, and leave a good-looking corpse." And he certainly did live and love fast enough. The coroner's report confirmed that his death on January 20, 1965, at the age of forty-three was due to complications from a damaged liver.

The music man who dedicated his life to the joy of teenagers and became their strongest ally died with little notice twenty days after collapsing at his Palm Springs home. During those last few months, he'd been unable to find work, was broke, and was still facing tax evasion charges. In a way, Freed was the ultimate reflection of this music genre. He was wild, reckless, and never boring. But even he could not survive the backlash of the payola scandals that crushed his career and, according to some, wiped out his zest for life.

In 1984, Freed was inducted into the Akron Radio Hall of Fame, housed in Quaker Square, in honor of his contributions to station WAKR. Two years later, the pioneer of rock radio received long-deserved acknowledgment when he became one of the first inductees into the Rock and Roll Hall of Fame and Museum (in the special "Nonperfomer/Early Influences" category). Today, Freed is honored in "The Big Beat: Alan Freed," a permanent exhibit on the second floor of the Rock Hall, just a few miles from his former WJW studio. And though Freed was not physically present to receive these deserved awards, rock and roll lovers of all generations certainly believe that he was very much there in spirit.

Bill Randle

> It was the energy that carried the record. Nobody created a hit. The hit was already there. All it required was exposure and availability.
>
> —Bill Randle, *Scene Magazine,* 1981

When it came to exposing the music and making it available to the public, Cleveland's Bill Randle was the man. No one knows if his knack for discovering the next big hit is by way of intuition, a good ear, or simply the fact that Randle is no dummy. Chances are it's a combination of all those things. Between his Cleveland and New York gigs in the 1960s, the scholarly record spinner took courses at Case Western Reserve University toward his Ph.D. in American Studies, which he received in 1966. Over the span of four decades, Randle has accumulated nine degrees, including a master's in mass communication and sociology, a master's in journalism from Kent State University, a master's in education from Cleveland State University, a law degree from Oklahoma City University, and an honorary doctorate of humanities from Bowling Green State University. "Not bad for a high school dropout," Randle has said more than once.

Bill Randle was always ahead of his time, one example being his opinion on drinking and drugs. An astute businessman, groundbreaker, and career maker, Randle claims he never turned to drink because he'd seen how heavy drinking can destroy major talent. (And when one thinks of all the great musicians now silenced by too much partying, Randle appears an acute prophet as well.)

Drug use among musicians is today as volatile as alcohol consumption was in the 1950s—and Randle surely wouldn't have tolerated it if he'd become Elvis Presley's manager, as he came close to doing in 1955. The connection with Elvis stemmed from the previous year when Randle and Tommy Edwards became the first deejays north of the Mason-Dixon Line to realize Elvis's star potential and play his records on the air. It was a controversial move, since back then even Alan Freed thought Elvis was more hillbilly than hipster. As deejays for Cleveland radio station WERE-AM 1300, Randle and Edwards took a gamble and played the rocker's first songs (Edwards played "Blue Moon of Kentucky" for his country fans while Randle played "Good Rockin' Tonight" for his diverse listeners). Thus began Randle's acquaintance with a future rock and roll king.

Born in Bellville, Illinois, in 1923, Randle grew up in Detroit during the Depression. His leadership qualities were apparent early on. At age seven when he had his first job, a paper route, he rose each day at 3:00 A.M. to beat out his competition for the best street corners. When he was a teenager, his interest in music blossomed, as did his appreciation for black artists. Living in a predominantly black neighborhood, Randle was exposed to blues and jazz, and to this day he is a staunch admirer of Bessie Smith. He and his family moved to Ohio in 1935, where ten years later Randle began his radio career as a freelance radio announcer, shuffling back and forth among Detroit, Chicago, Cleveland, Akron, and Youngstown.

Because he loved the music, Randle often played jazz on the air in the late 1940s, when he was expected to play the more mainstream pop "white" music. "I got fired nine times one year," he once boasted about the period when few jocks, if any, were playing "race" music. One Thanksgiving night, Randle played a black jazz version of Sister Rosetta Thorpe singing "Silent Night." He received such negative reactions from listeners protesting the "sacrilegious" music that the program director went ballistic and, once again, fired Randle. But this time WERE owner Ray Miller saved the day. Realizing the bold deejay was stirring things up, and attracting listeners, Miller rehired him and gave him permission to play what he wanted. It proved to be a wise move on the station owner's part. Over the next decade, Bill Randle was to take Miller and WERE to high and powerful places.

By the summer of 1955, Randle was well known in the music business and was hailed as the country's top disc jockey as well as the most powerful and influential record spinner in America. Then again, no one worked harder at it. Randle was, and remains, a workaholic. His radio show aired six days a week from 2:00 to 7:00 P.M. Then on Saturdays, he'd fly to New York to host a popular four-hour afternoon show on WCBS. In addition, he was fast becoming revered for his uncanny ability to forecast hit records and groups. Soon he was dubbed the "Kingmaker," for it seemed every musical act he touched turned to gold. By playing—and thus promoting—their records across the airwaves, Randle played an integral part in bringing Tony Bennett, Pat Boone, Johnnie Ray, the Four Lads, the Diamonds, the Crew Cuts, Bill Haley, and other favorite fifties artists to the forefront. Fats Domino has credited his northeastern popularity to both Randle and Freed due to the prominent deejays playing his early records in Cleveland. And fifties pop idol Johnnie Ray, once a struggling singer out of Oregon, became an overnight success as a direct result of Randle playing his records.

Randle was the antithesis of the 1950s manic, screaming, radio jock. It was his straightforward, down-to-earth style that signified his credibility. He had a keen sense for knowing what would and wouldn't work and for recognizing what listeners wanted in their music.

The Wizard of Pop

From the start of his career, Randle hand-picked the music and musicians he felt were star-bound, something he admits today's deejays no longer have the luxury of doing. With his track record for breaking new acts, Randle is one of the reasons Cleveland became known as a breakthrough city early on. His reputation was so powerful that record executives throughout the country scurried to Cleveland to bargain and seal deals with the influential deejay. "Promo men from all over the country would fly in to pay homage to Bill Randle," Steve Popovich, founder and president of Cleveland International Records, recounted in a 1995 *Cleveland Free Times* article. "You'd have to wait an hour to get in to see him, but he was heavy then and he's heavy now. Randle is still a genius at music; he knows it and loves it passionately."

Randle's natural intuition coupled with a savvy business sense proved reliable time and again. More often than not, the music man hit pay dirt. He is credited with several number-one hits during the '50s and '60s. Beginning in 1950, Randle pushed Johnnie Ray's "Whiskey and Gin" up the charts, quickly followed by Ray's "The Little White Cloud That Cried" and then the singer's biggest record, "Cry," which sold 4.5 million copies. Back-up singers on the record were four men from Toronto, who would later know their own success as the Four Lads. Their "Moments to Remember" sold four million copies in 1955 with the guidance of the Cleveland deejay. "Randle would only play the records he personally liked," recalls Bernie Toorish of the Four Lads. "Fortunately for us, he liked ours and was instrumental in getting our songs played on the air, and as a result we found success."

Bill Randle (*left*) with Elvis and Scotty Moore preparing for the October 20, 1955, concert at Brooklyn High School. The school was the first Cleveland rock and roll landmark designated by the Rock and Roll Hall of Fame and Museum. *Plain Dealer.*

In 1951 Randle started the "Mantovani craze" after making the Italian violinist, along with his forty-piece orchestra, a huge success with "Charmaine." "The Battle Hymn of the Republic" by the Mormon Tabernacle Choir was also a Randle success. But perhaps his greatest triumph was a Canadian group originally called the Canadaires who, at Randle's suggestion, changed their name to the Crew Cuts (to reflect their haircuts). In 1954 the deejay had the group cover a previously released song by the Chords called "Sh-Boom." At the time, it was becoming increasingly common for white groups to cover R&B songs, thus propelling them up the charts. And while the Chords's version did well, the Crew Cuts's recording made the coveted No. 1 spot in *Billboard,* remaining there through August and September and ultimately selling 1,500,000 copies. What's more, "Sh-Boom" is now considered the first bona fide rock and roll record. The group hit it big the next year with "Earth Angel," which peaked at No. 3. The Crew Cuts went on to be inducted into the Rock and Roll Hall of Fame in 1988.

Other high points for Randle included signing on the Diamonds ("Why Do Fools Fall in Love?" and "Little Darlin'") to Mercury Records. And in 1957 Randle was spinning the record that had everyone doing "The Stroll" on *American Bandstand.* He also delved into songwriting of sorts, rewriting the old Civil War song "The Yellow Rose of Texas" together with international songwriter Donald George. The song was then recorded by Mitch Miller in 1955 and rose to No. 1 that year.

Although radio rivals, Randle and Alan Freed developed a friendship that continued long after the controversial deejay took his Moondogs to New York. Randle met Freed soon after he arrived in Cleveland, when Freed was working as the TV disc jockey for WXEL. Their shared love for blues and jazz grounded the long-standing relationship. Both pioneers and standouts in their fields, the two men are excellent examples of Cleveland's early dominance over the country's radio industry.

All Shook Up

And then came Elvis. When Presley made his first trip up north with guitarist Scotty Moore and bassist Bill Black, the group was known as the Bill Black Trio. They were invited by country music deejay Tommy Edwards to come to Cleveland to perform at the Circle Theater for a Grand Ole Opry Jamboree–style show featuring favorites Kitty Wells and Roy Acuff. This was February 1955, and the Memphis teenager was as unknown as Southern grits in a Cleveland Heights diner.

Upon learning of Elvis's music (through Edwards and Arnold Shaw, then a successful record producer/promoter), Randle was afforded the opportunity of discovery. When the perceptive deejay began playing Elvis's songs on his show, the reaction was phenomenal. The phone lines lit up like stage lights, and Randle knew he was onto something big. Though just how big, no one—not even the Kingmaker himself—could have forecast. When an upcoming concert was to be filmed for inclusion in a short film chronicling Randle's exceptional career, Elvis was invited. The show's headliners were among the most popular of their day, with pop singer and heartthrob Pat

Boone heading the list. Other scheduled acts were Bill Haley and the Comets (whose "Rock Around the Clock" ultimately became the era's rock and roll anthem), the up-and-coming Four Lads, and Canadian singer Priscilla Wright. The concert took place early in the day on October 20, 1955, at Brooklyn High School, followed by a second concert at St. Michael's Hall that evening. Randle recalls telling Boone, "I got a guy who's gonna be the next big thing—Elvis Presley." But upon meeting the shy but kinetic teenager before the show, with his shirt collar turned up and hair slicked, Boone feared the boy's performance would be a catastrophe and joined many in doubting Randle's prediction. That is, until they witnessed the audience reaction once Elvis took the stage.

There was simply no stopping him. The kid from Memphis jumped into "Good Rockin' Tonight," "Mystery Train," "That's All Right," "Blue Moon of Kentucky," and "I Forgot to Remember to Forget." To the surprise of many, save Randle and Edwards, Elvis Presley's unforgettable stage presence marked the beginning of historic changes in our musical entertainment. And it could be said that Elvis, not the Who, was the first to smash his equipment on stage: When he broke a guitar string on stage that night, Elvis was so incensed that he threw the instrument to the floor, thrilling the crowd even more.

Footage of this concert was shot at both locations for the eighteen-minute documentary to be called *The Pied Piper of Cleveland*. Randle produced the show, having hired the starring acts and then summoning director Arthur Cohen and cameraman Jack Barnett to capture it all on film. But when Randle insisted Cohen and Barnett get shots of Elvis's performance, both refused to film "that hillbilly." Not one to give up easily, Randle responded by offering to pay them out of his own pocket. The two finally relented. Randle, in fact, still possesses three canceled checks, illustrating that he paid $200 to Barnett, $250 to Cohen, and $600 to the bandleader, Wendall Tracy. Years later, the film that included the skinny young singer with the odd stage movements became the earliest-known concert footage of the boy who would be King.

The Case of the Missing Movie

The film narrating the life of the country's most popular deejay was never released. Somehow it became lost, during which time it was often referred to as "The Case of the Missing Movie." Then, nearly forty years later, the mystery was solved. In 1992, the Merlin Group, a company of entrepreneurs based in London, found the film, along with fifteen canisters of unprocessed film from Cleveland-area concerts, in a vault at Universal Studios labeled "A Day in the Life of a Famous D.J." Randle, who possessed an excerpt of the original footage and had even shown it in classrooms at Euclid Shore Junior High and on WEWS Channel 5 news back in 1956, was now in the unique position to bargain for the rights.

"In a way, it was the world's biggest crap shoot," the veteran deejay told a newspaper reporter. Randle referred to the fact that the potential buyers had seen virtually none of the footage before vying for the rights. His intuition and insistence on the cameraman covering Elvis's performance that night in 1955 were now going to net him a substantial amount. A British tabloid reported that Randle sold the rights to the Merlin Group for an estimated $1.9 million, with the businessmen turning around and selling the film to PolyGram International for a reported $2.2 million. Although Randle denied the "ridiculous" price tag, he later admitted he was awarded a fair amount.

Why was the concert film never shown, but instead placed in a vault? Randle speculates it was because Colonel Tom Parker, upon becoming Elvis's manager a month after the Cleveland concert, enforced a movie stipulation that prohibited any previous footage of Presley from being shown. And once in the vault, the film was simply forgotten.

At the time Elvis was seeking a manager to replace disc jockey Bob Neal and had already approached the Four Lads's manager Mike Stewart during that Cleveland visit. When Stewart declined, Elvis approached Randle. A contract dated November 3, 1955, was presented to the Cleveland deejay by publishers Jean and Julian Aberbach with Hill and Range Songs, Inc., in New York, but Randle never signed it. Stating that he never had the right temperament to be a manager, Randle admitted to being tempted nonetheless. But WERE made the decision easy for him, offering Randle a substantial raise and part ownership of the station if he would stay in Cleveland. So Randle turned down Elvis Presley, and Colonel Parker, who was already very much in the picture, became the man who took over the singer's career on November 21, 1955. Still, Randle was chosen to introduce the twenty-year-old singer in his television debut on January 28, 1956. The show, a CBS-TV variety program called *Stage Show*, was hosted by big-band leaders Tommy and Jimmy Dorsey and produced by popular comedian Jackie Gleason.

Randle continued his starmaking quests through the rest of the decade. But his reputation made him vulnerable to the seedy side of the business. When the payola scandal was at its height, Randle was not exempt. In December 1959 a man and woman tried to extort $5,000 from the deejay, warning him that if he didn't pay up, the two would reveal "a 1953 police report" to the *Cleveland Press*. That report involved an incident in which a young singer and his manager offered Randle $500 to play the singer's record. In addition to the blackmail threat, Randle discovered a note under his door that read, "You're next." In fact, the *Press* had already known of the six-year-old report which turned out to be unfounded speculation. Randle claimed at the time that he merely advised the men on how to go about issuing a record and estimated the procedure would likely cost around $500. But when Randle then refused to play the record, the men threatened him. That's when the deejay filed the police report.

In view of this latest threat, Randle summoned police once again and then explained the incident to *Press* readers. "If I were taking money, I could have given the record the three minutes it would take and I could have gotten rid of them. It's just the opposite with me. I won't play a record if I'm pressured."

In a 1999 conversation, the straight-talking businessman elaborated on those dark broadcasting days. "People ask why I didn't take money. But why would I? Put myself in somebody's pocket for money? That'd take away all your independence. Plus, in '55 when that stuff started, I was making 600,000 real American dollars, that's about three million today. . . . It had nothing to do with ethics, though I do have that kind of an ethic. It had to do with the fact the taxes were enormous, and you had to pay. I mean, who thinks they can beat the Feds?"

Still in Command

After WERE changed its format in 1960, Randle quit the business for a time, concentrating on pursuing his degrees and teaching. He taught mass communication at Kent State University as an assistant professor and at the University of Cincinnati as a professor. It was while he was at Cincinnati that Elvis Presley stopped by one day to say hello. "I hardly recognized him," Randle recalled. "He looked terrible, but he still called me 'Mister' Randle."

Between his teaching stints, Randle worked for WCBS in New York. He returned to WERE-AM in Cleveland in 1965, remaining there until 1972. By the late seventies, he was a deejay for WBBG-AM, where he continued to make his presence known by sparking the national hit "The Pina Colada Song" by Rupert Holmes. Today, Bill Randle still reigns as Mr. Influential, working the afternoon shift at WRMR-AM 850, where ratings have doubled since he joined the station in 1992. The seventy-something deejay keeps busy juggling his radio show with various other interests. He maintains a law practice in Lakewood, has completed a book called *The Selling of Elvis,* and continues to discover new talent. In 1994 he produced a CD for jazz singer Terry Blaine. In 1996 he introduced a new Toronto act, the Spitfire Band, to America during a time when other promoters wouldn't book the group because they believed the act was a financial risk. The band quickly sold out their first public appearance with Randle at the business helm. Clearly, Randle still has what it takes.

In response to all he's accomplished over his lifetime, Randle comments in a way only he can: "I know more about this business than anyone alive, and I'm not interested in reminiscing about it all. I'm just not interested in my own history. I simply do what I like and stop doing it when I no longer enjoy it." The element of risk—or age—apparently has never occurred to him, and because of this Cleveland has been the fortunate recipient of this music legend's bountiful talents.

In 1998, the leaders of the Rock and Roll Hall of Fame and Museum decided to pay homage to the many historic landmarks in the Cleveland area. First on the list was Brooklyn High School, where Elvis performed his legendary concert forty-three years before. On October 21, an official plaque was placed on the building, designating it a national rock landmark.

Pete "Mad Daddy" Myers

> Howdy doody, little sneakers . . . my brain is pretty hot [sound of boiling water in background], yeah, you could hear it flow . . . so welcome to another . . . show.
>
> —Mad Daddy

"I can still hear him in my mind saying, 'This is Mad Daddy from the land of oobladi, ooblada,'" recalls fan Allan Brandenburg. "I listened to him every night in my room. He had a voice you couldn't forget."

"I was just a kid of about eight or nine when I listened to Mad Daddy when he was on WHK," recalls guitarist Chris Butler (the Numbers Band/Tin Huey/Waitresses). "I used to get in a lot of trouble when my parents caught me listening to that 'demon rock and roll.'"

If you ever heard Pete "Mad Daddy" Myers on the radio, you never forgot him. Myers had a style no one could imitate. Today he is hailed as a genius of words and rhyme. His rapid on-air delivery held his audience captive to his poetic rantings and ravings. Think pre-rap.

Although he certainly made an impression on his listeners, one person in particular was greatly influenced by Myers. Ernie Anderson, an equally eccentric disc jockey at WHK, earned a reputation from his many station firings throughout northern parts of the United States. And within a year, his stint at WHK would also be history, but not before his friendship with Myers made a lasting impression. Three years after Mad Daddy left for New York, Anderson adopted the wild and crazy antics of his mentor and became Ghoulardi, the wild and crazy host of WJW's Friday night *Shock Theater*. It became the biggest TV hit in Cleveland history. In 1966, Ghoulardi left the North Coast for Los Angeles and became TV's highest paid announcer during the seventies and eighties. His baritone voice is best remembered for introducing *Love Boat* and *America's Funniest Home Videos*.

But Myers was the first to host a horror movie in Cleveland on WJW-TV. He held court on Channel 8's late-night movie for a short period in 1958, but it seems the world was not ready then for that kind of maniacal TV host. Still, the memory of a crazed madman draped in a black velvet hooded cape remains etched in viewers' minds. (He was able to pull it off thanks to his schooling at the Royal Academy of Dramatic Arts in London.) While his career paralleled that of radio hero Alan Freed, Myers's on-air antics made Freed seem like a choirboy. Like Freed, Mad Daddy earned his broadcasting wings at an Akron station (WHKK), after a brief stint in San Diego. He took his name and wild persona to Cleveland's WJW in January 1958 and then to WHK five months later, before ending up in New York.

Although he was neither a Cleveland native (he was born in San Francisco in 1928) nor on the city's radio airwaves for more than a few years, Pierre (Pete) Myers is more a legend in Cleveland than anywhere else. He is fondly remembered by his audience as well as his coworkers. One coworker is former WHK and WKYC deejay Mike Reynolds (a.k.a. Michael Chadwick Bartholomew Reynolds III, "The Chaplain of Soul"), now residing in Phoenix. "I first met Pete Myers at a dance he was hosting at the Euclid Avenue Temple, which was Fairmont Temple at the time, in Shaker Heights," says Reynolds, who began his radio career pulling records for Bill Randle at WERE. "I believe he already had his 'Mad Daddy' radio show then. Myers was the best there ever was, that's for sure. Yes, you had Bill Gordon and 'The Doc,' Bill Randle. But the truth is, Pete Myers was the best disc jockey that ever came out of Cleveland, bar none. Nobody could hold a stick to him. I was just a kid when I started at 'HK, and by listening and watching him, Mad Daddy trained my ear."

Also in 1958, the eccentric deejay was offered a substantial pay raise to move to a radio station just down the street. His WHK debut was delayed, however, by a WJW contract clause that barred him from working at a competing station for ninety days. While he waited out his three months, the ever-inventive Mad Daddy, fearing his listeners might forget him, devised a publicity stunt well remembered some thirty years later. When his former WJW manager told Mad Daddy to "go jump in the lake," the deejay thought it was a great idea. He contacted the Civil Aeronautics Administration and the Coast Guard, telling them he had parachuting experience. They gave him the go-ahead, despite the real truth that this would be Myers's first-ever jump out of an airplane. At 3:00 P.M. on June 14, 1958, Mad Daddy jumped from a plane 2,300 feet above Lake Erie, reciting rhythmic chantings all the way down to the chilly sixty-degree water. When he returned to the airwaves that August on WHK, his prominence was not only intact, but he had gained even more fans. During his year at the station, Mad Daddy served double duty: From 2:00 to 4:00 P.M. he was the mild-mannered Pete Myers; from 8:00 to 10:00 P.M. he was the crazed Mad Daddy, whose chantings of "mellow as Jell-O" and "wavy-gravy" became catch phrases. The latter was taken from bluesman Andre Williams's tune "The Greasy Chicken," which the deejay played incessantly. Myers's uncanny ability to speak like a 45 RPM record on 78 RPM speed—entirely in rhyme!—earned him a legion of impassioned fans along the North Coast.

By the middle of 1959, Mad Daddy was such a household name that he thought he'd take his act to the "big time," to New York. To his thousands of admirers, the news was catastrophic. Mad Daddy had succeeded in giving his listeners the entertainment they'd been looking for since Alan Freed; now he, too, was leaving them. His last broadcast here, on June 26, 1959, marked the sad end to a historic radio figure in more ways than one.

He had secured a job at WHK's sister station in New York, WNEW, and was anxious to light up the Big Apple just as he'd done the North Coast. But there he had a different audience, one that saw no humor in his show. Behind-the-scenes politics kept Mad Daddy at arm's length, and he was forced to play it straight—which didn't suit him. In 1963 he moved to WINS. Like Freed, Myers had great expectations when he arrived at New York City's top station, but things were no different there; moreover his new boss was a former assistant, (a "go-fer," really) of his from his Cleveland days. So Pete Myers was no more than just another radio jock in New York. His failure to

"Mad Daddy" prepares to take flight to publicize his switch from WJW to WHK radio, June 14, 1958. He convinced the Coast Guard and Civil Aeronautics Administration that he had parachuting experience. He did not. *Photo by Herman Seid. Cleveland Press Collection, Cleveland State University.*

achieve the on-air celebrity he had once enjoyed took a toll on his ego. Some say that he turned to drugs (rumors of heroin addiction) to kill his inner pain; others cite his already unstable personality as the cause of his decline. Neither reason mattered when he decided to take his own life the morning of October 4, 1968, in his New York apartment. His dramatic exit garnered only a brief mention in the local papers.

This erstwhile, madcap deejay forever captured the hearts of radio fans and is still heard on a few elusive recordings (one included in the limited edition of *Cle* no.3x).

Phil McLean

Another radio personality, though not known as a rock deejay, helped get "the rock rolling" in the 1950s, deserves a mention. Like Bill Randle, McLean hailed from the Motor City, and the two met when McLean, who'd previously spun records at high school, was visiting the Detroit station where Randle was working. When the station manager in the next room overheard McLean's crisp, resonant voice, he offered him a job. Later, when Randle moved on to Ohio, McLean wasn't far behind.

At Randle's suggestion, McLean was hired at WERE in 1951, where he quickly drew a following by playing a wide variety of music on his program. By playing records by previously unknown singers and musicians, he launched the careers of many pop artists. Soon the former World War II navy fighter pilot joined the ranks of Cleveland's most powerful and influential deejays. And when rock rolled onto the scene, McLean helped promote the music and bring it to the forefront. In an article chronicling McLean's career here, *Cleveland Press* entertainment writer Harriet Peters wrote, "McLean and Bill Randle were teen idols and making hit records and creating record stars like Johnnie Ray. Along with thousands of other teens, I couldn't do my homework unless the radio was tuned to McLean or Randle."

McLean's most popular stint on the North Coast was as host of the city's own version of *American Bandstand*. *Cleveland Bandstand* debuted in 1955 on WJW-TV, Channel 8. One fan of the show, Walter Masky, often helped McLean choose the records he would spin, and upon graduation in 1958, Masky become music director at WERE, once again working with the popular deejay. The bandstand show aired for several years; but, unable to keep pace with the nationally famous program, it was canceled by 1960. Early that same year, new owners at WERE decided to "go another way" by changing formats and releasing all in-house deejays.

McLean found himself without a job. He left Cleveland for the New York, where he befriended many of the top artists of the day, including Tony Bennett and Rosemary Clooney. He was also engaged for a time to Patti Page. While hosting an overnight show there, he brought Barbra Streisand's "Happy Days Are Here Again" to his audience's attention, and the song became her first national hit.

The popular deejay returned to Cleveland in 1971 and worked first for WHK-AM/1420 and then for WWWE-AM/1100. In 1977, fed up with management changes that resulted in another firing, he decided to leave the business, accepting a management job at the Chagrin Falls restaurant Hunter's Hollow Tavern. Then by the decade's end, he moved to Hilton Head, South Carolina, where he returned to radio, working at stations WHHR-AM and WLOW-FM.

Phil McLean was one of Cleveland's prominent disc jockeys in the 1950s. Although he hadn't lived in the city for over a decade, his death from bone cancer on May 28, 1993, at the age of seventy, was duly noted in the *Plain Dealer*. McLean once had this to say about himself and his Cleveland coworkers: "What set us apart was we really cared about music. We weren't afraid of discovery. Every record I played was a 'good' record, something that may not have been a hit, but had the right to be one."

Tommy Edwards

Although known mostly as a country music deejay, Tommy Edwards had an undeniable rock connection. It began when the WERE deejay hosted his "Saturday Night Hillbilly Jamboree" at the Circle Theater, where he'd bring in various artists to entertain his audience of country music lovers. On Saturday, February 26, 1955, Edwards booked the Bill Black Trio, which was making its first trip north. The front man of the group was a dark-haired kid with the unusual name of Elvis Presley, who snarled as he sang. It was his voice, however, that got him noticed by Edwards.

The deejay had begun spinning the Memphis boy's records just months before, and one song, "I Forgot to Remember to Forget," was already making its way up the national country charts. And that prompted Edwards to bring Elvis and his band to Cleveland. There were already many native southerners who had settled in the blue-collar town because of the promising opportunities for work after the war. Coupled with the diverse ethnic groups (such as Slovenian, Polish, Irish, Italian, Finnish, and Jewish) making their homes here and the number of African Americans moving into

Music fan Patty Rowe picks a record for Cleveland Bandstand host Phil McLean. *Photo by Al Willinger. Cleveland Press Collection, Cleveland State University.*

the Hough district, Cleveland represented the melting pot of music in America. And Tommy Edwards had a feeling that the snarling Southern singer would make an impact in this industrial city. He was right.

That first visit was well received and got the expected crowd reaction. But it was when Elvis returned to the city several months later to promote his latest release, "Mystery Train," that Cleveland music history changed forever. Elvis played the Circle Theater jamboree on Wednesday, October 19, the night before he played an afternoon gig at Cleveland's Brooklyn High School and an evening stint at St. Michael's Hall.

Dave Nida, former distributor at Northern One Stop Records who counted Edwards among his clients, recalls the deejay telling him about that event. "I remember Tommy saying how the kids went crazy over Elvis that night at the Circle, and how the next day he drove Elvis to the Robert Hall clothing store in Collinwood because Elvis wanted to dress like Pat Boone, whom he saw at the Brooklyn High School [earlier that day]." Elvis was indeed a fan of Pat Boone's, and when the young singer showed up at St. Michael's that evening he was wearing a snazzy brown tweed jacket, red socks, and Boone's trademark white bucks. By that second northern exposure, the Memphis man was well on his way to success. But Hank LoConti, owner of the rock venue the Agora, remembers when Edwards brought Elvis to Cleveland that first time.

> Right after the Bill Black Trio played the Circle Theater that February night, Tommy brought them over to my place, then the Club 18, on E. 18th and Payne. Elvis went up on our stage, and he was just this incredible performer, even then. I remember he was a nice, shy kid who didn't drink, but I really didn't pay attention to his name at the time.
>
> Then about a year later, my wife and I are sitting at home and she says, "You gotta watch this TV show. This guy who was on last week is coming on again, and you gotta see him."
>
> Well, I started watching it [*The Tommy and Jimmy Dorsey Stage Show*, Elvis's first television appearance], and when I noticed his body movements I said to my wife, "Don't you remember him? That's the kid who was singing on our stage last year." That's when I found out his name was Elvis Presley.

The white guy with a blues soul, a hillbilly accent, and a mean right hip not only crisscrossed the musical genres, but he also had a phenomenal influence on those who reveled in them—whether rock, country, blues, or gospel.

Gonna Write a Little Letter

Tommy Edwards was born on March 27, 1923, in Milwaukee. After getting his start in radio at Spencer, Iowa, station KICD in 1945, he worked for a time at WOKY in Milwaukee before settling at Cleveland's WERE in 1951. He began staging many of the early sock hops that took place in high school auditoriums throughout the area. Among his many "firsts" was projecting slides onto a screen to accompany the music at those popular dances. He also was first to provide a weekly music newsletter, later emulated by *Billboard* and *Record World*. Renowned for his vast record collection and knowledge of the music industry, Edwards launched the *TE Newsletter,* a publication distributed to more than two hundred agency men, music publishers, columnists, and deejays across the country. Even *Billboard* itself credited the radio pioneer for being the first music man in the country to publish a newsletter. A September 1955 article in the *RCA DeeJay Digest* entitled "Nearly Everybody in New York Reads Tommy Edwards' Newsletter" called it "a weekly newsletter which is read as carefully by the entire music business as the big trade papers are read." In a 1980 *Scene* article, Edwards said of the newsletter, "I chronicled everything that happened during the week; who was in; what artists; what records looked strong; what promotion men called on us. And the letter had some impact. If a promotion man was in town and he wasn't mentioned in the letter he was most often called on the carpet when he returned to his base."

Edwards's interest in country music as well as pop tunes involved him in the North Coast success of several early '50s artists. His radio show aired weekdays from 10:00 A.M. to 2:00 P.M. and succeeded in filling a void for country music lovers. Along with his radio success, Edwards also recorded two songs himself, both in January 1957. "What Is a Teenage Girl" and the follow-up "What Is a Teenage Boy," made a noticeable, albeit small, dent on the national charts. In 1960, new management at WERE took over and subsequently released Edwards and other deejays, including Bill Randle. After abiding by a clause in his contract that barred him from working at any other station within a hundred-mile radius for two years, Edwards joined Akron station WADC. Soon after, however, he grew disillusioned with the radio industry and returned to Cleveland in 1962, not as a deejay but as a record store owner. He opened Tommy Edwards's Hillbilly Heaven on the corner of W. 25th Street and Denison Avenue.

"My premise was to sell only country music, which I started to do," Edwards said in the *Scene* interview. "Then I found that the parents who wanted country music would bring in their kids, and of course, they wanted the latest Stones or Beatles release. And I didn't have it, so I saw the handwriting on the wall and started putting those records in." Such was the beginning of what turned out to be one of the most successful record stores in Cleveland, one that was known nationwide. "I think part of Tommy's success was that he was a total gentleman in a world often full of rogues," Nida says. "He also personally did all the buying for his store. He was amazing when it came to that. He'd come in and actually sift through the warehouse bins of old or discarded records slated to go back to the manufacturer. He knew what his customers wanted and always went out of his way to provide for those customers." As a result, his shop offered not only the latest in popular music but also rare and out-of-print records, including the most complete selection of Elvis records available. It was not unusual for him to buy 300 to 400 records a day from the distributor. His reputation was such that even his competition would recommend his record store to fulfill a customer's needs. In 1973 Edwards moved his shop to 4237 Fulton Road, Cleveland, and changed the name to Tommy Edwards' Record Heaven.

In June 1981 the famous record proprietor and former radio personality suffered a stroke; one month later, on July 25, at fifty-eight, he died of a heart attack.

After Edwards's death, his family sold the business to Chuck Rambaldo. "I was always a regular customer at Tommy Edwards' store," Rambaldo recalls. "He would get any record you were looking for. So when he died I told my mother, 'I'm going to buy that store.' At first, she thought I was crazy because I had a real good job then. But my mom was healthy and needed something to do so we bought the store! It's been a real labor of love." Rambaldo has followed in Edwards's footsteps by supporting local bands and recording artists. "I'd have a lot of local guys play in my store," he says. "And that's how I came to decide to make a history out of it by producing a CD of these groups. Rambaldo released "Cleveland's Local Legends of Rock 'n' Roll, Volume 1" in 1999 and Volume 2 in 2000. "There'll be more," he adds. "You can be sure of that!"

Kemal Amen Kasem (Casey Kasem)

And the hits just keep on coming. Now for our request and dedication . . .
—from "American Top 40"

Today, the name and distinctive voice of Casey Kasem are recognized throughout the country, but it was in Cleveland that he fine-tuned his disc jockey style and developed that unmistakable voice and amiable persona. Detroit native Kasem had been a radio sports announcer in high school and acted in radio drama on the Armed Forces Network while serving in Korea from 1952 to 1954. From there it was back to his hometown, where he ultimately got a job at WJLB-AM playing R&B music and then at Detroit station WJBK-AM.

It was in May 1959 that twenty-six-year-old Kasem began what would turn out to be a short-lived career in Cleveland, but one significant in terms of radio status. He was hired for the night spot at WJW-AM 850, once the time slot of Mad Daddy. "On the last day of Mad Daddy's show [on WHK]," Kasem notes, "I remember local record promoter Bob Skaff and I were driving out to the [race] track, and he said, 'Wanna hear the no. 1 disc jockey in Cleveland?' He turned it on, I listened, and it was terrific. And I immediately knew that in order to fill his shoes, I had to have as much excitement going for me as he did."

From that first day, the new deejay in town dubbed his show "Casey at the Mike" and succeeded in winning over his audience with his good ear for rhythm and blues as well as his own creative style. He also began hosting *Cleveland Bandstand,* replacing Phil McLean, who had moved to New York. That simultaneous entry into Cleveland television and radio forever sealed Kasem's reputation as a media personality. *Cleveland Bandstand* was canceled soon after, but "Casey at the Mike" continued to gain a following. Kasem's strong, clear voice and easy-speaking manner began drawing a young audience every night at eight. By the end of his first ratings period, the station had jumped from the depths of zero to the number two spot. It was all due to word of mouth, since his presence was given little press notice. (In those days not much was reported on radio personalities.)

Just as Kasem was enjoying his new career in Cleveland, the payola investigations began crashing down, darkening many a bright career. Like hundreds of deejays during this time, Kasem too was approached: One day at a luncheon a record producer told him he wanted to give the deejay a present because he was playing a record others had refused. Kasem turned the man down, explaining that he played the song because he genuinely liked it and that he didn't accept gratuities. The next day the man sent Kasem a gift certificate from a local clothing store. The deejay, in turn, promptly sent it back. Three days later the payola scandals broke out in full force. Casey Kasem's promising career remained untarnished.

Holdin' Steady

While working his magic as a deejay, Kasem was harboring dreams of becoming an actor. But fate had other plans. After his successful year in Cleveland, Kasem moved on to Buffalo and then to Oakland before settling down in Los Angeles in 1963. It was in L.A. that Kasem's radio career took off nationally, and, not long after, his success extended to television when he hosted a TV dance show, *Shebang,* produced by Dick Clark. In 1970 Kasem began the syndicated radio show that would be his calling card: "American Top 40." These achievements in radio ultimately paved the way for the acting opportunities he desired, and Kasem had acting spots in several TV series throughout the '70s and '80s.

Today, Kasem is still heard on radio stations around the globe. His famous "Casey's Countdowns" have generated three separate shows: The long-running "American Top 40" has continued with the same tried-and-true format since 1970; "American Top 20" was designed a few years ago for the adult contemporary stations; and "American Hot 20" was formulated for the more up-tempo hits. Kasem is the youngest inductee to the Radio Hall of Fame; he has his own star on Hollywood Boulevard's Walk of Fame"; and he was given a Lifetime Achievement Award from *Billboard* in 1997— nearly forty years after making his name in Cleveland.

Payola Again

Cleveland was so big in the early '50s with Bill Randle and later with us at KYW that people in the business knew that if it was played here it would spread all over the country. It got so strong at KYW in 1957, I couldn't go to the bathroom without someone saying, "Here's a $100 and a Freddie Cannon record." It turned out to be "Tallahassee Lassie." But do you know what? I never played records that didn't become million sellers. Even with all this going on, I wouldn't play crap. At that time, there were no clear cut or active payola laws.

—Chuck Young, KYW's music director,
October 1956–December 1959 (*Scene,* 1990)

The Fabulous Fifties certainly didn't end that way for much of the broadcasting industry. Despite the fact that 1959 was a banner year for the record business, payola succeeded in rocking the entire music nation—and Cleveland, known throughout the country for its prominent role in radio, did not escape its wrath. Two deejays in particular suffered: Joe Finan and Wes Hopkins, both KYW employees. As the radio station's most successful disc jockeys, Finan and Hopkins were mainstays, enjoying the peak of their careers. By the end of 1959, however, paranoia among deejays was rampant. Payola, and everything it stood for, was responsible for killing many a radio career, particularly ones having to do with rock and roll. The congressional hearings into "Payola and Other Deceptive Practices in the Broadcasting Fields" began in February 1960 and succeeded in breaking open formerly common industry practices. Bill Randle gives an example.

Right before the payola scandal hit, Hill & Range [song publishers] once sent me a Mercedes for making a hit out of their song, "Butterfly." I told the executive who'd brought it here from New York that I didn't want their car. I said, "I already have nine cars, including a Mercedes [which he later sold to famed race-car driver Roger Penske], a Bentley Rolls Royce convertible, and a 300 SL with a sixty-gallon gas tank. What do I need this clunker for?" It was just a basic stock-standard Mercedes, and I didn't even like the looks of the thing. So the guy continued on and his next stop was Philadelphia. He gave the car to Tony Mammarella, then producer for *American Bandstand,* and during the payola investigations, the car was one of the items mentioned in his testimony.

The end result of those testimonies, after destroying hundreds of broadcasting careers, was to make it illegal for a disc jockey or other radio station employee to accept any kind of payment for playing a record. Also, these employees could not involve themselves in other areas of the recording business.

On that fateful day in November 1959 when payola rocked the radio industry, KYW's Finan and Hopkins were caught in the thick of it. Although six other Cleveland deejays were accused of payola practices and subsequently fired, these two popular record spinners were made scapegoats. News headlines such as "Wes Hopkins and Joe Finan Sue KYW for $2.5 million" merely added to the mess. It was an ugly time in radio history. The listening fans, however, were loyal advocates. "They are worth every penny they are paid," one twelve-year-old girl wrote to the *Cleveland Press.* "We admire Finan's interest in entertaining youth on the radio and record hops. What do you want from us cats? After all, we're hep." The following March Finan took the stand at the New House

Office Building in Washington, D.C. While under oath, he admitted to receiving various items as well as cash.

But time has a way of healing wounds, and Finan has continued his radio career, working for a time at one of the three musical musketeers of '60s Cleveland radio, WIXY-AM 1260. While Hopkins moved to Columbus, where he is believed to be today, Finan stayed closer, and since 1985 he has hosted a popular talk show on Kent/Ravenna station WNIR-FM 100.1. The radio veteran was inducted into the Akron Radio Hall of Fame in 1989. Chuck Young went on to start up a record distribution company, Cleveland One Stop, in 1978.

Although many deejays did not survive the repercussions of payola, the electrifying beat of the music, the phenomenal success of Dick Clark's *American Bandstand*, and the impending British Invasion all helped bring about an acceptance and/or tolerance of rock music. And the disc jockeys who knew what teens wanted in their music held fast and strong. Fortunately for early rock lovers, in those days deejays had ultimate control over what was played; and because they were allowed to personally program their own shows, these pioneering deejays were able to push the artists and songs they and their fans enjoyed. In the first decade of rock and roll, the deejays were king, and Cleveland ruled with the best of them.

Recommended Reading

Clark, Dick, and Richard Robertson. *Rock, Roll and Remember.* New York: Thomas Y. Crowell, 1976.

Escott, Colin, with Nartin Hawkis. *Good Rockin' Tonight: Sun Records and the Birth of Rock 'n' Roll.* New York: St. Martin's Press, 1991.

Guralnick, Peter. *Last Train to Memphis: The Rise of Elvis Presley.* New York: Little, Brown, 1994.

Jackson, John A. *Big Beat Heat: Alan Freed and the Early Years of Rock 'n' Roll.* New York: Schirmer Books, 1991.

Passman, Arnold. *The Deejays.* New York: Macmillan, 1971.

Shaw, Arnold. *Honkers and Shouters.* New York: Macmillan, 1978.

Smith, Wes. *The Pied Pipers of Rock 'n Roll.* Marietta, Ga.: Longstreet Press, 1989.

Worth, Fred L., and Steve D. Tamerius. *Elvis: His Life from A to Z.* Chicago: Contemporary Books, 1988.

2 It's Only Rock and Roll, but They Like It

The blues had a baby and they called it rock 'n' roll.

—Muddy Waters

By the dawn of the 1960s, rock and roll had secured its place in popular culture thanks to those early R&B musicians who played it, listeners who welcomed it, and club owners who opened their doors to it. Many black artists at first resented the growing trend of white singers recording their songs, and understandably so. Yet it was these cover versions that exposed the music and propelled it up the national charts. As a result, singers such as Little Richard, Fats Domino, Chuck Berry, Frankie Lymon, and others were able to gain their own deserved successes and create opportunities for future performers.

The '60s saw the excitement of rock music move into virtually every medium—radio, television, and journalism. Radio still dominated with on-air personalities and fresh music that sparked teen interest with its individual styles and sounds. Television got into the act, taking its cue from *American Bandstand,* and began airing more dance shows such as *Shindig, Where the Action Is, Hullabaloo, Soul Train,* and Cleveland's own *Upbeat.* Then came the magazines. In 1961, Liverpool, England, brought us *Mersey Beat,* the first "fan" magazine, and in 1964 the first official all-rock publication, *Crawdaddy,* was published in Boston. Of course, nothing came close to the popularity of *Rolling Stone* magazine, which debuted on November 9, 1967, with John Lennon gracing the cover. More than thirty years later, *Rolling Stone* continues to set the standard for rock journalism.

With so much happening at once in this embryonic world of rock, to chronicle the events of the era is like attempting to answer that old cliché: Which came first, the chicken or the egg? Whatever the case, America's youth now had an agreeable sound that was universal and that, despite the onset of war and civil unrest, bridged the gaps among races and genders. By this time, music was defined in a variety of terms: R&B, jazz, country, bluegrass, gospel, classical, rock, pop, and rockabilly. But no longer were any of these genres referred to as "race" or "colored" music.

Pop Rock Artists from Ohio's North Coast

Although Cleveland was a respected and influential radio market, the city's success in the industry seldom benefited its own artists. The reasons are as individual, numerous, and complex as the music business itself. Some artists had to go elsewhere for their success, while others copped local and regional hits yet failed to make a mark outside

The "Pride of Cleveland Past" poster that hung in the offices of WMJI. *Courtesy of Karen Cipriani.*

the surrounding area. The stories could fill *another* book. Nonetheless, the North Coast has always been rich with musical talent. Featured below are those rockers that made it and those that came oh-so-close.

Johnny Moore, Lead Singer for the Drifters

The Drifters, like countless other groups, changed members (thirty musicians came and went) over the course of its eleven years in existence. Founding member Clyde McPhatter chose the name because musicians often drifted from one group to another—a common practice today—and it became particularly fitting for this group

With McPhatter at the Helm, the group's first big song was "Money Honey," one of 1953's best-selling R&B songs. The following year they recorded "Honey Love," another big seller. Then the army beckoned McPhatter, who left the group in April 1954. The Drifters survived, filling the void with David Baughan, a former member whose voice was similar to McPhatter's. But Baughan's excessive drinking while on the road led the other band members to oust him, replacing him with Johnny Moore in 1954. By 1955 the group had returned to the chart with hits "Fools Fall in Love in a Hurry," "Adorable," "Ruby Baby," "Soldier of Fortune," "It Was a Tear," and "I Gotta Get Myself a Woman." But by spring, Baughan was back in and Moore returned to Cleveland and to his former group the Cleveland Quartet, which changed its name to the Hornets (whose recordings are available on a 1980 Pea Vine album, *The Hornets and the 5Cs*). In August, Moore was asked to rejoin the Drifters. The group then continued touring and frequently shared the billing with Cleveland native and shock-rock pioneer Screamin' Jay Hawkins. In the fall of 1957, Moore was drafted and replaced by Bobby Hendricks. A year later, this lineup disbanded.

But Drifters' original manager George Treadwell reinvented the group by hiring all new members, including lead singer Ben E. King (Benny Nelson). By 1959, they began a string of hits that included "There Goes My Baby," "Save the Last Dance for Me" (which made it to Billboard's No. 1 in October 1960), and "Up on the Roof." Moore returned in 1964, helping them garner more hits, like "One Way Love," "Under the Boardwalk" (re-released by Atlantic after it was suggested they "clean up" a controversial lyric, "we'll be making love"), "I've Got Sand in My Shoes," and "Saturday Night at the Movies."

When Treadwell died in 1967, his wife, Faye, took over management, and the group continued to record and perform. Johnny Moore, now the most recognized Drifter, remained in the group (which performed occasionally through 1993 and has since reformed with new members), with the exception of brief interludes in 1978, 1981–83, and 1986. The Drifters have had forty-seven American R&B/pop hits—fourteen of them in the Top 30 hits, and twenty U.K. hits. In 1987 the group took its rightful place in the Rock and Roll Hall of Fame.

Screamin' Jay Hawkins (Jalacy Hawkins)

Toward the end of the 1950s, a number of black artists were becoming known for their onstage antics as well as music's sometimes sexually suggestive lyrics. Chuck Berry had his "Maybellene" (later his "My Ding-A-Ling" would make "Maybellene" sound like a church gospel). Little Richard had "Good Golly, Miss Molly." Fats Domino crooned on his "Blueberry Hill." But Clevelander Jay Hawkins took it further with his rendition of "I Put a Spell on You," which was originally written as a love ballad in response to a break-up with his girlfriend but gave way to a wilder side during the recording session and became an unexpected hit in 1956. Legend has it that Hawkins's deep, intense "Spell" was the result of the singer's inebriated condition at the recording session and that because of this the tune became more commercially attractive. This forced Hawkins to learn to sing that way in order to perform the song live in the way his audience would expect.

Hawkins went on to repeat that early success in 1958 with "Alligator Wine," penned by the famous songwriting duo Jerry Leiber and Mike Stoller (most famous for many of Elvis's hits). But follow-up songs such as "Constipation Blues," "Bite It," and "What That Is" never came close to rivaling his prior hits.

Born in Cleveland on July 18, 1929, Jalacy Hawkins began his career as the singer/keyboardist in 1950s groups that included Fats Domino's band and Tiny Grimes and His Rocking Highlanders. He became "Screamin' Jay" purely by accident. One night as the flamboyant performer was giving a concert in Charleston, West Virginia, an intoxicated woman repeatedly heckled him to "scream, baby, scream" his songs. After constant badgering, Hawkins finally relented, taking on the nickname that became his calling card.

Screamin' Jay's performances are legendary. He opened his shows by being carried on stage in a coffin. He wore voodoo-style black satin suits with a matching cape. His companions carried skeletons, bats, rubber snakes, and a cigarette-smoking skull on a stick, named Henry. This bizarre performing style got him into trouble one night at New York's Apollo Theater, when he was on the bill with other R&B groups. It seems a couple of members of the Drifters (no one is sure whether Clevelander Johnny Moore was in on the prank) thought it would be a hoot to lock the eccentric singer in the coffin he used in his stage act. The show was then delayed as Hawkins attempted in .vain to push against the lid to get out. It was a screamin' moment indeed for Hawkins, one he'd prefer to forget. (He finally got out by rocking the box so hard it fell over, breaking open the lid.)

In 1981, he was asked to open for the Rolling Stones at Madison Square Garden. Realizing he'd have to give quite a show to keep diehard Stones fans at bay, he approached the stage wearing a one-hundred-foot rubber snake draped around his neck, a red and black full-length cape, and a yellow turban, complete with a plastic parrot on top. After this show, concertgoers were talking about the opening act as much as the headliner.

Because of his wild stage acts, Hawkins is considered one of the originators of what became known as shock rock. Although he'd play an occasional concert in Cleveland, he mostly performed in Europe, his songs in America all but forgotten. He did, however, get a lot of mileage out of "I Put a Spell on You." It can be heard in the 1978 movie *American Hot Wax* and in the 1984 film *Stranger Than Paradise*. The song has also been covered by various artists, most notably Creedence Clearwater Revival with lead singer John Fogerty.

After Hawkins's death in Paris on February 12, 2000, at age seventy, it was announced that this former flamboyant Clevelander is known to have fathered seventy-five children the world over.

Bobby Womack

This singer/songwriter/guitarist, who grew up on E. 63rd Street and Central Avenue, began singing almost before he could walk. By the time he reached tenth grade, he knew he wasn't going to last long at East Tech High School. "That school happened to be right across the street from the Majestic Hotel. I can still remember lookin' out the window of my history class, Room 15, and seein' all the greats, like Count Basie, goin' in and outta that place. And I remember my teacher, Mr. Washington. He'd be askin' me a question, and I'd be so engulfed in watching out the window that I wouldn't hear him, until he'd come by and whack me on the head and say, 'Hey, Womack, stop lookin' out there 'cause you ain't never gonna be in that hotel. If you be anything, you'll be the janitor.' But I knew what I wanted to be. And I wanted to be a singer goin' in and outta that hotel."

What the hopeful young singer didn't know, however, was that the Majestic Hotel employed two other ambitious teenagers—David Ruffin and Eddie Kendrick—who sang in the kitchen of the hotel's restaurant while washing dishes and dreamed of being stars themselves. Ruffin and Kendrick had a group called the Cavaliers. When they moved to Detroit, they hooked up with three other singers and realized their dream when they formed the Temptations.

Of course, Bobby Womack, too, would go on to worldwide fame despite his teacher's prediction. By age fifteen, he was already a member of a quintet with siblings Cecil, Curtis, Harris, and Friendly Jr., who called themselves the Womack Brothers. Staying true to their father's vision, the boys sang gospel tunes in churches and in auditoriums all over the Midwest, often sharing the bill with popular acts of the day like the Soul Stirrers, whose charismatic singer was named Sam Cooke.

We always sang gospel music 'cause that was my father's music. Sam took to us right away and one day he said to us, "You think your father would let you boys open up for me?" I said, "No way, he wouldn't approve." So Sam says, "Okay, I'll tell you what. We'll do some gospel, then we'll work something out." But soon as my father found out we were doing what he called "boogie woogie" music, he was furious and told us, "You can't stay here anymore," and he threw us all out of the house. When we told him, Sam said, "Your father can't be serious," and I said "Oh, he's serious as a heart attack." And Sam felt responsible 'cause we were all young yet.

While still part of the Womack Brothers, Bobby toured with Cooke as the soul singer's back-up guitarist. Then in 1961 he and his brothers signed to Cooke's own SAR label and took the name the Valentinos. By the following year, the Valentinos were on their way with the single "Lookin' for a Love," which peaked at No. 72 on the R&B chart. (The song was later recorded by the J. Geils Band and became one of their biggest hits.) At Cooke's suggestion, the former choirboys moved to Los Angeles to further their recording careers. Womack's association with Cooke remained close until the soulman's tragic death in 1964.

Now a Los Angeles resident, Womack began his recording success in earnest. While performing with the Valentinos as lead singer, Womack wrote and recorded songs that quickly hit the charts between 1962 and 1964, though the most successful ones, "I'll Make It Alright" (No. 97) and "It's All Over Now" (No. 94), never came close to the coveted Top 40. The latter song, covered by the Rolling Stones in 1964, gave the British band their first U.S. hit (No. 26) as well as their first No. 1 record (on U.K. charts). After Cooke's death, Womack left the band, and his brothers, to pursue solo efforts.

As a guitarist, Womack worked with such regal peers as Ray Charles, James Brown, Aretha Franklin, King Curtis, and the Stones, in addition to 1960s successes the Box Tops, Dusty Springfield, Joe Tex, Rod Stewart and the Faces, and Janis Joplin (he wrote her popular tune "Trust Me"). As a songwriter, he wrote numerous hits for his recording comrades, such as Leon Russell, Sly Stone, and George Benson. Wilson Pickett alone covered seventeen of Womack's songs, including "I'm a Midnight Mover" and "I'm in Love."

But it was as a solo artist that Womack found his true calling. An impassioned singer/songwriter, his reputation for conveying human angst is near-legendary. His soulful renditions of "Fly Me to the Moon" (which peaked at No. 52), "Love Has Finally Come at Last" (a duet with Patti LaBelle that reached No. 88), "That's the Way I Feel About Cha," "No Matter How High I Get, I'll Still Be Lookin' Up to You," "Woman's Gotta Have It," "No One Wants You When You're Down and Out," and "Where Do We Go from Here?" each made an impact on the charts. He made the Top 40 in 1972 with "Harry Hippie," which peaked on pop charts at No. 31 and on the R&B charts at No. 8. And in 1974, he re-recorded "Lookin' for a Love," which became his biggest U.S. success, hitting the No. 10 spot.

He continued pounding out albums throughout the 1970s as well as producing for friends, including Rolling Stone Ron Wood's debut LP *Now Look* (1976). However, in 1976 Womack's failed attempt to go country with the United Artists release *B. W. Goes C&W* caused the label to drop him. (The singer says his original title of the album was *Move Over Charlie Pride and Give Another Nigger a Chance*.) But Womack rebounded—first on Columbia, then on Arista—with his last albums of the decade: *Pieces, Home Is Where the Heart Is,* and *Roads of Life.*

The 1980s kept Womack just as active with a best-selling R&B album, *The Poet,* which peaked at No. 29. It was followed by *The Poet II,* which became his first platinum recording on the U.K. chart, reaching No. 31. In 1985, he appeared on *Late Night With David Letterman* to promote his album *So Many Rivers,* which became a hit both in the U.S. (No. 66) and the U.K. (No. 28). He also contributed guitar licks on the Rolling Stones's 1986 *Dirty Works* LP and sang with Mick Jagger on "Harlem Shuffle" and "Going Back to Memphis."

Womack describes himself as "the last of the soul men" (referring to the loss of such greats as Sam Cooke, Otis Redding, Jackie Wilson, and Marvin Gaye). In fact, his

Bobby Womack, "the Soul Man," in a 1985 Cleveland concert. *Photo by Janet Macoska.*

1987 release is called *The Last Soul Man*. The 1990s releases included *Resurrection* (1994) and *Back to My Roots* (1999).

With such wild associations as the Rolling Stones, Rod Stewart, and Sly Stone, it's not surprising that Womack's concerts can be extravagant at times. At one performance at the Front Row in Cleveland in the 1980s, this "solo" artist was accompanied by fourteen musicians, including a six-piece band, three female vocalists, a harp player, and four horn players. His attire for the evening consisted of a red uniform trimmed in gold with matching gold shoes and hat, and later he changed into a brilliant pink suit. With that kind of glitz to showcase his legendary songs and soul-penetrating voice, no one can forget a Bobby Womack performance.

"My father was really my greatest influence," Womack says of his early ambitions. "I used to say Sam Cooke and, yeah, he definitely was, but I never gave my father [who died in 1981] enough credit. He's the one who got me started in gospel music and he always told us kids, 'I could never afford to send you all to college, and that's why it's important that you sing because you can always entertain people. People love to be entertained so there'll always be room for you.'"

This homegrown superstar received a Pioneer Award from the Rhythm and Blues Foundation in 1996. And although it's been more than two decades since he left Cleveland, Bobby Womack listens when his hometown calls. In 1993, when it came time to break ground at the site for the Rock and Roll Hall of Fame and Museum, Womack was there. Five years later, when it came time to make a video welcoming the return of the Cleveland Browns, Womack was there again. "Being recognized as being from Cleveland means a lot to me," he says. "That's where my roots are, and the city is close to my heart. But back then, there was no way you could've made it there as a professional, especially as a black artist. But let me tell you, there is more undiscovered talent in Cleveland than Motown ever had."

Yet with all his accomplishments, awards, and undeniable influence on the music world, when it comes time for induction announcements for the Rock and Roll Hall of Fame, Womack's name is never there—an exclusion that is puzzling to many, most of all to Womack himself.

I don't know why I've never been [inducted]. I keep hearing that it's a political thing, and if that's true, that isn't right. I hope they're not waitin' 'til I'm dead. What good would that be? I remember sitting by Johnny "Guitar" Watson at the R&B ceremonies. We were both there for the Pioneer Award. I'm lookin' at him thinking, now, here's a guy who don't smoke, or do drugs. He's clean cut and has all this talent. And I told him, "You deserve the Pioneer Award, not me. I'm no pioneer. Why don't they give me some other kind of award? You *invented* music, man." A week later, he was dead. So you see, you never know. That's why people should get acknowledged while they're still living. I was so happy when Sam [Cooke] got into the Rock Hall, but I was sorry he wasn't there to enjoy the recognition.

But Cleveland deserves the Rock Hall. I think it's great, and hopefully it will give upcoming local artists greater opportunities as well. When I was starting out, there was nothing, just a few places you could play, like Gleason's [Musical Bar]. As an entertainer, people would say to me, "Hey, you're in the wrong city if you want to make it." Maybe that'll change now.

No matter what, though, Cleveland will always be a part of who I am.

The O'Jays (1957–)

The vocal and dance group the O'Jays formed in 1957 under the heavy influence of *American Bandstand,* the TV show that was the first of its kind to feature a black singing group, in this case a group with a hit song, "Why Do Fools Fall in Love." "Frankie Lymon and the Teenagers are what did it for me," recalls Walt Williams, one of the original members of the O'Jays. "When I was in the eighth grade, they came to do a show at the annual 'Shower of Stars' at Canton Memorial Auditorium [now Canton Civic Center]. That group was just about the most fantastic thing I'd ever seen. I think they influenced the whole area because suddenly singing groups started popping up everywhere."

Seeing a black group on national television inspired these young "doo-wop" singers. Although the teens grew up with gospel music, they were more influenced by the Drifters, the Coasters, Jackie Wilson, and LaVern Baker. Williams and his vocally strong classmates from Canton McKinley High School formed a group called the Triumphs. The members were all seventeen and under: lead singer Eddie Levert (age sixteen), William Powell (sixteen), Bill Isles (seventeen), Bobby Massey (seventeen), and Walter Williams (fifteen). They went on to call themselves the Mascots and recorded several singles for the Cincinnati-based King Records through the late 1950s.

Williams recalled the group's beginnings:

I remember the day Eddie and I were coming home from Cook's Park, not too far from where we lived in Canton. . . . We passed this little neighborhood grocery store owned by the Gervacis, and one of the sons, Lee, was outside. He came up to us and asked if we knew anyone who could sing some songs he'd written, to see if they were good enough to record. We said, sure, we knew someone. We could do it. So that night we rehearsed in the store after it closed. A few days later, he and his partner took us to Cincinnati and we auditioned for Sid Nathan in his office. We ended up recording some of Gervaci's material as well as some of our own.

But when it came time to sign a recording contract for his son, church deacon and choir director John W. Williams refused to give permission, because it would mean Walter would have to quit school for the road. To the group's good fortune, they had a conspirator in Williams's grandmother, who intervened and signed the papers herself. The group members subsequently left school and began their career in earnest.

It's important to note that accessible venues for black artists were few and far between. Back in the early '60s, black performers were not readily welcomed into white communities, no matter how talented they were. After honing their own style at the Urban League and YMCA dances, the R&B group found musical homes at the Baby Grand and the Bama Club in the Akron/Canton area, Cleveland's popular Call and Post Ballroom, and Gleason's Musical Bar. A few years later, the group changed its name and became regulars at Cleveland's top R&B club, Leo's Casino, which was known for featuring the hottest acts of the era, including Smokey Robinson and the Miracles, the Four Tops, Dionne Warwick, and the Supremes, to name just a few. "I can still recall one of our first gigs there," Williams says. "We were billed with other singers in a 'Battle of the Groups.' One of those groups, of all things, were the Temptations. I mean, we were hardly known outside of town, and here we were, sharing the bill equally with the 'big guys.'"

Before long, however, they would fit into that "big guys" category. After attracting audiences with their finger-snapping style, the quintet caught the attention of Cleveland deejay Eddie O'Jay at WABQ-AM, who hosted sock hops at the Call and Post. The influential disc jockey befriended the young men and helped steer them in the right musical direction by introducing them to Motown king Berry Gordy, who gave them some tips for making it in the business. To honor the man who paved the way to their success, the group changed its name to the O'Jays in 1961. A Greater Cleveland legend was born.

The group began recording singles in 1963 and for the next four years released hits such as "Lonely Drifter," "Lipstick Traces (on a Cigarette)," and "I'll Be Sweeter To-morrow (Than I Was Today)" for Imperial Records and they released their debut album, *Comin' Through,* with Imperial in November 1965. By then the group was singing and dancing across the country and was on its way to becoming an international success story. During that steady climb to the top, however, there was a change in lineup. Isles left the group in 1965 and moved to California, and Massey exited in 1972 to form his own record company in Atlanta. Massey's move was ill-timed, given that the group's first big hit, "Back Stabbers," was released later that same year. William Powell was forced to retire from the group in 1976 when he was diagnosed with cancer, though he continued to record with them. Powell succumbed to the disease in May the following year. In his place came a familiar name in the R&B world, Sammy Strain, who'd already made a name for himself with Little Anthony and the Imperials.

In 1968, the O'Jays formed a friendship with songwriters/producers Kenny Gamble and Leon Huff, who were founding fathers of the Philadelphia Sound. Their record firm, Philadelphia International, was established in 1972, and the O'Jays were among the first to record on that label. The duo's songs combined with the trio's distinct vocal sound turned the collaboration to gold; the group's debut effort on that label gave the O'Jays their first No. 1 hit record. Both the single "Back Stabbers" and the album of the same name sold more than a million copies in 1972, forever securing their place in R&B history.

After that monster hit came another. "Love Train" hit No. 1 on *Billboard* within weeks and ultimately became a platinum seller in 1972, making it their biggest success to date. The song was nominated for a Grammy in 1973 for Best R&B Vocal Performance by a Duo, Group, or Chorus, but lost to Gladys Knight and the Pips' "Midnight Train to Georgia." By then, there was no stopping these hometown heroes. "Put Your Hands Together," "992 Arguments," "For the Love of Money," "Let Me Make Love to You," "Give the People What They Want," "I Love Music (Part 1)," and "Use Ta Be My Girl" all made the U.S. charts. "For the Love of Money" was nominated for a Grammy in 1974 for Best R&B Vocal Performance, though Rufus's "Tell Me Something Good" nabbed the award. Then in 1978 "Use Ta Be My Girl" lost the Grammy to Earth, Wind & Fire's "All 'n' All." But the hits kept coming. The group's 1973 album, *The O'Jays in Philadelphia,* was yet another best-seller.

In addition to their recording success, the group was famous for its live performances. The O'Jays "vocal choreography," so popular with sixties Motown singing groups, put them on top as stage performers. Their fancy footwork, however, didn't come naturally. Working for Motown Records, Cholly Atkins's job was to choreograph and teach stage etiquette to young music groups who often came out of Detroit's inner city. "Cholly is just amazing," Williams comments. "And he never made it easy on us. The hardest thing is that he devises dance steps that are actually contrary to the music. Kind of like tappin' your head and rubbin' your stomach at the same time. But somehow he'd get us to do it, and it always ends up looking great on stage. We'd rehearse with him for eight weeks straight, seven or more hours a day. And it was always worth it. Cholly got us prepared, and no one does it better." Atkins also coached the Temptations, the Four Tops, Smokey Robinson and the Miracles, the Supremes, Gladys Knight and the Pips, and Marvin Gaye. Now in his eighties, the 1989 Tony Award–winning dance man continues working, staging shows for professional acts and teaching vocal choreography at dance companies and college universities. He also keeps tabs on such former protégés as the O'Jays, who still seek him out for new dance numbers. "I've spent twenty-four years working with the O'Jays," Atkins has said of the group. "And they're still one of my favorites to work with."

Throughout the 1970s, the singing group took its choreographed act on the road and met with sold-out shows wherever they went. Then there were the albums: *Ship Ahoy* (1973), *Live in London* (1974), *Survival* (1975), and *Family Reunion* (1975), which all went platinum. There was *Message in the Music* (1976), *Travelin' at the Speed of Thought* (1977), *So Full of Love* (1978), and *Identify Yourself* (another platinum winner in 1979). In the 1980s came *My Favorite Person* (1982), *When Will I See You Again* (1983), *Love and More* and *Greatest Hits* (1984), and *Let Me Touch You* (1987). Topping off the decade was *Serious,* which reached No. 7 on the album chart and featured the No. 1 hit single, "Have You Had Your Love Today." One could never say the O'Jays don't stay on top of trends. Thanks to Levert's son, Gerald, the 1989 O'Jays' single had the grooves and style of hip-hop, having been produced by the next-generation Levert, along with musical friend Marc Gordon.

In the summer of 1997, the group, which includes Clevelander Eric Grant, released its first album in nearly ten years, "Love You to Tears." That recording was also produced by Gerald Levert of the modern-day R&B success LeVert (see Chapter 15). The O'Jays continue to do weekend shows throughout the nation, carrying on a tradition of inspiring and entertaining capacity crowds, based on the simple fact that their songs, style, and vocal blends remain timeless.

On February 26, 1998, the O'Jays received the coveted and prestigious Pioneer Award in New York. As R&B's highest honor, it is bestowed to artists that have helped shape the music of that genre. "I've always said we'll be like the Mills Brothers in terms of longevity," Williams claims. "It's already been forty years, and we'll keep going because we still love it. It's just that simple."

The Short Cuts (1957–63)

Two sisters from Cleveland Heights were the darlings of the local pop circuit in 1959. Mary Ellen and Margy (often spelled Margie) Keegan were students at the Ursuline Academy of the Sacred Heart High School when they began their musical journey. "I had started a pantomime group with some friends," Mary Ellen Fath explains. "There were five of us then and we all had short hair, so I thought up the name Short Cuts, taking the idea from the Crew Cuts. We did songs like 'Little Darlin' by the Diamonds, 'Come Go With Me' by the Del Vikings, and Elvis's 'Teddy Bear.' I did a pretty good imitation of Elvis, too!"

From a family of five girls and one boy, Mary Ellen and Margy, closest in age at fifteen months apart, began singing together at home. Both recall that music was a big

The Short Cuts, Margy and Mary Ellen Keegan, 1959. *Courtesy of Mary Ellen Fath.*

part of their growing-up years. "Mom had a beautiful voice and would sing with her cousin at all the family gatherings," recalls Margy Lamb. "And her brother was a recognized opera singer in Cleveland, though he died at an early age. Our father's brother was in theater and radio in Chicago. So we have show business in our blood!" When the pantomime group disbanded, the sisters kept the name Short Cuts and began writing their own songs. "We loved that three-part harmony of the McGuire sisters," Mary Ellen recalls. "We were also influenced by the Lennon sisters and Andrea Carroll who we'd see on the 'Gene Carroll Show.' The Short Cuts began singing their original songs and the pop tunes of the day at record hops, county fairs, and local TV and radio shows, including Bill Randle's radio show on WERE. Soon they were shopping for a record deal. By this time they had graduated high school and had decided to take a shot at stardom. "We started making some demo records on our own," Margy says. "We rented the studio time ourselves [at Audio Recording] and we used our own musicians. Our friend Jo [Josephine] Ditchman played piano, and our cousin Tim McHenry played drums. Mary Ellen played the ukelele. Bill Randle liked our music, so we got him to pitch it for us, and he was instrumental in selling the master to Carlton Records."

The single, "I'll Hide My Love," with b-side "Don't Say He's Gone," ultimately sold 30,000 copies and made it on the regional charts. The duo then went on an eastern seaboard tour that included an appearance on Dick Clark's *American Bandstand* on May 18, 1959. "We were doing six appearances a day on that two-week tour," Mary Ellen recalls. "It was fun, but hectic. And of course, we didn't have any money. So our cousins, aunts, and uncles all pulled together and helped us financially to buy the proper clothes and things we needed."

The Short Cuts became merely a memory soon after Mary Ellen married in 1963, with Margy marrying soon after. Both women spent the next few decades raising their families. Today, Mary Ellen resides in the Cleveland area, while Margy lives in Atlanta. But their love of singing together remains. "Now that our children are on their own, we've been thinking about this new project," Margy says. "We'd like to put together a CD with some original songs written for our grandchildren. And, just for fun, put it on eBay for grandmothers, and their grandchildren, everywhere to enjoy!"

Poni-Tails (1957–60)

One of the earliest pop/rock girl groups in the nation was from the North Coast. The Poni-Tails consisted of three eighteen year olds from Lyndhurst's Brush High School. The singers, Toni Cistone (lead vocalist), Patti McCabe (low harmony), and Karen Topinka (high harmony, but soon replaced by LaVerne Novak from Regina High School), started performing at school dances in the late 1950s.

"It was really just a lark how we got together," says Toni (Cistone) Costabile. "When we were seniors, we sang in a talent show and soon after that, my neighbor suggested we go to Audio Recording in Cleveland and record a song, which we did. Then we had to decide on a name. The Crew Cuts were really big then, so we wanted to have a name

The Poni-Tails in Germany, 1959. *Left to right:* Laverne Novak, Toni Cistone, and Patti McCabe. *Photo by Dr. Herr V. Meister. Courtesy of Laverne Glavac.*

contrary to them and came up with the Poni-Tails. It was a problem at first because our hair was still short, and when we'd pull it up, there were these little stubs hanging down." Because Novak had a short bob when she joined the group, she would attach an artificial ponytail to her hair for every performance, in keeping with the group's namesake.

The teenagers recorded their first song, "Your Wild Heart," in 1957. Soon after, their manager, Joe Petito, negotiated a three-year contract with ABC Paramount (now MCA). It wasn't long before they had recorded ten songs for the label. One of them was "Just My Luck to Be Fifteen," which became a regional hit but failed to make the national mark. Then in 1958 the Poni-Tails recorded a song written by New Yorker Fred Tobias, a pop/rock ballad called "Born Too Late." Cleveland deejay Bill Randle gave it a spin and broke the Poni-Tails's career.

"That song went all the way up to No. 2 on *Billboard* charts by July of that year," Costabile says. "But we just couldn't bump 'Volare' by Domenico off the No. 1 position." Nonetheless, the song propelled the young girls to overnight success. This swift rise to national recognition may have benefited from the song's theme of a young girl's dreams of an older boy, which hit a teen-angst nerve.

Their popularity enabled the trio to travel around the world, performing with such '50s icons as Bobby Darin, Connie Francis, Nat King Cole, Frankie Avalon, Paul Anka, the Everly Brothers, Chubby Checker, and Bo Diddley. During an unforgettable European tour, the teens found themselves in Germany at the same time as Elvis Presley, who was serving out his army duties there in July 1959. For three starry-eyed girls from Cleveland, the memory would last a lifetime. "We not only met him, he invited us to the house where he was living," Costabile says, her voice rising a touch. "I couldn't be-lieve our luck. He told us how glad he was to see someone from the States and asked us all kinds of questions about what was happening back home. I remember we had pop and pizza while he sang 'Amazing Grace.' Then he shocked us by breaking into our own 'Born Too Late'! He asked us to come back the next day and of course we did. He was very hospitable and made us feel comfortable. Those were two pretty wonderful days!"

The group's sole hit is still played on oldies radio stations across the country. Rock historian and Cleveland native Norm N. Nite cites "Born Too Late" as one of his all-time favorite records from that era. As often would happen with bands in the uncertain pop/rock world, the Poni-Tails' follow-up record, "Seven Minutes to Heaven," did not fare as well, and Cleveland's first all-girl pop group broke up when their contract ended. But, anyone living in Cleveland back then recalls their short-lived celebrity.

Today, lead singer Toni (Cistone) Costabile and LaVerne (Novak) Glavac remain in the Cleveland area; Patti (McCabe) Barnes died from cancer in 1989. Glavac, who now sells herbal products for weight loss and wellness programs, can boast another rock connection. Her son Bob Richey (known as Kurtt Terdd) is a musician in his own right—the founding member of the '80s punk rock group the Pink Holes. Costabile is retired from the Mayfield School District, where she worked in special education, and she continues to sing—in her church choir.

The Poni-Tails are enshrined on the "One-Hit Wonders" wall in the Rock and Roll Hall of Fame and Museum. In January 1997 Costabile represented the group at a press conference announcing the Rock Hall's "My Town" exhibit, a tribute to Cleveland-area groups and musicians.

The Secrets (1961–64)

Coming on the heels of the Poni-Tails's success was another girl group that picked up where their '50s counterpart left off. The Secrets started out as a trio in 1961 with Karen Gray, Jackie Allen, and Carole Raymont, all eighteen years old and from East Cleveland's Shaw High School. "We basically began singing at things like mother-daughter banquets, WHK and KYW sock hops, and after-school functions," recalls Karen (Gray) Cipriani. "Once we graduated, Patty Miller from Eastlake North High joined in. By 1962 we were singing at places like the Green Darby and Hires Lounge on the east side and opened a lot for Tom King and the Starfires, who were really popular back then. And when we played the Chateau on the west side, we were the act following Barbra Streisand!"

It was the singing engagement at the French West nightclub in Parma in the spring of 1963 that got the young women noticed by a Philips West Coast artist and repertoire (A&R) man. Before long, the girls were signing a contract and recording in New York's

Bell Sound Studio, sharing the same label as Lesley Gore ("It's My Party"), the Shangri-Las ("Leader of the Pack"), and the Angels ("My Boyfriend's Back"). Their hit song "The Boy Next Door," written by Johnny Madera and David White (of Danny and the Juniors), sold 870,000 copies and peaked at *Billboard*'s No. 18 in December 1963. "That song gave us the opportunity to travel with some great artists like Bobby Rydell, Dionne Warwick, Lou Christie, Lesley Gore, Freddie 'Boom Boom' Cannon, Vic Dana, and we opened for the Dave Clark Five at the Civic in Pittsburgh—10,000 kids, our biggest crowd ever," Cipriani recalls. "But the time we opened for Connie Francis at the Palace Theater is probably our favorite memory. We thought she was a great entertainer and a real nice person."

The singing quartet also landed on *American Bandstand*. "Initially, we were scheduled to do the show the weekend of November 22, 1963. But of course, everyone knows what happened then. We got to our hotel and we saw all these people against the wall crying because they'd just announced President Kennedy had been shot. From that moment on, everything—the show's taping, a scheduled sock hop, even the air flights—were all cancelled. We spent the weekend in our hotel room watching TV and mourning with the rest of the country." The Secrets did manage an appearance on Dick Clark's show the following February; they were the last act to perform before the show moved its headquarters from Philadelphia to Los Angeles.

But, because their record fell short of selling one million copies, the Secrets were unable to make an album (a million-selling single was a prerequisite in the contract). Although the quartet recorded a few other singles, including "Hey, Big Boy," "Oh, Donnie," and "He Doesn't Want You," none reached that goal. The women decided to

The Secrets in harmony at the Chateau, where they shared the bill with up-and-coming star Barbra Streisand, June 1964. *Courtesy of Karen Cipriani.*

abandon their music career and parted ways in July 1964. Each got married, and their debut song retired to the land of one-hit wonders.

"One thing I'll never forget was the time we were playing Cobo Hall in Detroit in the fall of '63," Cipriani says. "We were the headliners, and one of the opening acts was this black girl group who was the lead-in act. Well, they did a couple little songs and I remember Carole saying to me, 'Well, their choreography is great, but they'll never make it.' That group was the Supremes!"

Andrea Carroll

Andrea Carroll had a busy childhood and most of it was spent in the limelight. Born on October 3, 1946, in Cleveland, Andrea Carroll began her performing career at age three when she first performed on the *The Gene Carroll Show* (no relation), an amateur talent show that was the longest running show in American TV history, airing 1948–79. The young singer also won such beauty contests as Little Miss Cleveland and Little Miss Ohio. At age eight she won the *Cleveland News* Star Night contest, after being chosen by an impressive judging team of Perry Como, Nat King Cole, and Patti Page. Her singing appearance at Cleveland's Alpine Village at age twelve got her more notice, and she later won the Walt Disney National Talent Contest. From 1949 until 1972, however, she was a mainstay on Gene Carroll's Sunday afternoon television show.

In July 1961, Carroll released "Young and Lonely" and "Please Don't Talk to the Lifeguard," which increased her local popularity, though neither song made a dent on national charts. Two years later, the seventeen year old finally grazed the singles chart with "It Hurts to Be Sixteen" (Big Top Records), but the fame was short-lived. And as luck would have it, in 1965 Dianne Ray covered "Please Don't Talk to the Lifeguard" and took the song up to No. 31.

Today, Andrea Carroll Hill resides in Burbank, California, and has a doctorate in clinical psychology.

Ruby and the Romantics (1962–71)

Originally an all-male group from Akron, George Lee (first tenor), Edward Roberts (second tenor), Robert Mosley (baritone), and Leroy Fann (bass) were known around the lounge circuit as the Supremes. But when they first heard Ruby Nash (Garnett) sing, the group decided her luminous voice was just what it needed. "I'd been singin' since I was three," Nash recalls. "But I never performed on stage until long after high school. They'd have these talent shows around Easter-time at the Akron Community Service Center (now the Urban League), and I started singing with a girl group there. I remember there were five of us, though I can't recall the name we used. But it was at one of these shows that I was asked to join [the Supremes]." It was 1961, and by then, Nash was already thirty years old.

The group played some area talent shows as well as local clubs, including the notable Leo's Casino. As their exposure broadened, Leroy Kirkland, an arranger for Kapp Records, took the group to New York. There, Allen Stanton, the well-known A&R director of Kapp Records, heard them sing and signed the group in the fall of 1962. Capitalizing on the boy-girl hook, Stanton suggested they change their name to Ruby and the Romantics. One day while listening to demos with Stanton, Nash took a liking to a song cowritten by songwriters Mort Garson and Bob Hillard. Knowing the song was special, Garson and Stanton questioned whether this was the right group to record it. Finally, after much insistence on Nash's part, the group recorded "Our Day Will Come," and the song quickly rose to the top, reaching the coveted No. 1 spot on March 23, 1963.

This smash hit was followed by other songs for Kapp, including "Young Wings Can Fly," "My Summer Love," and "Does He Really Care for Me." The group also recorded the original version of "Hey There, Lonely Boy," which was later covered by Eddie Holman, who changed the title to "Hey There, Lonely Girl." Though these did well, none came close to the success of that first record. But according to Nash, that didn't matter. They thoroughly enjoyed their glory days. "We traveled often during those years," she recalls. "We played a lot in Toronto but also went overseas. We performed in clubs in London, Germany, Bermuda, Bahamas, and even the West Indies. One of my favorite memories is playing the Apollo with all the various Motown acts. And through the years we played with every one of them. And the show we did at the Akron Civic Theater with Smokey Robinson and the Miracles was very special."

Today, only Ruby Nash Garnett and Ronald Mosley survive. "It's been written many times that I changed the group over the years, but it's just not true," says Garnett. "It was the same five of us throughout the whole time. And it's a shame there's only two of us left. And here, I was older than all of them!" Although past retirement age, the sixty-something former singer works full-time as a cashier for the Salvation Army. "We didn't get the royalties we should've gotten," she adds. "Remember, that was back when no one questioned what the record companies said or did." The group did, however, get just recognition when Ruby and the Romantics received the coveted Pioneer Award from the Rhythm and Blues Foundation in 1997.

Dave C. and the Sharptones (1956–71; re-formed 1982–)

Despite a ten-year hiatus, this group is the longest-running band in Cleveland rock history. Formed back in 1956 when drummer/singer Dave Cox from John Marshall High School got together with friends Harry Willis (guitar) and Gene Schokowski (saxophone), the Motown-inspired group included guitarist Bob Evetts, bassist Ron Lissinger, drummer Bob Pricing, and Rudy Purino on tenor sax. Influences include Chuck Berry, Jackie Wilson, Jerry Lee Lewis, and Elvis. "We got our name from Sears & Roebuck," Dave C. recalls. "That's where Willis bought his amp. It was a Silvertone, so one day we were trying to think of a name and we looked at the amp and said, 'That's called the Silvertones, we'll be the Sharptones.'

"We started playing some gigs on the west side and every Thursday night at Skateland at E. 93rd and Euclid. We then wrote and recorded an instrumental called 'The Skateland Bounce' [on the Goldleaf label]. The song did well locally and got airplay on stations like WJMO, which was the top black radio station at the time. That really helped it sell." The Sharptones also recorded "Diane" and "Black Pepper," local hits in 1964 and they continued playing on both the East and West Sides, at Deckers Lounge (at W. 120th and Lorain), the Tramend Lounge (Union and Broadway), and the Peppermint (W. 58th and Lorain, formerly Olsen's). From 1962 to 1963, the group was the house band at the Heidelberg on W. 25th, where they played every weekend. Monday nights they played at the Virginian Lounge in Shaker Heights, where they brought in fans of all ages, from twenty-one to eighty. By the late 1960s, Dave C. and the Sharptones was performing at the prestigious Leo's Casino. "Leo's was a very exciting place," Dave C. says. "We got to rub elbows with the best, like the O'Jays and all the big Motown groups. You felt really privileged to play there."

While WHK radio man and Peppermint Lounge owner Carl Reese was helping to promote the group, the club's manager, Walt Masky, got them their best gig of all—on national television. "We started playing on the *Upbeat* show in 1964," notes Dave C., who after seeing James Brown at the Cleveland Arena abandoned the drums for the microphone—front and center. "We got to see many greats on that show—everyone we admired, like Otis Redding and Joe Tex. And producer Herman Spero arranged for us to meet the Beatles at their hotel when they were in town. Now that was somethin'."

Members at one time or another included Bill Morris (guitar), Travis Pearson (bass), and Mike Geraci (sax). The group disbanded in 1971 when members either were drafted or got married. "It nearly broke my heart," Dave Cox says. He spent the next decade working in a factory, until 1982, when he found musicians interested in reforming the group. The New Sharptones are Dave C.; John Hemmings on drums, guitarist and group manager Doug Cowell, Matt Haller on sax, Tim Cernan and Tom Miller on keyboards, and J. D. Strader on trumpet. The band plays on both sides of Cleveland, most notably weekend gigs at places like Dick's Last Resort in the Flats, Light Rock in North Ridgeville, Sawmill Creek Resort in Huron, and Doc and Louie's on the West Side.

Bocky and the Visions (1961–65)

This early pop/rock band started out as a four-man group with no instrumentation (think Four Seasons). Robert DiPasquale (a.k.a. Bocky), the undeniable leader, quickly attracted fans with his powerful vocal style. Early members included Sonny Peters, Arnie Immerman, and Jimmy Randazzo, and there were also sax and horn players Mike Geraci and Vic Walkuski. In 1961 the group recorded "All Through the Night" and "Tell Me You're Mine." Those who remember that early rock scene, however, best

The all-vocal Bocky and the Visions Quartet, 1963. *Clockwise from top:* Arnie Immerman, Jimmy Randazzo, Robert Dipasquale (a.k.a. Bocky), and Sonny Peters. *Courtesy of Buddy Maver.*

recall Bocky's 1964 lineup, which included Richie Greene (a.k.a. Dick Whittington) on lead guitar, Tony Bodanza (also known as Tony Styles) on rhythm guitar, Don Schwartz on bass, and Buddy Maver on drums.

"We went to Cleveland Recording Studio right away," recalls Maver, who began drumming at age thirteen and joined the Visions four years later. "We recorded 'I'm Not Worth It,' 'Spirit of '64,' and a few other singles. It was an exciting time."

While playing at all the "in" clubs on both sides of Cleveland, Bocky and the Visions cut a deal with Philips record label, making it the first official Cleveland-area rock band to sign with a national label. "Spirit of '64" and "I'm Not Worth It," both written by Bodanza, got airplay on the top radio stations and became the group's biggest local hits. "Bocky and the Visions was the biggest [of the area groups at the time]," recalls fan and Outsiders member Sonny Geraci. "They had songs that hit the Top 10 in Cleveland. Kids, myself included, thought they were a national act because we always heard them on the radio."

During its four-year reign as Cleveland's top band, Bocky and the Visions opened for the biggest acts of the day at the "hottest" venues. At Public Hall they opened for Chuck Berry, the Rolling Stones, the Dave Clark Five, the Beach Boys, the Four Tops, and the Shangri-Las. They also opened for the Animals at the Cleveland Arena, and for Jan and Dean at Euclid Beach Park. They appeared on the *American Bandstand*–type dance show *The Big 5 Show* (pre-*Upbeat*). "That whole period was a gas," Maver says. "Opening for the Rolling Stones in 1964 was particularly memorable. It was all so low-tech. I don't even think the drums were miked. Charlie Watts was set up on the floor, and there was no drum riser at all. What I'll never forget about that show was a bunch of girls swarmed the stage, and one girl came behind Charlie, grabbed him from behind, and they both fell over backwards!"

When Bocky and the Visions broke up in 1965, members went on to other bands. Bocky wound up in Rastus, while Maver formed Richie and the Fortunes with Richie Greene, Bodanza, Schwartz (soon replaced by Jay Mohler), and sax player Terry MacLoud. "The musicianship was of the highest quality," Maver says of the Fortunes. "We were an R&B band and did seventeen James Brown songs when other bands were doing the Beatles. There was this one place—the legendary Sands—in Portage Lakes that was an old speakeasy. Every night . . . there was a line of people around the building waiting to get in."

In 1967 the group became Dick Whittington's Cats, the name they recorded under when their regional hit, Wilson Pickett's "In the Midnight Hour," was released. (The record, incidentally, was produced by Chuck Mangione.) A year later, Maver left to form the Charades (later Charade) with Bodanza. That lineup included guitarists Bill Hanna and John Vossos. It became one of the most popular dance bands during its two-year incarnation. The Charades played to packed houses at the Agora, the Plato, and the In Spot (Eastgate Coliseum, Mayfield Road). In 1970 the group signed with Epic Records and released "And You Do" shortly before disbanding.

Although members went various ways, they came together nearly two decades later when tragedy struck. In March 1988, Bocky was killed during an altercation on a city street. Within months, musicians throughout the area banded together to help his widow and children and to pay tribute to their friend. The result was the "Cleveland's Legends of Rock" benefit concert produced by Maver. The outdoor summer event took place in downtown's Mall C and included reunions of the best of Cleveland's rock from the past and present. Members from Dave C. and the Sharptones, the Twilighters, Rastus, the Choir, Michael Stanley Band, Rainbow Canyon, Wild Horses, and Beau Coup all participated. It was just one example of the camaraderie, not competition, that has always been a hallmark of Cleveland-area musicians.

The Grasshoppers (1962–66)

Today, the Grasshoppers are remembered as being Ben Orr's first band. Orr went on to be the bassist/singer and cofounder of the new wave group the Cars. But in the early 1960s, singer/guitarist Dante Rossi was the star of this West Side quartet. The original members included Rossi, Louie Pratelli (lead guitar), Jerry Zadar (bass), and Sid Turner (drums). The name came from the boys' fondness for leaping about on stage when they played. Those celebrated antics, along with their beaty, pop-style music, helped earn the group a faithful local following.

In 1964, Rossi left and was replaced by seventeen-year-old rhythm guitarist Ben Orr (born Benjamin Orzechowski) from Parma's Valley Forge High School. "When Benny was asked to join the Grasshoppers, well, that was like someone asking you to join the Dave Clark Five," recalls drummer Wayne Weston, who replaced Turner when the latter was drafted in 1966. "That was *the* band back then."

I met Benny at a Battle of the Bands at Valley Forge High. I was in the group, the Castles, with Rick Caon on lead and John Matuska on bass. The Grasshoppers had just done this *Upbeat* show in the auditorium earlier that day, and we were in the battle of the bands that night. As we started playing, we noticed Benny come in the side door. I remember we thought that was kinda cool, him coming to hear us play, because he was this local star. Afterward, Ben came up to us and said, "I like your band." Then the following week, he contacted us and said, "Hey, two of our guys just quit [Pratelli and Zadar] and we've got bookings." And Sid was getting drafted. So, it was like, boom, we became the Grasshoppers. What's funny is I always knew Ben as a rhythm guitarist, never saw him with a bass.

Orr had become a Grasshopper just in time for the *Upbeat* craze. The group was the hit show's house band, and by 1965 they had released two regional hits: "Mod Socks" and "Pink Champagne (and Red Roses)," the latter written by Orr. As a result of the band's TV exposure, their songs received some national attention, though it died down quickly.

In 1966, the Grasshoppers became Mixed Emotions and then the Colours after acquiring manager Ray Taylor (Taylor also managed the Choir). The group played often on the West Side, mostly at the Rolling Stone Club (later to be called It's Boss) on Brookpark Road. But just as the group was getting ready to sign a record deal, Orr was drafted into the army (though he received a deferment months later as an only surviving son), and the group disbanded.

About 1970 Orr left Cleveland and moved to Columbus. There he and friend Ric Ocasek formed several bands before ending up in Boston and putting together their most successful union, the Cars, in 1976. Two years later the Cars, with Orr on bass and often vocals, was voted *Rolling Stone*'s best new band and hit big with "My Best Friend's Girl" and "Just What I Needed." The Cars' self-titled debut album became a platinum seller. After a string of hits including "Moving in Stereo," "Bye Bye Love," "Candy-O," and "Drive," the group disbanded in 1987. Orr continued on with solo projects, which included his 1986 release *The Lace*. Although he never moved back to his hometown, the Cleveland-bred rocker kept in close contact with his family and friends until his death from pancreatic cancer on October 3, 2000.

The Grasshoppers, 1964. *Top from left:* Sid Turner and Jerry Zadar; *bottom from left:* Ben Orr and Louie Pratelli. *Photo by Diane Akins.*

But the Grasshoppers live on as a result of those few, but well-remembered, recordings still given airplay on oldies stations, like WMJI-FM. "When you consider all the bands around back then," says *Sun Newspapers* writer and WELW radio host Jeff Piorkowski, "I think the Grasshoppers captured the sound of the early '60s the best."

The GTOs (1966–69; formerly Joey and the Continentals; later Montage)

Although *Upbeat* fans will forever remember the GTOs as the show's one-time house band, loyal longtime admirers recall Joey and the Continentals. Over a period of ten years, four of the original members stayed together through three separate incarnations (quite possibly a record in this field). Formed in 1961, Joey Porrello (lead singer and trumpet), Ray Miller (lead guitar), Don Evans (bass), Gene Marotta (drums and vocals), and Dennis Slivco (sax, conga, and vocals) made a name for themselves on the local club circuit long before they were nationally known. Only the lead guitarist would change over time, with Walter Nims (Tom King and the Starfires, Outsiders), Jack Godzich, and Russ Wichert alternately sharing that position.

"We were playing this bar, Luccione's, on Chardon Road in Richmond Heights," Don Evans recalls. "Walt Masky heard us and liked us. He and Carl Reese [then deejay at WHK] were booking record hops around town at the time. So they started promoting us and got us jobs on both the east and west sides of town. It happened real fast."

Joey and the Continentals, 1965. *Left to right:* Walt Nims (lead guitar), Gene Marotta (drums), Dennis Slivco (sax), Joey Porrello (vocals), and Don Evans (bass). *Photo by Lynn Rebman. Courtesy of Don Evans.*

As Joey and the Continentals, their sound was a lively blend of R&B and jazz, with their recorded songs a mix of covers and originals. In 1964 they recorded "Linda," which was followed the next year by "Baby" and "No One Can Make My Sunshine Smile."

"'No One Can Make My Sunshine Smile' was an old Everly Brothers tune," says Gene Marotta, who was just fifteen when he joined the group.

> That song should've been a big hit for us, but we had the worst timing. You see, right away it played on local radio and was an instant hit, and soon became a regional hit—at one time to No. 4 in Akron. Because it climbed the charts here so quickly, in the Top 10, the record company suspected we were buying our own records [called "hyping a record"]. Then the week it was ready to break nationally was the same time the Beatles came to town, and the radio stations literally played nothing but the Beatles that entire week, which made our numbers drop so considerably, the record company decided we really must have been hyping our record and refused to distribute it nationally. It was too bad 'cause it was really a great song.

But luck did come their way in 1965 when Masky, who also produced the local TV show *The Big 5 Show*, hired them as the show's house band, changing its name to the more hip-sounding GTOs. When *The Big 5 Show* became the nationally syndicated *Upbeat*, the GTOs became national television stars. "That was probably the most exciting time of my life," Evans says. "But, of course, then I didn't realize just what we were in the middle of. We'd come into the studio and there'd be Jose Feliciano or Kenny Rogers. We were backing some of the most popular artists of that era, like James Brown, Bobby Vee, Chad and Jeremy; but make no mistake, it was real work. Fortunately all of us could read music, because we had to learn every artist's song, like Gene Pitney's 'Town Without Pity,' which was twenty pages long, a lot of chord changes, rhythm changes. . . . It wasn't like, 'Hey, we're on TV.' It was a real job."

Despite their television exposure, the GTOs would boast only one Top 10 hit. The Brian Wilson tune "She Rides with Me" brought the group brief national fame in 1966. The song stopped in its tracks at No. 90 on *Billboard* charts. Marotta explains why:

> When we were getting ready to record that song, we had a choice between going with Cameo Parkway, which was a bigger, more secure record company, or Frank Sleigh, who'd just started a new record label. Sleigh had produced, along with Bob Crew, the first few Four Seasons' hits, including "Big Girls Don't Cry."
> Sleigh also offered us a better deal, so we went with him. "She Rides with Me" became the "Pick Hit of the Week" at New York station WMCA-AM, which at the time was the biggest radio station in the country. Well, smack in the middle of that same week, Sleigh filed bankruptcy, which meant the master was tied up in it and we couldn't press any more records, couldn't sell or distribute it. And that was that.

The group left *Upbeat* in 1969, changed its name to Montage, and added female member Tampa Lann's vocal and keyboard talents to the group. (A few years later, Lann would play keyboards for the Bee Gees.) "Musically, Montage was the best the group ever was, a real cookin' band," Marotta notes. "Ironically, when we were the most popular, as the GTOs, we were probably the least talented." He admits that by 1971 time and changes took their toll, and the group disbanded for good.

Today, founder Joey Porrello is a successful audio/video producer in New Jersey, with ninety gold, platinum, and multiplatinum awards to his credit. Over the years he has worked with the O'Jays, the Isley Brothers, and Ben Vereen, among others. In 2000, he released a CD called *Cleveland, the Heart of It All,* which is being distributed through Cleveland Action Music. He recently told one reporter, "With all the positive changes that have happened to the city during the '90s . . . I felt compelled to let the entire country know about it."

The Baskerville Hounds (1964–73, 1980–82; re-formed 1999)

In 1964, singer/guitarist and ex-Grasshopper Dante Rossi formed this five-piece band, originally calling it the Dantes. Members consisted of Bill Emery (bass/vocals), Doug McCutcheon (keyboards/vocals), Larry Meece (lead guitar/vocals), and John Kirkpatrick (drums). When WHK deejay Ron Brittain took over as their manager, he decided to call the West Side group Tulu Babies.

As Tulu Babies they released "The Hurtin' Kind," which did well locally. In 1965 Jim Testa, who produced the record, became the group's manager and changed its name to the Baskerville Hounds. Two more local hits came their way: "Debbie" and "Space Rock, Parts 1 & 2." The former made it to No. 99 on *Billboard,* and the latter ultimately reached No. 60, because "Space Rock" became the theme song for the Friday night TV show *Ghoulardi.* Nearly every teen on the North Coast tuned in to watch Ghoulardi, played by the former WHK deejay Ernie Anderson. (Anderson's show was such a beloved ritual with teens that police claimed the city's street crime rate would actually drop during the show's time slot.) The Baskerville Hounds's upbeat rock sound often drew up to a thousand fans at their club gigs, and they opened for the Rolling Stones at Public Hall in 1965. They also opened both the North Ridgeville and the Mentor Hullabaloo in 1967.

A series of turnovers took place in the late '60s. In 1965, Kirkpatrick left and Michael Macron stepped in on drums (replaced by Bobby Dillinger in 1970). McCutcheon left in '66, replaced by Jack Topper. Meece left for the service in 1968 and was replaced by Roger Lewis, who was in turn replaced by Danny Cox. Tom Evans came in on bass but was later replaced by Roland Solomon.

In 1967, the Baskerville Hounds released a self-titled album that included "Last Night on the Back Porch" and "Caroline." In 1969 they recorded "Hold Me," which peaked at No. 88 on *Billboard* and rose to No. 1 regionally in cities such as Erie, Buffalo, and Tampa. Problems developed with manager Testa, but the group was bound to a contract.

By 1973, however, they had had enough and broke up. The group briefly re-formed in 1980 with Rossi, Meece, Emery, Macron, and McCutcheon, but by 1985 Rossi had turned country and spent the next decade playing various places catering to country music. Two of the bands, Quint and Rag and a Rose, included Baskerville buddy McCutcheon. Today, Rossi, owner of a hair salon in Parma Heights, has re-formed the band with Meece, Emery, McCutcheon, and Dillinger. "It's an updated version of Baskerville Hounds with a variety of new, all-original, good ol' rock 'n' roll music," he says. The group is playing the local club circuit and released a new CD, *Look at Us Now*, in 2000.

The Outsiders, formerly Tom King and the Starfires (1965–68)

In 1964, Shaw High School graduate and rhythm guitarist Tom King was enjoying local success with his group Tom King and the Starfires, which included guitarist Walter Nims, bassist Merton Madsen, drummer Howard Blank (who was replaced by sixteen-year-old Jim Fox, who then was replaced by Ronnie Harkai, later replaced by Dennie Benson), and sax player Dennis Slifko. The group always drew a sizeable crowd in the Cleveland area. At first their group sound featured instrumentals, with the focus on the horn section and occasional vocals by King. Then, like nearly every band that came after the British Invasion, the Starfires began concentrating on the English sound. With their unique blend of British and Motown, the Starfires became one of the area's top groups, playing popular clubs on both the East and West Side.

But King had even bigger aspirations—and an uncle who owned a small record company called Pama. Tom King and the Starfires recorded several songs on this label, including "Maybe Baby" and "Stronger Than Dirt." The latter was heard regularly on Ghoulardi's show. Meanwhile, baritone sax player Mike Geraci mentioned to his younger brother that King's band was looking for a vocalist. Eighteen-year-old Sonny Geraci, a recent graduate from John Adams High School, went to audition. His deep, smooth voice and dark, good looks fit the bill. By now, the band included King, Geraci, Madsen, Bill Bruno (replacing Nims at lead guitar), and Rick Biagiola (drums). As the new lineup was making headway with its contemporary style, King began searching out a bigger recording label. "It was a family situation, and I got into an argument with my uncle about it," recalls King. "I was soon deemed an outsider. So I decided to use it." The Outsiders became the new name for King's group.

At this time, King began dabbling in songwriting. With his brother-in-law, Chet Kelley, he penned a song titled "Time Won't Let Me." "Our new lead guitarist, Al Austin, played on that record, and he was terrific," recalls King. "He died in a car accident, and his tombstone says 'Time Won't Let Me.'" King and Mike Geraci contributed to the horn section on the song, which the group recorded at Cleveland Recording Company in the fall of 1965.

The Outsiders getting ready to record "Time Won't Let Me." *Left to right:* Bill Bruno, Sonny Geraci, Tom King, and Mert Madsen. *Courtesy of Ronald J. Harkai.*

In the meantime, their manager, Roger Karshner, signed the group to Capitol Records. For marketing purposes, Karshner labeled them as a California group, even in their hometown. (Karshner would later become vice president of Capitol Records. His 1971 book *The Music Machine* takes a cynical look at the record business and includes his history with the Outsiders under the name "the Misfits.") "During the time we came out," Geraci explains, "Cleveland radio stations frowned on playing local artists' records because they'd tried it before and nothing happened. So our manager told them we were from the West Coast, that Capitol was putting a lot of money behind us, and that we were going to be huge." True to Karshner's prediction, before the last blast of snow fell on Cleveland in March 1966, the Outsiders had a national hit record.

The group became a regular on *Upbeat* but soon were off on a national tour with pop idols Gene Pitney and the McCoys (with Dayton native Rick Derringer). "The first tour we did was a ten-day promotional tour for Capitol Records," Geraci recalls. "Time Won't Let Me" was "just breaking regionally. New York was the last stop, and we played on *Hullabaloo.* Chad and Jeremy ["Yesterday's Gone"] were hosting, and Bobby ["I Fought the Law"] Fuller was there, too. And there were screamin' kids all over the place. That whole experience was a real thrill 'cause we were just kids ourselves. Right after that, Dick Clark signed us to do one of his rock 'n' roll tours. That's when we realized we were definitely nationally known."

Geraci, whose influences include the Beatles, Dion, the Motown sound, and the O'Jays, recalls that first record, which has since become one of the great rock and roll classics. "We were ahead of everybody with that song. Over the years, a lot of successful people [in the industry] have sat eyeball-to-eyeball with me and said 'Time Won't Let Me' was a major influence for them. People in groups like Chicago [and] Tower of Power and James Gurcro, who produced hits for the Buckinghams, Blood, Sweat & Tears, and Chicago, all told me that song was their favorite track of all time."

The record had the perfect pop sound and produced what could be referred to as the true "Cleveland sound." But it was only the beginning in what proved a vintage year for the Outsiders. From their debut LP came the group's next hit single, "Girl in Love," which made it to No. 21 on the charts. This was followed by "Respectable," an Isley Brothers gem that made it to No. 15.

Then came a moderately successful single, "Help Me Girl" which was given to them by writers Scott English (who penned Barry Manilow's "Mandy") and Larry Weiss. Unfortunately, the songwriting duo had given the same song to British rock star Eric Burdon. Timing proved everything, indeed, when Burdon recorded "Help Me Girl" at the same time as the Outsiders. Burdon, who had just given a memorable performance at the famous Monterey Pop Festival, saw his version of the song peak at No. 29 while the Outsiders's interpretation stalled at No. 37. This unfortunate circumstance repeated itself when English and Weiss once again gave the Cleveland group a song called "Bend Me, Shape Me," which landed on their third album. The group declined to release it as a single. A year later, American Breed recorded the song, which hit the Top 10 in the U.S. Then Amen Corner did the same, taking "Bend Me, Shape Me" up the U.K. Top 10 charts.

Along with numerous concerts they played throughout the country, the Outsiders completed four albums for Capitol: *Time Won't Let Me* (1966), *The Outsiders, Album 2* (1966), *In* (1967), and *Happening Live* (1968). By the release of the fourth album, the group's members had begun swimming different tides, and it was soon clear the band was about to break up. The group dropped Karshner, and King took over the business end—a move made after band members received no royalties for their biggest hit because Karshner had taken over publishing rights. By 1967, however, King dropped out, but the band continued to tour with former Starfires guitarist Walter Nims and Rick D'Amato on bass. When Geraci and D'Amato left for California in 1968, King returned with a new singer, John Simonell.

In 1970 Geraci formed a new band in Los Angeles, with guitarist Jeff Hubbard of Minneapolis, bassist Doug Weimer of Indianapolis (later replaced by former Joey and the Continentals/GTOs/Montage bassist Don Evans), drummer Robert Neilson, and former Outsider bandmate guitarist/songwriter Walter Nims. This group recorded some songs under the Outsiders name, and King, who continued his band under the same moniker, was not amused. Before a lawsuit was issued, Geraci changed his group's name to Climax. In 1972 they recorded a song by Nims called "Precious and Few," which jumped to the No. 3 spot almost immediately and then catapulted to the coveted No. 1 position on *Billboard*. Because of continued radio airplay, the song remains a popular ballad decades later. "Precious and Few" became the group's signature song and its only major hit. In 1975, Climax disbanded, and Sonny Geraci returned home to Cleveland the following year. Meanwhile, Outsiders leader Tom King continued in the music business and today works in the production end of the industry.

After taking time off to live a "normal" life, working in his family's home improvement company and raising a family, Geraci returned to his musical roots in the mid-1980s. During that time, "oldies revival tours" became popular, and the veteran singer found himself back in demand. He began playing various package tours with other pop survivors such as Lou Christie, Lesley Gore, Billy J. Kramer, and Dennis Yost. Then, in the spring of 1997, a new recording, *Sonny Geraci—On the Verge,* was released on his own label, Precious Time Records. The CD, which was produced by Geraci and Cleveland musician Rich Spina (most known from his '70s band Love Affair), includes some re-recorded Outsiders songs in addition to new and cover material. Now in his fifties, Geraci continues to deliver on stage at various shows across the Midwest.

"Being in the Outsiders was the most fun I think I've ever had," Geraci notes. "Maybe because it was all new to me then and I was only eighteen. The ride going up was like a roller coaster, but it was absolutely a great ride. And it was a good experience traveling coast to coast. After that era, it all became more business-oriented. Today, especially, you've got to really hustle to keep your name out there. But really, nothing else beats it. Thank God for 'Precious and Few.' It remains on radio playlists across the country and it keeps us working. Seems no one gets tired of hearing it when we do our oldies shows."

Joe Jeffrey Group

In 1964, new Cleveland resident Joe Jeffrey began playing in vaious clubs around town. By 1969, the Joe Jeffrey Group hit it big with the song, "My Pledge of Love," which peaked at No. 14 on *Billboard.* The band is included in the "One-Hit Wonders" exhibit at the Rock and Roll Hall of Fame and Museum.

Our "Bubble-gum" Contributions: The Music Explosion and the Ohio Express

The late '60s introduced yet another music genre to American radio. The bubble-gum listeners trend lasted less than a decade, yet it spurred many fun-style groups and danceable hit songs. Bubble-gum could be described as a comeback of the sanitized version of early rock, as swimming against the rough tide of harder rock and roll sounds so prevalent at the time. Because of this, many of these groups were not taken seriously in the industry, and some failed to enjoy more than one hit. More successful groups include: Tommy James and the Shondells ("Mony Mony," 1968), 1910 Fruitgum Company ("Simon Says," 1968), the Monkees (their 1966 hit "Last Train to Clarkesville" was the first of many), and the "studio" group the Archies (debuted in 1968 with "Bang Shang-a-Lang" and copped a few more memorable hits before disappearing). The latter two groups were the brainchild of future rock concert host Don Kirshner, who developed and produced the bands' concept—their sound and their look. Strange as it is, the Archies weren't a real band but rather cartoon characters; the records were produced in a studio by various musicians, yet songs like "Sugar, Sugar" made it to No. 1 anyway. In turn, the Monkees were at least human, having been created specifically for a TV show about an American version of the Beatles. That group did manage to steer away from the bubble-gum image, and members proved themselves to be real musicians. By the mid-1970s, bubble-gum was replaced with disco, another short-lived craze.

On the North Coast, two groups from Mansfield—the Music Explosion and the Ohio Express—managed to ride this brief musical tide. The Music Explosion's one-hit wonder, "Little Bit o' Soul," made an impressive impact, reaching the No. 2 spot on May 27, 1967 (and it is still played with regularity on oldies stations). But it wasn't much later that the quintet disappeared from the charts. The Ohio Express fared better with three big hits. "Beg, Borrow and Steal" got the group into the Top 100 in 1967, while "Yummy, Yummy, Yummy" peaked at No. 4 on May 18, 1968, and "Chewy, Chewy" reached No. 15 on November 2, 1968. The group disbanded soon afterward. Both groups' records were produced by Jeff Katz and Jerry Kasenetz, who made hits for the 1910 Fruitgum Company as well.

Television Rocks: *American Bandstand*'s Cleveland Connection

If Dick Clark had had his way back in the fall of 1955, *American Bandstand* might well have gotten its start in Cleveland.

As Clark tells it in his book, *Rock, Roll and Remember,* he suggested a similar concept for Cleveland TV. While working as a radio announcer for Philadelphia's WFIL-AM FM-TV, Clark substituted once for Bob Horn, the original host of the then-local dance show *Philadelphia Bandstand,* and was immediately smitten with the job. Thinking he'd never get a chance for the cushy position in his hometown, the ambitious twenty-five year old called up the general manager of Cleveland's WEWS-TV, Channel 5, identifying himself as the "substitute host" of *Bandstand.* Clark then offered to do a copy version of the Philadelphia show for the Cleveland station. By then the industry was familiar with the show, and the manager did not hesitate in giving his answer. He responded by telling Clark, in no uncertain terms, that he would never "put that crap on the air."

A year after Clark's call to Cleveland, Horn was involved in a scandal and was fired from the show. Young Dick Clark was eagerly waiting in the wings. He took over as host just in time to get some experience under his belt before the show's national broadcast debut on August 5, 1957, as *American Bandstand.* This television program fast became an institution among the young viewers and part of a cultural lifestyle for generations to come. The show carefully presented rock and roll as being as American as bobby socks, apple pie, and the Edsel. It embraced innocence and good, clean fun. *American Bandstand* succeeded in making the music acceptable, despite those who deemed it a bad influence and believed it to encourage rebelliousness among the young and impressionable.

Airing weekday afternoons, the show was an after-school habit among teens everywhere. With its showcase of pop stars, danceable tunes, and "pick-a-hit" song forecasts, *Bandstand* was an adolescent's dream. It also allowed for them to observe their peers from across the nation, from fashions and hairstyles to dances and rock idols. The dance show served to showcase a slew of new artists and cultural movements. And for that, rock and roll buffs everywhere, including those on the North Coast, can be grateful.

Cleveland Bandstand (1955–60)

Even though WEWS didn't take Dick Clark up on his proposal, Cleveland soon boasted its own version of the popular dance show. The powers that be at WJW jumped on the *Bandstand* wagon and did their best to imitate the popular idea with *Cleveland Bandstand.* The show was hosted by area teens' favorite disc jockey, Phil McLean of WERE.

Already hosting a daily late-night TV movie show, McLean had fast become known for his distinctive voice and easygoing manner. His enthusiasm for music earned him the position as emcee to Cleveland's answer to *Bandstand*. "I remember the show was certainly a copy of *American Bandstand* in every way, highlighting the artists who'd sing and promote their records," recalls Cleveland TV veteran "Big Chuck" Schodowski. Schodowski, of WJW-TV, is half of the long-running Friday night movie program, *The Big Chuck and Little John Show*, which, having been on local airwaves for more than thirty years, has known a far better fate than the '50s dance show.

In 1959, deejay Casey Kasem arrived in town from Detroit, where he was hired as WJW-AM's nighttime personality. When McLean departed to New York for a job at radio station WNEW-FM, Kasem replaced him as host of *Cleveland Bandstand*. However, it became apparent that the local *Bandstand* paled in comparison to the popular, nationally syndicated version, and it was canceled by 1960.

The Gene Carroll Show (1948–79)

The Gene Carroll Show, though we kids would watch it basically to make fun, was important in that it created yet another outlet for musical creativity.

—Jim Fox, drummer and founder of the James Gang

Although certainly not a rock production, this local talent show did attract and highlight hometown pop artists such as Andrea Carroll, the Poni-Tails, and the Canadaires (later known as Bill Randle's discovery, The Crew Cuts). *The Gene Carroll Show*, one of the first shows aired on WEWS-TV Channel 5, became a Sunday afternoon ritual among viewers. The program enjoyed a lengthy run despite the fact it was virtually filled with human blunders and not taken seriously by anyone—except, perhaps, former radio man Gene Carroll himself.

The first half hour featured competing acts that used the show as a vehicle for getting exposure for one's talent and/or song, so it never lacked for promising guests, among them the Womack Brothers. "Gene Carroll to me was like Ted Mack [who had his own national amateur variety show in the 1950s]," Bobby Womack recalls. "He was really something. We'd be on his show and win so much, he'd get tired of seein' us. But he always did tell us we'd be famous." Another guest who went on to play in Cleveland rock bands E.T. Hooley and Jack Rabbit (with renowned rocker Chrissie Hynde) was Donny Baker. "I was on that show a couple times, as a solo act and with a band," Baker recalls. "The first time I was in grade school, about eleven or twelve years old. As a matter of fact, I still have the guitar I used on the show. It was a 'K,' which was a big acoustic jazz guitar of its day. My dad got it for me and I remember I could just barely get my fingers to reach around to the strings."

The second half of the hour-long program showcased professionals—talented regulars who, with their song-and-dance numbers, gave the program its needed credibility. To this day, viewers of this semi-amateur production remember it as fondly as Sunday evening's *Ed Sullivan Show*.

Bob Ready, a *Gene Carroll* regular who went on to represent many local and national artists, credits his years on the show for his future endeavors. "The show taught us about productions, timetables, and dealing with human conditions. Plus it was live, and there'd always be that camera in your face. Sometimes you couldn't even hear the music in the background as you sang, so that was certainly difficult. But personally, the entire experience helped me deal with adverse conditions later on in the business."

This show's long-running success was most likely due to a few factors. First, the program, which boasted a community flavor, offered a chance for those hoping to be the next big discovery. And for viewers, there'd always be someone familiar—a relative, neighbor, or friend's child—performing. The bottom line, however, was that the show was simply amusing to watch—even if for the wrong reasons. Nerves, stage fright, and panic afflicted many of the performers. Yet it was these painful, candid, all-too-human conditions that gave the show its character and, ironically, that kept viewers watching week after week for decades.

Most rock hopefuls, however, had to wait until the mid-'60s when *The Big 5 Show* (later *Upbeat*) came into view in order to further their budding careers. Unfortunately, like many of the earlier TV programs, there remains little footage of this wonderfully fresh and honest Cleveland broadcasting staple.

The Big 5 Show/Upbeat (1964–71)

This show was a hit from day one. Everything associated with the show played a part in making Cleveland the center of the world when it came to rock 'n' roll.

—Don Webster

The phenomenal success of *American Bandstand* inspired Herman Spero. "My dad's idea was to take what *Bandstand* was and do it in Cleveland, but he wanted to go a step further. Rather than having one or two acts appear, he'd mix several national and local ones together on the same show," recalls David Spero, who, at thirteen, was hired to hold up the cue cards and then later helped write the show.

The *Upbeat* story begins on August 29, 1964, when this music/dance show debuted as *The Big 5 Show* on WEWS-TV Channel 5 on Saturday afternoons at five o'clock. Its success was immediate, thanks to the program's success in featuring top rock artists, local deejays and bands, and the hottest songs of the day. It was also a precursor to other national music programs, such as *Shindig* (which aired a month later, in September 1964, and went the way of most 1960's dance shows, airing its final episode on January 8, 1966) and *Hullabaloo* (whose television life was even shorter). *Upbeat* outlived them all.

In the first season, Spero, along with associate producer Walt Masky, used deejays from radio stations (the popular WHK "good guys") as hosts with local groups as alternating house bands. Familiar faces on the show included deejay Ron Brittain, manager of the Baskerville Hounds, and "Empire Joe" Mayer, manager of the Grasshoppers.

During the conception of the show, producer Herman Spero approached syndicators, who turned him down, claiming rock music was a fad that surely wouldn't last. With such audience response that first season, however, Spero remained hopeful that national sponsors would change their tune. He just had to find a way to sell them on the idea. While vacationing in Toronto with his family, Spero observed the host of a TV dance show airing from Hamilton, Ontario. The charismatic emcee looked almost familiar with his youthful looks, easy manner, and skilled confidence—just like the host of *American Bandstand*. "That's it! We'll get our own Dick Clark!" Spero is reported to have exclaimed. Upon contacting the station, he learned that the man's name was Don Webster, and the savvy businessman made the young announcer an offer he couldn't refuse.

"It wasn't an easy decision," admits Webster. "My career was blossoming in Canada. I had started building a house and had young children. But after heavily weighing the pros and cons, I was off to Cleveland—wife and kids in tow."

With Webster as host, the premise not only worked, but it sold wary syndicators. A year after its debut, the black and white *Big 5 Show* switched to color, changed its name to *Upbeat,* and was watched in more than one hundred cities across the nation. "The show was put into a different kind of syndication—called 'bicycle syndication,'" Spero says. "They'd make ten copies of the show, and those would get sent to ten different cities. They, in turn, would air it, then send it on to ten more cities and so on. So, if you did *Upbeat*, you could travel for six weeks and see yourself every week, if you were in the right city. I don't know anyone else who did it that way, but it worked. And that's how records would get happening as well. For example, Tommy James and the Shondells would happen out of Pittsburgh, then move to Cleveland, then Chicago, Denver, San Francisco. Then it'd all come together."

A performance on *Upbeat* jump-started many a career. Simon and Garfunkel (their "Sounds of Silence" became the No. 1 record in 1965), Gary Puckett and the Union Gap ("Young Girl"), Billy Joe Royal (who, just starting out, had to borrow appropriate clothes from Herman Spero when he came in town to lip-synch his hit "Down in the Boondocks"), the Lovin' Spoonful ("Summer in the City"), Little Stevie Wonder ("Fingertips"), Question Mark and the Mysterians ("96 Tears"), Terry Knight and the Pack ("Better Man Than I"), and the McCoys ("Hang on Sloopy," —Ohio's unofficial state song) all got their first national exposure on the show.

Local acts got in the picture, too. "Playing *Upbeat* was just the best job in the world," says GTOs drummer Gene Marotta. "We got to meet nearly every great performer there was back then. The ones I enjoyed the most I think were Bobby Goldsboro, Freddy Cannon, and Wayne Cochran. Cochran's band really knocked me out." Local watchers remember the excitement they felt seeing their high school and college friends on the show, as members of the Choir, the James Gang, the Outsiders, and Damnation of Adam Blessing gained thousands of nationwide fans from their appearances on the show.

As a young employee, and the producer's son, David Spero met and befriended hundreds of celebrities during these years. His home was often visited by nonrock stars as well, such as Bob Hope and Johnny Carson's late-night sidekick Ed McMahon. Consequently his career has been more auspicious than the average Joe's. He's been a deejay (WXEN, WNCR, WMMS) and has managed several artists, such as the Michael Stanley Band, singer Harry Nilsson, drummer Joe Vitale, actor Ted Neely ("Jesus Christ Superstar"), former *Saturday Night Live* comedian Don "Father Sarducci" Novello, Joe Walsh, and Eric Carmen. Although he never had a free Saturday until he was twenty-one, on *Upbeat* Spero was just another kid having a good time. He also realized he was the envy of not only colleagues at school but his teachers. "I had this one teacher who was crazy about Joe Butler [drummer for the Lovin' Spoonful]," he recalls. "She told me if I introduced her to him, I wouldn't have to go to class the rest of the year. So when I knew they were comin' on the show, I told her to come down. I introduced her to him. I never had to take humanities again!"

But his favorite memories of the show were when Stevie Wonder would guest star. "Stevie was a big clown," Spero recalled. "He came on the show once, and just as he was about to do a take, he stood facing the wall to sing his song. Now mind you, he was just goofin' around; he knew exactly what he was doing. But in the booth, my dad and the technical guys were going crazy trying to figure out who was going to tell him! So they asked Stevie to step 'a little to the right,' and he'd move but just slightly. So then they'd say, 'Okay, Stevie, now give us just another turn,' and so on. And he'd always end up right back to the wall no matter what they said! He was great fun."

Webster had his favorites, as well. "There were so many great acts it's hard to pick favorites. But you'd have to include all those great Motown acts Berry Gordy would bring in. They were always very polished and ready to go. And I enjoyed Kenny Rogers. This was back when he was in the First Edition."

Many of the incoming groups scheduled performances at Leo's Casino and LaCave during their weekend stay. They would perform Thursday through Saturday nights and then tape *Upbeat* on Saturday afternoon, where they lip-synched their hit songs. Several popular acts, like the Fifth Dimension ("Up, Up, and Away") and Aretha Franklin ("Respect"), became regulars on the Cleveland dance show. As national groups performed before packed houses at these major clubs, word spread throughout the industry that these Cleveland showcases were the place to be.

Whole Lotta Shakin' Goin' On

Then there were the *Upbeat* dancers, who shook up many a young boy's heart. The girls came from area high schools and auditioned for the show. Some were chosen as dancers, others as "hand clappers" (who would clap to the beat of the songs while always looking enthusiastic). "I was just thirteen when I became a clapper on *Upbeat*," says Vera Lynn Nida, who was with the show for a year. "A bunch of us girls sent for tickets initially, but we were there so often, soon we didn't need tickets anymore. And that's when we were chosen as official clappers. I remember the house band at the time was the Puzzle People, and we got to see every major act from the Four Tops and Fifth Dimension to hometown groups like the Outsiders and Damnation of Adam Blessing. It was such a fun time, and always exciting."

Dick Blake, the show's original choreographer, taught and often created new dances to be imitated across the country. Blake was already known as a talented dance man and continues to show off his steps at adult education classes in Cleveland Heights. Jeff Kutash began as *Upbeat*'s choreographer in 1966 and remained there until 1970, when Hank Nystrom took over. "The most amazing thing about Jeff Kutash," says Webster, "was that he was a total natural. Here was a guy with these big feet who never took a dance lesson in his life, and he went on to be more successful than any of us." According to Jane Scott, Kutash's success includes teaching those infamous moves to John Travolta for *Saturday Night Fever* and the "Moonwalk" to Michael Jackson. He also became an award-winning choreographer in Las Vegas for his "Jeff Kutash Splash Review."

These were also the days of go-go girls, young dancers clad in tight micromini skirts and fringes who would wiggle and shake vigorously to the music while in discotheque cages at area lounges. The *Upbeat* dancers were decidedly conservative, usually wearing poorboy cotton tops, knee-length skirts or dresses, and white boots that were all the rage. They were thankfully spared the barred cages.

"*Upbeat* set the stage for other rock and roll dance phenomenons that followed in the mid-'60s," Kutash says. "When it comes to the dance moves, they all learned from what were were doing on that show."

Of all the happy memories produced by this legendary program, one show is sadly remembered by fans. On December 9, 1967, after taping *Upbeat,* Otis Redding ("Sittin' on the Dock of the Bay") went on to play Leo's Casino that night. It was to be the soul singer's last public appearance. That evening he boarded the jet that ultimately crashed in Wisconsin, killing him and other band members. Herman Spero was hesitant about airing the *Upbeat* tape until Redding's widow insisted they show it in the singer's memory.

After a successful seven-year run, the show stopped abruptly when changes in the industry slammed on the brakes. By the early '70s, the music had become more business-oriented, with rock concerts getting bigger and more costly. In addition, the media focused on controversial concerts such as Altamont and Woodstock, linking drugs to rock and roll. As a result, sponsors became leery of having their products associated with the music, making it increasingly difficult for programs like *Upbeat* to gain their support.

"It was like someone came in one day and said, 'Something's not working here, and starting tomorrow, it's you,'" Spero says, referring to the fact that no one on staff was given prior notice of the cancellation. "But it was probably time. I think my dad was getting fed up with the people he was dealing with. It used to be entertainers were thankful to be on the show and looked at it as a great opportunity. Then came the drugs, though contrary to popular belief, I think it was just pot at the time. Plus, now everybody was a 'rock star,' and people had attitudes and started coming in with a bunch of demands. It wasn't as much fun anymore."

Don Webster agrees. "What made it so fun in those days was everyone was young and there to have a good time. I mean, they took the music seriously, but not themselves. Then as rock got bigger, things started to change. But looking back, it's amazing to see how many of those young talents that were on *Upbeat* are now enshrined in the Rock Hall of Fame."

Upbeat breathed its last breath on January 9, 1971. But through the grace of video-tape (though not much), there were enough sections of the show to treat local fans to a thirtieth-anniversary program in 1994, highlighting the many memorable performances that had taken place over its seven-year run.

In September 1979, Herman Spero died of a heart attack while working on a new show in New York. A music lover all his life, he had been involved in the medium throughout most of his career and had friendships with many big names in show business. Before and during *Upbeat,* he also produced one of Cleveland's most popular Sunday afternoon programs, *Polka Varieties,* which aired on WEWS-TV from 1956–71.

"*Upbeat* was really ahead of its time," David Spero says.

It was before *Shindig, Hullabaloo, Don Kirshner's Rock Concert, Midnight Special*—all those type shows. And there were no perimeters as far as the music. Dizzy Gillespie did the show, [and] so did Gene Krupa, Iron Butterfly, Tommy Roe. The Supremes would be on the same show as, say, jazz organist Jimmy Smith. I think that was the real key to its success. There was such diversity in way of talent on each show. Literally every major band made an appearance, including the Beatles and Stones through taped interviews Don made with them. And I can remember James Brown flying in on his private Lear jet, which certainly left an impression on me. It was the first time I'd ever seen anything like that.

Without a doubt, *Upbeat* was special. On April 13, 2000, *Upbeat* was designated a Cleveland rock and roll landmark by the Hall of Fame and Museum. The ceremony began that morning with an unveiling of the landmark plaque, placed near the entrance of the WEWS building. That afternoon a celebration commenced at the Rock Hall, beginning with a lively set by the original *Upbeat* house band, Dave C. and the Sharptones. Later that evening, a sold-out *Upbeat 2000* show took place, with performances by Gene Chandler (of "Duke of Earl" fame), Mitch Ryder ("Devil with a Blue Dress On"), the Miracles ("The Tracks of My Tears"), Jerry Butler ("Only the Strong Survive"), Freda Payne ("Band of Gold"), Gary Pucket ("Young Girl,") Ben E. King ("Stand by Me"), Lloyd Price ("Personality"), Kim Weston ("It Takes Two"), and Gary Lewis and the Playboys ("This Diamond Ring"). The show was broadcast live on Channel 5—of course.

The Fab Four Come to Town

The Beatles' first American television performance was broadcast on *The Jack Parr Show* on January 3, 1964, by way of a film clip. But it was their appearance on the popular *Ed Sullivan Show* that propelled the British band to superstardom in a single night. On February 9, 1964, life as we knew it changed forever for this generation as well as the music industry when the Beatles arrived from Liverpool and played their new style of music on national TV. The group influenced nearly every way young Americans lived: the way they wore their clothes and hair, the records they listened to, their sudden interest in everything British, and their new appreciation for musicianship. If one is to believe all the Boomers' accounts, every TV set in America was tuned to CBS that night. (Yet aside from "Topo Gigio" appearances and maybe a circus act or two, teen-agers generally found this variety show boring, spending that hour in their rooms, leaving their parents sitting transfixed in front of the TV.)

But this show was different.

With the overwhelming success of their first U.S. release, "I Want to Hold Your Hand," the Beatles were already widely accepted by American teens, as evidenced by the greeting they received from 10,000 fanatic admirers upon their arrival at New York's Idlewild (soon to be Kennedy) Airport. Of course, this was not by accident; the event was orchestrated by New York deejay Murray the K, who had taken Freed's place at WINS and had been using the British act as a marketing tool for weeks, calling himself the "fifth Beatle."

The group captured the heart and soul of every teen watching that night. Boomers will eagerly tell you with surprising recollection how they were sitting in their living rooms crowded around their black-and-white television sets, watching intently while

Ed Sullivan introduced rock's newest sensation. And while the music was the reason for the group's success, the members' individual charm, wit, and definitive style (shaggy haircuts and pointed-toe ankle boots), captured an entire generation. From that day forward, cemented in stone—or, in this case, rock—the Beatles ruled.

That excitement was merely amplified on the North Coast when the Fab Four arrived on September 15, 1964. Ten thousand Beatle fans showed up at Cleveland's Public Music Hall to hear them play live. Screaming fans stormed the stage, prompting police to halt the concert for ten minutes while they tried to restore the peace. From that moment on, every boy (and, to their credit, some girls as well) from nine to nineteen began strapping on a guitar or grabbing a couple of drumsticks, holing up wherever they could get out of parental range to express themselves through the sound of this British-style rock and roll.

When the Beatles returned to Cleveland for a much-awaited encore on August 14, 1966, the city went wild. The media vied for interviews, radio stations held contests, and television crews fought to be first to cover the event by camping outside the band's

The Beatles play Public Hall, September 15, 1964. *Photo by George Shuba.*

room at the Sheraton Hotel as well as their mobile-home dressing room at the Cleveland Municipal Stadium the day of the historic event. Fans gathered to get a glimpse of rock's royalty. This, despite a media curve-ball—Lennon's statement that the Beatles were more popular than Jesus, which was taken out of context and blown out of proportion—that drastically reduced ticket sales to half of original expectations. Still, on that day 24,646 fans were waiting. "Of all the concerts I went to after the Beatles, none of them came close in terms of loudness and excitement. You couldn't hear one song they played; all you heard was screaming," recalls concertgoer Dennis Fedorko, then a guitarist for the Euclid band Faces in the Crowd. "It was sheer pandemonium, but I wouldn't have missed it for anything. The best part was at the end when my buddy, Don Nebe, ran out to the field as the Beatles were getting into the limo, jumped on top of the car, and managed to shake Ringo's hand before security guards nabbed him!"

The Hippie Movement Invades the North Coast

In the sixties San Francisco's infamous Haight-Ashbury district gave rock its headquarters and helped create a counterculture of epic proportions. But Cleveland teens didn't need to travel 2,000 miles; we had our own drop-in, tune-out, hang-out, hang-loose, happenin' place by way of Coventry Road. The Cleveland Heights street mimicked the famed California strip in nearly every way, boasting an array of diverse establishments to occupy the younger set. There was the well-stocked record store Record Revolution (which still exists), fashion trends at Bill Jones Leather Shop, the Generation Gap, the Dress Me Shop, the Coven-Tree (which sold jewelry and handmade clothing), and the Cargo Express import store. Hungry teens gravitated toward Irv's Deli, and as twilight set in the young crowd would venture over to the 1864 General Store, where they could hear live folk, blues, or jazz music while shopping for leather goods or antiques. For those old enough (and tough enough, since it was a designated Hell's Angels hangout), a night out in Coventry often included a visit to the See Saw Bar. But perhaps the most popular place, particularly on weekends, was the Heights Arts Theater, which hosted some rather outrageous midnight flicks on Saturday nights, most notably *Reefer Madness* (the '50s film warning of the dangers of marijuana that became a farce for this generation) and, in the late '70s, the *Rocky Horror Picture Show* (a bizarre spoof that encouraged audience participation and that had an unprecedented decade-long run).

"That street was like my second home, and I worked at a lot of the places there all through my teens," recalls Dan Landau, who still lives nearby. "The street always had a steady stream of regulars who hung out on the strip—the old beatniks who were carry-overs from the beat generation as well as the young hippies who came from every surrounding city. I remember visiting both the east and west coasts during that time, and people would hardly react if I said I was from Cleveland, but if I mentioned Coventry, they'd go, 'Oh, yeah, I've heard of that place!'"

Coventry Road was hailed by teens as the coolest strip on the North Coast, though most were barred from the area by parents who viewed it with much different eyes. Of course, that didn't stop hundreds of kids from frequenting the place every chance they got. The constant evolving fashion trends seen on Coventry Road reflected what was happening with the music. The styles were creative, individual, and uninhibited; most importantly, it was guaranteed that no logical-thinking adult would dare imitate the look. The entire movement was pretty much off limits to almost anyone over thirty.

Times They Are A-Changin'

From its inception, the only consistent truth about rock music is that it's consistently changing. By the end of the 1950s, the careers of many promising artists had been interrupted: The army summoned Elvis; the law seized Chuck Berry (charged with taking a juvenile girl across state lines for lewd purposes); Jerry Lee Lewis married his thirteen-year-old cousin (promoters were not amused); Carl Perkins was in a debilitating car wreck (he survived, but his career took longer to mend); and Little Richard disappeared from the charts as he took up preaching the Gospel. (He's since not only regained his rock status, but he tells all that he's the true originator—and emancipator—of rock music. And few can dispute this.)

But the most shocking event occurred on February 3, 1959, when a plane crash claimed the lives of rock's earliest influences and brightest stars. The beloved Buddy Holly, J. P. "the Big Bopper" Richardson, and Richie Valens were en route to a concert when horrid winter weather conditions caused their plane to crash in an Iowa cornfield. The event was immortalized by singer Don McLean's ballad "American Pie," in which he referred to the loss as "the day the music died." Then just a year later, on April 17, 1960, rock lost Eddie Cochran in an auto accident. Even with this tragedy, the music did not die but merely took up the challenge of the next era. Without a doubt, rock and roll was the ultimate escape, sounding off against Vietnam, racism, and the Establishment.

Recommended Reading

Allan, Tony, with Faye Treedwell. *Save the Last Dance for Me: The Musical Legacy of the Drifters, 1953–1993.* New York: Popular Culture, 1993.

MacDonald, Ian. *Revolution in the Head: The Beatles' Records and the Sixties.* New York: Henry Holt, 1994.

Pawlowski, Gareth L. *How They Became the Beatles: A Definitive History of the Early Years, 1960–1964.* New York: E. P. Dutton, 1989

Stambler, Irwin. *Encyclopedia of Pop, Rock and Soul.* Rev. ed. New York: St. Martin's Press, 1989.

Sumrall, Harry. *Pioneers of Rock and Roll: 100 Artists Who Changed the Face of Rock.* New York: Billboard Books, 1994.

3 The Clubs Where It Began

So when they say where it all began, for many of these performers, where it began for them was in Cleveland. They would get the support on the air, and they had some great people working in the radio stations. And if you came to Cleveland, there were plenty of opportunities for you to play.

—Rock historian Norm N. Nite (*Northern Ohio Live,* 1993)

Before it was rock, it was rhythm and blues. Despite the fact that few radio stations played R&B, Cleveland boasted numerous clubs that promoted this sound, contributing greatly to its popularity. In the 1950s, people were still venturing out to nightclubs more than staying home in front of TV sets. And music lovers had their pick of places for live entertainment on both sides of town. It was the day of the lounge, and many popular ones were found on or around the city's main strip along Euclid Avenue.

There was Moe's Main Street (7715 Euclid Avenue), which offered a variety of music from big bands and crooners such as Johnnie Ray to R&B; the Versailles Motor Inn's Penthouse Club (2901 Euclid Avenue), the site of many a business deal in the record industry; and the Alpine Village (1640 Euclid Avenue). And nearby were Lindsay's Sky Bar (E. 105th and Euclid), Theatrical Restaurant (711 Short Vincent Avenue), Majestic Hotel (2201 E. 55th Street), and, on the corner of Mayfield Road and Euclid Avenue Winston Willie's Jazz Temple, the ultimate "beatnik" club, which hosted such jazz greats as Miles Davis and Dizzy Gillespie. There was also Gleason's Musical Bar (5219 Woodland, near E. 52nd Street), a favorite hangout of Little Richard and many notable acts when in town, and the Ebony Lounge, located on Cedar Road, where the Orioles were favorite guests with their hit "Crying in the Chapel." And, of course, the Circle Theater was among the most popular music venues of the 1950s.

By mid-decade, more and more clubs were popping up around town. Though there were still R&B clubs and some folk clubs, or coffeehouses, many places were featuring rock and roll music. Astute club owners offered different choices on alternate nights to accommodate a variety of musical tastes.

One of the first clubs to play live rock music was at 26910 Cook Road in Olmsted Township, originally called the Olmsted Lodge. Built in 1949, it was yet another popular lounge-type club, frequented by West Siders in particular. But it found new life in 1961 after it changed its name to the Corral and began catering to the emerging rock scene. The club maintained its popularity until January 18, 1982, when it was destroyed by fire.

Otto's Grotto, located inside the Hotel Statler–Hilton at 1127 Euclid Avenue, was often referred to as the "mecca of joyful madness." Otto's was perhaps the classiest of lounges and catered to the after-work business crowd, particularly those in the music industry. Many national artists, while staying at the renowned Swingo's, ventured over to Otto's after playing gigs in other clubs. With its garish lights and loud music, one might say this hip venue was disco before there was such an entity.

The former Olsen's Lounge (5307 Lorain Avenue near W. 45th Street) was renamed the Peppermint Lounge after the popular New York venue. East Siders frequented the Green Darby (14126 Lakeshore Boulevard) and Hires Lounge (28833 Euclid Avenue) and the Orbit Lounge (37415 Euclid Avenue in Willoughby), which became the popular teen hangout the Utopia and offered a variety of music throughout the 1960s. For example, depending on the night, the Orbit highlighted rock, Motown, and even polka bands. Mentor had what started out as the Torchlight Lounge (7681 Mentor Avenue), which is more fondly remembered by Boomers as the Mentor Hullabaloo. The building changed hands and names often but never wanted for rock lovers and players through the '60s and early '70s.

Indeed, Cleveland never lacked for live—and lively—entertainment, as it consistently offered an array of great venues for musicians and music lovers of all makes, tastes, and styles. These northeast Ohio locals were instrumental in making the Cleveland area the fastest-growing market in the country for live bands, and many attest to the fact that no other city could compare with city's club owners' support of local musicians. Walt Masky, who ran the Peppermint Lounge with Carl Reese and later became associate producer of *Upbeat,* managed one of the most popular East Side lounge bands of the time, Joey and the Continentals, and often booked Dave C. and the Sharptones. Other choice groups in the late '50s and '60s who frequented these rock clubs included Bocky and the Visions, Frank Samson and the Wailers (an East Side "twist" band in which guitarist Glenn Schwartz played briefly), Richie and the Fortunes (later the Charades), Walt and the Marquis (founder Walt Tiburski later became a key player in Cleveland radio), Tom King and the Starfires (pre-Outsiders), and the Twilighters (with bassist and future record promoter Steve Popovich). At no time could a young person in the Cleveland area fall victim to musical boredom.

Coffeehouses: Musical Playgrounds

Present-day depictions of 1960s coffeehouses—smoke-filled rooms, guitar-strumming singers, bad poetry—pretty much capture how it really was. Cleveland's original coffeehouses were located mostly in and around the University Circle area, where musicians and music lovers alike congregated (sometimes in a church basement or in a nearly abandoned building) to listen to the mellow sounds of harmonicas, guitars, and folk singers.

Yes, they served coffee, but no one remembers consuming much of it. And since liquor was looked down on as the Establishment's drug of choice, marijuana, along with other "recreational drugs," was deemed king of the vices. Coffeehouse-goers would converge outside these buildings through rain, snow, sleet, or hail to bask in their own "mind-expanding" world that, to them at least, brought out the pureness in the musical sounds. From here on out, drugs and rock would forever be closely associated.

One of the original Cleveland coffeehouses was the Left Bank, housed in a basement of an old apartment complex. More cropped up as the fad took hold, offering relaxed meeting places for those too young for the bar scene, places where they could gather and share various talents and interests—all with no cover charge. Other popular coffeehouses were the Well and the Outpost, both in East Cleveland. Faragher's Back Room, on South Taylor road in Cleveland Heights, owned by Bill "Red" Faragher, was more of a club than a coffeehouse, yet its casual atmosphere resembled the latter. It was an early testing ground for budding comedians such as Bill Cosby, the Smothers Brothers, and Ohioan Tim Conway before it majored in the folk scene. That began when a young folk singer named Phil Ochs, then an Ohio State student, started playing and hanging out there during the summer of 1961. Ochs went on to become one of the most notable names in folk music, until his suicide in 1976.

But it was the appropriately named Coffee House, at East 115th and Euclid Avenue, that was frequented most and became the hippest place for aspiring musicians to hang out. Many of Cleveland's best started in this unpretentious environment: Glenn Schwartz (Mr. Stress Blues Band, James Gang, Pacific Gas & Electric), Jimmy Fox (James Gang), Bill Miller (Mr. Stress), Dan Klawon (Mods, Choir), Tom Kriss (James Gang), Donny Baker and Richard Shack (E.T. Hooley), Dale Peters (E T. Hooley, James Gang), and Dave Griggs (Griggs Blues Band), to name but a few.

A social and musical outlet, coffeehouses offered a place for musicians to hone their talent, for listeners to enjoy music and learn from others, and for folks simply to gather. These venues came back in vogue in the 1990s, but they are very different in that the atmosphere is more sophisticated and not nearly as colorful or intriguing (most are located in shopping centers or strip malls). The varying degrees of sounds heard in coffeehouses today are often a far cry from the traditional folk/rock and philosophy- and poetry-based songs offered up in the early days.

Leo's Casino (7500 Euclid Avenue 1963–72)

Leo's was a true melting pot of entertainment for the community at large. It was a small club, but Leo Frank and Jules Berger always booked top-notch acts. It was about the classiest place you could play in Cleveland at that time.

—Walt Williams, the O'Jays

Today, Leo's Casino is fondly remembered by musicians and comedians alike as having been the best place to play in Cleveland. For patrons, it was one place where blacks and whites could socialize freely, a rare opportunity in the racially tense 1960s. Comedian Dick Gregory called it "the most fully integrated nightclub in America." Freddie Arrington, former marine featherweight champion who frequently acted as emcee, said "Everyone seated nice there, just like a checkerboard."

In 1952, Leo Frank was a few years out of the navy when he bought a little bar on E. 49th Street and Central Avenue. After remodeling it, he dubbed it Leo's and began booking R&B acts along with his usual jazz fare. Acts such as Cannonball Adderly, Jimmy Smith, Ramsey Lewis, Dizzy Gillespie, and eighteen-year-old Aretha Franklin played there in the early days. In 1962, however, a fire broke out from the barbeque place next door, and the building burned to the ground. Undaunted, Frank merely took up residence in the rear of the Quad Hall Lounge Bar at E. 75th and Euclid Avenue, where he reopened Leo's the next year with the help of new partner Jules Berger. With its intimate (started with a capacity of 300, and later expanding to 700) atmosphere, good food, and array of entertainment, Leo's Casino became a stop for groups when they hit the North Coast.

"The place drew mixed crowds and yet everyone felt comfortable and enjoyed themselves," recalls Walt Williams of the O'Jays, a group that performed there regularly. "You could take the family and you knew you wouldn't be hassled in or outside the club. And they had a good policy there. Anyone below drinking age had to wear a Hawaiian lei around their neck so the waitresses knew not to serve them alcohol." Jules Berger's daughter, Shelley, remembers, "I was just seven when I started going there with my father. My mother usually stayed home, and my teenage brothers were interested in other things. I was Daddy's little princess, so I'd go see him often and pretty soon I was helping out there, such as counting the money and doing odd jobs. Everyone was always nice to me. I remember being in love with Jerry Butler [of the Impressions]. It was my first crush. I was only in second grade!"

"I used to get my dad to take me there before I was old enough to drive," recalls Jimmy Fox. "There weren't a whole lot of teenage kids there, but I'd go to watch those great jazz drummers who ended up being a big influence on me as a drummer. Leo's was just a great place to go and had such a unique atmosphere. There wasn't a jazz or R&B group who was popular that didn't play there at one time or another." Fox was there one night in the summer of '69 when Sly and the Family Stone ("I Wanna Take You Higher") played the club for the first time. Fox recalled the event in a 1981 issue of *Scene:* "Sly left the stage playing the harmonica and had the whole band follow him single-file, along with the four or five hundred people in the place. He marched us all out onto Euclid Avenue and up and down a couple of blocks, got onto a bus and drove away still singin' and clappin.' He left the entire audience standing there on Euclid Avenue!"

Throughout the 1960s, R&B and Motown shared the club's spotlight. Leo's Casino played host to countless talents such as Smokey Robinson, the Temptations, Little Anthony, Ray Charles (with newcomer Billy Preston, who opened for him), Dionne

Warwick, Gladys Knight and the Pips, Sam Cooke, Jackie Wilson, the Four Tops, the Supremes, Nancy Wilson, James Brown, Muddy Waters, Little Stevie Wonder, and soul man Otis Redding. The list goes on and on. And there was a steady stream of comedians as well, including Richard Pryor, Dick Gregory, Redd Foxx, and Flip Wilson.

"Flip got his start at my father's club," Shelley Berger recalls. "He became a close friend of the family, and I remember he always brought me flowers and sometimes jewelry. He was a remarkable guy, and not only did we keep in touch all these years, Flip remained one of my dearest and closest friends."

Indeed friendships were formed among both patrons and players at Leo's. Case in point: From 1965–70, Berger and Frank served as managers for the O'Jays who played regularly at the club. The Canton natives consistently drew large audiences in those early days. By 1970, however, working the club *and* managing the successful group proved too much for the club owners. One of the jobs had to go—but not before Berger and Frank hooked their friends up with Philadelphia International record producers Kenny Gamble and Leon Huff and former Cleveland deejay Ed Wright took over as the group's new manager.

One story about the Leo's Casino years stands out from the rest. It took place during a dark time in Cleveland history—the Hough riots in the summer of 1966. Shelley Berger, as usual, was at her father's club. "I'll never forget one night during those riots. There was all this fighting and violence going on outside, and the National Guardsmen were lining the streets. The Supremes were playing that night, with Flip Wilson as host. It was kind of bizarre . . . even more so thinking back to that time. But here were the patrons inside our small club, a mix of both blacks and whites, sitting peacefully together enjoying the entertainment, and havin' a great time. Yet right outside the doors racial havoc was being played out on the streets. I think that says a lot about the people that frequented my father's club. Even the riots didn't keep them away."

But the Hough riots and the "Glenville Shootout" two years later did ultimately affect the nightclub. By the end of the decade, patrons fearing the "rough" neighborhood looked elsewhere for their entertainment. The music scene was also changing. Acts began demanding more money for appearances and booking one-nighters as opposed to weekend performances. And artists were being wooed to newer, Coliseum-sized venues. Although Jules Berger, who bought out partner Leo Frank in 1970, hung on long after the glory days had ended; he, too, succumbed to changing times and in 1972 closed the doors on a part of Cleveland's music history. Leo's Casino was reborn briefly in 1983 when Frank and restaurant entrepreneur Jim Swingo reopened it in the main ballroom of the Statler Office Tower, with opening act the Four Tops. Not able to recapture its former allure, however, the revamped club closed the following year.

With virtually every popular act of the era playing Leo's Casino, it has indeed become a landmark in Cleveland club history. The "My Town" display at the Rock and Roll Hall of Fame in 1997 paid homage to the beloved nightclub with a pictorial showcase highlighting the club's most popular guests. And on July 24, 1999, the Hall of Fame designated the site a historic landmark by placing a large plaque on its bare grounds, facing Euclid Avenue, for all to see. The event took place outside on a makeshift stage.

Deejay Billy Bass served as emcee, and Martha Reeves sang "Dancin' in the Streets." Also on hand at the party were Dionne Warwick, Jerry Butler, Chuck Jackson, former Leo's emcee Freddie Arrington, and nearly a hundred guests.

"It's unbelievable," Leo Frank said of the honor. "I'm so grateful they did it while I was still alive." Many people echoed that sentiment when Leo Frank died two weeks later. "We were so fortunate to pay tribute to [Leo] so recently prior to his passing," Terry Stewart, newly appointed executive director of the Rock and Roll Hall of Fame and Museum told the *Plain Dealer*.

Although present at the opening of the 1997 Rock Hall display and the 1999 ceremony, Shelley Berger needs no "event" to remember her father's club: "I have only fond memories of so many artists before they got big. I can still see Marvin Gaye, Flip, and them playing poker with my dad after the club closed at night. I recall how they would confide in him; it was clear they trusted him. And they didn't forget him, either, after their careers took off, which most of them did. More than anything else, that's what brought my father the most satisfaction—to see those acts make it."

LaCave: "The House of Folk Music" (10165 Euclid Avenue, 1962–69)

This former pool hall, a 200-seat basement room, became one of the most fondly remembered venues in Cleveland music history. Known mostly as a folk club, LaCave in the University Circle area also played host to a variety of pop and rock groups.

Lee Weiss, Stan Heilbrun, and Nelson G. Karl opened the club in March 1962. By the end of that year, Stan Kain would also join the team when he purchased an interest in the club and served as manager (until 1967; Larry Bruner then was the club's manager from 1967–69). On September 27, 1966, the folk venue presented its first rock band, Terry Knight and the Pack, a Michigan-based group that later became Grand Funk Railroad. That event was followed by many firsts at the club.

Patrons were treated to such "unknowns" as Simon and Garfunkel, Judy Collins, Joan Baez, Jose Feliciano, and Richie Havens, each of whom won an early fan base after appearing at the famed club. LaCave also featured major musical acts such as Pacific Gas and Electric, Canned Heat, Iron Butterfly, James Cotton and the Chicago Blues Band, Janis Ian, the Youngbloods, the Paul Butterfield Blues Band, and hundreds of others. Keyboardist/vocalist Al Kooper first played there with the Blues Project, and by the late 1960s he was a frequent guest with Blood, Sweat and Tears. The Velvet Underground with Lou Reed performed there April 26–28, 1968. And blues vocalist Janis Joplin made her presence known when she and her band, Big Brother & the Holding Company, wowed the LaCave audience for two straight nights, August 6 and 7, 1968.

But the folk beat was the club's specialty. Over the years, LaCave greeted many notable balladeers such as Arlo Guthrie, Peter, Paul and Mary, Phil Ochs, Odetta, Josh White (an investor in the club), Tom Paxton, Tim Buckley, Joni Mitchell, and other great folk artists of the decade. And as with most club owners of the day, LaCave managers didn't neglect homegrown talent. While college folk singers from nearby Cleveland State were regular guests, so was the blues/rock favorite Mr. Stress Blues Band. And later the club was frequented by future punk/underground artists such as Peter Laughner (Rocket from the Tombs, Pere Ubu) and Jamie Klimek (Mirrors, Styrenes).

But, like many clubs of its era, LaCave fell victim to changing times, debts, and other troubles, and on July 10, 1969, it hosted its last concert. True to form, it went out with a bang by featuring top singer/guitarist Johnny Winter and the group the Man as its opening acts.

Cleveland Arena (3717 Euclid Avenue, 1937–77)

The Cleveland Arena, a 10,000-seat facility, was hailed as the "All-Sport Palace" and was generally referred to as simply the Arena. This was one of Cleveland's first indoor playgrounds, built to house the Barons, Cleveland's ice hockey team. During its forty-year history, it hosted basketball games, boxing matches (where Jimmy Doyle died tragically in a championship bout on June 24, 1947, and Cleveland rocker Screamin' Jay Hawkins won a Golden Glove championship, as did singer Jackie Wilson), the Ice Follies, and Barnum and Bailey's Circus.

The great hall also played host to many memorable concerts, and more peaceful ones at that. The Arena's Saturday afternoon concerts were popular among the younger set (most notably the Rolling Stones show, with the McCoys on June 25, 1966). Other memorable performances included the Bob Seger System ("Ramblin' Gamblin' Man") and the Jeff Beck Group ("Jeff's Boogie"). And of course there was the Moondog Coronation Ball of March 21, 1952, which put Cleveland on the rock and roll map.

But then came the new, attractive Richfield Coliseum in 1974, which romanced concert and sports promoters alike. Suddenly the modern, suburban Coliseum was in and the old, downtown Arena was out. After attempts to sell the Arena proved unsuccessful, the once-revered entertainment venue became a victim of the times and succumbed to a wrecking ball in early 1977.

Public Music Hall (1220 East 6th Street, 1922–)

This venue, located on the corner of Lakeside and East 6th Street, is made up of Public Auditorium (Public Hall, 500 Lakeside Avenue) and the Music Hall. The two share a stage that is divided by a partition serving as a back wall for each space. Both "rooms" continue to host some of the best acts in rock, although because of space today's bigger acts play Cleveland's newest concert venue, the Gund Arena. The 3,000-seat Music Hall, preferred by mellower patrons because of the intimate atmosphere, embraces acts such as James Taylor and Lyle Lovett.

Anyone over forty can recall the controversial "Beatles Ban" of 1964. The problem began with the famous Beatles concert that filled every one of Public Hall's 10,000 seats on September 15, 1964. Overzealous fans rushed the stage, interrupting the performance and creating general havoc. Parents, naturally, began questioning the safety of such concerts. Weeks later that concern was validated when, at a Rolling Stones concert, an excitable teenage girl fell from a balcony, prompting Mayor Ralph Locher to ban all British acts.

When the ban was finally lifted in the summer of '66, Public Hall rock acts returned and the rest of the decade saw the Who, Cream, Grand Funk Railroad, the Doors (right after the infamous Miami obscenities arrest [which is why this author wasn't

David Bowie's first U.S. performance, Public Hall, September 22, 1972. *Photo by David Spero.*

permitted to go]), the Jimi Hendrix Experience; Janis Joplin with Country Joe and the Fish; Crosby, Stills and Nash; Led Zeppelin; the Grateful Dead; the Moody Blues; and Dylan mates the Band. The Jackson 5 debuted there on April 10, 1971. In the 1980s came more favorites, such as John (Cougar) Mellencamp and U2. And one of the early glam-rock concerts featured a young, colorful David Bowie in his first U.S. appearance, which he made sure no one would forget. Clad in his Ziggy Stardust best, the tall, skinny Brit wore a black and gold jumpsuit with neon orange boots that matched the color of his hair. A rock and roll rookie, Bowie took to the stage like a pro and gave fans a memorable performance.

Jim Morrison and the Doors at Public Hall, 1968. *Photo by George Shuba.*

WHK Auditorium (5000 Euclid Avenue, opened as the Metropolitan Theater, 1913)

This building, which began as an opera house, is nearly a century old but is still put to good use as the famed Agora Ballroom. From 1950–75, this large auditorium housed the offices of radio station WHK-AM and for the last seven of those years, its sister station, the nationally hailed WMMS-FM. As home to early WHK-inspired pop concerts throughout most of the 1960s, the venue became Cleveland's first official rock residence. For a time in the late 1960s, the place was called the Cleveland Grande Ballroom, continuing its reputation for showcasing the best in rock. And when the old Hippodrome Theater closed in 1980, the auditorium became the New Hipp. The building stood empty for years after the radio stations moved out but was resuscitated in 1985 by Agora owner Hank LoConti, who took it over and remodeled the aging building.

Numerous talents and much electrifying music—from opera to rock—have passed through those doors. One of the most memorable concerts of the '60s took place when ex–Blues Project member Al Kooper played there with Blood, Sweat and Tears, one of the most popular groups of that time.

Allen Theater (1501 Euclid Avenue at Playhouse Square, 1921–)

Developed by Toronto brothers Jules and Jay Allen, this Italian Renaissance–style theater completed the cultural strip along Euclid Avenue, joining with the Hanna, Ohio, and State Theaters to form Playhouse Square. Like its neighbors, it showcased mostly plays and motion pictures. However, in the rocking sixties, many concerts were held at these theaters. John Mayall ("Room to Move"), the Yardbirds ("For Your Love") Eric Clapton's Cream, Steve Winwood's Traffic ("Mr. Fantasy"), Blue Cheer ("Summertime Blues"), the Byrds ("Mr. Tambourine Man"), Santana ("Evil Ways"), the Youngbloods ("Get Together"), and the Allman Brothers Band ("Ramblin' Man") all played there.

The Allen continued to play host in the 1970s to the best in rock by featuring the likes of the Grateful Dead (October 29, 1971, broadcast live by WNCR-FM), Pink Floyd, Mitch Ryder and the Detroit Wheels, Lou Reed, Uriah Heep, the New York Dolls, the Eagles, and newcomer Bruce Springsteen (February 1, 1974, opening for Wishbone Ash).

Cleveland nearly lost this beautiful building because of diminishing attendance, forcing the theater to close in 1968. Just when it was being scheduled for demolition in early 1993, the Playhouse Square Association saved it, signing a long-term lease to keep and restore the Allen to its former glory.

The Palace Theater (1701 Euclid Avenue, Playhouse Square, 1922–)

Part of Playhouse Square, this theater remains a good venue for shows as well as theatrical productions. When it was hosting musical acts in the sixties, the auditorium seated 3,100 and was one of the most prestigious places for musicians to play. Canned Heat and the Steve Miller Band were among the favorites there. And although the theater closed in July 1969, the Playhouse Square Association once again came to the rescue and saved it from demolition. After extensive remodeling, the Palace reopened in April 1988.

Teen Clubs: When Rock Was Young

Astute club owners past and present have had the business sense and personality to make their clubs attractive to young music lovers. Among the most notable club pioneers listed often in this book are Carl Reese (the Peppermint Lounge, the Rolling Stone, It's Boss); Dick Korn (D'Poos in the Flats, Viking Saloon); Hank Berger (Traxx, Phantasy Nite Club, Hank's Cafe, Liquid, Spy, Fishbones, and Wish); and of course, Kent's most famous proprietor, Joe Bujack (JB's).

The 1960s had a variety of dance places, called "teen clubs," that catered to the fourteen-to-twenty-one-year-old set. Until then, aspiring musicians had few places to hone their talent other than high school gyms, church halls (where "proper dress" was required), or the occasional teen house party (where parents were just a music chord away).

Northeast Ohio produced yet another first when the Hullabaloo Scene at 1380 S. Chapel in Louisville (suburb of Canton) became the first of the national chains of these young-adult dance clubs (which grew out of the NBC TV show "Hullabaloo"). Its popularity grew fast among the young teen set, and within months there were five Hullabaloos scattered across the area, providing teens fun and safe places to hang out with friends.

The scene was the same in every club. There were the dancers who quickly filled up the open floor at the first beat of the music. Then there were the "watchers"—a sea of teens positioned in front of the stage, staring at the bands as if hypnotized. The guys stood in awe as the talent performed in a way that always looked easy (and cool); the girls, when not dancing, stared down their objects of desire, usually the lead singer or frontman. "As soon as I got my driver's license I'd drive to Mentor Hullabaloo every weekend," recalls Lake County native Patty Holzheimer. "My favorite bands were Damnation of Adam Blessing, Freeport, and the Raspberries. It was during that time that Otto, the owner, formed what was called the 'Teen Board.' We used to hold group meetings and help out in the coat room or the pop stand. But we only joined so we could mix with the band members. My girlfriend, Kathy Curtis, worked at the Chesterland Hullabaloo as a dancer in one of those go-go cages they had there for a time."

But as with everything else in an adolescent's life, there were rules. In the case of the Hullabaloo clubs, a poster listing the dos and don'ts of proper behavior was strategically placed on a wall just inside the front door. It was a mere formality, however, and wasn't given a moment's thought by those for whom it was intended. Of course, there were the law-and-orders, whose ominous presence kept most rowdy teens at bay. Most of these blue suits mingled nicely with the young patrons, letting the kids be kids. They even managed an occasional smile.

Teen clubs served their purpose well. Young people had a fun place all to themselves, and young musicians had an outlet for perfecting their acts. And though many of these groups played the same club several times a month, no one, it seemed, ever grew tired of them. It was the music that attracted the patrons, not the club itself. Fickle in their choice of dance places, fans followed faithfully wherever their favorite bands played, be it East Side, West Side, or south to Akron or Kent.

"Those teen clubs were like a musical college," says Michael Stanley. "At first, I was going there to see the girls. But soon as I got there, I'd be standing front and center watching the bands." And though, unlike Stanley, many of these novice musicians and groups never made a record or hit the coveted charts, these inspiring young rock bands made their mark and sometimes even took the city by storm.

Ottopreneur: Otto Neuber, Pioneer of Northeast Ohio's Club Scene

Otto and Hank LoConti were the two most important people when it came to clubs and supporting local talent in the '60s and '70s.

—Rich Spina, former Love Affair frontman and veteran musician and producer

German-born Otto Neuber came to Cleveland in 1957 in search of the American dream. Within a few years, he not only realized it, but he owned it. Neuber is considered the first to meet the needs of rock lovers under eighteen by providing an outlet for their favorite music.

Neuber began his new life in America as a tool-and-die maker, working seven days a week at a Ford plant. But he still made time for his real love. His passion for music extended to guitar playing and composing. By 1963, he was managing his friend's 221 Club on Chagrin Boulevard (later known as the Balcony), turning it into the first rock-only club on the North Coast. He went on to acquire what became the most popular club east of Cleveland, the Mentor Hullabaloo, in 1966. He later changed the name to the Mentor Rock Shop, and the place flourished as it nurtured rock fans by booking some of the best bands in and out of town. "Cleveland was very supportive of rock 'n' roll bands, both local and national, in the '70s and early '80s," said Neuber, now retired. "Groups would come from all over, and the club rooms would be filled, and they were paid good—500 dollars a night—which they weren't getting in other cities."

"I had the Yardbirds there, Jeff Beck, Rod Stewart, Pacific Gas and Electric, Ted Nugent, Todd Rundgren with the Nazz, and all the big Detroit acts," he recalls. Although he named Alice Cooper as one of his personal favorites, he added, "But oh, what he did to my club! He had these big bags with feathers and had them connected with CO_2 tanks. At the end of the show . . . 2,000 feathers all over the club. I had a thousand people there and all I was serving was Coke. Now you know what happens when pop is spilled over the floor? Let me tell you, these feathers settled into the pop and the next day, I had a crew of four people working eight hours cleaning up that floor!"

A variety of local acts played Neuber's clubs as well, such as the Choir, the James Gang, Damnation of Adam Blessing, Eli Radish, Cyrus Erie, the Lost Souls, and more. Despite good business, Neuber was not immune to the realities of commerce. In 1970, Mentor city officials, responding to neighborhood complaints, warned Neuber about the noise level at the Rock Shop. After several altercations, city hall won the battle, with Neuber deciding to sell the business. Even after new owners remodeled, the city's building inspectors weren't satisfied, and the beloved dance club was never reopened.

But Neuber wasn't done. He purchased an Ohio club east of Cleveland in Geneva-on-the-Lake. Because it offered a venue for young rockers fifty miles from the city, Rush In was hugely popular on long weekends. Fate intervened once again, however, and a new liquor ordinance was passed, changing the former eighteen-and-over policy to twenty-one and over. "That law changed everything overnight," Neuber recalls. "Clubs were closing down at the rate of 50 percent. After all, a whole group of youngsters were being left out."

Rush In, which catered to an adolescent crowd, was history. By then Neuber had quit his day job as a tool-and-die maker at the Ford plant, freeing him to invest in more ventures. This time he took up residence in the then-obscure Flats district. Ironically, he purchased a club called D'Poo's Tool and Die Works but changed its name to Otto-Site. After that, he bought another Flats club, Tom Jones Backroom (Old River Road), which he renamed Otto's Backroom in 1972.

That same year, he also began a booking and management firm called Energy Talent/Solar Management, which helped direct aspiring musicians and bands. Among his clients were the Statesmen, the Monks (he changed their name to Sheffield Rush), Reign, Freeport, Champion, and a group originally called Skyport, which he changed to Love Affair. "That band was the closest I came to a national success," Neuber says. "But there are always so many factors that dictate if a group makes it or not, and sometimes it's a matter of sheer luck." Though the hard rock group fell short of national stardom, it earned a huge following on the North Coast through the late '70s and early '80s—much of it due to Neuber's management.

"One main reason why Otto was so good at what he did was [that] he took his job very seriously," says Rich Spina. "I'll never forget one night I was really sick with the flu and I told Otto, 'Hey, I just can't do it tonight, I don't have the energy to pull off Zeppelin [songs].' He looked and me and said simply, 'Well, Rich, you can't do it, I can find hundreds of singers who'll gladly take your place.' And I went up there and did just fine. Otto was driven, and if you wanted to work with him, you had to be, too."

Neuber attributes his achievements to one simple, and familiar, principle: "If you want to be successful, you've got to be willing to work hard. And I always spent my own money trying to get these bands nationally recognized. Not everyone can say that." Then he adds in his heavy German accent, "Yep, I came close a lot of times, but no ceegar."

Seasons in the Sun

There was always a great deal of activity along the North Coast, particularly during the summer season. In addition to the various outdoor parks and beaches that served as musical playgrounds, there were a few places that boasted the greatest allure and drew large music-loving crowds.

Musicarnival (4401 Warrensville Center Road, 1954–75)

Opening in the summer of 1954, Musicarnival was one of the first tent music theaters in the United States. The large circular blue tent, created to house musicals and theater productions, was designed by Cleveland architect Robert A. Little.

Located next to Warrensville Heights City Hall, this open-air venue became the perfect place for a summer rock party. As rock music gained acceptance, Musicarnival began hosting a few concerts, and soon visits from contemporary artists were commonplace. During the summer of '69 alone, the big blue tent took under its cover Procol Harum, Iron Butterfly, Led Zeppelin (with opening act the James Gang), Country Joe and the Fish, Frank Zappa and the Mothers of Invention, Pacific Gas and Electric, and others.

The local group Cyrus Erie, with Eric Carmen, Wally Bryson, and Bob and Mike McBride, had the honor of opening there for the Who. The popular quartet was befriended by Pete Townshend and company when the Who's equipment broke down and the young band members lent the British act their amplifiers. To the delight of these aspiring musicians, this act of kindness sealed the groups' musical camaraderie.

But the good times didn't last. Like the Arena, Musicarnival fell victim to changing times, with competition attacking from all sides. The outdoor concert venue Blossom Music Center became the tent's greatest threat as it started booking rock acts in addition to its Cleveland Orchestra concerts and other summer entertainment.

By 1975, the airy summer venue, which had hosted every form of entertainment from musicals such as *The King and I* to the eccentric Frank Zappa, had become a thing of the past. Today, the site where the "big top" once stood serves as the parking lot for Thistledown race track.

Blossom Music Center (1145 W. Steels Corners Road, Cuyahoga Falls, 1968–)

Blossom was conceived to fill the need for a summer festival program for the Cleveland Orchestra. Located on eight-hundred acres of pristine land in Cuyahoga Falls, it has more than served its original purpose. The unique and acoustically sound amphitheater, designed by architect Peter Van Dijk with architectural adviser Pietro Belluschi and acoustical engineers Christopher Jaffee and Heinrich Keilholz, was an answer to a prayer.

Named for arts benefactor Dudley S. Blossom of the Musical Arts Association, the amphitheater's musical events range from a Cleveland Orchestra concert to a Nine Inch Nails hard rock show. Over the years, Blossom has played host to every conceivable pop act of the day. Well-remembered sell-outs began with Frank Sinatra (the first artist to play there), followed by an interesting assortment of talents that included Pink Floyd, the Doobie Brothers, Meat Loaf, Journey, the late Harry Chapin, and regulars like the Moody Blues and Jimmy Buffett. The 18,700-capacity venue is also dear to the heart of Michael Stanley, whose band still holds the record for sell-out concerts at Blossom.

"Blossom, particularly in the seventies, was the greatest place to go," notes deejay Joe Cronauer. "I remember a friend calling me up at five o'clock on a Tuesday night and saying, 'Hey, I got an extra ticket for James Taylor tonight at Blossom. Wanna go?' That kind of stuff happened all the time. And it cost something like six bucks for a lawn seat, so it didn't break you. Then you'd bring in, like, a picnic table of food and fourteen coolers [exaggeration noted]. I remember being on the lawn, with all this chicken and watermelon, and listening to the music while laying on a blanket under the stars. It was incredible. I was an usher for one season just so I could be a part of that."

Cleveland Municipal Stadium (1931–96)

Cleveland Stadium, with its seating capacity of 78,189, was the largest outdoor arena in the world at the time it was built. The Cleveland Indians played their first baseball game there on July 31, 1932, and by 1947, both the Indians and the Browns called the place home.

In the mid-1970s the place became a concert haven when Belkin Productions introduced a new custom in outdoor entertainment. "The World Series of Rock" became the most coveted summer event ever, and everyone from the Rolling Stones and ZZ Top to Michael Jackson and Crosby, Stills, Nash and Young drew sold-out crowds (see Chapter 11). Suddenly, Municipal Stadium was known for more than cheers and jeers. It was now a rock and roll stadium.

It was appropriate, then, that it would host the biggest all-star rock concert ever commemorating the inauguration of the Rock and Roll Hall of Fame and Museum on September 2, 1995. The guest list included an eclectic group of musicians from every era: Little Richard, Jerry Lee Lewis, Chuck Berry, James Brown, Aretha Franklin, Sam Moore, Bruce Springsteen, the Kinks, Bob Dylan, Johnny Cash, Chrissie Hynde, John Fogerty, Al Green, George Clinton and the P-Funk All Stars, John Mellencamp, Melissa Etheridge, the Gin Blossoms, Alice in Chains, Soul Asylum, Slash, and Natalie Merchant. The historic concert lasted until the wee hours of the morning. The double

CD from that event, *The Concert for the Rock and Roll Hall of Fame,* is now available for all rock lovers to enjoy.

Soon after, Art Modell moved his football team to Baltimore. And with the Indians permanently housed in nearby Jacobs Field, the stadium that had seen so many hot dogs, peanuts, and beer lost its purpose and glory and was finally razed in 1996.

Part 2
The Battle of
the Sixties

4 Radio Stations and Deejays Fight for Listeners

I've lived in New York and California and I can honestly say that the North Coast is one of the hippest areas with the most musically conscientious people. In terms of rock music, I think a lot of that has to do with our early exposure to it. We had those great AM stations that were always battling to be the first to give us "world exclusives" whenever the Beatles, Stones or any of the big groups had a single out. So we heard a lot of the new songs before anyone else. And that helped produce all those bands that quickly learned the songs, then got to play them at the teen fairs and clubs around town. The combination of it all served to give Clevelanders the opportunity to enjoy the music probably more than anyone.

—Dave Nida, musician and record promoter

It was during the 1960s that deejays really started earning their wings. When teen reaction over the Beatles made headlines throughout the world, radio promoters opened their eyes as well as their pockets. Promotional advertising increased to new heights, as did the role of the disc jockey, who used every creative means to win listeners. At first the competition in Cleveland was between two pop stations, WHK and KYW (to become WKYC in 1967). In December 1965, another station, WIXY, skated onto the radio rink, making the fight still tougher. One result of these rivalries was that Cleveland-area listeners were treated to exclusive scoops, often being the first audience to hear a new record or group. This made for better music choices all around and only served to increase the city's reputation as "Radio Central." And even though things got pretty heated (bordering on nasty) at times, radio wars produced great on-air entertainment.

Since the dawn of radio broadcasting in 1909, teenagers have been the measure of its success. Sybil M. True of San Jose, California, wife of pioneer broadcaster Charles "Doc" Herrold and a broadcaster in her own right, was first to discover this truth. She noticed that each time she played new songs, young people wanted to buy the records. Today, at the beginning of the third millennium, this practice hasn't let up. Play a record a teenager likes and you've got yourself a winner. That radio fact trickled into the television medium in the 1950s when Dick Clark played his favorite tunes on *American Bandstand* and watched the songs shoot up into the Top 10 spot in a blink of an eye. In this fashion, Clark's program produced hundreds of teenage singing idols, making them (and himself) quite rich.

Using this philosophy in the 1960s, radio stations became obsessed as they strived to cater to the musical whims of youth, ultimately producing higher ratings than ever before. And like rock itself, this trend had begun in the Fabulous Fifties.

Why Cleveland Was Such a Hot Radio Market

We'd usually beat the trades (e.g., *Billboard, Cashbox, Record World*) as far as getting something on the radio. In fact, Cleveland was part of those that would be developing the numbers on the charts. I remember we used to meet up at a place like the Versailles [2901 Euclid Avenue] when that was big. There'd be 30 or 40 people there every night from 7 'til maybe 5 A.M.

—Record promoter Ron Iafornaro describing
Cleveland radio's heyday (*Scene Magazine,* 1981)

It was back in the 1950s that Cleveland became known as "Radio Central." Initially it was because of the city's prime location: located between New York and Chicago, Cleveland was the try-out point for new records, often receiving the platters first. Record store owners and radio deejays had ultimate control. The radio men were "pied pipers": When deejays played the records, their listeners and the industry followed. As a result, promo men and their artists flowed through the revolving doors of downtown Euclid Avenue buildings like the steady rotation of a 45. Most of the stations were located within a five-mile radius of each other, allowing easy access for these promoters to go about marketing their product. In a 1956 *Cleveland Press* article, a major record distributor proclaimed Cleveland to be the "Nation's No. 1 Pilot City" because of its ability to launch more records than any other market. At no time was this more evident than in these formative years. Bill Randle, of course, started this trend and was perhaps the main reason Cleveland was considered early on as the pop music hub in North

America. "I realized the music we were playing in Cleveland was on the cutting-edge of the musical trends—it was miles ahead of New York," Randle once told a reporter, referring to his weekly commuting trips. He recalled taking those popular records from Cleveland and playing them on his New York City weekend radio show. "They'd end up being big hits there. People thought I was some musical genius, but really, I was just shooting fish in a barrel. It was already a hit in Cleveland."

The growth of rock music prompted a whole new craze in radio. People with a keen business sense smelled opportunity and began scrambling to make their mark in this lucrative medium. Whereas before disc jockeys had been simply announcers, the popularity of Alan Freed's on-air antics forced them to become "radio personalities" if they wanted to attract the day's adolescents. Stations fought all-out for high ratings and teen affection. Competition was fierce. In recording studios, executives were always on the lookout for the next big hit and hitmaker, and radio forced the issue with its constant efforts to be the first to play that promising new hit.

Talking heads were spinning and the heat was on. This at times resulted in some stations being slapped with a "cease and desist" order from the Federal Communications Commission (FCC) when playing a new song without the record company's permission. No matter. It wasn't how you played the game, but who would ultimately win. As radio executive Carl Hirsch said of the business, "I don't get dressed to go to work. I get dressed to go to war."

Although business trends in the music industry have changed drastically over the years, Cleveland radio remains an important market to crack. Today, thanks to generating such mega-acts as the O'Jays, Chrissie Hynde of the Pretenders, Tracy Chapman, Nine Inch Nails, Bone Thugs-N-Harmony, and, most recently, Macy Gray, the North Coast continues to be a music mecca.

Music, Music Everywhere: The Mighty Transistor

In 1954, a new sound wave was developing, one that would capture the hearts of teens everywhere by the end of the decade. No longer did adolescents have to be confined to their rooms to listen to their favorite sounds. They were now able to take their music with them wherever they went—while walking to a friend's house, sitting on a porch, or, during summers on the North Coast, lying about on the beaches of Lake Erie. The development of the transistor radio forever changed the way we listened to music.

Today we have the boombox, the Walkman, and the portable CD player. But back then the hand-held transistor radio, which could be played for hours on a nine-volt battery, served us well and caught on as fast as the Twist. It also brought back to radio listeners who, since the novelty of television, had made TV their entertainment of choice. This miniature solid-state radio had much to offer. Not only was it easy to carry, tucking neatly into one's pocket (or, with the aid of earplugs, underneath the bedcovers at night), but it also fit perfectly into a teen's meager budget.

Norm N. Nite

> He was the guy standing yelling "Cleveland" at the top of his lungs at every free moment.
>
> —Dick Clark, referring to Nite's campaign to get the Rock Hall built in Cleveland *(Northern Ohio Live,* 1993)

During the exciting days of early rock radio, many radio kings were crowned. But one man stands alone when it comes to radio and music, and he was born and raised in the heartland. The name Norm N. Nite—"Mr. Music"—is legendary in the music industry. That legend began with his radio career, which has now spanned over thirty years.

Like many teens in the 1950s, Norm N. Nite was bitten by the rock bug while listening to Alan Freed. He was still able to pick up Freed's "Rock 'n' Roll Party" in his West Side home when the controversial deejay moved to New York's WINS. A music lover at an early age, Nite began collecting records of his favorite artists. "I would purchase 45s of Little Richard, Fats Domino, and Elvis. That was the real start of it," he recalls.

He became increasingly intrigued with how they arrived at their hits and with their journeys to stardom. Nite began compiling a notebook of these facts, noting the musicians and groups' formations and accomplishments. The file came in handy later when, as a WHK deejay in 1968, Nite would refer to this wealth of information in his evening "Nite Train" program.

Growing up on Lake Erie's shores in the Tremont section of Cleveland, the 1958 graduate of West Tech High School began his radio days in 1961. That's when he became involved with his college radio station, WOUB (Ohio University), prompting him to change his major from business administration to radio/TV. Rock music was still not taken seriously when this student wrote his thesis on rock and roll in 1965. After serving in the military from 1965 to 1967, Nite made what would be his first of countless television appearances.

> It was *The Mike Douglas Show.* I still remember the date—January 21, 1968. I was promoting a record album I narrated, called *Rock 'n' Roll—Evolution or Revolution,* on Laurie Records. That was the label that Dion and the Belmonts, Gerry and the Pacemakers, and a lot of other groups recorded for. It was an album of excerpts of songs with me telling the history of rock 'n' roll and was actually the first record ever done on rock history. I was on the show with Bobby Darin and Lesley Gore. That was a real treat for me. I'm very proud of the fact that my national television debut was over thirty years ago now, and I've done over forty national TV shows since then.

In 1970, Nite became a professional record spinner at station WGAR-AM. There he played '50s rock and enlightened listeners with his knowledge of rock trivia. It was during this time that he became known as "Mr. Music." Three years later, persuaded to go the way of most popular disc jockeys, he made the move to the New York.

The move east proved a good one for his career. Nite hosted a syndicated weekend show on New York station WCBS-FM, which brought his status as a rock historian to national attention. His radio shows included "The U.S. Hall of Fame," a weekend Top 20 countdown (which often rendered Nite the number-one spot in the Arbitron ratings), and "Solid Gold Scrapbook." By the late 1960s, Nite's loyal listeners were encouraging him to write a book that contained all the interesting bits he had acquired over his years as a rock historian. He gladly complied.

So for five years Nite collected data and conducted hundreds of interviews with recording artists from two decades of rock to produce his first book, *Rock On: The Illustrated Encyclopedia of Rock 'n' Roll* (1974). This volume became the first reference book to chronicle rock's history and was such a needed source that soon Nite was writing more. So far two other volumes have been added to the *Rock On* series (and there are sure to be more).

Not one to abandon his roots, Nite has spent the past few decades dividing his time between radio jobs in Cleveland and New York. From 1990 until 1995, he worked at both Cleveland oldies stations WMJI-FM and WCBS-FM. In addition, he has emceed numerous rock concerts during his long career. He continues his stint on WCBS and soon will celebrate his twenty-eighth year there.

Nite put his reknown as a radio personality and human database of rock information to good use when he became Cleveland's personal ambassador and campaigned vigorously to acquire for Cleveland the Rock and Roll Hall of Fame. The only radio personality to serve on the Hall's board of trustees, this pied piper led his tireless crusade because he believed no other city deserved the coveted museum. Nite was instrumental in luring disbelieving higher-ups to the North Coast to check out the possibilities for themselves. (See the full story in Chapter 19.)

Many Clevelanders believe, and rightfully so, that if Nite, their staunchest ally, hadn't lobbied during what became a ten-year odyssey, the Rock Hall might very well be gracing another coastline. Instead, thanks to Norm N. Nite and other notable leaders, and some hard-driving maneuverings, the city that embraced rock from its infancy will now enjoy it ever after.

Radio Wars

WHK and WKYC and WIXY were always battling it out. It was really fierce competition. But all of these people took great pride in being able to be the first to break a new hit single.
    —Steve Popovich, Cleveland International Records *(Cleveland Free Times,* 1995)

The "wars" were fantastic. The competition was so intense, we were beating each other over the head every day. And the ironic part was by doing that we made each other bigger, because we were bringing so much attention to what we were doing.

The wars created great radio and made it a market unique in the United States of America.

—Eric Stevens, former program director of WIXY-AM and
vice president of operations at WMMM-FM

WHK-AM 1420 (1921–)

WHK has the distinction of being Cleveland's first radio station. Radio began in earnest in America in 1920, and a Cleveland man named Warren R. Cox began operating a four-tube, 50-watt transmitter out of his home at 3138 Payne Avenue on July 26, 1921. During its seven-plus decades of broadcasting, WHK has remained a leader in the industry, despite, like its radio companions, its many changes. The station was known as 8-ACS until 1922, when the Department of Commerce made it unlawful for amateur radio stations to broadcast without a commercial license. Cox obtained one and WHK was born, making it the sixth station in the country to receive a commercial license. It was then chosen by the Cleveland Radio Association to broadcast its weekly hour of musical entertainment.

It's been a classical station, a rock station, a Top 40-station, a "beautiful music" station, a country station, a solid-gold station, and finally, in the 1990s, a talk-radio station. It has also had its share of colorful (to say the least) disc jockeys. In the '50s there was Bill Gordon (who later shared TV 5's "One O'Clock Club" with legendary newswoman Dorothy Fuldheim), the late Ernie Anderson, and Pete "Mad Daddy" Myers. And Carl Reese reigned from 1961–64. Reese is now a Cleveland radio legend, having done stints on AM stations WERE, WJW, WBBG, and WRMR, beginning in 1954 and continuing to the present.

Besides being one of the first stations on the air, WHK brought yet another first to the medium—"color radio." This was a term used to describe the style of radio that became the station's calling card throughout the 1960s: energized deejays, uninterrupted double/triple record plays, and, in the words of the "Big Chief," Norman Wain, promotions, promotions, promotions.

The 1960s brought Johnny Holliday (with his "Radio Oneders" basketball team, jocks who played for charity, including Roger Zenisek, Dan Mason, Scott Burton, Tom and John Sgro, and Mike Ziokas), Johnny Walters, Pat Fitzgerald, Eddie Clark, and Ray Otis). Then came the WHK "Good Guys"—Joe Mayer, Al James, Ken Scott, and Bob Friend. And long before Howard Stern touched his first soundboard, the North Coast boasted its own shock jock in the maniacal form of '70s deejay, Gary Dee Gilbert—Cleveland's most controversial disc jockey to date.

But Holliday, who was there from 1959–64, had a fast-talking, lighthearted style that made him the early rockers' most memorable WHK personality. "I'll never forget listening to Johnny Holliday's 'Top 40 Tunedex' when I was in high school in the early

'60s," says T.J. the Deejay (Thomas J. Studniarz Sr.), freelance disc jockey and avid record collector. "That was the record countdown he'd have everyday at 3 P.M. and play in the order of sales, from No. 40 up to No. 1. So sometimes you'd hear the same song at the same time of day depending on whether it moved either up or down on the charts. Holliday was one deejay I never missed. He had a great radio voice, very distinctive. And he always sounded so cheerful; it made you feel good just listening to him."

Those were the station's glory days, when it romanced the young and made a connection to its listeners by way of deejay appearances at high school record hops, charity events, and station-sponsored concerts. And in true color radio fashion, it stoked Beatlemania for all it was worth. In fact, its fanatic reputation was such that the Beatles' most creative and critically praised album, *Sgt. Pepper's Lonely Hearts Club Band,* had the radio station's call numbers on its celebrity-filled cover—the only station in the country to boast this prestigious honor. If one looks to the right of the album cover, there sits a doll wearing a sweater that reads "WHK Good Guys Welcome the Rolling Stones." WHK's early rock status is also highlighted in the 1997 film, *Telling Lies in America,* by Hollywood screenwriter and Cleveland native Joe Eszterhas.

The radio station, however, did earn its status in a rather devious manner. WHK didn't get where it was by simply spinning records. As far as northeast Ohio boomers are concerned, this station will eternally be remembered for pulling off the biggest coup in radio history.

With a Little Help from Their Friends

In 1964, AM stations WHK and KYW battled fiercely for the highest ratings. When word hit that the Beatles were coming to Cleveland on their first American tour, Round 1 had officially begun. Both stations had strong allies, and both wanted to secure sponsorship of this electrifying event. KYW boasted the most popular deejay in town, Jerry G., while WHK had "Emperor Joe" Mayer, a confirmed Beatlemaniac. But only one station would be deemed the "Official Beatles radio station."

The behind-the-scenes maneuverings began with three savvy salesmen: WHK's Norman Wain, Bob Weiss, and Joe Zingale. The trio realized, as did their competitors, that representing the Beatles on their American debut would ensure their success for a long time to come. So in anticipation of this event, Weiss and Wain kept control at the station while Zingale flew to New York to convince MCA (the tour's booking agency) to grant their station sponsorship.

But the salesman was in for a surprise. Soon after his arrival, Zingale learned KYW had beat him to the punch and already made a deal with MCA to bring the Beatles to Cleveland.

"We didn't know what to do," Wain explains. "So we cooked up a scheme. We told them [MCA] they could go with KYW, but that we were the only station that had Public Hall. Now, the truth was, we didn't have Public Hall."

When MCA management called their bluff and asked for proof, Wain once again consulted his staff. Within hours, he produced a bogus telegram stating that WHK had secured Public Hall for September 15, the only weekend the Beatles were available. Negotiations with KYW were promptly canceled. Norman Wain and friends succeeded in outsmarting the competition.

Hot Town, Summer in the City

Throughout the school year, radio personalities were everywhere, hosting charity benefits and record hops at area high schools and shopping centers. The events brought the fans closer to their radio and recording idols and, in turn, raised huge dollars for hospitals and other charities. It was not coincidental, certainly, that these dance parties served to provide huge ratings for the stations.

So, by way of "giving back" to loyal listeners throughout the year, stations sponsored outdoor "appreciation" concerts, all summer long, that were free (or close to it). Usually taking place at area amusement parks, WHK's "Freak Out" shows were among the most popular summertime events.

At one time or another, the Young Rascals, Paul Revere and the Raiders, Neil Diamond, Keith, the Blues Magoos, Tommy James and the Shondells, the Left Bank, Sonny and Cher, and other pop artists all generously gave their time and talent for these events. (The stars were happy to oblige in hopes of selling records, despite the fact they were paid very little for their performances—a practice unheard of in these "show me the money" days.) And big crowds were a guarantee. One particular WHK Day concert at Geauga Lake Park drew an estimated 125,000 people. At that event, the fans were so excited upon seeing Fabian that the pop star was forced to sneak into the park disguised as an ice cream vendor.

Walt Tiburski—whose own phenomenal career began with his high school band Walt and the Marquis and then expanded to executive positions with stations WMMS-FM, WNCX-FM, and others—recalls being influenced by WHK's key players. "My first radio contact was with Joe Mayer, soon followed by Ron Brittain. Brittain was the afternoon-drive jock, and he'd put a concert together in Cleveland called 'The Brittain-American Show,' which starred all-American acts like the Shangri-Las and Jay and the Americans. And when the Beach Boys played, I covered the story as editor for my high school newspaper. That's when I got firmly rooted [in the business]."

In 1967, WHK's popularity with adolescents changed drastically when management changed formats, deciding to become a "beautiful music" station—a far cry from its former incarnation. Yet despite the changes and overwhelming competition during its more than seventy-five years in broadcasting, WHK is still a presence in the industry. Today its "All News Plus" format, consisting of local, national, and international news and sports, weather and traffic reports, business news, and talk shows, is the only one of its kind in Northeast Ohio.

KYW-AM 1100

Although WHK may have had better business sense, KYW had a 50,000-clear-watt channel as opposed to WHK's 5,000. And KYW also had those VIPs (Very Important Personalities). Of course, KYW was the station that "lost" the Beatles, but that didn't stop deejays Jerry G., Jim Stagg, and Jay "the Jaybird" Lawrence from winning the Fab Four's friendship, even traveling with them at times (of particular note, to the group's famed New York Shea Stadium concert). By 1965, this celebrated association gave the station its needed edge over WHK, and as a result KYW was soon hailed as Cleveland's number-one Top 40 station. "Before the station changed to WKYC," Jerry G. says, "our last ratings for prime time, which was my 6–10 P.M. shift, was 33 shares [one out of three radios tuned to KYW]. That was unprecedented and will most likely never happen again. It wasn't me necessarily; it just shows how the music was such a part of young people's lives."

The station also had a sixteen-year-old music lover named Eric Stevens who jumped on the radio bandwagon while still attending Cleveland Heights High School. "I started out doing record hops with the VIPs in 1964. Unfortunately, those don't exist today, but back then they were big events. We'd travel over a one-hundred-mile radius of Cleveland. There'd be live bands sometimes, or we'd play records and it was not unusual to have 1,000 kids at a record hop, and I remember a hop near Cedar Point that brought out nearly 2,000," Stevens recalls. He also fondly remembers when Jim Stagg went on tour with the Beatles, and the teenager was appointed to take over the record hops in Stagg's place. "That was a truly special time," he says. "I was lucky enough to begin my career with KYW and the Beatles, and there's been nothing in my life more exciting before or since."

One of the most popular radio shows was the Sunday evening "Jim Runyan and Folks," which rode on the folk music trend. Stevens became producer of the show and interviewed folk artists of the day, including Bob Dylan, Gordon Lightfoot, and Ian and Sylvia, among others.

KYW became WKYC in 1967, but the change meant little to listeners. The station continued to attract an audience, particularly for its "Caravan of Stars." These concerts of up to eight very different acts that drew a variety of fans. Many of these shows were held at Euclid Beach Park on Lakeshore Boulevard near E. 156th Street, also a popular spot for political rallies. Although literally hundreds of rallies were held there, the most memorable by far was the John F. Kennedy Steer Roast held just two months before he was elected president.

But time and Beatlemania passed all too quickly. By 1969, the station's VIPs had moved to other jobs and soon WKYC would drop its rock and roll format. Like WHK, the station (whose call letters are now WTAM) focuses on news and weather reports. Yet, for a time it could still boast a rock and roll connection. Two of the most popular disc jockeys in Cleveland's rock history, Jeff and Flash, were air personalities from 1994–97, part of the AM station both grew up listening to.

Clearly it was those Very Important Personalities that made the station such a dominating force in sixties radio. And perhaps no one can recall them better than the young kid they influenced the most. "Every one of those deejays were fantastic," Stevens says. "They were truly extraordinary personalities, and what made the station so promotionally strong. There wasn't a weak link in the chain."

WIXY 1260 (1965–76)

I do motivational speaking around town. And when I give my resume at a meeting, I may say, "able to leap tall buildings in a single bound, have x-ray vision, and super powers," and people yawn. But when I mention I was program director for WIXY [1967–69], everybody just lights up. It's amazing the power that station had on people here as well as certain demographics.

—Eric Stevens

From the start, it had all the right elements: the brains of radio whiz Norman Wain; young, energetic deejays; and the ability to put a creative spin on the music it projected. Not bad for a 5,000-watt station. "We pulled out all the stops," Wain recalled at a 1997 radio forum at the Rock Hall. "You name a contest, we did it. You name a giveaway, we did it. We did anything you can imagine to give attention to ourselves. Plus we were fortunate to have some pretty great disc jockeys."

They also had important behind-the-scenes men who knew what kids wanted to hear. "We were way ahead of our time when George Brewer had me pre-program every record," recalls Stevens, who, at age twenty-one, started there as music director of the infant station. "For three years I not only picked every record, but chose the order in which they were played and when we played it. Nowadays that's no big deal, but back in '66 no one did that. In fact, my sound was so imbedded in my head that if there was a problem, the deejays would play the records out of order and I'd hear it in my car or something, and that's how I knew they needed me."

The designated playlist was Top 40 rock and roll at its best in the hands of original staffers Mike Reineri (morning drive), Larry "the Duker" Morrow (midday), Lou "King" Kirby (afternoon drive), and Dick "Wilde Childe" Kemp (7 P.M.–midnight). Other music men soon jumped on board, namely Big Jack Armstrong, Chuck Dunaway, and Billy Bass, and they became favorites as well.

With transistors being the hottest teen possession, the rockin' sounds of the musical call letters WIXY 1260 could be heard wherever miniature radios were clasped tightly to ears—be it the park, the beaches, or the street.

Then on August 14, 1966, the Beatles returned to Cleveland. But this time, circumstances were drastically different. Wain explains: "We were all set to sell 70,000 tickets [to fill the Municipal Stadium]. Then, a month before, Lennon made the remark about the Beatles being bigger than Jesus. It offended a lot of people, and a lot of them stayed away." That comment from Lennon that fans were more preoccupied with this pop group than they were with Jesus was meant as a complaint that the church was losing its connection with youth. The media, however, ran with it, adding fuel to the fire by taking the quote out of context and repeating the remark while failing to explain—or admit—that there was more truth than ego in Lennon's statement. Immediately, some radio stations and fans alike started bashing the Fab Four.

All the hubbub resulted in a ban of Beatles records and, of course, influenced projected concert sales. Within days of the statement, and weeks before the anticipated Cleveland stadium concert, even local clergymen got on the bandwagon denouncing the Beatles, causing ticket sales to move slowly. The timing couldn't have been worse. The controversial remark fell flat in the laps of Cleveland's promo men, who then had to do whatever they could to rekindle wounded fan interest and increase dwindling sales. Radio stations did their best to drum up excitement by sponsoring "Meet the Beatles" contests and spinning out Beatles tunes. Tickets were so accessible that WIXY Beatle coupons were advertised in the *Plain Dealer,* so fans could easily obtain tickets by mail. Two years before, that kind of offer wasn't feasible. Then, as the date closed in, deejay Al Gates prepared to fly to London to tour with the group and offered to personally deliver letters and gifts to the band members before arriving back with them for their scheduled North Coast concert.

The buzz helped. In addition, just three days before that appearance, Lennon made a public apology to all who were offended by the comment. By the day of the concert, 24,646 tickets had been sold (at $3 to $5 each!), but the concert itself was considered by promoters a dismal failure, for sales were nowhere near the targeted numbers and the stadium was only one-third full.

But those fortunate enough to attend the Municipal Stadium concert that night got to experience the show of a lifetime, particularly considering no one dreamed it would be the last concert tour ever by the Fab Four. The crowd, naturally, went crazy as the Beatles hit the stage (set up at the Indians' second base). And just as had happened hundreds of times before in hundreds of cities, as soon as the Beatles began playing, mass hysteria ensued. By the third song, the group was forced to retreat when 3,000 kids broke down a snow fence and rushed onto the field. Even the police were at a loss to stop the chaos. After a thirty-minute intermission, the crowd calmed down and the British band was able to conclude their ten-song set. Because of such chaos at every concert they gave, the Beatles later announced that they would tour no more.

But it was merely the beginning for WIXY 1260. The station's famous "world exclusives" made the deejays heroes in the eyes of young rockers. Eric Stevens recalls:

At one point we had a transmitter which was where the programming people were, and I wanted to get another Beatles exclusive. This one was "Penny Lane" and "Strawberry Fields." We worked it out with the Capitol Records promotion people that I would meet them downtown. They'd give me the record and I would drive out to the transmitter, then they'd go to 'KYC and 'HK and give it to them. Everyone would have to wait 45 minutes 'til I'd get over there. Well, what they didn't know was that we could feed audio from the downtown office to where the transmitter was. So in about five minutes, we'd yell, "Only WIXY has it!" And we'd play the songs for about a half-hour back-to-back while these guys were running to the other stations. I remember one Capitol promotion man got to 'KYC, and when he handed the record to the music director, the guy literally jumped up and down on it, he was so upset.

Still another memorable exclusive involving a Beatles single took place in April 1967. Fans on the North Coast can still recall hearing the Beatles' song "A Day in the Life" before anyone else in the country. Of course, this act resulted in an immediate FCC "cease and desist" order. But the damage—or, rather, the scoop—had been done.

WIXY Appreciation Days

The first big event, held on May 28, 1966, at Chippewa Lake Park, showcased the popular acts of the time: the Beau Brummels ("Laugh, Laugh"), the Vogues ("You're the One"), Cleveland's GTOs, and others. "My favorite one had to be with Neil Diamond and the Fifth Dimension, in the summer of '67," Stevens recalls. "I had the unique job of putting the acts together, and that, of course, was a lot of fun. That particular day it was pouring rain. We all got on a big bus and drove out to Geauga Lake. I remember Neil Diamond standing on stage singing, 'Girl, You'll Be a Woman Soon,' with the rain pouring on him and all the young girls grabbing for his hand as he was singing. It was really a dramatic moment because it was raining, and the crowd was huge and emotions were high. Then afterward we all drove out to the old Versailles and partied with the acts, and just had a great time."

Another annual event happened when WIXY got together with the *Cleveland Press* and hosted the Teen-age Fair Pop Expo at Public Hall. This festival, held annually at the end of summer, was a celebration of all the young acts and included performances by national artists as well as local groups such as the James Gang, Cyrus Erie (pre-Raspberries), Silk (with Michael Stanley), Damnation of Adam Blessing, and the Mr. Stress Blues Band. But perhaps the most popular attraction was the Battle of the Bands contests, which highlighted local groups with the most potential. "Those teen fairs were one of the biggest events in town," David Spero says. "Not only was it great for local bands to gain exposure, I saw everyone from Mitch Ryder to Van Morrison there. That's how those kind of bands built followings. And it served as a great outlet for young kids."

Without a doubt, WIXY was the hottest rock station in Cleveland by 1967. "Anybody who was anyone either appeared in concert or came by the WIXY studios," recalls Chuck Dunaway, WIXY program director from 1969–75. "WIXY was the number-one rock and roll station in the number one rock and roll city in America." The popular deejays brought out record-number fans wherever they made guest appearances.

It was also one of the first stations across the country to begin the regimented Top 40 playlist, a format now regularly used by both AM and FM stations. Although this move virtually marked the beginning of the end of the creative freedom enjoyed by deejays, who had previously ruled the turntable, the premise worked. "When we started Top 40 back then," Norman Wain recalls, "it was the top of each list in all genres, not just one. In other words, you'd hear the top songs—from rock to country music—across the board." Although not welcomed by the disc jockeys, the format caught on and helped propel WIXY to the top of AM radio. Through to the end of the decade, the station enjoyed high ratings and good times. (Who can forget those two-and-a-half-minute "Chicken-Man, the White-Winged Weekend Warrior" episodes, and the ongoing contests and concerts?) It also educated aspiring deejays with its WIXY School of Broadcasting, where for fifty dollars one could learn the ropes of the industry.

Although WIXY would remain a popular force in AM radio until the mid 1970s (when it changed to big-band station WBBG), FM radio would soon become the biggest media movement since television.

Break on through to the Other Side

Almost overnight, the same radio stations that were enjoying a honeymoon with young audiences discovered just how fickle this beat-driven generation was. FM radio came

WIXY supermen on Channel 5's *Morning Exchange*. Left to right: Jim Labarbara, Billy Bass, Lou "King" Kirby, *Morning Exchange* host Fred Griffith, and Larry Morrow. *Photo by Janet Macoska. Courtesy of Billy Bass.*

blasting onto the scene with its superior-quality sound. "Frequency modulation" used wider channels, enabling it to broadcast in stereo as opposed to AM's mono. It didn't take long for FM to catch Baby Boomers' attention.

Although it had been around for decades, the frequency had previously not been considered a viable medium. Many stations had simulcast AM and FM ("sister stations"), with FM simply duplicating the AM programs. In 1965, the FCC ordered FM sister stations in cities with populations over 100,000 to provide a different spin to its product, forcing it to be a separate entity from AM. This gave FM the edge it needed. Natural teen curiosity lured radio's biggest share of listeners to lend an ear. Suddenly AM radio was stagnant and boring. FM was for the more aware, the hip, the "underground" (innovative music promoting album cuts as opposed to hit singles).

Radio veteran Denny Sanders explains:

None of this development of FM would've ever happened if the five following things didn't happen all at once, by a sheer piece of luck. First, the FCC ordered to split AM/FM stations in 1965. So there you had the window. Number two, radio stations, still not believing this would create an audience for FM, therefore didn't take it seriously. So when young folks like myself came along proposing somewhat radical formats, station owners didn't care. They felt we were all a bunch of inexperienced kids they didn't have to pay much. To them, it was better than putting on seasoned professionals who would cost them money. All they saw was that we were cheap.

Third, in those days practically every other person was eighteen, when the post-war baby-boomer audience was peaking. Fourth, stereo recording of contemporary music was becoming more common, providing yet another reason that made FM more attractive. Not instantly, but planting the seeds. And finally, what I call the "sensory explosion"— like television going from black & white to color, people wearing psychedelic-oriented clothes, tie-dyed, paisley and lots of colors. Young people's experiments with sensory-enhancing drugs. Therefore the high-fidelity stereo transmission of FM was kind of cool. You could hear the cymbals and tambourines on the records—you could get it all in stereo.

FM radio also brought about significant changes in rock and roll. Whereas AM spun out spit-polished tunes from pop, soul, and Motown to rockabilly and the "lite-rock" sounds of the Top 40, FM featured the electric and "hard rock" sound never heard on AM. It introduced listeners to songs that seemed to go on forever, with sixteen-minute drum solos, extended guitar whines, and lyrics filled with sexual innuendos or obscenities. One long song—really a short story—was "Alice's Restaurant," sung by Arlo Guthrie, son of famed folk singer Woody. The song became something of a national anthem for the hippie generation. Thirty years later Cleveland rock stations WNCX-FM and WMMS-FM continue to air it in its twenty-two-minute entirety every Thanksgiving afternoon.

With its unbridled, often controversial sound, FM became the listeners' medium of choice. The years 1967–71 saw several Cleveland "progressive rock" programs establishing themselves in this new world of pop evolution. Martin Perlich jumpstarted the trend. "The first true underground radio program, irrefutably, was Martin Perlich with his 'Perlich Project on WCLV,'" according to Walt Tiburski. "Then came Billy Bass, who had a Sunday night program on WIXY. This was the first inkling of the bigger movement."

The bigger movement began in earnest with the development of Cleveland's first "official" progressive radio station. The "new groove" station, WHK-FM (which later became WMMS), went on the air on August 15, 1968. Its sudden marketability was the result of the FCC change, which helped WHK recoup former AM fans (now college age) while boasting the most progressive and pioneering deejays in the city. "The New Grooves" consisted of Martin Perlich, Doc Nemo (Steve Nemeth), Victor Boc, Billy Bass, Rick D'Amico, and Pat (McCoy) Mack. These charismatic personalities had bounced from one turntable to another in the 1960s, and though their individual talents merged well with the new station, changes were inevitable. By September 29, 1968, WHK-FM had new call letters—WMMS—and several new deejays.

Why did young record spinners switch stations so often? Because they could. Free-form FM stations in Cleveland were sprouting up everywhere: WZAK, where Doc Nemo introduced many to their first underground sound; WXEN, with former WRUW-FM deejay, Victor Boc, and David Spero; and WCLV, a classical station which nabbed the spinning and speaking talents of former WXEN deejay Martin Perlich. Perlich began grabbing up obscure records from the downtown discount store where he worked and thus pioneered the "alternative radio" format introduced in his Sunday evening "Perlich Project."

Then came WNCR-FM, another pioneering station that by 1970 had brought together all of these restless disc jockeys, including Bass, who was still number one to many listeners from his old WIXY 1260 days. "'NCR was the fun station," David Spero recalls. "We had total freedom. Plus, we could play more music [because] the commercials were in between the music. Now the music is kinda in between the commercials. [In the beginning,] the four of us [Spero, Nemo, Bass, and Perlich] were all on different stations doing kind of the same thing. And I didn't even know these other guys were on the radio, and they probably didn't know me. But we all just thought you should be able to hear a nine-minute Doors tune or Jimi Hendrix—someone that didn't have a two-minute song. So when we all got together at 'NCR, it was a great mix." Another notable disc jockey there was Jeff Gelb, who, along with Shauna Zurbrugg, hosted a morning show from 1971 to 1973. "It was a magical time," recalls Gelb, now director of information services at Radio and Records.

Money really had nothing to do with it; it was about your passion for the music. As a deejay then, you were really called upon to be a "radio magician," someone who could create an image, feeling, or audio environment by way of what you were playing. You were creating your own universe to share with friends whether you knew them or not, and the segue was all-important. I remember we kept our own segue books. For instance, if I were to play a Cat Stevens song, I'd go to the book and look up Cat Stevens and say, "Okay, this segues into a Rolling Stones cut." The fun was to surprise or thrill your audience by giving them something they hadn't heard before, and to make it seamless, so listeners never had the opportunity to turn off the radio because they couldn't tell where one song ended and another began. Unfortunately, those times are long gone.

Despite the fact that WNCR fast became a top FM market early on, the format didn't survive much into the decade. When management changes occurred in 1971, its most popular disc jockeys staged a walkout, led by Billy Bass. The former employees all went on to bigger and better things, and WNCR eventually switched formats. But none of these experimental, revamped stations would come close to the success of an up-and-coming station that flew past its competitors.

Cleveland's FM fate was sealed when its top guns—Nemo, Bass, Spero, Boc, and Perlich—all made WMMS their new home. This dynamic, innovative group exposed its audience to the underbelly of rock and roll, leaving the slow-to-change AM rock stations (as well as their FM brothers) in the dust.

Goodbye Yellow Brick Road

The unique aspect of radio in the '60s was the variety of sounds available to listeners: color radio, free-form, progressive—it was all that and more. *Broad*casting as opposed to today's *narrow*casting. For example, Perlich was allowed to play underground sounds on a classical radio station. And aside from WIXY, stations didn't use a playlist. Jocks wrote down what they played so the incoming deejay wouldn't use the same song on the next show. Today, a song is often repeated before the shift is even changed.

Those cruising the radio dials craved the new, the offbeat, the unusual. And FM stations provided it. This new concept not only welcomed unique music and artists but required it. In the beginning, the joke among AM jocks was that FM meant "Find Me." To their utter amazement, people did. And now the tables have turned. AM's popularity is about where FM's was forty years ago. Most of the credit for FM's success lies in the young deejays whose attitude was not "why?" but "why not?" They took risks playing those unusual, experimental tunes and as a result became major influences in the music industry.

But like everything else in the unpredictable, fickle music world, the creative freedom and offbeat style that made listening to the radio fun and exciting in the '60s would be lost in later decades' corporate culture. Today, radio is simply another business (owned by conglomerates as opposed to small, independently owned companies); music is secondary, and listeners' opinions don't seem to matter anymore.

But during those radio wars, the music was the bottom line, and everybody won. Alas, we're not in Kansas anymore . . .

Recommended Reading

Aquila, Richard. *That Old Time Rock and Roll.* New York: Macmillan, 1989.

Gillett, Charlie. *The Sound of the City: The Rise of Rock and Roll,* 2nd ed. New York: Pantheon, 1989.

Nite, Norm N. *Rock On: The Illustrated Encyclopedia of Rock 'n' Roll,* Vol. 1. New York: Harper and Row, 1974.

———. *Rock On.* Vol. 2: *The Years of Change.* Rev. ed. New York: Harper and Row, 1978.

———. *Rock On Almanac: The First Four Decades of Rock 'n' Roll.* New York: Harper and Row, 1989.

Santelli, Robert. *Sixties Rock: A Listener's Guide.* New York: Contemporary Books, 1985

Scott, Barry. *We Had Joy, We Had Fun.* New York: Faber and Faber, 1994.

Taylor, Derek. *It Was Twenty Years Ago Today.* New York: Simon and Schuster, 1987

5 Hail to the '60s Radio Wonders

During the 1960s, there were a number of dynamic on-air personalities in Cleveland radio. While many moved on and out of the area, several of them have maintained their North Coast roots and are still active in the industry. Included here are those deejays whose presence has not been forgotten by their audience. Most are native Clevelanders, while a few, though not born and raised on the North Coast, were Clevelanders at heart during their time here.

Jerry G. Bishop (b. Jerry Ghan, 1942, Chicago: KYW, WKYC)

Jerry G. and the Beatles rose to the top almost simultaneously. The deejay who arrived in Cleveland from WPGC in Washington, D.C., began a prominent career at KYW in November 1963, as the Beatles' first hit, "I Want to Hold Your Hand," had just hit the airwaves. His nightly "Beatles Countdown" was a delight to teens throughout the listening area: as a result, this deejay's popularity broke records. Jerry G. remembers:

> When the Beatles thing broke, we began doing the "Countdown." Every day we'd get anywhere between 800 and 1,000 postcards from fans picking their top seven Beatles songs, and we'd play them in that time period.
>
> It was also around that time I started the television show, *Jerry G. and Company* on Channel 3 [WKYC affiliate]. It was a live program showcasing stars like Sonny and Cher, Gary Lewis and the Playboys, and they'd lip-synch their hit songs. It was similar to the *Upbeat* show but a little looser, more like the *Mike Douglas Show* when

that was broadcast from Cleveland. We had high school kids sitting in the audience, and I'd even sing on the show. [One song, "She's Gone," was recorded and released locally.]

The power of radio back then was unbelievable. That was evident when we'd go out and do personal appearances, and hundreds upon hundreds of kids would show up to see the guys spinning their favorite records.

Largely because of Beatlemania, Jerry G. cites 1966 as one of his best years in the business. This was the year he was assigned to fly to England (accompanied by Jane Scott and a lucky young winner of KYW's contest—with her mother, of course) to meet the Beatles in their hometown of Liverpool. Jerry G. continued on with the Beatles entourage for the rest of the American tour, flying in their private jet. "I was one of ten reporters on that plane. We stayed at the same hotel and rode in the same limo. As a result, I got to be good friends with them, especially McCartney and Lennon. We got into some heavy conversations, about the war and philosophical subjects, which I think was a welcome break for them 'cause at the time all reporters wanted to talk about was their long hair." The Cleveland disc jockey ended up with five hours of taped interviews, which he later edited for a one-hour special for his radio program. He then put the tapes away. Thirty years later those tapes netted him a substantial amount of money when he licensed some of the material out to Apple Records for use in the Beatles Anthology broadcast.

Jerry G. was respected by his radio coworkers and fans alike. "What I remember most about Jerry G. was his 'alligator' counting contest," notes nightclub deejay T. J. "the Deejay" Studniarz, who has one of the few copies of the recording of "She's Gone." "He really catered to kids, and he'd make things fun for them. He'd have kids call up and tell him where they spotted an alligator. One would say under his mother's car, another would say in their neighbor's yard. It was silly but it kept them interested and listening." Says former WKYC colleague Jack Armstrong, "I always thought his sign-off was the best. He used to say, 'Stay calm, try to adjust.' Great words to live by."

In 1967, Jerry G. left town for a Chicago station, eventually winding up on the West Coast. He currently resides in San Diego and for years hosted a morning talk show, called *Sun Up San Diego,* on CBS affiliate KFMB-TV. And though he's stretched his wings and is now proprietor of two restaurants, the Greek Islands Cafe and Asagios Restaurant, the AM-radio king has not hung up his earphones. He is the afternoon deejay for big-band station KPOP. He admits to having gray hair now but alleges that he's still one of the handsomest deejays around—referring to KYW's claim that he was the "World's Handsomest Disc Jockey."

Jay Lawrence (b. Chicago; KYW, WKYC, WBBG)

"I was one of those cynical people who said the Beatles wouldn't last," Lawrence says with a laugh. "I figured it was all just a passing fad—here today, gone tomorrow. Then they ended up helping my career."

Like Jerry G., Lawrence got his first Cleveland radio job at KYW just at the height of Beatlemania in 1964. "To this day I tell the story of when Jerry G., Jim Stagg [who traveled with the group for that tour], and I hung around the Beatles when they were here in Cleveland. I can remember standing out in front of the Theatrical Restaurant, getting amphetamines for Lennon and girls for them. I tell people I was a drug dealer and pimp for the Beatles—but no one believes it!" Almost from their first on-air exposure, Lawrence (then one of the few black deejays in Cleveland) and Jerry G. befriended not only their audience but each other. "I happen to have one of those raucous, infectious laughs, and Jerry, on purpose, would get me started laughing on the air where I couldn't stop. Then one day someone recorded my laugh and it was used on the Ghoulardi Friday night horror movie show."

When Jerry G. left for Chicago in 1967, Chicago native Lawrence was chosen to take his place as host of the TV show. The format was changed to star—get this!—a horse named Ralph. "[*The Big Ralph Show*] was more a variety-type show centered around this horse called Big Ralph, who would never show up so I always had to sub for him. Yes, it was a bizarre concept, so bizarre I think it lasted about thirteen weeks, tops."

When KYW became WKYC in 1968, radio life wasn't the same for this amiable deejay. "The [new] management said I talked too much!" So what did he do? He ultimately became a talkshow host for KTAR-TV in Phoenix, where he resides today.

"But I will say, and I mean it sincerely, that the best times in my career was when I was in Cleveland. Not just in radio, but all those times Jerry and I would perform live in Halle's [department store] auditorium. We'd do shows together. We'd sing and play guitar, and everyone, especially the teen girls, had such a fun time. He and I always worked well together and we keep in touch to this day."

Mike Reineri (b. Pittsburgh; WIXY)

Reineri was among the first deejays to anchor on WIXY when it debuted in 1966. The morning-drive air personality stayed for just a year, but he returned to the station in 1969. For the next six years, Reineri gathered a lot of memories. His favorite? The promotions.

I remember the hot pants contest on Public Square that drew something like 50,000 people. Then there was Lady Godiva promotion. That's when I got this gorgeous girl to ride seminaked on a horse that had no clothes on whatsoever—from E. 40th Street and Euclid [where the station was located] to Public Square. It was like a parade; there were people five feet deep standing on the square. Though I don't recall much of the purpose behind that event other than it was tied to some tax we were opposed to. But I certainly remember the girl!

Another successful promotion was when we gathered a troupe of volunteers and called them "Reineri's Raiders." This was when people were becoming more environmentally aware, with the pollution, recycling and all that. We got people to come out and clean up Public Square. It was so clean afterward, I said you could fry an egg on the sidewalk, and to prove it I did!

In September 1997, Reineri returned to Cleveland for a WIXY weekend reunion sponsored by oldies station WMJI. He hadn't been back since he left in 1975. "I tell you, the city is pretty sharp nowadays, and the Rock Hall is just gorgeous," he says.

Reineri remains in the radio business. He owns a company called Morning Drive, Inc., which serves station WAXY in Miami. The call letters are similar to his old Cleveland station, he admits. "I still say WIXY on the air about once a month or so, even after all these years!"

Chuck Dunaway (b. 1934, Oklahoma; WKYC, WIXY)

Chuck Dunaway began his years in Cleveland in 1968 as the afternoon-drive jock on WKYC, having previously worked for a station in Houston. He found himself at the right place at the right time—the day Jimi Hendrix came to town.

Joe Eszterhas [Hollywood screenwriter] was a *Cleveland Press* reporter at the time. He was doing a stringer article on Hendrix for *Time* magazine. Because I was emceeing the show at Public Hall, he called to tell me Jimi was coming in the day before and asked if I would like to join him and Jimi at Otto's Grotto that night. Of course, I said "sure." Leonard Nimoy was also in town and ended up joining us as well. And Jimi got up and played that night; it was wild. And he was phenomenal—just took the place by storm. And thanks to Joe's photographer, I've got a great picture of us to remember it by [see p. 602].

Anyway, then comes the concert the next night. Jimi was nearing the end of his show, and he's getting ready to light up his guitar when the Cleveland Bomb Squad came in. There'd been a bomb threat. So we had to stop the show and everyone had to look under their seats for a brown paper bag. After a half hour of this, nothing was found and we resumed the show, and the second show went without incident. I was anticipating the article in *Time,* but when it came out there was no mention of Jimi's guest appearance at Otto's where he spontaneously got up and blew everyone away with his guitar, or about the fantastic show he gave the following night. It was all about the bomb threat. I thought that was a huge injustice.

Then WIXY came calling. Dunaway was hired as WIXY's program director in 1969, staying on until 1975. They were years Dunaway recalls fondly. About his former boss, Norman Wain, Dunaway says, "The man could sniff out a promotion a mile away." No one would dispute that. Like his former coworkers, Dunaway has his favorite WIXY publicity stunt. "That's when we got our own Francine," he says. "See, Francine was a very well-endowed lady who made her presence known on Wall Street, and made the newspapers all over the country. So of course, Norman Wain countered with our own

Francine, saying, 'Anything New York can do, we can do better.' So we advertised on the air for ladies to participate in our 'big boob contest.' First prize was $500, and boy, did we get the response. It was funny watching the people's reaction when this parade of big-chested women stopped traffic for over two hours!"

But it was meeting members of rock's royalty, like Hendrix and Janis Joplin, that Dunaway treasures most. When the station was sold to Globetrotter Communications in 1975, Dunaway was hired by the company to organize syndicated rock and roll shows, though the idea never materialized.

After returning to Houston, Dunaway didn't forget the power of Cleveland's rock scene. "When ZZ Top was just a local Texas band, I told their manager, Bill Ham, that they should play at the Cleveland Agora if they wanted a good shot at national exposure. Ham took my advice and called Hank LoConti and got them a gig there. Right after that, they really hit big. It was a great pleasure to bring my favorite Texas band together with one of my favorite music towns."

In 1997, Dunaway sold his four Joplin, Missouri, radio stations: KXDG (classic rock), KSYN (Top 40), KIXQ (country), and KJMK (adult contemporary). He is now enjoying his retirement traveling and spending time with his family. He is also enjoying the

freedom from everyday work stresses. "Maybe now I'll have time to come up and see the Rock Hall, which I've been meaning to do since it opened!" he says. Anyone who remembers this industrious disc jockey will welcome that homecoming.

"Big Jack Armstrong" (b. John Charles Larsch, 1945, Durham, N.C.; WIXY, WKYC)

> To be a successful jock, you have to be different, take risks, reinvent the wheel, so to speak.
>
> —Jack Armstrong

Beginning his radio career at age nineteen at Charlotte station WAYS, Armstrong quickly drew an audience with his unusual way of speaking. He was able to spew out an amazing 386 words a minute, earning him a place in the *Guinness Book of Records*. "That was in 1971," Armstrong recalls. "The significant thing about that was although [President] Kennedy was clocked at 500 words a minute, I was the only one who could talk that fast ad-libbing. The key is to be able to talk and think that fast on an ad lib basis." The title followed him all the way to Denver station KTLK, where he became known as the "fastest mouth in the West."

Armstrong joined the WIXY crew in 1966, just in time to meet the Beatles.

> I was there at the '66 concert at the Cleveland Stadium, when they had to stop the concert because things got so out of hand. I can still see those kids pushed up front against the fence, almost suffocating. It was a frightening thing to see. Even Ringo looked rattled. He was white as a ghost. It was John Lennon who decided to go back on stage, against our better judgment. But he was right in the end. There would've been more chaos and riots had they not returned to finish the set.
>
> I've met a lot of people in my career, though few who really moved me. But when Lennon walked in the room, he physically moved me. You could actually feel like a spiritual presence in the room, so much so that I felt the hair on the back of my head stand up. No one affected me like that, before or since.

In December 1966, Armstrong left WIXY for the 50,000-watt station WKYC. However, the change didn't net him the job security he was searching for, and he left Cleveland in December 1967. Over the years he worked in Boston, Toronto, Hartford, Buffalo, and Indianapolis before returning to North Carolina. But of his radio days, Armstrong says:

> I never made a distinction between AM and FM. To me it was simply radio. But FM succeeded because AM failed. Then they took the Top 40 format from AM to FM and made no changes. The same theories we were using in 1966, for forced fifteen-minute listenership, are precisely the same they're using today. Unfortunately, that

(*Opposite*) WIXY or bust. A mostly male audience enjoys one of many WIXY 1260 radio promotions, the "Big Boob Contest." "It was timed for the noon hour luncheon break," photographer Nehez recalls. "The well-endowed contestants used a ladder, as I did, to get to the platform as the crowd quickly spilled into the main intersections, blocking traffic. WIXY representatives introduced each contestant and took their measurements amid whistling and catcalls. Police were finally unable to control the crowd and the WIXY people were told to get." *Photo by William S. Nehez.*

limits what gets played on the radio. It's so competitive. People may be just listening to you for five minutes, so you better be playing a hit during that time. If you're playing anything the least bit marginal, they may never tune in again. So you better be playing a bona fide hit, no matter how obnoxious that may be. That's what radio has become.

I'm bothered about some of the songs that are so profane and violent, like how you should go out and shoot some cop on the corner. That's not what music's supposed to be about. It should be enjoyable entertainment. But too often it's used as a social statement. That's fine, but don't just throw the message out. Entertainment comes first. Give me something peppy with it, something I can sing along to and enjoy. The same goes with jockin'. You can put out your opinions, but be entertaining, funny, and creative.

Today, Armstrong lives in High Point, North Carolina, and works the morning-drive slot at oldies station WMQX-FM. He returned to Cleveland in April 1998 to be honored by the Rock and Roll Hall of Fame and Museum in celebrating twenty of the top legendary disc jockeys throughout the nation.

"When it comes to this business, you have to put things in perspective. Sure, I could be bitter about some things that's been done to me; people can be mean-spirited. But I just remind myself that I've done well, I've affected the lives of millions of people. I haven't had to lie, cheat, or steal to get ahead. I've just done the best I could do, and that's a gift in itself. You don't have to hurt people to be successful."

Larry Morrow (b. Lawrence Dale Joseph Morrow, 1938, Detroit; CKLW-AM, WIXY-AM, WWWE-AM, WERE-AM, WQAL-FM)

I walked into my hometown station, WXYZ, with an empty briefcase, but full of ambition and announced, "This is what I wanna do for the rest of my life. I've just come from the Marine Corps and have no higher education as of yet, but I've got a lot of soul."

—Larry Morrow

Voted the most popular deejay in his hometown of Detroit, Larry Morrow, then better known as CKLW's "Duke Windsor," arrived in Cleveland in 1966. He came here after being hired by former WHK salesman Norman Wain, who'd just become owner of the city's newest and most promising AM radio station, WIXY-1260. Although the new kid in town, Morrow was no stranger to the North Coast listening audience. Thanks to CKLW's 50,000-watt power, "the Duker" was already familiar to Ohio teens.

With more than three decades in the radio industry, Morrow has many memories. His favorite takes him back to Southeast Asia in 1969. "That was when the Vietnam War was at its height. It was a rough time for families, especially when Christmas was approaching. That's when I got the idea to fly there and 'bring the boys home for the holidays.'"

Between Thanksgiving and Christmas, Morrow sent taped interviews from over 200 soldiers in thirty-one bases to be broadcast on WIXY. That experience wasn't forgotten when he returned to Cleveland. Many GIs called the deejay when they got home to thank him for being there. And Morrow made it a point to visit those who came home only to be hospitalized.

While at WIXY, Morrow and then-wife Pam wrote a song called "Get It On," which another popular deejay, Dick "Wilde Childe" Kemp, sang. The song was given much local airplay, and with lyrics like "Jam up, jelly right, and peanut butter tight," it rode the bubble-gum wave for some time.

In 1971, Morrow won the *Cleveland Press* Best Disc Jockey Award. One of seventy-plus radio and TV personalities nominated, Morrow received more than one million votes of the total three million cast. From then on, he was Larry Morrow, King of the Deejays.

When Morrow left WIXY, he went to work at station WWWE, where he stayed for ten years. Then it was on to WERE before finally settling in at WQAL. The man who, in 1979, was deemed "Mr. Cleveland" by the mayor, led the city's bicentennial parade in 1996 dressed as Moses Cleaveland. After receiving the keys to the city from Mayor Michael White and Governor Voinovich, the respected radio man responded, "This is the jewel in the crown for me."

Three years later, in May 1999, the inevitable happened. Morrow was a victim of the 1990s trend of stations being bought up by huge corporations. He was abruptly let go when the station went "another direction." Morrow says it was time for him to go. "I'm happy to be away from it. So much of radio today has become trash talk, with many jocks who are unprofessional and immoral. I don't want to be a part of that."

His distinctive voice, professional manner, and "nice guy" persona helped earn him a place in the Broadcasters Hall of Fame in Akron. In 1994, he was nominated for the national Radio Hall of Fame in Chicago. While honing his radio talents, Morrow earned a business degree from the University of Michigan. Today he is forming his own business venture and says it is the most refreshing thing he's done in years. But one of the last of the great '60s jocks to leave radio, he is sorely missed.

Joe Mayer (b. 1925, Cleveland; WEOL-AM, WDOK-AM, KYW-AM, WHK-AM, WGAR-FM)

"Emperor Joe," as he was known, is most remembered as one of the WHK "Good Guys" who befriended the Beatles when they came here for the first time. Mayer recalled on numerous occasions how he came to party with John Lennon and company at the old downtown Sheraton Hotel (now the Cleveland Renaissance) during both their Cleveland visits (1964 and 1966). Over the years, rumors circulated that the Beatles did not actually stay at the hotel but rather at the deejay's Fairview Park home. Mayer's wife, Ginny, denies the claim. "The Beatles did not stay with us," she says, "but we did have George Harrison's sister staying here for a time. And Paul Revere and the Raiders stayed with us when they came to town."

Joe Mayer began his career in 1953 at Elyria station WEOL-AM, after serving as a radioman for the U.S. Army during World War II. While at WHK, Mayer hosted numerous rock concerts, including the Rolling Stones's first Cleveland appearance at Public Hall in 1964. As unbelievable as it seems today, the Stones drew a mere 1,000 people to the 10,000-seat auditorium The AM deejay was hired in the late 1960s at WGAR, then an adult-contemporary and easy-listening station. He remained there through the early '70s. By then the deejay was referred to as "Mother Mayer" and "Captain Kidney" for his generous contributions and ongoing work as Northeast Ohio's honorary chairman of the March of Dimes and for his participation in fund raising for the Kidney Foundation.

During his forty years in radio, he won recognition and fans wherever his voice took him. Mayer died of a heart attack on May 16, 1997, at the age of seventy-one.

Jim LaBarbara (b. December 1941, Pittsburgh; WKYC, WIXY)

In 1966, Jim LaBarbara was working at a radio station in Erie, Pennsylvania, when he heard of an opening in Cleveland.

> Record promoter Steve Popovich, who was working for Decca at the time, suggested I go see Bob Martin, then general manager at WKYC. So I took a tape with me and met with him in Cleveland. Just two days later, Bob calls me and I thought it was this other deejay in town playing games. So I promptly hung up on him. Then Bob calls back and says, "Listen, if you hang up again I won't call back, and I'm offering you a job at WKYC." Boy, I started apologizing all over the place!
>
> I was real excited to work there because it was a 50,000-watt station and I was able to listen to it when I was a student at Allegheny College. Jerry G. and Jay Lawrence were my idols. So soon as I got there, I developed a good friendship with them. They were really good at what they did and were great mentors to learn from.

WKYC also had a recording studio downstairs, allowing the deejays to be first to play new songs recorded there by artists such as Terry Knight and the Pack ("Better Man Than I") and the Lemon Pipers ("Green Tambourine"). And a fan of local band the Choir, LaBarbara played their single "It's Cold Outside" before anyone else. "That song was a giant hit regionally," he recalls. "It stayed No. 1 for over five weeks. I used to do a lot of record hops, especially at Painesville Armory where the Choir often played."

By January 1968, new management stepped in and started to "clean house." Everyone was fired. Like his coworkers, LaBarbara went out looking for a new job. And he quickly found one, just down the street at a fairly new station that was fast becoming the most listened-to station in Cleveland: WIXY 1260. LaBarbara was assigned the all-night show, and he'll never forget his introduction to the new studio—and coworkers: "I came in that first night, and there was Bobby Magic with a garbage can on top of his head. And he was yelling into it on the radio. Now I had made it there just in time to go on the air but didn't know how to run their equipment. But when I asked Bobby to clue me in, he said, 'Sorry, I can't stay. I gotta go. Don't worry, it's real easy, man. You'll get it, but I gotta go.' He had a date or something, so he took off, leaving me on my own." The debut went smoothly, and for the next year and a half, LaBarbara enjoyed participating in WIXY's numerous promotions.

In 1969, LaBarbara left WIXY for a position at WELW in Cincinnati, and he now hosts the afternoon show at Cinci's oldies station WGRR-FM. In 1994, Declamania, a club of radio fans from around the country, named both LaBarbara and Jack Armstrong among the top forty deejays of all time, and in 2000, he, along with Jack Armstrong, was inducted into the Radio/TV Broadcasters Hall of Fame in Akron.

Among the Missing

Dick "Wilde Childe" Kemp (WIXY), with his energized style, is probably remembered more than any other '60s deejay. But when Kemp left the city in the early 1970s, there were numerous questions and much controversy about his whereabouts. Stories abound regarding this colorful personality, who is suspected to be either dead or, as a reliable source suggests, "most likely living out his fantasy of 'living in da woods'" (his favorite saying). Yet other sources say he is still alive but prefers to be anonymous. Steve "Doc Nemo" Nemeth (WNCR, WMMS) was another well-liked deejay who seemingly disappeared after leaving the North Coast in 1973 for greener pastures and warmer weather. Lou "King" Kirby (WIXY) and his wife live in Cancun, Mexico, where they sell real estate. Jim Stagg (WIXY) was last known to own a record store in Illinois. Chuck "the Napper" Knapp (WIXY) was last known to be living in Minnesota and a member of the Promise Keepers, a group for Christian men. Last word was that Bobby Magic (WIXY) was making a living as a freelance club disc jockey in Los Angeles.

6 WMMS-FM: The Glory Years

Top 40 was ignoring rock. Album radio was ignoring current rock. They were content to play old Jeff Beck and old Led Zeppelin. We'd play Beck and Zeppelin if they had a new product out, but we also played a lot of the new bands. I mean, rock 'n' roll will live forever, but only if you keep finding new rock 'n' roll heroes.

—John Gorman, WMMS music and program director,
1973–86 (*Northern Ohio Live*, 1993)

If it weren't for my wonder years in Cleveland, listening to WMMS, I might not be covering music and entertainment now.

—Chris Willman, *Entertainment Weekly* writer
(*Plain Dealer Sunday Magazine*, 1996)

With its album-oriented music (long-playing, largely uncensored underground sounds), WMMS clearly defined FM radio. Its growing reputation for breaking innovative artists with unprecedented promotion and intense publicity paved the way for its contemporaries. Debuting in September 1968 (replacing WHK-FM), this counterculture station didn't really get off the ground until three years later. It was then that WMMS single-handedly captured the market, maintaining that prestigious position for the next two decades. And while the station has seen its share of struggles and changing voices, WMMS remains one of Cleveland's premier rock and roll stations.

Back in its prime, however, there was more than one force behind the success of this radio phenomenon. During its formative years, the young, ambitious radio staff boasted an eclectic group of talents: at first Martin Perlich, Billy Bass, Victor Boc, and Doc Nemo, and then Kid Leo, Jeff Kinzbach and Ed "Flash" Ferenc (known as Jeff and Flash), David Spero, Steve Lushbaugh, Matt the Cat, Len "Boom Boom" Goldberg, BLF Bash, and Boston natives Denny Sanders and John Gorman (who became the station's most influential program director). It was also one of the first stations—AM or FM—to put women behind of the microphone: Joyce Halasa, Shauna Zurbrugg, Betty "Crash" Korvan, Shelley Stile, Dia Stein, and Ruby Cheeks.

"During that infant period, WMMS was a magnet for creative types. We had a frightening array of talented individuals," says Walt Tiburski, who went from being the station's sales manager to station manager, and then vice president from 1973 to 1984. "First there was the owner, Milt Maltz, then Carl Hirsch, who was a brilliant radio executive, Denny Sanders, John Gorman, and these young energetic deejays."

As a group, those record spinners had the nerve to experiment as well as the freedom to play whatever moved them (which often included unknown songs and artists, ultimately leading to the breaking of several of today's rock legends). Each had a hand in catapulting the careers of Bruce Springsteen, David Bowie, Golden Earring, "Southside Johnny" Lyon, Roxy Music, John Mellencamp (then John Cougar), Pat Benatar (who later married Parma native guitarist Neil Giraldo), Mott the Hoople, Humble Pie, Yes, Grand Funk Railroad, and Genesis. These artists, among others, owe much of their success to Cleveland radio and its listeners.

Come Together

As sometimes happens, however, the tales told over the years fail to give credit where credit is due. Such is the case of the North Coast discovery of Bruce Springsteen.

While there's no doubt Leo heavily promoted Springsteen's once his career took off, the honors for the breakthrough of the Jersey rocker must be shared with Michael Stanley and David Spero. According to Spero,

Kid Leo and I were always getting into musical battles. He was into glam rock like New York Dolls, Roxy Music, Alice Cooper, that kind of stuff. And I was strictly a rock and roller, playing the Rolling Stones, Beatles, and the like.

So when the E Street album came out, Michael Stanley called me and said, "Have you heard this guy, Bruce Springsteen?" Now I'd seen him as a folkie down at Ohio University. He was one of the opening acts with Blood, Sweat and Tears, the Eagles, Joe Walsh, Billy Preston, and Dr. Hook. That was '74, when he'd just come out with his *Greetings from Asbury Park*.

Then once I heard the E-Street album [*The Wild, the Innocent, and the E. Street Shuffle*], I loved it and started playing it on the air. And I'd tell Leo, "You gotta play this guy." And he'd say, "Yeah, when you start playing Roxy Music." Finally I played a Roxy Music tune I thought was pretty cool, so then he had to play Springsteen. Well, shortly after that I left [the station], and eight months later *Born to Run* came out, and Leo is credited for breaking Bruce Springsteen.

Another misconception involves David Bowie. To this day Billy Bass is credited with the honor of introducing David Bowie to the North Coast, and the acknowledgment is certainly well deserved. Bass did succeed in bringing Bowie's music to light in northeast Ohio and is responsible for Bowie's first Cleveland concert (as his first stop on his American "Ziggy Stardust" tour with the Spiders from Mars) at Public Music Hall on September 22, 1972. But Bass himself will tell anyone who'll listen that it was Denny Sanders who initially turned him on to the Brit glamor boy. Sanders recalls that time:

> The RCA records man knew I was a bit of a music freak and gave me a test pressing of the "Hunky Dory" album just days before it was officially released. He played "Changes" for me, and he told me it was David Bowie, whose early music I remembered back when I worked in Boston [for station WNTN-AM]. But this was a more mature and focused Bowie. That album knocked me out.
>
> This was the era when Crosby, Stills, Nash and Young, the Band, James Taylor, and the Allman Brothers were the big sound. And songs were getting longer and longer, and looser and looser. Then here comes this guy with a four-piece band wearing colorful clothes and orange hair making these little two-and-a-half minute . . . gems. It was so refreshing to hear this new music with such basic rock 'n' roll values.

Sanders then played the album for Bass, and once he put it on the turntable, Cleveland rockers were immediately captured by the Bowie sound.

Evidently discovery of talent is largely a collaborative effort. And there is no better proof of this than the work of those pioneers at WMMS.

History of a Radio Icon

Originally housed in the former WHK auditorium, this Metromedia-owned company (the call letters WMMS stand for "Metromedia stereo") quickly gained popularity. The young, vital staff was not afraid to try new things, and because it was a new medium, there were no rules—ideal conditions for this rebellious generation. More often than not, this band of radio gypsies succeeded. In 1972, program director Billy Bass devised a resourceful new concept that quickly changed the way Clevelanders enjoyed live music.

The celebrated "Coffeebreak Concerts" (later with host Matt the Cat) became an immediate hit with listeners, despite grumblings from those who believed daytime rock concerts didn't stand a chance. The idea was to bring artists to the people when the midweek drudgery was at its peak (Wednesday), thus getting them over "the hump." And because of its afternoon time slot, the premise fit an artist's late-night schedule.

Initially the concerts were played live at the studio and featured folk and acoustic acts. Soon these "unplugged" concerts branched out into a full-fledged plugged-in stage show. After chatting on-air with the morning deejays, the rock stars would move down the street to the Agora Ballroom (E. 24th and Chester) by 11:00 A.M. (later 1:00 P.M.). They would then play in the intimate confines of this popular concert hall, cranking out one full hour of lunchtime music. By then, the Agora was making national waves among rock artists and fans alike, so it was the perfect venue for such groundbreaking affairs. No one seemed to mind these daylight performances; rather, the idea of partying midday seemed to delight concertgoers, who saw them as welcome breaks from what was often a dreaded routine. Indeed, many employee "sick days" were used up at Coffeebreak Concerts, particularly when a favorite artist came to town.

The unparalleled live weekly concerts highlighted progressive music and helped earn a faithful fan base for the artists as well as the station. These live—and free—rock shows featured a broad spectrum of the best artists of its time, including Lou Reed, Peter Frampton, John Cougar Mellencamp, David Sanborn, Bryan Adams, Cyndi Lauper, and a slew of other rockers. Listeners were indeed treated to some memorable performances.

Ch-Ch-Ch-Changes

Just as the station's breakthrough reputation was gaining notice, Metromedia decided to sell WMMS to Malrite Communications in late 1972. According to many sources, Milton Maltz wanted to buy WHK-AM partly out of revenge for having been fired from there years before; its sister station, WMMS, was simply part of the package. Some staffers believed that with the new ownership the station and all it stood for would be threatened.

Former PR director and deejay Joyce Halasa recalls:

When we all started with 'MMS, we had so much freedom. Plus we were such a diverse group, especially agewise. I was twenty-two, Billy [Bass] was thirty, Wilde Childe was around thirty-five, Martin [Perlich] was close to forty, "Tree" [Tom Kelly, the station engineer] was just sixteen or seventeen, David [Spero] was eighteen/nineteen.

And once we broke Bowie, then came Lou Reed, Mott the Hoople, and we knew we'd really started something. We had to continually come up with new projects because there was literally no budget to buy any advertising whatsoever. Billy and I were doing everything. He was program director; I was handling public relations as well as a ton of other things. But with the company sale, we were suddenly being challenged about everything. Things were being orchestrated differently. What it came down to was, it just wasn't the same station anymore.

A series of run-ins with Malrite management over promotions caused Bass and Halasa to retreat rather than conform, and they summoned their coworkers to do the same. They didn't.

And radio life went on. In reality, the station's hold on northeast Ohio listeners was only just beginning. For despite the loss of favorite late-night deejay Bass, another man would take control, one who not only successfully filled the hole Bass's departure left but brought to the station new blood. With Denny Sanders at the helm, WMMS took risks and made more changes—including the station's logo.

A Buzzard Is Hatched

By the spring of 1974, it became obvious that WMMS needed to alter the way it illustrated the station's identity. The popular, controversial mushroom logo was on its way out. The freestanding mushrooms were growing toxic amid questionable implications. With the call letters appearing on two mushrooms and a little martian leaning against one of them, smoking a thin pipe, it more than faintly seemed to advocate the use of drugs. John Gorman had a better idea.

Controversial logo for a contentious radio station, WMMS. *Original art by Jude Tiburski Elliot.*

"Gorman and I happened to have the identical poster on our office walls," Tiburski recalls. "It was a popular hippie poster showing two scrawny buzzards sitting on a wire looking at each other and one saying to the other, 'Patience my ass, let's go kill something.' And John envisioned that on the tombstone of what was then our biggest competitor, WGCL-FM."

The station hired American Greetings artist David Helton to expand on the idea. An avid fan of WMMS, Helton devised a symbol that perfectly represented the station's attitude: a hip-looking bird with a snarly, mischievous grin—the predatory buzzard. The first inception was of the lank-haired bird sitting on a tombstone in a graveyard with handbills for rival stations WIXY and WGCL in its beak. Before long, however, those handbills weren't necessary. WMMS and the buzzard stood alone.

When Helton left in 1990 to start his own graphics business in his hometown of Chattanooga, there was no question who would take his place. Brian Chalmers, art director for Cleveland's popular entertainment circular *Scene* magazine, had worked with Helton before and he knew how to draw the station's mascot and successfully honor the buzzard tradition. The buzzard's popularity was such that the sneering bird became a fashion statement, showing up on t-shirts, halter tops, hats, belt buckles, cloth patches, and sunglasses. Some fans even went as far as to get buzzard tattoos!

What's the Buzz, Tell Me What's Happening

By the mid-'70s, WMMS certainly ruled the airwaves of Cleveland FM radio. Its energetic personalities and savvy marketing extended the station's impact far beyond its hometown roots.

"I'll never forget when I was in Lithuania in 1991, halfway around the world, into the Soviet Union in search of my father's farm," recalls Johan, former Agora promotions manager. "I'm smack in the middle of 'countryville' and I drive up by this river and stop at the first farmhouse I see. I pull up to the driveway, and there's a car parked there, and it has a WMMS bumper sticker on it! This was in the middle of nowhere—the fields of Lithuania, for heaven's sake!"

But it was the Clevelanders who enjoyed all the benefits. Naturally, this internationally known rock station had an unrelenting drive to stay perched on the top branch of the industry. Denny Sanders explains:

In the great days when it all jelled and came together, 'MMS was a major national force, this being between '75 and the mid '80s. There were really four of us who were the major programming designing committee. That was John Gorman, who was program director and had a tremendous sense of determination; myself, who understood the mechanics of broadcasting; Kid Leo, who was music director, with a terrific ear and could spot a hit a mile away; and one of the unsung heroes at the station, Rhonda Keifer, who was programming coordinator and basic all-around assistant who would galvanize communication.

The 1973 WMMS staff with Linda Ronstadt: (*left to right*) Denny Sanders, David Spero, Ronstadt, Steve Lushbaugh, Burt Stein (Elektra/Asylum promo man), John Gorman, and (*top*) Jeff Kinzbach. *David Spero Collection.*

We loaded the radio station with production in the same way a Top 40 station would be. In other words, we had a pre-recorded slam-bang, top-of-the-hour "The *Home* of the Buzzard, WMMS, Cleveland," with the jet sound. We had what are called bumpers, that had the "Shuu-shuu-shuu—WMMS," all this stuff. Progressive or album radio didn't have any of that. They had this attitude where they weren't supposed to have production or pre-recorded "identifiers," that they were like a classical music station and had this certain dignity to retain.

I felt there needed to be electricity to the station, that the station itself needed to be as exciting as the music we played. And that's what made 'MMS different. We were probably the first album-rock FM station in America to utilize dramatic production. We had a more focused rock and roll attitude, a signature sound.

Back in 1972, Sanders was holding down two jobs at the station. He was on the air from 2:00 to 6:00 P.M. and also acted as program director. And it was killing him. Enter John Gorman.

Sanders and Gorman had worked together at WNTN-AM near Boston. Sanders knew his hometown buddy would be the perfect one to take over the music and, eventually, programming duties (Sanders wished to stay on as deejay), so he summoned his friend to Cleveland. Gorman shared Sanders's belief in the progressive music, and his philosophy merged perfectly with the tone of the station. His organizational skills were such that within two weeks he had the music office in flawless order. He was later appointed the new program director. "Once John had things in control, I went home and I think I slept for a week," Sanders recalls. Gorman led WMMS down a streamlined path of its own from 1973 to 1986. "More than anybody, John defined the attitude and the image of 'MMS—of an aggressive radio station that was determined to win, and he had an great sense of marketing," Sanders adds.

During this era, there was virtually no competition. WIXY was on its way out (if for no other reason than it was an AM station), and the remaining Top 40 stations were segregated. Some, like WGCL-FM, offered more pop sounds, while others safely remained mainstream. And "adult contemporary" stations offered soft-rock music and little else. So for fans craving the latest electric sounds, there was only one radio station.

In 1977, the company moved to 1220 Statler Office Tower on Euclid Avenue. Even with a change of address, the station never skipped a beat. WMMS not only dominated Cleveland radio, it owned it. When an industry survey came out noting more records were sold per capita in northeast Ohio than anywhere else in the country, there was little doubt that WMMS was the catalyst. Indeed, this rock station's reputation for cutting-edge progressive programming had much to do with that dominance.

But it was more than just the music they played, or the assortment of in-your-face advertisements. It was that array of colorful personalities that made 'MMS unique.

More than any of them, Kid Leo defined the station. He was in the same age group as his listeners, he was accessible, and he always maintained a working-class attitude. Clevelanders identified with him. And with his Italian charm and seemingly boundless energy, he was utterly likeable. Sanders says he'll never forget the day he met him. "This skinny little Italian kid walks in my office one day with this silly purple hat on. He talked a lot with his hands and was a very colorful character, and just loaded with energy. This was during the time I was searching out college radio stations to fill some openings. And Leo was just what I was looking for. He was streetwise, funny, and totally unpretentious, perfect for the attitude I wanted for the station. This crazy, funny kid ended up being the main musical air personality both on and off the station."

From 1972 to 1988, Kid Leo was everywhere. Listeners would hear him during the day on his radio show and see him at concerts and special events at night. His very presence represented the station. In many fans' view, Leo *was* WMMS—so much so that when he left Cleveland for New York, it seemed that the station lost some of its luster. To faithful listeners, the exit of Sanders and Gorman in 1986, then Leo in 1988, and finally Jeff and Flash in 1994 marked the end to a truly golden era in rock radio.

Without a doubt, in the glory days of WMMS, it was the deejays that got listeners tuning in each day and kept them coming back for more. There was the "voice" of WMMS, Len "Boom Boom" Goldberg, who continues to do the station's commercials after twenty years. There was a creative promotional team that included Malrite's John Chaffee, Sanders, Gorman; vice president Tiburski; and full-time promotional director Dan Garfinkel, who brought to the station his experiences from Playhouse

Square and the Cleveland International Film Festival. And no listener can forget the gravelly voice of BLF Bash (a.k.a. Bill Freeman), maintaining all-night partiers' attention on his graveyard shift from 1976 to 1998. And though Matt the Cat later left to work at soft-rock station WDOK-FM, he is still remembered for his easygoing, light-hearted manner that suited perfectly his midday hours, particularly the "Coffeebreaks."

The Get-Down Man

For a guy who was only on the air a scant five minutes a week, salesman Murray Saul, "The Get-Down Man," managed to make Fridays at 6:00 P.M. memorable.

"I was in seventh grade when I learned of the real power of that station," recalls Joe Cronauer, who later became a WMMS employee, along with partner Brian Fowler. "I particularly remember hearing kids on the school bus—I mean everyone, shouting 'Got to, Got to, Got to, GET DOWN!!!' And I thought 'What are they talking about?'" Cronauer soon found out. "I listened to 'MMS because I *had* to. I liked listening to other stations, but the pressure to tune into 'MMS was so great, you just weren't cool unless you did." Each Friday from 1974 through 1977, Saul's spirited chant officially kicked off the six o'clock hour with his "salute to the weekend."

As with many things that clicked with the station, this popular bit came about as a fluke. "Murray was an amusing fellow. He was older and a bit of a beatnik, a fun guy, " Sanders explains. "Well, one day he was talking to his elderly aunt on the phone. She was hard of hearing, so he had to talk loud and repeat things a lot. And he was saying, 'I'll see you on Tuesday. No, Tuesday, TUESDAY, TUESDAY.' We got to ribbing him about this and pretty soon, TUESDAY turned into FRIDAY, FRIDAY. We started putting him on the air because he was so unusual. Here was this older fellow who was just as wild as we young folks, and was into the same things we were." "Through the week, Murray and I would work on the script," John Gorman recalls. "It usually began with something that had made the local news. It was sort of a 'welcome to the weekend' commentary on what was going on politically and socially, et cetera."

Tuning into the "Get-Down Man" became a Friday after-work habit for 'MMS listeners. And though the weekend greeting ran its course after three years, it remains one of the most memorable skits associated with the station. In the spring of 1999, Gorman and Saul released a CD of everyone's favorite "Get Down" episodes. Now in his seventies, Saul remains in the Cleveland area and recently retired as account executive for *Scene.*

We Belong

(*Opposite*) A 1977 poster announcing the much-anticipated Springsteen concert. *Courtesy of Jim Kluter.*

With the free-form style of FM radio came another first: female disc jockeys. (Of course, there were also the behind-the-scenes women: promotion coordinator Gina Iorillio and Rhonda Keifer.) By the mid-1970s, WMMS had at least one woman deejay in its

WMMS 101 FM
PROUDLY PRESENTS
THE ROCK AND ROLL EVENT OF THE YEAR
THE CLEVELAND BOYS
WITH SPECIAL GUEST
BRUCE SPRINGSTEEN

SIX NIGHTS ONLY
AT
THE COLISEUM

MAY 9, 10, 11, 12, 13, 14, MONDAY thru SATURDAY   8:30 p.m.

TICKETS: $6.50 in advance $7.50 at the door

TICKETS AVAILABLE AT ALL TICKET-TRON OUTLETS,

J. P. SNODGRASS, CLEVELAND TUX,

and all RECORD THEATER LOCATIONS

John Mellencamp celebrates his fortieth birthday at the WMMS studio, 1991. *Photo by Brian Chalmers.*

employ. Joyce Halasa began as the station's public relations director; between promotions, she took over as morning deejay for a time before taking her talents to the Agora Ballroom. Shauna Zurbrugg started at WNCR-FM, and then followed coworker Billy Bass after he switched stations. Zurbrugg was lively and used her acting ability to don a persona that brought new listeners to the station. She left for L.A. in 1972. Debbie Ullman, a friend of Denny Sanders from Boston's WBCN, stayed until a serious car accident laid her up for several months. Upon recovery, Ullman went to work for Akron station WCUE. Shelley Stile joined 'MMS in June 1975 and served as music director from 1976 to 1978.

By the time Betty "Crash" Korvan came on deck in 1976, WMMS was at the starting gate, and this energetic woman was there to enjoy the ride and the high ratings. "Betty was a very interesting person," John Gorman notes. "She was never probably a great on-air personality in terms of wit or persona. Her talent was that she was well-read and absolutely loved the music. It wasn't what she said, but how she crafted the music." Even for those who never stayed up nights listening to her show, Betty Korvan's name was well-known thanks to the slogan that graced many an 'MMS T-shirt: "I go to bed with Betty Korvan and wake up with Jeff and Flash." She remained at the station until moving to Deadwood, S.D., in 1984.

In the early 1980s, another rising star came on board after meeting Kid Leo at a party in Florida. Already working in broadcasting, Dia Stein was actively seeking something different. She found it at the Cleveland rock station. Although she only worked weekends and left after just a few years (for New York's NBC radio), she is one of the women deejays fondly remembered and associated with the station.

Jumpin' Jeff and Flash

No pair in the history of Cleveland rock radio has had a greater impact, created such exciting programming, or been so revered by listeners than Jeff and Flash. During the station's most successful run, deejay Jeff Kinzbach and newsman Ed "Flash" Ferenc ruled the roost as the anchor team for what became known as the "Buzzard Morning Zoo." Their popularity was largely due to their zany humor, obvious compatibility, and

Frequent Cleveland visitor Todd Rundgren hams it up with WMMS art director and photographer Brian Chalmers, 1993. *Photo by John Quinn.*

uncanny sense of what would best entertain their audience. With that winning formula, the two set out on a trailblazing partnership that, despite their sudden 1994 exit from WMMS, endured all the trials and tribulations of the industry.

The Jeff and Flash show was anything but dull. "We hosted toga parties [inspired by John Belushi's *Animal House*], 'bare as you dare' stunts, and went on vacations with over two hundred listeners to Jamaica for a week at a time. And we did a lot of spur-of-the-moment things on the show. We'd use sound effects and fresh ideas. We let the current events in Cleveland dictate what we would do in the mornings," Kinzbach says, adding that both he and Flash married blondes they met on one of their cruises. Be it by way of the Token Jokes (where listeners called in with the "dirty joke of the morning") or Spousal Arousal (a rather dangerous segment in which a spouse would inflict a practical joke on his/her mate on the air), listeners knew to prepare for the unexpected.

And then there were the Blow-ups, perhaps the most popular segment, according to Kinzbach. "That all started as our response to the numerous car blow-ups occurring back then. It seemed every week another car was being blown up and a mob figure killed. So we were sittin' around one morning talking about it and asked listeners, 'If you could blow something up, what or who would it be?' And it really took off. Folks would call up and say, 'I wanna blow up my ex-wife, or my boss, or my landlord—we'd get tons of responses for that one.'"

The Token Jokes started much the same way: A vehicle to get audience response. "We didn't want to be a typical show and just joke around all the time, so we summoned our listeners to call up with their own jokes, and that way everyone was having fun," Kinzbach says. "In that respect, we gave listeners a sense that they owned part of that show, and that made it all the more special," Ferenc adds.

Like many radio success stories, this partnership came about by accident. Ferenc arrived at the station as an intern from Cleveland State University, having worked at the campus station WCSU (as did Kid Leo, Betty "Crash" Korvan, and Matt the Cat). Beginning as a news assistant, the college student soon became the station's news editor, which is how he earned his nickname. Kinzbach says Ferenc had the nerve-wracking habit of completing a news story just seconds before morning deejay Sanders needed to report it on the air. Employees began remarking how Ferenc always delivered his copy "like a flash." One day, after a particularly close call, Sanders used the name on the air: "Oh, here comes 'Flash' now." And the name stuck.

In January 1974, Ferenc began reporting his own copy, reading the news on the air. But there'd be several changes before his future partner, Kinzbach, would join him. When Sanders switched from mornings to afternoons, Debbie Ullman arrived to cover the morning rush-hour shift. When she left to recover from her car accident, the station was without a morning person. Charlie Kendall was then hired to fill the 6:00–10 A.M. slot. Kendall had been brought to the station in 1975 by John Gorman, who had heard him on Framingham, Massachusetts, station WVBF-FM, where Kendall worked with another future WMMS alumnus, Bill "BLF Bash" Freeman.

"Working at 'MMS was an incredible experience," says Kendall, now at WYBB in Charleston, North Carolina. "Three days after I got there was Bad Company's premier performance at the Agora. Right after that, they took off. Then there was Roxy Music at Public Hall, the biggest venue they'd ever played. I remember being so impressed with Cleveland music fans. They were incredibly astute. They knew the bands and recognized quality. And boy, if we made a mistake on the radio, they let us know. On the other hand, if we did something good, they let us know that, too." Kendall was familiar with breaking acts. He is credited for being the first disc jockey to play Aerosmith, on WVBF. After he gave "Dream On" and "Mama Kin," a spin, the Boston group became one of the biggest American acts in rock history. The morning deejay left WMMS in 1976. "When Kendall left, Steve Lushbaugh took over the spot," Kinzbach says. "Then he took off for WMMR in Philadelphia. That's when they gave it [morning shift] to me." Kinzbach was working as the station's production engineer at the time, but because he often filled in for other deejays, he had earned on-air credentials. On December 28, 1976, the enthusiastic deejay and the fast-moving newsman—both nineteen—were officially dubbed "Jeff and Flash," WMMS's new morning team.

In January 1987, at the height of the Buzzard Morning Zoo, the pair gained an unprecedented 20.4 share of the listening audience in the Arbitron ratings—a feat unheard of in today's market. Compare this to the show that came in second, WQAL's morning show, with its 6.7 share (more of the normal range in a ratings period). Such was the impact of these two young dynamos. "And we were just having fun," Kinzbach says in response to that phenomenon.

In 1981, a Cleveland Indians baseball strike forced the cancellation of a much-anticipated All-Star game. In response to their listeners' disdain, Jeff and Flash summoned their audience to Municipal Stadium to stage a "Big Boo" in public protest. When the time came, 15,000 people made the trip downtown and then booed so loudly in unison that, according to Ferenc, it was "way above the threshold of pain." The incident was covered by newspapers across the country and was yet another example of the off-the-wall antics that consistently brought the deejays high ratings and national recognition.

The "Big Boo" was evidence of the tremendous bond these "zoo keepers" had with their listeners. But just as it seemed nothing could jinx the pair's good fortune, Lady Luck was about to deal them, and the station, a lousy hand. In 1979, *Rolling Stone* began conducting an annual national readers' poll to cast their vote for the number-one radio station in the country. For nine consecutive years, WMMS was the big winner, and the station's call letters became familiar with rockers around the world.

But in 1988, the station was accused of stuffing the ballot boxes to ensure its continuing reign as the national radio king. On February 25, a front-page story by Michael Heaton and David Sowd ran in the *Plain Dealer:* "A top executive at Cleveland's highest-paid radio station admitted this week that station personnel stuffed the ballot box to win this year's Rolling Stone Magazine reader's poll." The article also included a copy of a memo by the WMMS promotions director that contained instructions to the business manager to pick up copies of the magazine with the ballots and have a part-time promotions staffer "do them." In response to the questionable tactics, *Rolling Stone* withdrew the station's last title and promised to do away with the Best Radio Station category. (However, *Rolling Stone* managing editor, Jim Henke, reinstated the category on the ballot in the magazine's December 1, 1988, issue. "The feeling here," he told the *Plain Dealer,* "was that we get a lot of promotion from the radio stations, and there's no reason to alienate them.") As a result of the controversy, which made headlines throughout the industry and across the country, this one-time powerhouse lost much of its credibility, which in turn affected future ratings.

Not Their Lover

The biggest in-house upset was in the mid-1980s, and was the result of a decision that, to this day, not everyone involved agreed with: WMMS, always known and revered as an album-oriented rock (AOR) station, began leaning toward a Contemporary Hits Radio (CHR) format by playing Michael Jackson's "Billie Jean."

"It was very frustrating being in the business and watching it [the station] slowly deteriorate because they put more and more restrictions on us [in terms of creative decisions]," Kinzbach says. "Then came the day they decided to play Madonna and Michael Jackson and go Top 40. That was the day the credibility of that radio station died."

John Gorman sees it differently. "I never felt we were standard AOR, but rather a pop culture station. So when artists like Jackson or Prince's popularity went beyond urban contemporary, I felt we should extend the format."

However the personal and professional feelings differed, one irrefutable fact remained: When "Billie Jean" hit the national airwaves, none of the Buzzard's faithful listeners expected to hear the pop tune on *their* progressive music station. And when they did, the rock station's dedicated following felt betrayed.

"You should've seen the phones light up after that song played," Kinzbach says. "After all, that was *their* radio station, *their* music. And suddenly it wasn't just theirs anymore. What it did was bring in a whole new group of listeners." "That movement hurt the core audience, the ones who'd grown up with us," Ferenc remarks. "Yes, it brought in other listeners, but I feel it damaged the foundation, cheapened the product."

Alternately, Denny Sanders observes:

There was a whole new musical movement which reached maturity in the early '80s, spearheaded by groups U2, Duran Duran, INXS, Tears for Fears, etc. Michael Jackson had just given a critically acclaimed performance on the Motown 25th Anniversary TV show, Eddie Van Halen played on Jackson's *Thriller* album, Prince burst on the scene with some knockout stuff, and Madonna's material was played at every party I went to. WMMS was at a crossroads. If we ignored the whole thing and continued to emphasize Pink Floyd and Led Zeppelin, our audience would eventually age and drop out of the eighteen to thirty-four demographic. WMMS's trademark was to break new bands and performers. By 1982, WGCL, who was playing all of this new music, beat us in the ratings for the first time. We were doing Foreigner block parties, so it's no wonder! Some of us, the more music-oriented deejays, felt the station was missing the boat and sounding behind-the-times. We never went "Top 40" in the technical sense. We merely blended the more rock-compatible new stuff in with the more traditional AOR material, albeit carefully, depending on the time of day or night. After three or four months, the ratings exploded. We got more women listening in great numbers for the first time, while our male audience still had their traditional AOR. From late 1982–87, WMMS had the highest ratings of its history. We became to radio what *Rolling Stone* magazine was to print: a universal creation which was able to deal with nontraditional rock subjects with a rock 'n' roll attitude.

New Moon on Monday

By 1986 the station had seen several personnel changes. VP Tiburski had departed in 1984 to start his own national media company, Win Communications, Inc. Gorman, operations manager for both 'MMS and its sister station, WHK-AM, and Sanders left to usher in a new station, WNCX. Then, after sixteen years of being the station's prime afternoon jock, Kid Leo called it quits on December 16, 1988. Though he admits it was a difficult decision, Leo had been given an offer he couldn't refuse, at Columbia Records. And if losing Leo took veteran fans to their knees, what came a few years later forced them to the ground. On April 15, 1994, it was announced that Jeff and Flash would no longer be a part of WMMS. To thousands of loyal listeners, the buzz was now gone forever.

But the station picked itself up, dusted itself off, and began a new life with a new generation. WMMS, now located in Tower City, continued to acquire vital talent, such as another successful radio duo, Brian and Joe, who cut their teeth on the very team they replaced in 1994, Jeff and Flash. Today, like most stations in this area, WMMS continues changing managements and deejays and experiments with various rock formats.

The early, formative years of Cleveland's media powerhouse is the stuff of history. It's unlikely that such a phenomenal radio success story will ever be repeated. "We grew right along with our listeners," Ferenc says. "During those decades we went through it all together—good and bad. The phenomenal music, the deaths of Keith Moon, Lynyrd Skynyrd, Joplin, Hendrix, Morrison, John Bonham, John Lennon. And, of course, what was happening right here in our city—the '79 default, the '81 baseball strike, the bad river-burning jokes. Our listeners knew we were all-Cleveland no matter what, because this was our hometown."

In recalling their near twenty-year history at 'MMS, Ferenc and Kinzbach have similar thoughts on their successful run. "One thing we've always done was we stood up for Cleveland," Kinzbach notes. "People recognized that and stood up for Cleveland with

The Buzzard today.
*Concept by Jim West.
Design and illustration by
Brian Chalmers. Digital
illustration and
production by Joe Molnar.
Electronic imaging and
printing by Davies Wing.*

us. I truly believe all that support helped bring back the city. It made us respectable again." Flash adds, "We cheered for Cleveland, we cried for Cleveland, we worked for Cleveland. And through it all, we managed to have one hell of a good time!"

Denny Sanders, however, best summed up that golden time in radio. With a touching account of an unforgettable time, Sanders describes what it was like behind the scenes of a beloved radio "family."

It was sort of like the Beatles. In that, I mean it was a very good band. We were all very lucky to be in the right place at the right time. But eventually we all grew up, did our own solo albums, and the band could no longer stay together. But it was really wonderful while it lasted.

There's a sort of bittersweet line from the Woody Allen movie *Radio Days* that's sad but true. It goes something like this: I loved these people. They were my friends and I worked with them for many years. We shared great times. They were so much a part of my life. But sadly, as the years go by, as I try to remember what we did, their voices become dimmer and dimmer . . .

7 The Blues Connection

Blues is the foundation of all American music. Everything comes from blues—jazz, rock, funk—it all comes out of the blues.

—Robert Lockwood Jr.

Once people hear the blues, they want to hear more. The blues' 12-bar rhythm and bridge is what gave rise to rock 'n' roll.

—Jim Nisenson, founder of the Ohio Blues Society
(*Plain Dealer,* 1986)

Along with the rapid growth of rock and folk in the 1960s came a new generation of musicians who were giving a contemporary twist to the early style of "race music." White teens were catching on to the music that spiced up their musical taste buds. The blues was born in the Mississippi Delta, where black slaves and sharecroppers sang of pain and troubles as they worked the fields. Later, blues artists took their music to the streets, back alleys, and urban watering holes. As the music filtered its way north, the blues was welcomed by white musicians just as rock was making headlines. Interest reached as far as London, where it was particularly embraced. It is often said that if it weren't for American blues, there would've been no British "invasion" of artists such as John Mayall, Eric Clapton, the Rolling Stones—or, for that matter, any rock and roll.

With the influence of bluesman Buddy Guy, who popularized the mixing of blues sounds with the electric feedback of rock and roll in the late '50s and early '60s, Chicago became the epicenter for blues in the North, and the music became known as "Chicago blues." During that era, the Windy City produced some of the best harp players and blues guitarists—among them Otis Rush, B. B. King, Muddy Waters, Howlin' Wolf, and Robert Lockwood Jr. Since the '60s, Cleveland has bred a host of blues talents, such as Colin Dussault's Blues Project, Travis Haddix, Blue Lunch, Austin "Walkin' Cane" Charanghat and the Skydogs, Blue Taxi, and Blues DeVille, as well as those profiled below.

Robert Lockwood Jr. (or, as early fans remember, Robert *Jr.* Lockwood)

> There's a totally unique flavor to Lockwood's music. It's distinctive; nobody can do what he does. On a personal level, the man taught me how to maintain your dignity as a human being on the road surrounded by rats.
>
> —Jimmy Ley, Cleveland musician

Now well into his eighties, legendary bluesman Robert Lockwood keeps his name and his music in the limelight. He still plays at various clubs and festivals around Cleveland, continues to pump out record albums, and even lends his talents to the occasional musical theater production, such as for the Rabbit Run Theater in the eastern suburb of Madison.

Born in 1915 in Marvel, Arkansas, Lockwood had an edge early on. His two cousins taught him to play his grandfather's pump organ; but it was his mother's boyfriend, renowned Mississippi Delta blues pioneer Robert Johnson, who introduced him to the guitar and passed down some unique licks to his teenage protégé. Johnson died in 1938, but by then Lockwood had become a blues guitarist in his own right. When the family moved to Chicago in 1951, he quickly picked up on the "South Side" blues style of the northern plains. The combination of the bluesy South and electric guitar sound of the North gave the thirty-six-year-old a style all his own. It's a curious blend that is not all blues but not quite jazz—just simply the Lockwood sound.

In Chicago, the blues player was hired as session guitarist for the small independent label Chess Records. His electrifying chords can be heard on songs by Chess artists Little Walter and Sonny Boy Williamson. Embracing a more jazzy style, Lockwood became frustrated with the limitations of the Chicago blues scene. In 1961, he accompanied Williamson to Cleveland. But when Sonny Boy moved on, Lockwood stayed put. A trip meant to be just a pit stop turned into a lifelong residence for Lockwood, who is now considered a bona fide Clevelander.

Over the years, this guitar legend has played with the best of the best: Muddy Waters (who was also inspired by Robert Johnson), John Lee Hooker, Sonny Land Slim, Eddie Bord, Willie Mabon, Otis Spann, and Little Walter, with whom he toured for many years. Lockwood was also instrumental in launching other careers, most notably that of a young man who became known as B. B. King. Born Riley B. King in Indianola, Mississippi, the fieldhand grew up listening to the "King Biscuit Flour Hour" on Helena, Arkansas, radio station KFFA-AM, whose powerful airwaves spanned three Southern states. Lockwood's masterful sounds came through the radio King listened to on his lunch hour. When the bluesman came to perform in King's hometown, the two became acquainted, and Lockwood began working with him on the rudiments of the guitar. It wasn't long after that B. B. ("Blues Boy") took his guitar talents and his distinct soulful voice and launched a lucrative career that has sustained him well into the dawn of the new millennium. No doubt the man who served as his mentor had much to do with that.

Although others have staked their claim in blues history, Lockwood seems content to let his music speak for itself rather than embrace celebrity status. Though he keeps a low profile nationally, this blues wonder hasn't been forgotten by his colleagues. In 1980, along with buddy Johnny Shines, he received the W. C. Handy Blues Foundation award for Traditional Blues Album of the Year for *Hangin' On*. Jim O'Neal, editor for *Living Blues* magazine, once wrote about Lockwood: "He's one of the guitar players who shaped the modern guitar sound and one of the few who understands the breakthrough spirit of the [blues] music." In 1995, Lockwood recorded *Swings Live in Tokyo*, which sold tens of thousands of copies; and in 1996, British magazine *Mojo* named Lockwood one of the Top 100 greatest guitarists of all time. Aside from *Hangin' On*, there's been *Steady Rollin' Man, Contrasts, Does 12, Mr. Blues Is Back to Stay*, and *What's the Score*. In 1982, *Plays Robert and Robert*, which features a mix of Lockwood's and Johnson's compositions on 12-string guitar, was issued by the French Black and Blue label. It's a real find for any blues lover.

As with many blues artists of the '50s and '60s, Lockwood influenced the music of his white counterparts and affected those who simply appreciate his talent. "One night we were playing a gig" at the Red Creek Inn in Rochester, New York, recalls Jimmy Ley, who met Lockwood in 1970 and has toured with him many times over the years. "We all noticed this guy standing there way in the back of the room. He was wearing a black hat, black jacket, and black beard. We figured he was just some obscure blues fan. He stood there the entire night, watching and listening—never spoke to a soul. Then, as we were packing up after the last set, we noticed he was gone. That's when the owner came over and said, 'Did you guys happen to notice that guy standing in the back? That was Bob Dylan.' Apparently he'd been a big fan of Lockwood for years and just wanted to see him play without being hassled. He made the owner promise not to say anything until he had left."

Lockwood has had a substantial influence on Cleveland's young white musicians in particular. "I'm daddy to a lot of white boys," he's been known to quip. Younger associates who have played with him over the years include brothers Glenn and Gene Schwartz. And just as Robert Johnson did for him, Lockwood groomed a protégé of his own in the form of Mark Hahn (a.k.a. Cleveland Fats). A guitarist who studied with the "King of Cleveland Blues" and played with him for fifteen years, Hahn has become Cleveland's newest blues wonder. Another Lockwood fan moved all the way from London, Ontario, to be near his idol. Mr. Downchild (Steve Brazier) and the Houserockers was a top blues band in Canada when the group first played at the Mistake, filling in for a traveling Jimmy Ley. While in Cleveland, Brazier checked out his inspiration. And by 1985, Downchild decided he liked the North Coast as much as Lockwood and moved his family to Cleveland. Since then he has shared the stage with his mentor and has acquired his own following as a club-circuit regular.

It was thus appropriate that Lockwood would be invited to play at the Rock and Roll Hall of Fame's tribute to Robert Johnson on September 17, 1998. The following year, a city street near Settlers Landing in the Flats was named "Robert Lockwood Jr. Road," just in time for the blues icon's eighty-fourth birthday. And the bluesman continues to do what he does best at various Cleveland venues, including every Wednesday night at Fat Fish Blue.

The Mr. Stress Blues Band (1966–)

Back then there was very little blues activity in Cleveland as opposed to places like Chicago, so we had to make our own environment.

—Bill "Mr. Stress" Miller, speaking of his early blues career in the 1960s

I have the greatest respect for "Stress." He's always remained true to himself and his music through the years. He never sold out.

—Butch Armstrong, Cleveland musician

The Beginning of Blues Rock

In the early sixties, folk music was defined by songs like Woodie Guthrie's "This Land Is Your Land," Pete Seeger's "Where Have All the Flowers Gone," and Peter, Paul and Mary's "If I Had a Hammer." By mid-decade, however, with electric guitars entering the musical mainstream, folk and blues music inevitably produced a new offspring.

It took root at the heart of the folk music scene, New York's Greenwich Village and its famed coffeehouses: the Gaslight Cafe, the Night Owl, and the Bitter End. Smack in the middle of the folk heyday, musicians such as Bob Dylan were discovering the unique sounds of the Paul Butterfield Blues Band, the first white blues band to hit nationally. Before long, Dylan, the ultimate hippie folk king, had gotten himself some musical backup in the form of a group of blues musicians he simply referred to as "the Band." To many folkie diehards, this was the ultimate disgrace. Dylan had gone electric.

Other folk-style musicians soon followed Dylan's lead. John Sebastian formed his Lovin' Spoonful, John Phillips gathered up some Mamas and Papas, Roger McGuinn took flight with the Byrds, and so on. This interplay of folk, blues, and rock produced a new sound, called "electric blues" or "blues rock."

In Cleveland, young musicians began experimenting with this new mix in the University Circle area. One man in particular, who, like Dylan, was greatly influenced by Paul Butterfield, was twenty-two-year-old Bill Miller. "I discovered the Paul Butterfield Blues Band when they came out with their debut album in 1965," he says. "And I began to mimic what I heard on my first harmonica/mouth harp, an American Ace. I really got into it then. Butterfield was to me what the Beatles were for a lot of rock players."

"I met Bill when he answered an ad in the *Plain Dealer* my friend Pete Sinks placed for a musician," recalls keyboardist Mike Sands, who was a member of the band from its inception. "We were just out of high school back then. It was a mutual discovery, because not too many were into that kind of music. So Pete and I were delighted to find another comrade. We were immediately impressed with Bill, and the three of us got together and just started jammin' at places around town." Cultivating his own musical style in Cleveland's coffeehouses, Miller helped produce blues enthusiasts on the North Coast by showcasing the music throughout the area.

Miller, soon to be referred to as "Mr. Stress," began his ascent into blues rock before there was such a thing. Although born to a music man who played as many as nine different instruments during the Big Band era, Miller credits his earliest and greatest influence, WLAC, a station out of Nashville. "From 1948 to 1960, my family lived in the Cedar projects at E. 30th and Cedar Avenue, due to my parents' divorce a few years before. My black neighbors would listen incessantly to this one station that was just pumpin' out blues. It got to a point where I had to get my own radio so I could listen for myself to the sounds of Muddy Waters, Howlin' Wolf, B. B. King, Slim Harpo, Little Walter. I became obsessed, so much so that hearing Lazy Lester and Lonesome Sundown sent chills down my spine."

In 1965, Miller, who had received violin lessons from his father and took high school band courses in piano, trumpet, and clarinet, began playing acoustic harp with the folk singers in places such as the Well in East Cleveland. "At the time, the blues was the alternative music of its day. Hell, if you didn't play Motown or Top 40 in the '60s, you had a tough time getting jobs." On the national scene, Paul Butterfield made the harmonica hip again. In Cleveland, it was bluesman Bill Miller. And for years, Miller was the only white guy offering it.

Naming themselves "Mr. Stress"—the code used at psychiatric hospitals for alerting staff when a patient's out of control—Cleveland's first white blues band was born. The first group of musicians to perform under the Stress name was comprised of guitarist Glenn Schwartz, bassist Wayne O'Neill, keyboardist Mike Sands, and drummer Pete Sinks.

Although the band started playing the very java clubs where they hung out at, before long they were traveling around town to teen clubs and summer festivals. Their reputation as the only group playing that style of music led them to bigger venues, such as the renowned LaCave, where they set an attendance record for the biggest crowd drawn by a local band. Soon they were opening for national acts that played there, such as Ted Nugent and his band the Amboy Dukes.

But it was their first official (i.e., paid) gig at the Coffee House on E. 115th and Euclid Avenue—on Thanksgiving night 1966—that marked their beginning as a bona fide music group. (And it's the date the band commemorated for years with a performance at the Euclid Tavern, the club they played every weekend for nearly two decades.)

Got Their Mojo Working

Miller inadvertently became "Mr. Stress" simply because he was the frontman. "I didn't set out to be a singer, I was chosen by default—no one else wanted to do it," he says. Miller also was the voice and soul of the group, and the one who kept the band together throughout its many changes.

"It was a vibrant scene for musicians back then," he says of the 1960s. "In those days, a lot of musicians would perform with ones from other bands. Whoever was around would play together. And a white man could hang out in black bars. And we could play blues there—as long as we played it well. We had some really great jam sessions."

The list of area musicians who once played with Stress over the years reads like a Who's Who of Cleveland-based talents. They include drummer Jimmy Fox (with whom Miller, Tom Kriss, Rich Kriss, and Schwartz made a recording that was never released), Lud Hrovat (onetime drummer, Dave C. and the Sharptones), Donny Baker (guitar, E. T. Hooley), Dale Peters (bass, E.T. Hooley, James Gang), Vito San Filippo (bass, O'Jays, Tower of Power), Dan Klawon (Mods, Choir), Alan Greene (Jimmy Ley), Glen "Stutz Bearcat" (Generators, Armstrong Bearcat Band), and Greg Nelson (guitar). In 1972, guitarist Peter Laughner (Pere Ubu founder) came to play. "Pete was with us about three months," Miller recalls. "Then his musical taste started changing, and he got really into the Velvet Underground, a precursor to punk. He could definitely be considered the founding father of the New Wave scene in Cleveland." And in 1975 an aspiring young drummer played with them for a time, eighteen-year-old Anton Fier. He, too, became a leading figure in punk underground as a member of the Electric Eels, the Styrenes, Pere Ubu, the Feelies, and Golden Palominos. Rumor has it that the band, which played regularly at the Cellar Door on Cedar and Taylor Roads in Cleveland Heights, was joined on stage one night by a singer from Akron who later became one of rock's most prominent and enduring performers—Chrissie Hynde. Although Miller confirms it, Hynde claims to have no recollection of it.

Making a name for themselves among musicians, the Mr. Stress Blues Band began touring and opening for the most popular acts of the day throughout the late '60s and early '70s. At Detroit's legendary Grande Ballroom in 1969, they opened for Steppenwolf, Cream, and MC5. "That was a real highlight," Miller recalls, "The Grande was *the* rock emporium in the Midwest."

Luck wasn't always with them, however. One of Miller's greatest disappointments was when the band prepared to open for Led Zeppelin at the Grande, only to be bumped off the bill at the last moment in favor of an unknown band called Golden Earring (who, of course, went on to become national recording stars). And by the mid-1970s, the lifestyle was taking its toll on Miller. "In the early days, my voice was pretty high, I could reach falsetto notes, but after singing regularly and smoking like a chimney, I ended up having a biopsy on my throat in 1975 due to scar tissue. But as Aretha Franklin says, 'If you're a singer and don't have scar tissue on your vocal cords, you ain't shit.'"

In 1969, the band (Miller, Sinks, Donny Baker, and bassist Duane Verh) was offered a contract with Capitol Records. After reading the paperwork, however, Miller turned down the opportunity. "I realized it was for union scale per master and for 8 percent of the wholesale price. It was nothing," Miller explains. "I was to produce the session in Cleveland with no help. In other words, they wanted it done cheap. Plus there was no guarantee they'd release it or promote it. There's always a point in a musician's career when you think that maybe, given the right elements, you can make it big in this business. I thought that, too, in the '60s when we were touring and opening for the big-name groups. But by '75, when the band split—again—I came to realize that wasn't going to happen."

Although the group never achieved national recognition or secured any decent recording contract, they were an important presence in Cleveland's music scene for decades.

Further on up the Road

From 1972 to 1974, they were the house band for the Brick Cottage on Euclid and Mayfield Roads. They also had another weekly gig at the Cellar Door (later Peabody's Café, and now the Rhythm Room). All the while members came and went and came again: "Over the years, I kept shifting the same guys in and out because we never parted on bad terms. When someone left, it was usually because of job, marriage, or some other personal commitment," Miller says.

In February 1978, Mr. Stress was hired to play Wednesday and Saturday nights at the Euclid Tavern. The old club, which had been a bar since the 1890s, was located five miles east of downtown. With its old wooden bar and tin ceiling, the "Euc," as it's affectionately called by regulars, was, dark, smoky, and intimate— the perfect venue for a master blues band. Once word got around about this white blues band, blues enthusiasts packed the Euc' to capacity every Saturday night from 1978 through the late 1980s. During most of the time, the lineup consisted of Miller, Sands, guitarist Tim Matson, and drummer Nick Tranchito. "That was probably the most authentic blues group I ever had," Miller says.

The blues band's most successful album to date was its first, *Stress—Live at the Euclid Tavern,* recorded one Saturday night in 1980. By this time, of course, Mr. Stress was synonymous with the Euclid Tavern. As a bar band that offered something other than pop rock music, it was also a saving grace for local blues lovers.

As the '90s came into view, the earthy music began enjoying recognition nationally with such artists as Stevie Ray Vaughan, Buddy Guy, Robert Cray, and Blues Traveler. Today on the North Coast, acts like Robert Lockwood Jr. and Mr. Stress are the veterans among the many younger blues musicians who dominate the area. And there are several clubs that offer nothing but the blues, certainly a change from previous decades.

The Mr. Stress Blues Band, although continuing to shift players, has maintained a faithful following for more than three decades. Despite the growing numbers of contemporary blues musicians locally, the band has been chosen as Best Blues Band in the annual *Scene* readers' poll more times than any other group.

In October 1994, Miller suffered a heart attack while en route to a gig. (The band's newest album, ironically named *Killer Stress,* had just come out.) Three weeks later, the Euclid Tavern owners, along with Miller's friends, held a benefit to cover the veteran bluesman's hospital expenses. In addition to the eleven bands that showed up to play, Miller's numerous and longtime friends and fans were there too—as was Miller, though this time in the audience. Although his health problems set him back for awhile, the esteemed music man and his harp continued to entertain, playing approximately three nights a week on both the East and West Sides. His 1999 lineup included Dan Mahoney (drums), Robin Montgomery (piano, replacing Sands), Hoss Ostrunic (bass), and Greg Nelson (guitar).

"It's truly an honor to be in this band," Nelson says. "I've played in fifteen different bands from rock to jazz, country to blues, and done over 2,000 gigs. But when the drummer is peeling the paint off the walls, the amp tubes are so hot your choked B string on your Roadhouse Strat screams 'til next Tuesday . . . there's just nothing better. And that's despite the fact bar owners pay amount hasn't changed much since the Kennedy administration!"

Now in his fifties, "Stress" is known to educate his audience between sets by recounting what the rock and roll capital was like thirty years ago and how literally hundreds of talented musicians played a part in bringing it all to light. "Anyone here

Bill "Mr. Stress" Miller poses with thirty years of club memorabilia. *Photo by Deanna Adams.*

remember the old Coffee House, D'Poos in the Flats, or the Hullabaloos?" he'll ask, to many smiles and nodding heads. "Yeah, that's where we all started playing—Jimmy Fox, Joe Walsh, Glenn Schwartz. Those were great days. You know, a lot of talented people have passed through this city, some who aren't even alive anymore. None of us made much money, but we sure had a lot of fun." Then he breaks into a rendition of Sonny Boy Williamson's "Don't Start Me to Talkin."

Glenn Schwartz

For more than ten years, the Schwartz Brothers, Glenn and Gene, have been Thursday-night regulars at Hoopples Riverbed Cafe, drawing a transgenerational crowd. They come to see a phenomenon. And that's what they get. A sweaty Glenn Schwartz winces and contorts his face while driving home R&B riffs few have seen executed this way. The standing-room-only crowd is spellbound. And while his disciples listen and watch his vibrating fingers, the guitar god seems oblivious to all but his stringed instrument. It is only when he takes a break that bar patrons resume drinking, conversing, moving.

Occasionally conversation in this West Side bar touches on the guitarist's history. "Yeah, he once played in the James Gang." Or, "I read where Jimi Hendrix called Glenn Schwartz one of *his* favorite guitarists!" Or, "He's had more influence on local guitarists than anyone else." Or, "I heard this guy's a living legend."

They are all right. When it comes to cataloging guitar geniuses, the name Glenn Schwartz is cited time and again, and not just on the North Coast. As guitarist for the L.A.-based Pacific Gas and Electric, and a featured artist at the 1969 Miami Pop Festival, Schwartz was a major influence on musicians on both coasts.

His beginnings, however, were modest. Born and raised in Cleveland, he only picked up the guitar at his father's urging. The eleven year old began taking guitar lessons at nearby studios, but he soon became better than his teachers. "His first guitar, I believe, was a Gene Autry acoustic," his brother Gene recalls. "It was during that time Glenn started listening to a lot of the old blues records. We'd go to the Giant Tiger [department store] and go through all these records in the used record department and find albums by B. B. King and Jimmy Reed, all for about a nickel apiece. He started playing out at about twelve in polka bands at the old Slovenian Home [Cleveland's East Side]."

He "interned" in early '60s bands—Frank Samson and the Wailers and the Sensations—until the army called. Glenn spent from 1965 to 1967 in Germany, where with military comrades he formed his own band. Upon release from the army, word spread quickly about Schwartz's return to Cleveland, and Jimmy Fox hunted him down to get him to join his band the James Gang (see Chapter 8). Schwartz gained the band local celebrity by playing the guitar with his teeth (before Hendrix!) and by playing while hanging upside down from guitarist Bill Jeric's shoulder.

Then Glenn decided to take a trip out West. "He was driven out there by a friend," Gene recalls. "He got dropped off on a corner with just a suitcase and his guitar. At one of his first gigs out there, Duane Allman saw him and asked him to join the Allman

Glenn Schwartz at the
Miami Pop Festival, 1969.
Photo by Butch Armstrong.

Brothers. But he was already putting together his own band, Pacific Gas and Electric, and turned him down."

In 1970, Glenn returned to his hometown and convinced Gene to learn bass so the two could perform together. The Schwartz Brothers, usually accompanied by a drummer, began playing often at Faragher's, a popular club in Cleveland Heights. "Whenever they advertised that we'd be playing there, every table got reserved," Gene notes.

In 1972, Gene Schwartz met Robert Lockwood Jr. and joined his band. Glenn turned to religion and joined a commune for the remainder of the decade. Although he spent most of that period as a recluse, he managed to complete three albums of his own. He reemerged onto the scene in the early eighties, and with his brother by his side, the two began touring with Lockwood.

In 1989, they began what has become a Schwartz tradition: Thursday nights at Hoopple's. They continue to attract large crowds, including many celebrities and old friends. Sometimes they're one and the same. "After Joe [Walsh] was inducted into the Hall of Fame, he came into town," Gene recalls. "He showed up at the bar in a limo and surprised us. We hadn't seen him in years. After that, he and Glenn kept in touch, and last Thanksgiving [1998], he stayed at our house, where he and Glenn practiced all day and jammed together later that night at Hoopple's. It was quite a night!" What became the bar concert of the year, witnessed by a crowd of stunned and excited customers at 1:00 A.M., received much press and was talked about for months after.

But for as much as he's known for his guitar wizardry, Glenn Schwartz is also famous for using the stage as a podium to warn his flock of the evils of the world and to condemn the sins of mankind. Few seem to take it to heart. "Just as quickly as he can fill a room with this playing, he can empty it when he starts to preach," one musician notes. No matter. His rantings don't last long enough to detract from his playing. Besides, watching Schwartz execute his demons with his guitar is indeed a religious experience!

Jimmy Ley (James Michael Leyava)

There are three things I regret ever doing: alcohol, drugs, and getting paid for playing music. They've all led to a lot of misery in my life.

—Jimmy Ley

The John Mayall and the Blues Breakers tour wasn't the only reunion taking place that spring night in 1981 at the Front Row Theater in Richmond Heights. The opening act, the Jimmy Ley Blues Band, had returned to Cleveland after disappearing from the local scene five years before. As the group's members made their way down the aisle to the stage, the audience rose in a standing ovation.

This was music to the ears of singer/songwriter/pianist/guitarist/harmonica player Jimmy Ley. After more than twenty years of playing the blues circuit throughout the North and South, the struggling music man had finally "arrived." His hometown fans not only remembered him but were obviously glad to see him back. After long years of trying to keep the music together—despite revolving band members, the traveling, the near misses with stardom, and drug and alcohol abuse—Ley was finally able to realize his elusive dream. The guy who had "blown it" so many times before was now basking in admiration and appreciation. And most importantly, this welcome-home by his peers reaffirmed his reputation as a prominent and serious blues musician. But, the good time wouldn't last. "Three months later, I couldn't *buy* a gig in Cleveland," the blues player says.

His story is a musician's nightmare. Jimmy Ley was living out the songs he played: He was the epitome of the down-trodden, hard-livin', all-night-boozin' bluesman. And he had no one to blame but himself.

James Michael Leyava was born in Cleveland on March 10, 1948. In 1956, at age eight, he started his own band, the Ivy Leagues, while attending Parma's Renwood Elementary School. He taught himself to play piano and drums, and he listened to Nashville's WLAC on his radio. "I heard all kinds of stuff on that station," Ley recalls. "I loved the music of Jimmy Reed, B. B. King, and went nuts over Bobby 'Blue' Bland when he sang 'Little Boy Blue.' I don't remember ever hearing a term associated with the music; it was just what they played."

In 1961, Ley was attending Brecksville Junior High School when he formed a five-piece band called the Mutations, and soon the adolescents were playing gigs at high school sock hops, private parties, and "tons of small halls." They often opened for top local headliners Dave C. and the Sharptones as well as for Joey and the Continentals. "We were working like crazy but having a great time. We played some Elvis, early Top 40, and songs like Slim Harpo's 'Scratch My Back.' I got even more into blues and started the repetitive chanting like some of the bluesmen I heard on the radio. I remember we got five bucks a man, but I'd have done it for free. We were ready to break, I just knew it. Then that damn Beatles thing hit." Suddenly everyone in the North wanted to hear the Fab Four's music. So Ley became a blues traveler. Over the next decade, he toured through Europe and across the southern states, and for a time was a Washington, D.C., resident, playing regularly at downtown clubs. Anything to keep playing the blues.

In 1970, he returned to Cleveland. "One day Dick Korn [owner of D'Poos in the Flats] calls me up. At the time he was managing Otto's Grotto in the Statler, but he was getting ready to open this new club and asked me to get together a house band for him. So I got two guitarists, Bill Jeric and Alan Greenblatt [Greene], bassist Rick Magic, and drummer Doug Bacik, and we formed the Jimmy Ley and the Coosa River Band." That spring, Ley's newest blues band (which included Donny Baker) debuted at the downtown club Viking Saloon. "It was an invitation-only night, and it was really something," he remembers. For the next two years, the group had a regular gig at the club that became a groundbreaker for many local musicians. From 1972 to 1976, Ley and company played weekly at the Mistake, formerly Vikings Den, an after-hours club just downstairs from the Agora on E. 24th Street.

But for every memorable gig, there were more that remain a blur to the bluesman. "I started drinking and doing drugs pretty much when I started playing. By the time I was in ninth grade, I was working five nights a week in places like Hires Lounge on Euclid Avenue. So I was always in a bar. When I was working the Mistake, a lot of the [Agora] headliners would come downstairs—Bob Marley, Eric Burdon, Edgar Winter, Bad Company members, Elvin Bishop, some really impressive people. But I hardly remember any of it. Though I do remember the night Al Kooper came on stage to jam with us and literally blew up Al Greene's amp. That night stands out because [Kooper] just smoked it, then left. He never even apologized, or compensated Al for it. But Hank [LoConti] went out and got him a new one."

North Coast City Blues

By 1977, Ley's drinking was affecting his performance, and he watched the crowds dwindle. Soon, Jimmy Ley and the Coosa River Band had played their last gig at the Mistake. Ley then moved on to Charlottesville, Virginia, where, for a time, he had his own blues radio show. In 1980, he toured with Robert Lockwood and Johnny Shines. He was so content with his life then that he turned down an offer to be keyboardist for the late Stevie Ray Vaughan (before Vaughan became world famous). He stayed there until his return to Cleveland and that fateful comeback at the Front Row. But once again, booze inflicted its wrath, and his reputation as an unreliable alcoholic erased all hopes of getting gigs at any number of area clubs. Finally, on August 29, 1983, Ley signed himself into a detox hospital and a new way of life. He sold his equipment to Bill "Stress" Miller and vowed never to drink or play ever again.

But before long, offers to play started trickling in. Determined to live a normal life, Ley turned them all down, refusing to return to that lifestyle. He was convinced he couldn't play music straight.

I was terrified to get back into that scene again. I didn't play at all for three years. Then Hank LoConti called. He said, "Look, I got this blues gig coming up with Robert Jr. Lockwood and the James Cotton Blues Band. I know you can play sober." I told him, no way, I won't do it. But he kept after me. Finally, I said, "Okay, I'll come and do six or seven songs, but then I'm outta there."

There was Alan Greene on guitar, John Daubenspeck on bass, and Jimmy Hoare on drums. And we tore the place up! I was really proud that I could play sober, but I still figured it was just for one night.

Not long after, Stress called because he needed a piano player one night at the Euclid Tavern. And before he knew it, Jimmy Ley was back on the music circuit. Since then, he has continued to hold down a day job while playing a few gigs a month, often traveling out of town. But now when he orders a drink at the bar, it's coffee.

From his years of working with some of the best musicians Cleveland had to offer, Ley has nothing but admiration for his fellow bluesmen. "Robert Lockwood is simply a unique human being," he says. "He doesn't drink or carouse. He's there to play his music, then he leaves. He taught me a lot in that respect. And Stress—well, no one plays 'Mojo' like he does. Then there was Dave Griggs [of the Dave Griggs Blues Band] who, when he was sober, was the greatest damn guitarist. He was a great showman, too. He could have a drink in his right hand and do a whole solo with his left, snappin' his fingers and talking, all at the same time. But he left for L.A. in 1970, and I heard he died of a heart attack in '86. It's too bad because he was phenomenal."

Today, Ley can look back on forty years of playing, and living, the blues. The man who's worked with a slew of musicians, including the late blues pianist Otis Spann, is back on track. After years of "thinking about it," Ley finally recorded his first album in 1988. *Northcoast City Blues,* with his band the Funk Pumpers, was released on the band's own Funkomatic label. A second album, *Two Sides to a Story,* came out on in 1991. And then there's that 1991 songwriting award. Ley won third place in the R&B division in *Billboard*'s worldwide songwriter's contest. The song, what Ley calls a basic musician's lament, is titled "Pay Me in Cash."

I don't need no fancy stretch limo
I don't need no cocaine or hash
I don't need no 3 A.M. bimbo
I just need you to pay me in cash.

For that he got no cash, but he did receive a $1,000 Gibson guitar.

In 1996, he released another album, *The Stalker,* on Slippery Noodle Records. "For the past five years, I've been playing at the Slippery Noodle Inn in Indianapolis. A few years ago they started their own label and I was the first out-of-town artist they signed on." His latest lineup includes guitarist Jason Green from Parma Heights, bassist Tony Fortuna from Mayfield Heights, and drummer Mike Wardrope from Lakewood.

Frankie Starr

Frankie plays every song like it was the last one on earth.

—Glen "Stutz Bearcat"

Before there was a Jonny Lang or a Kenny Wayne Shepherd, there was Cleveland's guitar prodigy Frankie Starr. In 1989, eighteen-year-old Starr was being hailed as a local blues phenomenon. Aside from obvious talent and nimble fingers this musician is not what blues legends are made of. He doesn't drink, smoke, or do drugs, and by all accounts he appears to be a happy guy. So why the blues?

"It's honest music," Starr says. "That's what attracted me right from the start. I liked the soulfulness of the music. It was easily digestible for me, not bombarding you with a thousand notes, like rock. And I didn't get the same type feelings when I heard rock as when I heard guys like B. B. King. But I didn't have anyone to share that interest but my mom, who got into it because she grew up listening to Chubby Checker, Little Richard, Chuck Berry. All my buddies were listening to Ozzy Osbourne, Aerosmith, AC/DC. I was the oddball when it came to music."

Joni Starr was her son's first musical influence. "My mom plays keyboards, and when I was nine I started playing drums in her band," he recalls. "It was like an all-occasion band. We played in bars, lounges, weddings. At about eleven I started getting interested in the guitar, so my mom got me this Ventura-type electric guitar, an Aria. But I had a hard time playing it because the strings were real heavy, and it hurt my fingers. Then a friend of ours got me an acoustic guitar and the strings were much softer. That's when I really got into playing it."

Then one day Frankie's mom presented him with a musical gift. "My mom picked up this record collection," he recalls. "She and my dad were divorced so we never had much money. She found these old albums somewhere and traded in her wedding ring and some silverware to buy this great blues collection with Freddie King, Bobby Blue Bland, Albert King, B. B. King. A lot of ones you don't find anymore. I played them so much I wore them out. I never gave thought to preserving them." Included in that collection was Jimi Hendrix's *Are You Experienced?* thus expanding his guitar education.

The self-taught musician began playing the guitar in local clubs.

Playing in my mom's band, I was thrown into situations that forced me to do songs I didn't know or never played before. Although I didn't know the mechanics of music, I caught on fairly fast. I played by ear.

We also formed a blues band at that time, a side project called Frankie and the Rising Stars. At that point, the only job you could get playing the blues was in the black neighborhoods. We were going into these real rough bars where we were the only whites in the place. I remember this one bar had a sign in the window that read, "Frankie and the Rising Stars" and underneath it said, "Whites Playing The Blues!" That became our drawing power.

Ever the promoter, Joni Starr would take her son to various venues and talk the headlining act into letting the young teen sit in with them. Sometimes it worked, even with such notables as Albert Collins, Robert Lockwood Jr., and James Cotton. Other times it didn't. "I remember going to see Little Willie and the All-Stars at this bar on Miles Avenue," Starr says. "My mom introduced me like I was the hottest guitar player in the world, but he just said 'no.'"

But then came his introduction to his next major influence, local guitar hero Glenn Schwartz. "When Little Willie was killed [by his ex-girlfriend], the Palomino [on Lorain Road] staged a benefit for him. I'll never forget that night. I got to see all these great musicians, including Glenn Schwartz. He had this strange aura about him. We thought, now this is a different kind of dude. When he started playing, we just went 'whoa.' He was amazing. We became friends, and he'd come over to the house and show me different riffs and how to take proper care of a guitar." But the friendship began to wane when praying took over playing. "Playing music with Glenn meant you also had to pray with him," Starr says. "I'm a Christian, but he started pushin' the religion more than the guitar-playing. I just wanted to play guitar."

By then Starr had secured a manager. "Vicque [Fassinger] had some good ideas on how to promote me," he says, "and pretty soon we had a gig almost every night. One club we were known for was Mirenda's [now City Blues, on Pearl Road in Parma]. We packed that place every time we played, there'd be lines of people outside waiting to get in." Starr also got noticed when he participated in the 1988 and 1989 Hot Leads guitar contest, held at the Flats's Peabody's DownUnder. The first year he won first place in the junior division (eighteen and under). The next year, he placed second in the adult division, losing to metal guitarist Neil ZaZa. He then formed Frankie Starr and the Chill Factor with bassist Glen "Stutz Bearcat," rhythm guitarist/vocals Scott Dykstra (who coined the band name), and drummer Greg James. They played everywhere—from Cleveland's Euclid Tavern to Kent's JB's to Akron's Schwanies.

Fassinger, who many viewed as a control freak, molded Starr into the guitar prodigy he became known as but subsequently alienated some bandmates, as well as his family and friends. As a result, the Chill Factor got off to a chilly start, with members drifting in and out. "I liked playing with Frankie. He was really talented and a nice guy," says Stutz Bearcat, whose resumé includes Generators and the Mr. Stress Blues Band. "I just couldn't handle Vicque taking over our lives. I recall one time we were on break at this one club, and I was actually stooped down in a corner so she wouldn't see me having a beer and enjoying myself!" Fassinger and Starr parted ways in 1989 when the guitarist decided to handle his career himself.

When Bearcat left, Starr recruited Joe Arthur, the bass player who came in third in the 1989 Hot Leads contest. Other notable members through the years include bassists

Fred Toby, Joe Mazz, Lennie Fatagadi, Jeremy Ilenin, and Phil Mercan. Drummers were Toby Packard and Mike Deilia. For a time, the group also boasted harp player Ron "the Reverend" Wietecha. Despite the turnovers, the band managed to play more than two hundred gigs a year. Some jobs included opening for artists Albert Collins, Lonnie Mack, B. B. King, Robert Cray, Johnny Winter, Edgar Winter, Joe Walsh, Leon Russell, and Stevie Ray Vaughan. "We were opening for Stevie at the Veterans' Memorial in Columbus," Starr recalls. "He stood off to the side while we played. I can still picture that smile on his face. He was grinning from ear to ear and I remember how

Frankie Starr feels the blues at Scorcher's in Stow, 1998.
Photo by Joni Starr.

freaked out I was he was there. The next day, we were getting ready for another show, and we got to talking. He ended up giving me this note that read, 'Keep playing from your heart. You're really an inspiration.' I have it in a frame now."

By 1995, Chill Factor was no more. Joe (Joseph) Arthur went on to become a successful singer-songwriter in New York, with a 1999 debut solo effort, *Come to Where I'm From,* receiving an "A+" from Entertainment Weekly. In 1995 Starr released his self-titled CD. A second, *Heaven Help Us,* followed in 1996. His current lineup in the Frankie Starr Band includes Packard, Fatagadi, and Deilia. The CD, *Boogie 2000,* was released in October 2000. Starr gives lessons on his craft at Cuyahoga Community College, and he continues to learn as well. "Rich Holsworth has been my guitar teacher the last three years," he says. "I learn a lot of new, cool stuff from him. I hope I'll be able to continue making a living at this because I love what I do."

Recommended Reading

Bane, Michael. *White Boy Singin' the Blues.* New York: DaCapo Press, 1992.

Kiersh, Edward. *Where Are You Now, Bo Diddley?* New York: Doubleday, 1986.

Lomax, Alan. *The Land Where the Blues Began.* New York: Pantheon, 1993.

Palmer, Robert. *Deep Blues.* New York: Penguin, 1981.

Santelli, Robert. *The Big Book of Blues: A Biographical Encyclopedia.* New York: Penguin, 1993.

8 Battle of the Bands: The Early Rock Groups

The Age of the Guitarist

If you really want to taste some cool success, you better learn to play guitar
—John Mellencamp, from the *Uh-Huh* album

They were all going to be the next Beatles. With the Fab Four phenomenon, garages and basements around the country were turned into studios for ambitious young musicians honing their craft, with their neighborhood pals often their sole audience. Although drummers were certainly necessary to achieve the right sound, when it came to rock and roll, the guitar was king. Slung over one shoulder and gripped close to the player's belly, the guitar moved with the body. The very physicality of the guitar represented the rebellion, abandon, and sexuality associated with the rock and roll generation.

In the Cleveland area, music stores such as DiFiore's Music (Lorain Avenue), Petromelli's Music and Sodja's Music (both on E. 185th Street), Arrowhead Music (conveniently located from across Mentor Avenue's Hullabaloo), and Westgate Music (Center Ridge Road) experienced a surge of business during this time both in sales and in lessons. The guitar was the instrument of choice. In addition, teen rockers were teaching themselves to play the stringed instrument simply by listening and imitating their favorite artist's recordings, practicing at every conceivable moment. And if talent was apparent, these novice guitarists were soon producing sounds all their own.

But it wasn't until the players got on stage that they came to realize what it took to be successful. Not only did they need acceptance from their peers, but there was the defining moment when they would have to compete against their musical allies during the "Battle of the Bands." Surprisingly, these sessions were regarded as fun rather than serious competitive events, for most participants were just glad to have the chance to play. It was, indeed, all about the music—not money, managements, or contracts. The competition was nothing compared to what young musicians must contend with today, where musicians are a dime a dozen and that coveted record contract is as elusive as a 45 record.

Before John, Paul, George, and Ringo, it was 1950s musician Les Paul who popularized the electric guitar. The country-western-turned-jazz performer created the solid-body guitar that Gibson made available in 1952. By the late '60s, young guitarists everywhere were trading in their Rickenbackers for a classic Les Paul guitar, which remains a favorite among many musicians. The legendary innovator and performer, who also invented multiple-track recording, was inducted into the Rock and Roll Hall of Fame in 1988 as an Early Influence.

One Way or Another

In a band, it was usually the lead guitarist who garnered the most attention. While the drummer sat in the background, the guitarist (who often sang lead as well) was front and center. (Many musicians admit they started out in a band solely "to get the girls." That premise appeared to work. How else can one explain the near-frenzied attraction female audiences have with seemingly unattractive rock stars?)

Since the dawn of the electric guitar, America and the U.K. have produced many guitar geniuses, each of whom in turn became a major influence on future artists—Chuck Berry, Duane Eddy, Eric Clapton, Jimi Hendrix, Jeff Beck, Pete Townshend, Stevie Ray Vaughan, Jimmy Page, and Eddie Van Halen are all considered the greatest among rock guitarists.

And northeast Ohio also contributed its share of exceptional guitarists. Joe Walsh, Glenn Schwartz, Phil Keaggy, Wally Bryson, Neil Giraldo, Butch Armstrong, and Alan Greene have all been hailed as gifted musicians. After years of playing gigs throughout the area, these musical heroes ultimately became mentors for a new generation of area guitarists—some of whom are their own sons. For example, former Raspberry Bryson undoubtedly influenced son Jesse, whose band, Qwasi Qwa, tied for first place at a 1997 Battle of the Bands at the Odeon in the Flats and now plays the local circuit. Glass Harp bassist and former Michael Stanley member Dan Pecchio has a son, Ted, who also plays bass (most notably for the now-defunct Mr. Tibbs). Now fathers, and even grandfathers, each of these veteran guitarists continues to play music today. But back when they were just aspiring musicians, they learned and fed off each other, which produced more of a bond than a rivalry. True, each wanted to be the best; but their egos weren't so fragile that they didn't appreciate a colleague's greatness. Of course, there were always the inevitable "creative differences" that popped up within a band. In some cases, these internal conflicts proved healthy and made for a better, tighter group. Other times, however, they destroyed the band's nucleus. It's that inner artistic tension that remains the biggest factor in a band's breakup.

The 1960s saw hundreds of notable musicians and bands performing along northern Ohio shores. Although many never became nationally recognized, those listed below are ones Cleveland fans remember most—with a fondness that lingers more than thirty years later.

The Mods/Choir (1964–70)

> I remember our first gig. We played at Mentor Beach Park and were paid $5 apiece. At sixteen years old in 1965, I thought that was big money! I've always wanted to play music and I'm just as happy staying local and playing our own tunes. I'll still be playing when I'm fifty.
>
> —Wally Bryson, guitarist for the Mods, Choir, and countless other bands

When it comes to the history of Cleveland garage bands, the Mods lead the pack. As rock migrated into small-town USA, the music filtered from TV's *American Bandstand* into the city streets. And in the somewhat rural, suburban Mentor, Ohio, lay the foundation of one of the most enduring and beloved early rock groups on the North Coast. Like many young bands across the nation, this group's history was born and cultivated in the family garage.

"My buddy and I were about ten or eleven when we used to ride our bikes in the summer and head towards this one house in Mentor," recalls Jeff Adams. "You could hear the music long before you got there, which got us peddling faster. We didn't know they were the Mods then. It was just cool to go watch this rock band practice over and over."

In the beginning, it was just a matter of something fun to do. It was 1964 when these four restless Mentor High School teens decided to put a band together. Led by Dan Klawon (originally the drummer), the Mods was made up of guitarists Dave Smalley and Dan Heckel and vocalist Tom Boles. Within months, however, Boles was ousted; Wally Bryson replaced Heckel; Klawon stepped up front with his rhythm guitar; bassist Dave Burke joined in; and Jim Bonfanti came in on drums. Klawon recalls those early rock and roll days:

> I had a jump on Beatlemania because this girl in my neighborhood went to England and came back with the "Meet the Beatles" album and the single "She Loves You"

with "I'll Get You" on the B-side. That was before it was released in the States. Plus I saw the Beatles on the *Jack Paar Show* before they played *Ed Sullivan*.

So we began playing songs by the Beatles, the Who, Stones, Zombies, Troggs, and Moody Blues. If they were from England, we played it. We had this song list that was unbelievable. We used index cards with a repertoire of about one hundred songs on them. Then we'd go into rehearsal, quickly learn, like, seven new songs, and play 'em out that weekend. The PA systems back then were so underdeveloped it didn't matter if you didn't have the words down pat—no one could hear the singing anyhow.

We probably played a song from every band from the British Invasion, and some American songs like "Johnny B. Goode," "Farmer John," "Wipe Out," and Johnny Rivers's songs. And everybody alternated instruments, depending on the song. We'd have that written on the cards, as to who played what on what song.

"Dave Burke usually played bass," adds Randy Klawon, who became the Choir's lead guitarist in 1968. "But he'd also come out and play guitar, and he was a really good guitar player. Wally played bass, too, and I also remember Wally going on the drums a few times."

The group's musicianship and versatility brought the teenagers to the attention of Decca Records promo man Ray Taylor, who became their manager and booked them wherever their peers would congregate. With its hometown identity, the Mods became Cleveland's answer to the Beatles, quickly attracting a following among the eighteen-and-under set. Since teen clubs had not yet been established, the band was a constant at high school dances, armories (for awhile they were the Saturday night house band at Painesville Armory), and roller rinks. The group also opened for national acts like the McCoys, Terry Knight and the Pack, and even "white-bread" performers such as Bobby Rydell.

Competition then was almost nil, since the group's greatest contenders, the Outsiders, were off touring America with their national hit "Time Won't Let Me." It wasn't long before rock bands saturated the music scene, with teen clubs opening at the rate of one every couple of months. Yet despite the fact that the local rock scene was growing fast and furious, the Mods remained the darlings of Cleveland's East Side.

What Can a Poor Boy Do, 'cept to Sing for a Rock and Roll Band?

More and more bands began peppering the teen landscape, each one catering to a specific group of fans. In the '60s, teenagers fit into one of three categories. There were the mods, where both girls and guys wore their hair long, dressed in "Beatle boots," peace medallions, tie-dyed shirts, and paisley, hip-hugging bell-bottoms. On the opposite end of the spectrum were the greasers, who kept the 1950s fashions and attitude alive (later characterized in the movie *Grease*). The guys wore slicked-back hair;

ankle-length, straight-legged pants; and leather jackets, while the girls were recognized by teased hair that, according to some unwritten law, had to be at least three inches high to qualify. Then there were the collegiates, who seemed to miss the era's great movement all together. Ridiculed for their academic achievements and straight-laced clothes (button-down cotton shirts and penny loafers), collegiates pretty much kept to themselves, wisely staying clear of the intense rivalry between the leather-clad greasers and the mods in all their Carnaby Street glory. These rivalries also extended into their choices of music. Greasers preferred the R&B and Motown sounds and mods the music of the British Invasion.

Through their music and fashion styles, the Outsiders attracted greasers, while the Mods attracted, well, mods. And whenever both groups showed up at the same youth dance, the place would indeed rock and roll. "When all that was going around, there were places the Mods couldn't play because of their long hair and style of clothes," recalls Dennis Carleton, rhythm guitarist for another early group, the Lost Souls. "Somehow we crossed that bridge because although we played rock 'n' roll, we also did the Motown sounds and R&B. So we could play places where the Mods probably would've gotten beat up!" Wally Bryson also vividly recalls those days. "I remember one time we had a Battle of the Bands with a group called Danny and the Satins at this K of C Hall on Vine Street [in Willowick]. It was pretty much their club, a greaser club. So we not only lost [the contest], but our girlfriends were getting their hair singed with cigarettes and stuff. Another time we got jumped at a Manners Restaurant when we were in the Cyrus Erie. It was pretty wild."

The Establishment wasn't too hip on "longhairs" either. Stories to confirm this came by way of the local Lake County newspapers in 1966, when Bryson was expelled from Mentor High School because his hair was too long. (If only they could see him today, with completely grey hair worn waist-length!) Not one to back down, Bryson simply went on to complete his high school education at Griswold Institute in Cleveland, a school that had a record number of students in the '60s because their long hair wasn't against the rules. And similar cases abound. Mods drummer Jim Bonfanti recalls being so ridiculed on his school bus that he could no longer ride it home. In addition, that same year, Carleton was thrown out of St. Joseph High School in Euclid when his long hair was "discovered." He jokingly blames the incident on *Plain Dealer*'s Jane Scott: "At school, I'd grease my hair behind my ears, so no one realized how long it was. Well, then Jane comes out with an article about kids with long hair. And she uses a BIG picture of me as an example. Next day, I was called into the office and they suspended the whole band." With only three months until graduation, Carleton and his band members appeased school officials and "trimmed" their hair. The guitarist went on to graduate and today makes his living as a professional musician and teacher.

In 1966, the Mods changed their name to the Choir. Seems a group from Chicago, the Modernaires, had shortened their name to the Mods and were the first to lay claim to the title, thus forcing the Cleveland group to make the switch. No matter. By any other name, it was still the same group of teenage boys who would soon have themselves a hit record. The song, "It's Cold Outside," recorded on Canadian-American Records and later released on the more successful independent label Roulette is perhaps the most identifiable record from this era in Cleveland music. Penned by sixteen-year-old Dan Klawon, it became an immediate success, particularly in Cleveland, where radio airplay made it a regional No. 1 hit for five straight weeks. The record also graced *Billboard*'s Top 100, peaking at No. 68. "I used to write quite a bit then, and one day I was thinking of some sort of theme to use with the moon/spoon, girl/boy lyrics," the author explains. "I decided to go with a weather analogy." Living in Cleveland, Klawon no doubt thought "cold" seemed a fitting comparison.

During its six years, the Choir saw several member-shufflings as it formed, re-formed, and reinvented itself. Reasons for the turnovers varied. One of the most common was the enforcement of the draft in the late 1960s. Whatever the reason, the music itself survived the frequent band member shifts and, in most cases, was the better for it. Beginning in 1966, the Choir was showing up everywhere—from local TV programs to the Music Hall stage, where a year later they opened a show featuring the Who, Blues Magoos, and Herman's Hermits. "I'd been a fan of the Who since their first album," Bryson recalls. "And to be playing on the same stage as them was a real thrill." That thrill was nothing compared to a few years later at Musicarnival when, with his group Cyrus Erie, Bryson lent their amps to their Brit heroes after theirs blew up. It wasn't so much a measure of kindness, according to Bryson. "I just wanted to hear them finish the set."

As a result of the live performances and their national hit single, the Choir became popular with not only with the average fan but with other aspiring musicians as well—musicians like South Euclid–native Eric Carmen. In fact, one of Carmen's earliest ambitions was to share the same stage with Choir guitarist Wally Bryson. A few years later, the future singer/songwriter of the Raspberries would indeed realize his dream, just as he would come to learn the true meaning of the adage "Be careful what you wish for." For as Carmen (who never did make it into the Choir but later joined with Bryson to form Cyrus Erie) and the Raspberries would discover over the next decade, one of the biggest problems in being a musician is not making music but contending with individual egos.

Still, the Choir sang. This despite the ever-changing cast of musicians that included, at one time or another, lead guitarist Jim Anderson, keyboardist Kenny Margolis, bass players Jim "Snake" Skeen, Denny Carleton, and Bob McBride, former organist (and James Gang alumnus) Phil Giallombardo, guitarist Rick Caon, and lead guitarist Randy Klawon. At age fourteen Klawon had filled in on drums for his "missing" brother Dan on the Ghoulardi show when the latter didn't make it back in time from attending a Stones concert in Detroit. He was just sixteen when he joined the Choir, replacing Anderson in 1968.

The Choir released another single in 1970, "Gonna Have a Good Time Tonight," though the song didn't make much of an impact. Finally, in the summer of 1970, the group called it quits, leaving its talented musicians to move on to other bands and glories.

Cyrus Erie (1967–70)

We were just dying to make a record, and when we did it and heard it on the radio, it was the biggest thrill. 'Cause you listen to the radio all your life growin' up and suddenly something you've done is playing on it. . . . Well, it's a thrill you never forget. And no matter what happens in your career, they can't take that away from you.

—Wally Bryson

Even with the unusual name (coined after a bulldozer), this band worked—for a while. Within a year of its formation, this group's songs of young love and teen angst took it to near cult-level status among Cleveland youths. The lineup consisted of two of the area's most admired musicians: Eric Carmen, who had gained a following with his Sounds of Silence group, and guitarist Wally Bryson, who was fast becoming one of the most renowned guitar players on the North Coast. (Bryson, having left the Choir in late 1967, replaced guitarist Marty Murphy, Carmen's best friend, shortly after the group formed.) The young girls fell for Carmen's looks and lyrics, while the guys (all of whom secretly entertained dreams of being rock stars) watched every movement Bryson made as he alternated between a six-string Gibson or twelve-string Framus. Along with brothers Mike (drums) and Bob McBride (bass) and Donny Young (keyboard), the group covered songs by the Beatles, Moody Blues, Left Banke, Small Faces, and Rolling Stones. Cyrus Erie also opened for the Byrds, Strawberry Alarm Clock, and the members' idols, the Who, who once called the band one of the finest groups they'd ever performed with (placing them in the same status as the James Gang). "That night we played with the Who at Public Hall, Pete Townshend taught me to play the intro to 'Substitute,'" Bryson recalls. "So I was the only guy in town who knew how to play it right. I was in awe because I'd been a fan of the Who since day one. And it was truly amazing to watch and hear Townshend play guitar."

The group consistently set attendance records at every teen venue it played, and as a result, manager Don Ladanyi changed the name of his North Ridgeville Hullabaloo club to Cyrus Erie West. Although equally talented, the group's greatest rival, the Choir, now didn't stand a chance against the Carmen-Bryson union.

Their appeal was such that in 1969, Epic Records execs took notice and flew the band to New York to cut a record. The single, "Sparrow," was recorded at Columbia Studios, but it was its B-side, "Get the Message," that got the most radio airplay. The release did well regionally but failed to have an impact on the rest of the nation. In addition, inner tensions made it increasingly clear that it was time for a change. In the winter of 1968, Bryson was replaced by Terry Lehman. Over the next few months, Bryson would rejoin the group only to depart once again. By spring of the following year, in one last-ditch effort to survive as a group, Cyrus Erie members Carmen and the McBride brothers united with former Choir members Randy Klawon and Kenny Margolis. Within a year, however, Margolis returned to the Choir, with Bob McBride joining him. Soon after both bands called it quits. Eric Carmen and Dan and Randy

Klawon formed the Quick, which disbanded within months, although they did manage a sole recording, "Ain't Nothin' Gonna Stop Me."

But Cyrus Erie is well remembered by fans as well as those who have credited its merits over the years, including Jeff Beck, who once said that Cyrus Erie's version of "Nights in White Satin" was better than the original by the Moody Blues. And Eric Carmen himself has stated that Cyrus Erie was the best band he was ever in—including the more successful Raspberries.

The Lost Souls (1964–68)

The Lost Souls was born out of an unlikely band of five Catholic boys. "One day a school buddy, Larry Tomczak, approached me about starting a band like the Beatles," recalls guitarist Dennis Carleton, who was fifteen at the time. "So we all went and took music lessons at Sodja's Music on E. 185th Street for only about nine months. Luckily, everyone in the band was pretty good, particularly for our age."

Members consisted of Carleton, Tomczak (drums), Ed Gazoski (guitar), Rich Schouenaur (sax and flute), and Chuck McKinley (bass). The quintet called themselves the Lost Souls, and in no time at all these kids from Cleveland's St. Joseph High School became a hot musical commodity. During this pre-Hullabaloo era, the group played every weekend at the typical teen hangouts as well as at "every Catholic parish on both the East and West sides of Cleveland."

With the addition of guitar teacher Dennis Marek, the group rose to a higher and more polished level by 1965. Their unique combination of guitar, bass, drums, flute, sax, and mandolin made them popular and accepted by all teens, breaking the often-stubborn barrier between mods and greasers.

Aside from the Mods, the Lost Souls were the top East Side band at the time. The group opened for acts such as the McCoys at Bedford's K of C Hall and the Shangri-Las at Boston Mills Ski Lodge. Their career highlight was performing at the Cleveland Stadium right on the heels of the Beatles' concert in 1966. "Everyone was still reeling from all the excitement of that," recalls Carleton, whose mother made all his stage clothes in those early years. "I remember we opened for Bobby Vee, the Lemon Pipers, and the Poor Girls. Soon as we came out of the dugout, the crowd saw our long hair, and all these wild girls came after us screamin.' We were just mobbed! It was the first and probably only time I was actually scared to death. We all thought we were going to get crushed. Of course, now when I look back on that, it's funny. And I think, wow, that was pretty neat!"

The young band thought they were on to something when Choir manager Ray Taylor took them into Cleveland Recording to make a tape of ten original compositions with renowned engineer Ken Hamann. But before the Lost Souls could acquire a label, the group disbanded. Subsequently, in 1984 Carleton released the tape on his own Greenlight Records and Tapes label, and the cassette was favorably reviewed by notable San Francisco writer Richie Unterberger of *Option* magazine: "A super collection from previously unreleased tapes from mid-'60s Cleveland sensations, the Lost Souls," it read in part. "These guys were one of the most eclectic pop/rock groups; in attitude, they recall the Left Banke. There are echoes of folk/rock, British Invasion, Motown, garage, hard/rock distorted guitar, and even some jazzy tempo changes. Lost Souls, indeed—this is one of the great lost groups of the '60s, and one of the best reissues of 1984."

The group broke up in 1968 when its members went off to college. Carleton, then nineteen, went on to join the third version of the Choir with Phil Giallombardo, former James Gang organist. That lasted less than a year, at which point Carleton moved on to various bands during the following decades.

Despite all the changes, Carlton has managed to make a living as a musician. The list of groups includes a theatrical rock group called Moses, the short-lived but memorable Milk, the Inner City, the Fa Band, and the late '70s group the Pagans (one of the first to come out of the Cleveland punk scene). Throughout his career, Carleton and his bands have opened for Alice Cooper, Iggy Pop, Ted Nugent and the Amboy Dukes with Ted Nugent, MC5, and the Hello People.

"Moses was just a fantastic band," he recalls. "We did all these crazy things. We'd turn off the lights and play out a nuclear bomb scare threat, then the lights would go on and there we'd be, wearing these grotesque masks and Brian Sands [Kinche] on guitar singing 'Great Balls of Fire'—a very cultish, Frank Zappa-ish band. We played all over northeast Ohio and a lot in Pittsburgh." With Dave Alexy's mad drumming and Jimmy Page–like solos by Randy Klawon, Moses gave its audience a show not soon forgotten. Carleton likens the unique act to a mix of *Beggar's Banquet, Magical Mystery Tour,* and the *'60s Rock 'n' Roll Circus.*

Today, Carleton plays folk music at various coffeehouses and festivals. He also teaches guitar at the Willoughby School of Fine Arts. But looking back at his long-standing musical career, he admits there was nothing like those early days. "Back then there was a *real* music scene here when you think of the phenomenal talents that were around us. When people think of the '60s, they often think of the psychedelics and the drugs, but for the most part, it was an innocent and fun time."

The Poor Girls (1965–69)

This rock band was not only among the first to be made up of all females, but it was also the first of note to come from the Rubber City—Akron, Ohio.

"I started taking guitar lessons from a guy named Joe Ciriello," recalls bass player Debbie Smith. "He was a local guitar player who had a rock and roll band, the Chambermen. At one point he suggested forming an all-girl rock band. Now, this was during the Hullabaloo days, when it seemed everyone was in a band. I had just moved from Detroit and was familiar with all-girl singing groups, but girls with guitars and drums? Mentally I couldn't picture it. But we did it anyway."

And it was surprisingly easy. Sue (Schmidt) Horning says,

I'd been playing folk guitar for a year or two and listened to music by Dylan, Joan Baez, and Peter, Paul & Mary. But as soon as I heard the Beach Boys, I wanted an electric guitar.

Debbie Smith had just moved to Akron from Detroit and we started hanging around together at Litchfield Junior High School. The two of us, along with Pam Johnson, were taking guitar lessons from Ciriello, who lived just down the street from us. When he suggested we form a band, we thought, why not? We knew another student, Esta Kerr, played drums, so Debbie sent her a note in study hall asking if she wanted to be our drummer. I remember she had this huge Slingerland drum set.

Johnson, Schmidt, Smith, and Kerr started practicing on weekends in Johnson's basement. They played songs every teen with a guitar and drums played: "Little Black Egg" (the Nightcrawlers), "Wipe Out" (the Safaris), and "Pipeline" (the Ventures). "A year later we still did them but started changing the arrangement," Horning notes.

The Poor Girls. *Left to right:* Esta Kerr, Sue Schmidt, Pam Johnson, and Debbie Smith. *Courtesy of Susan Schmidt Horning.*

"There weren't a lot of songs sung by women, so we usually had to change the lyrics, or at least the pronouns."

Their name also came easily. "WHLO 40 AM deejay Bob Ansel thought of it," Smith adds. "At the time the big thing in fashion was the Poor Boy sweater. So he said, 'Why don't you call yourselves the Poor Girls?' And that was it."

After weeks of rehearsals it was time to secure management. "My sister, Cindi, modeled for a local agency," Smith says. "This was when the go-go girls were popular on shows like *Shindig* and *Hullabaloo*. There was one fashion show she did in Cleveland that was in conjunction with a rock show. She mentioned to the promoters, Rich Bedrick and Jack Vopal, that her sister had a rock band and told them they should hear us. First thing they did as our managers was throw out everything we were doing and had us learn new songs. So we started playing a wide variety of songs, from the Supremes and Sam and Dave, to the Beatles and Traffic."

Then they began acquiring jobs and dressing for the part. "We started getting a lot of jobs at clubs like Mentor and Chesterland Hullabaloos, and Painesville Armory," Smith recalls. "We did some Battles of the Bands and played Otto's Grotto during summer when school was out. The fashion then was 'mod,' so we wore custom-made matching black and white Houndstooth suits with black leather boots."

As the only area female rock band, the Poor Girls attracted a heavy male, as well as female, following. The group garnered several mentions in the press. Jane Scott included them in a *Plain Dealer Sunday Magazine* feature on the burgeoning local rock scene, "The Rock 'n' Roll Beat Goes On."

"Certainly, it was hard being women musicians in a male rock world," Horning says. "But we took music seriously, which I think led others to take us seriously as a band, not a novelty act, and were respected by other musicians. I remember a gig at Kent's Fifth Quarter when we played with Joe Walsh's early band, the Measles. It was only our second gig there, and we didn't have a bass. Debbie played bass on a Stratocaster! I mean, we were *just* starting out. I remember Joe and the other guys were so nice to us. They lent us their amps and were very encouraging. We really appreciated that. Years later, when I applied to Berklee [Boston's College of Music], Joe wrote a letter of recommendation to help me."

Although Akron's most famous female rocker, Chrissie Hynde, attended Firestone High School with them and was a close friend, she was never a member of the Poor Girls, contrary to long-fed rumors (which probably started because Hynde often accompanied the group to their gigs).

Soon after graduation, the group disbanded when Johnson and Kerr left the rock and roll business. Schmidt and Smith continued their musical odyssey as members of a short-lived basement band with future First Light drummer Rod Reisman, Cinderella's Revenge, Friction, and the Akron New Wave band Chi Pig. But there was something special about the times of the Poor Girls.

"We opened for Cream at Akron Civic Theater in '67 with the James Gang, and that was certainly phenomenal," Smith recalls.

I also remember playing Otto's Grotto one night when the Who, Herman's Hermits, and the Easybeats all came down to hear us. We thought nothing of going up and talking to them, even those who were much more successful than we were. There weren't the barriers then. We were all musicians so we had this common bond. The music scene wasn't corporate then. It was so much more intimate and accessible.

Though none of that would have happened had we not been blessed with such supportive parents who encouraged us, and two men who worked hard for us for the simple love of music. We were fortunate.

Today, Debbie Smith is an Akron lawyer, and Horning is completing her history Ph.D. at Case Western Reserve University.

The Damnation of Adam Blessing (1968–74)

Being a part of that band remains the single greatest experience in my life. I'm really proud of what we did.

        —Jim Quinn, who now runs a music marketing company

The Damnation of Adam Blessing was the hardest rock band one could find on the North Coast in the late 1960s. "We did some cover tunes from our favorite bands like Jimi Hendrix and Cream, but mostly we did original stuff," recalls Jim Quinn, rhythm guitarist and founder of the group. "Adam [a.k.a. Bill Constable] wrote most of our songs, but each of us had a hand in bringing it all together."

It was originals such as "Morning Dew" and "Back to the River" that earned the group national recognition. The young musicians were barely out of their teens when vocalist and guitarist Bill Constable, his brother Kenny, and Quinn (from area group Society) teamed up with bass player Ray Benich, lead guitarist Bob Kalamasz, and drummer Bill Schwark (from Dust) to form a rock group that would parallel the James Gang in local popularity. "We were just kids when we all started playing in bands," notes Bill Constable. "I started out at fifteen playing polkas," he adds with a laugh. It was a far cry from the acid-rock music he and his musical cohorts became known for.

"The name came about after I read a book called *The Damnation of Adam Blessing,* and I thought it'd make a great name for a band," Constable says. The book included an intro that read, "and once again, I dreamed I was Billy," thus launching the transformation of Bill Constable into Adam Blessing. "Not long afterward, I met the book's author at the Village Gate in Greenwich Village, New York, and she was thrilled we were using her title."

The five-piece band's timing was thrilling as well. They emerged at a peak time, when hard rock and marathon songs were the flavor of the day. Damnation's hard-edged electric sound (likened to Grand Funk) perfectly captured the rebellious mood of the late 1960s. "One song, in particular, we became known for at concerts and always drew big cheers," Constable recalls. "That was a cover by Jimi Hendrix called 'You Got Me Floatin,' which we played at every set. It highlighted a solo by each player, and depending on how we felt at the time, would last anywhere from thirty minutes to an hour. My one biggest regret to this day is that for some reason we never recorded it."

After playing all the area teen clubs, high school auditoriums, *Upbeat,* the Agora, and winning virtually every Battle of the Bands contest they entered, the group was ready for the big time. Under the management of former WIXY music director Eric Stevens, who then operated Brilliant Sun Productions, the quintet took their hot sounds into the recording studio.

With a new United Artists contract, they recorded their self-titled album, which quickly became a national bestseller. Included on that 1968 album was the five-minute, fifteen-second version of "Morning Dew." This version was often played in its entirety on FM stations, while AM stations cut the song to fit into the preferred two-minute standard format. Either way, the song was a hit, climbing into the coveted Top 10. In Cleveland alone, the group's debut album sold close to ten thousand copies within months of its release.

After that, it was on to the road, where the band opened for the some of the biggest acts of the decade: Janis Joplin, Uriah Heep, Derek and the Dominos, Jefferson Airplane, Alice Cooper, Iggy and the Stooges, the Faces (with Rod Stewart), Grand Funk Railroad, Stevie Winwood, and hometown buddies the James Gang. The band played such famous venues as L.A.'s Whisky a Go Go, New York's Village Gate, nearly all the big city stadiums, and Cleveland's Musicarnival—a 1968 playdate singer Constable won't ever forget.

We were opening for Vanilla Fudge, whose song, "You Keep Me Hangin' On," was in the Top 10. Their plane was late, so each time we ended the set, our manager would make us go back out and keep playing until they arrived. Well, after about three hours and four sets, we ran out of songs, and there were fifty that we knew. So we finally started playing "You Keep Me Hangin' On," and the crowd went crazy. And the band members arrived just as we were completing the song, and we got a standing ovation! Afterward, the guys from Vanilla Fudge actually thanked us for keeping the crowd entertained all that time and said they thought it was great we played their song as well as we did. Even they appreciated that it had been a great moment in rock time.

Another great moment in this band's history happened on an air force base in Kentucky. "It was a Toys-for-Tots Benefit concert with about 60,000 people in what was the biggest arena in the country at that time," Constable notes.

Well, as we were playing, Jimmy [Quinn] was egging me on to go offstage and out into the audience. Which I did. And again, it was during the song, "Floatin'." Well, suddenly I realize the microphone's been ripped out of my hands, and I motion to these marine guards, who acted as security, to make a path so I can get back to the stage. With these huge spotlights shining down on me, the whole thing seems surreal, like a dream sequence. I look up at Jimmy on stage and he must've been fifty yards away.

Now all across the front of the stage, on long card tables, were these lightweight vocal columns, which were the sound systems that all bands used in clubs back then 'cause they were portable. There was probably about a hundred of them. So the guards cleared a path all the way to the stage, and I ran straight down the aisle and jumped between the columns, and that's where I hit—right where the two card tables came together. So the tables went up in the air and so did all the columns that were on them; it was like a big teeter-totter. And all the technicians were trying to grab them, as Jimmy reached down and just barely grabbed me by the hand, pulled me up and turned me around. Just in time for the chorus of the song and we picked it right up—like it was planned! We spent a lot of time talking about that over the years!

There was yet another memorable moment for the band, but for different reasons. This took place at the Cincinnati's Riverfront Stadium in front of 72,000 overzealous fans in 1972. Constable remembers:

Damnation of Adam Blessing in the Flats, 1969. *Left to right:* Adam Blessing (Bill Constable), Bill Schwark, Ray Benich, Jim Quinn, and Bob Kalamasz. *Photo by George Schuba.*

This was one of those all-day outdoor concerts that started at ten o'clock in the morning and lasted 'til about midnight. Everyone who was anyone in rock was playing there that day. There was Grand Funk Railroad, Mountain, Stevie Winwood and Traffic, Alice Cooper, Iggy Pop—I can't even remember them all. We were about the fourth group to go on. Now we'd been set up on this huge stage on second base. There were these snow fences all the way around. So we were ending the show, of course, with "Floatin." Now by this time, the crowd had been pushed back all the way under the grandstands. As usual, throughout the song, there are lead sections, like a lead for guitar, a lead for bass, and so on. Now we were coming back out of the drum solo and back into that main chorus, where there's full-blown harmony. That's when the crowd proceeded to knock down the snow fence and rush the stage. I'd about had a heart attack. It was kinda like being in the middle of an open field in front of a buffalo stampede!

The group survived the very sort of ordeal that explains why the Beatles quit touring. The Damnation members also recall being asked to perform at Woodstock; because of previous commitments they were forced to decline.

In 1970, Damnation released their *Second Damnation* LP for United Artists. The single "Back to the River" peaked at No. 3 on local charts. "That song remains my all-time favorite," Quinn admits. "Maybe because it was our biggest hit, or perhaps because it was about the war that was so prevalent in our lives back then. That song had a lot of impact."

But like thousands of talented bands, their days were numbered. By the time their third album, *Which Is Justice, Which Is the Thief,* came out in 1971, the spotlight had dimmed. The album did not fare nearly as well as its predecessors (due to management conflicts). The group disbanded in 1974 just a year after releasing a final album, recorded under the name Glory.

Constable, now living in Houston with brother Kenny, talks about the last days.

The whole thing just started getting tedious; the spark was diminishing, and we all wanted to try other things. Plus, times were changing. We were into playing hard rock, while the rest of the music world was turning out light rock/pop. We weren't willing to play that, nor wait for it to come full circle, which of course it did.

But it sure was a great band, and when you think of all the changes bands go through with members, we were unique. The five of us stuck together throughout the life of the band. We were virtually inseparable.

But clearly, it's not the greatest way to make a living, and certainly not conducive to marriage. But when you're young all that doesn't matter; you just wanna play your music. You don't think about how much money you're gonna make or about business deals. You think about how the audience reacts to you.

The former Adam Blessing sums up the life of a rock star in true Dickensian terms: "When it's working, it's the best of all worlds. But when it isn't, it's just about the worst."

Most of those who have been there would likely agree. Yet, both Constable and Quinn admit that the life of Damnation, which took place during an era filled with uncertainties, was for them the best of times.

On September 27, 2000, members reunited for a concert at the Rock and Roll Hall of Fame and Museum after twenty-six years. The show was in conjunction with the reissuing of their first three albums, in a boxed set on the Italian label Okarma.

The Eli Radish Band (1968–73)

They were country when country wasn't cool. They were country rock when there was no such thing. Eli Radish practically defined the term "alternative." While their musician colleagues were all playing rock, members Tom Foster (guitar and pedal steel), Danny Sheridan (bass), Skip Heil (a.k.a. Skip Towne drums), and Kenny "the Rev" Frak (lead vocals) were making music that was hard to come by on the North Coast in the late 1960s. The group played few covers (Neil Young's "Down by the River" and some country-western standards), preferring to focus on original material, including a few songs by local musician Nankar Tillis, relative of Mel Tillis. Their originality got them booked with groups like Country Joe and the Fish, the Doors, the Who, Grand Funk Railroad, and the Kinks.

"I called up Foss [Tom Foster] one day and said, 'Let's start an insane band,'" Sheridan recalls. "We struggled for months searching for ways to put rock grooves under country, or country blues, material . . . blending traditional country and western with rock 'n' roll roots. If we'd had the sense to call it 'country rock,' we would be legends now. We chose to call it 'country-acid,' a takeoff from the psychedelic music of the era—truly an ill-fated moniker." Danny Sheridan had just left his first band, Spontaneous Corruption (signed with Philips-Mercury Records), which had included drummer G. G. Greg and guitarist Ken Hamlin. The bassist became Radish's greatest asset when it came to promotion.

"We were just six months into it when I got a call from Roger Karshner [national VP promotions manager for Capitol Records] who had heard about us out in L.A.," notes Sheridan. "He called me in the middle of the night and asked if we wanted to make an album."

Eli Radish had already been making waves on the local club circuit and college campuses with its different style of music. They were known for the protest songs and antiwar sermons singer Frak would inject into them, suiting well the political activism of the day. As a result, Frak was nicknamed "the Rev." Because of the band's unique style, Karshner, who had taken the Outsiders to national fame, saw a fortuitous opportunity.

"Roger had all this sheet music from the first and second world wars," Foster recalls. "He said, 'I want to put this to country music and have you maniacs play it.' So we

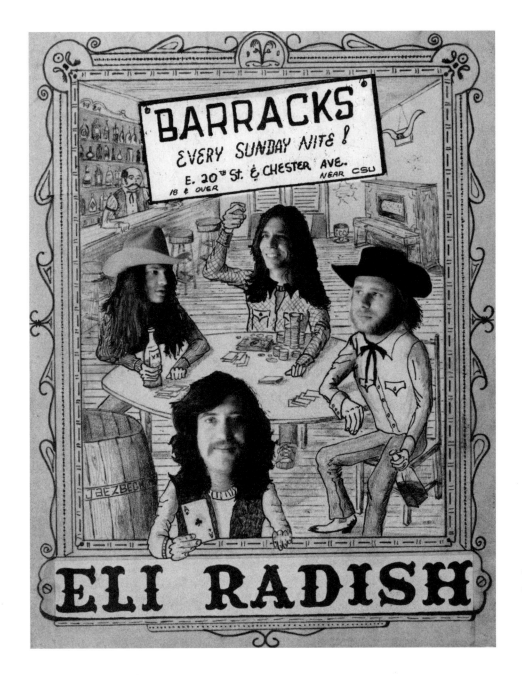

An Eli Radish poster— a common sight at Barracks in 1970. *Courtesy of Danny Sheridan.*

spent the next couple weeks learning all the songs off the sheet music, and put 'em down and made the album. It was an exciting time. Capitol flew us out to California, putting us up in the Hollywood Hawaiian Apartments. They gave us a practice studio, which happened to be next to the room the guys from Poco were in. Then we signed on to Capitol Records. It was great. They gave us transportation, any instruments we wanted, amps. That was back when the Sunset Strip was really hot. So we'd practice all day and hang out on the strip all night."

The result was the appropriately titled *I Didn't Raise My Boy to Be a Soldier.* The LP contained ten famous war songs, such as "When Johnny Comes Marching Home" and

"Ballad of the Green Berets," but done in a very different style. "We purposely performed off-beat and out of tune," Sheridan recalls. "We thought it was funny and helped put our antiwar message across. But the label just didn't get it." Despite limited radio airplay, the album caught on fast with the college circuit and ended up selling 50,000 copies nationwide. Through the years, Sheridan has heard that Boston station WBCN plays the LP every Fourth of July.

In 1970 Eli Radish was the first to bring in crowds to the Flats area when they became the Thursday-night house band for the Harbor Inn. (As the bar's first live band, members had to build their own stage.) In no time at all, the inn proved too small for the group's audience, and the band became weekly regulars at Tom Jones Backroom. Popularity with the local college set increased, and the band picked up a Sunday-night gig at Barracks (later Viking Saloon), just a stone's throw from Cleveland State University. They also added the Cleveland Agora to their list of venues.

Local entrepreneur Dan Gray, founder and president of the Creative Studios of Daffy Dan's (a multimillion-dollar company selling T-shirts, coffee mugs, and basic Cleveland-related memorabilia), served as roadie for the band. "Those were the most outrageous times," he says, referring either to the band or the decade, or both. "One moment that stands out was when the band opened for the Doors at the Allen Theater. I remember Jim Morrison had locked himself in the dressing room, and it took this big, black guy to finally break down the door to get him to come out! And then there was the time Eli Radish toured with the Who. Because it was my job to get the trucks to the events early, and I was the last to leave after the bands played, I was known for scoping out places to go and party. Keith Moon, especially, was always seeking me out 'cause he, of course, always wanted to party, and he knew I was the man to see."

In 1970 Eli Radish members welcomed a true country boy into their fold: David Allan Coe. "We met David when we were playing in a club in Akron," Sheridan recalls. "He was fresh out of prison and had just released his first album, *Penitentiary Blues*. He had heard about this crazy band. And after the gig, we got to talking. Not long after, he started opening for us at gigs in Kent, then joined in once we started playing. We did some Nashville recordings and some shows. He played with us until '71 when he started writing his string of hits in Nashville."

The inclusion of ex-con Coe (see Chapter 15) merely added to the group's bad-boy image. "We had kind of a wild reputation," Sheridan notes with a laugh, "which, of course, we promoted and encouraged! There were a lot of local musicians who didn't want to hang around us. There were parties where the host would say, 'Don't let those guys in!'"

By 1971, this "radical/country/hippie/biker/rock band" had added women to their formation. Fiddler Eva Karasik, a San Francisco native attending the Cleveland Music Institute, was first to join. "I wanted her to lose some of her symphonic polish," Sheridan recalls, "so I taught her to drag her bow across the strings, like a saw. It worked great. Her father, a first chair viola in the San Francisco Symphony, came to see us when we were opening for the Who. He saw her 200-year-old instrument covered with silver roadie tape to hold a contact microphone over an F hole, and let's just say he was not amused!"

Soon after, Starr Smith (vocals and guitar) and Barbara Merrick (vocals) joined the band after singing background vocals with the national group Pure Prairie League. Among all the rock groups on the North Coast landscape, this band stood out, and its unique musical style was a welcome change for many. Despite just one released recording, the group earned a large following beyond Ohio's border, with their hard-country-boogie sound and war protests.

Although this eccentric band broke up in the spring of 1973, their impact was strong. Gray recalls the band's significance.

> Eli Radish was an important band because they fit right in to the sign of the times. Just think: If it wasn't for our generation questioning everything going on back then—the environmental concerns, the war, human rights—where would we be today? After all, the powers-that-be at the time thought everything was just fine. The war was justified, nothing wrong with pollution, etc.
>
> No one, even people from that era today, realizes how important that free-thinking of ours was. And it came out in our music, our lifestyle, and made people more aware of what's really important. I'm afraid what's happening today is kids are more concerned with just themselves and are totally accepting of things. No one questions anything anymore.

Perhaps in this respect, the music of that era, which often focused on questioning authority, did accomplish this generation's goal to change, or at least make an impact on, the world. And in its own small, disparate way, Eli Radish served to open the eyes and minds of its young audience.

More than thirty years later, band members are widely scattered. Tom Foster is presently an insurance property and casualty adjuster in the Cleveland area. Skip Heil continues to play country music in California. Ken Frak's whereabouts are unknown. Danny Sheridan is involved in various aspects of the music business. The bassist toured with Coe from 1974 to 1978. He also became manager for then-girlfriend actress/harpist Nina Blackwood, who became one of the original video disc jockeys on MTV (see Chapter 15). He wrote music for TV shows *Fame* (along with Cleveland musician Jonah Koslen) and *CHiPs,* in which he made a guest appearance. Through the years, Sheridan has produced albums for musician friends and during his eight-year marriage to Bonnie Bramlett (of Delaney and Bonnie fame) restarted her career as well. The couple spent two seasons on *Roseanne,* where Bramlett played a biker waitress and Sheridan played Hank the bass player. Sheridan also composed the song "Roll on Down," sung by David Crosby in one episode on the show. He currently runs CrisisManagement and Associates, an entertainment/multimedia company in L.A. He also manages the jazz group Native Vibe, which hit *Billboard* charts in May 1999. He says he still runs into people all over the country who fondly recall the eclectic Eli Radish.

The Case of E.T. Hooley (1967–70; 1971–74)

Named for an old Scotland Yard case, this early hard-rock band featured several impressive talents. Its original lineup included bassist Dale Peters, guitarist Richard Shack (both of whom were later in the James Gang), guitarist Donny Baker (Jack Rabbit with Chrissie Hynde), drummer Paul Konowski, and lead singer Chip Fitzgerald (Pacific Gas and Electric). Fitzgerald and Baker's first band, the Disciples (also with future Numbers Band and Tin Huey member Chris Butler), were already well known in Cleveland. But E.T. Hooley was notable in its own right.

"We formed back in '67 and started playing around town, mostly teen clubs," Richard Shack recalls. "As a kid, I was into the blues, then caught onto folk music. But when I heard the Beatles, that was it. I started playing guitar and Jimmy Fox, who went to my high school [Cleveland Heights High], and I started jammin' together." That friendship resumed a decade later when Shack joined Fox in a later version of the James Gang. Although E.T. Hooley's fate was less prosperous than its counterpart, it made its presence known on the North Coast and beyond. The group, which played material by Jimi Hendrix, Cream, and Eric Clapton in addition to original songs, filled every area venue it played. So it was only natural that this Cleveland band was eager to move on to bigger cities and greater opportunities. The band performed at New York's Electric Circus and even spent a few months playing at several "hot spots" in Puerto Rico. "We had a good time traveling around and playing some fun gigs," Dale Peters recalls. "But I can still remember walking the streets of New York literally looking on the ground for money. It was an experience, I'll tell you, and one that opened our eyes." And so they returned to Cleveland. But the homecoming didn't last long. Konowski decided to call it quits, and Baker followed. "Donny felt, without Paul, the structure of the band would be greatly altered," Chip Fitzgerald notes. "Paul had a unique style of playing and, in a big way, defined our sound." The others, however, weren't ready to give up. For the second formation of the band, vocalist Fitzgerald took over on guitar. They found their new drummer, Kenny Mills, fresh from Ted Nugent's band. Then the quartet headed to L.A.

"We pulled into town, hadn't even unloaded our stuff when this guy comes up to us and asked if we wanted to play at this antiwar rally," Fitzgerald recalls. "We had no idea where it was or how large it would be. The next night we're at this mammoth place, where they make the floats for the Rose Parade, and find out we're opening for Led Zeppelin!" After that, the group had no problem getting gigs around town, including at the Whisky A Go Go. But for the most part the musicians, just barely out of their teens, found the rock road long and steep.

When the band returned to Cleveland to play a teen fair at the Convention Center in 1970, no one but Shack wanted to go back to California. He did, and the band split up. Soon after, Fitzgerald took Glenn Schwartz's place in Pacific Gas and Electric, where he stayed until deciding to reform E.T. Hooley in 1971. Newcomers included bass player Dave Snyder, drummer Tommy Schrontz, and sixteen-year-old guitarist Todd Sharp. "A friend of ours, Bill Dearango, knew I was looking for a good guitarist.

He told me, 'You gotta hear this kid play guitar.' Well, I'd been around Jimmy Page and Glenn Schwartz, so I wasn't easily impressed. But Todd just fried me, he was amazing."

Dearango was Sharp's guitar teacher. Through his Cleveland Heights High School years, Sharp worked partime at Record Rendezvous and was a go-fer for Billy Bass during the deejay's early WMMS years. Bass returned the favor years later, when he became the guitarist's manager for a time. When E.T. Hooley disbanded, Sharp, a singer-songwriter as well, went on to perform with Bob Welch, formerly of Fleetwood Mac. He then recorded with Mick Fleetwood for his 1981 solo LP. From 1981–84 he toured with Hall and Oates. He also cowrote Christine McVie's "Got a Hold on Me" and "Love Will Show Us How" and toured with Rod Stewart. His own debut album, *Who Am I,* was released in 1986.

The last E.T. Hooley continued to play all the local clubs until 1974, when band members called it quits for good. Fitzgerald went west, first to Colorado, then back to L.A. Today, he resides in Cleveland. Shack eventually reunited with high school buddy Fox for one of the last incarnations of the James Gang.

"Despite all the ups and downs, it was an amazing time," Shack says of this band's early history. "And you never forget your debut performance. Ours was at the Old Bohemian Hall. I remember after it was over, Fox [then in the James Gang] comin' over to me and saying, 'Remember, you're still the *second* best band in town!'" Shack and Fox have remained close friends and enjoy reminiscing about what they consider to be rock's "glory days." Said Shack,

Jimmy and I were talking the other day about those times. We agreed that, in retro-spect, the best times and the most fun shows were those old hometown gigs like "It's Boss" on the West Side and all those great Hullabaloos. There was a lot of stuff goin' on then. Cleveland and Detroit were really hot when it came to the music. I remember going to the Grande Ballroom [in Detroit] and seeing their local bands like the Rationals and MC5. And we had our own Cleveland Grande [the former WHK Auditorium], where we once opened for Deep Purple. But once you get into albums and go touring and stuff, there's a tremendous amount of pressure.

Back then, it was just pure fun. The kids loved it, we loved it. It wasn't even about the money. It was about playing the hottest tunes and really getting into it. And the great thing is people still remember us. Just a few years ago, this guy came up to me at a gig in L.A. and said, "I remember you,'" and I said, "Oh, from the James Gang." He said, "No, I didn't know you were in the James Gang. I meant the Case of E.T. Hooley. I remember seeing you guys in New York and I thought you were just the coolest band that ever happened!"

And you know, it still feels good to hear.

The James Gang (1966–76)

When most fans think of the band whose hits include "Funk #49," "Walk Away," "Midnight Man," and "Woman," they think of Joe Walsh. But in fact, the James Gang began and ended with Jimmy Fox. "Guitarist Ron Silverman and I started the band in 1966," recalls Fox, who briefly played with Tom King and the Starfires at sixteen. "He's the one who came up with the name, just out of the blue one day. Though for years we'd tell the press the name came about because Jesse James was a distant relative or some such story, but it was really that simple."

They all came out of Kent State, which became known for its array of musical talents, evident by the slew of excellent local bands playing regularly at Kent's showcase taverns. When not playing in their college backyards, the band was doing gigs at all the teen clubs, such as the Mentor and Chesterland Hullabaloos and Agora Alpha, the first Agora club.

The James Gang in 1967. *Left to right:* Ron Silverman, Glenn Schwartz, Tom Kriss, Jim Fox, and Phil Giallombardo. *Courtesy of Ron Silverman.*

Like most rock bands, the James Gang experienced various incarnations. The first lineup included drummer Fox, guitarist Silverman, bass player Tom Kriss, and keyboardist Phil Giallombardo. Another early member was Greg Grandillo on guitar, who later became a member of the '70s band Rainbow Canyon. Grandillo left the band before its first gig and was replaced by guitarist Dennis Chandler. Chandler was a good choice; he had spent much of his youth in Detroit as a student of Bo Diddley and Lonnie Mack.

Walk Away

"Then there was a guy called Mouse," Fox recalls.

> I don't think we ever knew his real name. But the significant thing about Mouse was that he could never remember the names of the songs, so he was always about four bars late into it, 'til he figured out what they were. During this time we heard Glenn Schwartz was out of the army looking for something to do. I'd never heard Glenn play but I'd heard rumors about him and how talented he was. He was quite a bit older than us—Phil and Tom were just in tenth grade at this point.
>
> Finally I caught up with Glenn one day and asked him to come and hear the band. At first he rejected it, then finally agreed. He came to listen to us at the English Grille, two doors from the LaCave. At one point during the set, Glenn came up on stage and started playing "Jeff's Boogie" with us, and of course, he was phenomenal. About halfway through the song, I noticed out of the corner of my eye Mouse packing up.
>
> And we've never seen him to this day!

From that moment, Glenn Schwartz was a James Gang member. Cleveland guitarist Butch Armstrong recalled his first impression of Schwartz for a 1996 *Scene* article.

> They were playing at the Chagrin Armory in Chagrin Falls. The James Gang broke into their first song, "The Nazz are Blue," by the Yardbirds with the famous Elmore James signature lick intro. Within seconds, Glenn was pouring wet with sweat and saliva singing and attacking the guitar in every way and form. We were in shock! His enormous hands pulled and tugged the strings as if they were rubber bands. He vibrated his notes with his fingers! Incredible!
>
> Glenn proceeded to play every song from Jimi Hendrix's "Fire" and "Purple Haze" to Cream's "Sunshine of Your Love." He finished the set with Jeff Beck's signature song, "Jeff's Boogie," in his own way, and it was better than Beck.
>
> He later became known for sustaining a feedback note with vibrato for a long period of time, while leaning back, placing the back of his right forearm over his forehead as if in distress, and hanging upside down while on guitarist Bill Jeric's shoulder!
>
> That night Glenn became the biggest inspiration of my life.

Meanwhile, Ron Silverman had been drafted, replaced by Bill Jeric, who was fast becoming a popular member of the group. "Bill was one of those guys with a tremendous desire to learn everything about playing guitar," Fox says. "And he had an endless amount of energy. He and Glenn hit it off big."

But Schwartz didn't stick around. Several months later he left for Los Angeles, where he became a celebrated member of the West Coast acid-rock group Pacific Gas and Electric, playing many memorable rock events, like the famous Miami Pop Festival.

Then came Joe Walsh, who'd just come off a popular Kent band called the Measles. "I was going to Kent State by then," Fox says, recalling the spring of 1969. "Glenn had just left the band on a Sunday, and that Monday this guy knocks on my apartment door and says, 'I hear you need a guitar player,' and it was Joe. Talk about word of mouth! So he came to rehearse with us and we liked it and things went on from there." Went on they did. Within months, the James Gang, now a power trio consisting of Fox, Kriss, and Walsh, burst out of the starting gate with *Yer Album,* which charted a respectable No. 83 on *Billboard.*

The story of this midwestern band typifies that of the true American rock and roll fantasy. Their unique, distinctive sound—best described as gritty, funky, and the epitome of what became known as hard rock—was their claim to fame. And through a series of fateful events, this college-bred, small-town rock band emerged into a full-fledged national recording act—with "gold records on the wall."

"We were really playing because it was fun and were surprised when we actually made money," says Dale Peters, former E.T. Hooley bassist who replaced Tom Kriss in January 1970. "Besides the albums, I'm probably most proud of playing Carnegie Hall. Nowadays you can just rent it but back then, in '71, you had to be invited to play." That concert was recorded live and became one of several of the band's gold albums.

The trio toured with the Who and, back home, gave a memorable performance at Musicarnival, opening for Led Zeppelin in the British group's first Cleveland visit. During its decade of existence, the James Gang played with some of rock's greatest. There were performances, as well as a few parties, with Grand Funk Railroad, the Kinks, the Who, Humble Pie, Led Zeppelin, and Eric Clapton. The 1970 European tour, opening for the Who, helped the Gang hone its particular style and forever established it as a band to be reckoned with.

Dale Peters recalls his "battle of the basses" with John Entwistle. "We got into a lot of jams on that tour. One night Entwistle started mocking how I played an old Yardbirds tune, 'Lost Woman.' I returned the favor by mocking his playing 'My Generation.' We had some great times with those guys."

An encounter with the Beach Boys, however, proved less successful. A prospective weeklong tour with them was abruptly shortened to one night. The Ohio trio was thrown off the tour by Beach Boy Mike Love. "We'd just come off of that Who tour and were into getting kinda crazy like them. You know, jumping off our amps, smashing equipment, creating general havoc," Peters recalls with a laugh. "Well, we had these flash pots with flash powder which we wanted to use for the show. Well, I guess it was

A poster of the most familiar James Gang lineup, 1971. *Left to right:* Joe Walsh, Dale Peters, and Jim Fox. *David Spero Collection.*

a little too close for comfort for Love, who was into his Indian vibe at the time and had these expensive Oriental rugs on stage. I guess he was afraid we'd burn them or something." Nonetheless, the James Gang's travels with rock's prominent players earned the band greater respect and, in their own words, taught them to be better musicians.

When their second album, *James Gang Rides Again,* hit record stores that fall, the single "Funk #49" reached No. 59, while the album itself peaked at No. 20 on *Billboard,* giving its members their first gold disc. Right on the heels of that came the group's *Thirds,* featuring the catchy tune "Walk Away," which won still more loyal fans. The single peaked at No. 51, while the album itself reached No. 27. Another memorable hit, "Midnight Man," made it to No. 80.

In November 1971, Walsh left the group to move to Boulder, Colorado, where he re-emerged as part of a power trio called Barnstorm. And even with Walsh's celebrated years with the Eagles, beginning in 1975, his early association with the James Gang were not be forgotten by the thousands of fans whose best adolescent memories are laced with the music this distinctive band made.

Walsh made his last recorded James Gang appearance on the group's *Live in Concert* (from the Carnegie Hall performance), but a 1973 compilation LP, *The Best of the James Gang Featuring Joe Walsh,* peaked at No. 79 on U.S. charts. And while Walsh went his separate way, the James Gang kept riding. Guitarist Dominic Troiano replaced Walsh, and the group added Roy Kenner on congas and vocals. The James Gang, now a quartet, released a new LP, *Straight Shooter,* in 1972.

One of this new formation's most thrilling performances was at the Akron Rubber Bowl on June 16, 1972; the band completely filled the stadium's 70,000-seat capacity. Also on the bill was Three Dog Night, who insisted that two 14-by-20-foot screens be erected to allow the entire audience a front-row view of the event. A major innovation in rock concerts, this has now become the norm at outdoor shows.

In 1973, Troiano left to join another well-known group, the Guess Who (just after recording the James Gang's *Passin' Thru* LP), and Tommy Bolin (later a Deep Purple member, now deceased) took his place. After two more releases on Atlantic Records, *Bang* (1973) and *Miami* (1974), the lineup changed once again, now with Fox, Peters, Shack, and guitarist/vocalist Bubba Keith. A year and one album later (*Newborn,* 1975), that formation broke up as well. But this sturdy, determined band of musicians wasn't done just yet. In one more attempt to recapture the band's former glory, the James Gang reemerged with Fox, Peters, Giallombardo, and guitarist Webb (who played with Stephen Stills) to record *Jesse Come Home.* Several singles from the album received airplay, but not enough. After a decade of riding out numerous storms, the band took its final journey into the sunset. "It basically came down to the fact we just never could get back the old sound once Walsh left," Peters says, "and we finally had to realize it was time to move on."

"I made a bad career decision late in the game," Fox admits. "Eric Clapton had invited me to do some session work with him. I recorded with him on his *461 Ocean Blvd.* album but had to decline his offer to join his band permanently because we were wrapping up an album at the time and had a tour starting the following day in Indiana. It was booked and the equipment had already gone ahead, and Clapton says to me, 'Of course, you'll stay?' and I said, 'Well I can't.' I mean, that was my band and I just couldn't walk away. Of course, now I think back . . . . You could definitely say that is my biggest regret."

Through the years, former member Chandler made a name for himself as well. During the 1960s, the keyboardist/guitarist befriended B. B. King while frequenting a Cleveland club, Gus's Showbar (E. 69th and Superior Avenue). Years later, he began a campaign on King's behalf. As a salesman for Gibson guitars, Chandler initiated a drive to win endorsement for King's own signature guitar (after all, Les Paul had his own model). The Gibson Model ES 355 TDSV is now called "the Lucille." The hard-won efforts of the Cleveland musician were not lost on King, who often has Chandler accompany him on stage and who calls him his "adopted son." Through the decades, Chandler has either backed or played with recording artists such as the Temptations, the Supremes, Smokey Robinson, the Four Tops, Little Richard, Chuck Berry, and Jerry Lee Lewis. His songwriting skills have brought him many projects, including authoring jingles for local television and radio.

But it took twenty years and a U.S. president to produce a bona fide reunion of Fox, Walsh, and Peters. A diehard fan of the group, Bill Clinton brought them together to perform during his 1996 campaign. The historic event was held at the Cleveland State University Convocation Center. They reunited once again to play for the Presidential Inaugural Ball in Washington, D.C., the following January. "That experience was unreal," says David Spero, Walsh's manager. "Who'd have ever dreamed back in the '60s, the James Gang would be playing at a presidential ball?"

Ever since that exciting, and too brief, reunion, rumors of a comeback of the James Gang remain as persistent as those ever-hopeful of a Beatles reunion. And surely there's always room for hope. After all, as the reuniting of the Eagles, Motley Crue, and Fleetwood Mac, among others, certainly confirms, there is no such thing as "never again."

Recommended Reading

Pollock, Bruce. *Hipper Than Our Kids: A Rock and Roll Journal of the Baby Boom Generation.* New York: Schirmer, 1993.

———. *When the Music Mattered: Rock in the 1960s.* New York: Holt, Reinhart and Winston, 1983.

Shaughnessy, Mary Alice. *Les Paul: An American Original.* New York: William Morrow, 1993.

Part 3
It's More Than a Job; It's an Adventure

9 The Agora: A Rock 'n' Roll Institution

That concert in '78 when Bruce Springsteen played the Agora for WMMS's tenth anniversary was just a fabulous, magical night. One of the highlights of that era.
—Denny Sanders

On the West Coast, it was San Francisco's Avalon Ballroom and the Fillmore and L.A.'s Roxy. On the East Coast, it was New York's Bottom Line and Max's Kansas City. On the North Coast, the premier place to be seen, heard, and ultimately noticed in the rock world was none other than Cleveland's Agora.

Just ask such rock artists as diverse as Bruce Springsteen, Ted Nugent, Bob Seger, Meat Loaf, Sting, Paul Simon, Joan Jett, John Mellencamp, ZZ Top, Pat Benatar, Alice Cooper, Roxy Music, Southside Johnny, Eric Carmen, Todd Rundgren, Bad Company, Yes, Kiss, Sheila E., and Nine Inch Nails's Trent Reznor, as well as tens of thousands of rock and roll fans. "I was told that if you want to break the Northeast, you have to play the Agora," ZZ Top manager Bill Ham once told Agora owner Hank LoConti, who ended up booking the unknown act in 1974 for $200.

No truer words were spoken. And it all started with a jukebox junkie. "I was twenty when I started helping my brother on his jukebox route," LoConti recalls. "Then in '51 I got a job with Leaf Music at E. 17th and Payne. Within three months I surpassed the boss's son's route and the owner asked if I'd do both routes, which I thought was great. 'Course I never realized he should've paid me extra for it!"

Those routes were where teens hung out in those days—drug stores (with soda fountains) and hamburger drive-ins like Kenny King's and Big Boy Restaurants.

"I knew what people liked in their music and bought directly from the large record companies—RCA, Mercury, King, Columbia, Decca, MGM, and Capitol, which were all located within a few miles of each other. In the '50s, there were a lot of good pop-oriented artists. I'd buy anything by Nat King Cole, Sinatra, Tony Bennett, the McGuire Sisters. And Johnnie Ray was really hot then, too." While on his daily jukebox routes, LoConti noticed high school kids invading places meant for college students; because of this, "they were becoming real 'punch palaces,'" he says. Soon LoConti was entertaining thoughts of a private venue strictly for college students, where they could enjoy their favorite music. Such was the idea that led to a future as a rock entrepreneur.

His vision became the first Agora club, called Agora Alpha, located near Case Western Reserve University. With one partner and $20,000, LoConti opened the club on February 27, 1966, and local rock band Selective Service played that historic event. The club owner served only food and milkshakes until he acquired his beer license nine months later. The license allowed him to serve 3.2 beer and stay open until 12:30 A.M. "The club was an instant success," LoConti recalls proudly. "And I immediately realized we were in the wrong place. It wasn't big enough [200 capacity], there weren't enough parking places [exactly twelve], and residents were complaining."

Because of the hordes of college students invading the city block each weekend, LoConti searched for a new building, finding it just down the street from Cleveland State University. "It was a large building with 16,000 square feet on the first floor, 8,000 on the second, and 4,000 in the basement." On July 7, 1967, the Agora Beta opened to the public. December's Children got it all started. "It was a real thrill to open that club," recalls guitarist Craig Balzer, whose brother Bruce also played guitar in the band. "It meant a lot to us, because Hank LoConti was always supportive of the local bands." The club soon became known as the Agora Ballroom.

From the start, the downtown nightclub was one of a kind, offering the best in local talent: the Choir, James Gang, Damnation of Adam Blessing, the Raspberries, Glass Harp, Charade, Rainbow Canyon, and the Case of E.T. Hooley. The nightspot drew huge crowds every weekend. Kids began congregating hours before the doors opened in order to be guaranteed a seat. "In the beginning I was opening at 6:00 P.M., but then I started opening two hours early so the kids wouldn't be forced to wait outside," LoConti says.

"We were strict. We caught a lot of high school kids signing up to get in," LoConti recalls. "So we'd find out how old they were, and they had to bring their college I.D. with them. But a lot of kids would take their brother's or sister's I.D., so we didn't just take the I.D., we checked it out by actually calling their house and asking their mothers. It was a good method, and it worked. Then if they passed, they'd get a membership card with their picture on it, and [be] given a pewter mug [for the 3.2 beer] with their name and number on the handle, which we stored there for them." Another rule allowed members to bring a guest, but in doing so, they were required to sign a "responsibility form" that, in essence, said the college student was responsible for his or her friend's behavior. This made one think twice about who they chose to bring. And the ominous sign posted above the bar—"There is nothing more frightening than ignorance in action"—provided food for thought for any guest. That, and the equally threatening presence of big, beefy security guards.

"Hank was a great guy but very serious about his business, which is why it ran so well," says Kevin Dugan, former stage manager and technician for Rainbow Canyon and the Raspberries. "He was the absolute nucleus of Cleveland's rock scene." (Cleveland-native Dugan has an interesting rock history himself. When the Raspberries disbanded, he went on to become part of the road crew with the Beach Boys and has since served as production manager, technician, and/or coordinator for rock celebrities such as Eric Carmen, Fleetwood Mac, Bob Welch, Guns n' Roses, Poison, and Ratt. Today he is the personal technician for Van Halen bassist Michael Anthony.)

The reason for the gravitational pull of young clientele was, of course, the music at the Agora. Along with the diverse selection of local acts was the appearance of national ones, or those that would become national as a direct result of the Agora exposure. Acts like the James Gang. "We were just starting out when I approached Hank about playing the Agora," drummer Jim Fox recalls. "Now this was back at the first one, down by University Circle. It was always a great, fun gig. The audience seemed to appreciate what we were doing, and I always felt they were with us 100 percent. We could play what we wanted and everyone had a good time. We played, they listened and danced."

Over the next seventeen years, this North Coast site became a music institution and the place where every musician around the country longed to perform. The club consistently offered an eclectic array of acts by showcasing every type of rock—pop rock, hard rock, glam rock, heavy metal, punk, reggae, and rap/hip-hop. And at the heart of it all was an unpretentious man who, like San Francisco's Bill Graham, became a pioneer in the business of rock and roll.

A polite, amiable businessman with an engaging manner, Hank LoConti, now in his sixties, is thoroughly liked in a business so often known for rogues. The respect and affection musicians have for him is recounted time and again. "Hank was very encouraging, always greeted us warmly and paid us the going rate," Fox says. "I remember it was a real family business, with his mom taking the money at the door and paying us at the end of the night. I think a big part of Hank's success was that he was always willing to take a chance [by hiring unknown acts]. And he was actively involved in the music, more than just the business. He paid attention to it, listened to it, understood it, rather than [being] a person who just booked gigs."

"When we first became the Raspberries," guitarist Wally Bryson recalls, "'Uncle Henry' bought us the suits we wore for our debut at his club. I can't say enough about the guy. He did what no one else was doing at the time, and he did it without screwing anyone over."

"The man never stopped," bluesman Jimmy Ley recalls. "He'd be working something like fifteen-hour shifts. And you always wondered if he got your messages. Well, one day we decided to make sure. Hank had a habit of going into his office at some point in his day. He had this big leather chair behind his desk where he'd lean back, lock his hands behind his head, kick his feet up on the desk, and just stare at the ceiling for a few minutes. That was his way of relaxing. So we started taping the messages to the ceiling, so as he leaned back, he'd look up and he'd be sure to see 'em!"

Over, Under, Sideways, Down

The basement of the Agora was fast becoming a musical hot spot as well. From its inception in 1968, the downstairs club (originally called the Viking's Den), with its 350-seat capacity, offered an intimate atmosphere. In the early years, it often showcased the groups not quite ready for primetime and became a breeding ground for those hungry for the alternative experience. Throughout the 1970s the venue saw jazz, reggae, blues, and punk bands. Pere Ubu, the Dead Boys, Chrissie Hynde, Devo, and Rocket from the Tombs gave their audiences early punk experiences here. On June 8, 1972, the Viking's Den was renamed the Mistake. But considering its habit of featuring cutting-edge acts and after-hour visits from the headliners upstairs, the Mistake was anything but one. And though it changed its name to the Pop Shop in 1983, its new wave tradition lived on.

Still, the Agora Ballroom was king. By 1970, LoConti prepared to open another club in Columbus's Old State Theater on the Ohio State University Campus. "I had some college students helping me get the place ready, and they were telling me that making it a membership-only club wasn't going to fly down there. This was the era where young folks were hell-bent on equality, and right before the Kent State riots. They suggested making it an eighteen-and-over club." LoConti agreed, with one exception: He opened the club to girls eighteen and over and guys twenty-one and over. And because he'd earned the young people's respect, when all hell broke loose just days after the Columbus club opened (the shootings at Kent State on May 4, 1970, sparked many riots on other campuses all over the country) and businesses were being damaged all around him, LoConti's club remained untouched.

According to Hank Jr., it was the Columbus Agora that first earned national recognition.

My first memory of the Agora was the Columbus venue where I saw the Grateful Dead in '71. I was ten years old at the time and it was like culture shock, 'cause here I was a young city boy coming from a "greaser" era, then suddenly thrown into this campus "hippie land." And this was during the Vietnam protests and all that. It definitely left an impression.

Back then, more nationally known bands played at Columbus because the place was a lot bigger, with a 1,700-seat capacity, and, in some respects, Columbus was ahead of Cleveland, particularly for those "hippie-style bands" like the Dead and Procol Harum, mostly because of the 60,000 Ohio State students across the street. It was a real college town, so it drew a lot of bands.

Aside from the regular Friday and Saturday night parties, there were "Welfare Wednesdays," which offered draft beer for ten cents; the unprecedented Wednesday afternoon "Coffeebreak Concerts," which became internationally known for legendary performances of the "Who's Who of Rock"; "Golden Sundays," named for the regional talents it continually showcased (such as the Raspberries); and what fast became the most successful weeknight concert event of all, "Monday Nights Out at the Agora." The Monday night concerts, which were taped and subsequently sent to nine other stations on its radio network, debuted on April 16, 1973. Shrewdly, LoConti decided to open his club on a night all others were closed. "It just made sense to me," he says. "The kids don't care what night it is as long as you're offering their kind of entertainment." Once again, his business instincts were right on the money.

In 1971, Cleveland's grand entrepreneur pioneered yet another great musical concept. Hooking up with progressive rock station WNCI, the Columbus Agora began producing live radio broadcasts of concerts, beginning with Ted Nugent. Not long after, the Cleveland Agora got on the bandwagon and began airing the broadcasts with sister station WNCR-FM (later expanding to include OSU's college station). The "Live from the Agora" concert series became the first weekly radio program of its kind. When WNCR changed formats in January 1973, WMMS was there to pick up where 'NCR left off. In fact, upon the announcement of the series, the Agora sold out the first

Rain never stopped Cleveland rock fans. Here, the line extends down the block for a Southside Johnny and the Asbury Jukes concert on May 2, 1977. *Photo by Janet Macoska.*

thirteen shows. Not coincidently, within months of broadcasting these live concerts nationwide, WMMS became the number-one FM radio station in Cleveland.

The electric pairing of these two media giants of radio and rock club inspired Ian Hunter, of Mott the Hoople fame, to write the song "Cleveland Rocks," emphasizing what deejay Billy Bass had already said about the city being "the Rock 'n' Roll Capital of the World." Also in 1973, television brought the Agora to fans outside city limits when the Columbus Agora and Craciun III Productions joined forces and produced a recording of a TV special called "Music, You're My Mother." The radio/television mix became the first nationally syndicated rock and roll simulcast in concert club history. And there was more. Sansui of Japan sponsored the radio program "New World of Jazz," the first of which was a Ronnie Laws (formerly with Earth, Wind and Fire) concert. The shows were syndicated to over fifty stations in the United States, the United Kingdom, South America, Asia, and Australia.

Then, on October 21, 1978, came "On Stage at the Agora," the first production to be broadcast live on television. The shows became a monthly feature, simulcast on WMMS and WJW-TV Channel 8 (the CBS affiliate at that time). The first group to

Todd Rundgren wows his fans at the world-famous Agora, August 1978. *Photo by Janet Macoska.*

headline these concerts was Springsteen's New Jersey buddies, Southside Johnny and the Asbury Jukes.

Notes "Southside Johnny" Lyon,

> But that wasn't the first time we played the Agora. Our debut performance there was in 1976. It was our first big "hey, we're getting out of Jersey" gig. When we walked in, it was sold out and we were totally amazed. The place was packed! The noise and the crowd was incredible.
>
> You see, prior to that, we'd been doing all right in our hometown, but we certainly weren't nationally recognized. But in Cleveland, we were starting to hit it big as a direct result of that lunatic Kid Leo playing us on WMMS. And unbeknownst to us, he'd been hyping us like mad for the Agora concert. So when we got up on stage, we could do no wrong. We pulled out all the stops and were even doing songs we didn't know—it was crazy. We were just having a ball up there!

One of the more memorable concerts Southside Johnny and his fans recall was when Bruce Springsteen, having just finished a two-and-a-half-hour set at the Coliseum, rushed over to the E. 24th venue to jump on the Agora stage and jam with his friends.

TV specials continued, with concerts featuring Todd Rundgren, Ian Hunter, Eddie Money, Toto, Meat Loaf, and others. These broadcasts were made possible because the Agora was one of the few nightclubs in the country to boast its own on-site recording studio, Agency Recording. As a result, LoConti has a library of over four hundred taped recordings of concerts from 1972 on.

Here, There, Everywhere

By its tenth anniversary, the Agora owner learned at a *Billboard* convention that his was considered the country's finest nightclub. And by the early 1980s, Agora clubs had multiplied to now total thirteen: Cleveland (1967–), Columbus (1970–84), Toledo (1972–80), Youngstown (1972–80), Painesville (1977–81), Akron (1980–84), Atlanta (1978–84), Dallas (1978–91), Houston (1980–84), Tampa (1980–82), and Hallendale, Florida (1980–81). There were also clubs in Hartford and New Haven, Connecticut (1981), both of which never quite got off the ground.

"Each club had its style and character," LoConti says. "I have to say, though, that out of all the clubs, Cleveland was number one. Despite some of the other markets where the economy was stronger, they just didn't beat Cleveland. It was a unique club. I haven't found a duplicate yet. That's why I decided to get rid of the rest and concentrate on Cleveland." And it is the Cleveland Agora that remains today. This despite the fact that the E. 24th location closed due to fire in 1984 (the same year the equally popular Columbus venue closed its doors). Within a year, LoConti found a new home for his club. Coincidently, it was the most appropriate place one could imagine—the old

WHK Auditorium, where much of Cleveland got its rock reputation in the first place. The present Agora is alive and well at 5000 Euclid Avenue and is being rediscovered by a whole new generation.

But in those first seventeen years, when rock was young, the grand old Agora played host to virtually every rock group known to fans. The Agora's reputation was such that part of the 1979 movie *One Trick Pony,* with Paul Simon, was shot and produced there and made cocktail waitress Mare Winningham a star.

But then, there were the horror stories.

"Iggy Pop almost put us out of business when we'd just started at the downtown location," LoConti recalls.

When he played there, I was busy taking care of things in Columbus. Now, at that time we used to put chairs on the floor right in front of the stage. There was a kid sitting up in front with this girl. Iggy comes out on stage wearing a jock strap, and he jumps off the stage, turns around and moons the girl, spreading his cheeks right in her face. The kid, in turn, pinched him so hard he probably still feels it today, then his friends start in on him [Iggy]. It took every security guard we had to break it up and get Iggy back to the stage.

So two o'clock in the morning, my brother's doorbell rings and it's this kid telling him what happened. Then I get a phone call in Columbus and my brother tells me the story. Now I'd already booked in a string of acts—Alice Cooper, MC5, Bob Seger, Ted Nugent—but I ended up telling the booking agent, "That's it, cancel everything in Cleveland 'cause I'm not there to watch it, and can't guarantee anything."

And when I returned to Cleveland, I immediately took out those chairs by the stage!

Wendy O. Williams, lead singer of the hardcore punk band the Plasmatics, caused even more problems with her group's concert on January 21, 1981. While on stage, Williams, sporting a Mohawk haircut and little else, performed topless (black tape and shaving cream covered her nipples) while cutting up a guitar with a chainsaw. The punk diva was consequently given a pandering obscenities charge that drew national press attention. And although she was acquitted, the famed Cleveland concert club wasn't. The Agora was slapped with violating three lewdness regulations, and the State Liquor Commission withdrew its license for three weeks. But Wendy's presence that night stayed in the minds of all, especially Johan (Linas Johanson), there on his first night as the club's promotions manager. He quipped: "If this is what rock 'n' roll is all about, count me in!"

Stories abound, of course, and fortunately most are of a positive nature. But given a choice of fans' favorite moments, one show wins hands down, according to those lucky enough to have experienced the historic North Coast event either live or by radio. Not surprising, it was another Agora first. The concert considered the greatest show on rock and roll earth came via live broadcast on WMMS on August 9, 1978. The headliner was a man *Plain Dealer* rock writer Jane Scott had predicted would be a "superstar" years earlier: Bruce Springsteen.

Backstage Pass

If it was music for the young—or young at heart—Hank LoConti offered it. Even his own mother was a captive fan, especially of that Jersey rocker. "My mother was seventy-nine years old when Springsteen played our thirteenth anniverary show [in conjunction with WMMS's tenth anniversary]," LoConti recalls.

> She'd been around entertainment her whole life, so she'd seen lots of shows and got along well with the groups.
>
> Now Springsteen wanted a stage with a T-shaped ramp where he could walk out into the audience. And we sat my mother right by the corner of the T. Well, she sat through both of his shows that night. And of course, he was just incredible.
>
> Afterwards, I took her backstage and introduced her to him in the dressing room. She stood there, told him how much she enjoyed his shows, and added that she thought he was absolutely good-looking!

The Agora was indeed a family affair. "I remember I was ten years old and watched my mother backstage doing this guy's makeup," recalls Henry LoConti Jr. "I found out later it was Alice Cooper!" "When I was a kid, I never wanted to work anywhere but the Agora," says Johan. "It kinda represented that aura of Bill Graham, like you could get close to what was happening. One thing that amazed me back then was when you'd come up at the box office, Grandma or Aunt LoConti was always there to greet you at the door. They'd be like, 'How ya doin,' how's school, you got your grades up?'"

The concert venue served more than typical rock fans. Many began lucrative careers behind the scenes, working as light and sound engineers, stage managers, record and radio promoters, roadies (called the "Rowdy Roadies"), and managers.

As a regular at the club, Johan, a 1977 Eastlake North High graduate, began an internship there on weekends in between classes at Cleveland State University. He interrupted the flow in 1982 by moving out to Newport Beach, California, in an effort to latch on to the L.A. music scene. "But when I came back for a visit, the place was abuzz about the Rock Hall coming here, so I knew this was the place to be." By then it was 1985, and LoConti was getting the new building ready to open after the former Agora had burned down. Johan was hired as public relations and promotional director. "Working at the Agora is not just a job or a business," he says. "It's, in every aspect, a labor of pure love for anyone who works here. Every artist that ever played here will tell you how the LoContis treat them like family. They even have a washer and dryer available for them to do their laundry when they're in town, and, believe me, that's a real luxury for them. And when Pappy [Agora's chief security guard] died, we even held his funeral there because this was his family, too."

Dennis "Pappy" Fagan worked at the Agora from 1970 through 1995, but his close association with the club went beyond that. After graduating from South High School in Willoughby in 1968, Pappy (who earned his nickname through his mentoring of younger Agora staff members) was roadie for December's Children. "But he was more than just a roadie," adds Craig Balzer. "He was our security guard and our friend. Both he and his brother Ed were an integral part of that band." As member of Miami Security, a colorful group of security guards and roadies for the Agora circuits, he was an ongoing presence and faithfully maintained his post at the backstage door throughout the years. His heavyset frame intimidated anyone who entertained a thought of getting between him and the rock stars.

"But he was really just a big teddy bear," Johan insists. "He protected and treated the Agora like it was his home. And in a sense it was." So when he died from a heart attack in 1995, there seemed no more fitting location for his funeral than the place where his beloved memory lives on with those lives he touched.

The House of Rock

"The reason Cleveland's Agora stood out," says LoConti, "is most likely due to rock's attraction to the North Coast, resulting from its open-minded audiences that crave the innovations and creativity of an artist." Today, the third-generation Agora plays host to acts ranging from death-metal acts, like Entombed, Cannibal Corpse, and Marilyn Manson, to the melodic blues of Bobby Blue Bland and Blues Traveler. The ballroom itself, with bar and table seating, has a capacity of 700; it shares the building with the Agora Theater, which has a capacity of 1,800. Both are wired to the building's ninety-six-track JBH Recording Studios (for recording of concerts). The ballroom and theater often serve as the last stop before a band goes on to larger, arena-sized venues.

Although he enjoys reminiscing about those groundbreaking years, Hank LoConti takes what he has learned and puts it all in perspective.

If you're going to survive in the lower end of the business, like I've been all my life, you've got to promote the smaller acts. It's the lower end, but the most exciting and gratifying. You get to see the artist before people realize they're stars. You get to bring them when only a handful of people want to see them. Then one, two, or five years later, thousands are clamoring for tickets and you're wondering, where were these people back then? You knew all along they were going to be big. Take Springsteen. First time I saw him on stage, I said, "There's a superstar." There was no doubt in my mind where this man was going. The quality was there. Huey Lewis, another excellent entertainer. Pat Benatar, too, was terrific. I happened to catch her once at rehearsal at my Atlanta club. I was up in the mezzanine and heard her as she did a soundcheck a capella—no music, and she had this incredible voice.

If you want to measure success by performance and operation rather than monetarily, then I guess you could say I'm successful. I've had a good education over the years in all the different markets, listening to the different music and buying records for different cultures and people. That's what's been satisfying.

In 1979 LaConti received *Billboard*'s Steve Wolfe Memorial Award for his immeasurable contributions to the music and entertainment industry.

In 1995, LoConti handed over the business to his son, Henry Jr., now president of Agora Productions. But that didn't mean he retired. "I could never retire," he says. Proof of that statement is a quick glance at his agenda. He remains active in the entertainment insurance business as well as the Buckeye Music Center, the venue he helped establish back in the mid-1970s. (Similar to Blossom Music Center, Buckeye is a 55,000-capacity outdoor concert venue located forty-three miles east of Columbus.) He also can easily oversee Agora activities from his office over the club. In addition, he is an active partner in Agora Promo West Promotions, an entertainment company.

But foremost on his mind these days is his newest venture in St. Petersburg. That's Russia, not Florida. "I never planned on opening a night spot in St. Petersburg. The opportunity simply presented itself," he says. On a business trip there with his nephew in 1995, LoConti was asked to build an American-style discotheque there. The challenge was too great to turn down. Grand opening for this auspicious new club was April 1997; Debbie "Blondie" Harry performed. The St. Petersburg venue, called "Hollywood Nites," is now a popular nightclub for Russian adolescents.

Recommended Reading

Marsh, Dave, and James Bernard. *The New Book of Rock Lists*. New York: Simon and
    Schuster, 1981.

10 Cleveland's Prominent Rock Journalists and Publications

When rock music first broke on the scene in the 1950s, anything connected to it was not considered worthy of mention in the mainstream press—unless it was to report a riot or something downright horrifying, as in the case of Alan Freed's first rock concert or Jerry Lee Lewis marrying his thirteen-year-old cousin. Items like these were front-page fodder and TV and radio's top stories—and precisely how rock earned such a dishonorable name in its infancy.

But a woman reporter from Cleveland changed all that. With her "Young Ohio Page" covering rock's positive side, the excitement and lively adventures of the music and times, Jane Scott put a different spin on the perception of rock, and with bold stroke of her pen, she wiped out the flaws and provided the punch. Other writers quickly caught on to her beat, and by the mid-1960s rock was at last considered a viable news item. On the North Coast, big-city newspapers, as well as a few weekly indie papers, were capturing rock's moments in print as well as through the flashbulbs of a select group of photographers who caught all the pomp and circumstance as well as the rowdy and ragged.

The Journalists

Jane Scott, *Plain Dealer* Reporter and First Lady of Rock Journalism

> Forget the kooky image and all that "world oldest teenager" crap. She's sharp as a tack—and the hardest working reporter I've ever met. The woman will not be denied.
>
> —Michael Heaton, *Plain Dealer* columnist (*Cleveland Magazine,* 1993)

She's been described as "Jammin' Jane," "Amazing Jane," but never "Plain Jane." There's a reason for that. "Plain" would not describe the life of one who has interviewed eccentric rock stars such as Michael Jackson, Alice Cooper, Ice-T, and Iggy Pop (and outlived numerous others, including Jimi Hendrix, Keith Moon, Otis Redding, Kurt Cobain, Bob Marley, Stevie Ray Vaughan, Wendy O. Williams, and Stiv Bators). Nor does it accurately describe a journalist who still attends more than a hundred concerts a year and maintains a weekly "What's Happening" column, despite the fact she has already celebrated (in fine fashion) her eightieth birthday.

Jane Scott is probably the only rock reporter who carries her Golden Buckeye card alongside her backstage passes. With her trademark glasses (trifocals) and large canvas tote, Jane often gives people the wrong impression. "Someone once described Jane as looking like a woman who just got off the bus in the wrong town," *Plain Dealer* reporter Michael Heaton said in an 1996 *Avenues* article. But a quick glance inside her oversized bag dispels the myth. She does pack peanut butter sandwiches, earplugs, tissues, and a small flashlight—preparations for what could be an overnight bus trip. But further investigation also discloses a plastic hair cover, ever-ready pen, and reporter's notebook. The contents all come in handy when attending a rock concert: The sandwiches save time and money, the earplugs protect against the high-decibel sounds as heard from the front row, the flashlight (which she often holds in her mouth) aids in notetaking when stage lights grow dim, the hair cover comes in handy for rainy days at outdoor venues like Blossom and Nautica, and the tissues are for when the bathrooms run out of toilet paper. "Which they always do," says Jane.

Little in her past suggested Jane Scott would earn her living—and a good one at that—meeting and writing about rock and roll stars. Certainly not the generation she came from. Growing up during the Great Depression in the West Side city of Lakewood, she enjoyed listening to all kinds of music, particularly the Big Band sounds of Glenn Miller, Tommy Dorsey, and Artie Shaw. And her all-time favorite Christmas gift was a small, wind-up Victrola she received as a young teen. The first thing she played on it was a song called "Sent for You Yesterday, and Here You Come Today" by Jimmy Rushing, who sang with Count Basie. That's when she fell for the boogie-woogie beat.

Reading and writing were also passions. A high school classmate recalls her hiding a teen music magazine under her Latin book, a hint at the direction fate would take her. After graduating from Lakewood High, she attended the University of Michigan, where she studied journalism and became a staff writer for the *University of Michigan Daily*.

In 1941, Scott graduated with a Bachelor of Arts degree and a teacher's certificate, ready to make her mark in the media world. But then the Japanese attacked Pearl Harbor. She enlisted, instead, in the new women's branch of the navy, the WAVES (Women Appointed for Voluntary Emergency Service), becoming one of the first in Cleveland to do so. She became Lieutenant Scott, handling confidential reports until the end of the war. Jane then began pounding the pavement for that longed-for newspaper job. "It took ten years and three tries to get a job at the *Plain Dealer*," she says. Her first application was when she was still in high school. Then after her navy stint, she tried again. No opening. So she started small. She worked at the *Chagrin Valley Herald* before her third application at the big-city paper proved the charm—in ways no one could have imagined.

Jane Scott, at age thirty-three, was hired as assistant society reporter on March 24, 1952, three days after rock and roll's infamous debut at the Cleveland Arena with Alan Freed as host. But even if she'd been working at the paper at the time, the lady journalist would have never been hired to cover that rocking event. Female reporters were limited to senior activities, wedding notices, and women's luncheons. Besides, then rock and roll was considered base, tasteless, a subject no serious city journalist would dare take on.

But in 1958, the feisty reporter added the "Young Ohio" section to her beat when the previous columnist left to have a baby. The teen-oriented page was devised in 1952 by the *Plain Dealer*'s Sunday editor, Phil Porter, but Jane soon made it her own. By now, she was covering both ends of the society spectrum, a double duty she referred to as her "pimples to pensions" beat. And that's when Jane discovered a new outlet for her pen: rock and roll.

As the *Plain Dealer*'s teen editor, she had covered the Beatles's first Cleveland visit in 1964, but that was before the term "rock critic" was invented. Scott went on to cover the 1966 Beatles tour by flying to England with WKYC deejay Jerry G. and reporting on the group's former Liverpool hangout, the Cavern. "I began at the top," Scott remembers. "My first rock press conference was with the world's biggest rock group, the Beatles, who I interviewed just before their August 14, 1966, show at the Municipal Stadium."

"But rock was still not taken seriously," she says, "In fact, the idea of putting too much focus on it was sneered at [by the supervisors]." Still, the forty-something woman persevered, literally creating her own beat as an official "rock reporter," helping turn the tide as the music entered society's mainstream. However, the word "critic" is erroneous in her case. The unbiased journalist simply reports. Because Jane Scott took rock seriously, her professional colleagues—and wary bosses—did likewise. After that Beatles encounter, Scott's next big scoop came in the form of rock's ultimate "bad boys," the Rolling Stones. She still counts the disheveled band of maniacal rockers as one of her favorite groups, as well as among her many celebrity friends. She admits Keith Richards, the most notorious Stone, is her favorite. "I guess opposites do attract," she says with a girlish giggle.

Over the next four decades, this "amazing Jane" took a musical journey that rivals no other. She has interviewed nearly every name in the rock industry and has the photos to prove it. These she displays throughout her home, a condominium overlooking Lake Erie, located in the same town she grew up in. The Cleveland journalist is known nationally thanks to exposure from appearances on MTV, ABC-TV's *Good Morning America,* and NBC-TV's *Entertainment Tonight.* She has been profiled in *Rolling Stone, People,* and the *Wall Street Journal* (front page, of course).

And that's not all, Jane notes. "I was also in a pornographic magazine," she told a captive audience at the 1997 Rock Hall's "An Evening with Jane Scott." "I'll never forget the day someone came up to me and said, 'Jane, I saw you in *Chic Magazine.*' I didn't even know what that was, but I rushed to the store and purchased one. And sure enough, there I was! Apparently, the article in *Rolling Stone* was syndicated to other publications. . . . But the most embarrassing part about that was when I purchased the magazine, I ran into a member of my church. I felt I should explain myself so I said, 'Oh, I didn't buy this to read it—I'm in it.' Well, that didn't help much!" But it did expose her legendary sense of humor.

Then there's her list of past and present acquaintances. John Lennon and Yoko Ono (who gave Jane with one of her scarves and a pair of her signature sunglasses), Paul McCartney, Jim Morrison, Keith Richards, Bruce Springsteen, David Bowie, Michael Jackson, Bob Seger, Sting, and hundreds more have all considered Jane Scott a personal friend. Today whenever pop stars arrive in Cleveland, one of the first questions they ask reporters is "How's Jane?"

Cleveland's favorite rock writer, Jane Scott, backstage with Billy Joel at the Coliseum in 1984. *Photo by Janet Macoska.*

In 1989, when finally nailing an interview with one artist she longed to meet, the elusive Bob Dylan, the consummate reporter and world's oldest rock writer was rendered speechless. In a piece for the *Plain Dealer*, Scott recalled all the times an exchange with the legendary singer had eluded her: "The years flashed by. . . . The time in February 1974 that I spent my own money to fly to Indianapolis, then rented a car to catch his Indiana University concert in Bloomington. That 1986 [*sic*] day I flew on my own time to Live Aid in Philadelphia, where he was appearing. The questions I'd always wanted to ask. The many times his management turned me down for interviews . . ." So when the fateful moment came to pass, it seemed fitting that the auspicious occasion took place in none other than her hometown. Meeting him backstage at Cleveland's State Theater, Scott found herself tongue-tied. "I finally murmured something about his new album. I reached out to shake his hand. That's when he kissed me. Once on each cheek." He then went on stage and dedicated "Like a Rolling Stone" to her. Unfortunately, she didn't hear the honor. "I hate to say this, but he does mumble a bit."

When it comes to the history of rock and roll, Jane Scott has seen it all. And only a few interviews have eluded her. Most notably, one with Janis Joplin (she was moody before the concert, too stoned afterward) and another with Michael Jackson (he was eleven, and it was past his bedtime). She made up for the latter several times since. Her biggest missed opportunity, however, was having never interviewed Elvis—though she claims to have not given up on him!

Her rock and roll stories would indeed fill a book—one people have been urging her to write for years. She has, however, recounted some of these experiences in various published pieces.

In 1968 she accompanied Hendrix to Blaushild Chevrolet on Chagrin Boulevard in Shaker Heights, where the guitarist purchased a gleaming new Corvette for $8,000 cash. That same year she got to interview her favorite soul singer, Aretha Franklin, in the dressing room at the old Arena, where the regal lady was dressed in a ten dollar terry cloth robe ("But looked just as queenly," Scott says).

She was at the media party at downtown Swingos Keg and Quarter, where she witnessed the mischievous Who drummer Keith Moon handcuffing a stunned (and none too happy) Kid Leo to an unidentified woman as his fiancée looked on. (Moon did release the two before evening's end.)

She developed a friendship with the Lizard King himself, Jim Morrison, and a routine phone interview turned into an intimate conversation about the singer's views on life. Another time, she stood by as singer Alice Cooper, visiting Cleveland in 1986, wrote out an excuse for a seven-year-old fan who skipped school to attend a media luncheon. The letter said in part, "Raymond was absent from school today for a very good reason. He was learning about the evils of rock 'n' roll."

On July 20, 1969, Jane was covering the Led Zeppelin concert at Musicarnival while her peers were home watching the historic Neil Armstrong moonwalk on TV. And Jane was there for the first Live Aid Concert on July 13, 1985, at JFK Stadium in Philadelphia—an event she says she wouldn't have missed for the world.

Scott's friendships with Cleveland rockers have brought her to near-regal status among musicians of all ages and styles. The veteran reporter has had a hand in helping the careers of hometown heroes such as Joe Walsh and the James Gang, the Raspberries, the O'Jays, the Michael Stanley Band, the Dead Boys, Pere Ubu, Beau Coup (who wrote a song, "Jane," in her honor), Trent Reznor, Tracy Chapman . . . The list goes on. And it includes blues musicians. "Jane has been the best friend a musician has in Cleveland, especially in the early days," Jimmy Ley says. "It'd be really something. You'd be making small talk with her on the phone, and unbeknownst to you, she'd be writing out a whole story on you as you talked. She did more to help the local music scene than anyone, particularly for blues when blues wasn't as popular."

She also encourages aspiring rock photographers. "I was one of Jane's 'Young Ohio' reporters back in the early '70s," recalls Janet Macoska. "She'd send us out to press conferences whenever famous people came to Cleveland. I got to interview and photograph Leonard 'Mr. Spock' Nimoy, Pat Paulsen (who was doing *The Smothers Brothers Show* then), and Spanky of Spanky and Our Gang, and others as well. It was a great experience for a student, and Jane realized that early on. In fact, she was the first person who did that for young people. . . . I personally owe a lot to her."

But alas, the pioneering journalist has no time to write her autobiography. While her aging peers have long since retired, taking life easy with grandchildren, golfing, or knitting, this fiercely independent, never-married reporter is too busy keeping up with the world of rock music. She rushes to the office five days a week to gather information and write her weekly column. When not at work, you'll find Jane front and center at any number of concerts, ranging from Hole, Bone Thugs-N-Harmony, and Green Day to Mariah Carey and the Backstreet Boys. And for the most part, she claims, she genuinely likes all the music.

Jane in the Twenty-First Century

I was done in, along with three young things, by a three-letter word: Mud. I not only slipped on a little hill the second day, but couldn't get enough traction to stay up. A kindly photographer retrieved my mud-covered glasses and led me through the tent cities to the press area.

—Jane Scott, describing her Woodstock '94 experience

And still, Jane writes on—despite the eight decades she's seen, despite being nearly crushed by a herd of overzealous fans rushing the stage at Lollapalooza '95, despite being swept down a muddy hill at Woodstock '94 or being accidentally locked in a ladies' room at the Cleveland Stadium. She endures it all in the name of rock. But it nearly all came to an end in 1987, when the editors she had written for since the early 1950s decided it was high time she retired—or at least, get out of the rock scene, perhaps to cover gardening, or maybe suburban theater.

When word got out that the *Plain Dealer* was looking for a more youthful replacement, there was pandemonium. The media blitz began with 126 of her newspaper colleagues signing a petition to retain her royal rock beat. It peaked with a front-page profile in the *Wall Street Journal*, a generous mention in *People Magazine,* and appearances on *Entertainment Tonight,* MTV, and *PM Magazine*. She was even featured on an Australian TV show called *Sunday Today*. After all that worldwide attention, the *Plain Dealer* hierarchy wisely decided to let her be.

In 1997, still writing her column and music reviews, Jane Scott was honored by the Rock and Roll Hall of Fame with a wall displaying photographs of her interviewing rock celebrities. The "wall of fame" was on the museum's second floor, appropriately next to the "My Town" exhibit, which paid tribute to Cleveland's rock scene. Many felt the temporary exhibit was overdue and too short-lived. Indeed, her fans and friends feel Jane Scott deserves a permanent place among the music honorees.

Although she's been asked many times why she doesn't retire, she always patiently answers, "What would I do?" her tone full of surprise. The surprise comes because those who ask apparently don't get it.

In the 1992 *Plain Dealer* piece "Backstage Pass to Rock Memories," Scott explains the motivation that keeps her rockin': "Well, yes, there are a few little evils. I've had my trifocals and my big red hat knocked off accidentally by over-exuberant fans. I've even gotten used to young things calling me 'grandma' behind my back (they change their tune when they see that precious backstage pass pinned to my blouse). I may be older than their mothers, but when the beat begins and the excitement builds up, I feel a bond with all of them." At a 1996 young writers and musicians forum that took place at Wilbert's Bar and Grille in the Flats, the legendary Cleveland rock journalist showed up wearing a simple black skirt, comfortable black flats, and—what else?—a black Pearl Jam T-shirt.

Rock on, Jane.

Bruno Bornino, *Cleveland Press* Reporter

Jane Scott wasn't alone in her quest to report on the rock scene. The *Plain Dealer*'s competitor, the *Cleveland Press*, boasted its own reporter and music critic, Bruno Bornino. Although there were other *Press* reporters covering the music and teen scene, such as Harriet Peters and Judy Prusnek, readers of this paper turned to Bruno's updates for the latest and greatest in rock and roll.

Graduating from Ohio University, Bornino began his newspaper career at the *Cleveland Press* in 1960. He, along with Jane Scott, was there to cover the Beatles' Public Hall appearance in the fall of 1964.

"The Beatles really set the tone for everything in rock," Bornino notes. "I think literally every group—local, national, and international—was influenced by them. They led the way, not only in music but in fashion, lifestyle, everything. When you think they were only together about six years, that's phenomenal. If *Billboard* would've allowed it, they'd have dominated the entire chart. As it was, I think they had like twenty-two out of one hundred [top singles] at one time. The Beatles was probably the only band that was universally accepted. That itself was unique."

So, like his *Plain Dealer* colleague, Bornino was there to capture and chronicle all the crazy, hazy days of rock and roll on the North Coast. And right alongside him at most of those early rock concerts was *Press* photographer and friend George Shuba.

Bruno always gave us the opportunity and liberty to shoot what we wanted to shoot. Given that freedom, you inevitably got the better pictures.

As a writer, he was very meticulous in that he did a lot of research on his subjects beforehand. And he had a whole different way of expression. Like, he'd take the songs the artist sang and relate it to stories of that individual in his column. You'd discovered a whole new side of the artist who sang the song. His pieces were interesting because you always learned something new.

We had a great time in those days. I think that whole ten-year period from the mid-'60s to mid-'70s was the most creative and most exciting time.

In the summer of 1966, Bornino began his own rock column, "Bruno's Big Beat," and quickly earned the youths' interest and trust. He knew his stuff so well that he could often predict the outcome of a concert—despite evidence to the contrary.

For example, in October 1970, Led Zeppelin was among the hippest groups, according to teens and the media. Although they had yet to have a hit single, both their debut album and second LP, *Led Zeppelin II,* had achieved gold-record status. The group was scheduled to play Public Hall with opening act Grand Funk Railroad. Yet Bornino predicted, "Don't be surprised if Grand Funk Railroad steals the show." The latter was playing its first Cleveland gig and had a Top 10 hit, "Time Machine." Most fans were looking to the much-ballyhooed Led Zeppelin to top off the evening. But the *Cleveland Press* rock reporter had hit the nail on the head. Grand Funk Railroad, according to many who were there, were so "energized and amazing" that the crowd chanted for their return toward the end of Led Zeppelin's set (see Chapter 20). Bornino was indeed a rock forecaster. "That lineup was a good one," he says. "But I knew Grand Funk put on great live shows. Plus, I knew their manager, Terry Knight, and I really believed in what he was doing. The band had a lot of talent—very high energy and entertaining, and they proved it in their concerts."

But his career in rock journalism would not be as fortuitous as that of Jane Scott. By early 1982, the *Cleveland Press* was experiencing problems, and it showed in the entertainment section, "Go" (formerly "Showtime"), which included information on fashion, lifestyle, motor sports, and radio and television. Where before the section always included articles on the local scene, written by local reporters, it was reduced to generic entertainment pieces, usually off the UPI wire. However, in his last few articles, the venerable rock reporter managed to provide rock news of a local interest with a feature on Cleveland's hottest band, the Michael Stanley Band, and he was the first Cleveland reporter/writer to announce the wedding of singer Pat Benatar to Parma-native guitarist Neil Giraldo in the spring of 1982. His articles ceased soon after, and the *Cleveland Press* folded in June of that year.

Fans missed Bornino's input, knowledge, and entertaining writing style. For a while he did freelance pieces for the *Akron Beacon Journal* and Sun Newspapers. Although Bornino no longer writes about rock music, he says he'll never forget those rockin' years. "I always liked the music, and that kept it interesting. And I liked nearly all the local acts in the '70s—the James Gang, Eric Carmen, and the Michael Stanley Band in particular. And I honestly believed those local bands like MSB, Love Affair, [and] American Noise were going to make it big. Cleveland was very rich with talent in that period."

Rock Writers Abound

Thanks to pioneering journalists Scott and Bornino, there are now several area rock writers who keep fans abreast of what's happening in the world of rock and roll. Special mention goes to Michael Norman (*Plain Dealer*), John Soeder (*Plain Dealer*), John Petkovic (*Plain Dealer*), Laura DeMarco (*Plain Dealer*), Joanne Drauss Klein (Sun Newspapers), Jeff Piorkowski (Sun Newspapers), Carlo Wolff (freelance writer), and Robert Cherry (freelance writer).

Local Rock Publications

Scene Magazine: Northeast Ohio's *Entertainment Weekly* (1970–)

"To leisure connoisseurs of all ages, welcome to '*The Cleveland Scene.*' You'll learn about leisure-time activities you're not likely to read about elsewhere locally. If it's the best of times you're after, '*The Cleveland Scene*' will guide you to it [*sic*] week after week."

This is what the publishers promised in their debut issue on July 1, 1970—and they didn't disappoint. Despite some expected financial and artistic growing pains, the small, local publication quickly became *the* resource for northeast Ohio music lovers, filling what was once a pronounced gap in entertainment media. Initially, the free weekly guide covered every aspect of the world of diversion (current films and theater)—with music coming in a distant third. Not for long. It was soon apparent that readers wanted to know more about the music scene, particularly rock, in all its varied forms. And so it began. The paper expanded its readership to include the Youngstown and Akron-Canton area, consequently dropping the "Cleveland" from its title.

Born in an old building on Libby Road in Maple Heights, *The Scene* (which became simply *Scene* in 1975) would soon move to a warehouse at E. 124th and Euclid Avenue (then known as a hippie neighborhood). The small (eight pages) independent paper consisted of pieces written by college students and aspiring musicians, some with no journalism background. But it wasn't about *how* they wrote, but about *what* they wrote. Until then, rock enthusiasts relied on the two big-city newspapers, the *Plain Dealer* and *Cleveland Press*, whose Friday sections—"Action Tab" and "Showtime," respectively—

related the wheres and whens of regional entertainment. Still, because of limited space, even reliable columnists Jane Scott and Bruno Bornino were confined to a page or two a week. There was also a local independent paper called the *Great Swamp Erie da da Boom,* which was short lived. (Could it have had something to do with the title?)

Where the newspapers left off, *Scene* picked up—doing so a day ahead, distributing the week's issue on Thursdays to ensure first readership. It worked. Before long, the publication was the major source of what was happening in the music world; and by its twentieth anniversary, it was producing copy in the polished offices of the historic Playhouse Square building at 1375 Euclid Avenue (appropriately, the same one in which Alan Freed gave credence to rock and roll).

Yet, from the start, entrepreneurs Rich Kabat and friend Joe Puleo knew this new venture was risky business. "But the timing seemed right," Kabat says. "I had started a marketing company, MRP [Market, Research and Promotions], which involved several aspects of marketing, like sign-painting, printing and advertising specialties. It was an advertising friend of mine who told me *Cleveland After Dark* was folding and suggested we pick up the slack. Joe had marketing and advertising experience, and I'd attended John Carroll University for journalism, so we thought, let's give it a shot."

The ill-fated *Cleveland After Dark* was an entertainment weekly run by the publishers of *Boston After Dark* (which at one time included Ray Riepen, founder of the first underground club, Boston Tea Party, and instrumental in the early FM rock format at WBCN). Simply put, the Boston natives producing the Cleveland paper didn't have the passion for what was happening on this music-minded North Coastline and wanted to return to the East.

Kabat had no problem filling positions, though he saw many faces come and go that first year. Indeed, the staff was diverse and ever-changing, comprised of a good blend of academic students and streetwise rock and roll lovers. Puleo and Kabat hired Harry Reminick as editor. After just a few issues, John Richmond (former *Cleveland After Dark* jazz critic, now executive director of the Northeast Ohio Jazz Society) took over as editor, while former *Cleveland After Dark* writer/photographer Anastasia Pantsios became assistant editor. When Richmond left in 1971, Carmie Amata (former *Cleveland After Dark* film critic) became editor. (Amata went on to her own column for the L.A.-based *Cableviews Magazine.*) There were indeed some rough starts until things stabilized when Jim Girard (who had joined the staff in 1971) became editor the next year.

"After having several people work for me whose primary interest was film," Kabat says, "Jim brought in some music background, which was what we'd been looking for. That was one aspect that caught my interest in him. The other one was he was willing to work cheap! Jim agreed that rock wasn't being covered enough in the local publications, and that's what we wanted to focus on."

The publisher admits that the hardest part in the early days was getting sponsors to have enough faith and bucks to front a new publication, and an alternative one at that. He was constantly hustling to convince backers that this was no fly-by-night paper, "hustle" being the operative word. "We went directly to the bar owners to sell an ad and were very business-minded," Kabat says. "They [*Cleveland After Dark* staff] were all journalists who wanted to write about great things but lacked the advertising to back it up. You can't just want to go out partying, getting free tickets and drinks. You have to always be aware to sell some advertising to survive."

By its second year, *Scene* was hitting its stride. The weekly paper was fast becoming a respectable source of music information, with record and concert reviews, celebrity interviews, and updates on the band-hopping among musicians. And, with Girard's "Sez Me" editorials, the paper was a given source of entertainment.

"Most of that column was written at three o'clock in the morning after hitting the downtown clubs," says Girard, who remained editor until 1977, when he became general manager. "There were many times I was so inebriated I'd no idea what I wrote until the copy came out, then I'd go, 'Man, where was my head at?' But apparently, no one was really reading it, or those who did were in the same state of mind!"

Then came the most-read and talked-about column: The gossip section of the paper, which was originally written by a character named Crocus Behemoth—a.k.a. David Thomas. While Thomas would eventually go on to front Pere Ubu, in the early '70s, he was just a "punk" teenager who had a penchant for heavy-metal music and vodka. "I started at *Scene* in 1971 doing layout in the old warehouse office at Euclid and E. 124th Street," he said in the paper's twenty-fifth anniversary issue. "Tuesday night was layout night. I brought a bottle of vodka to work and charged up the hot wax spreaders. I started writing about music and doing reviews because I could, and they needed somebody to do it." Thomas would remain a colorful fixture with *Scene* from 1971–74.

The "Making the Scene" column debuted as "The Phlorescent Crocus and Rickie" (for staffer Rick Nelson, who left soon after and was replaced by Mark Kmetzko). Then it became "Making the Scene with Croc O Bush." (The "bush" referred to Kmetzko's hairstyle, and the name became a popular drink within local pubs.) By 1974, the section became simply "Making the Scene" and until 1986 was headed by another character who went by the name of Peanuts (and, as record reviewer, by the elusive "D. B. Cooper"). He continues to be a local music writer/publicist and still declines to reveal his real name.

The music-oriented section detailed the who, what, where, when, how, and sometimes why of the current music scene. During this mid-1970s era, when punk rock was erupting onto the scene, and disco was lurking in the background, nearly every big city had an "alternative paper." While most didn't last, *Scene* hung in there—either through sheer luck or Kabat-inspired determination.

"Rich and [brother] Dan [Kabat, who often assisted financially] never lost sight of the importance in what we were trying to do," Girard says. "There were times we were living literally issue to issue. There were weeks when, to get the issue out on Thursday, they had to collect money from advertisers on Wednesday. And when push came to shove, Rich would always do the right thing morally. He wouldn't do anything 'shady-business'-wise. By the same token, he'd do what he had to to survive, and that was often a real fine line. And somehow he always made sure people got paid."

Also, what kept the paper alive was the young, energetic staff of admitted social butterflies. Or was that barflies? "We got kidded a lot for always being in a bar," Girard says. "Lunches and after-work hours were spent in Pat's Tavern when we were on E. 124th Street. And Swingos Keg and Quarter was where all the big names stayed when in town, so I'd be there at 8:30 in the morning getting an interview before they [the artists] started drinking. At night we'd be at places like the Smiling Dog Saloon, the Viking, or Agora. But a lot of decisions and ideas came when we were in the bars, more than at the office. It gave us a more relaxed atmosphere to discuss our work and do some troubleshooting. But yeah, I'll admit it, we did party a lot back then!"

Just like the lively crew at WMMS, *Scene* employees were part of a way of life among Cleveland Boomers. Both groups were seen regularly on the nightclub circuit. While the deejays were there to showcase the music, the young journalists were there to do "in-depth research" on the club scene.

In a particularly—or characteristically?—wacky moment, Girard and Crocus formed a band (of sorts), calling themselves the Great Bow Wah Band. The pair would join local group Ambleside (and sometimes other bands, such as Granite, Atlantis, and Dragonwyck) on stage at clubs like the now-defunct House of Bud and Viking Saloon and, sometimes, the elite Cleveland Agora. "It was definitely a 'theater of the absurd,'" recalls guitarist Craig Balzer, then of Ambleside. "It was Crocus's idea that everyone go on stage dressed really strangely and do wild, wacky stuff. We'd just have fun, playing songs like 'Louie, Louie,' and everyone played a part in it. Crocus sang, and I think Girard provided the liquor or something! It was really a vehicle for Crocus, and how he actually got his first band, Rocket from the Tombs."

In 1972, Kabat and company set up shop in the heart of Cleveland's cultural district, Playhouse Square. The move allowed the staff closer access to radio stations, clubs, and the Flats, where young music lovers were migrating several nights a week. By its fifth anniversary, the paper filled twelve pages, had twenty full-time employees, and boasted a readership of 45,000. It was clearly hip to be *Scene*.

The year 1975 saw more stability among the staff as well as a marked increase in credibility. The latter came with the addition of Keith Rathbun, an Ohio University graduate and the first to come with a bona fide journalism degree. "I hadn't exactly set my sights on working at the *Scene* after graduating, I just fell into it. And once there, I certainly didn't expect to stay more than a year or two," admits Rathbun, who served as editor from 1978 to 1981 and publisher from 1998 to 2000.

I'd been working as a stringer for the *PD* and bartending at the Boar's Head restaurant when one of the waitresses told me *Scene* was looking for freelancers. I started reviewing films, music, sports, and one thing lead to another and I became a full-time employee.

I really liked it from the start. You have to remember, this was the ushering in of the alternative newspaper era, so we were filling a true need. Plus there were great people here, and you were given such freedom as a writer. And you got such response when you'd visit the clubs. People would come up to you and were so passionate about the music and what we'd write about. That, above all, made you feel you were fulfilling your purpose because readers really cared about what you were doing.

Also on the masthead in 1975 was Raj Bahadur, a University of Washington graduate. Although he majored in political science, the Cleveland native decided a political career wasn't for him. Instead, his friends Jim Girard and Bob Ferrell coaxed him to *Scene* as a music critic. "Joe Perry [of Aerosmith] was my first interview," he recalls. "Afterward I thought, now this is a way to make a living!" He began covering movies in the early '80s, and despite moving to New York City in 1985, Bahadur continued writing film reviews for the Cleveland paper until 1999.

Clearly, one attraction for readers of any publication is artwork. *Scene* provided that, too. For photos of concerts and general happenings, Bob Ferrell was there, camera ready, to capture the moments. "It was 1974, and I'd just graduated from Cleveland State, when Jim Girard told me *Scene* needed a photographer," recalls Ferrell, who was teaching history during the day while moonlighting for *Scene*. "It was less complicated in those days as opposed to now, when you must sign a release saying you won't do anything with the photos and are limited to a couple of shots. Back then they'd give you your photo pass, you'd go in the pit, and you were pretty free to move around and do your job. I remember shooting the Led Zeppelin concert, and Jimmy Page would look at the camera and actually hold the pose until he knew you got what you wanted. How cool is that?"

For the next decade, Ferrell, who also served as *Scene*'s sales manager, acquired hundreds of high-profile photos and sold several to national publications like *Creem*, *Rolling Stone*, *Billboard*, *Hit Parader*, and even *Playboy*, which in 1987 published his photograph of Kid Leo when he was nominated for Best Deejay in America. "I left *Scene* in '85 to do more photography work because the sales position was taking up more and more time," Ferrell says. "But it was a great place to work. And you can't get away from *Scene* people, even though many of us have gone on to other jobs and places. It's like an Old Boys' Club. Our own version of the Ivy League—without the ties." Today, Ferrell freelances for Belkin Productions.

Mark Holan, who came on board in 1979, was an anthropology major at Cleveland State University who considered music and writing merely a hobby before *Scene* beckoned.

"I was always a music buff. I grew up listening to my older brother's favorites, like Bob Dylan, the Animals, Cream, Hendrix. But the Beatles were it for me. There was no bigger Beatles fan than I was—still am. And living in Cleveland, we had those great deejays like Joe Mayer, Doc Nemo, Jerry G. And we had our own Wolfman Jack in the form of WMMS's BLF Bash [Bill Freeman]. So I was first a music lover who entertained thoughts of being a writer. And I was always a *Scene* reader, so when I read an ad that they were looking for a delivery guy, I answered it. Then I started doing some reviews for them. Next thing I know, in 1981, I became the editor." Holan remained the editor until Kabat sold the publication to New Times, Inc., in 1998.

Today it's *Cleveland Scene* once again, though it barely resembles the *Scene* of yesterday. It remains a free paper and continues its alternative theme, but its focus on the local music scene has greatly diminished.

Many of its former employees continue to be a part of the media. Among its alumni are an impressive list of those who used their *Scene* experiences to achieve successful careers. Former staffers include Liz Ludlow (former *Cleveland Magazine* editor), Joanne Draus Klein (writer/columnist for Sun Newspapers), Kymberli Hagelberg (*Akron Beacon Journal* reporter), "Peanuts" (who, using the handle "Host of the North Coast," works as a freelance writer and publicist), and art director, photographer, and now WMMS illustrator Brian Chalmers. Chalmers began working with original Buzzard creator David Helton in 1986 and took over in 1990. Joanne Drauss Klein, assistant editor from 1983 to 1984, fondly recalls her time at *Scene:* "I was the paper's first intern while attending Kent State University. It was really exciting as a young girl in my twenties, seeing and talking to all these rock celebrities who would saunter in and out of that office." Klein writes two columns for Sun: "On the Rocks," which highlights the renowned artists in rock history, and "First Word," which keeps readers on top of what's happening in the Cleveland area.

Through trials and tribulations, music and personnel changes, and less and less bar time, the paper matured along with its staff and is now among the oldest weekly indie papers in the country. Two credits to their journalistic talent and credibility that stand above the rest: In 1981, *Scene* writers worked doggedly to educate their readers on Cleveland's rich rock and roll past and produced the "History of Cleveland Rock, Part I," published that January, which was followed by Part II in February 1982. Hailing the movers and shakers that made Cleveland the "rock capital," *Scene* captured the highlights and subsequent changes that earned the city the title.

On September 20, 1996, as part of Cleveland's bicentennial celebration, copies of both those supplements, along with *Scene*'s twenty-fifth anniversary commemorative issue, were secured in a time capsule and ceremoniously buried at the Star Plaza on Playhouse Square. This Cleveland Rock and Roll Time Capsule contains other cherished North Coast rock artifacts as well, including an original poster from the Moondog Coronation Ball, an Agora thirtieth-anniversary T-shirt, the *Concert for the Rock and Roll Hall of Fame* CD, and a boxed set of Pere Ubu CDs. The capsule is to be opened at the city's tricentennial in the year 2096.

AP/Alternative Press (1985–)

There'll always be an alternative to everything. *AP* is not meant as alternative music, 'cause when it came out, "alternative" was not termed yet. But we've always considered ourselves an alternative to *Spin* and *Rolling Stone*. Our whole premise in each issue is to first entertain, by doing articles on groups readers are familiar with, and then to educate, by including info on the up-and-coming bands.

—Mike Shea, publisher

Growing up in Aurora (approximately thirty miles south of Cleveland) with three older brothers and sisters and parents who loved music, Mike Shea was exposed to classical, Big Band, and early rock/pop. "As corny as it sounds, I have to say my soul was moved by music from birth on," he says. "As a kid I always had lots of energy, so my mom would throw on Herb Alpert records and I'd stop, go right in front of the speakers—you know, those huge ones from the '60s—and just sit there and zone out on Herb Alpert. Music was the only thing that kept my attention. And in the summer, my mom would have on those AM stations blaring by the pool, in the days of Neil Diamond and the Fifth Dimension."

But once he hit adolescence, he wanted to be separate from the pack, particularly in his musical taste. With brothers and sisters on the tail-end of the boomer generation, Shea was force-fed Peter Frampton (his brother's favorite), the Beatles (sister's favorite), and Barry Manilow (other brother's favorite). "Although I enjoyed listening to those types of music, I think I got into punk and alternative out of self-defense. I wanted my own music."

So as a teen in the early '80s, it wasn't surprising that he gravitated toward the likes of heavy-metal bands such as Judas Priest, Time, Iron Maiden, and Blue Oyster Cult. From then on, life as he knew it would never be the same. "Thank God," he says. And it was around that time he met hardcore punk enthusiast Jim Kosicki who, with his eight-inch-high purple Mohawk, hung around the culture-rich Coventry area. Kosicki introduced Shea to a whole new brand of rock music. "Jim really influenced my musical taste buds," he says. "He's pretty much responsible for bringing me to where I am today. He's the one who first turned me on to WCSB [Cleveland State University] and WRUW [Case Western Reserve University] morning radio shows. Now that's where I found music I could call my own."

In his freshman year at Kent State, Shea was frequenting clubs like the Pop Shop in the basement of the old Agora and the Underground in the Flats, both venues that featured punk and alternative music. His favorite bands were Tuxedo Moon, the Smiths, Alien Sex Fiend, and Bauhaus. But at the peak of his clubbing and partying, Shea contracted mononucleosis.

Forced to sit home for months, he became bored and restless. "There was nothing remotely good on TV. And forget anything about new music. The only local rock publication was *Scene,* which didn't cover much on the punk scene. Neither did *Rolling Stone* and *Spin.* And you weren't hearing it on WMMS. So that's when I got the idea to put together a much-needed alternative fanzine. I knew there must be others like me who wanted to know what was happening with groups like the Smiths, the Cure, Sonic Youth, Love and Rockets, as well as industrial bands like Test Department and Nick Cave and the Bad Seeds."

Alternative Press
publisher Mike Shea.
Photo by Deanna Adams.

The debut issue of the free *Alternative Press* (or *AP,* as it is now known) hit the streets in June 1985 and resembled a college-type newsletter. The six pages were jam-packed with key information on what was happening in the world of the "new music." Its front page told readers about the Smiths' first U.S. tour (although Cleveland was excluded) and had concert reviews of the Madonna/Beastie Boys appearance at Public Hall and Frankie Goes to Hollywood at Music Hall. There was a short eulogy on the Pop Shop, which had perished by fire, and a first interview with local punk band Death of Samantha, who went on to become a national underground presence by the end of the decade.

Of his early writing experience Shea says:

I'd been the editor of my school newspaper. I also had worked as entertainment editor for *Our Times* [later to become *New Times* of the Greater Cleveland Poet's League], where I shadowed Jane Scott. So of course, I picked up a lot from her. And Jimmy [Kosicki] was a sweet talker, so I'd send him out selling ads to local flower shops, bakeries, boutiques, anywhere we could get some money up front.

I remember going to one flower shop at Green and Mayfield Roads. I showed the owners a copy of my school newspaper saying, "It's going to look something like this," and these older ladies thinking, "Oh that looks nice, conservative," and the paper comes out and here it's this punk publication! But everyone was good about it. Sure, we lost some [advertisers], but we gained some too, like record stores and college radio stations, who jumped right in.

My major goal was to be totally objective about everything, whether it was punk or hard-core, skinhead music, or new wave—whatever. I didn't want to be a negative magazine, or biased. And it really wasn't hard getting help. I was literally having people come up to me saying things, like one guy who worked at a photo studio, "Well, I can take photographs and sneak in when my boss doesn't know it and develop them myself." And I'd say, "Okay you're the photo editor." Another one would say, "I'm really into skate music." Bing! You're the skate editor.

Another said, "You know, I'm really into fashion." Bing, Bing . . .

So there we were, just these kids with separate talents merging together for one common purpose. We printed up one thousand copies of that first issue and passed them out at a punk show at the Cleveland Underground. Every one of them went.

Word spread quickly through underground channels, and Shea began getting phone calls from people in Columbus, Detroit, and Pittsburgh, all wanting to get the word out about alternative bands in their areas. "Suddenly, *AP* was this major outlet for punk bands."

Still, finances had the last word. After the eighth issue, Shea was forced to suspend publication. "We had no idea what we were doing," he admits. "We were just a bunch of kids and were quickly running up expenses. It was costing like $3,000 for one issue. It got crazy." That was October 1986. Thinking he'd gone as far as he could go with it, Shea got a more stable retail job and left behind his brief fling with journalism.

Then about a year later, one of my former writers calls me and says, "How 'bout putting together a reunion issue? I think a lot of people would like to see it." Well, I told him how much it would cost, and he said, "I'll front it." I said, "Really? Well, how am I gonna pay you back?" He said, "Don't worry about it. I loved writing for it so much, I really want to do this." I said, "Cool!"

I started calling up all these labels in New York and told them we were putting out another issue and they said, "Oh, thank God, you're back. You were really filling a void on a national level." We hadn't realized how well known we'd become.

And in no time we got like $8,000 in advertising revenues—three times more than we'd ever gotten before. So we started back up again and just went from there.

The second time proved to be the charm, and the small idealistic group was on a mission. The comeback issue came out in June 1988 with a cover story on Love and Rockets. And each subsequent issue got bigger and more colorful—in various ways.

By then, a music lover from Greenburg, Pennsylvania, had emerged on the scene. "Around the fourth or fifth issue, I'd written a review he didn't agree with, to put it mildly," Shea says of his first encounter with Jason Pettigrew. The disagreement was about former Bauhaus singer Peter Murphy's rendition of Pere Ubu's single "Final Solution." Shea thought it was "pretty decent"; Pettigrew thought it "sucked."

"So here's this guy calling me at home telling me how totally wrong I was. That it was the stupidest piece of reasoning he'd ever heard. So after this big discussion, I said, 'Okay, if you think you can do better, send me some of your stuff.'" From that moment on, Pettigrew became a regular contributor. Readers liked his raw sense of humor, and Shea liked his writing style. "The first thing that impressed me about Jason was he went about things very professional," Shea says. "And he wasn't only knowledgeable about the music; he could really write well. Our magazine immediately went up a few notches when he began writing for us."

By 1989, Pettigrew was the senior editor, and soon he packed his things and moved to Cleveland. He has since gained the reputation as one of the nation's top music critics. "Historically, Cleveland has always been hipper than Pittsburgh, with more shows, more bands," Pettigrew says. "So I'm glad to be here."

I remember coming to Cleveland a few times when I was younger because things were happening here. Like, I saw XTC at the old Agora in '82, and other groups that just didn't play in my hometown.

My primary job at *AP* is news—some group breaks up, has a new record coming out, a celebrity drug death, or some type of political thing. And because we're a magazine with a two- month lead time, that means I have to dig harder. But I have moles, I have contacts. . . .

Then there's the "Low Profile" section where I give readers a reference guide to new groups that are interesting but radio's not going to play them, and you won't read about them in *Rolling Stone*. For that column I'll usually frequent places like the Euclid Tavern, the Grog Shop—wherever independent rock is happening.

Because of his love of and belief in the underground music scene, Pettigrew started his own record label, Carcrashh, in 1994. Since then the indie company has released several recordings by local artists, including Gem, Coltrane Wreck, and Prisonshake, as well as New York's Nicole Blackman and England's Slag Dog Ensemble.

By the end of the 1980s, *AP* grew into a professional-looking magazine and was no longer free. In 1992, the widely distributed publication made its competitors take notice when it became a full-fledged corporation with an actual board of directors, and its full-color glossy-covered issues became available at newsstands around the world.

"We're now considered the number three music publication in America," says Shea, who dropped out of college during his sophomore year to devote all of his time to the magazine, "even though our circ is nowhere that of *Spin* and *Rolling Stone*. Ours is 110,000, *Spin*'s is 450,000, and *Rolling Stone* is 1.3 million. Still, it's a situation where *Spin* comes out and says something like, 'We want to do a cover with Courtney Love, and we don't want *Rolling Stone* or *AP* getting it before us. They don't mention *Details* or *Entertainment Weekly*, they say *AP*. That says something. I'm a thorn in somebody's side." And the Cleveland-based publication is respected enough for *Rolling Stone* senior features editor Anthony DeCurtis to call *AP* "the country's leading alternative rock authority."

"I remember when *AP* was just a fanzine, wasn't even what you'd call a newspaper," recalls the Agora's Johan.

At the time I was managing a band called Separate Checks, which featured Laura Ferrell [who now reports metro traffic]. I thought it was a really cool paper that filled a void. I first met Mike [Shea] at the Euclid Tavern when he came to review the group, and then we decided we wanted to help him out financially. So we did a benefit for him at the Phantasy, raising over a thousand dollars.

I was so gung-ho on the publication that Laura and I took several bundles to the New Music Seminar in New York in late '85, and that's how *AP* got out of Cleveland. We distributed it in the trade show, we had it in the lobby. I wanted to show the rest of the country this other part of Cleveland's music scene and became a real catalyst for the paper. I mean, I was Mr. *AP* back then.

Still, I never would've dreamed how big it's gotten. What's amazing is that many people to this day don't realize this beautiful and informative publication comes out of Detroit Avenue in Cleveland. Yes, *Rolling Stone* and *Spin* are well respected, and I read them both, but *AP* is undoubtedly *the* hippest magazine on the newsstand.

Shea says,

AP has been fortunate. We've never had a huge turnover, and I think it's because it's a fun place to work. Yes, we are a corporation, with corporate stock and all. Yet it's two sides of a coin. It's laid-back but aggressive. Professional but with a personal touch. And most important, we really believe in what we're doing here. From the beginning, I always wanted *AP* to be for that kid in class, high school or college, who wanted that inside scoop on his or her own music scene. And I want to be the guy who informs them about it. I try to always peruse other publications and decide what I like and don't like about them and use that as a guide. Plus, we try to give short pieces so readers can flip through and make it easy for them and less time-consuming to read.

Shea credits three particular assets that keep his vision afloat. "Someone once told me that to have a successful business you need a good lawyer, a good accountant, and a good mentor. I've followed that advice." One of his mentors is John Malm, president of Nothing Records and manager for Nine Inch Nails. "We came out of the same scene, so we can relate to one another, both on a business level and a personal one. He's helped me a lot. But, of course, you've got to put out a product people really want or it just won't sell. Hello? I mean, look at the Edsel for instance. . . . We grew because we give readers what they want in a magazine and info they can't find anywhere else."

In July 1995, *Alternative Press* celebrated its tenth anniversary with a two-day weekend blowout at the outdoor Nautica Stage in the Flats. Bands included Helmet, Prick, Catherine Wheel, Medicine, the Verve, XC-NN, Girls Against Boys, Flaming Lips, Smoking Popes, Everclear, Gene, Jawbox, Soul Coughing, and Luna. "It was a great weekend," Pettigrew says. "And backstage, it was really interesting. The bands were so disparate in style—heavy-metal, funky, psychedelic, and hard-charging punk bands. Yet there they were all sharing thoughts, exchanging ideas, and stories. Actually, it paralleled what the magazine is all about: a common ground of music fans."

CLE (1977–81; resumed 1995)

In 1977, before *Alternative Press* was even an idea, an offbeat publication that highlighted Cleveland's cutting-edge rock scene was making waves on the North Coast. The debut issue of *CLE* magazine hit the underground streets in the winter of rock's discontent, capturing the attention of locals and, before long, new wave enthusiasts around the world.

It was the onset of the punk era, when the New York Dolls were glittering across the East Coast and the Sex Pistols were taking England by storm. But radio was formatted and mainstream, so the sounds of the Velvet Underground, the Stooges, and Akron's own Devo were being slighted on the airwaves in favor of pop stars like Elton John, Journey, and Billy Joel. "There was this whole other music scene a lot of people weren't aware of," says *CLE* founder and publisher Jim Ellis. "There was hardly anything being written about it or heard on the radio. Yet there were these good, interesting bands coming out, like the Ramones, Television, Talking Heads. And, in Cleveland, you had Rocket from the Tombs, the Electric Eels, and Mirrors, who were all so far ahead of their time. But the music remained very underground. None of the rock stations would play it, and most clubs had bands that only played covers."

At the time, Ellis was an eighteen-year-old John Carroll University student and avid record collector who worked part-time at Hideo's Discodrome, a record store that was fast becoming an exclusive hangout for underground music fans. A devoted reader of *Rolling Stone*, *Circus*, and *Crawdaddy*, Ellis felt his hometown should have more press coverage on the music that had a fast-growing and dedicated fan base.

He approached twenty-two-year-old Gary Mollica, a psychology graduate of Case Western Reserve University, who was a deejay at the college's radio station, WRUW, and a fan of the music as well. Together they produced that first fanzine, *CLE* (the name and logo came from the luggage tickets used at the Cleveland Hopkins airport), which received positive press from Jane Scott and drew interest as far afield as New

York. That first effort filled twelve pages, with stories on the up-and-coming Devo and the Dead Boys as well as news on both the local and national scenes.

"My interest in music that was different stems back to when I'd listen to Doc Nemo on Sunday nights on WXEN," says Ellis, a 1976 Euclid High School graduate.

This was his pre-'MMS and 'NCR days, when he'd play all kinds of disparate music. Nemo was the one who introduced me to a lot of the underground stuff, and I got hooked into that psychedelic scene. I didn't even realize most of it was drug-induced. I just thought it was cool. It was definitely not reality—in any way, shape or form. Then again, when you're in seventh/eighth grade, how much reality is going on anyway?

In high school I was heavy into the prepunk bands like Velvet Underground and MC5. Then I started collecting records and buying singles and albums of anything that caught my interest. I can still remember the day I was standing at the counter of Record Theater and saw this new single there. I picked it up to read it, and it was by a local group I'd never heard of before. So I bought it for a buck, went home, and put it on my turntable. And boy, what I heard coming out of it was the craziest sounds! I'd never heard anything like it before. It was wild, weird, and I loved it. The song was called "30 Seconds Over Tokyo" by Pere Ubu, and I thought, wow, this bizarre, cool stuff's comin' out of Cleveland?!

I began stopping by this other record store, Hideo's Discodrome, because it was on the way to my job. I always had time to kill between my classes at John Carroll and Cleveland Trust, where I worked at the time. It was kind of a hippie-type record store, and they always had this batch of great selections where you could buy an album for, like, two dollars. One day I was talking to the clerk there and told him I was really into this new group, Pere Ubu. He looks at me and says, "Pere Ubu? I'm *in* Pere Ubu!" Here it was guitarist Peter Laughner, who was working there. From that point on, we were good friends.

Because of that friendship, Laughner talked the boss into hiring Ellis. "Peter told John [Thompson (a.k.a. Johnny Dromette, the store owner], 'Hey, the guy's in here all the time and he knows the music, you might as well pay him!' And it turns out I lasted longer than he did."

Laughner, barely out of his teens, was already a veteran of the local music scene, having played in several groups that were well received in the area (see Chapter 14). As a writer for *Creem* magazine, Laughner frequented the New York art/punk scene and thus began importing various punk material and ideas into the Cleveland area. It's been said that, alongside New York and Detroit, Cleveland had the largest and most influential underground movement in the nation at the time. "Every time Peter came back from New York," Ellis recalls, "he'd enlighten me about what was happening there, what concerts he saw, and was always bringing back these fanzines that were dedicated to the New York scene. That's where I got the idea Cleveland should have its own." The scene itself almost demanded it.

The Drome, as the record store was known, became a hangout for those whose musical tastes veered from the norm. David Thomas also worked there for a time. The location was as attractive as its colorful employees and clientele. As Ellis recalls,

That store sat at the top of Cedar Hill [by Fairmont], right where the traffic light was. So John would have these incredible window displays with these bizarre-looking mannequins holding up the Sex Pistols' album, or anything that attracted attention. And he changed it all the time, and each one was enough to stop someone dead in their tracks. Probably my favorite display was when he created a reenactment of *Hollywood Squares* with the nine squares featuring local celebrities like Ghoulardi, Dorothy Fuldheim, and our own Crocus [David Thomas].

Now, in New York, it would've been a blip on the radar screen. But this was Cleveland—the Midwest. People didn't expect that. So after awhile, residents around the area were referring to the store as "The Hideous Drome." To be sure, there were a lot of strange-looking characters wandering in and outta that store. The displays alone were just totally out of left field!

It was precisely that atmosphere that helped usher in the area's formidable punk rock scene and give birth to Cleveland's first publication celebrating that lifestyle. Soon bands themselves were not only hanging out at the Drome but often practicing and performing there. As such, Ellis and Mollica soon felt they just had to write about it.

While putting their thoughts and ideas together for their publication, the two entrepreneurs weren't expecting to write an obituary in its debut. But on June 22, 1977, Peter Laughner died from acute pancreatitis at the age of twenty-four. Issue 1 of *CLE* paid homage to their friend.

The young publishers found a printer and produced 500 copies in the basement of the established Cleveland newspaper *Call and Post*. "They offered it to us dirt cheap, but it wasn't worth it," Ellis admits. "They used the cheapest material, so the issues were flimsy and of poor quality. They actually started turning yellow after a few months. So by the time we were ready to print [Issue] 3A [Summer 1980], we found another printer we were happier with. Those are done on beautiful stock which made it look more like a real magazine."

It took a full year for Issue 2 (Fall 1978) to be released, as did each subsequent issue until the first incarnation folded in 1981. But in those five annual issues, *CLE* was chock-full of current information on new wave groups, and featured intriguing drawings by local artists as well as photographs. Issue 2 featured a story on the Electric Eels, a group that had played out only a half-dozen times before disbanding in 1975. Issue 3 appeared in the summer of 1979, with Akron favorite Tin Huey and memories of the old WHK Auditorium. Peter Laughner was once again the subject of Issue 3A, with a tribute to his life and comments on how he influenced the North Coast punk scene. Issue 3B (Spring 1981), featuring another Akron punk favorite, Lucky Pierre, was *CLE*'s final issue. At least for the next fourteen years.

"Each issue of *CLE* got more and more complex," says Ellis of the fanzine's initial demise. "More people started getting involved and we added more artwork. Plus, the music and scene were changing, getting into that hardcore music that was replacing the original punk. See, I was initally attracted to it because it had an artistic and literary feel to it, more of a high-bridge style of rock. But when I saw it turning into the slam-dancing and the mosh pits, with everyone slammin' into each other, and the music came secondary, I bowed out of that whole scene. Besides, I had just quit/got fired at the Drome and had to find a real job. I did, then I also went back to school and eventually got a degree in computer science."

Graduating from Case Western Reserve in 1982, Ellis began his career as a computer systems analyst. Gary Mollica, a 1977 Case graduate, moved to Pasadena, California, after Issue 2 was published.

The second wave of *CLE* was a surprise even to the publisher. In 1995, Ellis's old friend David Thomas (now a bona fide rock star, particularly in England) called him from his London home looking for rare Pere Ubu tapes for the band's new boxed set, *Datapanik in the Year Zero.* Digging through his past, Ellis found material that was never touched on in any of the issues. Listening to his old tapes of the Mirrors and the Electric Eels, he realized how contemporary the former bands still sounded. He then thought of all the new bands emerging out of 1990s Cleveland that were receiving little press. His interest restored, he put together Issue 3X.

The publication had a more professional look than previous issues. It contained a timeline of Pere Ubu, reflections on the short life of the Mirrors, and an article on Kent's current phenomenon, Cruel, Cruel, Moon. It also included a fascinating look at Pete "Mad Daddy" Myers. The story, originally printed in *Cleveland Magazine,* was yet another Cleveland rock history lesson. 3X had also caught on to a revolutionary idea: publication plus CD. To coincide with the magazine's subjects, a twenty-song CD was included in the packaging. "I wanted subscribers to hear what they were reading about," said Ellis.

The early recordings made of Mad Daddy are clear and crisp, capturing the essence of his voice, ghoulish laughter, and appeal. There are vintage recordings of Pere Ubu playing at Cleveland's Pirate's Cove in 1977 and other music to keep new wave fans entertained. Ellis's computer background came in handy when it was time to digitally master the recordings to CD. He admits the hardest part was unearthing good recordings of Mad Daddy at work. But the end result is clearer than those who remember listening to him back in 1959 recall.

Issue 4.0 proved the biggest seller, with eighty-four pages packed with information and articles highlighting, once again, the old scene, such as local band Death of Samantha and memories of the Pop Shop. It also featured the current college radio scene. Issue 5, with a two-CD set of nineteen songs, focused on current bands like Gem and Craw.

For now, Ellis is debating the future of the magazine. "It takes a lot of time and money to do it yourself," he says. Yet readers' interest might sway him to continue. He regularly receives hundreds of letters and subscription requests from fans as far away as England, Australia, and even Africa, thanks to word of mouth and the Internet.

Cleveland's Rock Photographers

George Shuba

> Jane Scott once called me the "grandfather of rock photography," and I'd say that's a pretty fitting title. I was the first in Cleveland to be called a "rock photographer," where before there was no such thing. But boy, in no time, the rock really started rollin'.
>
> —George Shuba

Imagine . . . You're a twenty-three-year-old college student who's always been interested in photography. You've been in the air force and the national guard, and you've entertained thoughts of becoming an industrial psychologist. But your passion for photography is a constant lure, ever since taking classes while in the service. Then, suddenly, you're in the right place at the right time. You cop your first professional assignment in the field. And it's a job photographing bugs. George Shuba, now a veteran photographer, will never forget his career debut.

I used to frequent this little studio in the Old Arcade owned by two sisters, Mary and Grace Driscoll, who were the first women photographers in Cleveland. I was there the day in '64 when WHK radio man Jim Lowe came in looking for a photographer. I said, "I'm a photographer." He said, "Are you any good?" I said, "Sure, I'm damn good!"

He proceeded to say he had this photo assignment for the Beatles. I said, "Well, I could do that," all the while thinking, now why would he want me to photograph beetles?

So I went home and looked in the dictionary and read. Beetles. Bugs. There's twenty-five million types, et cetera. See, I hadn't heard of the group yet because . . . you have to understand, back then rock didn't get a lot of press—well, maybe in the teen section—but of course, I didn't read that. And I hadn't seen them on *The Ed Sullivan Show*.

But I managed to obtain a lot of information quickly and went down to meet the Beatles where they were deplaning, at the old Cadillac tank place [now the I-X Center in Brookpark]. Then it was on to the press conference, and for the next few days, let me tell you, it was quite a baptism into a career! I'd never seen anything like it. I witnessed these absolutely hysterical girls shaking and crying and the mass pandemonium that ensued. I had no idea how big the Beatles were until that Public Hall concert. What a bath! I was told to snap "a couple of rolls" of film, which resulted in about ten pictures. Had I known . . .

The only way to describe that concert was it was like being in a darkroom and suddenly there's these thousands and thousands of bright lights from the flashbulbs popping everywhere. And the nonstop screeching . . . and kids rushing the stage. You just can't imagine what it was like unless you were there.

He and the WHK staff were set up at the Sheraton Hotel that weekend in the executive suite, one floor below the Beatles (who stayed in the presidential suite). By sheer happenstance, and despite heavy security, Shuba ran into Ringo in the hallway when the twenty-two-year-old Beatle was attempting to sneak off by himself to see the city. Shuba, cameras in tow, was delighted for a chance to talk one-on-one with the world's most famous drummer.

"But we didn't even touch on rock and roll, just about my cameras and my job, which he seemed genuinely interested in," Shuba says. "And there were teenagers everywhere in the building trying to get a glimpse of any of them. We even found a few fans hiding out in our room and had to call security. It was that crazy. But the most important moment during that assignment, and one I'll always treasure, was when I was shooting them as they were leaving the concert in the limo. Paul McCartney waved to me through the window, and I got a shot of it. . . . Paul waving to little ol' George, his way of saying 'thank you.' Now that is a special photograph."

From that historic first came a quick succession of photo assignments for Shuba, mostly from the old *Cleveland Press*. Many of these jobs were at Public Hall, the center for rock concerts at the time. Shuba's lens captured them all, including the Dave Clark Five, the Rolling Stones, Paul Revere and the Raiders, the Beach Boys, the Who, Jimi Hendrix, Janis Joplin, and the Doors with lead singer Jim Morrison. "When I saw Morrison, I tell you, he was so drugged up you could see the back of his head—inside—through his eyes, they were so dilated. Finally at one point in the concert, he passed out on stage and I have the photo to prove it. Though no one would admit it, that guy was, without a doubt, ODing. They immediately dragged him off stage and no one saw him afterward." But for the most part, he says, the stars kept their act together. And through the next decade, Shuba saw and photographed hundreds of them.

It was during the mid-1960s that WEWS-TV 5 was airing *Upbeat,* which was syndicated to more than a hundred major markets. Now known as "the Beatles photographer," Shuba was the natural choice to capture the stars and events. "I did all the publicity shots for the show on a freelance basis right up to the cancellation [in 1971]. That was a terrific job." Because of his alliance with Channel 5's popular music program, Shuba was kept busy shooting for approximately twenty-two record labels as well as working with top AM stations WHK, WIXY, and WKYC. Those were the days when stations held summer concerts at area amusement parks.

"I remember meeting Neil Diamond at the '67 WIXY Appreciation Day at Geauga Lake. He was a genuinely nice guy. We got to talking over hot dogs and Cokes for about two hours before the concert. Then during his show, there was an electrical storm. But he kept going, despite the heavy rains and the mud, and gave a truly memorable performance. And because of that, I don't think his fans paid much attention to the weather, either."

Among all the celebrities he's photographed over the years, he says his top favorites have to be Diamond, Aretha Franklin ("she's not just the 'Queen of Soul,' she's the 'Queen of Personality'"), and James Brown. "I can still see him [James Brown] in his room before his show, suits all lined up across the bed," said Shuba. "He'd let his hands drag across them, feeling the material and fabric of each one, until he decided which one he'd wear. And then he'd sweat so profusely during his performance, that suit would be totally ruined afterwards."

While making his living taking pictures, the James Ford Rhodes High School graduate who never got around to finishing credits at Ohio State was attending the police academy. In 1966, he became a reserve captain with the Cuyahoga County sheriff's department. "When I started working in narcotics, the doors to my career in rock were shut very quickly. I mean, just think what I'd been witness to backstage. My new status certainly wasn't conducive to a career in rock and roll. So needless to say, although I was the first, I had a short-lived stint as a rock photographer. But nevertheless, a memorable one, to say the least."

Shuba continued his photography, switching gears from rock to weddings, business shots, and the occasional media event. From 1965 to 1983, he served as official photographer to renowned television journalist Dorothy Fuldheim. Over the years, Shuba claims the faces he's captured through his lens would total "around a million people, and that's absolutely factual." His photographs have been used in various publications around the world and are featured in several books, including *Morrison: A Feast of Friends,* by Frank Lisciandro (1991), and *The Hendrix Experience,* by Mitch Mitchell and John Platt (1998). There's also the 1997 MCA Hendrix compilation CD *South Saturn Delta,* which includes a booklet containing one of Shuba's photographs of Hendrix during his sole Cleveland visit. He shares photo credits there with fellow photographer Linda McCartney. "I felt privileged to be included with her work. And just a few weeks before her death, I was going to write her a letter telling her so. That taught me a lesson about doing things when you think about it."

Shuba knows the importance of advance planning when it comes to shooting his subjects. That's precisely how he gets the shots he wants. "A millisecond can make or break you," he says. The millisecond that counted most was when Shuba was shooting the Who concert at Public Hall in 1968. "I was over at stage-left, and I was to meet with them for an interview after the concert. I was on my way backstage when someone called out, 'He's throwing the drums into the audience—Get that picture!' Back I ran, didn't even have time to focus, and at full gallop got by the edge of the stage curtain just as Keith Moon picked up the drumhead and threw it. And I got the shot. If I'd wanted to stage that, I couldn't have done any better."

Over the years, Shuba has received various awards for his work, including journalism awards and some prestigious ones at the May Show in New York. However, he says the real reward comes when he shares his images with other people, sees his photographs on the wall, or most importantly, hands over a cherished photographic memento. "Just recently I was at a record convention and was introduced to this girl from the Ukraine. She was sixteen and loved the Beatles. I gave her two photographs of them, and just to see the expression on her face. That's the reward. Or when we donated one of the Beatles' pictures from their press conference here to Ronald McDonald House, and they got $350 for the print. It's an honor to share my legacy with others."

Shuba, who served on the advisory board of the Rock and Roll Hall of Fame,

A typical Who concert. Keith Moon's drum set gets tossed into the audience at Public Hall, ca. 1966. *Photo by George Shuba.*

recalls another special memory from his rock photography days. "We were at a gathering in honor of what would've been Jimi Hendrix's fiftieth birthday. It was held at the Crawford Auto Museum [University Circle]. I took a poster of Jimi which we made from black and white to color, had it framed, and presented it to his father on behalf of the Rock Hall. When we gave that photo of his son to him, "Hendrix had tears in his eyes. There's no prize in the world that could compare to how I felt at that moment."

Several of Shuba's prints have appeared at the Rock Hall, and his studio was used for most of the publicity photos prior to the September 1995 opening. Today, Shuba and Associates on Pearl Road offers various forms of photography, including commercial, advertising, and slide presentations. He also photographs for Sun Newspapers of northeast Ohio.

Looking back on those historic music days, Shuba reflects, "I've gotten to meet celebrities most people only dream of. Probably my only regret was I never asked for an autograph, because as a professional, it's not something one's supposed to do. But now I sure wish I had. So many are gone already—Jim Morrison, Hendrix, Joplin,

Keith Moon, Sonny Bono . . . . But I've got a lot of treasures via that camera. And those you just can't put a dollar amount on. It's the privilege of preserving history."

Janet Macoska, Writer/Photographer

Some people dig out old photo albums or vintage slides of those who have touched their lives to show friends and relatives. But imagine having your hostess whip out piles of huge photo books filled with celluloid prints of rock and roll's greatest and most influential artists. Imagine discussing decades of rock with a woman whose viewfinder has captured its energy, live action, and pronounced attitude. Or hearing about the unpredictability that permeates the performances of music legends such as Paul McCartney, David Bowie, Madonna, Elton John, Bruce Springsteen, Sting, Billy Joel, Michael Jackson, Garth Brooks, and Aretha Franklin.

"Ever since I was nine, I'd dream of meeting Paul McCartney, and that thought alone encouraged me to become a rock photographer," Janet Macoska says. "I figured that way I could possibly—maybe—with any luck, gain access to him." It didn't take long for Lady Luck to shine on her dreams—on both counts. By age thirteen, Macoska was a bona fide published photographer, and ten years later, in 1977, she came face-to-face with her beloved rock idol on a London street.

I was visiting London and was determined to meet McCartney. I knew where his house was and had it all figured out. I took some photographs I had from the Wings tour and I had Linda's first book, *Linda's Pictures,* so I figured I'd get Paul to sign his pictures, give him a book of my photos of him, and have Linda sign her book. I came prepared.

Well, I'm walking down their street, and here they both come out their door heading towards their car. I had to think fast before they got into the car and drove off. So I called out, "Linda, wait." Well, they were so stunned that someone asked for Linda instead of Paul, they both just stood there and waited 'til I caught up.

We had a great conversation, but I spent most of it talking to Linda 'cause I was too nervous to talk to Paul. And the funny thing about that was Paul stood there winking at me the whole time 'cause I wasn't paying attention to him!

The elements of fate were all there, beginning with the Beatle's Invasion. That's when ten-year-old Macoska discovered her parents' camera, a Kodak Duaflex they never used. She started taking pictures of everything—the house, her friends, the family dog. Then came the disc jockeys she'd listen to on her transistor radio.

I used to call up Jerry G. and "Big Jack" Armstrong, my favorite deejays at WKYC, and talk to them a lot. Coincidentally, my father, who was a lawyer, worked in a building near the radio station. So I'd go downtown with my mom, then make haste toward the station, taking my camera with me, of course. I started helping Big Jack with his fan mail, like sending back autographed pictures of him, things like that. In exchange, he'd give me records, which I thought was a pretty fair deal! I started taking pictures of the stars who would come there to be interviewed.

It was a very relaxed scene back then. I mean, here was this young kid walking into WKYC, one of the biggest radio stations in Cleveland, and the receptionist would just wave me on, and I'd proceed on up in the elevator. That's something you could never do now.

It was during her time at WKYC that Macoska snapped a color photo of Sonny and Cher taking phone calls on the air and promptly sent it to the national publication *Teen Screen Magazine*. "I was thirteen and so excited when they published it. The magazine promised to pay the grand sum of two dollars—and they stiffed me!" But that did little to deter the teen photographer.

After graduating from Lourdes–St. Steven High School, Macoska enrolled in Cuyahoga Community College, where she joined the school newspaper staff. When students failed to complete assignments or articles, Janet suggested filling the space with music reviews.

I'd contact the people at Belkin Productions, who were quite supportive of college students. I not only got to go to the shows, I'd interview the groups backstage. You didn't need photo passes then; anyone could bring in a camera. I started out using the old Twin-lens Reflex ones that you'd have to look down into but soon realized they were impractical for concerts because of the low lighting. That's when I went out and purchased my first 35mm camera.

I took one beginner's black and white photography course at Tri-C [Cuyahoga Community College] but basically learned just by doing it. I remember photographing Bruce Springsteen with Wishbone Ash at the Allen Theater [when the Jersey singer was just breaking in on the North Coast]. Unfortunately, the photos didn't turn out well. But I learned from the mistakes and the experience.

She made up for that show a decade later when she snapped a captivating close-up of Springsteen jamming with musical cohorts Clarence Clemons and Nils Lofgren at the Richfield Coliseum. The photo has since been used in several displays of her work.

By 1974, Macoska had abandoned plans to attend Northwestern University for a journalism degree. She was too busy covering rock events with her camera. "My first real concert was when Walt Tiburski, then with WMMS, got me into Public Hall to see the Beach Boys, who were the headliners, but also on the bill were Electric Light Orchestra and Linda Ronstadt. I got to watch the whole show from the side of the stage, and I was hooked. After that, I'd go to any show people gave me a ticket or a pass for. Sometimes, that meant seven days a week, or even two or three concerts a night. Oftentimes I'd go from Public Hall, then head straight to the Agora. There was always a choice of great shows to hit in Cleveland."

It was at the Agora that Macoska made a friend for life. "I covered the Sensational Alex Harvey Band when they played the Agora in 1974. I was so overwhelmed by his show, I wrote this tremendously biased article of what a great performer Alex was and how he was destined to be a superstar. His management was so thrilled with the review, the publicist sent me to shoot their concert in Louisville, Kentucky. Alex was the first person to believe in what I did and actually pay me money for my pictures. Up until then, I'd been doing it basically for tickets to get into the shows."

The two developed a close friendship—so close that in 1977, at the Scottish rocker's invitation, Macoska traveled to England and stayed at the family home. Even then, it was a working vacation. "I covered the Alex Harvey Band at the Reading Festival, where they headlined this huge concert. They were really big in England. Soon after, Alex hooked me up with my first agency, London Features International." Since Harvey's death in 1982, Macoska has maintained family ties, flying to England each summer to visit with his widow and son.

In those early years, she served as photojournalist for Cleveland's *Exit* magazine, and in 1976 she began her own Columbus-based music magazine, *Focus*. She didn't drive, so she relied on buses for the three-hour trip. As far as getting her driver's license, she didn't feel the need. "I never had a problem with people driving me to concerts," she says. After a year, however, the biweekly trips took their toll, and she went on to other ventures.

Macoska's work has been on display in galleries around the globe. Her proudest moment came when her favorite print of McCartney (playing at New York's Lyceum Theater in 1989) was chosen to hang in the permanent collection of London's National Portrait Gallery. She also had five portraits on display at the first Cleveland Hopkins Airport Community Portrait Gallery. And throughout the opening month of the Rock and Roll Hall of Fame and Museum, in 1995, she had her own exhibit, "Fame—The Photographs of Janet Macoska," at the Ninth Street Gallery in downtown Cleveland, which serves as her home base. At this writing there are nearly a hundred of her photographs housed in the Rock Hall, most of which have yet to be displayed, though her Jane Scott contributions hung on the wall beside the 1997 "My Town" exhibit.

Her photos have appeared in *Rolling Stone*, *Creem*, *Sports Illustrated*, the *New York Times*, *The Times* (London), *People*, and virtually every national music and teen publication in the U.S., including the venerable *16 Magazine*.

"Janet was freelancing in the '70s when she started sending her work to us," recalls Randi Reisfeld, former *16* editor and author of *This Is the Sound: The Best of Alternative Rock*. "I was struck by not just the quality of her photos but how she was able to capture the personality—the essence—of the performers through her camera. She'd take the time to write out captions on the back of the photos on everything you needed to know and what was going on then. She got us great shots of the popular '70s bands like Cheap Trick, Styx, REO Speedwagon, and Bay City Rollers. Because of her professionalism and talent, I started giving her various assignments and sending her to L.A. to shoot teen idols like Shawn Cassidy, Kiss, and, later, Luke Perry [an Ohio native] on the *90210* set. She did photos of Michael J. Fox for us when he was filming *Light of Day* [filmed partly at the Euclid Tavern]. And she did the very first—and best—shot of Leonardo DiCaprio."

In 1975, Macoska shifted gears from rock to sports, shooting fly balls as a staff photographer for the Cleveland Indians. She remained with the team until 1986. Between Indians games, she worked concerts throughout the 1980s. But times had changed. There were several reasons it ceased to be fun anymore, she says. One was the two-song restriction the artists and their management impose on photographers, limiting the chances of seizing a candid moment. Another was the change in the rock scene itself. The industry that began as pure entertainment became corporate big business and lost some of its allure and energy. Not only that, the mosh pits that became so popular in the 1980s became downright dangerous for anyone in the way.

Macoska has shifted her focus to the country music scene, which reminds her of the early rock days. In that genre, too, she has captured the best, everyone from George Jones to Garth Brooks. In addition, she's garnered photo assignments for television, such as for *Home Improvement* and *Beverly Hills, 90210,* and has gone on location for movies, including *Shout* with John Travolta and *Uncle Buck* with the late John Candy. "I've met some amazing people because of my job," she says. "I've been at Paramount Studios and was as wide-eyed as a young girl meeting the likes of Jimmy Stewart and Steven Spielberg. Those were priceless opportunities."

Renowned Cleveland photographer Janet Macoska has fun with WMMS's Jeff and Flash and Julian Lennon, 1992. *Photo by Brian Chalmers.*

Regrets? She's had a few. One involves Paul McCartney. "I certainly regret never seeing the Beatles in concert. The first time they came to Cleveland, tickets were distributed by a lottery system, and I wasn't one of the lucky ones. The next time, in '66, my family was taking a vacation to Michigan, and I was held captive against my will! But at least I've gotten to meet Paul and photograph him. I'll never forget the last time I saw him. It was 1989, just before a press conference in Chicago. I had some photos to give him, and as I did so, it suddenly struck me that I was looking at this former Beatle who is now middle-aged. Yet for a few minutes there, time stood still, and I was transformed back to this ten-year-old girl with this huge crush on a Beatle."

In 1990, Macoska was covering the Grammy Awards for *16 Magazine*. It so happened McCartney was receiving a Lifetime Achievement Award that evening, and the Cleveland photographer and ultimate McCartney fan was there to witness the auspicious occasion firsthand.

For her, the years have gone by swiftly, like a flash from her ever-present camera.

Particularly in the early days, the biggest advantage of being a rock photographer in Cleveland, when the city had such a reputation for breaking bands, was that many times an artist would kick-start his or her tour here. People like Bruce Springsteen almost always would start his tour in Cleveland. This was because bands felt the audience here was more receptive, rather than in towns where the crowd tended to be more jaded. My pictures sold better nationally because I often had the first pictures from the tour. So magazines like *Rolling Stone* would pick them up so readers could see what the stars were wearing on that particular tour, and things like that.

Back then there was much less competition. There were really only three or four of us in Cleveland at the time covering it all. I do miss the freedom photographers used to have—when you didn't need anyone's permission to shoot pictures, and you could shoot as many as you felt were necessary. Because the secret to getting a good shot at a concert is waiting for the right moment. Waiting for the lights to be right, the right movement by the performer. In the course of watching a show through the lens, there's like a rhythm to it. You have to know where and how the performer's going to move. And you can't always pick up on that rhythm when you're limited to two or three songs, which is now the standard. Today there are contracts to adhere to, and restrictions that limit what you can do, which diminish the creativity. Unfortunately, photographers starting out now won't have those same opportunities I did.

Macoska's work is now syndicated worldwide by Retna Pictures of New York and London. Aside from galleries, her work appears in several rock books and on record sleeves, most notably on Led Zeppelin's CD boxed set and on the reissue of David Bowie's live double album, *Stage*. In 1997, Macoska's work was included in the art exhibition "Art Rocks," in Pasadena. She was in good company. Other exhibitors included Graham Nash of Crosby, Stills, Nash and Young, the Who's John Entwistle, and Linda McCartney. That same year she was recognized by the Akron Art Museum when it procured six of her rock photographs for its permanent collection: shots of David Bowie, Ted Nugent, Kiss' Gene Simmons, Akron natives Devo, and Michael Hutchence. And in 1998, the Hard Rock Cafe secured several of her snapshots to be hung in their various restaurants around the world.

But there'll always be a share of Macoska's works displayed right in her hometown, enabling North Coast rock fans to bask in the photographic memories she imparts through her lens.

Anastasia Pantsios, Photojournalist

Anastasia Pantsios's father, a chemist whose hobby was photography, was the first to introduce her to the world of pictures. He taught her photo processing in the darkroom, but it had always remained a hobby for her. "I started getting more interested in photography around 1969," says the Chicago native. "I didn't get serious about it, though, until the mid-'70s when I did yearbook photography at Case. By then there were many concerts taking place in Cleveland—nearly every night. There were few professional photographers to capture it all."

It was while attending CWRU for her master's degree in stage design that her love for dramatics began taking a back seat to photojournalism. Between her daytime classes and nighttime concert shoots, Pantsios began writing for local publications, such as *Cleveland After Dark*, the *Exit*, Akron's *Zeppelin*, and *Scene* (where she was associate editor during its first two years). In 1974, she was given her own weekly column in the *Plain Dealer*'s Friday entertainment section, called "Rock Beat." It featured newsworthy items about happenings in the rock scene, both locally and nationally. And there was always something happening, particularly at the smaller concert venues. "My favorite place was the old Agora," she says. "I was so familiar with the layout, I'd know just where to stand to get the best shots."

Through the years, Pantsios captured action shots of bands of various music genres, including punk, new wave, and heavy metal. Her photographs have appeared in significant publications around the country, including *Rolling Stone, Esquire, Spin, Creem,* and *Circus*. Her work has also been published in numerous books, such as Norm N. Nite's *Rock On Encyclopedia,* and have been used in music television specials on MTV and VH1.

In 1978, the three primary female rock photographers in Greater Cleveland— Pantsios, Janet Macoska, and Akron native Stephanie Janis (who left the business a few years later to start a family), each in her early twenties—merged their talents and formed Kaleidescope Productions. The premise of this collaboration was twofold: to provide rock photographs for various publications and to dispel the myth that "if you're a woman in the rock industry, people immediately think you're a groupie," Pantsios wrote in one of her articles. "It doesn't matter how experienced or professional you are, they think you're there to get close to the bands."

These female entrepreneurs had no problem proving themselves to be serious professionals. Jobs were plentiful as the trio dominated the area's rock scene, capturing exciting moments in Cleveland's rock history. By 1982, however, the three had started phasing out their company. Janis was gone, and Pantsios's and Macoska's interests were veering off in different directions. Pantsios was shooting more heavy-metal groups, while Macoska was involved in teen rock and was serving as staff photographer for the Cleveland Indians.

In 1988, with rock always her main focus, Pantsios, together with *Scene*'s Mark Holan, founded the Cleveland Music Group, an organization to help musicians further their careers and find camaraderie.

"My initial idea sprang from reading about music groups in other cities," she says. "This was during the time when South by Southwest was started by the Texas Music Association, and there was WAMA [Washington Area Music Association] in Washington, D.C. This was at the point when the Cleveland music scene was rather isolated, everyone was kind of off by themselves, and no one was aware of what the others were doing. So I thought something like this could bring all the disparate parts together."

The group's focus was to provide exposure for local bands and musicians and to help them in acquiring recording contacts. Some of the members over the years included Keith Rathbun of *Scene,* Jim Clevo of JCP Productions, tavern owner Dewey Forward, writer Cindy Barber, Belkin Productions public relations assistant Donny Young, and musician Michael Stanley. Pantsios resigned from the group in June 1993.

Today, Pantsios continues to freelance, both as a writer and photographer, for local publications, such as the *Plain Dealer.* From 1992 to 1998, she was a senior writer for the *Cleveland Free Times* until a change in ownership. She also wrote for the now-defunct *U.S. Rocker* magazine. Her photographs are still in demand by national publications. In October 1999, Pantsios had her first exhibition at the Kelly-Randall Gallery in Cleveland's Tremont area.

Recommended Reading

McDonnell, Evelyn, and Ann Powers, ed. *Rock She Wrote.* New York: Bantam, 1995.
Russell, Ethan A. *Dear Mr. Fantasy: Diary of a Decade, Our Time and Rock and Roll.* New York: Houghton Mifflin, 1985.

11 Record and Concert Promoters

An essential, though largely unheralded, group of music lovers made it their business to discover and market new sounds and artists: the record retail business owners and concert promoters. While early rock deejays often get credit for discovering new talent, behind-the-scenes musicmen were really responsible for merging the sounds with the fans and, together with the radio personalities, kept the music spinning. Without the record sellers, deejays would be out of a job and music fans would be denied savored moments.

Leo Mintz, proprietor of Record Rendezvous, was one of the first to recognize the need for a downtown store exclusively for the phonograph-buying public. Yet there were other music caterers, as well, who helped push contemporary sounds to new heights. George Freeman, founder of the Northern One Stop record store, the first of its kind in Cleveland, was another early influence. Ron Schafer, of Piks Record Distribution (a nationally known polka distributor with World's Renowned Sounds and a three-time Grammy winner), explains the concept of the One Stop store: "With the One Stop store, Freeman enabled jukebox record buyers to buy from several labels like Columbia, Capitol, MCA, et cetera, and get everything they need under one roof [rather than going to all the individual warehouses]. He, of course, charged a premium for that convenience, but it certainly saved time and made things easier for the buyers."

Paul David is another big name in record promotions. He founded Stark Records in 1960 and pioneered the idea of putting records in department stores. In 1978, David opened the first Camelot Records, in North Canton. Today there are twenty-seven Camelot stores across Ohio. Tommy Edwards, in addition to being one of Cleveland's most popular deejays in the 1950s, opened up his Hillbilly Heaven record store in 1962. It later changed its name to Record Heaven and ultimately became known worldwide.

There were also notable record distributors—such as Henry George and Sanford (Sandy) Beck of Custom Distributors, Phil and Bob Skaff of Liberty Records (Skaff later became Paul Anka's manager), Harvey Korman and Ron Schafer, of Piks Record Distribution (later part of Mirus Music, Inc.)—who had a hand in making Cleveland the largest distribution market in the Midwest. Prominent record promoters include Carl Maduri, president of Sweet City Records, now of Maduri Productions in Florida; Marty Mooney, who now works for record mogul and former Columbia A&R man Steve Popovich of Cleveland International Records; and Ron Iafornaro of the now-defunct Mirus Music. One of the first production companies to come out of Cleveland, Sweet City Records (1978), was associated with Belkin Productions. Auburn Records (with owner/president Bill Peters) was renowned in the 1980s for its concentration on the heavy-metal scene. And the 1990s brought John Malm's Nothing Records, the company that first produced Nine Inch Nails.

A record promoter sells the songs. A concert promoter sells the artists. Both see opportunity early on and, through diligence and dedication, provide lasting musical experiences.

Record Promoters

Leo Mintz

In 1939, there were no television sets; radio and phonograph records were the greatest source of in-home entertainment. Knowing this, Leo Mintz opened his first record shop in a small building at 214 Prospect Avenue. Then the assistant manager at an army-navy store, Mintz had been driving down the road one day listening to his car radio when the idea hit him. How great it would be to own a record store—not just a store in which one walks in, buys a record, and walks out, but a place that catered to the musical cravings of its customers. With $500 and a dream, Mintz set up shop selling used jukebox records, adding new ones to his inventory as finances allowed.

He made weekly—sometimes daily—trips to a Columbus warehouse to purchase records by artists his customers craved. In addition, he gave shoppers complete access to these records by openly displaying them along the walls and in bins throughout his store (prior to this, records were kept behind the counter, available only upon request), a move that attracted customers from all over Ohio. Mintz was also one of the first to provide listening booths so that prospective buyers could preview a record before making a purchase. Largely because of these progressive practices, customers came in droves.

It was in 1951 when Mintz began noticing that his business was attracting suburban white teenagers who would sift through boxes stuffed with R&B records. Mintz at first was baffled. The white adolescents chose to listen to records by black artists like Bessie Smith, Fats Domino, Ruth Brown, Amos Milburn, and Charles Brown. They'd spend hours singing and dancing to the jazzy sounds, yet they always left empty-handed. And Mintz knew why. "Race music" was simply not accepted in the white community. He knew that parents would have been horrified if their children came home with such records. So the businessman's mental wheels began turning. If only he could change how this music was perceived . . . if only he could get these records played on the radio.

Mintz's answer came one day in the form of Alan Freed. He was in Mullins Bar on Euclid Avenue, a popular downtown lunch and after-work hangout, when he struck up a conversation with Freed. The two discovered their mutual interest in music when Freed explained his forced hiatus from Akron radio (see Chapter 1). Mintz told Freed he had some pull at WJW-AM radio, as one of its major sponsors, and promised to get his new friend a job there, enabling Freed to resume his disc jockey career.

Mintz had an ulterior motive. After inviting Freed to his record shop to check out the scene, the store owner convinced the disc jockey to play some of the records so popular with his customers during his nightly broadcast. Although hesitant at first (his program was basically a classical format), Freed knew not to "bite the hand that feeds you." And after spinning the tunes of Della Reese, "Big" Al Sears, Red Prysock, LaVerne Baker, and Ivory Joe Hunter, among others, he was hooked. The music had exactly the kind of energy the young deejay himself personified, and before long, he was playing nothing but it. It became immediately clear, however, that the music, favored by both black and white listeners, cried out for a new, more marketable name. So they called it rock and roll.

Mintz's initial plan to commercialize, and thereby bring a wider acceptance to, the music exceeded expectations. This behind-the-scenes record man is perhaps the most overlooked person in Cleveland rock history. While many recognize and honor (though posthumously) Freed's considerable contribution in the birth of rock and roll, there are more, including a surprising number of Clevelanders, who are unaware of the vital part Leo Mintz played in this history. But as a successful store owner, he seemed content to continue working hard for customer satisfaction and for the music. Those who grew up on the North Coast during this era clearly recall his Record Rendezvous stores.

"I can remember from 1950 on, my mother would take us downtown," recalls blues veteran Bill "Mr. Stress" Miller. "We'd be walking down Prospect Avenue, and you always knew when you were getting close to Record Rendezvous because you'd hear the sounds of those R&B records blasting out of these old scratchy speakers outside. I remember seeing black as well as white teenagers going in and out of the place because it was located near the trolley bus stop where East Siders from Cedar Road, Woodland, and neighboring areas would come downtown." He adds, laughing, "I also recall my mother complaining about the music every time we passed it. 'Course, she was into Big Band music. And the music coming out of Record Rendezvous certainly wasn't her cup of tea! Yet, that is precisely where I got my first taste and appreciation of rhythm and blues."

The store was ahead of its time in the '60s as well. "That store became a meeting place for philosophical discussion and a place to hear the latest musical innovators," notes its long-time manager and one-time Pere Ubu guitarist, Jim Jones. "On any given day you could rub elbows with locals Peter Laughner, Anton Fier, Chrissie Hynde,

David Thomas, and most of the future Ubus. There were radio deejays, poets, artists, even visiting musicians like Keith Moon, Tom Waits, Elvis Costello, Lenny Kaye, and other bands and personalities that have since come and gone. It was a rare and charged atmosphere."

Because it filled a definite need, Mintz's business began growing by leaps and bounds. Realizing he needed larger space, he opened a Record Rendezvous at Public Square, then another one at Richmond Mall in Richmond Heights by the late '60s. Although there were other popular record stores at the time, like Melody Lane (originally located on Detroit Avenue in Lakewood, followed by stores in Parma and Rocky River) and the Music Grotto across from the campus of Cleveland State University (which boasted colorful album covers painted on its outside walls and an astute manager, Billy Bass, who became one of Cleveland's best-loved and legendary deejays), the Record Rendezvous was king.

Until the time of his death from cancer on November 4, 1976 (at age sixty-five) Mintz managed to singlehandedly keep control of each of his three stores (Prospect, Public Square, Richmond Mall), with help from family members. With five locations by the end of the '70s, the stores dominated the North Coast area.

After Leo's death, son Stuart took over the company and expanded it to include stores at Randall Park Mall in North Randall and Great Lakes Mall in Mentor. But soon after, unforeseen circumstances occurred that led to the demise of each store, one by one. Through a serious of unfortunate, controversial events, the first and last Record Rendezvous closed in June 1987. The reasons are varied and complex. At the top of the list was the recession and high interest rates of the early 1980s (the company's credit interest rates skyrocketed from 6.5 percent to 23 percent). Also, the record industry—internationally, nationally, locally—experienced a marked decline that affected overall sales. In a 1987 *Cleveland Magazine* article, "The Day the Music Died," author Stephen Sawicki discussed yet another problem: "One of the store's greatest problems, though, had little to do with outside forces. A threat lurked within, humming and clicking in the basement of the Prospect store. It was Stuart Mintz' Sperry Univac computer. . . . Much of the information the computer churned out was either incorrect or came too late to be of use. Mintz spent most of his time in the basement, developing and refining new programs. In the stores, the computer made it difficult for managers to order their records until the last possible minute before the busy weekend. Further, they had trouble stocking the stores because of credit problems with the distributors." The poor credit was the result of internal problems.

Consequently, conflicting business dealings between Stuart and his new business partner, Joseph Simone, and subsequent disagreements about distribution of finances led to the final fall. Simone had started his own record distribution business in 1970, and Leo Mintz became an enthusiastic customer. By decade's end, Simone's Progress Record Distributing was the most prosperous independent record distributor in the United States, and its president was a millionaire. In 1983, Stuart realized he couldn't go it alone and made Simone a full partner to help keep the record stores afloat. What happened instead was, according to the *Cleveland Magazine* article, "Simone started opening doors to his warehouses and sending us stuff he couldn't do anything with," said one manager. "He was cleaning out stuff that was marginal to unsalable." The article also cited other business tactics, particularly concerning bank loans, that were "extremely curious."

In June 1987, nearly half a century after its birth, the historic and beloved Record Rendezvous died an unceremonious death (with little media coverage), its founder largely forgotten by its rock-and-roll-loving former customers. A year after the store's demise, Simone filed for bankruptcy.

Several months before the closing of the last store, the Rock and Roll Hall of Fame and Museum's special projects director, Chris Johnson, announced plans to include exhibits of the store in its museum. The idea stemmed from a 1985 tour of the city by the New York Rock Hall board of directors (led by Cleveland native and rock historian Norm N. Nite; see Chapter 19). The group had chartered a bus and stopped at Record Rendezvous so that Atlantic Records founder and Rock Hall exec Ahmet Ertegun could purchase some records as souvenirs from the historic store. At the time of printing, fans and patrons of the store still await the promised exhibit.

Steve Popovich, President of Cleveland International Records

Steve Popovich loves music. All kinds of music—gospel, country, R&B, polka, and, of course, rock and roll. He came by it honestly. "There was always music playing in our house," he says. It was this passion for the music and an instinctive business sense that has made Popovich one of the most recognized names in record promoting. And not just on the North Coast.

Born on July 6, 1942, and raised in the small town of Nemacolin, Pennsylvania, this coal miner's son began playing bass guitar during high school in a band called Ronnie and the Savoys. The group, which he describes as "hillbilly," released the local hit "Slappin' Rods and Leakin' Oil." After graduating from Cumberland Township High School in Carmichael, just outside Pittsburgh, he, his mother, and his sister moved to Cleveland (his father died in his senior year). It was in Cleveland that Popovich found his musical niche. Today, this legendary and highly respected record promoter's past and present are firmly rooted in the city that not only boasts a rich rock and roll scene but a varied ethnic one as well.

"My musical interests are all over the place," he says. "Cleveland, with its great diversity, fits right in. In ethnic music, I've always loved the accordion. People used to laugh because I like polka music. But nowadays more musicians are using accordion accompaniment, and that music is growing in popularity." (Proof of that is the success of *Frank Yankovic & Friends: Songs of the Polka King, Volume 1,* on Popovich's Cleveland International label.)

Soon after moving to Cleveland, Popovich joined a band called the Twilighters, which played numerous gigs on both sides of Cleveland (most regularly at the East Side venue Hires Lounge, in Wickliffe). The group's single, "Be Faithful," was included on WKYC's popular playlist and peaked at No. 13, one notch above Sonny and Cher's "Baby, Don't Go." That was in 1962 when the twenty-one year old was working days in a Columbia Records warehouse for thirty dollars a week. Except for a brief stint in sales and promotion at Decca Records, Popovich remained with Columbia's Cleveland branch until 1969. While there, he worked his way up, and soon became promo man for the company, booking acts for the *Big 5 Show*. He would arrive at the airport each weekend to escort the celebrities to the studio.

"It was a great time in the music industry, especially in Cleveland," he says. "Everybody who was anyone played that show. You had Paul Revere and the Raiders, Sonny and Cher, Neil Diamond, Otis Redding, Simon and Garfunkel. . . . All that coupled with the exciting competition between the big AM radio stations WHK, WKYC, and WIXY. Not to mention radio kings like Bill Randle, Carl Reese, Joe Mayer, and others. Those were the days when there were more talents and less egomaniacs."

Over the next few years, the enterprising young man learned as he went along, and by 1969 Popovich had moved to New York and become assistant to Columbia's head of promotions, Ron Alexenburg. There the ambitious, but decidedly midwestern, boy found things were done differently. "I thought I was gonna get there and the record business would be just like in Cleveland. That it'd be exciting and you could get things done," he said to the *Free Times*. "I soon found that wasn't the case. I discovered that whole scene Cleveland had didn't exist anywhere but in Cleveland."

Nonetheless, Popovich dove right in, wasting no time discovering new talent he felt had star potential. In 1970 he became the youngest vice president of promotions at CBS Records (Columbia's parent company), and in 1974, he became head of Epic Records' A&R department, where he was responsible for signing and developing various artists. He was named top promotion executive in the country by *Billboard* for 1973 and 1974. Because of Popovich's flair for musical discovery, Epic (Columbia's sister label) went from a $15 million company to over $100 million. The man who claims a person need not have a "business head" to be a successful music promoter ("just a natural instinct for what's good") was largely responsible for the success of national pop stars such as Ted Nugent, Boston, Cheap Trick, Wild Cherry, Southside Johnny and the Asbury Jukes, Boz Skaggs, Billy Joel, REO Speedwagon, Ian Hunter, and Michael Jackson (his Epic contract produced the platinum-selling *Thriller*). He was also instrumental in the development of Chicago and Blood, Sweat and Tears, two of the leading recording groups of the 1970s, as well as England's David Essex, Danish act Michael Learns to Rock, and national country artists the Charlie Daniels Band and Kathy Mattea.

Perhaps more than anything else, Popovich is nationally known for his brilliant promotion of one who initially appeared to be an unlikely rock star, Marvin Lee Aday— a.k.a. Meat Loaf. That was in 1977, four years after Meat Loaf had recorded an album that had been turned down by every major record label. It was also the year Popovich made a risky career move. Yet, by the end of that year, both he and Meat Loaf would break into the music industry like a bat out of hell.

Backstage at the Cleveland International Record Artists Showcase show at the Agora, November 1978. *Left to right:* Mick Ronson, Karla DeVito, Meat Loaf, Ellen Foley, and Ian Hunter. *Photo by Janet Macoska.*

Cleveland International Records: The Early Years, 1977–84

By 1977, Popovich, growing weary of the rat race in the Big Apple, decided to return to his North Coast roots. Taking all he'd learned from the bigger record companies, he forged his own independent label called Cleveland International Records. For that, Popovich summoned two successful CBS executives, Sam Lederman and Stan Snyder, who became his partners while maintaining their base in the New York office. With backing from Epic (in return for distribution rights), Popovich acquired several of the company's acts—including Ronnie Spector (formerly of the '60s girl group the Ronettes), Nino DeLeon (a New York singer), and country singer Eddie Middleton—and set up an office in his Willoughby Hills home.

It was during this time that New York attorney David Sonenberg brought Popovich a tape of a guy he was managing who was going by the name "Meat Loaf." Upon first hearing the recording, the former A&R man was not overly impressed. But after listening to the songs (penned by Jim Steinman) several more times, the music exec felt his intuitive antenna go up. But none of the radio commanders-in-chief shared his response. And who could blame them? Here was a big—no, rotund—singer who clearly lacked the requisite sex appeal, who had a rather off-the-wall album full of melodrama and operatic overtones, who went by the name of a blue-plate special, and whose past credits included an acting stint in the bizarre film *The Rocky Horror Picture Show.* In addition, one of the songs on his album was a song called "Paradise by the Dashboard Light," which was deemed too long (eight minutes) and too risque (a teenage boy and girl having sex in a car) for radio airplay. But after hearing Meat Loaf sing live in a New York studio, Popovich and his small staff were convinced and signed him to Cleveland International. The album was remixed to add clarity and accentuate the boisterous sound, and *Bat Out of Hell* was released on Cleveland International Records in November 1977.

Undaunted by the negative response from radio programmers, Popovich and company prodded and pushed to get the album noticed. It did, but only by Cleveland's WMMS, Omaha's KQ-98, and New York's WNEW listeners. "We knew we had a hit," Popovich says. "But it was very difficult convincing others in the business. But once [John] Gorman and Kid Leo [of WMMS] agreed to play it, things started to happen."

What happened was a sold-out show at Cleveland's Agora that same month, which "brought the house down" and resulted in another sold-out performance weeks later at Cleveland's 3,000-seat Music Hall (broadcast live on WMMS). Not bad for a new and largely unknown artist. Meat Loaf, along with the equally big-voiced Karla DeVito and their entertaining theatrics, had captured an audience already known for its musical awareness. Within weeks the debut album (by then also being played on Cleveland stations WMMM 105 and WGCL 98) was flying off record-store shelves—at least on the North Coast.

And thanks to WNEW deejay Scott Muni (who had worked at Akron's WAKR-AM 1590 in the 1950s), East Coast sales were brisk as well. Soon, Canada and the U.K. caught the buzz, when Cleveland International launched a music video of Meat Loaf performing three songs from the album (before there was such a thing as MTV). In Australia, the album surpassed the previous top seller, *Saturday Night Fever.* In Holland, *Bat Out of Hell* became the country's biggest seller in its record history.

All this without much support from Epic. Because sales were less than remarkable in the rest of the U.S., particularly on the West Coast, the company started pressuring Popovich to stop at the $200,000 mark in record sales and proceed onto the next project. "But we didn't give up," he says. "It's not like we had something else to promote at the time. And besides, I knew the potential [the record had]."

Meat Loaf's debut album, produced by Todd Rundgren, went from gold (500,000 copies sold) in May to platinum (1,000,000 copies sold) in September. On September 6, 1978, while Meat Loaf was performing at Blossom Music Center, CBS president Walter Yetnikoff appeared on stage and presented the robust singer with a platinum album certification for worldwide sales topping four million.

Although the recording continues to sell (according to *USA Today*, it ranks as the third largest-selling album of all time, after *Thriller* and *Saturday Night Fever*), the success story between Popovich and Meat Loaf does not have a fairy-tale ending. In September 1995, Popovich filed a lawsuit against Sony Entertainment, claiming he was defrauded out of millions of dollars in royalties from the *Bat Out of Hell* album sales. In February 1998, the suit was settled out of court for an undisclosed sum.

During Cleveland International's first incarnation, Popovich signed on pop singer Ellen Foley (the lead female vocalist on the debut Meat Loaf album), Chicago band the Boyzz, and Cleveland's own Euclid Beach Band. He also discovered, produced, and managed Joe Grushecky's Iron City Houserockers ("Have a Good Time, but Get Out Alive") and arranged the release of Ronnie Spector's single "Say Goodbye to Hollywood," recorded with the E Street Band (produced by Stevie Van Zandt and Bruce Springsteen). The latter, however, failed to hit Top 40 (author Billy Joel's cover of the song received more airplay and ultimately fared better). Then Popovich ushered in Southside Johnny and the Asbury Jukes, resulting in a long-standing friendship with Johnny Lyon and "Miami Steve" Van Zandt (who gave him an Asbury Jukes jacket with "Cleveland Steve" embroidered across the front). In 1980, Cleveland International released the long-awaited second Meat Loaf album, *Dead Ringer,* quickly followed by *Midnight at the Lost and Found,* which was the final Meat Loaf release on the label.

In 1986, Steve Popovich was offered the senior vice presidency of Polygram Records in Nashville. Knowing the opportunities were wide open in country music at the time, he closed up his rock business, eager for a new challenge. True to form, he immediately made his stellar presence known by signing Johnny Cash, the Everly Brothers, and Kris Kristofferson, and within three years he brought Polygram's country division to major-label status. His work there complete, Popovich returned to the North Coast in 1995, where he reactivated his label.

Cleveland International: The Later Years (1995–)

The first year of the label's comeback saw the release of ten albums. Among them were Ian Hunter's *Dirty Laundry: Back from the Dead,* a live album by local country singer Roger Martin, and *Polka Time: 20 of the Best,* by eleven-time Grammy nominee Eddie Blazonczyk. One release in particular gave Popovich a lot of satisfaction: *Cleveland International Records 1977–1983* includes cuts by artists close to his heart, such as Southside Johnny and the Asbury Jukes, the Iron City Houserockers, Ellen Foley, Ian Hunter, the Euclid Beach Band, and Jim Steinman. The CD continues to be one of the biggest sellers in the Rock Hall's record shop.

And Cleveland's current events weren't lost on its top music exec either. When Browns owner Art Modell was making his way to Baltimore, Cleveland International responded in record time. In November 1996, the five-song CD *Dawg Gone* was released with titles like "Go to Hell, Modell" and "Lies." Proceeds from sales were donated to the Save the Browns Foundation, which helped the city retain the team's name and assisted in getting a new football stadium built. For Indians fans there was "This Is Next Year," a CD featuring local band Sittin' Ducks (with Wally Bryson and Dan Klawon), songs by country artist Roger Martin and national sports songwriter Terry Cashman. Cashman sings his "Talkin' Baseball (Baseball and the Tribe)" and "The Battle of Herb Score" on the record.

In 1995, the *Cleveland Plain Dealer* named Steve Popovich one of Cleveland's twenty-five most influential people, sharing that honor with notables like Henry Mancini, Bob Hope, Phil Donohue, Paul Newman, and Chrissie Hynde.

Former WIXY program director Chuck Dunaway remembers working with him in the 1960s: "'Intense' would probably be the best way to describe Popovich. Out of hundreds of record industry people I've dealt with over the years, he ranks as one of the most profound I've ever met. And I'm sure that's why he's where he is today." Southside Johnny Lyon, who's been in bands since 1966, adds, "We sent him a demo tape of four songs including 'Fever' and 'I Don't Wanna Go Home.' That was the start of it all for us. Popovich signed us to Epic and immediately got into that lunatic promotional thing he does so well."

The late country singer Roger "I Am Cleveland" Martin never failed to credit Popovich for giving him a chance when others would not. "He has given me great guidance and advice over the years. I was making money in the business before signing with a label, but there comes a time when you have to do it professionally, and if anyone knows how to do that, it's Popovich. For someone like me who's been bounced around from pillar to post in the industry, it takes a lot for me to trust anyone in the business. But that man's been a mentor and a great asset to me."

For now, the music mogul plans to stay close to his roots, saying that with the technology today, he can easily do business in his small office in the same building that now houses the famed Agora. And one can bet money that he'll continue to keep an open ear for the next big hit—no matter the genre. Because of his own diverse interests, Popovich has been the subject of articles in *Billboard, Goldmine*, and *Wall Street Journal*. He received a Grammy in 1986, along with Joey Miskulin, for producing Frank Yankovic's album *70 Years of Hits;* that was the first year polka music was considered among the awards.

"If it's good music," he says, "who cares if it's rock, polka, instrumental, or reggae? The song's still the key." It's precisely that attitude that has made him a success.

Jim Clevo, President of JCP Complex

His official bio reads "a one-man music micro-empire . . . author, speaker, panelist, technical consultant, A&R consultant, business advisor, and noted figure at national and international music conventions." Simply put, Clevo is a master at bringing underground music out of the holes Cleveland-area bands often find themselves.

There is perhaps no one more passionate about his work than Jim Clevo, who dove headfirst into the local music scene in 1985. Since then, this music lover and loyal Clevelander has been a familiar face at record conventions everywhere—New York City, Austin, Berlin, Cannes, to name a few. He's been the subject of articles in *Billboard, CMJ* (College Music Journal), *Goldmine, Pollstar, Option, Playboy, High Times, Musician,* and, locally, *Scene, Plain Dealer, Cleveland Magazine,* and *Northern Ohio Live.*

Born James S. Chlebo, the 1975 John Marshall High School graduate's ascent into music production began when he enrolled in the Ohio School of Broadcasting in 1979; while attending Cleveland State University. The novice disc jockey did the usual "paying your dues" stints on college radio (WCSB) and at stations in Cincinnati (WOXY-FM) and Ashtabula (WFUN-FM) before going on to California. By 1985, he had hung up his headphones, returned to Cleveland, and become a music writer for the start-up magazine *Alternative Press*. That's when his interest in the local music scene took hold.

With little more than ambition and a belief in the Cleveland music scene, Clevo began to make things happen. He started his own business, Jim Clevo Presentations, a "multimedia" empire (albeit small scale), in 1987. He began producing compilation discs and passing them out at local clubs so patrons could get a taste of what the rock and roll capital had to offer. Also that year he set up a booth at the annual CMJ Marathon, and the next year he was the first regional promoter to produce a CD for distribution there. That New York record convention, while focusing on college radio and promotions, showcases live music as well. Clevo made sure he brought his best samplings of Cleveland rock and arranged for these groups to perform at nearby CBGB. Since then he has traveled to numerous music conferences and conventions, including an annual trip to Austin, Texas, for South by Southwest.

Presently his list of compilation CDs of Cleveland musicians include *From the Eerie Shore, Join Rivers, Another Listen . . . Is in Order! Killer Blow, Northcoast Blend,* and the double CD *Clearing the Air.* Bands that have benefitted from Clevo's dedication include Terrible Parade, the Vivians, Indian Rope Burn, the Walk-Ins, Hot Tin Roof, Death on a Stick, Hostile Omish, and, his biggest success, Mushroomhead.

As this one-man operation got more press and increased band interest, Clevo was forced out of his home office and into rented space on Lorain Road, near Kamm's Corners. Thus, JCP Complex was born. The venue features the Jim Clevo Stage, an intimate setting that welcomes North Coast bands and musicians. Clevo puts on several concerts a month, all local talent, and uses his company for seminars, videotaping, and rehearsals. Thanks to his stage shows, this entrepreneur has raised money for the Lakewood Beck Center of Arts, Cleveland Public Theater, the Northcoast NORML (National Organization for Reform of Marijuana Laws), the City Mission, St. Herman's House, and the Cleveland Music Group, for which he served as president and chairman beginning in 1990.

Others attest to his dedication. "A one-man wrecking crew," says CMJ Music Marathon directors Dave Margulies and Joanna A. Green. Jim Testa of *Jersey Beat* magazine puts it this way: "He's either a lunatic or a saint. . . . I just wish someone like him lived in Hoboken."

Jim works hard. And that, along with interest, has been in short supply in the decade in which he has promoted local music. "People spend more time complaining that we don't have a Top 40 radio station than about what is happening on the local music club scene," Clevo says.

There is a definite lack of interest in local music compared to sports here. It's very frustrating to me, who's been witness to a wide spectrum of incredible talent, to see it being blatantly ignored. It's not anywhere near the music city that I observed when I began this venture. And it was a poor scene then—that's why I got into it.

There was an incident in Detroit in 1997 where local musicians, some record label people, and others collected a few thousand signatures and marched in front of their local rock radio stations demanding that the program director come out and tell them just when they were going to play local music. And it did result in some sort of compromise. That's the kind of direct activism Cleveland has yet to exhibit. Apathy being the most serious reason why.

But if anyone can change that, it is Jim Clevo, who has coauthored a book, *Networking in the Industry,* for those seriously interested in helping promote music. "The legacy of Jim Clevo is his ability to teach bands how to promote themselves, giving his take on the business, and making the performance space available by offering his services," says Alan Grandy, formerly of several local bands and owner of his own label, Sound of the Sea. "He's the one who taught most of us that if we all work together we can accomplish so much more. He really sacrificed to be able to do what's he's done [for the Cleveland music scene], and I'm glad the table's finally balanced for him. To live the lifestyle he led for so many years to do that, and to the degree in which he did, you have to give credit where credit's due."

Mayor White declared Clevo's fortieth birthday, December 15, 1997, "Jim Clevo Day" in Cleveland. The proclamation was in honor of "his work on behalf of Cleveland musicians."

The Concert Promoters

A lot of today's promoters are what I call producers. They're not promoters; the music is not in them. They are producing a show and thus are producers. It's not the same as being a promoter. A promoter is someone who takes an act that can't be sold and develops an audience for that act. A producer takes an act that already has an audience. As Bill Graham [famed San Francisco concert promoter] once said, "Anybody can take a poster of Led Zeppelin, put it in the bathroom and sell a show. A promoter's the guy who takes the act that just got signed to a record company, that has a following of one or two hundred people, and brings in another four or five hundred." Or when a show is not doing well, the promoter goes out and does everything he can to make the show happen—and doesn't give up. That's a promoter.

—Hank LoConti, Agora founder

A concert promoter books the acts; secures the date; rents a venue; buys insurance; hires security, stagehands, ushers, and technical staff; handles ticketing and advertising; and orchestrates the setting, sound crew, and stage lighting. Perhaps most tedious of all, the promoter must court the artists, whose sometimes quirky demands add to the already hectic schedules. Sinatra (whom the Belkins brought to Public Hall in 1969) required a dressing room with the comfort and allure of Caesar's Palace. Aerosmith's Steven Tyler has a passion for wheatgrass juice. Bob Seger requests ashtrays and salt shakers from White Castle restaurants. Then, of course, there are the limos and catered buffets . . . .

Hank LoConti

The success of Hank LoConti is substantial. For three decades LoConti has been instrumental in promoting countless rock acts on the North Coast through his Agora clubs (see Chapter 9) and other notable venues. And the events, stories, and prominent rock names who played have been recounted many times. "You could spend weeks talking about just one club, let alone all the others," LoConti says. Although the basic mission is the same—to provide the best in music for fans—the club owner agrees that the methods and protocol of accomplishing that goal have changed considerably since the club's infancy. LoConti says,

I think nowadays the promoters and the industry are making a terrible mistake. They see an artist sell out a show, see advertising dollars go up, and so goes the prices. Well, these are the executives who can afford it, so they don't care. But the *real* public that buys the album, the public that stands for hours in line to buy the tickets, or camp[s] out the night before to try and get up close, they are the ones who get cheated because all the good seats are being held.

And because the scalpers were getting big dollars, this created your gold-circle tickets. The promoters, or producers, figure if people will pay a big amount for good seats, they'll reserve those seats and charge a higher price. And you know, there really isn't anything wrong with that, it's not illegal. But they're forgetting one important thing. The people getting those seats usually aren't the real fans. The kids [who lack connections] are. They forget it's those fans who create the energy of the show and buy the music. If you want to sell something, you need the build-up, the heightened energy only they can provide. So I've never allowed the record people to be seated in front of the stage. I always put the kids down front and the industry people on a platform in the back. This way the fans create the energy, the record execs see it and thus are encouraged to go out and sell to them. It always made for a better, and more successful, concert all the way around.

It was the true music fans who Hank LoConti had in mind when he began his mission to provide top entertainment, or a place where novice musicians could develop their craft, at a price within young people's means. That began in 1966 with the first Agora club. But things didn't always fall in place for LoConti. In 1972, as the Agora grew in reputation and locations, he and his biggest competitor, the Belkin brothers, forged a business union in an attempt to resurrect an old but popular club just down the street, the Plato at E. 22nd Street. The two best names in promotions cooperated with Plato owner Chuck Zingale to remodel the downtown venue, renaming it the Threshold. But the night after its opening, the building burned to the ground. Club life went on, though, and LoConti continued to take risks for his well-defined ambitions.

"One thing a lot of people don't know is that Hank was the first guy to stage an outdoor rock concert at an army base," recalls Kevin Dugan, former technician and stage manager for Rainbow Canyon and the Raspberries. "It was held at Fort Campbell, Kentucky, with Jack Craciun Productions. It was a real interesting bill, with Barbie Benton, the Earl Scruggs Review, Pure Prairie League, Chaka Khan and Rufus, and Joe Cocker. When it came to bringing music and people together, Hank played an integral part."

LoConti didn't miss out on the disco craze either. Along with partners, he opened the Rare Cherry in 1977. Later that year LoConti turned his Toledo venue into the disco club Touch of Class. Both became premier places to dance the night away. And together with record/radio/television producer Walt Masky, he also ventured into a new record company, Agora Records. But after a few years, the concert promoter realized his true love was the Cleveland Agora and eventually dropped his other businesses.

LoConti relied on investors to help him financially, in addition to hiring trusted family members. His brother, Nick, handled affairs and liquor orders for the Agora, and his mother and wife were familiar faces at the club, helping in a variety of ways. But more than anyone, it was LoConti who called the shots.

In 1980, LoConti and Belkin Productions joined forces once again to present rock shows at Legend Valley (now Buckeye Lake Music Center), a 55,000-capacity outdoor concert venue and camping facility. With its open, rural atmosphere, Legend Valley was a desirable place for music for both artists and fans. Today, Buckeye Lake, located thirty miles east of Columbus, is solely a LoConti–run business.

"I'd have to say the biggest years I had were in the '70s, a great decade for entertainment," LoConti says of his lifelong career as a promoter. "The record companies were signing and supporting acts, and a lot of music was made. But the bottom dropped out in 1981. The record companies stopped all support because money was tight, interest rates high, and they couldn't afford the tours. It didn't affect the superstars so much. They could go out because they didn't need the support. But the smaller acts weren't getting signed and in turn couldn't tour. We probably missed out on some good artists back then because of it."

In 1997, LoConti opened a new club in St. Petersburg, Russia, beginning a new chapter in his career, and life. "If someone had told me a few years ago I'd be opening a club in Russia, I'd have said they were crazy," LoConti says. "I had no interest in opening another club. Over the years, I must've turned down thirty offers to build or be a partner in a club. But my nephew went over there to buy an insurance company, and one day his partners asked him if he knew someone who could make this closed-down restaurant into an American-style dance club. He thought of me right away."

Hollywood Nites, not surprisingly, was an instant success, providing young Russians an opportunity to experience what Americans have enjoyed since the Beatles era.

"It's almost like the '60s all over again," notes son Henry, who has accompanied his father there several times. "They don't have anything like it in Russia. So having a nightclub like this is truly pioneering. My dad is constantly amazing me—what he can do. I was too young to observe the evolution of the Agora, but this one I can watch grow from birth on. So for me personally, it's very exciting."

At an age when most men are retired, Hank LoConti is on the road to new business adventures, and they always involve music. "One thing about the entertainment business," he says, "you can change it along with the music and keep the same building. If you do it right, there's no reason to ever close a venue, just as long as you keep up with the music and the changing times."

Jules and Mike Belkin

There are several main reasons why acts made a point to play Cleveland in the early years. The biggest are Hank LoConti and the Belkins having the guts to book bands that not a lot of people had heard of. And many times their instincts proved right and those acts went on to national fame.

—David Spero

Mention the name "Belkin" to any rock and roller—musician or fan—and the recognition is instant. Since 1966, the Belkin name has been synonymous with music. The Belkin organization now includes several family members, but it literally began with two brothers, Jules and Myron (better known as Mike).

The beginning of the Belkins' careers goes back to a retail store at W. 25th and Clark Avenue, where rock and roll was far from their minds. After all, their business was clothing; they worked at their father's Belkin's Men's Shop, and musically, their interests veered more toward Big Band and folk music. It began when an associate of Mike's, who owned an outlet store in Ashtabula and booked music acts to supplement his business, hired him to help with upcoming Glenn Miller and Tommy Dorsey Orchestra concerts at Ashtabula's Swallows Ballroom. Not finding the job too difficult, Mike Belkin started promoting more acts into the eastern suburbs; eventually agencies suggested he (and later brother Jules) start bringing acts into Cleveland. The first official Belkin concert took place on February 5, 1966, at the Music Hall with the Four Freshmen and the New Christy Minstrels. The two groups were chosen mostly because they were the new promoters' personal favorites at the time. As such, the brothers began booking acts they felt were winners—a gamble, to be sure, but the odds were good.

Despite Cleveland's reputation for breaking records, there was virtually no one in the city who made it his job to persuade the artists to come and perform here. And the Belkins knew that. By 1967, Belkin Productions was a full-fledged entertainment company. Almost immediately, the brothers discovered their niches. Jules began handling the public relations area and booking acts, while Mike became the negotiator with the acts' management. They soon earned a reputation as the ones to contact for concert appearances and just as quickly cornered an uncharted market.

For many, a Belkin booking was an artist's first exposure to the North Coast. Bette Midler, who began her career singing in gay bars, turned to Belkin for her Cleveland debut. So did Barry Manilow, who often accompanied Midler on the piano in those early days. The brothers were soon welcoming other successes to Cleveland: the Doors, Jimi Hendrix, the Guess Who, Jefferson Airplane, Chicago, America, and David Bowie.

"In 1968, I was working at WKYC when I got a call one day from a friend, Ron Sunshine, who was working for a booking agency in St. Louis," recalls former WKYC deejay Chuck Dunaway.

> He wanted to know if I'd like to book a hot new act called the Jimi Hendrix Experience. I said, "Wow, absolutely." He sent me the contracts and I cleared the date at Public Hall. I then went to Dino Iani, 'KYC's manager at the time, who said I'd have to clear it with NBC Legal. Well, they said, "No, it's a conflict of interest." So I asked around to find out who the local concert promoter was, only to find Cleveland had no major promoter. I guess that's why Ron called me. There was one name, though, that was mentioned—Belkin—who I'd heard about when they had Gary Lewis and the Playboys play in the parking lot of their clothing store.
>
> So I called Mike and told him who I had a contract with. They took the show, and the tickets sold out in less than two hours! They were wise enough to add a second show, and before long that sold out too. From then on, the Belkins were in high gear.

Belkin Productions, Inc., took promotions a step further when it joined forces with local AM radio stations such as WJW, WJMO, and the "big cheese," WIXY 1260. A WIXY Belkin show proved a winning combination. The Belkins organized, booked, and brought in the acts, and the deejays on Cleveland's most popular rock/pop radio station, lauded for its outrageous promotions, would scream "concert" across the airwaves. Between the two, Cleveland music fans were treated to nearly every act listed on the *Billboard* chart—and more.

And when WIXY died its sad death due to the popularization of FM radio, the Belkins hooked up with WMMS and began a marriage that has stood the test of time (despite their other rock radio mistresses, such as WNCX and WMJI).

Meanwhile, the Belkins, together with Belkin Productions vice president Carl Maduri, branched out into management (Belkin-Maduri Management) and record producing (Sweet City Records). Their first client? The James Gang.

"We knew we needed some management, and the only professional people in the area were the Belkins," Jimmy Fox recalls. "This was in '69, so they weren't known for artists' management at the time, but they were already an important part of the industry, so that was good enough for me. I gave Mike a call and he said, 'We can't do anything for you until you get a recording contract. But when you get one, give me a call back.' And true to his word, soon as we secured a contract, Belkin became our manager." That relationship continued after the group disbanded in 1976, as Fox soon joined the promotion team at Belkin Productions. He remained there until 1982. Belkin-Maduri Management oversaw the early careers of Joe Walsh, Donnie Iris, Maureen McGovern, the Michael Stanley Band, vocalist Samona Cooke (daughter of soul legend Sam Cooke), and local favorites such as Wild Cherry and Breathless. They continually added more credibility to their growing empire.

But it was in the seventies era when the brothers Belkin really showed the stuff they were made of. Never limiting themselves to rock, they promoted a constant string of concerts in assorted venues for every musical taste. Performers ranged in musical styles from mainstream artists such as Liza Minnelli, Frank Sinatra, and Burt Bacharach, to pop acts like the Jackson 5, the Osmond Brothers, and Chicago.

The opening of the Richfield Coliseum in 1974 paved the way for still more Belkin bookings and for the biggest rock acts, most of which performed there at least once until the venue closed in 1994. The Coliseum replaced former popular venues such as Public Hall and the Cleveland Arena, becoming the "happening place" to see a favorite act, and the Belkins were more than happy to provide it. Working with owner and developer Nick Mileti, the first Belkin presentation at the Coliseum was on October 28, 1974, with Stevie Wonder. From then on, the venue, with the promotion wizardry of the Belkins, provided a place to rock for acts like Deep Purple, the Rolling Stones, Prince, Kiss, Cyndi Lauper, Led Zeppelin, ZZ Top, Black Sabbath, Van Halen, Michael Jackson, Bruce Springsteen, and Metallica. Billy Joel visited most often, with eleven concerts in fourteen years. And of all the acts that played there in its twenty-year history, Cleveland's own Michael Stanley Band broke and held the attendance record with a packed house of more than 20,000 fans. The last Belkin/Coliseum concert was September 1, 1994, when Roger Daltry of the Who brought "A Celebration: The Music of Pete Townshend and the Who." The Coliseum became a mausoleum when Cavalier owners George and Gordon Gund moved their basketball team to a new downtown Cleveland facility, the Gund Arena. The building was razed in late 1998.

The North Coast promoters didn't limit themselves to Cleveland; they took their booking talents to more than a dozen major market areas throughout Ohio as well as to cities like Buffalo, Chicago, and Grand Rapids. Until others got on the bandwagon toward the end of the decade, Belkin Productions ranked as one of the three biggest promotional companies in the country.

They were also pioneers in promoting the outdoor rock concert—at least on the North Coast. It began in a big way, at the Akron Rubber Bowl in 1972, with none other than the Rolling Stones and opening act Stevie Wonder. That debut was without a doubt the event of the summer, if not the year. Although the facility seated 35,000, no one minded taking to the field; the show brought in more than 40,000 exuberant fans. With that overwhelming response, as well as the success of another outdoor concert at Lakewood's Edgewater Park the previous year, the Belkins began a summertime series of rock and roll events all fans remember—because of the phenomenal bands who played, the many rain-soaked afternoons, or the vicious hangovers the overindulgent experienced the next day.

Every summer for six years, the Belkins hosted several Saturday concerts at the Cleveland Municipal Stadium on the lakefront. The shows, always featuring four to five top names, usually began at noon and ended sometime after sunset. Often an elaborate fireworks display topped off the evening. The first "World Series of Rock" kicked off on June 23, 1974, with Lynyrd Skynyrd, Joe Walsh, REO Speedwagon, and the Beach Boys. It drew a sizeable crowd, with more than 33,000 rock fans in attendance (after all, by this time the Belkins were pros at promoting a concert). That debut turned out to be its lowest draw. Most shows (despite the stage usually taking up most of the bleacher section) would pack in 80,000 or more rockers. On August 30 of the premier year, a record 81,316 rock and roll lovers showed up for Santana, the Band, and Jesse Colin Young. But the real lure that day for music fans was the headliner: the legendary Crosby, Stills and Nash. That attendance record was surpassed only once: the Rolling Stones sold-out show was estimated to have drawn 82,500 people to the July 1, 1978, stadium concert. However, the afternoon edition of the *Cleveland Press* that day boasted a few thousand more: "City Becomes Rocktown as 86,000 Fans Roll In."

Joe Walsh performs before a sold-out crowd at the June 1974 "World Series of Rock" concert. *Photo by Janet Macoska.*

The Series grew bigger (and rowdier) each year and featured such notable acts as Pink Floyd, Rod Stewart, Fleetwood Mac, Bob Seger and the Silver Bullet Band, Peter Frampton, the J. Geils Band, Aerosmith, Southside Johnny and the Asbury Jukes, Joe Walsh, Yes, and Todd Rundgren's Utopia. And no hometown rock event would be complete without offering Cleveland's hometown favorite, the Michael Stanley Band. From the start, these concerts (which ranged in price from $8 to $12.50) were anticipated throughout the long, cold winters as signaling the true start of summer on the North Coast.

Despite many successful concerts that left both fans and promoters happy and satisfied, the annual rocking events were, toward the end of the decade, viewed by many as a "drug haven." Alcohol and drug usage became more the draw than the acts themselves. Even concertgoers who didn't partake were looked on suspiciously. "My girlfriend and I were there for the 1978 ELO [Electric Light Orchestra] concert," notes one fan, Doug Ruth of South Euclid. "It was really hot that day, hotter than expected. And the potato salad we'd brought probably shouldn't have been eaten. So after awhile, feeling ill, my girlfriend went to the Free Clinic to get something to calm her stomach. Well, those working there insisted we had taken some bad drugs. They kept saying, 'Okay, now, what did you *really* do?' It was so bizarre, they just refused to believe the culprit was simply potato salad!"

The main hospital tent was equipped with several doctors, nurses, and more than seventy staff volunteers, as well as five satellite tents for each event. There was also the onslaught of ticket scalpers. For every concert, there were the highly visible "capitalists" wandering through the parking lot, selling tickets for well above the advertised price to those who lacked "good"—or any—seats. A notable example of this practice took place at the July 20, 1978, ELO show, when 400 fans were turned away at the gate because the tickets they'd purchased weren't worth the paper they were printed on.

Although many sellers were caught and subsequently arrested, it was impossible to catch them all. In addition, violence began to plague the concerts, exacerbated, perhaps, by the deafening decibels and the general rowdiness that is part of any large rock event.

On July 28, 1979, however, the situation took a disastrous turn. Thousands of fans had camped out the night before the show, and the early morning hours were marked by muggings, a stabbing, and a fatal shooting. Despite its beginnings, however, the concert that featured Ted Nugent, Aerosmith, AC/DC, Thin Lizzy, and Journey went off without a hitch. Though as *Cleveland Press* writer Bruno Bornino reported, "Its billing as the 'loudest-ever rock concert' turned out to be the understatement of the year. One family in Parma reportedly took shelter in their basement because they thought they heard a tornado. Actually, a tornado isn't as loud."

For the next concert, Belkin beefed up security, barred overnight guests on the stadium property, and prosecuted those caught with alcohol, drugs, fireworks, cans, and bottles. By the following year, it apparently all seemed like too much trouble. After one last summer fling in July 1980 with Bob Seger and the Silver Bullet Band, Eddie Money, J. Geils, and Def Leppard, the World Series of Rock ended.

By 1977, Belkin Productions, Inc., had moved to more plush offices on Chagrin Boulevard in Woodmere and garnered a qualified staff of musicians and music lovers. Jimmy Fox, Chris Maduri (son of record exec Carl Maduri), Joey Porrello (formerly of Joey and the Continentals), and Barry Gabel (whose wife was a former *Upbeat* dancer) were all on the payroll. But the 1980s found the Belkins changing some strategies to keep on top of trends in concert promoting. With the sudden popularity of the Flats, Belkin became the exclusive booking agency for the Nautica, Cleveland's first permanent outdoor theater, located along the Cuyahoga River. This semicircular venue has 1,500 reserved and 2,500 bleacher seats. For its opening concert on June 20, 1987, Belkin Productions welcomed one of the city's all-time favorites, Southside Johnny and the Asbury Jukes. "We felt privileged to be the first band to play there," Southside Johnny says. "It rained like crazy; everyone got soakin' wet and had a great time. It was yet another special memory I have of playing Cleveland."

As Donald Trump has maintained through the years, one can't be successful without being tough. Even relentless. There have been times the Belkin operation has been looked on as being a corporation of hard-nosed executives who have created a monopoly through stringent business dealings. In a 1991 *Plain Dealer Magazine* article, Dallas entertainment promoter Ross Todd said, "If a regular promoter from Des Moines wanted to book ZZ Top in Cleveland, Belkin would stack the week before and after with [acts of] even a cheaper ticket price to dry up the financial market. The promoter would lose his butt and never return to Cleveland." But many who have had close contact with them disagree. Former Cleveland deejay Tim Byrd says, "In the twenty-nine years I've been in the business, I've dealt with a slew of concert promoters. And I have to say Mike and Jules Belkin were the most helpful, professional, and cooperative of the lot. . . . The Belkins are the class of the class." Speaking to their business reputation, Mick Jagger said that there were only two promoters he'd ever accept a check from: Bill Graham and Jules Belkin.

But it's a trade-off, and even the business-minded Belkins have been known to be on the losing end a few times. Like when they booked the '60s pop group the Mamas and the Papas for Music Hall and the group canceled a week before. They rescheduled, only to cancel again the day of the concert because Cass Elliot was ill.

Concert promoting today has even more issues. Even with the increased competition, and with the stars increasingly calling the shots (with a standard contract of a 90/10 basis, the bulk going to the act), Belkin manages to get most of the big acts that come to the North Coast to perform at the Gund Arena, Nautica, and the Odeon. And when it came time to orchestrate the Rock and Roll Hall of Fame concert, the New York board of directors turned to the Belkins to fill the 26,000 unsold seats (out of 57,000) four weeks before the scheduled event. Once Belkin got involved and used the promoting methods for which they were famous, the show was a sell-out.

Their thirtieth anniversary party was another successful production. With a crowd of 1,070 guests, the sold-out party was held at Public Hall (appropriately, the same venue as their first introduction to concert promotion) where they were presented with the prestigious Tree of Life Award from the Jewish National Fund.

Today, Mike Belkin's son Michael is executive vice president, and Jules's daughter, Jamie, is vice president of special events. In 1998, Michael Belkin received the prestigious Bill Graham/Promoter of the Year Award presented by *Pollstar*, the leading concert industry magazine. He was selected by more than one hundred members of the nominating committee representing every area of the concert industry.

And the company has expanded its wings. It co-owns both the Polaris Amphitheater in Columbus and the Orbit Room in Grand Rapids, Michigan. In 1996, it acquired the Odeon concert club in the Flats, which, with its dark, cozy atmosphere and 1,000-person capacity reminds many of the former E. 24th Street Agora. With clubs of various sizes, Belkin can take an unknown act from the bar scene to a club atmosphere and—if the stars line up just right—to the 20,000-seat Gund Arena.

Recommended Reading

Clevo, Jim, and Eric Olsen. *Networking in the Music Industry.* San Diego: Rockpress, 1993.

Glatt, John. *Rage and Roll: Bill Graham and the Selling of Rock.* Seacaucus, N.J.: Carol Publishing Group, 1993

Schwartz, Daylle Deanna. *The Real Deal: How to Get Signed to a Record Label from A to Z,* New York: Billboard Books, 1997

Verona, Paul, Carlo Wolff, and Eric Olsen, eds. *The Encyclopedia of Record Producers.* New York: Billboard Books, 1999.

Part 4
Cleveland Rocks

12 The '70s: Any Ol' Way You Use It

As idealistic as the late 1960s were, the early 1970s was a time of tremendous uncertainty. The Vietnam War seemed to be lasting forever, and it was affecting everything—the economy, the politics, and the music.

In a frank interview with *Rolling Stone* in 1971, John Lennon told editor Jann Wenner, "I no longer believe in the myth, and the Beatles is another myth. The dream is over. I'm not just talking about the Beatles. I'm talking about the generation thing. It's over, and we gotta—I have to personally—get down to so-called reality." Lennon had turned thirty just months before making that statement, and his reaction made sense. After all, for years his generation lived by the motto "don't trust anyone over thirty." And now he and thousands of his Boomer brothers and sisters were facing unknown territory where maturity was expected. Did that mean in the music as well?

Music defined this generation, reveling in its freedom and drawing no lines. With a new decade, it seemed as though rock was suddenly playing it safe. This generation was growing up, and much of the music was mellowing. *Billboard* charts featured the music of Barry Manilow, James Taylor, Cat Stevens, Carole King, Bread, the Eagles, Crosby, Stills, Nash and Young, the Carpenters, and John Denver. This trend seemed to be trying to recapture the light pop sounds and calming effects that characterized rock's early innocence. But there were also those in denial. The bands and musicians who refused to accept growing older took their rebellious attitude a step further. These rockers were playing it safe as well, but safe to them meant refusing to mellow. Long drum solos continued, electric guitars whined, wild antics survived. The Stones kept rolling. The Who kept smashing. Led Zeppelin kept amazing. All was right with the rock world.

(*Opposite*) The Who's Pete Townshend jumps into action at the Coliseum, mid-1970s. *Photo by Bob Ferrell.*

(*Overleaf*) Led Zeppelin's Robert Plant and Jimmy Page at the Coliseum, mid-1970s. *Photo by Bob Ferrell.*

(*Above*) Clarence Clemons, Bruce Springsteen, and Nils Lofgren jam at the Richfield Coliseum on July 8, 1984. *Photo by Janet Macoska.*

As was the case with much of the nation, the '70s brought a whole host of changes to the city of Cleveland. City government was plagued by financial insecurity (even before Dennis Kucinich), and the media caught wind of the Cuyahoga River catching fire (as did Mayor Ralph Perk's hair, another overblown tale that flew across the nation like lake-effect snow). And it wouldn't let up.

Two decades later, those events are *still* brought up now and then. The backlash of all this, of course, was that Cleveland's credibility gave way to national jokes that scarred the North Coast for years.

But like rock music, this city has strong and stubborn roots. Cleveland not only survived but thrived. And it was music that saved the day, for it was in the dark midst of all the city's problems that Cleveland earned the lofty title, "The Home of Rock and Roll."

The 1970s brought continued diversity in rock music. Gone were the sock hops and beatnik coffeehouses and teen clubs. In their places appeared uptown and downtown

(Photo, page 251, cont.)
Photographer Janet Macoska says, "A photo journalist works to make a photo that captures an emotion, tells a story, freezes a moment in time. It also helps if the lighting is right, and everything's in focus. Sometimes you get all those components and more. This shot, for me, was a homerun."

bars that offered everything from old-time rock to punk, funk, and disco. Most of these clubs in and around the Cleveland area provided an outlet for every local band worthy of a listen. Throughout the decade, there was a smorgasbord of musical offerings, with something happening somewhere every day of the week.

Many Cleveland rock lovers still mourn the losses of groundbreaking clubs like the Viking Saloon and the Smiling Dog Saloon. There were the weekends at the Round Table and Wednesday's "Rolling Stones" night at the Mad Hatter. And there were the bands—Reign, Sweetleaf, Fully Assembled, Freeport Express, the Maxx Band, the Pamela Moore Band, Bazooom, Peter Panic, Snake Eyes, 1Yere, Rapscallion, Alarm Clocks, Freewheelin', Buck Shot, Pig Iron, Left End, Easycrossin', and many others.

The Musicians and Bands—Cleveland

Because the North Coast was such a rock mecca, there were hundred of bands that made the club scene. The artists discussed in this chapter meet two criteria: First, they were (and many still are) hugely popular with their audience; second, the featured musicians or groups recorded their music and had some songs hit the charts, if only regionally.

The Raspberries (1970–75)

> When you come to hear the Raspberries, what you can expect not to see is hair down to our waist. Beards. Torn Jeans. Mustaches.
>
> Here's what you can expect not to hear: Long, boring, drawn-out guitar solos. Long, boring, drum solos.
>
> Here's what you can expect to hear: three-and-a-half-minute pop-rock, go-get-'em songs. That's it. Elvis, Little Richard. The Beatles. The Stones. Chuck Berry. Nothing else.
>
> —from a poster written by Eric Carmen

For a band in existence for a mere half-decade, the Raspberries had a genuine impact on the music scene. More than twenty years since its break-up, this often-underrated group is continually being rediscovered and, finally, appreciated as the talented rock quartet it was.

Ironically, what made the Raspberries work became the group's downfall. What made this band the darlings of power pop—with Beatlesque harmonies, a Beach Boy–like appearance (clean-cut, short hair and matching suits), and lovestruck songs—also placed them into an "uncool" category. Their image as a teenybopper group garnered more media attention than did their combined musical mastery. And by 1975, after being featured in all the teen magazines rather than the more serious rock publications like *Rolling Stone* and *Crawdaddy,* it was that identification that succeeded in destroying the band's credibility.

But this was the early '70s, not the early '60s. Led Zeppelin and Pink Floyd were the hot rock bands, and even the former Beatles had long been "psychedelicized." And while some mellower sounds were filtering onto the charts in other places, Cleveland rockers would have none of it. But in the beginning, the Raspberries were tops—in and out of Cleveland: from the Cleveland Agora and Kent's JB's to New York's Carnegie Hall and L.A.'s famed Whisky A Go Go. Carmen coined the band's name after running out of ideas and, exasperated, said, "Aw, raspberries," a term often used by Froggy in the *Little Rascals.* The band determined it was just quirky enough to catch on.

The Raspberries' story begins in 1970, but the formation started long before that. Lead singer/guitarist/songwriter Eric Carmen, a John Carroll University student with a classical music background, had been in bands since he was fifteen: the Fugitives, the Harlequins, the Sounds of Silence, then on to the Cyrus Erie, where he hooked up with guitarist Wally Bryson. Bryson, too, was a young (age fifteen) starter with his group, the Mods, in which he pioneered the way for other area rock bands. Drummer Jim Bonfanti originally played in the Choir with Bryson, and bassist John Aleksic had been in bands GangGreen and Fortega (a short-lived band that also featured Bryson).

Their first gig was on October 16, 1970, at the Cyrus Erie West, the very club named after Carmen's and Bryson's former band. "We kicked off that night playing the Beatles' 'I Got a Feeling,'" recalls Bonfanti. "It reflected our overall mood of the group."

With each member having established a reputation through previous bands, the Raspberries secured a solid fan base. Bonfanti recalls those early times. "Within weeks we got regular gigs. We played JB's [Kent] every Thursday night. It became to the Raspberries what the Cavern was to the Beatles. It was this little dive college bar but a great place to play your music and get listener response. But I think our best job was Sunday nights at the Agora, where we played for about a year and a half. It was always packed, and everyone had a great time."

Six months after forming, in March 1971, the group recorded four demos at Agency Recording, the studio above the Agora. By then, Aleksic had been replaced by former Mods/Choir guitarist Dave Smalley, who joined upon his return from Vietnam. Smalley proved to be a talented songwriter as well and collaborated with Carmen on many songs. The group's greatest asset was its ear-pleasing, perfectly blended harmonies that matched the smooth, rhythmic vocals of the Beatles and the Beach Boys. Word of this talented band got around the industry fast, and the demos caught the attention of Jimmy Ienner. Ienner was quickly becoming a respected producer in the industry with an award-winning album for the band Lighthouse, as well as albums for Grand Funk Railroad, Three Dog Night, Isaac Hayes, and, later, Poco. Excited by the group's melodic and commercial sound, he persuaded executives from big recording companies such as Columbia, MCA, Mercury, and Capitol to go to JB's one hot summer night to check them out. They did more than that. The top record execs started a bidding war, each vying to catch this group on the way up. Fittingly, Capitol, the American record company where the Beatles began, signed them.

Suddenly backed with an exclusive contract with a reputable record company, it appeared the Raspberries' success would indeed come to fruition. Armed with the talents of Ienner and engineer Shelly Yakus, the Raspberries first entered the famed Studio B at New York's Record Plant studio (W. 44th Street) in the spring of 1972 and emerged with their self-titled LP. The first single from the album, "Don't Want to Say Goodbye," reached No. 86 in *Billboard*. But it was the second single that got the band noticed. "Go All the Way" shot up to No. 5 within weeks, giving the North Coast musicians a gold record after selling 1.3 million copies. The group made its way to television, playing on notable rock programs such as *Don Kirshner's Rock Concert* and the *Midnight Special*. The album itself peaked at No. 20 and spent twenty weeks on the charts.

But from the beginning, management decisions took the band in a direction that veered far from where members wanted to go. "We really took ourselves seriously but didn't realize all the press in the teen magazines was not going to get us noticed as a really rockin' rock and roll band," says Bonfanti. "In retrospect I think we should've chosen good managers as opposed to people we liked. We were too young to realize the difference between friendship and business."

Perhaps a good idea at the time, their debut album's cover was accompanied by a marketing gimmick: a "scratch-and-sniff" sticker that carried a strong raspberry fragrance. Then there was the "foxiest Raspberry" contest Capitol pitched, which offered a "Raspberry Rollswagon," a car especially made for the winner. Again, it was the teen magazines that promoted it, encouraging their readers to cast their votes for their "faves."

"When 'Let's Pretend' came out as a single, the jacket for the 45 was the entry form to the contest," Bonfanti explains. "There was a promo shot of us standing around the car, and people mailed in ballots stating which of us they favored." When all the ballots were in, drummer Jim Bonfanti was proclaimed the "foxiest." "That was pretty wild," Bonfanti adds. "They drew a name for the winner of the car, and I was sent to Florida to present the car to the girl who won. They had a little parade and I was given a key to the city from the mayor. Had to give a speech and everything. Yes, we were highly promoted!" All these elaborate marketing strategies, however, turned off some listeners, who began to view the group as being too corny or bubblegum. (It didn't help that the sponsor for their promotional tour with the Grass Roots was Carefree Sugarless Gum.)

But the songs had the last word. The group consistently sold out shows, including the 93,000-seat Los Angeles Coliseum in 1973. But in Cleveland the rock fans who initially embraced the group did an abrupt about-face at the same time the Raspberries were becoming international stars. "I think the record company misrepresented the group," says Lakewood attorney Hugh Carlin, who once wrote a letter to *Scene* in defense of the band. "They portrayed them as a 'teenybopper' group, and it became cool if you *didn't* like the Raspberries. I also think it was partly the matching white suits and the light pop tunes they played. A lot of young hippies couldn't relate to that. Clevelanders at that time were into David Bowie and hard-rock bands like Led Zeppelin and the Stones. But I knew better. They were a great sounding group, and I think they produced better music than any band in Cleveland—before or since." The change of hometown loyalties was evident when the group returned from playing sold-out venues across the country and failed to fill their hometown's Music Hall. "I think part of that was 'cause people were used to seeing us at the Agora and paying like a dollar, so why should they pay five dollars to see a local band, which was how they viewed us," Bryson notes.

Despite its healthy start, the quartet agreed that their first effort was "technically awful." They returned to the studio, determined to capture on vinyl what they had mastered on stage. The second album, *Fresh,* was released seven months after the first, in November 1972, and it drew a positive response from critics. It contained "I Wanna Be with You" (which reached No. 16 in the United States) and "Let's Pretend" (charting No. 35), which captured the diversity and musicianship reminiscent of their influences. "We were often accused of ripping off the Beach Boys and Beatles because of the covers we played and the way we looked," says Bryson. "That's when I became adamant about us ditching those suits and steering away from that early Beatle image."

In fact, the Raspberries, as has been confirmed posthumously, had a distinctive sound and was continually pumping out original music. All four participated in the writing and often shared vocals. Wally sang on most harmonies and played lead guitar (Rickenbacker twelve-string, Gibson Flying V, Gibson Double Neck 6 + 12, Fender Strat, Les Paul Custom, Standard Les Paul, and Gibson Blueridge acoustic) as well as most of the recorded rhythm parts. Eric, lead singer and frontman, played guitar and keyboards. Dave Smalley, the bassist, also sang, as did drummer Jim Bonfanti on several cuts.

On the heels of the release of that second album, the group was hired to open for the Hollies on their national tour. "Herb Belkin, then vice-president of Capitol, told us to 'go out there and blow them away,'" Bonfanti recalls. "And we did. The crowd loved us. They were screamin' for encores. Of course, that didn't go over well with the Hollies, who'd already made comments about our trying to look like the Beatles back in the hotel. So after a few playdates, we were kicked off the tour."

But the band was having too much fun to take offense. "We were all over the place in '73," Bryson adds. "We went on a European tour which included England [where "Go All the Way" was banned for "suggestive lyrics"], Germany, and France. And we were on both German and French TV. Back home we were opening for the Beach Boys, the Doobie Brothers, Three Dog Night, the Grass Roots, Little Feat, Sly and the Family Stone, Kiss—a lot of great bands. And in turn, we had people like Bob Seger opening for us. That was in Hollywood, Florida, and I remember our truck broke down and he lent us his amps."

On September 26, 1973, the Raspberries headlined Carnegie Hall. Armed with their diverse musical talents, harmonizing, and well-written songs, the group set out to dispel the rapidly growing bubblegum myth. Eric Carmen told *Goldmine* in 1993,

I knew we had an audience full of rock critics and non-believers and a lot of skeptics out there. I thought, what would be the most frightening, goofy thing to do to create more attention in that place. I thought, "play a Beatles song." After all, as "Beatle-wanna-bes"—that would be the last thing anyone expected us to do. So we opened up the show with the first four bars of "Ticket to Ride," and there was an audible gasp. They could not believe we were going to do it. You could hear it and feel it.

We just did the four bars, then launched into "I Wanna Be with You." It was kinda like we teased them and they dug it. We owned the place from those four bars on.

But there were problems. From the start, bandmates felt Carmen was taking too many liberties with what should have been group decisions. Back when Carmen suggested the band wear matching suits and sport short hair, the other members resisted the idea. But Carmen persisted and wore them down. According to Bryson,

It was Eric's idea that we wear suits in the beginning. We went along with it, but I particularly was against it. And after a while, we had to dump the suits. It got to be too much. I mean, you can take an idea past its logical conclusion. Same with the Beatle comparisons. Sure I was influenced by the Beatles. Who wasn't? But I never wanted us to sound like a cover band. I knew we had enough talent and writing ability of our own to define our own sound. And I think we did in songs like "Overnight Sensation" and "Party's Over." But, yeah, some of the other stuff probably sounded too much like the Who and Rod Stewart, and that, more than anything else, was a detriment to us and ultimately resulted in the death of the band.

Plus, Eric started making all the decisions, like what songs would go on the album. And although I got writer's credit on the album for my guitar intro on "Go All the Way," Eric had my name taken off the single, claiming you can't copyright a guitar intro. So I didn't get any royalties from our biggest hit. That, right there, was a sore point with me. And when Jim and Dave left the studio when we were working on *Side 3* to go hunting, Eric got really pissed and felt they were being irresponsible. That was pretty much the beginning of the end of that first incarnation.

Side 3 met with critical acclaim. It remained on the charts a mere eight weeks, however, and peaked at No. 54. Two singles from that effort, "Tonight" and "I'm a Rocker," did not do as well as expected, the former reached No. 69, the latter, a disappointing No. 94. And the group's differences were taking their toll. Soon after the release of that album, Smalley and Bonfanti were out of the band. "Actually what happened was Ienner flew me to New York for a meeting because Eric was planning on letting Dave go, saying he wasn't holding his own," Bonfanti explains. "They knew Dave was my best friend and were afraid I'd leave if Dave went. And they were right. Once Dave was fired, I quit."

Despite the loss of two vital bandmates, and despite their own conflicts, Carmen and Bryson weren't ready to call it quits themselves. When Bonfanti and Smalley left the band, the determined duo summoned former Cyrus Erie drummer Michael McBride to join in and Smalley was replaced by an ambitious guitarist and Raspberries fan, Scott McCarl.

McCarl (who was born in Omaha but spent his early youth in Cleveland) recalls,

Back in October 1972, I'd gotten the idea to send out some tapes of mine to various people in the business. Because I was a big Raspberries fan, I sent one to Eric. There were three songs on it, and one he particularly liked was "Don't Make Me Sad." Well, three months later, he called me saying how impressed he was with my music, and that just blew me away. I mean, this was a guy I really looked up to, and there was some talk about him producing me some time down the road.

Then the conversation started changing. Rather than talking about producing he was saying things to me like, "If you were in a band, what would you do in this situation?" I was a bit confused until Wally and Eric called me and asked me to come to Cleveland. I auditioned for them and they asked me to join the group. Here, this was one of my favorite bands, so to be asked to be in it was like a dream come true. I was just high as a kite.

Reenergized by the new formation, the Raspberries went back into the Record Plant to record the appropriately titled *Starting Over* album. That's when the group came face to face with one of their idols—John Lennon. "We'd been recording down the hall from where Lennon was producing Harry Nilsson's album," recalls Bryson. "I was sitting outside the studio in the hallway waiting between takes, and here comes Lennon. He was dressed all in black, had the tall, black witch hat on. I said, 'Hello,' and he smiled and in a real jovial tone said, 'Good Morning!' with his British accent. I tell you, I was just dumbstruck, couldn't think of another thing to say. I mean, this was a Beatle!"

Upon the next album's release, in April 1974 (which included Jeff Hutton on keyboards), it seemed the Raspberries could do no wrong. The single, "Overnight Sensation," became an immediate hit, peaking at No. 12 and remaining on the *Billboard* chart for eighteen weeks. At the end of the year, *Rolling Stone* named *Starting Over* best album of the year (despite it never charting higher than no. 123). With this sudden acclaim came a gig at L.A.'s Whisky A Go Go, where Keith Moon, the Who's zealous drummer, was in attendance. Before the Raspberries left the stage, Moon came up and played with them.

"We were playing 'Go All the Way' when suddenly I felt somebody banging on one of my tom-toms, playing along," McBride recalls. "It was Keith Moon. He then took his scarf off, put it around my neck and pulled me down. Then he proceeded to sit down at my drum kit. Of course I didn't mind. This was my hero. He played the entire next song, which was 'All Right Now.' It was pretty wild."

"That was an unforgettable moment," Bryson adds. "There we were, me, Scott, Eric, and Jeff [Hutton] jammin' with Keith Moon! There was also a guitar player, Stan

The Raspberries play the Agora, 1974. *Left to right:* Eric Carmen, Mike McBride on drums, and Wally Bryson with his double-neck guitar. *Photo by Bob Ferrell.*

Webb, from the English band Chicken Shack on stage with us. . . . It was great getting to play with one of our heroes."

There was also the time the group shared billing with John Lennon and Harry Nilsson at New York's Central Park, where a crowd of more than 150,000 fans showed up. "That was the largest crowd we'd ever played for," Bryson says. "But the biggest thrill was when both Lennon and Nilsson came up on stage to say hello to the crowd. That was awesome until the crowd surged forward and climbed on top of our equipment truck to get a look, and it smashed in the top of the truck!"

Although the fourth album garnered the Raspberries due admiration, the band was falling apart. The ongoing tension between Carmen and Bryson culminated in a physical confrontation one night after a gig outside a Chicago club. "It all came to a head that night," explained Bryson. "I'd had a real problem with Eric concerning some of the songs on that last album. There were three actually. Once again, one sounded too much like a Beach Boy tune, another was too close to Rod Stewart, and one had riffs too closely related to a Who song. And I had made him promise me, after Jim and Dave left, that we'd go off in our own direction and he wouldn't try to emulate anyone else. I told him, just be Eric. Because he certainly had as much talent as any of those people he idolized. But after a year, nothing had changed. He went back on his word. And between all the touring and stress, I just lost it." It was that old-fashioned fistfight that severed any chances of reconciliation. Afterward, Bryson spent two weeks in a hospital suffering from nervous exhaustion. "Everything was falling apart," he says. "The management had gotten rid of Hutton, who I thought added so much to the group. The album wasn't meeting expectations. The paychecks stopped coming from the record company because they knew we were ready to split up. We were getting bad press. By the end of it all, I was exhausted and penniless."

With the advantage of hindsight, Bryson says neither he nor Eric realized back then that they weren't alone in their disagreements. "We really thought at the time that something must be wrong with us because we disagreed and fought so much. It wasn't until years later we realized all the great collaborators did. Lennon and McCartney, Jagger and Richards, Townshend and Daltry. It's actually a fairly normal thing."

Former Rainbow Canyon guitarist Billy Hanna took Bryson's place for the band's last two scheduled jobs. On April 19, 1975, the Raspberries played their final gig at a club in Scranton, Pennsylvania.

But that's not the end of the story. A belated fan from Fort Washington, Pennsylvania, single-handedly helped bring the Raspberries back to the forefront when he produced what he calls "the ultimate fan book" in 1993. *Overnight Sensation: The Story of the Raspberries* (Power Pop Press) was largely an accumulation of newspaper reprints chronicling the history of the band throughout its career, but it also included in-depth interviews with all six members. The author, writer and musician Ken Sharp, never saw the band play live, having only discovered them years after the group's demise.

I got turned on to the Raspberries late—in the early '80s. I was still in college and working at Philadelphia rock station WYSP-FM. The production director knew my musical tastes veered toward the Who, Beatles, and Beach Boys and one day played "Starting Over" for me. I thought, *wow, this is great music*. Pretty soon, I was digging up every Raspberries tune I could find. To me, the Raspberries epitomized some of the most perfect music made. They had those amazing melodies, the virtuoso energy, the great harmonies. I began collecting everything I could about the band and tracked down all the members, which resulted in a cover story on them for *Goldmine* magazine. I got such great response from that, and had accumulated so much material by then, I decided to put out a book.

The self-published 352-page biography on a group now referred to as the "pioneers of power pop" came out in November 1993. The book brought renewed interest from fans all over the world, particularly in Japan, where, according to Sharp, Eric Carmen has a cultlike following.

After the group disbanded, the members went on to various careers. Carmen immediately began a solo career and wasted no time rising up the charts with "All by Myself." That song has since been covered by no fewer than six artists, including Celine Dion.

Wally Bryson moved to L.A. in late 1975 and formed a band called Tattoo with his old music buddies Dan Klawon, Jeff Hutton, Dave Thomas, and Thom Mooney. The next year Tattoo was signed to Motown's "white label," Prodigal, which released their one and only album. "We were happy with the tracks," Bryson notes, "but they mixed it without us there and literally killed any chance of it getting airplay. It was pretty terrible and got horrible reviews."

Tattoo members decided to disband rather than take Prodigal's offer to try again. But Bryson was a musician at heart, and when guitarist Gene Cornish asked him to audition for a new East Coast band called Fotomaker, he wasn't about to turn down the opportunity. Fotomaker consisted of Cornish and drummer Dino Danelli, both of the legendary '60s group the Young Rascals; guitarist/vocalist Lex Marchesi; keyboardist Frank Vinci; and Bryson. The group released two albums in 1978.

"I was real happy playing in that band," Bryson says. "I've played with some excellent musicians, but Danelli, Cornish, Frankie, and Lexy from Fotomaker were just the best musicians I ever played with—bar none. The only reason I left that band was due, I'll admit, to a little paranoia. At the time I didn't know if our third album would get picked up. And after my experience in the Raspberries and Tattoo, I didn't trust managers. Plus, certain incidents made me feel I was getting the run around again and I got scared. I had a family to think about—a daughter and a son on the way. So I quit."

Bryson returned to Cleveland, playing in various bands until he formed Sittin' Ducks in 1989. The band includes former Choir members Dan Klawon and Kenny Margolis, together with Ed Brown on drums and guitarist Ron Ondercin. Local musicians agree that Wally Bryson's guitar abilities deserve to be in the same class as many of the great guitarists. "I remember when I was in band as a teenager in Omaha," McCarl recalls. "We loved 'Go All the Way,' but of course we had the chords all wrong. When I finally met Wally, it was like, 'bow down,' because there's no one on earth that knows how to play those chords but Wally. His guitar intros in particular are fabulous."

Former Raspberries Eric Carmen and Wally Bryson reunite on stage, after twenty-four years, for Jane Scott's eightieth birthday. *Photo by Bob Ferrell.*

Scott McCarl, who lives in Santa Barbara, recently returned to music, releasing his first solo CD, *Play On,* on Titan Records in 1998. Two of the seventeen songs on the CD are ones McCarl had played on that demo tape he had sent Carmen twenty-seven years before. Former bassist Dave Smalley lives in Arizona and works as a respiratory therapist. And after abandoning his drums for more than ten years, Jim Bonfanti became reacquainted with the instrument when he caught "the bug" again in 1994.

Several artists have acknowledged the Raspberries as an influence: Bruce Springsteen, Tom Petty, Kiss's Paul Stanley, Axl Rose of Guns 'n' Roses, and the late punk rocker Stiv Bators of the Dead Boys. Dave Smalley perhaps sums up the legend of the Raspberries the best: "It's not stuff like the suits, the hair, the hype, all that kind of crap. That stuff goes away, and the only thing left is the music. That's what people listen to and that's what you're remembered by. So I would tell any musician today that the most important thing is the music."

On July 18, 1998, that statement was confirmed when Wally Bryson, Dave Smalley, Jim Bonfanti, and Scott McCarl came together again on the Odeon stage to promote McCarl's new CD. But it was Jane Scott who brought the original Raspberries out of retirement. At her eightieth birthday party, held May 6, 1999, at the Odeon, Eric Carmen and Wally Bryson shared a stage for the first time in more than twenty years. It was worth the wait.

The Michael Stanley Band (1974–87)

We are the most successful unsuccessful band in America. But it was our hometown fans that always kept us going.

—Michael Stanley

If Michael Stanley is "Cleveland's favorite son," he's also the country's most elusive rock runaway. The Rocky River native may not have reached the rock and roll dreams of his youth, but he's done one better. Through three decades of making music, Michael Stanley has managed to escape the internal excesses, endure the trials and tribulations, ditch the bitterness, and have "one helluva time."

Partial credit is due to the musician's sense of humor. For example, while working on the ninth Michael Stanley Band (MSB) album (all eight previous ones were number one hits locally but missed nationally), Stanley entertained thoughts of calling it *We've Never Heard of You Either,* a reference to their decade of national anonymity. He settled for *You Can't Fight Fashion.* And after a massive heart attack in 1991, the singer/songwriter/ guitarist said it was almost a welcome change to hear people ask, "How are you feeling?" instead of, "Why didn't the Michael Stanley Band hit nationally?"

That question is as enduring as the band itself. But you'll not find the answer in their music. The solo efforts on MCA, the three albums on Epic, the two on Arista, and the four on EMI will only confuse the listener more. And the numbers won't tell either. The group had a Top 20 *Billboard* hit ("He Can't Love You"), a Top 30 ("My Town"), and one Top 40 ("Lover"). And contrary to popular belief, it's not entirely true that the band is unknown outside its hometown. In St. Louis and San Francisco and in parts of Colorado, Florida, Texas, and New York, those MSB classics ring a bell, even if the group name doesn't.

It is widely agreed that this band had every quality necessary for rock and roll superstardom. Yet its popularity has remained largely where it began. But, as the frontman himself will tell you, that's not been such a bad thing.

"When I started in this business, all I was hoping for was a chance to play music and maybe make a record I could actually hold in my hands," Stanley says. "I didn't even care at the time if I heard it on the radio or even if anyone bought it. I wanted to be able to hold something that I created. 'Course, as things went along, those sights were raised. . . . But I have no regrets. The Michael Stanley Band was a great band with great musicians, and considering 99 percent of those in this business don't make it past the bar scene, I'd say we did okay."

Some would say they did better than that. The group has sold hundreds of thousands of records, was the first local band to headline the 20,000-seat Richfield Coliseum, has sold out every regional venue it has played, and, more than a decade after disbanding, retains a devoted fan base. Stanley still can't walk down any street in the Cleveland area without someone excitedly waving hello. After all the career stresses, the disappointments, and the shattered dreams, this consummate musician has the last laugh—a perfect example that the journey itself is often more meaningful than reaching the destination.

The journey of Michael Stanley and his beloved North Coast band reflects every note on the rock music scale—every high, every low. It is not, however, the tale of yet another rock band failing to "make it big." Rather, it is a story of a group of talented musicians who have given their hearts (but not their souls) to millions of people.

Like most aspiring rock musicians, Michael Stanley Gee was heavily influenced by the Beatles and the Rolling Stones. But his initial introduction to the music came through *their* influences—Chuck Berry and Buddy Holly. "I remember we were on our way to Florida for a family vacation when I heard 'That'll Be the Day' on the car radio," he recalls. "I just thought, now this is music! It was a pivotal point in my life. After that I got into Elvis and the Everly Brothers. 'Course, this was pre-Beatles. Once they hit, well, that was it for me."

He was fourteen when he got an acoustic twelve-string guitar "after seeing some guy on *Hootenanny* with one." Formal guitar lessons were promptly dropped, however, after a few months. "The teacher got absolutely livid when I asked him to teach me the main Chuck Berry riff. To him, that wasn't music. Go figure." The teenager taught himself instead. And like most beginning rockers, he formed a garage band in high school. First the Sceptres, then the Tree Stumps. After getting a favorable gig on the Sunday-night roster at the prestigious Otto's Grotto, the Tree Stumps caught the attention of Bill Szymczyk, A&R man at ABC Records and future Eagles producer. "He was there visiting with his old college roommate, Dick Korn. I don't think he was there on business, just to have a good time. But the more buzzed he got, the better we sounded," Stanley recalls, laughing. "By the end of the night, he thought we were the best band in the world!" Changing their name to Silk, the band recorded "Smooth as Raw Silk" on the ABC label at the Hit Factory in New York City. Then Silk broke up.

Turning down an offer to replace Tom Kriss in the James Gang, Stanley decided to pursue a degree at Hiram College while contemplating his future. He graduated with a BA in sociology and comparative religion in 1970. But music never took a back seat. While working as a manager at Disc Records, Stanley recorded two solo albums, one self-titled (with the single "Rosewood Bitters"), the other called *Friends and Legends* (with "Let's Get the Show on the Road"), both produced by Bill Szymczyk. The former LP included the talents of Joe Walsh (lead guitar/vocals) and Todd Rundgren (clavinet). The latter was recorded in Colorado with Walsh, Joe Vitale on drums, David Sanborn on alto sax, Kenny Passarelli on bass, and Dan Fogelberg and Richie Furay on vocals. "That was such a cool experience," he says. "I'll never forget how shocked I was when Walsh simply picked up the phone and called Dan and Richie, who lived nearby, to be on the album because we needed more vocalists. I'd been a fan of Richie's from his Buffalo Springfield days. And here he was going to be on my album. That was great."

The LP was part of a three-album release by MCA. As luck would have it, the other two were Elton John's *Goodbye Yellow Brick Road* and the Who's *Quadrophenia*. The Cleveland guy didn't stand a chance. "The salespeople never worked it because they weren't on a commission basis and got paid either way. So there wasn't a lot of incentive to promote it. They were busy enough with the other two," he says of the record company.

His solo efforts did well enough, but soon Stanley was ready for the camaraderie of a band. That same year he got together with songwriter/guitarist Jonah (né Gary) Koslen and bassist Dan Pecchio in an attempt to form an acoustic band. "We had first met through [then-manager] David Spero, who wanted me and Jonah to play with Michael on *Don Kirshner's Rock Concert*," recalls Pecchio, who had just come off a five-year stint with the acclaimed Glass Harp. "The three of us played together at Michael's house and it worked well. But Jonah and I wanted to get a drummer right away, and Michael wanted to stay acoustic."

Although they did not do the TV show together (Michael played with Walsh and bassist Passarelli) the trio toured briefly, opening for such acts as Richie Havens, King Crimson, the Eagles, and the Nitty Gritty Dirt Band. The tour complete, it was finally agreed that they needed a good drummer.

"For a long time, I wasn't sure I wanted to commit myself to a full band," Stanley says. "I mean, once you get a drummer you gotta get a truck and become a real working band. But they finally browbeat me into it. So one night we went to the Agora to hear Circus's drummer, Tommy Dobeck, because we'd heard a lot about him. Well, he'd just had an operation on his left wrist, and it was in a cast. So we thought, 'well, forget that.' But after hearing him play about four songs, we were really impressed. They were doing these Allman Brothers tunes that wasn't [*sic*] exactly easy on a drummer. We said, 'if this guy's this amazing with his hand bandaged up, he's got to be dynamite with it [the bandage] off!'"

Dobeck was in. But it took a little convincing on Dobeck's part, as he recalls.

One of the reasons I was playing like a wildman that night was it'd been two weeks since I'd played, so it felt great to be back. Plus I was on Percodan for the wrist pain, so I didn't really feel anything. I was havin' a good time. I saw Michael, Pecchio, and David Spero there but didn't know they were there to check me out. I remember doing "Mustang Sally" and Michael came up and sang, but he kept staring at me all night. So when you've got that attention, you tend to give people a real show.

But when they asked me to join them, I wasn't sure. But all these people kept saying, "Are you crazy? This is a once-in-a-lifetime opportunity. Look at the people he's involved with—Joe Walsh, record producer Bill Szymczyk, and Barnstorm drummer Joe Vitale." And Michael kept after me until I said okay.

The first of what would be hundreds of concerts in thirteen years was held at the Cleveland Agora on September 2, 1974. From that moment on, North Coast rock fans would never be the same.

The first incarnation of the Michael Stanley Band landed a recording contract with Epic. The quartet pumped out two LPs back to back: *You Break It, You Bought It* (with "Gypsy Eyes") in 1975 and *Ladies' Choice* ("Strike up the Band") in 1976. The band was on the road ten months out of the year, opening throughout the country for top acts including Joe Cocker, the Doobie Brothers, the Eagles, Bruce Springsteen, and Kenny Loggins. In turn, musicians of this caliber were opening for MSB on the North Coast, such as Billy Joel (who opened for them at the Akron Civic Theater), Cheap Trick, and John Cougar (who opened for them at the Richfield Coliseum).

"Probably the best time ever was when we were recording with Bill [Szymczyk]," Pecchio says. "He's such a talented guy who really believed in us and put his money into us. He was absolutely convinced we were going to be the next Eagles."

The album which was expected to break the group nationally was *Stagepass,* a live, double LP recorded at the Agora. The group had a studio album already planned, but the record company had other ideas. "We already had songs ready for a new album when Epic was threatening to drop us," Stanley recalls. "So I talked to Steve [Popovich, then head of A&R] and said, 'Come and see us play live and maybe you'll change your mind.' We were playing at the Youngstown Agora, and he loved us. So afterward we all went to the International House of Pancakes, and he suggested we do a live album to capture the energy and excitement he felt was best heard during our live performances." The twelve-song *Stagepass* was a favorable mix of old and new compositions, including two songs that would become MSB classics: "Midwest Midnight" (penned by Stanley) and Jonah Koslen's "Nothing's Gonna Change My Mind."

Although this critically successful album brought added attention and new fans in the heartland (selling in excess of 300,000 copies), it failed to capture the rest of America. "All we need now is a good hit single," Stanley told one reporter. And while fans, and the musicians themselves, might argue that there had already been several that should have "made it," the group ultimately lost its Epic contract.

Not to be deterred, the quintet (now with keyboardist/vocalist Bob Pelander) sent a three-song demo tape to Arista, who signed them. So in 1978, the band had a new label; a new manager, Mike Belkin; and a new guitarist, Youngstown native Gary Markasky, who replaced Koslen when he left to form Breathless. That same year, MSB released *Cabin Fever.*

"At first I thought we'd lost a lot with Jonah's absence," Stanley says. "He was such a good musician and great writer. That was a tough period, recording-wise. We spent over two months in this rusticlike studio in Wales with a new producer [Robert John "Mutt" Lange, who lived in Britain] and new members. To top it off, Bob temporarily lost his voice for some reason that's still a mystery, so I was forced to sing more than I had previously. But by some miracle, it turned out to be a good album. And Bob turned out to be a good songwriter." The Stanley/Pelander ballad "Why Should Love Be This Way" was the most promising album cut and a fan favorite. But still, not much happened to shake the industry.

Same thing with album number five. Like the others, *Greatest Hints* (1979) had promise. "That was my wall-of-everything period," Stanley says. "It was 'Michael Stanley Pretends he's Phil Spector,' where I had this musical attitude that involved a lot layering of different bells and things. Bob calls it the 'bells from hell' album. There was a lot of

The Michael Stanley Band, 1975. *Left to right:* Dan Pecchio, Michael Stanley, Jonah Koslen, and Tommy Dobeck (hidden) on drums. *Photo by Michael N. Marks. David Spero Collection.*

chiming and clanging and jangling. Still, I like the album, even today. But after it was complete, Clive Davis [president of Arista Records] hated it and said he wouldn't promote it, even though he had picked out all the songs and the producer."

Despite strong, upbeat tunes like "Promises" and "Last Night," and the harmony-driven "We're Not Strangers Anymore," the album, with little promotion, failed to garner that one hit single. "Plus, I think the title worked against us. We were using a play on words, but people thought it was a greatest hits album."

Meanwhile, with its catchy songs and melodic ballads, MSB was enjoying success on the North Coast. Everywhere the group performed, it broke attendance records. But with no Top 40 hit from either of the last two albums, Arista informed the band it was dropping them—ironically, on the very night it set an attendance record at the Richfield Coliseum. For the first time since the band's inception, the thirty-one-year-old musician entertained thoughts of giving up. "Without a label behind you, it's nearly impossible to tour," he says. "And without touring, you're not getting the needed exposure."

In the end, it was Dan Pecchio who packed it in. "Michael and I had been disagreeing a lot on some key issues," says Pecchio, who went on to pursue race-car driving. "One was that he always believed the record company should pick the single. I strongly felt it should be our decision. But all that aside, Michael and I really liked and respected one another. He once told me if he ever crashed in a plane and [was] left on an island with one other survivor, he'd want me there because he knew somehow we'd get out of the situation, probably because we do think differently. It is the highest compliment anyone ever paid me."

With Pecchio out, the group searched until they found bassist Michael Gismondi to replace him. They also added another keyboardist, Kevin Raleigh. With members Pelander and Dobeck, this lineup would remain stable (with the exception of Markasky, who departed in 1983 and was replaced by guitarist Danny Powers) until the band's break-up in 1987.

Energized by the new blood and creativity, it seemed, finally, that MSB was on a roll. The re-formed group kicked off with a new major label, EMI, and churned out an album members felt was more commercial friendly. Immediately, the *Heartland* LP got heavy radio airplay (especially on WMMS, a station that from the beginning was the band's greatest advocate), and, once again, "we toured our asses off." At the same time, technology seemed to be working for them as well—in the form of Music Television. "We were one of the first bands to play on MTV," Stanley says. "We got a lot of video play for while, because at first there weren't so many bands competing for it."

This time the group, as well as the fans, thought their time had finally come. *Heartland* boasted some of the group's best work. With songs like "Lover" (with Clarence Clemons on sax) and the national hit "He Can't Love You" (written by Raleigh), surely the rest of the nation would fall in love with the group just as thousands of North Coasters had. When it failed to happen again, everyone—from the local media to the fans to the band members themselves—was speculating as to what went wrong. Even Kid Leo admitted he hadn't a clue as to why the rest of the world "didn't learn what we knew," but he theorized that it may have had something to do with the fact that MSB's creative peak ran parallel to Cleveland's poor national image, musical and otherwise. Nonetheless, they continued on with three more releases: *North Coast* (1981), *MSB* (1982), and *You Can't Fight Fashion* (1983).

But in its hometown, the Michael Stanley Band was as big as the Rolling Stones. The group continually sold out the Coliseum, and there were annual summer sell-outs at the 18,700-seat Blossom Music Center and consecutively packed houses at the 3,200-seat Front Row Theater. Yet despite MSB's touring of the Midwest, the vigorous exposure, and the undeniable good songs, the rest of the world remained in the dark.

"We were the most down-to-earth band in the world," says Dobeck. "Probably because although we'd play in Cleveland to a crowd of thousands, we'd go on the road and play to only about 400–600 people. And to Michael's credit, he never let us slack off. I'll admit there were times I was tempted to just go through the motions because I'd be tired and part of me would say, 'Well, this is just a small audience.' But Michael wouldn't hear of it. He always insisted we give it our best no matter what type show we played. Michael was really the leader in that."

In 1984, MSB made two independent releases, *Inside Moves* and *Fourth and Ten* (recorded live at Blossom). Still, hometown fans were the biggest buyers. By 1986, the answer as to why "it" never happened didn't seem to matter anymore. When the group was dropped by EMI, Michael Stanley felt ready to move on. After nearly two decades of being just one hit away from national stardom, it was time to say goodbye.

"It was like getting a divorce," Stanley admits. "I was the one that made the decision, but the day I called a meeting to make it official was the hardest thing I'd ever done in my life. Particularly because we weren't breaking up 'cause we hated each other or couldn't make music anymore. We all got along and worked so well together. But I had fifteen people on the weekly payroll, supporting fifteen families. It was getting just too hard to stay afloat. But making it final. That was terrible. It broke my heart."

But in true MSB style, the group went out with a rock and roll memory not to be forgotten. "To everyone's credit," the leader notes, "it was like, 'we've got to make the last shows the best, not just go through the motions.' We'd leave our fans with a great memory of the band. And at first we were going to do just a couple of shows at the Front Row. But then they sold out so fast, we added a few more, then a few more, until we ended up with twelve straight shows. It was almost like having a regular job. You got up, went to the Front Row . . . it was incredible." Indeed it was. The shows were a hit not only with fans but also with critics. Jane Scott called her experience "one of the most heartfelt concerts I've ever seen." Anastasia Pantsios applauded the group for its diversity and showmanship.

Within weeks, Michael Stanley became a local TV star and radio host. From 1987 to 1991 he was co-host for the former magazine-style television show *PM Magazine*, on WJW Channel 8. He also hosted a weekend show on WMMS until leaving to become the afternoon-drive deejay on WNCX in 1992, where he is today.

And the music is still in him. In 1994, Stanley formed the Ghost Poets, which reunited him with Koslen and Pelander and brought in the vocal talents of Jennifer Lee.

That band produced a CD but then broke up two years later. Michael Stanley keeps playing on and returns each year to perform with old and new members, most often for summer concerts at Nautica in the Flats and New Year's Eve at the Odeon. There have been four Michael Stanley releases since MSB officially disbanded: *Right Back at Ya* (1991), a greatest hits CD celebrating the band's rich musical history, was followed six years later by *Misery Loves Company* (a greatest hits part two), both on the Razor and Tie label. In 1996, Stanley released *Coming Up for Air,* his first solo effort since his pre-MSB days. In 1998, his two-CD set, *Live in Tangiers,* was released. The CD includes many favorite Stanley hits, acoustic-style.

For any fan who lived on the North Coast during the era of the Michael Stanley Band, there's a memory that merges a song with a personal event—a "soundtrack" of our lives. From "Rosewood Bitters" and "He Can't Love You" to "My Town," every fan has fallen in love, made love, lost love, or remembers a love to an MSB tune.

That's what a musical legacy is made of.

We're an American Band

While other promising bands on the North Coast never quite reached the stature of a Raspberries or MSB, many came close. And the array of talented musicians in this decade each served to provide entertainment and abundant good times throughout the area.

Circus (1970–74)

In March 1971, a Cleveland-based group won a Battle of the Bands contest sponsored by the May Company department store and *Upbeat* producers Herman Spero and Walt Masky. It wasn't a surprising win. The group—with Phil Alexander (lead singer), Mickey Sabol (rhythm guitar), Tommy Dobeck (drums), Dan Hrdlicka (lead guitar), and Frank Salle (bass)—was already making a name for itself through contemporary cover songs, as well as originals that sounded just as modern.

Tommy Dobeck, better known later as the drummer for the Michael Stanley Band, recalls how Circus, his first group, was formed. "I'd already known Phil Alexander, who was in a band in Solon, and I was a roadie for him," he recalls. "And Frank Salle and I lived in the same neighborhood around Shaker Square. Then a friend of ours introduced us to Dan Hrdlicka and Mick Sabol, who lived around Fleet Avenue. We decided to get a band together, and as I recall, Phil stole the name from another band that had just broken up." Dobeck was influenced early in his career by drummers Ansley Dunbar (of Mothers of Invention), studio musician Steven Gad, and Bobby Colombi (Blood, Sweat and Tears).

(*Opposite*) Michael Stanley, "Cleveland's favorite son," in concert. *Photo by Janet Macoska.*

"I first wanted to play guitar, but I have very small hands. The guitar my parents bought me was an old acoustic type with steel strings, and no one told me to lower the

bridge on it, so I used to have these bleeding fingers. It was horrible. So I thought maybe drums would be more fun. Of course, you have to have very understanding parents to be a drummer. Still, as soon as I saw my father's car pull in from work, that was it, drums were over!" laughs Dobeck, who studied under well-known Parma Heights instructor Bob McKee and later at the Cleveland Institute of Music.

The prize for the Battle of the Bands contest was an RCA recording contract and $1,000. As an added bonus, the quintet secured Spero and Masky as managers. They went into the studio and recorded several songs, including "Stop, Wait, and Listen." The song (penned by Hrdlicka) not only played on regional radio stations but also was a personal favorite of New York's renowned deejay Murray the K, who played the song on his top-rated show. It peaked at No. 6 on local charts and at No. 85 on *Billboard*'s Top 100.

"The original five members, including myself, worked hard and long on our craft and our band for three years," Hrdlicka says. "Our popularity grew from a strong high school/college base. We played a mix of AM/FM hits from bands like the Rolling Stones, Grand Funk, CSN&Y, Spirit, etc. We worked our original music into the mix and were pleased when people liked it. We had great vocals, and a great frontman in Phil Alexander."

Circus became the Wednesday-night house band at the Agora in 1971 and, despite lineup changes, was a fixture there until the band's break up in 1974. Throughout its four years, the group was repeatedly voted Best Band, Best Male Vocalist, and Best Original Material in *Scene*'s reader's poll (in which nearly 10,000 readers participated).

In October 1973, their self-titled LP was released on Metromedia, the same company that owned radio station WMMS at the time. Besides "Stop, Wait, and Listen," another original tune, "Feel So Right," received local airplay. By then, the band's make-up began to change, with the exit of Hrdlicka (who joined Magic, later the Eric Carmen Band). He was replaced with well-known area guitarists Bruce and Craig Balzer, formerly of December's Children and Ambleside. And so the group's identity changed as well.

"We wanted to be more musically involved," says Craig Balzer. "So we brought in songs by the Allman Brothers, Todd Rundgren, and Humble Pie." And Dobeck recalls,

That's when we started having to dress up. The Balzers was really into a serious "image" thing on stage. They were adamant about us wearing satin suits and these red platform leather shoes. Me, I was a t-shirt, jeans, and tennis shoes kinda guy. And every night we were donned in all this satin, and I was wearing these red platform ruby slippers. It was so not me! And the really weird part about that was we were doing about 70 percent Allman Brothers tunes. So here's this glitter-looking band playing songs by the Allman Brothers, who had waist-long hair, cowboy hats, and boots. Now what's wrong with this picture? So it was around this time Michael Stanley was pushing me into joining his band, and every time I had to wear those clothes, I started thinking, gee, Michael said if I joined his band, I could wear anything I pleased. It started sounding better and better.

Shortly after Dobeck left, the Balzers were next to go. "Towards the end, there were a lot of problems," Bruce Balzer recalls. "It kind of got ugly with management, and we got disenchanted with the whole thing. One of the last things we recorded in Circus was our own version of the Dusty Springfield cover 'I Only Wanna Be with You.' We sent it to New York, and Capitol producer Jimmy Ienner heard it and thought it was a good idea. So he gave it to the band he was working with at the time—the Bay City Rollers!"

In an attempt to keep the band going, Circus singer and ringleader Alexander hired lead guitarist Al Globekar to replace the Balzers and bassist Norm Isaac in place of Salle. A series of drummers followed, but none matched the style of the original. By late 1974, Alexander called it quits.

Locally they are well remembered—not only by those old Agora fans but also by the radio listeners who continue to request "Stop, Wait, and Listen" on a regular basis.

Rastus (1969–73)

"Rastus was more popular outside of Cleveland because we actually started playing in Chicago at a place called Rush Up," recalls Mike Geraci. "It was a real popular place where acts like Chicago, Chaka Khan, and Ike and Tina Turner played."

At times the nine-piece band Rastus was best known for its distinctive "sax vibrations," executed by former Bocky and the Visions sax players Geraci (tenor sax) and Vic Walkuski. Initially, this group consisted of other Bocky alumni, including Bocky himself, drummer David "Smokey" Smelko, guitarist Tony Corrao, and bassist Don Nagy. Bocky soon left and was replaced by Mark Roman (vocals/trombone), then Danny Magalen (vocals/baritone sax) and Johnny Taylor (trombone). The well-orchestrated group was often compared to the brass blues/jazz sounds of Blood, Sweat and Tears and Chicago.

"It was more a 'listening band' than a dance band," notes Geraci, whose brother Sonny was lead singer in the '60s hit group the Outsiders. "We did mostly originals and were more a concert-type band. No one danced; they sat on the floor and listened. At home, we played a lot at Tom Jones Backroom in the Flats, the Plato, and some Kent clubs like the Dome. We also did a concert at the WHK Auditorium. But mostly we traveled the country. We were the first group in the city to have our own bus, trucks, roadies, and our own PA system. Then we acquired a producer from Detroit, John Rhys, who helped us put together an album of originals."

Rastus's self-titled double album gave the group added exposure (with the help of "Rastus" billboards appearing in cities across the country) and helped sell out venues in and outside their hometown.

"Soon as the album came out, it got a lot of airplay," Geraci recalls. "It made the Top 10 list in both Indianapolis and Chicago." Walkuski adds, "I don't recall the numbers, but we got on WIXY Billboard Chart, *Record World,* and had a nice write-up in

Billboard magazine. Then we made a second album, *Steam'n'* [1971], but soon as it came out, the record company went through some changes and put our album on the back burner. That killed us."

The group promoted the album all the way to Los Angeles, where, for a time, they were the house band at the famed Whisky A Go Go. They also played often at the L.A. Forum. "That was memorable because we got to open for Sly and the Family Stone and Tower of Power, which were groups we particularly liked," Geraci says.

When Carrao left, he was replaced with George Sopuch, who, toward the end, was replaced by Geraci's family friend, Joey San Filippo (a.k.a. Butch Armstrong). The group disbanded in 1973. The frequent question at the time was why this popular group would break up. Walkuski explains,

> With ten guys in the band, we became split. We had an option to be a Vegas band, but half of the group had families so they needed money but didn't want to travel. The others said screw the money, we just want to keep on rockin' and rollin.' When it came down to deciding, there was a fifty-fifty tie. It was nobody's fault.
>
> It's a shame we didn't get the success I think we should have. We were ahead of our time as far as the horns and playing very aggressive. We felt the music. But we didn't have the money behind us. We were street boys trying to get things happening, and there was no one to back us up. It all contributed to the fall.

Today Geraci continues to play in various venues. In the summer of 1998, he released a two-song CD, *Saxappeal.* Armstrong is currently in Armstrong Bearcat Band.

Walkuski built a recording studio in his home where he works on original material, such as gospel recordings. He currently plays in Nightbridge, a band on the "tuxedo circuit" (country clubs and executive nightclubs). He then switches gears and plays in blues bands at "biker bars."

Tiny Alice (1969–73)

"The Grateful Dead of Cleveland"

—Jim Girard, *Scene*

Talk about eclectic, this group was in a class of its own. Starting out as a jug band, its repertoire was a musical melange of original compositions and rock, jazz, country, blues, and folk covers. The group used nearly every instrument available, including horns, violins, metal washboard, blues harmonica, flutes, kazoo, piccolo, percussion, electric harp, trombone, guitars, drums—and humor. (One song on the self-titled album was "I Lost My Heart on the Stock Market of Love.")

"Originally, the lead singer was a small blonde girl named Alice Popovich, who looked like Alice in Wonderland, and that's how we got the name," recalls bass player and keyboardist Tom Marotta, now a Cleveland attorney who gigs on weekends in the band Indiscretions along with another Alice alumnus, David Krauses.

Although the band went through several membership changes in its time, the most-remembered lineup included Peggy Cella (vocals, acoustic guitar), George Woideck (guitar, vocals), Krauss (harmonica, electric autoharp, vocals), Norman Tischler (sax, trombone, flute), Danny Mazza (drums), and Marotta (keyboards and bass).

"We were quite politically motivated," Marotta says. "We did some antiwar songs, but it wasn't like lectures; we were too good-timey for that. Most of the material was fairly tongue-in-cheek, more along the lines of Country Joe. And we played a lot of benefits. I remember this one event for some cause or another, in Oberlin, where there were two rival factions of socialists and they started getting into it, with one guy trying to knock out the other by grabbing Norman's saxophone! But mostly, it was just a good time playing at local bars like the Viking, the Smiling Dog, and the Kent clubs." The band shared the same manager, Ed Goodgold, as the nationally known Sha Na Na, and thus frequently toured with the popular '70s group.

In 1971, Tiny Alice got its first (and ultimately final) recording contract with Kama Sutra (the Lovin' Spoonful's label) and recorded a self-titled album of mostly originals. Holding true to their eclectic mix, songs ranged from jazz to country to rock and blues. The LP was produced by WNCR disc jockey Martin Perlich. With the album's release, the band went on tour, which included a play date at New York's famous club the Bitter End.

But consistency was a problem for the band—with members as well as with music. "Over time, the band became increasingly electric, and members changed frequently, if not weekly," says Marotta.

Tiny Alice in 1972. *Front, left to right:* George Woideck, Norman Tischler, and Randy Benson. *Back, left to right:* Peggy Cella, David Krauss, Tom Marotta, and Dan Mazza. *Courtesy of George Woideck.*

So our sound inevitably changed. A common joke at the time was that when the band decided to become electric, we traded our metal washboard in for a Maytag. Towards the end, Peggy left, replaced by Betsy Marshall, then George left, replaced by Alan Echler, who in turn was replaced by Tom Luticia [jazz guitarist].

It's ironic. We were capable of doing so much because of the instrumentation, yet I think that's precisely what did us in. One minute we did straight out country-western, the next, kinda schlocky nightclub jazz. Each member came from such a diverse background—like, Norm grew up playing in bands in the Catskills. Randy [Benson, a later member] was a classical violinist.

By the end of 1972, the group lost its recording contract, and members agreed to go their own ways. "I think," Marotta concludes, "that with all the differences and the extensive touring, we just succumbed to that classic case of rock and roll burnout."

Rainbow/Rainbow Canyon (1972–75)

Longtime drummer Buddy Maver (Bocky and the Visions, Richie and the Fortunes, Dick Whittington's Cats, Charades, Mushroom) headed up this band. Rainbow's original lineup featured names already familiar to Cleveland-area music fans: bassist Chester Florence (who played briefly with the O'Jays), guitarist Greg Grandillo (once with the James Gang and Fully Assembled), guitarist/singer and trumpet player Billy Hanna (formerly of Charade), and keyboard player Norm Cotone (from the first Pig Iron lineup).

"From our own separate experiences, we decided not to jump in and write and record originals before we got used to each other. That had proved a mistake in the past," Maver says. "So we had a plan. We were going to learn great cover tunes and put a show together. We ended up with a dynamic stage show. Almost immediately, we became the Sunday night house band at the Agora, after the Raspberries hit big. We always sold out and got encores every time we played there."

Ultimate Rainbow fan Carol Jo Palladino agrees. "The place was always packed when Rainbow played," she recalls. "They were so good, and everybody danced. It was an exciting time for all of us. I would follow them wherever they played. Didn't matter if they were in Cleveland or the Columbus or Toledo Agora. We were there. I felt it was important to support the local bands." (Palladino was so devoted to the group that she formed a Rainbow fan club, whose membership grew to two thousand within months. "We'd advertise in the local publications like *Scene*," she says. "For two dollars you got a newsletter, picture of the band, and a T-shirt. You couldn't go wrong!")

When it wasn't playing area gigs, the group was performing throughout the Midwest. In an offbeat move, Rainbow took a job in Roselawn, Indiana, that the band will never live down—as the Sunday afternoon musical entertainment at the Mr. and Mrs. Nude America pageant, held at a nudist colony. The band did, indeed, undress for the occasion.

"We thought that would be a fun publicity stunt," Maver recalls. "And it worked. We had a picture of us playing in the nude [safely covered by their instruments], and it was printed in publications across the country!" (Unfortunately, not all the band members would give permission to reprint the photo in this book.)

With the dynamic Belkin-Maduri Productions as their management, Rainbow began writing its own material and soon secured a deal on Capitol Records in 1973. The following year the band released *Rollin' in the Rockies,* an album produced by Jimmy Fox. They recorded in a state-of-the-art studio in the mountains of Nederland, Colorado. Caribou Ranch Sound Studios was owned by James William Guericio, manager and producer of the group Chicago, and it was often used by other artists, such as Joe

Rainbow Canyon in concert, 1973. *Left to right:* Billy Hanna, Greg Grandilllo, and Norm Cotone. Not pictured: Buddy Maver (drums) and Chet Florence (bass). *Photo by Carol Palladino. Courtesy of Buddy Maver.*

Walsh, Stephen Stills, Elton John, and Michael Stanley. That's when the group decided to change its name to Rainbow Canyon.

Though the album did well locally, it was a disappointment nationally. With the realization that Cleveland was perhaps not the best place to make it big in the music industry, Maver suggested they try L.A. "Some of the members didn't want to go," he says, "So Norm and I reformed the band with Jay Mohler [Charade], and Donny Baker [Case of E.T. Hooley]." However, the newly reformed group didn't stay together long enough to see if they could make it. A year after the move, they disbanded.

In January 1977, Maver became the new operations manager and partner at the Cleveland Agora. The position involved overseeing and coordinating the ever-growing Agora chains, media projects, and the Agency Recording Studio, located above the Cleveland club. By 1980, Maver was vice president and talent buyer for the Agora as well as manager of the national band, Artful Dodger. Two years later, Maver once again made L.A. his home. He got a job as talent buyer for the Country Club in the San Fernando Valley. There he worked with owner Chuck Landis, who, along with Lou Alder (who orchestrated the 1967 Monterey Pop Festival and produced artists like the Mamas and the Papas), owned the famous Roxy nightclub.

Today, Maver is a real estate investor. In 1996, he began the first of what would become an annual Rainbow reunion at his Chagrin Falls home. Originally only former members and roadies were invited (including Palladino, of course). But as word spread, so did the invitation list. The third reunion boasted a Who's Who of Cleveland-area musicians that totaled some two hundred guests. Usually held in September, it has become one of the most anticipated end-of-summer events on the North Coast.

Dragonwyck (1969–75)

Lead man Bill Pettijohn formed this popular bar band, named for the book by Anya Seton. Other members included guitarist Tommy Brame, bassists and vocalist Michael Gerchak, drummer Jack Boessneck, and keyboardist Kenneth Stabb. The band's music was often considered rather dark (pre-punk), with a heavy Black Sabbath influence; but Pettijohn claims that their main influences were the Moody Blues and the Doors. From the start, Dragonwyck drew crowds at the teen clubs like the Hullabaloos, at suburban venues such as Admiral Bimbo's (Westlake), or downtown at D'Poos Tool and Die (later Otto-Site). It also made a name for itself in more than just the local area, thanks to a *Circus* magazine write-up that touted Dragonwyck as a band to keep an eye on in the city that was becoming the "next Liverpool."

"That was my first serious band," says Pettijohn, a Lakewood native whose Jim Morrison stage act is known throughout the country. "We played a lot at D'Poos, which was the first rock club in the Flats. We also did original material from the start. It was a young band and we were rarin' to go. That first year we formed, we put out what we call our 'white album.' It was distributed to deejays, club owners, friends, and a few record companies, though none of them picked it up." That limited vinyl pressing (seventy-five copies) was recorded at Cleveland's Audio Recordings and Garfield Heights' Landon Magnetic Sound. Now a collector's item, it is rumored to be worth between $1,800–2,500. "And I don't even have a copy of my own! My ex-girlfriend and her sister have my last ones."

The lineup changed when Stabb (now deceased) left the group in 1971 and keyboardist John Hall took his place. "That's when we really started becoming well known," Pettijohn says. "The first two sets we'd do mostly Moody Blues, including one whole side of *Days of Future Passed,* which would just blow people away. And John was so great. He had this Farfisa organ with an echo chamber and would make it sound like a mellotron. We sounded like this rock orchestra. John was a master at that. The third set we'd do our originals, written by myself and Tommy Brame. Then the fourth, we'd do all Doors, which eventually led to [the Doors' cover band] Moonlight Drive."

Once their popularity grew, the band started opening for various groups that headlined the Agora, including Foghat and Dan Hicks and His Hot Licks. In March 1973, Dragonwyck opened for Edgar Winter at John Carroll University, and Pettijohn remembers partying backstage at the Columbus Agora with Gene Simmons of Kiss. "We were opening that night for Golden Earring, who had their hit, 'Radar Love.' Kiss was playing the next night but were there to check them out. So after the show all of us sat backstage together, partied, and had a great time. This was back in October 1974, and if I recall correctly, it was the first big tour for Kiss."

The group was also something of a house band at the Viking Saloon, the site of its first live performance. The club would later be destroyed in a fire, leaving Dragon-wyck to seek other musical homes. But, just as the band was getting national attention by way of the *Circus* article and one in *Rock* magazine (Summer 1975), the group called it quits.

"There were some group problems," Pettijohn says of the breakup. "But basically, I wanted to continue my acting classes, which I did. And thankfully that has paid off down the road." Pettijohn has acted in several movies and is currently involved with the Cleveland-based Guerrilla Productions.

Fayrewether (1974–94; 1997–)

What made this group stand out from the others was its decidedly alternative playlist and unique theatrical show. And though members took pride in their original material, they also realized a working band needed to play familiar cover tunes if they wanted to secure club dates. According to singer/founder Paul Fayrewether,

> We decided right from the start we weren't going to play the typical stuff like Humble Pie and Led Zeppelin. We opted for the more obscure, like Genesis, Alex Harvey, and the Tubes. And we did album-oriented rock, like Bowie and Elton John tunes you didn't often hear on the radio. Plus, I knew a lot of theatrical people in the Elyria area and was always intrigued by it. At age three, I was singing and perform-ing on the playgrounds. When I attended Duquesne University I sang and danced with the Duquesne Tamburitzans. I wanted to instill some theatrics into the band because not many were doing that back in the mid-'70s. So I'd have these friends of mine design wild costumes and props for our shows.

One such example was when the frontman wore a handmade silver TV set on his head for their song "Don't Let the Television Turn You On." He also made entrances dressed as a James Cagney–type character, with pin-striped suit and Panama hat, and with a black stocking mask for his version of the Alex Harvey song "Man in a Jar." He's played an eighty-six-year-old man on stage, a bat man with five-foot wings, a tough New Yorker, and a hunter (for Genesis songs "Musical Box," "Watchers of the Sky," "Back in NYC," and "Squonk," respectively) and a dreamer for the Pretty Things' song, "Joey." Fayrewether was the first theatrical rock band in the area. After touring throughout the northern half of the U.S. and into Canada, the quintet earned a dedi-cated following based on its likeness to the groups it emulated.

The band formed in 1974, but after playing their first gig at the 301 Club in La Grange, Ohio, they decided they weren't ready for prime-time taverns. "It took another year to get our act together," Fayrewether notes. "Then we started playing in clubs like Shillings, Stoney's in Elyria, and Big Dick's in Lorain, which was a really hot rock 'n' roll club." Things caught on quickly, and before 1975 was over, Fayrewether was a favorite

Paul Fayrewether singing "Don't Let the Television Turn You On." Fayre-weather was the first theatrical band in Cleveland. *Photo by Brian Chalmers.*

at the Agora. Along with the lead singer, who also played flute and sax, the original lineup included co-founder and drummer Michael Graves, Dennis Geib (keyboards), Steve Sanders (bass), and Jay Kaltenecker (guitar).

In 1976, the group recorded "Don't Count Me Out," written by Emery Kapple, who had been in a previous band with Paul Fayrewether and Michael Graves called the

Book of Strawberry. A former L.A. resident, Kapple was a prolific songwriter who had written songs for artists such as Long John Baldry and the Captain and Tennille. The record made it into the hands of WMMS deejay Jeff Kinzbach, who began playing it regularly. Two years later, the single was included on the LP *Fayrewether (Picture Disc),* released on their own Gangster Records label. The 1,500 copies sold out before the record was even made available in stores, giving it collector status today.

By 1981, Fayrewether decided to change management. "We were being labeled as a Genesis tribute band, which I hated. We wanted to stand on our own material." More changes occurred when Graves and Geib left and the group found keyboardist Steve Musichuk and drummer Vince Broncaccio (replaced by Kevin Hupp, then Rick Mc-Clain). Nine months later, Sanders, Musichuk, and Kaltenecker departed and were replaced by guitarist/songwriter Geoffrey Moore, bassist Gary Simmons, and keyboardist Jeff Hutton (who'd already made a name for himself when he toured with the Raspberries a few years before). Through the next decade, Fayrewether, with the help of Moore's writing talents, released four albums and three singles.

The first release was a single called "Everything's OK," written by Moore, with "Poltergeist," written by Fayrewether and Hutton, on the flipside. "The funny thing about that," the band leader recalls, "is the A-side was about the potentiality of nuclear war and how people were just blowin' it off. The B-side we titled 'Poltergeist' because it means ghostly noise in German, and that's how one can perceive rock 'n' roll. But exactly one week after its release, the movie came out, so of course people thought we were ripping off the movie. But the irony proved beneficial and we actually sold a few of those!"

The group thought they'd get national recognition when they were signed to the Miller Brewing Company Rock Network in 1984. "It was good and bad," the frontman says. "On one hand we were getting our name out there; on the other, we weren't getting any royalties from it. They released several compilation albums which we were on, and we'd go on stage and promote their product. So it did give us jobs and exposure.

"We traveled a lot, too. We played in cities like Chicago, where we had a huge following, and Syracuse, Buffalo, Toronto, Milwaukee, Minneapolis, St. Louis, Louisville, Indianapolis, and all points in between."

Although the group had loyal fans, members knew they weren't going to be "the next big thing," nor did they particularly aspire to be. "We basically wrote and played to please ourselves, not some record exec. I can recall many incidences when A&R people would come out and see us play but couldn't understand why no one was dancing. But we weren't that kind of band. Our fans understood and appreciated what we were doing, but the record companies just didn't get it."

The final Fayrewether release was *Rough Cuts,* a 1993 compilation of the band's live performances over the years. In 1994, the group disbanded, citing family priorities and the lure of "regular jobs." Club dates had become increasingly difficult to obtain. "Throughout the '80s a lot of clubs went under," Fayrewether explains. "It started right after the new drinking laws went into effect because most of the clubs' business came from young people, ages eighteen to twenty-one. That had a snowballing effect. There were now less places for bands to play. We had families to support, and most musicians can't afford [health] insurance. So reality started hitting us in the face, and we had to get stable jobs."

By late 1997, however, Fayrewether was back on the music scene. "One day in March '97, I met up with Michael Stanley, who said, 'So when are you playing your next date?' I said, 'I don't have any plans.' He said, 'Well, you should.' Next thing I know I'm talking to Mike Belkin Jr., and he suggests a gig at the Odeon. So I got a group of musicians together and we played that November, and got a great response."

The 1997 group included guitarist Mike Maciejewski, bassist Eroc Sosinski, keyboardist Paul Christensen, and former members Hutton and Broncaccio. The band now does an annual show every November at the Odeon. "I'd love to get back into the studio," Fayrewether admits. "I've been talking to a number of people about it. Now it's a matter of me making that move—and of course fan interest."

Slaughter/Raven Slaughter (Slaughter, 1973–76; Raven Slaughter, 1977–79, 1981–97)

Touted as one of Cleveland's first all-original bar bands, Slaughter's rapid fan development defied the trend of cover bands. Band leader Raven Slaughter, who was influenced by English group Mott the Hoople, explains:

> That happened because, at the time, my voice and guitar chops weren't good enough to do cover tunes like the other bands that were dominating the scene then. Since I couldn't do that, I was forced to do my own stuff, which was writing straight-ahead rock 'n' roll. As a matter of fact, it was Stiv Bators [later of the Dead Boys] who first told me I should sing my own songs. He had auditioned for the band and I told him his singing sucked, so he said, why don't you sing then?
>
> There was a bit of a surprise when this band that did their own material would pack the English Disco [later Jiggy Zarr's]. We had the shiny, glittery costumes and platforms. I had the raven black hair; all the other guys had dyed blonde hair. The guitars and amps were all white. I had a custom-made guitar in the form of an S for Slaughter. I'd gotten that idea after seeing Ian Hunter at the Allen Theater, and he had one in the form of an H. We were into the shock/glam rock basically because Top 40 was so boring.

The rest of Slaughter included Joe Haver (guitar), Eugene Reardon (drums), and Greg Vrabel (bass). Despite their fan appeal, most club owners were not receptive to the group.

> My whole thing was, I was in it for the show biz and to make money. It was a career for me. So when I was approached by Marty Thau of the New York Dolls, or

people like that, they couldn't do anything for me I wasn't already doing myself. I was booking our own shows along the East Coast and renting out small halls for teen clubs.

Then I got blackballed by most clubs because one management company would tell the owners, "Slaughter does only originals, no covers, and that'll kill your business." Then the union started getting on me, and I was actually getting death threats. I finally said screw music, and went to Florida.

Rocker Raven Slaughter on stage in 1974 at Jicky's English Disco. Note his signature s-shaped guitar leaning against the drums. *Photo by Bob Ferrell.*

The 1971 West Tech High School graduate took off to Daytona Beach in 1977. There he reformed his musical namesake, and then talked bandmates into legally changing their names. Members included Frank Parnello (bassist, a.k.a. Robyn Slaughter), Robb Wormer (drummer, a.k.a. Robb "Harpy" Slaughter), and Chris Cremona (guitar, a.k.a. Snake Rock Slaughter). "I'd already been know as Raven Slaughter around town," the guitarist says. "People used to see us perform and started calling me that 'ravin' maniac from Slaughter.' Then I had a song called, 'Ravin' Maniac for Your Love,' so people started calling me Raven. My parents had branded me with a name they thought I could live with. But Raven suited me more."

In Florida the group quickly earned a reputation with their showmanship and original tunes, which ranged from dance tunes to heavy rock and glam rock. Because their style had elements of punk rock's drive and energy, they were sometimes branded as such. But Slaughter fought the image. "We didn't hate anybody; therefore we didn't belong in that punk rock category," he says. "And I think the glam tag was also contradictory, because I wore my hair long as opposed to short and spiky à la Bowie."

The band returned to Cleveland in 1979, and Paul Michael replaced Snake (who had formed his own band) on guitar. By 1980, the lineup included Jeff Cuebas on drums (when Robb left to form the Adults with Paul Michael; see Chapter 15). Now a three-piece with Raven, Robyn, and Jeff, the band continued to play clubs in Cleveland until Raven left for the West Coast in 1984. In 1986, former members Robin Slaughter and Jeff Cuebas joined Raven in L.A., and the group began playing notable clubs such as the Whisky A Go Go and the Roxy.

Then a 1991 truck accident put Raven—and the band—out of commission. For the next four years, a recuperating Raven produced and submitted songs for other bands. He returned to Cleveland for the opening of the Rock Hall and decided to put the band back together—again. With Cuebas he did just that, but he phased it out by 1997.

Raven Slaughter then formed the Electric Ghoulardis with Cuebas in honor of Ernie "Ghoulardi" Anderson. One of the group's biggest fans is Ron "the Ghoul" Sweed, who has taken that persona to a new level. With the late TV icon's famous beard and various props, Sweed has revived his idol's memory with a local radio and TV career, much like that of the original. Guitarist Slaughter has since formed Raven Slaughter Guitar Whores, playing rock standards and, of course, original songs.

Love Affair (1976–84)

This band started out as Brick, with three ambitious West Side teens from Ford Junior High in Brook Park. Wes Coolbaugh and John Zdravecky played guitar and Wayne Cukras played bass. By the time the trio attended Berea High School, they'd found a willing drummer in Michal Hudak and changed their name to Skyport. Within months, the group changed its moniker again, to Stairway, and it now included Midpark High student Rich Spina as the singer/frontman. Stairway fast earned a teen following by playing weekends at clubs like the Chesterland Hullabaloo and Cyrus Erie West.

In November 1976, the band became Love Affair, and that's when things took off. In addition to their musicianship, the quintet had another thing going for them: an astute manager named Otto Neuber. Neuber was best known as owner/manager of Otto-Site, Otto's Backroom, and teen club the Mentor Hullabaloo (changed to Mentor Rock Shop). He managed local bands as well, including Jasper, Satellite, and, later, Sheffield Rush, Reign, and Champion.

"Everything I've been able to do in my career, I owe to my supportive parents and to Otto's direction," Spina says. "He had that old-fashioned work ethic, so he wouldn't give into your ego. He always made us work hard. Looking back, I see that's the most important thing to learn, and the earlier the better."

Neuber was also instrumental in getting the group jobs at all the popular venues in town, often five nights a week. The group's regular gigs were Wednesday nights at the Akron Agora, Thursday nights at Kent's Filthy McNasty's, and every Sunday at Cleveland's popular West Side club the Corral. "That was really our home base," Spina says of the Corral. "We played there steadily from 1976 to 1980." Love Affair is also remembered for its crowded shows at the Cleveland Agora.

With a nice mix of catchy cover songs (with a lot of Led Zeppelin) and originals (mostly penned by Spina), the group entertained its audience with a vast repertoire. "One of the first songs I wrote in ninth grade, 'Queen of the Lovers,' was later used in the band," Spina recalls. "Then Otto began writing with me, and I found we made a good team."

Indeed, with teamwork, the five-man band and their hands-on manager went to Florida to record their debut album. The 1980 self-titled LP was released on the independent label Radio Records and was produced by the band members and Peter Schekeryk, husband to singer Melanie ("Brand New Key"). The single "Mama Sez" charted on *Billboard*'s Top 100. It also got extended play on WMMS and several radio stations around the country. Spina says,

We had big success in Florida. In Little Rock, Arkansas, the album debuted on the charts the same time it did on 'MMS. We were also a big import in England. But what really blew my mind was when I was recently playing with Gary Lewis and the Playboys ["This Diamond Ring"] in this place in North Dakota. This woman came over to interview us and asked if we were ever in other bands. I said, "Yeah, a Cleveland band called Love Affair." She looked at me and she said, "Really? I have that record, 'Mama Sez' at home." And I went, "Wow, and I've never even played around here before!" I was really surprised.

Even though it didn't get more recognition, we're still happy with that first album. It seemed to have really captured the essence of what Love Affair was as a live band—a true power pop rock band.

The group made a second LP, *Doyawanna,* that met with a lukewarm reception from both its audience and its own band members. "That second album was produced by an A&R man for the label who thought we should be a more heavy-rock band," Spina explains. "Then there were people there who wanted us to be a lighter pop band. So there was no direction, and the whole album ended up in disarray." (Nonetheless, some twenty years later, both albums are in demand by fans.)

By 1983, the quintet (with Youngstown native and guitarist/keyboardist Jim Golan replacing Zdravecky) had decided to change its name once again for what became the final album. But the group, now called Unknown Stranger, became just that with its fans. The band members decided to return to Love Affair (with Mark Best replacing Wayne Cukras) but soon called it quits for good.

Today, Spina divides his time between active studio work (he contributed to and produced Sonny Geraci's latest CD, *On the Verge*) and serving as musical director for the re-formed Gary Lewis and the Playboys. Lewis (son of comedian Jerry Lewis) moved to the Cleveland area in 1980. The Playboys is now made up of all Clevelanders—keyboardist Spina, guitarist Billy Sullivan (formerly of Beau Coup), bassist Paul Sidoti, and former Love Affair drummer Michal Hudak.

Easy Street (1970–88)

With its longevity, Easy Street can boast nearly fifty members throughout its history. Its first lineup consisted of founder/vocalist/keyboardist "Westside Steve" Simmons, vocalist Gary Krizo, lead guitarist John Marsek, rhythm guitarist Robin Harris, bassist Robert Martin, and drummer Robert Wallace.

For eighteen straight years, Easy Street performed all over the North Coast, particularly at Akron's Flying Machine (formerly the Draft House), Kent's Filthy McNasty's, Cleveland's Spanky's, and the Painesville Agora. The group played every Thursday night at the Cleveland Agora from 1976–1982, making it the club's longest-running house band.

Steve Simmons's nickname, "Westside Steve," came about when the group was opening for one of Cleveland's favorite national bands, Southside Johnny and the Asbury Jukes. "The first time I met him, he came up and said, 'Hi, I'm Southside Johnny.' So I said, 'Hi, I'm Westside Steve,'" Simmons recalls. "We had a laugh about it, and the name stuck. But through the years, people always thought it meant the West Side of Cleveland. But since I lived in Akron at the time, it actually refers to the west side of Akron."

Aside from the Michael Stanley Band, whose popularity no other band could rival in Cleveland, Easy Street and Love Affair were the top two bands in the city throughout the late '70s and early '80s. Simmons notes that the competition was friendly.

Both bands played so often at the Agoras, each of us would take turns writing dirty stuff about the other on the dressing room walls. 'Course, that was before we knew each other. The first time we actually met them, they had just finished playing the Dallas Agora, and we were coming in for the next week. We sat around drinking together and had a ball talking about some of the comments we'd written about each other—and which ones were better!

One thing about the bands was we all got along great. During that time there were enough clubs in the area to support all the bands that were around, so we all were making good money and havin' fun. I suppose it would've been different had there only been one or two clubs, or one that had a band only one or two nights a week. That would have made for tight competition. Then we probably would have hated each other.

Among the numerous Easy Street members were "Diamond Jim" Madden (keyboards), Russ Hagler (guitar), Gary Bonham (guitar), Dave Buyers (guitar), Kevin Hupp (drums, later with Edgar Winter), Rich Van Natter (vocals), "Broadway Joe" Morris (bass), Robyn Slaughter (bass), Sammy Merendino (drums, later session drummer for Hall and Oates), Ron Gillard (drums), Donnie Thompson (drums, bass, and vocals), and Tommy Dobeck (former MSB drummer). The horn section included, at various times, Larry Kane (sax, formerly with Wild Cherry), Ricky Bell (former sax player with MSB), Norm Tischler (sax), and Big Jim Means (trumpet).

The group, whose vast repertoire included both original songs (mostly penned by Simmons) and covers of songs by the Rolling Stones, Bruce Springsteen, Southside Johnny, Tom Petty, and Motown bands, played to packed houses in the Tampa and Hallendale (Florida) Agoras, as well as those in Atlanta, Houston, and Dallas. They often traveled the "hotel circuit" in various parts of Canada, including Ottawa, Toronto, Sudbury, Cochran, and North Bay. Playing their popular covers mixed with originals, Easy Street was a hit in the Great White North. "We did a bunch of songs by a bunch of different guys," Simmons says. "During the band's heyday, we had a great horn section, so we were able to execute a number of various sounds."

Growing tired of doing other artists' material, Simmons began getting serious about his songwriting. In 1982, the band released its self-titled LP that included the Simmons/Madden–penned "Love Tries," which was added to the WMMS playlist and made it in the Top 25 record sales in Cleveland. "For one week there, we outsold Bruce Springsteen and Robert Plant," Simmons notes. "Now that was something in Cleveland." Yet by the time band members reached their forties, and as the '80s drew to a close, it became increasingly difficult to stay together. According to Simmons,

We were getting too old to care about current music anymore. But more than that, the club scene in Ohio had gotten really bad. The worst thing to happen was when they changed the drinking age, because it's the eighteen, nineteen, and twenty year olds who would frequent the clubs, drinking their 3.2 beer. They're the ones to want to go out to a club the most and see a band. They're the ones to faithfully follow a band wherever it was playing. When they killed that, they killed that whole scene. I think now would be a perfect time to resurrect those teen clubs like we had in the '60s so the young kids would have a decent place to go see a band. I think that's why there aren't a lot of young bands nowadays—because they have no place to play. And that's really sad.

It was also sad when this group decided to call it quits. "We were in Canada when I blew up the band," Simmons recalls. "I knew it was the last time around. The last lineup with Morris, Dobeck, Thompson, and Andy Hawkins sounded great. But there were too many factors against us."

Westside Steve has gone solo, often entertaining in Florida during the fall and winter. In spring and summer, fans can see him at Cleveland and Akron venues and at Ohio's Put-in-Bay resort. His wife, Kymberli Hagelberg, a former *Scene* writer, is a journalist for the *Akron Beacon Journal*. At home, Simmons spends much of his time producing his own material. "I've got a home studio and I write a lot," he says. "But I find people want to hear the familiar, so that's what I give them. And I'm perfectly happy doing that."

Wild Cherry (1970–79)

This group, which burst onto the scene with a No. 1 hit song its first time out, originated in Steubenville (ca. 140 miles southeast of Cleveland) but had a definite North Coast connection. The quartet was the first act to record on the Cleveland-based Sweet City Records, a label owned by record producer Carl Maduri and concert promoter Mike Belkin. It also played the area so often that it was considered a Cleveland band.

Wild Cherry is a perfect example of the adage "timing is everything," but also proof that the chances of getting a second hit are, despite obvious talent, a matter of circumstances. Anyone who listened to popular music in the 1970s—even those who are unfamiliar with the group itself—remembers their danceable R&B tune "Play That Funky Music (White Boy)." The song played incessantly in discos throughout the nation and is still heard on radio and TV wherever '70s nostalgia is the theme.

The first incarnation of Wild Cherry formed back in 1970, with founder/guitarist/vocalist Robert Parissi and several fellow high school students. The group played area venues before disbanding in 1974. "I remember when we first formed," Parissi says,

I was beating myself up trying to find a name and nothing sounded good. I was so frustrated. Finally, when I was in the hospital getting checked for ulcers and the guys were visiting, pestering me again to come up with a name, I happened to be holding a box of cough drops. Looking at the label, I said, "For all I care, you can call it Wild Cherry," and they went, "That's it!" And I said, "Oh, come on, no way."

Well, we had a job the next week, so we used the name. I was still not sold on it until the guys brought up these girls to the stage saying, "Wow, we really love that name," so that was good enough for me.

When that early formation dispersed, Parissi wasn't ready to call it quits. The following year, he rounded up a new band with musician friends Bryan Bassett (guitar), Allen Wentz (bass and synthesizer), and Ron Beitle (drums). And he kept the name. "I was excited about the new formation, and the fact that dance music was really making a comeback," he says. "You know, David Bowie was big and disco was just emerging. I wanted our band to capture songs with that danceable beat."

According to Wentz, Ron Beitle came up with the lyric "Play that funky music, white boy": "We were playing at this club and were between sets. When Bob heard Ron say that, he got all excited and started scribbling on a napkin. I think he wrote the entire song in that one sitting."

In 1976, Parissi met studio musician Marc Avsec through Carl Maduri, who suggested Wild Cherry add the talented keyboardist to the band. "Bob asked me to join just as 'Play That Funky Music' was coming out," recalls Avsec, who went on to play in Breathless and Donnie Iris and the Cruisers. "I knew it was a good opportunity because I felt the song had a big chance of making it big because of its beat, and dance music was so popular then."

The song did indeed make it big. In the summer of '76, the record hit No. 1 on the R&B charts in *Cashbox*, and No. 4 in both *Billboard* and *Record World*. The song became one of the biggest hits of 1976. With such hype, their adopted town of Cleveland even designated August 24, 1976, as "Wild Cherry Day," and they were given a proclamation by then-mayor Ralph Perk.

Throughout the history of rock, there have been few white artists who successfully crossed over to the soul arena. Scotland natives Average White Band topped that short list. So when Wild Cherry began emulating their soulfulness, it made perfect sense for the Ohio group to open for the Scots at the Coliseum in 1976. "They were a definite influence on us," Wentz says. "We ended up playing with them several times and toured with them twice. It was a good billing."

Despite the fact that Wild Cherry was considered an R&B group, most fans recall it as a "disco band." Its members understand the connection but cling to their R&B and rock roots. "Straight disco was that four-on-the-floor [drum beat] with the kick drum, and we weren't *that* extreme. We were kind of a mix," Avsec says. "I mean, we were right in there with KC and the Sunshine Band, the Isley Brothers, Average White Band, the Jacksons, Rufus—all of whom we toured with."

The year 1977 saw Wild Cherry performing its hit song on the Grammy Awards; that year the band received a Best New Artist nomination. It didn't win (Starland Vocal Band took that honor for their hit "Afternoon Delight"), but all agree that the experience was reward enough.

"It was probably the most exciting time in my career," says Avsec, now a Cleveland-based entertainment lawyer. "I was a Barbra Streisand freak, so I was looking all over for her 'cause this was the year of *A Star Is Born*. I saw her but, of course, never got a chance to say anything to her. But I did get to talk to Henry Mancini, which was a thrill."

Allen Wentz will also never forget that night. "It was a thrill for me personally to meet Ringo Starr, Les Paul, Paul Simon, Jim McQuinn, and Linda Ronstadt, who I particularly liked. But it's important to note that the two guys that really made it happen for us was Chris Maduri and Joey Porrello at Belkin Productions. They spent hours in one room, with one phone, promoting the hell out of that song. They, above anyone else, got it going."

When the group entered the studio for its second album, it found it had been locked into a mold. "I was ready to do a straight-out rock 'n' roll record," Parissi says. "But they wanted a Funky Music, Part 2. So naturally, all the albums after that couldn't measure up." "We were really a rock band," Wentz adds. "But that disco thing was getting bigger and bigger. So here we had this huge disco hit and got stuck there. In the end, it killed us. By the third album, I'd had enough."

Wild Cherry had such a loyal following, and their hit was so well known, that there were others who wanted to be them.

"I'll never forget one day in the summer of '97," Wentz recalls. "I was in a music store in New York and overheard a conversation about Wild Cherry. Here it's nearly twenty years later, and I'm listening to this sales rep telling people in there all about his 'days in Wild Cherry when I was the bass player.' I stood there not believing what I was hearing and biting my tongue not to say something. I didn't want to embarrass the guy. But if only he'd known the *real* bass player of Wild Cherry was right there listening to this! But it was really funny. I remember thinking how pathetic for this guy to have such a no-life he's pretending he was in a one-hit-wonder band!"

"What's particularly frustrating is I've seen some one-hit-wonder bands" he says, "and, yeah, they should've had just one hit. But we were really a good, tight band with talented players. We didn't get a chance to be all we could because we were locked into that mode. But we sure had a good time while it lasted. And you still hear our song everywhere you go, so there's some consolation in that."

Wentz, now a New York resident, took a hiatus from the music business when he opened a computer store. He recently returned to his first love and released a full-length CD on his independent label. Avsec went on to join Brethren.

Wild Horses (1974–89)

On May 24, 1974, Wild Horses kicked off what would be the first of more than 3,000 gigs. As their name suggests, the members of this quintet were rabid Rolling Stones fans whose set list was filled with much of the British band's material—except the actual song from which they took the name. No matter. Wild Horses developed a steady following after playing in local clubs, starting with Cellar Door (later Peabody's Café). The list of venues includes Monopolies in Lorain (owned by WMMS deejays Jeff Kinzbach and Ed "Flash" Ferenc), the Flipside (Mayfield Road), both the Cleveland and Akron Agoras, and downtown's Piccadilly, Round Table, Last Moving Picture Show, and the Pirate's Cove.

The group began with co-founder/vocalist/keyboardist Bill Buckholtz, co-founder/bassist Roger Kleinman, lead guitarist Andy Leeb (later replaced by Steve Jochum), rhythm guitarist Robbie Golbfarb, drummer Rick Sostaric (later replaced by Tony Mazzone), and Dennis Christopher (sax, percussion).

Buckholtz recalls those early days:

Dennis would always come by and see us play. He was quiet but definitely a fun guy. Our first gig was this club in Fort Wayne, Indiana, and Dennis volunteered to play the tambourine. He gets on stage, and before the end of the first song there's nothing left to it. He had gotten so excited, got so into it, that it was just in shreds. So I gave him these things called claves, which is basically indestructable pieces of wood, and by the end of the second song, they were completely splintered. By the third song I gave him a cow bell, and by the end of the night it was all dented. But I think partly because of Dennis, the kids went wild over us. From that day on, Dennis was our frontman. Then he started saying he was going to bring in a saxophone. The other guys would tell me, "Oh, don't let him do it." But I wanted a saxman in the group. But when he first brought it in he could barely eek out a note and didn't even know what a C-note was. It was the hardest thing I've done in my life, but I worked on him for months, and he became a great sax player.

Word got around, and Wild Horses began getting gigs at college towns as well as at Cleveland's best clubs. In 1980, Wild Horses became known as more than just another cover band. When Jochum joined the group, he introduced original songs to its repertoire. One tune, in particular, became an overnight success. The upbeat single "Funky Poodle" became Clevelanders' favorite song. Not since the Choir had a North Coast band sold so many records locally in such a short period of time. The popularity and airplay spread to radio stations from San Francisco to Boston, and the record ultimately sold more than 15,000 copies, despite the decline of record sales due to the sluggish economy. As its composer readily admits, it wasn't Bach, Tchaikovsky, or Beethoven. But the tune was catchy, and its reggae beat was fun to listen and dance to. The single was included on the band's debut album, *Unbroken*. The album did reasonably well, but it was that Funky song that kept the fans coming to sing along.

"Actually, 'Funky Poodle' was not indicative of what we did," Burkholtz says. "Our playlist was filled with tunes by the Stones, Allman Brothers, the Doors, Santana, Manfred Mann—classic rock before it was even called that. We played almost every night of the week and our style never changed. I think that's what kept people coming back night after night."

"Probably my favorite Cleveland band was Wild Horses," says Joe Cronauer of the disc jockey team Brian and Joe. "My senior year, 1981, I was student-government president, and we got Wild Horses for a concert at Normandy High School. I remember having to compete with the class before that who got Michael Stanley Band to play there. People were still talking about that. And in 1979 I attended a Breathless concert at another high school. So I was under a lot of pressure to bring in a really good local band. And Wild Horses fit the bill. They were great."

Two years later, Wild Horses was still riding high. It had been voted Best Band two years in a row in the WMMS/*Plain Dealer* Rock Poll. In 1983, the group released its second album, *Bar Wars*. The title derived from the superhit 1979 movie *Star Wars* as well as from the band's response to the ailing club scene due to the change in liquor laws.

The lineup altered a bit through its fifteen-year history, but the fans stayed loyal. The group became the Monday night house band at the Agora. Celebrating its tenth anniversary in June 1984, Wild Horses hosted a party at the Agora, attracting old and new fans. In honor of those long and numerous nights, the band displayed a "survival book" filled with pictures and various memorabilia of the band's decade-long existence. Included in the book was an essay by Kleinman that read in part:

> By all normal standards we shouldn't have lasted a month. Wild Horses does everything a band is not supposed to do. We played oldies when everyone was playing Top 40. We played originals when everyone was playing covers. We played covers when everyone was supposed to be playing originals. We rarely change our material when everyone *knows* your song list must be completely overhauled every three months. We've got the world's worst light show. No one dresses the same, looks the same, acts the same, talks the same, or wants the same things out of life.

Wild Horses. *Left to right: Bill Buckholtz, Steve Jochum, Rick Sostaric, Dennis Christopher, and Roger Kleinman. Photo by Anastasia Pantsios. Courtesy of Bill Buckholtz.*

Yet in spite of all this and maybe because of this, we survived—even prospered. Why? Because with all our problems, we knew how to touch the people who came to the bars and frat parties, or whatever, with our music.

Euclid Beach Band (1978–80)

The story of how this band emerged is one of the more unusual ones. It began as a result of a typical Cleveland conversation piece—the weather.

"Rich Reisling, at the time, was one of the delivery guys for *Scene,*" Jim Girard explains.

I was standing with Rich outside by the trucks one wintry day. He was looking around and suddenly said, "There's no surf in Cleveland." I said, "Ya know, that'd be a cool idea for a song." He said, "Yeah, that [line] is in one of Eric's [Carmen] songs. And actually I've been thinking about writing a song about that."

So he called Eric up and asked if he could use the phrase. He said fine, and Rich came up with the music and I came up with the words, like, in a day. Then we approached Hank LoConti to use his studio. Next we talked to the director of the Red Cross and told him we wanted to do this for charity, a "pro-Cleveland song" for their disaster relief fund, and of course they were thrilled.

But in order to record a song, they had to come up with a group name. "Because it was a take-off of the Beach Boys, we wanted a name similar but not too much so," Girard recalls. "But it had to have the word "beach" in it. We all used to go to Euclid Beach a lot, so we thought, 'Okay, we'll be the Euclid Beach Boys. But again it sounded too much like that other band. Finally we settled for Euclid Beach Band."

Guitarist Reising and backup vocalist Girard, both Beach Boys and Abba fans, envisioned the song having strong vocalization. They summoned friends John Hart and Pittsburgh native Pete Hewitt, whose voices were eerily close to the Beach Boys, and also included former MSB member Jonah Koslen. "About two-thirds into the recording, we started having trouble with certain sounds and things," Girard explains. "So Eric Carmen came in and helped us finish it. But it took ten months to complete."

The single "No Surf in Cleveland" was a surprise success, immediately receiving heavy radio airplay (particularly on WMMS) and selling 10,000 copies within weeks. "We treated the record [recorded on the "*Scene* label"] like a campaign," Girard says. "And because *Scene* had a T-shirt company called Scene Graphics, we had T-shirts and pennants made up. It cost [*Scene* publisher] Rich Kabat about $3,000, but he was behind us 100 percent. And in truth, the record would never have been made without him. He allowed me to do whatever I wanted within the confines of the paper. If it was cross-promoting something, he let us go for it."

The song became so popular, it forced the musicians to form a *real* working band, in order to perform outside the studio. Reising and Girard rounded up various long-

time musicians, including drummer Buddy Maver and Koslen, and the Euclid Beach Band went from a studio band to a live rock and roll band.

When former Columbia A&R man Steve Popovich heard the song and offered to release the single on his new label, Cleveland International Records, the novelty tune gained international attention. The band, with producer Eric Carmen, flew to New York to re-record it with session musicians (including David Sanborn on sax). Reising re-mixed it back in Cleveland.

"That's when things really took off," Girard says. "We did at least six TV shows and played the song on the beach for Channel 5. Walt Tiburski even played the record for his friend, Mike Love of the Beach Boys, and he loved it! The song did amazingly well in L.A., too. And because of the Beach Boy/Abba vocals, it was a big hit in Scandinavia. By then, Popovich wanted us to make an album, and this fun little thing started becoming a job!"

The group had another single, "I Need You," which reached No. 81 on *Billboard*'s Hot 100 singles chart on March 31, 1979. But by early 1980, what started out as a fluke became demanding, veering far from the individuals' goals. The group disbanded, but the tune continues to "shoot the curl" on local radio stations.

The Euclid Beach Band films a video along Lake Erie's shores to promote its 1978 release *There's No Surf in Cleveland*. Photo by Bob Ferrell.

Musicians and Bands—Kent

Glass Harp (1968–73)

> There were so many great groups in the area throughout the '70s that if they'd been from New York or Los Angeles, they would've made it—no doubt. A perfect example of that is Glass Harp. As far as I'm concerned, no group could touch them.
> —Hank LoConti

Probably no other band on the North Coast in the early 1970s was more destined for greatness than Glass Harp. Yet, as for thousands of others who came oh-so-close, life's circumstances got in the way.

Glass Harp was formed in 1968 by a promising young guitarist named Phil Keaggy, his schoolmate John Sferra (drums), and Steve Markulin (bass), all Youngstown natives. In 1969, bassist and Youngstown State University student Dan Pecchio replaced Markulin. And though Sferra and Pecchio would go on after the lead guitarist's departure in 1973, it is Keaggy whose presence in this band still reverberates nearly thirty years later. For it was his distinctive, skillful guitar riffs that set this power trio apart from other area bands and quickly produced a fan base of near cultlike proportions.

Glass Harp performs at an Edgewater Park concert on May 20, 1972. *Photo by Ellen Bowen. Courtesy of Dan Pecchio.*

"Anybody who ever heard Phil play knows he belongs in the Rock and Roll Hall of Fame alongside Clapton and Hendrix," Pecchio says with conviction. Quite a statement, but one few would dispute. Keaggy, who was seventeen when he founded the group, made good use of his unique talents in spite of an accident that occurred when he was four in which he lost part of the middle finger of his right hand. He never considered it a handicap. "I just learned to work around it," he has said, adding he often uses a pick. By plucking the string while pulling the volume with his pinky finger in one fluid motion, he produced a violinlike tone that became known as "the Keaggy sound."

With comparisons to '60s supergroups Traffic, Cream, and Kent's own James Gang, Glass Harp got its first gig at JB's in northeast Ohio's favorite college town. But the band attracted few listeners its first time out. "We basically played for the bartender," Pecchio recalls. That would soon change.

When house band the James Gang went on the road, Glass Harp (which got its name from Truman Capote's *The Grass Harp*) was chosen to take over the Wednesday-night spot. The group soon attracted not only college students but also rock music lovers from nearby Akron and Youngstown, as well as Clevelanders. But it was a Canton radio station's Appreciation Day at Chippewa Lake Park that got the band noticed and signed by Decca/MCA Records. By 1970, their debut release, *Glass Harp,* was out (recorded at the Jimi Hendrix's Electric Ladyland studio in Greenwich Village), and the trio was opening for Grand Funk Railroad at Public Hall and headlining local concerts, such as a rare and popular outdoor gathering at Lakewood's Edgewater Park.

"Then we went on tour playing places like Boston, Detroit's Grande Ballroom, New York's Central Park," Pecchio recalls. "We hit the West Coast as well, playing in Berkeley and Winterland in California." The trio was also among several notable acts to play the legendary Fillmore East during its final week of existence. "That was really special," says Pecchio. "We played with Alice Cooper, who we'd first played with at JB's. And we were on the last poster made for the club. It's a great poster that lists all the groups that played the Fillmore over the years. That's a real treasure."

Then there was that memorable November 1971 night at the prestigious Carnegie Hall when they opened for the Kinks. "We were all really excited about playing there, and more than a little nervous," Pecchio says. "But you know, once we got to playing, we were too busy getting into what we were doing to think about anything else. We were well received and got a standing ovation. It was an unforgettable time."

The concert was recorded but not released to the public until April 1997. Rumor has it that the original master tape was destroyed by fire at Electric Ladyland. However, a reel-to-reel copy of four of the five songs was unearthed by recording engineer Ralph Moss. Also located was a copy of the twenty-eight-minute "Can You See Me." The CD, *Glass Harp Live! At Carnegie Hall,* renewed fan interest. As a result, the original members reunited for two performances: The first was held at the Rock and Roll Hall of Fame and Museum to commemorate the "My Town" exhibit; the second was at the Akron Civic Center, with a portion of the proceeds benefiting Akron Children's Medical Center.

By 1972, the trio was also known for its strong, well-blended vocals. *Synergy* and *Makes Me Glad* met critical acclaim and brought the group a broader fan base. Singles from those releases included "Village Queen," "Children's Fantasy," "Just Always," and "Whatever Life Demands."

The latter ended up being all too prophetic, however, for just as the band was on its way to national recognition, the heartbeat of the group suddenly called it quits. Twenty-one-year-old Phil Keaggy, a born-again Christian, decided his destiny rested with Christian music, and he left the band to pursue recording contemporary gospel tunes. And true to form, the virtuoso guitarist has become a successful artist in contemporary Christian music. Over the past twenty-five years, he has produced more than twenty albums. Besides writing, recording, and touring, he does session work as well.

Although Glass Harp lasted another year with Keaggy replacement Tim Burks, and added a fourth member, violinist Randy Benson, it was soon obvious the group had lost its synergy. By the end of 1973, Glass Harp had disbanded. John Sferra went on to play in other bands, while Pecchio cofounded yet another remarkable group, the Michael Stanley Band.

Still, when recalling the short-lived but long-remembered Glass Harp, one element is mentioned time and again. As Hank LoConti recalls,

I'll never forget the night I had Ted Nugent in for the Columbus Agora, with Glass Harp as the opening act. At the time we had no dressing room backstage, so Ted was in the office, which was up in the balcony. Well, we were sitting there talking when suddenly I realized I'd lost his attention, and without saying a word, he gets up and walks out the door. I'm thinking, What the hell did I say? I get up and follow him, and he's standing by the railing looking down at Glass Harp play. You could tell he was listening to that guitar. After the band was done, he turns to me and asks, "What's that kid's name?" I said Phil Keaggy. And he replied, almost in awe, "that kid is doing what most guitar players only dream about." I'll never forget that.

"When I first met Phil," Pecchio adds, "it was freakish to see this small-built kid of fourteen playing this guitar so skillfully. You couldn't help [but] be impressed. The thing with Glass Harp was we were in constant progression. From doing high school, then clubs, then the bigger halls. And I'm proud to say, there was never a time when Glass Harp didn't get an encore or standing ovation. And that's no matter who we played with. We opened for groups like Humble Pie, Yes, the Kinks, Traffic. It was good while it lasted."

All the former members have continued making music. Currently a Nashville resident, Phil Keaggy plays in a Christian band that travels the country. Sferra, residing in Warren, came out with his first solo album in 1997, *North Bound,* and plays in the band the Motion. When Pecchio left the Michael Stanley Band in 1980, he did a five-year stint in auto-racing in the 1980s. Afterward, Pecchio managed his son's band, Funkomatic (later Mr. Tibbs). He is currently contemplating forming another band, perhaps gospel-inspired with contemporary R&B overtones.

15-60-75, the Numbers Band (1970–)

If nothing else, this Kent-based band is a survivor. It has persevered through more than three decades of changes in the music and club scene; fires that wiped out two of its musical homes (the Kove and JB's in 1976); two missed opportunities for recording contracts; an unexpected kidney transplant for its frontman (in 1990); a van theft that left its members without their instruments; and club dates where the audience members said to friends, "Check them out, they're older than your parents!"

Through it all, their fans have always been able to count on the Numbers Band for the best blend of blues, jazz, and R&B. They've even been dubbed the "pre-alternative alternative band" of northeast Ohio.

"In the beginning we played only blues," sax player Terry Hynde says. "That right there made us different. Back then, in 1970, there weren't a lot of choices in music. You had the psychedelic thing and a little leftover soul thing. But not many people were doing blues. I think that hippie element or whatever was going on at that time really caught on with us, and as a result, we developed quite a following early on. It was something the audience could really plug into." (Aside from being a longtime member of this Kent band, Hynde is just as much known for having a little sister named Chrissie; see Chapter 15.)

An Akron native, Hynde moved to Kent in 1965 and, five years later, met up with guitarist Robert Kidney and joined a band that would be an integral part of his life for years to come. It didn't take this group long to get a steady job. The band played all along Water Street, where the college town offered up a variety of atmospheric, intimate tavern venues. The band became regulars at the James Gang's old stomping ground, JB's.

And like that Kent band that hit it big, the story begins with a guitar. "I got turned onto the guitar because I was pretty much of a misfit, so I spent a lot of time by myself anyway," recalls Kidney, who got his first guitar for his sixteenth birthday. "A friend of mine played the guitar really well, and one day we were sitting up in his room when he started playing it. Well, when the sound from that guitar came across the room, I tell you, it hit me square in the chest! That's what told me what I wanted to do with my life. When my mother bought me a classical guitar, I totally ruined it within a month by putting metal strings on it. So I earned money from my paper route, my mother gave me the difference, and I went down to Akron Music on Front Street in Cuyahoga Falls and bought an acoustic, which I still use today for all my composing."

Kidney and that guitar started entertaining at various coffeehouses so prominent in the '60s. "I was doing duets with my friend Gary Hawk," he recalls. "We started playing this notorious club in Cleveland called LaCave." It was at LaCave that Kidney honed his stage experience by opening for acts such as sixteen-year-old pop/folk star Janis Ian, the Jim Kweswein Jug Band, and young singer Linda Ronstadt, whose group, the Stone Poneys, had just had a hit song called "Different Drum." "You didn't get paid for opening for a band, but it was good experience," he says. "I remember Linda Ronstadt telling me backstage that she liked my music but I'd be more successful if I looked at the audience when I sang. I still don't do it. So maybe she was right!"

When Kidney went into the service, he was stationed in Chicago, where he became enamored with the Chicago blues—Muddy Waters, Howlin' Wolf, Buddy Guy, and Junior Wells. But he notes that his favorite bluesman since childhood has always been Robert Johnson. His brief stint in the navy over, Kidney was eager to try playing the blues.

When I got out of the service [in 1969], I learned Hawk had formed a band. So I arrived at their rehearsal ready to go and found out Hawk had just quit. So they asked me to front the band. I figured if I was going to front it, it should be my band, with a name I chose.

After obsessing over names, I thought, well, maybe I'll use numbers. No one uses numbers. Now, in those days, a lot of people, my friends included, were having their phones tapped by the FBI—not an unusual occurrence back then. So I thought, now this is really appropriate. I felt it would signify that period in history. The numbers I chose were 15-60-75, which I got out of a book by a British musicologist. It was called *The Blues Fell This Morning* and was a study of numeric consistency in blues. There was a whole chapter on blues songs that used numbers.

(They are best known as the Numbers Band, however, because no one seems to remember the exact numbers.) After deciding on the name, Kidney thought about getting a saxophone player to add to their blues repertoire. He found one where he was least expecting it. "I was at Blossom Music Center for the Janis Joplin concert in early summer of '70," he explains. "My date and I were in the audience when she points out to the crowd and says, 'Hey, there's Terry Hynde. He's a really good sax player. Why don't you ask him to play in the band?' I did, and we've been playing together ever since."

Their first gig was July 4, 1970, at Kent's Kove, dubbed "Home of the Blues in Ohio." Members included rhythm guitarist/vocalist/lyricist Kidney, Hynde on alto sax and harmonica, Hank Smith on guitar and keyboards, Tim Hudson on drums, and Greg Colbert on bass. The lineup, which has always included Kidney and Hynde, would soon change to include guitarist Mike Budnour, bassist Jerry Casale (replaced by Drake Gleason when Casale formed Devo in 1973), drummer David Robinson, tenor saxophonist Tim Maglione, and Kidney's brother Jack on sax and harmonica. The seven-man band was an immediate hit with its audience, playing many standard blues tunes. While many area bands relied on cover material only, Kidney began introducing his own songs into their sets, striving to be separate from the pack. The group became the house band at the Kove, attracting a crowd as diverse as its music. College students, professors, hippies, fellow musicians, bikers, and regular townspeople all gathered together to listen and dance to the Numbers Band until closing hours. And when they weren't playing the Kove, they were often next door at JB's.

On October 3, 1975, the band (now with Michael Stacey on guitar and Chris Butler on bass) made its Cleveland Agora debut, opening for Bob Marley and the Wailers. That show resulted in the live album *Jimmy Bell Is Still in Town.* Unfortunately, one month after that successful Cleveland concert, a fire forced the Kove to close for a time. A few months later, fire struck the Kove again, completely destroying it. The blaze spread to nearby JB's while the Numbers Band was performing. Though part of JB's was burned, the legendary bar was rebuilt and open within the year and became the Numbers Band's new home.

Meanwhile, the blues band distributed nearly all of the 2,000 copies of its first LP to various record labels, hoping one would sign them to a contract. The album garnered the band plenty of press in a variety of rock publications, including *Creem*, *Rolling Stone*, and *Spin*. By 1977, the Numbers Band had never sounded tighter. It was unique and in sync, and a recording contract was long overdue.

But by 1978, the college scene that had embraced the James Gang, Glass Harp, and 15-60-75 was replaced by a different generation with changing musical tastes. "The club owner started giving us a hard time, and we were taking a lot of shit from people that were surrounding the New Wave craze," Kidney explains. "We played blues, and many considered that 'old music.' Even our originals were looked upon as uncool because they sounded too much like the blues. We were already being considered old men. We were put downstairs, with the more current bands upstairs. The upstairs bar was on the street level, so it was the preferred place to be. It was a bitter time for us."

Two opportunities for recording contracts opened up, and the band was ready. After receiving copies of the group's records, Karin Berg, A&R person at Warner Brothers, expressed interest in hearing the band play live. The group packed up for New York to play the ultra-hip club Traxx, and Berg promised to be there. Determined to impress, Kidney and his band played one of their best shows. But by evening's end, Berg was a no-show. The band got rave reviews, but it didn't soften the blow.

Months later, the Numbers Band had another chance. Or so members thought. On April 21, 1978, Karin Berg brought her boss, Warner Brothers's record producer Jerry Wexler, into JB's. However, they weren't there to listen to the Numbers Band, but rather a New Wave group called Tin Huey. Chris Butler, now of Tin Huey, had become acquainted with Berg through *Village Voice* writer Robert Christgau. Wexler, who arrived that night in a white limo, is known for signing Aretha Franklin and Wilson Pickett to the Warner Brothers label. Berg had just signed New York bands Television and the Dictators.

"I was standing at the door to greet Jerry Wexler," Kidney recalls. "I shook his hand and said, 'You might like to come downstairs some time this evening and see my band. We've done some pretty interesting modernization with R&B.' Which was a very true statement. But he never came down."

"To this day, I don't understand it," Butler admits.

We kept telling them to go down and check out the Numbers Band because they were much higher in rank than we were, and because of Wexler's R&B leanings. We couldn't understand why they were interested in us, a weird little cough syrup–driven art-rock band that couldn't attract ten people at the time.

The sad thing about that was there was a lot of grumbling about me. Like I had something to do with them not coming down to see the Numbers Band. Nobody was responsible for blocking anything. But I think Kidney is still mad at me, and maybe all of us. But what he fails to realize is that, in our minds, he was God. Everybody in the band used to honor and credit him. Practically every record I've done I've included a thank-you to him. And yet, in a way, I can understand the bitterness.

Nonetheless, Tin Huey secured a recording contract. 15-60-75 remained a lonely number.

The 1980s found the Numbers Band playing on while continuing their attempts to secure a recording label. In 1982 the band released its first studio album. However, Kidney says the self-titled LP was doomed because the record was mismastered, causing it to skip in places, affecting the quality and, ultimately, the sales.

The 1983 Numbers lineup included Kidney, brother Jack, Hynde, Bart Johnson (bass, who soon left and was replaced by Fred Trabuzzo), Stacey (rhythm guitar), and Robinson (drums). That same year, Kidney's friend David Thomas of Pere Ubu produced the group's next release, a 45 called "Here in the Life," with the b-side "It's in Imagination." Thomas, in turn, included the latter title on Pere Ubu's boxed set, *Data Panik in the Year Zero,* in 1996.

Kidney's friendship with Thomas and former Pere Ubu bass player Tony Maimone started early in their careers while playing hometown gigs. But while Kidney's band remained local, Pere Ubu drew an international following. "One good thing that has come out of that period when we were getting pushed aside by newer bands was my friendship with Dave and Tony," he says. "They had been coming to see the band regularly, and when things started coming down on us and we were getting dissed, they supported me. That meant a lot and is a big reason why we're friends today."

Then came Kidney's association with former Pere Ubu drummer Anton Fier. "Sometime during this period, Anton came to see the band. I don't even know when it was. But one day I get this call from him and he's asking if his new band, Golden Palominos, could record a song of mine called 'Animal Speaks,' which was on our first live album. He ended up putting it on their 1987 *Blast of Silence* album with the lyrics sung by John Lydon [a.k.a. Johnny Rotten, formerly of the Sex Pistols]. Later they re-released it as an EP with Jack Bruce, former bass player for Cream, singing it on one side and John Lydon's version on the other."

In the interim, the Numbers Band recorded its third release, *Among the Wandering* (with new bassist Steve Calabria), which got big reviews but little airplay. Kidney then joined the Golden Palominos on the group's North American tour. Afterward, Anton Fier sought Kidney out for his group's next album, *Vision of Excess.* This time Kidney sang his own song, "The Push and the Shove." Other Kidney-penned songs—"Lucky," "A Letter Back," and "Wild River"—were also included on the group's CD *The Dead Horse.* Still another inclusion, "Begin to Return," showed up on the Golden Palominos' *Drunk with Passion* in 1990.

It was in 1990 that Kidney discovered he needed a kidney transplant. When local musicians realized the severity of the uninsured frontman's situation, they banded together and raised enough money to cover expenses. His operation was successful. Then in 1996, when the band's equipment was stolen out of Kidney's van on a city street, former Kent resident Joe Walsh called Kidney to offer his help. Walsh said he would offer an autographed guitar in exchange for the stolen merchandise. The equipment miraculously turned up, but no one claimed the reward.

In 1991, another live recording, *Blues by the Numbers,* featured remakes of their most popular songs. A twentieth-anniversary CD, *15-60-75-Twenty,* was also released that year. In 1992 came their *Hot Wired* CD, with current members the Kidney brothers, Hynde, former bassist Bill Watson (replaced in 1995 by Frank Reynolds), and drummer Frank Casamento.

In April 1998, David Thomas, now a London resident, arranged for the Numbers Band to play at England's South Bank Festival. The group returned again in January 1999. Kent's legendary band was even the subject of a *Wall Street Journal* article.

Through more than its share of ups and downs, Numbers Band members have ridden the waves like the seasoned professionals they have proven themselves to be. The band lives on and remains highly regarded by colleagues and fans. It continues to send material to record companies despite constant rejections. "Not commercially viable" has become the pat answer, with one producer actually telling Jack Kidney, "I don't see my Mercedes in this music."

The group that has worked more than 3,000 gigs simply likes to make music. Like the North Coast itself, 15-60-75 is a melting pot, boiling with a musical infusion of blues, jazz, rock, and R&B. Now in their early fifties, these fathers and grandfathers don't play out as often, but when they do, their longtime admirers make sure to be there.

Kidney says, "Sure, I wish things would've worked out differently, that I had done things differently. There's a lyric in a song I wrote that I live by. It goes, 'He was just a man who refused to live without regrets.' Because you can't move forward if you don't look back. You have to take responsibility and learn from it. I believe if you ignore your own history you're bound to repeat yourself."

On Their Own

Eric Carmen

In 1973, Eric Carmen, along with fellow Raspberries members, was in a New York recording studio when he ran into John Lennon—literally. "I'll never forget it," Carmen recalls. "I was headed toward the bathroom when I bumped into this guy whom I've admired from day one. When I realized it was Lennon, I was speechless. He looked up, recognized me, and said, 'Hey, I like your music'—and then he was gone."

That encounter, however brief, marked one of the greatest highlights of this singer/songwriter's career. To hear his idol say he liked the band and its music was the ultimate vindication. The Raspberries' "bubble-gum" label—a media tag neither welcomed nor accepted—wore on its members. And though nothing would change with Lennon's coveted approval, it did provide a salve for the rash of wounds stinging the group's reputation.

As the Raspberries frontman, Carmen was becoming the rock idol he'd often dreamed himself to be. He and band members Wally Bryson, Dave Smalley, and Jim Bonfanti had copped a No. 5 hit in 1972 with "Go All the Way," which sold more than 1.3 million copies and launched them to national rock fame. With the group's international popularity and its singles rising on *Billboard* charts, Carmen's clearly defined dream of success appeared to be coming true.

After years of struggle in this precarious business, these talented musicians' hit songs and clever marketing tools were finally making them the talk of the industry. But by the time they'd reached that New York studio to record their fourth album, *Starting Over,* the tightly knit band was beginning to unravel. Within the next few years, the North Coast group would disband in an ugly manner. First, after the recording of their third album, bassist Dave Smalley and drummer Bonfanti left the band, to be replaced by former Cyrus Erie drummer Michael McBride and guitarist Scott McCarl. Then, in late 1974, tensions were unleashed in a brawl between Carmen and Bryson in a parking lot, destroying any hope of the group's recovery. The varied circumstances that caused the group to disband forced Carmen to go on his own.

Eric Howard Carmen was born on August 11, 1949. His career began with a doorbell. "Every time the doorbell rang, he'd yell B-flat!" his mother recalled in a 1989 interview about her son at age seven. By this time, the precocious Lyndhurst resident was already a student at the Cleveland Institute of Music, where he was (and remains) the youngest ever (age three) to enroll at the school. At age six, he began playing violin, taught to him by his Aunt Muriel, a violinist with the Cleveland Orchestra. That instrument, however, was quickly replaced by the piano when he turned eight and got hooked on classical music, particularly that of Rachmaninov, whose Piano Concerto No. 2 in C Minor helped spawn his biggest hit, "All by Myself." But that love affair came to an abrupt halt when the twelve year old discovered the Beatles. From then on, it was the Byrds, the Rolling Stones, and the Who—whose influence prompted Carmen to take up the guitar and songwriting. By age fifteen, he was playing in teenage rock bands. Although not completely enamored of the idea of her son becoming a rock star, Mrs. Carmen gave him his first electric guitar (a Guild Freshman) and small Ampeg for his sixteenth birthday.

It was during this time that a popular local band caught his attention. The group seemed to be playing everywhere, from school dances to roller rinks to teen clubs. The Brush High School graduate would frequently go to watch them play, amazed by their musical abilities as well as their repertoire (Beatles, the Who, Stones). The Choir, which had garnered a recording contract and some success with its 1966 national hit "It's Cold

Outside," was the one group Carmen was determined to become a part of. And so he doggedly pursued its manager, Ray Taylor.

According to both Choir drummer Jim Bonfanti and guitarist Dave Smalley, Taylor was getting hounded by phone calls from "this guy, Eric, who was telling him he was the best musician in town, the best keyboard player, that he could sing higher and lower than everybody in town." This less-than-humble approach only made the band members steer clear of this self-promoter they came to refer to as "the Wonderboy." Despite that first impression, however, a viable friendship would eventually form between Bonfanti and Carmen that, despite a brief estrangement resulting from their Raspberries stint, has remained constant to this day.

Never accepted into the Choir, Carmen, then a John Carroll University student, persevered, deciding that if he wasn't going to be in his favorite group, he'd "have the best band in Cleveland, a band that would blow the Choir off the stage." That happened the moment Carmen stole two Choir alumni, Bonfanti and guitarist Wally Bryson, and formed Cyrus Erie. That band succeeded in becoming its rival's greatest competitor, and it even managed a recording contract with Epic Records. The single "Get the Message" was well received regionally. But, as with most local bands, the group—still hailed today as one of the best of its kind during its reign—went unnoticed by the rest of the rock world. When Cyrus Erie disbanded, Carmen approached Bonfanti about forming a "Beatles" band. It was to be a "power group," which meant only one guitarist was good enough, Bryson. Bryson brought in bass player John Aleksic, and the Raspberries were born.

It was apparent early in his career that Eric Carmen was going to make a name for himself. Not only was his musical talent evident and strengthened by his early influences and experiences, but he wanted—and needed—stardom. That was evident from his first moment on stage as a young teenager. According to those who knew him (and Carmen himself has referred to it in interviews), the multitalented musician would "pretend" on stage to be either Paul McCartney, Rod Stewart, Roger Daltry, or Mick Jagger, depending on the songs he played. Even back when he was in Cyrus Erie, fans recall how Carmen's entire persona, as well as his voice, would metamorphose into an image in such a manner that even his own audience would temporarily forget it was actually Carmen performing before them instead of the idealized rock idol. Everyone enjoyed the fantasy, and the act succeeded in winning Carmen many female hearts.

Things *looked* promising with the formation of the Raspberries. But looks were deceiving. The decision to try to bring back the innocence of the Beatles and the Beach Boys worked against the band. For just as the group's popularity was peaking, glitter rock came on the scene with its slicker version of hard rock. This trend shared the spotlight with psychedelic rock hippie bands like the Grateful Dead and Jefferson Airplane. Soon sterile, "white bread" rock images were going the way of '60s love beads and transcendental meditation.

And nowhere was the group's declining appeal more evident than in its hometown. As it made the rounds touring the United States, each time the band returned for a

Cleveland gig, it met with lukewarm responses. One of the biggest reasons was Carmen himself. Where before one of the band's greatest assets was his self-assured confidence, Carmen's hometown reputation for being "cocky," "conceited," and "remote" became a liability. When confronted by this, Carmen defended himself, saying he wasn't about to change his poised personality for what he deemed would be for the worse, meaning the "post-Beatles/drug/heavy-metal music trip" that was becoming the focus in '70s rock. Yet those issues served to underscore the idea that the whole marketing of the Raspberries was based on perception, rather than content. That misconception overrode the group's musical talent—talent that, twenty years later, placed the group at the top of the list of best power pop bands ever.

"Although the Raspberries really got a lot of flack, especially in Cleveland, and despite their reputation as a bubble-gum band, that group could really rock," says guitarist Al Globekar. "Anyone who ever saw them play live knew that."

The greatest irony in this story is that the biggest conflict between Carmen and Bryson was a result of Bryson's badgering his friend to steer away from emulating his idols and rely on his own musical merits. Yet, it wasn't until the band broke up, and Carmen made his debut solo album, that his individual talents emerged to the fullest. Apparently, what he couldn't accomplish with a group, he managed to perfect on his own. Little compensation to the Raspberries.

Immediately upon the group's demise, Carmen was offered a recording contract with Arista. And he wasted no time. Spending six months writing all the lyrics and music, and hiring local band Magic as his backup, the solo artist emerged with his self-titled album that was hailed everywhere as "superb" and gave him two Top 40 hit singles. "Sunrise" reached No. 34 on *Billboard* and "Never Gonna Fall in Love Again" peaked at No. 11. But it was the dramatic ballad "All by Myself," which rose rapidly to the No. 2 spot on *Billboard*, and No. 1 on *Cashbox,* that ultimately became his signature song. By April 1976, the song was certified gold and became a genuine classic, with musical greats such as Frank Sinatra, Paul Anka, Hank Williams Jr., and Celine Dion covering it. The album itself became a platinum seller in October 1977.

Realizing that timing is everything, Capitol Records jumped on the Carmen buzz and released *Raspberries Best Featuring Eric Carmen* in June 1976, which fell short of expectations, peaking at No. 138 on *Billboard*. But Carmen's creative juices were flowing. Hooking up with producer Gus Dudgeon (who was also Elton John's producer), he returned to the studio to record *Boats Against the Current*. That album, however, was delayed when "creative differences" once again interfered and Carmen was left alone to produce the album himself. The LP, released in October 1977, did well, reaching No. 45 and sparking a Top 40 hit single "She Did It" (No. 23).

From there he continued with two more solo efforts on Arista. *Change of Heart,* released in December 1978, peaked at No. 137, and his final album on that label, *Tonight You're Mine* (1980), got no higher than No. 160, with its biggest single, "It Hurts Too Much," reaching No. 75 on *Billboard*.

Carmen then took a five-year hiatus, with the exception of co-writing with Dean Pritchford "Almost Paradise," the love theme for the 1985 hit movie *Footloose*. Also in

Eric Carmen performs at the Music Hall in 1975. George Sipl is on keyboards. *Photo by Brian Chalmers.*

1985, Carmen signed with Geffen Records, releasing another self-titled album, which peaked at No. 128. A single from that LP, "I'm Through with Love," reached No. 87.

After the mediocrity of his last few albums, Eric Carmen hit pay-dirt early in 1988, ironically with a song he hadn't even written and, with former Raspberries producer Jimmy Ienner. Ienner called Carmen up one day asking if he was interested in singing a new song for a movie called *Dirty Dancing*. The song, written by John DeNicola and Frank Previte, was "Hungry Eyes." Upon hearing it, Carmen agreed it had hit potential and recorded the tune in five days at Beachwood Studios. The movie ended up grossing more than $50 million, and the soundtrack charted No. 1 for nine weeks on *Billboard* and went quadruple platinum in both the United States and Canada. "Hungry Eyes" peaked at No. 4, and Carmen spent the rest of 1988 on the *Dirty Dancing* tour, performing with Bill Medley (best remembered as half of the Righteous Brothers), and Merry Clayton and the Contours. Eric Carmen was back on top. Of course with his recharged career, Arista came out with *The Best of Eric Carmen*. That release included a new single, "Make Me Lose Control," which gave Carmen another Top 10 hit (peaking at No. 3) and sold more than fifteen million worldwide.

As far as his North Coast fans are concerned, however, Carmen's most important contribution rested with a song he penned solely as a tribute to his hometown. In 1986, talk of the Rock Hall being built in Cleveland was making regular headlines. While the jury was still out as to what city would be home to the coveted museum, Carmen and his brother Fred wrote "The Rock Stops Here," which many believed certainly helped the decision along (see Chapter 19).

The 1990s were filled with change for Carmen. First, in 1994, after years of jet-setting back and forth from Cleveland to Los Angeles, he and his wife moved back to the North Coast for good. The following year, after decades of enjoying a tremendous following and fan club in Japan, he signed with Japanese record label Pioneer LDC, on which he released his 1998 LP *Winter Dreams*. And in August 1997, he became a father for the first time. Now in the fifth decade of his musical life, Eric Carmen is working on yet another recording, continuing to produce the music that began with Rachmaninov and the Beatles.

Joe Walsh

Joe Walsh is one of the most intelligent and talented people I know. After all these years, the guy still amazes me.

—David Spero

Though neither born nor raised here, Joe Walsh will always be considered a Clevelander—and a Kent State University student. Forget the fact he's lived infrequently in the city. Ignore the trivial matter he spent a total of six years at Kent but never graduated. And don't even bother to speculate about who his dorm roommate might have been. In response to this persistent rumor, he admitted to the *Plain Dealer*'s Jane Scott, "I must have lived in practically every house in that town at one time or another. And I've got a lot of good memories."

The real truth of Cleveland's love affair with this legendary guitarist (who was actually born in Wichita, Kansas, on November 20, 1947, and raised in Columbus, Ohio, and New Jersey) is a lot simpler. From the very first day that youthful, blond, ambitious Joe Walsh stood on stage wailing his reverberating harmonics as only he could, the people of northeast Ohio have embraced him as their own. In the seven years he was a North

Coast mainstay, playing everywhere from Kent's trendy JB's, selling out the Akron Rubber Bowl and Blossom Music Center, and filling the 80,000 seats in the now-defunct Cleveland Stadium, Walsh's faithful local fans and his music have been intertwined. "It's an honor and privilege to say I'm from Ohio," he told the audience and the world at the Eagles' induction into the Rock and Roll Hall of Fame in January 1998.

That goes both ways. For this beloved musician has given Ohio enough rock and roll memories to last a lifetime. Throughout his lucrative career, Joe Walsh has been a musical wonder. He started playing rhythm guitar with an instrumental band called the G-Clefs while still attending his New Jersey high school. During this time Walsh got a job answering phones in a Cadillac parts department in Upper Montclair but was let go because he was always playing his guitar instead of working.

As was the case for every teen in America in 1964, Beatlemania captivated the seventeen year old and led him to form his first rock group, the Nomads. But it was when he moved to Kent in 1965 and established the Measles that his reputation as a gifted guitarist began. The young band quickly became a local favorite in the college town, playing Catholic Youth Organization (CYO) dances at St. Patrick's and the ever-popular Water Street taverns—Fifth Quarter, the Kove, and JB's. The group also hit the northeast Ohio Hullabaloo clubs and summer festivals.

"When they used to tape my dad's show *Upbeat* on the road to amusement parks like Geauga Lake, Euclid Beach, and Chippewa Lake, the Measles was often the opening act," recalls David Spero, now Walsh's manager. "And that's when I first met Joe. One afternoon the group was playing at Chippewa, and Joe and I started talking, and we've been friends ever since."

By 1968, however, Walsh left the Measles to join Choir members Dave Burke and Dan Klawon to form the Power Trio. But by April 1969, that group, too, would separate. That's when he joined the James Gang.

"Walsh fit in immediately," drummer Jim Fox recalls. "I remember he and guitarist Bill Jeric would spend something like twelve to eighteen hours playing in the basement—routinely."

The group recorded its first album that same year. *Yer Album* made it into *Billboard*'s Top 100, hinting at things to come: Within a year, the James Gang, and Walsh in particular, would be nationally known.

Indeed, 1970 proved a big year for Walsh and company. With former E. T. Hooley bassist Dale Peters stepping in to replace the departed Tom Kriss, the trio began taking their music on the road. By the time the James Gang opened for the Who in Pittsburgh that May, it was unabashedly clear: Joe Walsh was as remarkable as his guitar licks. It was at this concert that Townshend heard Walsh playing from his dressing room and rushed out to get a better earful. Townshend was so impressed by Walsh's performance that he dedicated the Who's next set to him and proceeded to invite the band to join them on their European tour. That exposure helped propel the group's talents across the British landscape.

That same year, *James Gang Rides Again* hit record stores and topped at No. 20 on *Billboard*. The biggest single from that album, "Funk #49," reached No. 59, and Walsh's musical genius was largely credited for that. The album turned gold. And 1971 saw still more hits. "Walk Away," from their *Thirds* album, reached No. 51 by June, followed by another hit single, "Midnight Man," which made it to No. 80. The album itself peaked at No. 27.

Although the James Gang continued for four more years, Walsh decided to spread his own wings in 1972—all the way to Boulder, Colorado. Turning down Steve Marriott's offer to join Humble Pie, Walsh got together with Kenny Passarelli and old Measles buddy Joe Vitale and formed Barnstorm. They toured extensively throughout the United States that year and into the next. Their debut album, *Barnstorm,* which focused mostly on Walsh, reached No. 79 in the fall of that year. Soon after, Barnstorm added keyboardists Rocke Grace and Tom Stephenson.

In 1973, Barnstorm released *The Smoker You Drink, the Player You Get,* which gave Walsh his first gold record with "Rocky Mountain Way" (Bill Clinton's all-time favorite tune). However, once again industry and media attention focused solely on Walsh. This inadvertently caused the end of Barnstorm. Over the years Walsh has expressed his frustration with the record company continually marketing him while ignoring his equally talented band members, particularly when the *Smoker* LP came out and the cover featured Walsh flying solo in an airplane. "No one understood what we were trying to accomplish, so why do it?" Walsh has said on the subject. "I wanted to be a band, not a solo artist. Vitale, especially, should've gotten more credit 'cause it wasn't all me. When Vitale and I work together, that's how we got those songs. It was in every aspect a collaborative effort." Disillusioned by how Barnstorm was perceived, Walsh decided to move on rather than fight industry and media waves. It was yet another new beginning.

That same year, 1973, Walsh moved to Los Angeles. He spent the following year using his producing talents for Dan Fogelberg's *Souvenirs* (resulting in the singer's first gold record) and Joe Vitale's *Roller Coaster Weekend.* In 1975, Walsh's live solo album, *You Can't Argue with a Sick Mind,* was released by ABC, and by the spring of 1976 it had peaked at No. 20, giving the enterprising musician yet another gold record.

In the meantime, he had already teamed up with a band whose members he'd used for several cuts on his 1974 *So What* LP. By the end of the 1975, the Eagles had landed in Walsh's backyard. And as was readily apparent, the electrifying presence of Ohio's favorite was just the spark the country rock band needed. Walsh replaced lead guitarist Bernie Leadon just in time for the Eagles' new release, *Hotel California.* The album, which quickly garnered multiplatinum status, became the band's most successful ever when it hit No. 1 in the summer of 1976, with four million copies sold. Its biggest hit was "New Kid in Town," which also shot up to No. 1. Over the next few years, the Eagles (Walsh, Don Henley, Glenn Frey, Randy Meisner, and Don Felder) saw more hits and tours and platinum sellers, *Eagles Live* and *The Long Run,* both in 1980.

Still, Walsh continued to produce solo efforts. In 1978, his *But Seriously, Folks* hit it big, reaching No. 8 on U.S. charts and No. 14 in the United Kingdom The best-loved single from that album was "Life's Been Good" (No. 12 U.S.), a humorous look at the life of a rock star. It remains a favorite on classic-rock radio stations.

When the Eagles broke up quickly and bitterly in 1980 (claiming "Hell will freeze over before we get back together." They did; it didn't), each went on to record solo. The breakup didn't seem to faze Walsh, who made good use of those years. He still had lots of creative talent to use and lost no time doing so. Throughout the 1980s he produced three successful solo works: *There Goes the Neighborhood* (originally titled "Days of Lines and Noses") was released by Asylum in 1981; *You Bought It, You Name It* was released by Full Moon in 1983; and *The Confessor* (Warner Brothers) came out in 1985. His distinctive guitar riffs are also evident on his colleagues' recordings, including Michael Stanley's 1973 debut LP *Michael Stanley* and its follow-up *Friends and Legends,* Richard Marx's *Don't Mean Nothing* (1988), and Bob Seger's *The Fire Inside* (1991). In 1980, Walsh became a Grammy nominee for his contribution on the recording of *Urban Cowboy.* Other notable artists on the record included J. D. Souther, Boz Scaggs, Dan Fogelberg, and Bob Seger.

Over the years, Walsh has been acknowledged by Eric Clapton, Pete Townshend, and Jimmy Page as one of the finest lead guitarists in rock history. And yet Walsh remains amazingly unchanged from that young guitar genius so many Ohioans recall.

"My first memory of Joe is this skinny, blond kid playing a blond, twelve-string Rickenbacker guitar, legs dangling over the edge of a bunk bed, strumming out the tune 'Norwegian Wood,'" recalls radio exec Walt Tiburski. "He played briefly with a Kent band I was in called the Motley Odds, and he was so immersed in his guitar, all he ever wanted to do was practice all day and night. He was a real slave driver and even back then wanted to concentrate mostly on original music rather than covers."

His passion for music and his legendary sense of humor have helped Walsh withstand the test of time in a career that is, for many, fleeting. Perhaps more than his musical mastery, his Cleveland-style brand of humor is most likely what has prompted North Coasters to claim him as their own. His on-stage attire often is worth the price of admission alone. He's shown up wearing everything from patriotic red-white-and-blue stovepipe hats to white dog bone earrings, coonskin hats, propeller beanies, and, when in Cleveland, an Indians jersey and hat. And fans can bet on being greeted with his usual murmur, "Hey, how ya doin'?"

Even his often-hinted-at inebriated condition is rumored to be more show than tell. Critics have described his concert appearances over the years with comments such as "lazy, slurred speech and droopy eyelids," "looks like he just woke up," and "looking pale, frail and out of it at forty." Yet most agree the act is at least slightly put on, because he "knows what he's selling and to whom"—particularly nowadays, since Walsh has claimed to have been sober for several years. Nonetheless, he knows how to endear himself to his audience. As one reviewer said, describing a typical Walsh crowd, "They'd have been happy if he just stood center stage and smiled for ninety minutes."

In addition to participating in several rock benefits, such as Farm Aid and Rock Against Hunger, he came through when his birthplace of Wichita experienced a tornado. He played two acoustic concerts for the area's relief fund. He was also one of the first to volunteer to play a benefit concert in 1986 to raise funds for the Kent State memorial to mark the May 4, 1970, shootings (which Walsh witnessed).

Through the years, Walsh has flirted with acting as well. He made a cameo appearance as a prisoner in the 1980 hit movie, *The Blues Brothers,* with Dan Akroyd and the late John Belushi, and he gave a memorable performance on *The Drew Carey Show* in January 1997, particularly when he broke into "Rocky Mountain Way." Thereafter he became a semi-regular on the show. Carey, in turn, was in his hometown to introduce Walsh at the guitarist's 1997 Cleveland Nautica concert.

After more than thirty years of friendship, David Spero probably has the best stories on this rock and roll legend. He recalls the time in 1992 when Walsh, ever the instigator, nearly cost him a traffic ticket. Walsh was touring with Ringo Starr for his All-Starr Band, and Spero picked the two up at the airport for their Cleveland concert. "It's 1:00 in the morning and we're leaving the airport, and we're sitting waiting for this light that won't change. And there's Joe and Ringo in the back seat going, 'Come on, just go already.' So finally I went. That's when a police car pulls up. I start to explain to the guy when he shines his flashlight in the back and suddenly goes, 'Holy shit! It's Joe Walsh and Ringo Starr,' and I'm saying, 'Yeah, they made me do it!' He did end up letting us go—after he got their autographs!"

But perhaps one story best illustrates the magnitude of Walsh's massive talent. "One day, Joe was sitting around with Ringo," Spero says. "And he was goofin' around with his guitar and he starts playing the Beatles song 'And Your Bird Can Sing.' Well, Ringo looks at him and says, 'How did you do that?' And Joe says, 'What do you mean?' So he had Joe play it again and Ringo says, 'But how'd you do that?' By now Joe's getting aggravated and said, 'What do you mean? That's what's on the record.' And Ringo says, 'Yeah, but it took *three* guitars to play that on the record!' And Joe goes, "Well, shit! No wonder I had such a hard time figuring it out!'"

Joe Walsh is over fifty now. And it appears that this guitar hero adopted by Cleveland so long ago has gone through all the changes and musical pairings a rock and roller can be expected to. Yet there seems to be no stopping him. He'll always find ways to amuse himself and others.

In the meantime, the Eagles (all seven of them, including Meisner and Leadon) were inducted into the Rock and Roll Hall of Fame on January 12, 1998, in New York. And true to form, Walsh, always one to stand out in a crowd, stood alongside his tuxedo-wearing colleagues clad in a show-stopping orange brick patterned outfit that drew a hearty applause as he approached the microphone to speak. "I'd like to thank the people of Akron, Kent, and Cleveland, Ohio, for believing in me," he said.

Joe Vitale

Canton native drummer Joe Vitale has played with Ted Nugent, Joe Walsh, the Eagles, Dan Fogelberg, and Crosby, Stills and Nash. Not a bad resume.

The son of a musician, Joe Vitale got turned on to music early. Even though his father played keyboards, young Joe was mesmerized by drummers. "I got hooked onto guys like Gene Krupa and Max Roach," he says. "But my all-time favorite was Spike Jones. So when I was six, I talked my parents into letting me take private lessons."

It was money well spent. By the time Vitale was a music major at Kent State University, he was playing in one of the many local bands in the college bars on the weekends. And it was there he met up with a young guitarist named Joe Walsh. "There was quite a few bars around the area, but the Kove and JB's were the two biggies. This was in 1968, and Joe was playing in both clubs in a band called the Measles. I got to know him then, and we used to jam together every so often in each other's bands. But just as I joined the Measles, he left to go with the James Gang."

The two hung out when not in class, and both were on campus during the tragic Kent State shootings. Soon after, Walsh went touring with the James Gang, and Vitale was hired by Ted Nugent when the singer saw him play at JB's. It wasn't until late 1971 that the two Kent alums met up again.

> I was on the road with Ted Nugent and the Amboy Dukes. And one of the concerts we did, we opened for the James Gang—talk about a small world. It was great to see Joe again, and after the concert, he invited me to his hotel to talk. He said he was leaving the group and moving to Boulder, Colorado, to form a new band, and asked me if I was interested. Of course I was. By the time all this came about, it was 1972. We looked around for a bass player for quite a while. Then we met Tommy Bolin, who was playing at this one place we always went to hear the local bands. He was a great guitar player. Well, he turned us on to Kenny Passarelli, and the three of us formed Barnstorm.

As Barnstorm, the trio recorded a self-titled album (on ABC/Dunhill Records) and toured throughout the year. In 1974, *So What* was released, which included backup by the Eagles members, sparking rumors of a new addition to the popular West Coast group. The rumors became reality when Walsh joined the band that had once opened for him, marking the official end of Barnstorm. However, Vitale would play on several cuts in Walsh's later solo efforts in addition to concert performances.

Meanwhile, back in Colorado, circa 1973, Vitale (again with Walsh) sat in on several tracks of Michael Stanley's second solo LP, *Friends and Legends,* including what became an MSB staple, "Let's Get the Show on the Road." Upon returning to Ohio in 1974, Vitale wrote the music and lyrics for his own solo album, *Roller Coaster Weekend* (Atlantic Records), which included guitar licks from Walsh, Phil Keaggy, and Rick Derringer. Although critically praised, the album barely grazed the Top 100 on *Billboard*. But by this time Vitale was everywhere. He drummed on Dan Fogelberg's album as well as for Stephen Stills's short-lived group Manassas. And for a time, Vitale had his own band, the Joe Vitale Orchestra, with former Barnstormer Passarelli, keyboardist Tom Stephenson, guitarist Bob Webb (once a Measles member), and percussionist and conga player Guilla Garcia. But he is most known for his association with CS&N, as he recalls:

> From 1976 to the present, I've been with Crosby, Stills and Nash [and sometimes Young]. One interesting thing about working with these guys is that this particular

group recorded—and Neil Young wrote—"Ohio." And I was there when the shit happened—you know, May 4th [1970 Kent State shootings]. I remember we were under martial law and wasn't supposed to go outside, and of course Joe [Walsh] did, and I think he got arrested because of that. But it's funny how many questions the band has had over the years about those couple of days. So to do that song live with the band that made that song famous is really special to me. It's such a great song, and of course, I have a particular emotional tie to it. I still get chills about it.

. . . But whenever they [CS&N] didn't work, I'd work with Joe or Dan [Fogelberg]. So I was always busy. I also toured with Peter Frampton for two years, right after his big live album. It was so hot then, it was a real whirlwind tour.

But when his old Kent buddy calls for musical help, Vitale is there. As an Eagles member, Joe Walsh often summoned the drummer to join them on tour. So in 1979 and 1980, Vitale was on the Eagles' *The Long Run* world tour.

The Walsh-Vitale bond continues. "It's always been great working with Joe," Vitale says.

We're Ohio guys, we share a bond, along with guys like Michael [Stanley] and Eric Carmen. I mean, all the people I've worked with over the years—British guys like Frampton and John Entwistle and the West Coast people like Beach Boy Al Jardine—they're all wonderful. But their roots come from a different place. The only thing we really have in common is the music. But we midwesterners, we share more than just the music. We grew up in the same climate, share the same childhood stories, the same weird sense of humor—the whole personality of the Midwest. And there's the small towns, like Kent. Now that, right there, was a big part of our lives. It truly was the best of times and the worst of times. The best 'cause we were all young with these incredible dreams and visions. Full of energy, innocent, and maybe a little crazy. Kent was a very healthy place musically back then. There were so many good bands that came out of that environment.

But it was also the worst of times. We were at that age [when] you were not only struggling with life itself but had that huge darkness called Vietnam hanging overhead. Every day you'd wake up and things would be fine until you'd remember this could be the day you got called up. We were just kids, living with this horrible fear. But I think that made us put all that passion and feeling into our music and probably made us better musicians.

And though it's actually good to be involved with people from other walks of life, it's so comfortable to work with guys you went though all that with, who you have this identity with. It's what makes playing with these Ohio guys all the more special.

When talking about his rich musical history, Vitale emphasizes how important it is to give credit where credit is due most: "My wife, Susie, and I met back at Kent State University in 1969, and she's been there with me through it all. She's been incredibly supportive. We've been through the depths and the peaks of the business, and she stayed by my side the whole time—dragging her around the country, getting the great gigs or losing the great gigs. She's been the common thread through it all. It may sound like one of those Oscar speeches, but I understand where they're coming from. She's the reason I've been able to survive this crazy business."

And like father, like son: Joe Vitale Jr., began drumming at an early age and now, in his early twenties, is already a veteran. "He's been on tour with me, playing with Crosby, Stills and Nash," recalls the proud father. "Joe Jr. also sat in and played 'Woodstock' with CS&N at Blossom Music Center in 1996. When he was sixteen, he played twice with both me and Joe [Walsh]. One at the Ohio State Fair and another at a military base concert. Both times the keyboard player didn't show, so I played keyboards and my son played drums. And he did a fantastic job." Vitale Jr. also made an appearance at a November 1992 concert at Cleveland's Palace Theater. There he took his dad's place on the song, "Live It Up," which his father wrote in 1985. The second-generation drummer is currently a music major at Mount Union College in Alliance.

Neil Giraldo

The songs "You Better Run," "Treat Me Right," "Fire and Ice," and "Hit Me with Your Best Shot" all sound familiar to rockers. But few know that the distinctive guitar licks that give those tunes their unique rockin' sounds come from a Cleveland boy. This Parma High School graduate helped compose other Pat Benatar hits such as "Promises in the Dark," "Hell Is for Children," and "We Live for Love."

"I started getting into music around age seven," Neil Giraldo says.

I took guitar lessons at Hudak's Music for three years. Then my uncle, Tim Manak, who was five years older than I was, started coming over with all these rock albums and taking me to various shows and concerts. He'd sneak me into places like LaCave when I was underage, and I'd see all the great acts there. I really liked Damnation of Adam Blessing. I used to jam with [Damnation guitarist] Bob Kalamasz's brother Jimmy, who was a drummer in another band at the time. When I was about fourteen, my uncle took me to see the Who when they played Musicarnival, with Cyrus Erie as their opening act. Now that was a phenomenal show. It really left an impact on me. I went home that night, looked at my little amp thinking, "Now wait, I can crank this thing up and it'll sound like this. . . ."

That was the beginning.

One of Giraldo's first bands was called Kneel, with his Uncle Tim as singer. But it was the next band, Lover's Lane, with well-known West Side singer A. J. Robey, guitarist Al Retay, Mark Cerio, and drummer Tommy Amato, that got things rolling for the aspiring guitarist. From 1972 to 1975, this group played many local venues, particularly the Viking Saloon and Jiggy's After Dark.

It was kinda silly. Robey became "A.J. Lane" and I became "Buddy Love," hence Lover's Lane! We used to rehearse at the Viking and became the house band. Dick Korn [owner] would always throw us the keys at the end of the night and say, "Put the empty bottles on the bar and lock up when you're done."

This was when Cleveland was right on the fringes of the punk scene. I remember we couldn't play the schools because we didn't play Top 40. We played the more obscure things, like quirky, offbeat cover songs by Alex Harvey, and our own material that was quirky as well. We never did the commercial stuff. It was then I became friends with Stiv Bators, back when he was in Frankenstein. Then came Rocket from the Tombs and the Dead Boys. I loved what they were doing; the energy, the attitude. And we were like that, too, though somewhat different. If you could describe our band in today's terms, I guess in a way, we were like frontline alternative back then. We weren't exactly punk but we weren't contemporary, either.

I think that's why when my wife [Pat Benatar] and I got together later on, it was a perfect marriage both personally and professionally. She was much more contemporary and I veered more toward punk, so we met halfway. I was coming from the left and she pulled me toward the middle. It really worked great.

In 1975, Giraldo and Frank Amato formed Thrills and Company. "My brother was always having guys over to play in our basement," recalls Tommy Amato (not the Lover's Lane member). "So after a while, I never paid much attention. Then one day, I'm in the kitchen and I hear this guitar. I was just seventeen but I'd never heard anything like it. I ran downstairs and it's Neil playing. After he was done, I told him, 'Man, that was something else. You're going to be a star someday." He just laughed and said, "Get outta here,' and looked at my brother and said, 'Who is this crazy kid?'"

Thrills and Company moved to L.A. soon after but disbanded when Amato returned to Cleveland. Giraldo eventually returned to Cleveland as well and formed a short-lived band with Roger Lewis and Kevin Raleigh. "That was only time I was in a commercial-type band doing contemporary Top 40 cover songs," Giraldo says.

Our plan was to be more business minded and get some money together to enable us to record. Then a crazy thing happened. Although I played guitar, I could also play piano and bass. So Tracy Coats [musician/businessman] mentioned me to Dan Hartman, who was putting a band together in New York and needed a bassist. He called me to audition, and though I'm really a guitar player, I went. When I got to New York, on my way to Hartman's audition, Tracy said, "[Rick] Derringer's here, they're looking for a guitar player, why you don't audition for him?" I thought, great, I'm a guitar player. It was funny because when I went to audition for him, I ran into Roger Lewis, who hadn't wanted anyone to know he was auditioning for Derringer. And I ended up getting the gig. I think because, although [Rick] auditioned up to 100 people, he liked me because I played other instruments as well. Plus he thought I was funny!

That was in 1977. After a year of touring and playing piano on Derringer's *Guitars and Women,* Giraldo was planning to head home to Cleveland. But fate intervened. "I got this call," Giraldo says. "The A&R man from Chrysalis Records was looking for an arranger/guitarist to put a band together for this female singer they had just signed. I was looking for work, so I said sure, hoping it would work out. And boy did it. I never went back to Cleveland."

In 1979, Pat Benatar and company released the album *In the Heat of the Night* with singles "Heartbreaker" and "We Live for Love" that both hit the Top 40. The next year brought the Grammy Award–winning *Crimes of Passion,* which rose to No. 2 and reached quadruple platinum with the hit single "Hit Me with Your Best Shot." Throughout the '80s, the New York–based band continued to produce hit after hit. Their success extended to their personal life as well when Giraldo and Benatar married in February 1982.

It's always fun to come back to play in Cleveland. I always see people I haven't seen in years. We'll be playing Blossom, for example, and signs will pop out of the audience saying, 'I was in 3rd grade with you,' or 'I sat behind you in tenth grade.' It's great. Pat gets a big kick out of it.

Guitarist Neil Giraldo on stage at Blossom Music Center, 1982. *Photo by Brian Chalmers.*

Back in the '70s, Cleveland, to me, seemed so underground. And it was great. There was a real scene happening then; I wouldn't have wanted it, the music and bands, any other way. We were part of that whole subterranean scene. Now Cleveland definitely seems above ground.

Today, Giraldo is involved in composing film scores, producing for various other acts, and putting together a new album. He and Benatar are planning to form a record company.

Alex Bevan

I was kind of a passing tome in the Cleveland rock scene. I don't think anyone really knew what to do with me because I was very acoustic and had this life on the road where I'd go to colleges and play concerts. Then I'd come home and be like this larger-than-life cartoon where everyone just wanted to hear "Skinny" and see the crazy side. It took me a long time to resolve the bar personality versus the concert personality.

—Alex Bevan

He's been playing music and recording albums for the past three decades. But to fans throughout northeast Ohio, this singer/songwriter/guitarist will forever be known as that "Skinny Little Boy from Cleveland, Ohio." That 1976 signature song, "Skinny Little Boy from Cleveland, Ohio (come to chase your women and drink your beer)," propelled Bevan to instant celebrity status, albeit regional. It sold more than 20,000 copies in his hometown alone and earned the folk singer long-due respect.

That song was written after a late night gig in Bryn Mawr, Pennsylvania. It was one of those socialite kind of parties where the person running the party told us, "Now here are the rules. You're not to talk to the guests, or drink with the guests, and you'll play for exactly forty-five minutes." Of course, this was nothing like we were used to. But we thought, okay, we'll play our gig and get the heck out.

Well, after we finished and started packing up, the guy approached us and said, "We want you to play some more. What will it cost?" Now we were a pretty free-wheelin' bunch, so we said, "Okay, we want to be able to eat and drink with the guests and talk with the guests, and a certain amount of money will have to change hands." So we played and drank and hit the shrimp bowl. At the end of the night I'm talkin' with this one gal for a time, when she asks where I'm from. I said, "Cleveland." Well, she looked at me like some foul air had suddenly come into the room.

So, while driving home, I was thinking about that and got into this revenge fantasy mode, and began putting this song into my head. It was like a joke, a song written à la Zapp comics, a kind of headstone fantasy. We got to my friend Marshall McCormick's house, and I completed it in his kitchen in about twenty minutes.

It's basically the twelve-bar blues form, and the baseline is like "Hit the Road, Jack," or "Give Me Fever."

The song was included on Bevan's second album, *Springboard*. The success of that self-produced recording was the vehicle that sent him on his way to becoming a household word along the North Coast. Unfortunately, as it did for hundreds of equally talented musicians, national recognition eluded him. But the 1968 Shaw High School graduate managed to make a living from his music and has the albums to prove it.

Beginning with *Truth to Sell* in 1971, his recordings include the aforementioned *Springboard* (re-released on CD in 1992), *Grand River Lullaby* (re-released in 1997), *Alex Bevan and Friends Live* (with bassist Marty Block, guitarist Steve Downey, and drummer John Beatty), *Come for to See You, Come for to Sing* (a live charity album to aid Camp Cheerful for handicapped children), *Simple Things Done Well, Tales of the Low Tech Troubadour* (Vols. 1 and 2), and *Best-Kept Secrets* (highlighting his "electric" era with the band Cuttlefish, with whom he produced *Deco World*). The 1990s brought *Water Songs, Who Killed the Dragon* (an ecological fairy tale about the healing of the earth), *Magic Moments from the Children's Nature Schoolhouse* (for Lake Metroparks), *South Shore Serenade*, and *All the Rivers Run* (for the National Parks Service). He also won an Emmy in 1987 for the soundtrack of the NBC documentary *Rustbelt Blues*.

Influenced by Bob Dylan, Paul Simon, and Gordon Lightfoot, Bevan began playing guitar in his junior year in high school and soon after was hanging out at the popular folk mecca LaCave. He then started frequenting the Well coffeehouse in East Cleveland with bluesman Bill "Mr. Stress" Miller, where both copped their first live gigs. From there the young singer graced all the intimate North Coast venues, and appeared on Ohio college campuses. He was a house regular at the Needle's Eye in Kent from 1968 to 1970.

Although his debut album showed potential, in-house problems occurred with its producer, and Bevan decided to do his own producing and marketing on all future albums. His second effort proved his instincts right, particularly with the little ditty he wrote on the way home from that memorable party. But then, he admits to getting a little help from his friends.

"'Skinny Little Boy' never would've gone anywhere without the 'MMS Coffeebreak Concerts," Bevan says. "That's how I got to know Steve Lushbaugh, Jeff Kinzbach, John Gorman, and Joyce Halasa—back when the Coffeebreaks were held in the 'MMS studio. In the fall, winter, and spring, I'd be on the road doing the college coffeehouse circuit and opening for acts like the Nitty Gritty Dirt Band, Pure Prairie League, the Earl Skruggs Review, and even once for Ike and Tina Turner. So I played the Coffeebreaks in the summer and the song [which got heavy airplay on the FM station] ultimately became like a summer anthem."

Bevan wrote another winning single in 1978 after watching the eleven o'clock news. Hearing about city officials and a circumspect forty-day rollover of city notes that led to Cleveland's default, Bevan penned "Another Laugh on Cleveland Blues (Who's Fault Is the Default?)," maintaining, "We've been a butt of so many jokes, we've got to keep our sense of humor." The song begins with "Cleveland is the best location in the nation / temporarily caught up in a bad situation," and ends with the lines "And we know that we're going to make it through, / Proud and smiling, too / We can laugh at ourselves. / How about you?" The song, which denotes an attitude long associated with Clevelanders, was written and recorded overnight with mikes thumbtacked to the ceiling. Perhaps breaking a world's record for fastest time between conception and radio airplay, the recording was played the following morning on WMMS. And for months afterward, it was the station's most-requested song.

Bevan experimented with broadcasting for a time by way of his WMMS friends. He hosted a weekend morning show on the radio station and for a time wrote musical quips about the Cleveland Browns, usually as a commentary about a recent game. He also had a hand in behind-the-scenes production for the Morning Zoo. Yet despite everything else he's done over the past twenty years, the name Alex Bevan remains synonymous with "Skinny Little Boy." "I think 'Skinny' became truly a folk song," he says of its lasting appeal. "I still get fan mail and orders for it, from people as far as Japan. Why, just the other day I got an order on the Internet from a guy in Australia. I've gotten postcards from guys in Iceland who had tapes of Coffeebreak Concerts with 'Skinny Little Boy.' It won't go away!"

Through his thirty-year career, the self-proclaimed low-tech troubadour has never veered far from his folk ballads, clear tenor voice and slide guitar. He admits to having no regrets that he didn't become the next Dylan and acknowledges that he's content to have been able to make a living by expanding on his creative outlets. "The perception of a folk singer is the music's there for the music's sake, as opposed to just generating income. One of the things about being a songwriter and creative artist is making sure I know what the purpose of the song is. If it's a jingle, I know the purpose of the music is to enhance the image of a product and introduce that product to someone. If I'm writing for an audience, what do I want to say to that audience? Or is it a song just for me? It can be an artistic dilemma at times—a carpenter with a different hammer."

Today, the singer/songwriter has become increasingly involved with environmental education, as evident in his recent recordings. He also continues to entertain all across Ohio's musical landscape, playing various restaurants and taverns as well as school concerts and YMCAs. In 1998, Bevan came out with yet another release, *Rules of the Road,* a ten-track CD recorded live at the Grand River Winery in Madison.

The former University of Akron English major, who, ironically, flunked classical guitar, credits his wry sense of humor in coping with the highs and lows of the music business, as well as life in general. "There comes a point when you have to, in self-inspection, laugh at yourself a bit. I've known some very serious artists with whom I still, every now and then, talk off the ledge. Particularly when you're a musician, it's important to have friends and community because you lose perspective on your life. And it's your friends who help bring you back in. I have a dear friend I go kayaking with, whose motto is, 'It's not the rivers you paddle, but who you paddle them with.' That pretty much says it all."

We Are the Champions

By the end of the '70s, the hippie culture was gone, disco was fading, and punk rock was taking its underground music to great heights. America was trying to deal with Iran's Ayatollah Khomeini as hostages were kept waiting. Cleveland was in financial default (beginning on December 15, 1978); mob-related bombings were rampant throughout the city, and the phrase "Help Me, I'm Dying" had been spray-painted across a Lake Erie pier, visible along the Memorial Shoreway for all to see. (And for years, despite the Clean Water Act of 1972, which led to the rescue of Lake Erie, no one cared enough to paint over it.)

Despite all this, there remained one bright spot, one lone day when this North Coast city made positive national headlines. In September 1979, the *Wall Street Journal* printed an article titled "Cleveland: Rock Music Capital of the World." It had taken seven years, but the phrase coined by former WMMS disc jockey Billy Bass was confirmed and made legitimate. Among the reasons noted were the city's top position in record sales, with Cleveland branches of record companies such as WEA (Warner, Electra, and Atlantic) outselling branches in New York, L.A., and Chicago. The article noted the ever-rocking Agora, with its reputation for featuring acts both large and small. It mentioned the exclusiveness of WMMS, whose ratings were rivaled by no other in Cleveland—or anywhere else. And perhaps most telling of all, it revealed the continuing recommendation of rock's biggest stars, who claimed Cleveland fans were the most supportive and enthusiastic. The article ended with one irrefutable fact that sealed its musical claim to fame: "If an act bombs in Cleveland," one record executive noted, "it can be its epitaph."

Recommended Reading

Clayson, Alan. *The Best of Rock: The Essential CD Guide.* San Francisco: Collins, 1993.
Dagnal, Cynthia. *Starting Your Own Rock Band.* Chicago: Contemporary Books, 1983.
DeCurtis, Anthony, James Henke, and Holly George Warren. *The Rolling Stone Illustrated History of Rock and Roll: The Definitive History of the Most Important Artists and Their Music.* Rev. ed. New York: Random House, 1992.

13 Cleveland's Rockin' Deejays of the '70s

The Top Brass of Progressive Rock

Martin Perlich (b. 1937, Cleveland; WCLV-FM, WHK-FM, WNCR-FM, WMMS-FM)

Before there was such a thing as alternative radio, there was Martin Perlich, who pioneered the format on the North Coast. As a deejay for classical station WCLV, his show, "The Perlich Project," which began in 1964, featured the lesser-known music of the day.

His interest in music began early—he started playing piano at age four—and eventually became a way of life when he got a sales-clerk job in 1959 at Discount Records near Public Square. Within a few years, he became manager, remaining there until 1970. Here, his close proximity to unique and "unknown" records served him well, providing him with material for his Saturday (10:00 P.M.–2:00 A.M.) and Sunday night (8:00 P.M.–midnight) radio shows.

"I always listened to his Sunday night program," Dennis Fedorko recalls. "His show was so entertaining because the records he'd play you knew you would never hear anywhere else. One that sticks in my mind today was a record of just water dripping in a bucket through the whole song. We were really into bizarre stuff like that back then!"

The connection Perlich felt with his audience inspired him to coin his popular phrase "people's radio," which referred to an attempt to democratize the playlist of the station, giving listeners what they wanted to hear. Listeners could call in and make requests and weren't restricted to just one format or type of music.

Perlich continued his "people's radio" concept during his stint at WHK-FM (pre-

WMMS) and WNCR. By the time he moved to WMMS in 1971, his growing audience knew to expect an education in underground music as well as commentary on the social concerns of the day. "I was always very vocal about students' rights, women's rights, gay and lesbian rights, democratic rights. And the music back then reflected and advocated those issues," he says. "When Billy Bass and I got together at 'NCR, and then at 'MMS, we shared a counterculture perspective. We were against the war, we were for freedom of speech, and Ohio was fairly repressive in those days. So we were quite socially conscious. But then, most young people were at the time, and I like to think we led that march."

Billy Bass recalls another aspect of those pioneering radio days: "During the early 'MMS Coffeebreak Concerts, when they took place inside the studio, Martin Perlich did the best interviews. In the beginning [when deejays would interview the artist before they played the record], we didn't know what to do besides a straight question/answer show, and unless Martin was available, it was a fairly dull interview. But Martin would get a fresh story from the person and new information, other than what he found off the press releases. He had a quick, investigative mind, so he could get that person to talk about something he/she hadn't planned on talking about, and that always made it interesting."

Today, listeners on the West Coast are enjoying the deejay's eclectic tastes in music as well as his extensive knowledge of the subject. Soon after he moved to Los Angeles in 1973 (to station KMET-FM), Perlich made his presence known *off* the radio as well: his decision to pose nude for a centerfold in the *LA Star* (a swinger's paper) got him fired from the radio station. But that just found him seeking other opportunities. For the next year and a half, he became co-producer for the NBC-TV music show *The Midnight Special;* he then left for public television, where he served as producer and host of the documentary *Rock Around the World.*

When not on the airwaves or on television, Perlich is a writer. He has written a biographical novel based on the life and death of his friend Tom "Tree" Kelly. Kelly was a Lakewood native who worked at WIXY as Billy Bass's production assistant before going to WNCR and WMMS. He moved to L.A. along with Perlich, where in 1979 he was shot and killed in his Hollywood studio apartment.

Perlich made a rare return to Cleveland in 1997 for a gathering at the Rock Hall that included some of Cleveland's top deejays from FM's "golden age."

Today, Perlich works at the University of Southern California's classical music station, KUSC-FM.

Billy Bass (b. 1941, Cleveland; WHK-FM, WIXY, WNCR, WMMS)

He was the guide that took us in the right direction.

—David Spero

In the 1950s, it was Alan Freed and Bill Randle. In the late '60s and into the '70s, the man of the hour was Billy Bass. Like the two radio kings before him, Bass has been regarded over the years with tremendous respect and admiration. Yet his auspicious radio career began almost as a fluke.

It was 1964, and the Beatles were invading American music and culture. Bass was working at the Woolworth's in the Van Aken Shopping Center in Shaker Heights when he decided to display the pop group's singles and albums at the end of the aisle instead of in the middle of the aisle, as was customary. "I placed the Beatles' records at what they called the 'end caps,' where normally things like hair spray were placed," Bass explains. "So it was the first thing you saw when you walked into the store. No one had thought of doing that before in a five-and-dime. And when everyone started buying them up like crazy, they thought I was some merchandising genius!" As a result, Stark Records, the wholesaler selling the records to Woolworth's, took notice and hired Bass to manage record stores. Himself an enthusiastic rock and roll fan, Bass sold music to his customers at Music Grotto in record numbers. Within months, Bass had sold more Beatles singles than anyone else in Cleveland.

This record store experience served him well when, in 1968, he became a disc jockey at the first "all-progressive" radio station, WHK-FM, which hoped to follow the concept of the progressive rock formats of New York's WNEW and San Francisco's WSAN. Station program director Pat McCoy approached the sales manager about this new age in radio. As Bass recalls, "Pat came in the record store one day. He said, 'Look, I've got these deejays who don't know much about this new music we're supposed to be playing. Could you help me out?' Then he added, 'You know, you've got a great voice. How'd you like to be a disc jockey?'" Bass's voice was indeed special—soft yet vibrant and friendly, and it was instantly recognizable. He also was one of few black deejays on the radio. But what made him truly credible and appealing to listeners was his extensive, and current, musical knowledge.

Although the progressive-rock format of WHK-FM lasted less than a year, it was just the beginning for the Glenville High School graduate. He joined the hot deejays at WIXY in 1969 and was soon deemed the nighttime radio king. Many Clevelanders recall listening to "the Bass," with their transistors hidden under the bedcovers. When not on the airwaves, Bass kept in touch with his fans at the numerous public appearances, many of which were charitable events.

When Bass moved to WNCR-FM in 1971, he shared mike time with other radio pioneers Martin Perlich, Shauna Zurbrugg, and David Spero, who became friends. So when Bass decided to go to then-infant WMMS, all three followed suit. As Bass tells it, when he first arrived at WMMS, the station was playing a lot of Southern rock—the Allman Brothers, the Marshall Tucker Band, Leon Russell. Bass saw more potential in progressive rock and, as program director, turned the station in that direction. "Billy was always there, knowing the right thing to do," says Joyce Halasa.

He began by introducing Cleveland's progressive radio listeners to the glam rock movement of the '70s, a sound previously only familiar to ultra-hip New Yorkers. He played much of the East Coast–London mix—Lou Reed, Mott the Hoople, the New York Dolls. And when coworker Denny Sanders brought singer David Bowie to his attention, Bass began playing Bowie's music regularly on his show. So much, in fact, that it caught the attention of the Belkin brothers, who were just beginning their promotion wizardry. The result was Bowie's first American concert—which was in Cleveland, at the Public Music Hall, on September 22, 1972. With the phenomenal success of that show, the Belkins quickly booked another Bowie performance just months later. Both concerts sold out within hours.

It was also during this time, too, that Bass unwittingly saved the reputation of his hometown. "One day I was in the office on the fourth floor and Bass was on the radio," Halasa recalls. "And believe me, when Bass was on the air, the whole city was tuned in. Suddenly I hear him say, 'Here, in the rock 'n' roll capital of the world . . .' and I thought, did I hear right? So I ran down into the studio and said to him, 'Where'd you hear that?' He said, 'I made it up. People need something to be proud of in Cleveland.'"

He was right. At the time, the city was being dubbed both "the worst location in the nation" and "the mistake on the lake." Bass recalls it well.

Back in 1971–72, Cleveland was considered the "armpit of the world." There was nothing happening that made us look good. The Indians weren't exactly doing great, nor were the Browns, and people were *still* talking about the river catching fire. There was really nothing we could be proud of—except the radio. Clevelanders were really attached to the music. Maybe it was a carryover from Alan Freed or Bill Randle or the WIXY days. But whatever it was, the audience felt they were important to the development of rock.

At 'MMS, we were always looking for things to get listeners excited. So one day I got on the air and said, "Look at it this way, we live in the rock 'n' roll capital of the world!" And just from that one time, I got instant feedback of some thirty to forty calls, at least. People would call up and say, "Yeah, that's right. We're the rock capital, without a doubt." I tell you, they ran with it!

Bass also came up with the Coffeebreak Concerts. "Now, the Coffeebreaks were really a prelude of MTV *Unplugged,* long before there was such a thing," he says of the studio concerts that debuted on March 22, 1972, with singer Jackie DeShannon. "We had a prime opportunity. All kinds of acts were coming into Cleveland to perform. The artist would come into the studio, sit down, grab a guitar and play. It was much better than doing your average interview." These mini-concerts were soon taken out of the studio and into the Agora Ballroom, where every Wednesday for more than a decade live concerts sponsored by WMMS were played during lunchtime. Bass's presence and vision had yet again succeeded in further defining and strengthening WMMS's identity and reputation.

And that wasn't all. He was also first to put a woman on the air, an adventurous young broadcasting student named Shauna Zurbrugg. "Billy, along with Martin Perlich, was very receptive toward me," recalls Zurbrugg, who had been studying at the Spec Howard School of Broadcast Arts. "Billy allowed me the freedom to play what I wanted.

He really trusted my instincts." Bass was also known for playing music that was rarely heard anywhere else. He once referred to it as "rebellious programming." His fans just called it "hip."

But in 1973, the deejay left WMMS when the station changed ownership, resulting in conflicts of interest between Bass and management. He moved to Dallas, then New York, and finally L.A. He explored the music industry, serving as promotion director of Chrysalis Records, working for RCA (Bowie's label at the time), managing R&B singer Luther Vandross (1991–94), and developing his own company, Raven Entertainment.

Twenty-five years later, in the fall of 1997, Bass returned to Cleveland as a deejay for the city's top oldies rock station, WMJI 105.7. He often says, "I was getting tired of the business end of the music industry. And when Denny [Sanders] offered me a job, I thought, why not? I was ready for a change and I really missed Cleveland—despite the weather." He moved to a studio apartment within walking distance of the station and close to where his Cleveland rock roots began. Within six months of his return, the evening disc jockey had taken over the listening audience in the thirty-five to fifty-four age range, becoming No. 1 in the Arbitron ratings.

However, with radio the only constant is change. In May 1999, Bass was let go from WMJI. Not off the air for long, he moved on to WZJM-FM, the "Jammin' Oldies" station.

On April 2, 1998, Bass, along with radio pioneers across the country (including colleague Denny Sanders), was honored at the Rock and Roll Hall of Fame to celebrate the facility's new "Legends of Rock and Roll" exhibit entitled "Dedicated to the One I Love."

David Spero (b. 1951, Cleveland; WNCR, WMMS, WMMM)

"I always wanted to be a disc jockey," says the son of *Upbeat*'s producer, Herman Spero. "In '68, I was working part-time at Man Talk, which was *the* hip clothing store in town. The owner, Chuck Avner, bought the midnight to 2:00 A.M. shift at WXEN, and I got to be the deejay and play whatever songs I wanted. 'Course, I didn't know what I was doing and was scared to death. I just kinda learned as I went."

But, as seems to be the case with the 1969 Beachwood High graduate, he caught on quickly. Spero earned his radio wings there before going to work at what became his favorite station, WNCR. After a year, Spero left 'NCR to rejoin his buddy Billy Bass at the new rock station WMMS.

"The thing I remember about David," recalls Denny Sanders, "was his appreciation for pop music. That is, well-done pop music. He also had a bit of a folk rock side. He really loved Joni Mitchell and Stephen Stills. He had this great passion for music. That was David."

In August 1974, Spero took a break from radio to concentrate on his new position as manager for a young musician named Michael Stanley. Four years later, Spero decided to give radio another try and went to work for WMMM 105. He describes that experience with less enthusiasm: "'NCR was the fun station. With 'MMS, it was becoming a real job. By the time I got to M-105, it was an ordeal. You were no longer able to be creative because of the playlists, and that took the fun out of it." And so ended his radio days.

When Spero became disillusioned with the radio business, he decided to go another route. He got a job as manager-director for the Midwest branch of Columbia Records, where he remained for the next thirteen years. By 1991, the company was planning to move to Chicago and take Spero with them. But Spero didn't want to go. "I wanted to stay in Cleveland for several reasons, but basically because I feel it's the best place to raise a family." He was then offered a position on the staff at WNCX, but last-minute negotiations fell through, leaving Spero clueless about what to do next. The answer came that same day in a phone call.

David Spero at WMMS studios. *David Spero Collection.*

"Joe Walsh had left a message with my secretary. So I call him back and he's telling me about this new song, 'Ordinary Average Guy,' that he was really pleased with. He asked me if I could book some tour dates for him, and I said, 'Why don't you have your manager do that?' He then tells me doesn't have one and did I know someone who'd be interested? I said, 'Boy, Joe, I don't know,' and he goes, 'I was thinking of you, idiot!' I said, 'Oh! Okay!'" Spero accepted. Through the years, he has also managed Michael Stanley, Joe Vitale, Ian Hunter, Father Guido Sarducci (the priest from *Saturday Night Live*), Harry Nilsson ("Without You"), and Eric Carmen. And in the summer of 2000, he accepted a position as VP of education and public programming at the Rock and Roll Hall of Fame and Museum.

Denny Sanders (b. 1951, Boston; WMMS, WNCX, WMJI)

"I was fascinated by radio at a very early age," Denny Sanders says. "I spent a lot of time in my room, with radio as my companion. I'd dial around listening to different stations and what was left of network programming, this being the late '50s, early '60s. Even then, I knew I wanted to be in radio."

So before the Beatles made their historic American debut on *The Ed Sullivan Show*, it was radio that brought rock music to the young Sanders's attention. The stations he listened to ran the East Coast gamut—New York's WINS, WABC, and WMCA and Boston's WBZ and WMEX. It was across these airwaves that Sanders discovered such breakthrough disc jockeys as Arnie Ginsburg, Murray the K, and Mad Daddy.

While still in high school, Sanders made his on-air debut in 1968 on the college radio circuit at the Massachusetts Institute of Technology (MIT). "I wasn't a student there," he says, "but back then they allowed anyone who was interested to go and do a show there. So it was a great opportunity, and I picked up on it." From the start, Sanders was progressive. He had the novel idea of flipping over the 45s normally played to hear what was on the other side.

After high school, he went to work at two Boston stations, WBCN and WNTN, before making a life-changing decision. A chance opportunity opened up, and twenty-year-old Sanders decided to come to Cleveland in 1971 to work at a little-known station called WMMS. "I started there in October," he recalls. "Then a few weeks later, along comes Bass, Spero, and Perlich from 'NCR. I think the music background of all four of us gave WMMS its first solidified credibility with its audience."

And they made the station popular, too. The former WNCR deejays brought with them much of that station's listening audience. Sanders earned new ones. "But we were absolutely not taken serious by the guys at WHK[-AM]," he says.

When WHK split the FM station, they had us build a different set-up and assigned certain WHK engineers to run the boards for the 'MMS crew under union contract. Well, those people hated it. They felt it was a personal insult to be engineering for a "bunch of kids" who played music they despised, in addition to doing a service which none of them felt would ever go anywhere!

One night, an engineer, who'd had a few drinks, stood in the control room, screamin' at me, "Don't you idiot kids know nobody's gonna listen to FM? There's no future in FM, the big money's in AM."

Then I'm on the air one day, and I look through the window and see an empty chair, and the record's fading away. The engineer had walked away, obviously 'cause they didn't take us seriously. And now there was dead air. Well, I had run my own boards back in Boston, so I rushed around the corner and started the next record, which was already waiting. Just then the engineer came up and screamed, "Hey, what are you doing?" I said, "I'm saving my show, that's what I'm doing."

Well, I got written up because of it. No one seemed to give a damn about the fact the program was interrupted. They cared so much about the rules, they'd rather let the programming go down the toilet than save the show. Fortunately, come 1972, we were all running our own boards.

And 1972 brought other changes as well. Sanders explains:

When Metromedia announced the sale of the station in the fall of '72, WMMS was just about breaking even moneywise, so the buyers [Malrite] let it be known they weren't interested in keeping the current format. Soon a letter-writing campaign to the FCC was launched [to keep the current format], and Malrite, not wanting to blow the sale because they were more interested in WHK anyway, acquiesced. But then-general manager David Moorhead left to go to KMET in Los Angeles, taking Perlich with him. Bass became acting general manager until the sale, and I became program director. But because Billy and Milton Maltz didn't see eye-to-eye on certain issues, Billy left soon afterward.

But Sanders wanted to stay. "I then went into Milton's office and basically said I thought, as program director, I could help keep the station going and bring it success, and so on. He agreed. But now in the course of two months, I needed to put together a new staff and bring a facelift to the radio station."

Where to get a group of disc jockeys willing and eager to work for the new management for minimal pay? The answer, Sanders quickly surmised, was just down the street at the Cleveland State University radio station. "In those days, WCSU was a closed-circuit radio station, only heard around campus, not the FM station you hear today. I remember going there and posting a notice on the bulletin [board] that read, 'Looking for people to audition to go on WMMS.' And I was fortunate enough to get some really great, raw talent from that pool. Kid Leo, Matt the Cat, Ed Ferenc, and Betty Korvan. And Jeff Kinzbach was a friend of our production director, Tom 'Tree' Kelly, so he returned from Michigan where he was attending college to come work for us." And that is when WMMS took off, and for years that Home of the Buzzard soared above—and well past—its competitors.

Meanwhile, Denny Sanders was fast burning out while trying to juggle both his on-air time and his job as program director of a station that was exploding in popularity. When it all got to be too much, Sanders gave a call to his Boston buddy John Gorman and convinced him to come aboard. Gorman became program director, and throughout the '70s Denny Sanders's radio life was like a dream.

But the '80s woke him up. Although WMMS still ruled the airwaves, several turns of events left listeners switching the dial. It started when the station slowly began changing its format from basically album-oriented rock to more contemporary hit rock, and the result was a loss of listener loyalty. By 1986, Sanders and Gorman, along with six others, decided to leave the station they had helped pioneer to join the former WGCL, now WNCX-FM 98.5, in hopes of sparking a new flame. (Sanders coined the call letters, which meant "North Coast Express," and his afternoon on-air time pitted him against his WMMS friend Kid Leo.) But a short five months later, the station's owners, Metropolis Broadcasting, switched the format to "classic hits," later "classic rock." John Gorman was ousted, and soon after Sanders was gone too.

In September 1988, Denny Sanders joined WMJI 105.7, hosting and programming a nightly rock and roll oldies show called the "Goodtime Rock 'n' Roll Show" on the (then) adult-contemporary station. Due to the ratings success of this weeknight show, WMJI switched to a full-time rock format in the fall of 1990. John Gorman came in as program director the following year and remained there until 1996, when he left to program Detroit station WKRK. Sanders was then appointed program director, and under his watch the station flourished. In 1998, WMJI received an "Oldies Station of the Year" nomination from *Radio and Records Magazine* and a prestigious Marconi Award nomination for "Large Market Station of the Year." The station is still Cleveland's number-one rock/pop station and features veteran radio voices Chris Quinn and John Lanigan.

A self-described broadcast freak, Sanders earned a 1977 Armstrong Award for broadcast excellence and has an honorary "Doctor of Radio" degree from Kent State University. He is included in the Rock Hall's display of the one hundred most influential music radio personalities of the past fifty years as well as in the "Legends of Rock and Roll" exhibit.

Sanders cites several fond memories of his nearly thirty-year radio career:

David Bowie—1972. That's was when Bowie was first touring with his Ziggy Stardust act. He was just fantastic and so dramatically different from what was happening in those days. His debut at Public Hall was certainly an important time in Cleveland rock history. It was his first U.S. concert and obviously a new beginning in music. And we were there, unafraid to play this wild guy from England. We were all over the Ziggy Stardust album.

I remember going up to Boston around this time to visit friends, and they were still getting excited about the Band and thought Bowie was superficial. They were like a beat behind. We [WMMS] were his gateway to America, and it was great.

And anyone there won't forget the 1978 Springsteen concert at the Agora for

'MMS's anniversary show. To see him in the intimate confines of that club—well, it was truly a fabulous, magical night.

Probably my most cherished memory is when I interviewed John Lennon in 1974. I talked with him for a half hour or so. I remember he talked about Julian that night, who was eleven at the time, and who no one heard much about back then. Lennon was saying how Julian was "messing around with musical instruments. I think he might want to get into the business." It was maybe the first hint that Julian was getting serious about music. That conversation was certainly a high point.

In a business so fraught with changes and instability, Sanders survived—and succeeded—when many did not. "You have to be a fighter if you choose this business," he says. "If not, you better quit and find something else. Because you'll often find yourself up against management interference, as well as listener indifference. You have to make people care, and you have to understand what you can do to be the best. But, bottom line, you have to have the passion for the music."

Kid Leo (b. Lawrence James Travagliante, 1950, Cleveland; WCSU, WMMS-FM)

As much as he loved me, he loved 'MMS.

—Jackie Travagliante, Kid Leo's wife
(*Plain Dealer Sunday Magazine*, 1990)

To many, Kid Leo *was* WMMS. For sixteen years, he was the pulse of the station, pumping music, and life, into the veins of North Coast listeners. He not only played the music, he embraced the music. He educated people about the music. He opened doors for the music makers. (He even named his son after '60s singer Dion.)

Initially, Kid Leo thought he was going to be an architect. After graduating from Our Lady of Lourdes Central Catholic, he took civil engineering classes at Cleveland State University. But his love of music and fascination with radio lured him into the broadcasting booth at his college radio station, WCSU 89.3 (then broadcast from the school cafeteria) and then led him to switch to Arts and Sciences, which included the Radio and TV major. Weaned on WJW's Alan Freed and Pete "Mad Daddy" Myers, Kid Leo instinctively knew the energy that drives the disc jockey and attracts the listener.

"Back then, the deejays *were* the music," he says. "Their voices and energy would jump out of the speakers at you. As a teenager I listened to all the AM rock stations, but I remember the KYW team best. I can even recall the lineup—there was Martin and Howard in the morning, followed by Jim Runyan, Jim Stagg, Jerry G., and Jay Lawrence. Then WIXY came along with all those great deejays like Jack Armstrong, Lou 'King' Kirby, and Billy Bass. And I remember Joey Reynolds distinctly because it was when the Stones' '19th Nervous Breakdown' came out. He played it nineteen times in a row, and I listened to it the whole time, not believing he would really do it."

While spinning others voices at his college station, Kid Leo found his own. At the same time, WMMS program director Denny Sanders, actively searching out deejays, felt Leo's brusque vocal cords and streetwise attitude were the perfect mix for what he wanted at WMMS. The twenty-two year old already had a cocksure nickname (courtesy of a senile nun at his high school, who, thinking he was someone else, started calling him 'Leo' instead of 'Lawrence'—and it stuck). While he was just "Leo" on the air at WCSU, upon arriving at WMMS he was told that, as a professional disc jockey, he needed to use both names.

Today, ethnic names are quite common on the air. Then, they weren't. "Travagliante" certainly wasn't anything you heard on the air at the time. But I was adamant about changing my last name, out of respect for my late father. So I started thinking of an alternative.

I was a boxing fan, and "Kid" at one time was a popular boxing name. There was Benny "Kid" Paret, "Kid" Gavillan, and Elvis had made a boxing movie called *Kid Galahad*. Besides, "Kid Leo" sounded cool. So they were just about to assign me a name when I suggested to Denny Sanders that instead of changing my last name, I'd use Kid Leo. He said, "Well, as long as you have two names, I don't care. Go with it."

He did. And radio man Kid Leo was born.

From the moment his voice first aired on WMMS (Valentine's Day, 1973), his confident style and love for and knowledge of the music began luring progressive radio fans (some who had turned away with the loss of Perlich and Bass). The hip-talking deejay with the deep, sanguine voice quickly gained an audience on his all-night shift, and his Saturday night show was high in the ratings. But he soon found the midnight–6:00 A.M. shift was not conducive to "a normal life." So when David Spero left the station, Leo asked for the 2:00–6:00 P.M. shift and got it. Within a year, and for many years afterward, Kid Leo continually won the afternoon-drive ratings.

He took his job seriously. While playing tunes during the day, the inspired deejay would sift through records at night, having taken home those he felt had potential. There he'd sit listening for hours, gauging which new sounds his audience would take to. He knew a hit when he heard one. He quickly earned his listeners' trust. They relied on the Kid's instincts; any new music the astute disc jockey introduced on his program was immediately welcomed. He increased the station's record library in the mid-1970s to an estimated 15,000 titles, the largest in the country at the time. He was instrumental in Cleveland becoming the "breaking" point where unknown artists won national recognition. Some of those who have Kid Leo to thank for their careers are John Mellencamp, Pat Benatar, Roxy Music, Cyndi Lauper, Eddie Money, and New Jersey rockers Bruce Springsteen and Southside Johnny. Leo is given mention on the sleeve of the 1976 Southside Johnny and the Asbury Jukes debut album, which refers to the Cleveland deejay as "Kid (why wait for the album) Leo." Southside Johnny explains:

I had sent a demo tape to Steve Popovich, who had just signed us to Epic. We were pretty much a local band in New Jersey, working on our first album. Now I didn't know anything about *Billboard* magazine other than it existed. I didn't know radio stations reported on hot new records they were playing—heavy rotation and all that crap. So one day I was in the studio working on the album, and some guy comes and says to me, "You better look at this magazine." I take a look and here's this lunatic deejay from Cleveland on this radio station I'd never heard of, reporting "The Fever" in heavy rotation. I said, "What the f— is this? How can that be?" What happened is Popovich was a friend of Leo and had sent him the demo. Leo loved it and immediately started airing it. Unfortunately for Leo, and he heard this from me loud and clear, the demo was made just to show Popovich what our songs sounded like. It was made with sixteen-year-old high school kids in the horn section because we didn't even have a horn section complete yet. And all of a sudden, here it was, blasted over *Billboard,* and I thought, "Oh my God." I called Leo and threatened his life!

But it all worked out well. We became fast friends because he's almost a surrogate New Jerseyan, same style guy. And with Leo hyping us like mad, that became the start of our popularity in Cleveland. So by the time we played our first show there [at the Agora], the place was mobbed.

Kid Leo helps Joe Walsh celebrate his fortieth birthday at WMMS studios. *Photo by Brian Chalmers.*

Because of his enthusiasm for the music, Kid Leo was promoted in 1977. As music director, he found his niche, ferreting out unknown talent and revealing it to radio listeners. As a result, in 1980 he was named in *Rolling Stone*'s "Heavy Hundred: The High and Mighty of the Music Industry." By this time, it was well known in the business that WMMS's Kid Leo was *the* radio jock you wanted to reach if you had any hope of securing a gig at the equally prestigious and important Agora. If Leo believed in you, he paved the way for others to believe in you. It was what he did.

Another of Leo's passions was sports, which he managed to work into his music show.

If I loved two things growing up, it was sports and rock 'n' roll. So, early on, I always tried to combine them in my show. This was in the days we called our format "progressive radio," and sports was a no-no because that format grew out of the anti-establishment feelings of the era, and sports represented "the Establishment." So when I first talked about sports on the air, internally, there was some sidelong glances. But the phones lit up. So I realized normal people like normal things, and radio deals with the masses. So bit by bit, I started bringing it up and the reaction was good. Eventually it led to a regular Friday feature with the Cleveland Browns, where I'd bring in guys like Tom Cousineau, Tom Darden, and Bob Golic to talk about the upcoming games.

The sports talk sparked a new segment in his show, "The Bookie Joint."

It was one of the best things I came up with. What I'd do was take the Vegas Line printed in *USA Today* that morning, and I'd take the Browns or their opponent, plus or minus their respective points. Then I'd put up something for offer, or barter, if you will. People would call with what they had to offer. We'd give really nice prizes like autographed stuff from either rock stars or sports figures. I'd never take money or things of great value; rather, I'd accept donations to worthy charities. Though I did get to play on some great golf courses at private country clubs! I have to say, I had a pretty good track record. It was always a lot of fun, and I met a lot of good people in the community as a result.

The sports segment drove his ratings even higher.

By the time he was appointed operations manager in 1986, however, Kid Leo's hands were tied as far as discovering and playing new artists. Changes were happening in radio. One big industrywide change occurred when the FCC deregulated the airwaves, making it possible, and profitable, for corporations to purchase a large number of radio stations and then turn around and sell them to the highest bidder. Prior to this, owners had strict limitations on the number of stations they could own, and they had to keep ownership for a minimum of three years. So the passion for the music was replaced by a passion for money, and radio became a Wall Street commodity. (The controversial Telecom Act would come later, effectively reducing the role, and influence, of the disc jockey still more.)

Throughout the 1980s at WMMS, there were shifts in ownership, management, format, and deejays. With each change, Kid Leo, along with his fellow music lovers, realized those "golden days" were gone, and radio would never be the same. Yet despite the downward spiral of his radio station, Kid Leo still managed to be named "Best Disc Jockey in the Country" by *Playboy* magazine in 1987. Unfortunately it wasn't enough.

"I don't want to get into the logistics of it all, but it wasn't a good time. Certainly a share of business politics was involved. Bottom line was, I left WMMS when I was still on top, and that's something I always said I'd do. I'd rather go out like Joe DiMaggio than go out like Willie Mays, trying to snag fly balls I had no business trying to catch. It leaves a better memory." When Leo left the station, he was ready to make new grooves in the industry. He accepted an offer from Columbia Records to become vice president of album promotion, a job he'd long been preparing for. While at WMMS, Kid Leo came into contact with just about everyone who was anyone in the music business. As a result, his name became well known beyond Cleveland. And he made friends all along the way.

So it wasn't surprising that his last day on the air, Friday, December 16, 1988, consisted of one celebrity phone call after another. Among them were Huey Lewis, Billy Joel, Joe Walsh, Bon Jovi, REO Speedwagon, and of course, Southside Johnny and Bruce Springsteen. Kid Leo's final show was just as it had been for years. He played Springsteen's "Born to Run" and told his faithful blue-collar listeners that it was time to "Punch out, wash up, come back, and wrap it up." But for Leo it would be the last time.

A decade later, Kid Leo is still working for Columbia, now as vice president of special projects and artist development. "I'm grateful to be still working in the music field," he says. "I still deal with music for music's sake. It's creative, at times aggravating, often flying by the seat of your pants. But it's never boring. Sure, today it's big biz. But it's still show-biz."

Jeff Kinzbach (b. 1953, Cleveland; WMMS, WTAM)

Anyone who remembers Jeff Kinzbach also recalls his radio partner, Ed "Flash" Ferenc. They were Cleveland's answer to *Saturday Night Live*'s "two wild and crazy guys." For eighteen years, this lively duo kept morning listeners tuned into WMMS and continually broke records in their ratings period. Though Flash was not a deejay, he was an integral part of WMMS's "Morning Zoo" radio show with his witty repartee. A newsman, Ferenc could be counted on to bring listeners the local news as well as provide humorous anecdotes. The successful teaming of these two was a boon for 'MMS; the respect these partners had for each other could be felt across the airwaves.

Jeff Kinzbach grew up listening to Cleveland's best AM rock and roll stations. "In the summer I'd go swimming at Lakewood Parks pool," he says. "They always had a radio station blasting. That was during the battles between KYW, WHK, and WIXY, so they'd have one of those three stations on. You heard all that great music and those terrific deejays."

His passion for radio was such that, at one point, he and his neighborhood friends put together a bootleg station that extended its airwaves to roughly a mile. And while attending Lakewood High School, he managed to get an after-school job answering phones at one of his favorite stations, WIXY 1260.

I was in tenth grade and knew I wanted to work at a radio station. So I started calling up every one I could. Then I talked to Bill Sherard, then program director at WIXY, and was hired by his assistant, Marge Bush. I don't think Marge ever got enough credit for what she did at that station. She was so much more than just a secretary; she pretty much took care of everything. Billy Bass was there at the time, and he was a great mentor to me. Once I started working there, I brought in two of my high school buddies, Tom "Tree" Kelly and Steve Lushbaugh.

When he entered the University of Michigan in 1971, majoring in psychology, he continued to pursue his interest in radio. After working part-time jobs at WCAR in Detroit and at CKLW in Windsor (a station Clevelanders were familiar with thanks to its 50,000 watts), he decided to leave college: "Initially I pursued radio to work my way through college. Then I realized I could finish up my psychology degree and work at a restaurant, or I could be a disc jockey. The latter was certainly more attractive to a twenty year old." He left college and returned to Cleveland to work at WMMS, a station still in its infancy.

When he and Ferenc joined forces in December 1976, they secured their place in Cleveland radio history. One of their many antics was dubbed "Go Back to Bed." This involved readers sending in postcards with their name, phone number, place of employment, and boss's name. Every morning they'd call up a boss and ask if they'd give their employee permission to "go back to bed." While most employers got a kick out of it, as well as a mention of their company on the air, a few would tell Jeff and Flash just where to go.

"My personal favorite thing we did on the radio, though," notes Kinzbach, "was the 'Easy Money Birthday Contest.' That's where we'd give away anywhere from $5,000 to $25,000, just for it being your birthday. There was something really exciting about giving away money to people."

This comedic duo also succeeded in bringing a new community awareness and camaraderie to the city of Cleveland with Flash's many news commentaries and their relentless drive to get the Rock and Roll Hall of Fame and Museum finally built. "We got so frustrated at one point," Kinzbach recalls. "Flash and I were on the air, and we decided we'd go and dig the hole ourselves! So we went down [to the proposed site], and here there were all these construction guys with tractors, bulldozers, front-end loaders—ready to help. It was great." Once the Rock Hall was built, however, the disc jockey and his comrade were unduly forgotten when it came to mentions of and appreciation for those who helped bring the celebrated Hall of Fame and Museum to Cleveland (see Chapter 19).

In 1994, Jeff and Flash were let go by the station's new management. Together, they moved to an AM news-formatted station, WTAM, where they stayed until 1997. Today, Kinzbach is a private investor and has no plans to return to radio. But he looks back at his colorful radio career with no regrets.

"I think back on all those years, getting up every morning at 3:00 A.M., and I wonder, *how did I do it?* But it was so much fun, such a great era in Cleveland rock history. Everything was so free. The music was free, there were no formats, no playlists, radio was owned by small companies, not huge corporations. And Cleveland had Hank LoConti. I have a lot of respect for him. He had so much to do with that whole music scene. He was willing to take risks. He and the Belkins made things happen."

And a whole generation who grew along with WMMS would say Kinzbach did his share in making things happen as well.

Len "the Boom" Goldberg (b. 1932, New York City; WMMS)

For more than twenty-five years, Len Goldberg has been the voice of WMMS. And it was his booming voice that got him into broadcasting. Goldberg tells the story:

It was about 1968 when I first came to Cleveland. At the time I was traveling quite a bit, producing teen shows in places like Denver, San Jose, and Sacramento. Before that I owned a teen club in Denver called the "Rug-ged Room" because it had this big rug in it. It was a converted billiard parlor (which was prevalent in those days). It was a huge room, something like 6,000 square feet. We built a stage and had acts come in. The most notable groups who played there were probably Herman's Hermits ["Mrs. Brown, You've Got a Lovely Daughter"] and the Turtles ["Happy Together"]. But no matter who played, if the room wasn't overcrowded, the kids weren't happy. They had to be like sardines.

I also had an ad agency and booked concerts. When the teenage fairs came to Denver, I was asked to help with that. I was then offered a position to produce teen fairs all over the country. I sold the club to travel and eventually made it to Cleveland to do a ten-day fair at Public Hall. By then I had a family and it was getting harder to be on the move. I decided to settle in Cleveland.

Around the same time, WMMS program director Billy Bass was looking for an overnight deejay. Afternoon-drive disc jockey Martin Perlich was leaving for Los Angeles, forcing a shift in air staffing. Bass called Goldberg and asked him to come to the station and to consider a new career. But Goldberg was doubtful about becoming a disc jockey.

"I had no on-air experience. Plus, I felt I wasn't that up on the music. Bass said, 'Don't worry about that. You can play anything in the studio.' Tree [Tom Kelly] was doing the all-night shift at the time. So one night Denny Sanders had me come to watch him work. Then, at something like three in the morning, he put me one the air for a half an hour. Afterward, Denny said, 'Okay, you start tomorrow.' "

That was in May 1972. When Malrite took over the station in December, Goldberg was switched from the all-night show to the midday 10:00 A.M.–2:00 P.M. slot, which included hosting the famed Coffeebreak Concerts.

By that time, Goldberg was reluctantly being called "the Boom," or Len "Boom Boom" Goldberg. "In those days, we still had some of the old equipment, powered by tubes rather than transistors, in the production studio. They were mounted on the walls. Well, my voice was so low, especially in the mornings, it would boom and shake the equipment. Everyone was getting a name, like Matt the Cat, Kid Leo, Betty 'Krash' Korvan. Most of that came from the ingenious brain of John Gorman. I don't know anyone who has more feel for the business than John had. But when he first suggested calling me 'Boom, Boom,' I didn't want it. But Gorman, in his infinite wisdom, convinced me to go with it."

That voice was so recognizable that "the Boom" was chosen to do many of the commercial identifiers and sweeps for the station. When Matt the Cat took over middays, Goldberg stayed on doing behind-the-scenes jobs (in 1989 he was promotions director) and fill-ins for vacationing deejays. "I was the pinch-hitter on the bench," he says.

But the 1990s were not good for most of the WMMS deejays. Jeff and Flash left in April 1994, leaving Goldberg and night owl BLF Bash. The station's ratings plummeted because of the "revolving door" ownership. For a short time between 1992 and 1993, Goldberg, too, got the boot when Malrite, now a major corporation, sold the station to Shamrock. Goldberg took that time off to have bypass surgery; so by the time WMMS was sold to Omni America Corporation, a recuperated Goldberg was asked to return. Presently, fans can still hear that booming voice on his "Boom 'til Noon" Sunday show. He admits, however, that there was nothing like the "old days."

I liked working with everyone, particularly David Spero and Denny Sanders. When I started there, I used to watch them to learn the art of radio. David always amazed me because he could keep the show going—two turntables cued up all the time—and talk on the phone while doing it. And Denny, he always did everything at the last minute. He would have thirty seconds left on a tune, and this was before CDs when you had to find the right groove on the record, and never miss a beat. He had to get the other album, find the cut he wanted, cue it up, and he did it in the nick of time—fluid motion. He never ceased to amaze me.

Probably my best memory of working at 'MMS was doing segues. That was the ability to go from one record to another and make it so you'd be listening to one song, then, lo and behold, comes another one, and you never heard the transition, it was so smooth. For example, they had come out with the moog synthesizers and started recording works of music like Bach, Beethoven, and such [on the synthesizer]. There was a record out called "Switched on Bach." And somebody put out an electric version of "Rhapsody in Blue," but they copied the original, note for note. So I'd start them both on the turntable, only one on air, and I would fade from one to the other, back and forth. This was, of course, during the all-night show.

I remember one night, right after I'd started, Milton Maltz and John Chaffey, who were Malrite, were driving from Michigan to Cleveland to visit the facility because they were getting ready to take it over. They heard it and told me they thought it was fantastic.

Doing those segues gave me such a sense of accomplishment. It was one of the biggest thrills of the gig.

Thousands of WMMS fans got their thrills listening to the entertaining blend of the music and creative talents that made up the successful rock station. And that signature voice that immediately identified it continues to be as legendary as the Buzzard itself.

BLF Bash (b. William Lionel Freeman, 1942, California; WMMS)

When Bill Freeman came to WMMS from Boston's WBVF-FM in 1976, he was already a radio veteran. Before coming to Cleveland in 1976, he had worked at stations all over the country, including KFYR (K-Fire) in Bismarck, North Dakota; KIKX in Tucson, Arizona; WABB in Mobile, Alabama; WNAP in Indianapolis; KQWB in Fargo, North Dakota; and WVBF in Boston. That considered, it's a wonder "the Bash" stayed at the same Cleveland radio station as long as he did. But this was a city long renowned for its radio gentry.

William Lionel Freeman's youth was spent surfing and reveling in the music of the day. In the 1960s he gravitated toward the Beatles and Stones, of course, but he also liked the sounds of Blue Cheer ("Summertime Blues") and Sam the Sham and the Pharoahs ("Woolly Bully"). He learned to play the drums, and for a time he thought of forming a band. Although the army interfered with those dreams, it was in the barracks that this music lover got hooked on radio for good.

After listening to late-night disc jockeys during his tour of duty, and through years of graveyard shift jobs thereafter (one as a master baker), Freeman decided he could do just as well, if not better. After taking classes at Minneapolis's Brown Institute of Broadcasting, he knew he'd found his niche.

"My first radio job was at WFYR in Bismarck," Freeman recalls. "To this day, that was one of the best gigs I ever had. It was one of those old-time regional powerhouses you hear about. I'd be there at night getting calls from San Francisco, Seattle, and Omaha. That was in '65, and it was obvious to me there was more than the Beatles going on, that there was this incoming glut of music that wasn't going to be processed on the average Top 40 station. So I negotiated in my contract to be able to play one album of my choice an hour. I was the all-night hard-rock guy. And it's what I've always been about."

In the days rock jocks had catchy radio names, Freeman decided to use his initials plus a word that described "a party, or a good smash in the pop sensibility." During the next twelve years, BLF Bash worked at nine different stations in as many cities—on purpose. "It was to my advantage to be on as many stations as I could to hone my musical chops when it came to being a broadcaster. So the more I learned, the more I could apply down the road."

The road ultimately led him to Cleveland. WMMS program director John Gorman first called Freeman in the summer of 1975 to ask him to join his staff. Freeman turned him down.

I was making good money working in Boston at 'VBF. Plus I was in the midst of planning a trip to Fargo to see old friends. When I told John this, he enticed me by saying if I stopped by in Cleveland on my way, he'd get me press tickets for the upcoming Stones' World Series of Rock concert at the stadium. Well, I was a big Stones fan, so I said sure.

I went to Cleveland and met everyone at the station. I liked the crew and spent two or three days in town. John knew I liked Mexican food so he took me to the Mexican Village restaurant, and we threw ideas around. I left with the notion that when things unraveled at 'VBF, which I knew was inevitable, I'd consider going to 'MMS. A year later, the station went disco and I left for Cleveland.

In September 1976, BLF Bash began his tenure at what became the nation's top rock radio station. "It was at the peak where all this new music was coming in and we had our ears to the ground," he says of that time. His gravelly voice fit perfectly on the graveyard shift, and listeners knew right away what station they'd tuned in to when they heard that deep rasp. Freeman would conduct his entire shift standing at the mike with shoes off. His night-owl hours kept him from partying with his work crew, so he maintained stronger ties with his audience than his coworkers did. Whether it was the combination of his keep-to-himself personality or working those after-bar hours, BLF Bash remained a mystery to his colleagues.

"Bash was always a puzzle to us, but we all loved him so much," former WMMS deejay Dia Stein recalls. "He was certainly a bit of a loner, but what a great guy. I thought the world of him, and he really knew his stuff. If I ever had to put together a radio dream team, there'd be no doubt Bash would be my all-night guy. He knew how to keep his audience."

That talent for maintaining listeners was the direct result of his musical knowledge and his rapport with callers. "Bash had great taste in music," recalls regular listener Jeff Adams. "He played your requests, which is not so common in today's radio. And if he really liked the song, he'd start a conversation with you about the group, as if it was just the two of you talking in your living room."

Over the next two decades, BLF Bash experienced and survived all the station's many changes and controversies. But by September 1998, the station was sold once again (the fifth time in as many years), and the last of the creative geniuses of WMMS was informed that his services were no longer needed—after twenty-two years. As with everything else, Freeman took it in stride and refused to get overly sentimental about it.

As I cleaned out my locker that last day, I looked around and said to myself, "Ya know, Bash, that was a job well done." I showed up to work every day. I did my best to entertain the people. And I got along with everyone I worked with, I didn't get into their business. And I stayed on top of what was happening with the music. So I left with a satisfying feeling.

I'd counsel anybody who wanted to get into broadcasting to have some clue as to why they're getting into it. Don't do it for the ego-trip, the parties, or other accesses. Approach it as a profession in broadcasting. Because it should be for the music that you get in it for. Not to be some esoteric-dimpled-delight who doesn't know anything about what's happening in today's music.

Matt the Cat (b. Matthew Lapczynski, 1953, Belgium; WMMS-FM, WNCX, WDOK-FM)

"[Kid] Leo and I had this bizarre idea of making demo tapes and submitting them to WMMS." Such was the beginning for two college kids who had dreams of breaking into Cleveland radio.

Matt the Cat was just another English student at Cleveland State University when he joined his college radio station. "I hadn't been a huge radio fan, per se. The fast-talking, motor-mouthing didn't appeal to me." The late 1960s, however, turned him around. "I had an appreciation for roots music, like Carl Perkins, whose music I became acquainted with through the Beatles covering his songs. Then I discovered album cuts, FM radio, as well as the new artists being introduced. Listening to Martin Perlich, Doc Nemo, and Denny Sanders made me realize you can develop your own deejaying style, and I thought it might be interesting work for awhile."

The CSU stint turned into actual employment in April 1973 when Matt joined WMMS as a weekend announcer, eventually becoming the popular midday jock. (His name was tagged by John Gorman because "it just sounded good.") The deejay with the mellow, "cool cat" radio voice became a celebrity in his own right when he began hosting the Wednesday Coffeebreak Concerts.

"The Coffeebreaks were always an adventure," he recalls. "There's something really exciting about broadcasting live. Anything can happen, and you had to stay on your toes. But that was the whole buzz. There were so many good concerts throughout that time. The one with Harry Chapin comes to mind. He liked having his audience participate in his shows, and he let me share the stage with him and made me sing a song with him. The man just wouldn't let me off the hook. He was a great guy and a great entertainer."

Many thought the same of Matt the Cat as well. "Matt was my favorite jock at 'MMS," says Dewey Stevens. "There was something about his delivery and the sound of his voice that appealed to me. And it's funny, after I became a deejay, people were saying how much I sound like him, so I must have picked something up from listening to him all those years."

In 1992, as a result of management, and budgetary, changes, the longtime deejay was unceremoniously released from WMMS. He became the weekend fill-in announcer at WNCX from 1993 to 1994 and then joined WDOK-FM in September 1994 as its morning announcer. Although WDOK's "easy-listening" was worlds apart from WMMS, the tempered voice of Matt the Cat fit in well with the station's format. In June 1997, he was let go when the station changed direction.

"Radio has always been a medium of change—music, format, management, ownership, and audience," he says. "These days, the changes that deregulation and consolidation have brought mean that the kind of approach we took at 'MMS is no longer possible in the new corporate culture."

The Pioneering Female Rock Deejays

Shauna Zurbrugg (b. 1951, Canton; WNCR, WMMS)

"Growing up, I planned on being an actress. That was always my main focus," recalls Shauna Zurbrugg. "I was on stage in one form or another in school and various regional and local community theaters. I was very much into music as well, and played the trumpet. I really wanted to play the saxophone, but I was turned away at the music store from buying a sax because the man said it was a 'male' instrument." That was her first taste of the very sexism that she'd later set out to change.

"I was very caught up in the culture of the '60s, and what was happening," she says. Her musical taste was "all over the map, though I particularly liked the Beatles, Stones, Mamas and Papas, Donovan, Jefferson Airplane—and Motown was a real big influence." But acting remained her focus.

In the summer of 1969, the Marlington High School graduate entered Indiana's Culver Military Academy. The choice was partially because other members of her family had gone there, but also because she'd heard of their notable theater department. "That was bizarre. I was a hippie, yet I was marching in a very country club–like military setting in the middle of Indiana in 1969!" Zurbrugg then attended Penn Hall Junior College for Women that fall in Chambersburg, Pennsylvania. The following year, she left to attend Kent State's Stark Campus, where she took classes in journalism and psychology. It was during this period that a radio announcement altered her goals.

I was driving home from class one evening and heard an advertisement for the Specs Howard School of Broadcast Arts on WNCR. This was just when 'NCR had started. And not to sound too clichéd, but a little light bulb did go off in my head. I was immediately aware that becoming a disc jockey could be an easy way to make a name for myself and thus break into acting. I was aware of the women's movement dominating the news in the early '70s—the burning of the bras, Gloria Steinem, et cetera. But no women were on the radio except behind the scenes, or reporting the news or weather.

Now really, I'm not that shrewd, but it did occur to me that my chances for getting on the air were good because the big news was that women were not being promoted and something had to be done. The consciousness was already out there and here was the key. So I dropped out of college and took the class.

Her teacher was Walt Tiburski, WNCR's sales manager and a veteran of the Cleveland music scene. "Shauna had a great knowledge and appreciation of the music," recalls Tiburski, who had also taught at the WIXY School of Broadcasting. "I was immediately impressed with her voice. As we say in the business, she had great pipes. And she was very hip in that she had an eloquent way of presenting her thoughts on the culture. She was able to parlay her talents with great focus and a smooth presentation. Her style was perfect, especially for those times."

Then there were the other rock radio pioneers whose influence were not lost on Zurbrugg.

The primary deejays were all associated with my favorite radio station [WNCR]—Martin Perlich, David Spero, and Lee Andrews. I asked Walt if I could go up to the studio sometime and watch everyone at work. I'd go a few times a week. Then came the pivotal moment of my entire career. Billy [Bass] had just left WIXY and had come to 'NCR [as program director/deejay]. Billy wasn't happy with the husband/wife team doing the morning drive time. One day while I was in the studio, Billy said, "You know, you got a good voice, why don't you make a tape for me?" I was thrilled! I put together a demo tape and brought it in to Billy.

Now this is a great story. Billy took me down to the production room and he was listening to the tape when all of a sudden he jumped up, twirled me around, and screamed, "You're the girl I've been looking for all my life!!" It was total Billy Bass! That was a beautiful moment, and the highlight of my career.

"Shauna was special in many ways," Bass says. "For one thing, she had a great voice. She also had a sense of humor and a good sense of the music. It was quickly apparent she had talent; she knew how to program the music. All these things combined won her a connection with our target audience. She was a perfect fit to what we wanted."

Zurbrugg and Jeff Gelb ("who looked just like Frank Zappa") became WNCR's new morning drive team in May 1971. Within a few months, Zurbrugg was given her own show full time, including her own Saturday night program, making her the first female disc jockey in Cleveland to have a solo show. But it also got her more male attention than she wanted—which made her a pioneer in yet another way. Today it's called "shock radio." Billy Bass recalls,

> Shauna was getting very frustrated by guys constantly hitting on her. So one night while we were listening to her show, I heard her invite the audience to come real close to the radio. She said, "Listen, guys, I want you to know I'm not interested in you whatsoever—do me a favor, have your girlfriends call instead."
>
> I said, "Oh my God, what is she doing?!" I came in the next morning, ready to give her a tongue-lashing because I didn't know how the audience would take that. Then I noticed the phones never stopped ringing. She was more popular than ever—but the general manager was having a heart attack! Everyone was going crazy. It ended up being an important moment for me as program director. It caused me to make a decision to just let her go with it. And really, she wasn't doing anything wrong; it just happened because she'd gotten tired of the harassment.

Zurbrugg continued to give listeners reasons to tune in. "Things became real interesting when I started calling myself the 'Screaming Queen Bitch' and 'The Crazy Lady.' I developed a tough persona. I created a character. It was fun, and my ratings went up. Much of what I did and said on the air that summer of '72 was simply for shock value. And it worked. We kept expecting the FCC to come down on us any second, but they never did!"

Chances are the FCC execs weren't even listening. In the early seventies, FM progressive radio was still not taken seriously by anyone except the hippies whose lives centered around the eclectic music and those who played it. It was during this time that the art of the segue was introduced to the listening public. Zurbrugg recalls:

> I remember Billy was blown away when I did something no one in FM radio had done before. That is, in the middle of the Stones, Cream, Free, Joni Mitchell, Jackson Brown, or the Dead, etc., I threw in a song like Aretha Franklin's "Ain't No Way." I remember Billy was driving around in the city, heard it, and said he had to pull over, and he started to cry. You see, he'd just ended a romantic relationship and had been feeling vulnerable. Hearing this tear-jerker touched him deeply. He also realized how effective such diverse programming could be.
>
> That kind of experimentation was so exciting because we could play Gershwin back-to-back with the Stones if segued correctly. For example, there would be a piano riff at the end of a Stones' tune, and that was in the same key as a Gershwin piece that began with a similar piano riff. That's the genius and beauty of a segue. To blend music so that, for a moment, you don't notice the shift from one artist to another. I don't think creative programming exists in many markets any more. Our

particular group—and I really give the credit to Billy and Martin—influenced me phenomenally. Then I took it a step further by adding R&B. We often tried to top one another with our segues. It was so wonderfully creative. To me, it was the most exciting thing about what we were doing, and it enabled me to exercise the artistic part of myself. Of course, the Cleveland audiences were always so open-minded; they were sophisticated and educated about music. This allowed extraordinary flexibility and versatility in their tastes that didn't appear to exist in many radio listeners in other parts of the country.

When her friends Bass and Perlich left for WMMS in early 1972, Zurbrugg was right behind them. She worked there with Joyce Halasa, another woman who had ventured into the male-dominated industry. Although these two women were immediately accepted by both their audience and their peers, it would take until 1976 for the FCC to take the movement seriously. This occurred when the Cleveland chapter of the National Organization for Women (NOW) filed a formal complaint charging discrimination against women in the workforce. That resulted, almost immediately, in more women achieving higher status in their jobs—radio in particular. Within weeks, Kent State University graduate Christy Phillips became the first full-time female disc jockey in AM radio (at station WMGC, formerly WIXY 1260, later WBBG).

A new era had been ushered in. But by December 1972, the first woman deejay in Cleveland's FM radio decided she could go farther in L.A. "Former WMMS general manager David Moorehead was now at L.A.'s KMET [where Martin Perlich worked] and said he'd find a slot on the air for me, but I knew that meant getting rid of someone else, and I wouldn't let him do that. So I ended up at KLOS, which was the number-one rock station in L.A. at that time, working on weekends." Her experience there was not what she was used to, however. "In Cleveland, I felt very much like I was a person. I had been accepted and appreciated for myself. It was a different story in L.A. I felt like I was the token woman disc jockey and quickly became aware of the kind of corporate thinking that was so much a part of radio in larger markets."

She resigned from KLOS in 1974 and moved to KMET until 1975. There she worked with Rachel Donahue (whose husband, Tom, had introduced progressive radio to San Francisco rock stations KMPX and KSAN) and KSAN alumna Mary Turner. But once radio playlists reduced the disc jockey's role to preselected records, Zurbrugg left the business. "It wasn't fun anymore," she says. "Because of the playlists, it became very stilted. The creativity in radio was gone."

After leaving radio in 1976, she tried a number of ventures. At the end of the decade, she worked for *Billboard* Flight Services, hosting a jazz show for TWA and a rock show on Air Canada. Throughout the 1980s, she helped usher in NBC-TV's *Entertainment Tonight,* where she produced music segments. In 1984, she became senior producer of Ted Turner's Cable Music Channel, the first cable attempt to compete with MTV (which Turner eventually sold to the owners of MTV). She also worked on a variety of celebrity-oriented and music-related TV shows.

Today, Shauna Zurbrugg works as a staff audio producer for Dove Audio, Inc.

/New Star Media, Inc., where she also abridges books for audio, and as a freelance book editor. She received two Grammy nominations in 1996, both in the Best Spoken Word/Children's Field category, for producing *The Wonderful O* (which Melissa Manchester read) and *Treasure Island* (read by Michael York). Although she never got around to becoming an actor or singer, Zurbrugg realizes she simply used her performance talents in other ways.

Joyce Halasa (b. 1949, Cleveland; WMMS, WMMM)

In addition to being one of the pioneering women in Cleveland FM broadcasting, Joyce Halasa has also been a photographer, a journalist, a public relations director, a promoter, and a manager for rock and roll bands. And according to her, it all seemed to "just happen." Perhaps she was at the right place at the right time; but certainly she had the brains and drive to make a place for herself in what were considered male vocations in the early 1970s.

"My interests were always vast, especially in music," she says. "I was never big into one particular artist. I liked rock but also enjoyed listening to blues, country, and folk—everything from Rod Stewart, Leon Russell, to Laura Nyro."

Halasa's connection with Cleveland rock history began before she was old enough to appreciate the new culture.

I was a real downtown kid. My mother worked at the Ritz Hat Company [later Barbara Anne Bridal], so I was down there all the time. Norm N. Nite's father worked upstairs blocking hats, making them into different styles, and the shop was located right around the corner from Record Rendezvous. My mother knew Leo [Mintz] well, and I became very familiar with that record store. In fact, all my old albums are in Record Rendezvous boxes.

At home, my mother always had the radio on. So I grew up on Bill Randle—starting at two and three years old. She listened to him every day. Then in high school [St. Stanislaus], I had this great job at Appliance City at E. 9th and Prospect, where I sold Nikons to the photographers from the *Plain Dealer* and the old *Cleveland Press*.

While attending Ohio University, Halasa studied the art of photography. She was photographer for the college yearbook and attended concerts to shoot the Who, the Grateful Dead, Simon and Garfunkel, Peter, Paul and Mary, and hometown bands Damnation of Adam Blessing, Glass Harp, and Tiny Alice. She graduated with a BFA in 1970, just in time to practice her skills and talents on Cleveland's lively rock scene.

There was so much going on then, especially around University Circle and downtown. You'd walk around there and run into people like Martin Perlich, David Spero, and Billy Bass. That was right around the time WNCR was going on the air.

I was working at Case Western Reserve as a university photographer and met Jim Mauk from the *Great Swamp Erie da da Boom* paper. I became a photographer and writer for it. Then I started tending bar at Socrates Cave [later the Mad Hatter]. That's how I met a lot of the band members. So everything was jelling at once.

The summer of 1971, Halasa was offered a job in public relations for an arts and crafts festival that became a historic milestone on the North Coast. The Crooked River Revival, sponsored by WNCR, became the first public event in the downtown Flats area. "Before then, *no one* went down to the Flats," she says. "We decided it was the perfect place for this event. We were hippies looking for an out-of-the-way place. We picked the Flats because it was convenient. There was all this room, plenty of parking space, no cops, no adults over thirty. And we got incredible coverage because it attracted some 50,000 people. I took photos, which were picked up by both the *Plain Dealer* and the *Press* with full-page spreads. That was the true start of the birth of the Flats."

By January 1972, Halasa's growing friendship with Billy Bass resulted in her becoming the first on-air female disc jockey on WMMS. "Billy had left 'NCR by then, and for a few months he just hung out with me at Case [Western Reserve]. Then he got an interview for program director at 'MMS. I'll never forget when he came back to see me that day. He was so excited and announced, 'Got me a radio station!' So Martin Perlich and David Spero followed him, and he hired me to do the PR. That was when 'MMS had no budget whatsoever. We did it all."

"All" included every promotion the young music enthusiasts could think of. The station sponsored a "Transcendental Sunday" at the Allen Theater, which showcased various new-age music groups. Interestingly, one of the bands included Shakti, a nephew of 1960s musician and meditation guru Ravi Shankar. The success of that event led to a series of concerts and benefits. One concert in particular—on May 20, 1972, at Edgewater Park (featuring Glass Harp)—was so successful it got front-page notice in the *Plain Dealer*.

WMMS was on the map, and Joyce Halasa was soon on the air. Bass hired Halasa for the 10:00 A.M.–2:00 P.M. shift. A few months later, she was promoted to the morning drive.

"I had no desire to be a deejay," she says. "I was scared to death, and I was so raw. But I know why Billy did it. He knew I really cared about the music; I had a real grip on the culture, and I understood what he was trying to accomplish. But it was a hard way to learn how to swim! To be a progressive disc jockey meant you had to go home, listen to five, six hours of music, find new tunes, sit down, and craft the segues. All I remember about that time was working constantly. I was deejay, promotion director, operations director, public service director."

She also had competition. Her air time, initially, was directly opposite WNCR's first lady, Shauna Zurbrugg. The two, however, became friends. "When Shauna was working at 'NCR," Halasa recalls, "we'd go a lot of places together. People couldn't believe we were friends because we were on competing radio stations. I guess they figured you had to be enemies." Zurbrugg recalls their friendship. "Maybe because we were the only women doing this at that time, Joyce and I shared a real camaraderie. She was incredibly supportive and a wonderful friend to me during that time. When I came to 'MMS, there were so many artists coming out at once. It was like an explosion of music. And here we were, able to have influence and bring it all about. We each had our own distinctive style, yet we blended perfectly."

But the glory days at WMMS ended for Halasa early in 1973. When Metromedia sold the station to Malrite Communications in December 1972, Halasa and Bass suddenly found themselves with little control over the music and a lot less freedom. As Halasa explains,

> Metromedia was a big national radio station chain which owned five of the key progressive stations. There was KSAN and KMET in California, WMMR and WNEW in New York, and WMMS/WHK in Cleveland. So when they sold ours to Malrite, which had two or three small radio stations—none in any major city—it was a big deal.
>
> There were only eleven of us at the time, and they weren't hiring any more. Our hands were tied every time we tried to do something to promote the station. Also, there were times we didn't know if we'd get paid. It was a mess.

Halasa and Billy Bass felt they were fighting a losing battle. Both were gone by March 1973.

Not wishing to try another station, Halasa began working at the Agora Ballroom, where she used her promotions and public relations experience to organize concerts and open new Agora clubs across the country. And with her close proximity to the bands, Halasa began to manage musicians, such as folk rock artist Alex Bevan and Bazooom (with guitarist Alan Greene), and did PR work for Circus, Youngstown's Left End, and one of the first New Wave bands in America, Rocket from the Tombs.

Halasa returned to radio in 1975, this time for WMMS's newest competitor, WMMM (M-105). "I'd work at the Agora during the day, then go on the radio from midnight–6:00, Fridays and Saturdays. By then I was more comfortable about being on the radio, and I loved the shift. You had much more freedom, no one was around, so you could really concentrate on the music. And working with [program director] Eric Stevens was a great experience. He had so much energy. He really kept us on the ball."

But by 1978, her radio stint at M-105 came to an end when her responsibilities at Cleveland's premier rock club increased. She was hired to book and promote the summer outdoor concerts at the Agora-affiliated Legend Valley in Licking County (later known as Buckeye Lake). "That was really a full-time job. In the winter, I'd go to other cities and open up new Agoras. Then in the last few years, I ran the Cleveland club again until it burned down. Then I continued to work at Legend Valley for another year."

Through the next decade, Halasa used her photography talents to capture the local bands of the era. Her portfolio most notably includes the earliest shots of Rocket from the Tombs. In addition, she wrote for the Akron indie paper the *Zeppelin*. She also worked at the Richfield Holiday Inn and wrote a series of articles on Cleveland's rock history for *Scene*.

Of her various duties and responsibilities in the industry, she says: "It certainly wasn't all glamorous. There were the disappointments, the loss of loyalties, the bad blood. On the other hand, it was extremely exciting to be in progressive radio when everything was happening at once and you knew you were on the cutting edge of music history. That whole scene was a once-in-a-lifetime event, and I'm glad I was a part of it.

Other Notable Deejays

Eric Stevens (b. 1948, Cleveland; KYW, WIXY, WMMM)

Eric Stevens was just sixteen and attending Cleveland Heights High School when, in 1964, he got a job at AM pop station KYW. "They call it a 'gofer' because basically you go for this, go for that. But that was okay with me. I was learning the craft and having fun with it, especially when I started doing record hops with those great VIP disc jockeys. It was a terrific breeding ground for what I eventually went on to do."

When the station changed to WKYC in 1967, Stevens was let go. He immediately started pounding the pavement.

I'll never forget when I called this one station, WPVL in Painesville, looking for a job, and was told, "Son, we only hire pros here." That made me angry, because although I was young, I'd been active in the business for three years, and had worked at what was then the number-one Top 40 station in Cleveland!

So I applied at WIXY, which was a new station. Because I'd already had experience in production when I produced "Jim Runyan and Folks," a Sunday night folk show at KYW, I was immediately made production director. Within weeks I was made music director, which allowed me to program all the music and choose the order in which it played. By the time I was twenty I was program director. That was when we beat both WHK and WKYC, going from like zero to number one. We had ratings that were not only extremely good then, but generally unheard of in today's market.

While at WIXY in 1967, Stevens was nominated for music director of the year. "WIXY broke a ton of records then; it was truly a powerhouse station. I didn't win. Someone from a New York station did. But it was still a real kick to be nineteen years old and not only be nominated but get flown to Las Vegas."

In 1969, Stevens left the station to form his own management company, Brilliant Sun Productions, which handled Alex Bevan and Damnation of Adam Blessing as well as the popular Detroit band Brownsville Station. (Stevens was instrumental in making their 1973 single, "Smokin' in the Boys Room," a No. 3 *Billboard* hit and $2 million seller.) "I must've done a helluva sales pitch," he says, "because I got a United Artists contract for Damnation without the record execs ever hearing the group!"

By 1973, WIXY lured him back as program director. "That's when I learned there's no such thing as returning to 'splendor in the grass.' It just wasn't the same, and the station was clearly dying [largely due to the popularity of FM radio]. [Owner] Norman Wain knew it every bit as I did." Stevens left WIXY to become vice president and operations director at new station M-105 in March 1975.

"We had a great group. There was Winn 'the Mud' Rosenberg in the morning; Eric Lawrence, midday; Bill Stallings, afternoon drive; and TR [Tom Rezny] at night. It was a real good mix of personalities."

Stevens also made the most of his experience from WIXY to promote his new station. There was a continuous stream of promotions, including doing live broadcasts from local high schools and broadcasting from a lucky listener's bedroom (which included breakfast in bed and a limousine ride to work that morning). As a result, M-105 became the fastest-growing station since WIXY.

"We had great ideas for promotions and ways of promoting our air personalities," Stevens recalls. "But aside from that, our slogan was 'the home of continuous music' because we'd pack in as much music as possible. For our third anniversary, we celebrated by playing 105 of the most requested songs and most requested live concert music."

Within three years, M-105 became one of the top-rated AOR stations in the country. It was also known for hiring women. Eighteen-year-old Suzy Peters had just graduated from Lakewood High School when Stevens hired her in 1977. (She'd go on to work for the Agora.) Music director Ellen Roberts and WMMS alumna Joyce Halasa also worked at M-105. Halasa says, "Eric was an extremely motivated person and talented man. The way he manipulated the M-105 hourly clock—it was masterful. He kept that station running smooth, and his energy was contagious."

By February 1980, however, Stevens decided it was time for a change. He began his own marketing/consulting firm, which he continues to this day. His business is broad based but centers on marketing concepts for products as well as producing television commercials. He is also a partner with Mike McVie, with whom he does radio consulting.

"I feel privileged to have been a part of the embryonic stage of rock radio," he says. "The whole experience has helped me continue to do things I love."

Tim "the Byrdman" Byrd (b. 1953, Chattanooga; WIXY, WGCL, WZZP, WHK)

When Tim Byrd was fifteen years old, he walked into Johnston, South Carolina, radio station WJES and announced to program director Jim Calk, "I want to be a disc jockey." Sensitive to the young boy's earnest enthusiasm, Calk told him to make an audition tape and work on his pronunciation. Within two weeks, "the Byrdman" was on the air.

Before he turned sixteen, Byrd had his third-class license, and by the time he was twenty, the young deejay had worked at stations in Greenwood, South Carolina (WCRS), Hickory (WIRC) and Charlotte (WAYS), North Carolina, and Jacksonville, Florida (WAPE). And he was on his way to Cleveland to work at the city's number-one radio station, WIXY.

"Whenever I thought of Cleveland, I recalled my favorite deejay, Jack Armstrong, who had honed his career there," says Byrd, currently working at WRMF in West Palm Beach, Florida. "I used to listen to Big Jack in the late '60s when he was on WKYC, which I was able to pick up in South Carolina."

At WIXY in 1973, he worked with some of the best personalities in Cleveland radio at the time—Mike Reineri, Dick "Wilde Childe" Kemp, and Paxton Mills. "That station was highly personality-driven, while at the same time not alienating or ignoring the music. That, I believe, is harder to do than getting on and just talking, like today's talk radio, or what's now become radio jukeboxes. The music is now regulated by playlists,

Tim Byrd with '70s teen idol Leif Garrett. *Photo by Janet Macoska.*

and deejays are forced to read from liner notes rather than letting their personalities show through."

But his WIXY days were short lived. A year later, Byrd was lured to Winston-Salem, North Carolina, station WAIR where, at age twenty-one, he became the youngest program director in the state. While there, he changed the station to "Fresh AIR" and received seven gold records for breaking hits. Then, in 1976, it was back to the North Coast at "contemporary music" station WGCL 98.5 (G-98), where his talent for picking hits continued as he netted five more gold records.

"That station was a lot of fun, and a lot of hard work," Byrd recalls. "I remember the charity works we did, like the Byrdman's Christmas benefits at Fagan's, and the deejays I worked with who became good friends. There was 'Little Stevie' Kritzer and 'Doctor' Matthew Frail, who was a real riot. And Tom Kent and I still keep in touch even though we haven't worked together for nearly twenty years."

During his G-98 days, Byrd recorded an old Bobby Womack tune, "Nobody Wants You When You're Down and Out," with fellow North Coasters Mark Avsec (later with Wild Cherry and Donnie Iris), Joey Porello (Joey and the Continentals, then of Sweet City Records), and Jackie Cooper (drummer for the O'Jays) at Cleveland Recording. "It was something I'd always wanted to do. Realizing how open-minded Clevelanders were about music, I knew it would be a good place to do it. And for a local 45, it did pretty good!"

Byrd was in Cleveland when disco invaded the nation's music culture. And though he hosted regular disco nights at the Brown Derby's "Luv Pub" in Rockport as well as at the most popular West Side disco, the Dixie Electric Co., his favorite place to go in town was a club that was short in life but long on memories. "Nite Moves was Cleveland's playground during that time," he says. "It was really on the same level of any of the classy New York City clubs, and we all just had a ball there."

The private disco would soon become the site for another venture in Byrd's career. Aside from his distinct voice on radio, many recall the Byrdman as host of TV's *Weekday Fever*. Because of his increasing popularity, when Cleveland TV station WKYC was looking for a suitable host for a new dance show, the Byrdman came to mind.

"WKYC-TV called and asked me to audition for this new show, and three days later they called to say I had it," he recalls. "Fred Silverman was running NBC network and had to give the final okay. So I viewed that as a high compliment. But when they told me the audition tapes were shown in a viewing room full of women, and they picked me out of all the others, well, that was the ultimate compliment!

"The show was just the greatest fun in the world," he says of the TV program that aired from 1978–79. "I remember when Nina Blackwood [Cleveland native and later MTV video jockey] and I were crowned the king and queen of Nite Moves. This was when she was playing at various clubs around town as a harp player."

He also shared the spotlight on the show with Nanci Glass (later host of WKYC-TV's magazine-format show *American Journal*), who would educate the audience on disco fashions, makeup, manners, and dance tips. The show was cancelled at about the same time that his days at WGCL were numbered.

In the spring of 1979, Byrd was offered what seemed to be a dream opportunity as program director for WZZP (Zip 106), but that stint proved ill fated by the fall. But Byrd wanted to remain in Cleveland, so he went from disco to country and took a job as program director for WHK-AM, which then had a country music format. He stayed with country music even after leaving Cleveland in 1980 for New York's WKHK-AM. He would remain in the Big Apple for the next eleven years. After moving to WNBC in 1983, Byrd worked with another Cleveland native radio veteran, Don Imus, as well as an up-and-coming controversial deejay named Howard Stern.

"I was there and watched that whole Howard thing unfold. Howard's antics were always getting him into conflicts with management. But of course, once they saw how successful it was, they caved in. After that, he pretty much could do anything. Then I got him together with his agent, Don Buchwald, and after that, things really got going for him."

In 1984, Byrd switched New York stations. While deejaying at WPIX-FM, he was offered another TV job—this time for VH1.

"When [the station] was first being conceived, they approached me because they were looking for my prototype to sell to the executives," he says. "Then they went out and hired everyone *but* me! They hired Don Imus, Rita Coolidge, Frankie Crocker, and Bowser from Sha Na Na. But over the next year, I started filling in for some of the veejays and ultimately got my own Saturday morning show and, later, a full-time show," in which he had a video countdown and did movie and book reviews.

The veejay returned for a Cleveland visit one weekend in the fall of 1986, when he promoted a "Guest VJ" contest sponsored by new Cleveland rock station WNCX, which, coincidentally, had replaced his former employer, WGCL. "It was great to be back, even for such a short time," he says, "I've always had a warm spot for Cleveland."

Further proof of that statement came in 1986 when Byrd voted for Cleveland in that famous *USA Today* Rock Hall poll. "I was a true New Yorker by then, but I really wanted Cleveland to get it. I felt [the city] deserved it. Cleveland had some noted influential people like Steve Popovich and the Belkins. I thought those two alone were great examples of real stand-outs in the industry, and class acts. And I tell you, I was thrilled when I heard Cleveland actually got the Rock Hall."

Tim Byrd now resides in West Palm Beach and continues his radio career at WRMF-FM, where he is hosting the afternoon drive. And on weekends he continues to play music people want to hear as deejay at the Krome and Monkey clubs.

Tom Kent (b. 1954, Winston-Salem, N.C.; WIXY, WGCL, WMJI, WRQC)

A true radio fan, Tom Kent grew up listening to deejays Rick Dees and Scott Shannon (both of whom went on to distinctive radio careers) on station WAIR in Winston-Salem. He was also able to tune into Chicago's WLS, his particular favorite. So it wasn't surprising when this avid young listener won a radio station contest: a trip to Washington, D.C., to see the Beatles.

"I remember looking at the ticket stub and it read $8, and I couldn't believe they'd paid that much for a ticket!" Kent recalls. "I'll always remember the date—August 8, 1966, right after my twelfth birthday. By then I already knew I wanted to be a deejay."

Kent recalls just how strong his desire to be a deejay was—and a deejay in Cleveland, no less.

In 1974, I was working at Memphis station WHBQ with program director George Klein, who was Elvis Presley's longtime friend. The story behind their friendship was Presley and Klein became best friends at Humes High School, where, because Klein was Jewish, he was not well received by classmates, and everyone thought Elvis a geek because he combed his hair funny and wore weird clothes. So because they were both teen outcasts, they pretty much became each other's only friend. After college, Klein went on to work at WHBQ, which ultimately became the first station to play Presley's records.

Anyway, I was this real screamin' wild nighttime manic deejay, going by the title "Truckin' Tom-Cookin' Kent." There was something about radio that gave me high energy, so I really got into it, having great fun with it. Well, one night George comes in the station and says, "I just came from Elvis's mansion, and he was listening to you on the radio while he was working out, and he thinks you're just the coolest thing, and he wants to meet you." Well, I was just blown away. I mean, even though I was of the Beatles era, I had tremendous respect for the King. Now the way one met Elvis was you got invited to meet him at the Memphian Theater, which he rented out for midnight showings [of movies]. Then if he liked you, you got invited to the mansion.

Well, I'd just gotten this great offer to go work at WIXY and had to jump on it because everyone knew about WIXY—all over the country. I mean, that station was legendary. So I was thrilled with the opportunity to do nights on WIXY. So, here I told Klein I had to pass on this once-in-a-lifetime chance to hang out with Elvis because I was going to Cleveland!

Kent admits that he wasn't overly fond of the city initially. "Cleveland in 1974 was, to a Southern guy like me, this dark, dirty, cold, dismal place. It was a real culture shock. On the other hand, I was working with a phenomenal radio team. Wilde Childe was doing middays, Mike Reineri was doing mornings, Paxton Mills on afternoons. Tim Byrd was on early evenings, me late-nights, and Mike Collins overnight."

In 1975 he received a "better job offer" from KLIF in Dallas (a 50,000-watt station as opposed to WIXY's 5,000) and promptly left Cleveland.

After Dallas, I was working at a Top 40 station in Miami and was really happy. But then came a decision I had to make. Because I'm a devoted Christian, I refused to advertise this one commercial about a nude nightclub. After all, my listeners consisted of a young audience and I was not comfortable about promoting that. My bosses said, "You have to play it." Well, that night came and I just couldn't do it. I was promptly fired.

Well, I was devastated. Then I read this verse in the Bible that Jesus said, "If you give up anything for me, I'll restore unto you a hundred-fold." Next thing I know, I get this call out of the blue from Bob Travis in Cleveland, offering me a job at WGCL, and they offered me exactly double what I was making at the Miami station—a hundred fold! It was wild. But though I was certainly relieved to get another offer at this time, in thanking God in my prayers, I had to ask him, "Oh, God, why Cleveland?"

Yet it ended up being the absolute best thing to ever happen to me. I loved working at 'GCL. When I started there they had something like a 3 share, bottom of the barrel, and 'MMS was the big station. Two years later, we had a 15 share and I'd beaten Kid Leo in afternoon ratings! Plus I'd fallen in love with my wife here and, amazingly, fell in love with the city, too. So when I got an offer in 1980 from WLS, my dream station since I was a kid, I couldn't pass it up, but I hated leaving Cleveland.

He was back in Cleveland in 1982, however, to work at WMJI, only to be sent to WAVA in Washington, D.C., soon after. In 1988 he and his wife returned once more to Cleveland when he became program director for WRQC ("Hot 92"). But two short years later, budget cuts and other changes forced Kent into a decision. "I decided to get out of radio then. The business had changed too much. You were no longer able to have your own personality anymore. They wanted you to read, blandly at that, from these liner cards. You weren't allowed to loosen up and have fun."

Kent became the regional promotion manager for Elektra at Cleveland-based WEA, where he remains today. "I'll never want to live anywhere else," he says. "The music fans in Cleveland are the best anywhere. I've worked in cities like Memphis, which of course is very music intensive, and Philadelphia, but neither compare to Cleveland. And of course, I think that's a big reason why we have the Rock Hall here instead of those other cities. You know, twenty years ago, I'd never believe I'd ever say this, but I truly love Cleveland!"

14 Punk Rock: A New Wave on the North Coast

Rock rolled into the music scene on a decidedly defiant note. Punk rock took that defiance to a whole new level. Punk fans reveled in the rebellious music that spawned a subculture that thrived on shock, anger, and apathy.

"It's a 'hell-with-it' feeling," described the late Stiv Bators of the Dead Boys. With lyrics like "There is no future" (from the Sex Pistols's "God Save the Queen") and song titles such as "Life Stinks" (from Peter Laughner's title track) and "Search and Destroy" (Iggy and the Stooges), punk's philosophy was anything but upbeat, jovial, positive. Punk's sound grew out of the extremes of hard, heavy-metal rock and then took on a life of its own, adding to the scene the extremes of an equally hard lifestyle. Lou Reed's 1973 hit "Walk on the Wild Side" became an anthem to later punk rockers, as did the Ramones's "I Want to Be Sedated," fueling the perception that the participants'—and music's—main nutrient was heavy doses of drugs, heroin in particular (which was later called the "common cold of rock death") and that punk music was all about debauchery and self-destruction. But it was this very counterculture appeal that attracted so many bored and disaffected teens in the late 1970s. Out of the punk scene came new wave, which was decidedly more toned down and less antagonistic yet still original and unquestionably "alternative."

Interestingly, this movement appealed primarily to young people from upper-middle-class families. Perhaps while impoverished or underprivileged adolescents live every day with chaos, death, and destruction, and therefore the themes executed in punk music were nothing new to them, rebellious teens who lived "the good life" were looking for a lifestyle alternative to the stable humdrum of their secure lives.

This new musical genre exploded onto the rock scene. While it did produce some classics, it took some prisoners, too, claiming its share of rock and roll deaths, not unlike those of previous generations. Among them were rock writer Lester Bangs and such notable artists as Sid Vicious (Sex Pistols), Johnny Thunders (New York Dolls, Heartbreakers), Jerry Nolan (Dolls, Heartbreakers), and Cleveland's own Peter Laughner (Rocket from the Tombs, Pere Ubu).

It is widely assumed that punk rock originated with Britain's Sex Pistols and its frontman, Sid Vicious (a.k.a. John Simon Ritchie). But in reality, punk was born in the United States, and the term was popularized by New Yorker Eddie "Legs" McNeil. In 1975, when attempting to find a suitable theme for their publication, he and friends John Holmstrom and Ged Dunnen founded *Punk* magazine, which featured a style of music and scene that was just beginning to infiltrate New York City's infamous bar CBGB (which stood for Country, Bluegrass, Blues, though the theme soon changed). This club on the Bowery, owned by Hilly Kristal (later manager of the Dead Boys), was, like another popular New York club, Max's Kansas City, a haven for eccentric types like Andy Warhol and became a breeding ground for such punk precursors as the New York Dolls, Lou Reed, Iggy Pop, David Bowie, Patti Smith, the Ramones, and Television.

The first genuine punk concert is attributed to the Ramones, who played their debut with Richard Hell's group Television in the spring of 1974. Then came the Patti Smith Group, with Television as their opening band, at CBGB's in March 1975. Word of the concert spread through the underground, and CBGB became New York's newest trendmaker, and in June 1975 the club hosted its first Summer Rock Festival, featuring the Talking Heads. By November, England had caught on to the punk scene and welcomed the Sex Pistols on stage at St. Martin's Art College in London. A new genre of rock music was born.

Meanwhile, back on the North Coast, a similar scene was attracting audiences. Just as the Ramones were igniting audiences in New York, and Iggy Pop in Detroit, one eccentric, talented guitarist was blazing a new trail in his own hometown: Peter Laughner.

The Cleveland Punk/New Wave Pioneers

Peter Laughner (1952–77)

Musically, Laughner had a wide influence. His record collection included pop/jazz artists like Clevelander Albert Ayler and bluesmen such as Willy Dixon, Robert Johnson, and Leadbelly among the obscure sounds of the '60s underground pioneers Captain Beefheart and the Velvet Underground. Former *Scene* editor Jim Girard recalls,

> Laughner had great musical tastes. He really understood good music. He liked Dylan and Lou Reed and, of course, was very much into the Stooges, MC5—that whole Detroit scene. But he also liked Merle Haggard and the Flying Burrito Brothers, when it was way uncool to like anyone like that.
>
> I knew about him before I even met him. We were enemies because I was going with this girl he had dumped on pretty bad. Then once I started going with her, he tried getting back with her. We didn't go to the same high school, but we ended up at a lot of the same parties. People would say to me, "Oh, Peter Laughner—yeah, he's really cool." But when I finally met him, he still had acne and was not stereotypically handsome like I expected. I remember thinking, "This is the guy everyone thinks is so great?" But once I got to know him better, I understood. Peter had a lot of charisma. Musically, he was way too artsy for me. I mean, he was so into the Velvets, where I really liked the Who.

The Velvet Underground, which played fairly often at LaCave during the late '60s, had the greatest influence on Laughner. He and Mirrors guitarist Jamie Klimek managed to get backstage a few times to chat with Lou Reed. "Actually, they became good friends," Girard recalls. "Peter and Lou would party together a lot when he was in town. I remember Peter would fly with Lou to Buffalo or Columbus, wherever he was playing."

Another strong influence was renowned *Creem* magazine writer Lester Bangs. Laughner became acquainted with Bangs after he wrote a letter to the editor of the Detroit-based magazine. According to Bangs's own account, the two had an unsteady relationship (fueled by each other's drinking and drug habits). However, upon Laughner's death, Bangs wrote a eulogy for his friend that was first published in *Creem* and then later reprinted in Bangs's 1987 book, *Psychotic Reactions and Carburetor Dung*.

Laughner's first band, Mr. Charlie, came together in 1968 and consisted of some Bay High School classmates. The young band played mostly cover material of the Rolling Stones and Yardbirds variety until its leader got exposed to the art-rock/blues style of the Captain Beefheart band. Laughner grew up in the upper-middle-class neighborhood of Bay Village, the city where, in the 1950s, Dr. Sam Sheppard was accused of murdering his wife, Marilyn (the case on which, supposedly, the TV series *The Fugitive* was based). His comfortable, free lifestyle allowed him to experiment with his creative energies and enabled him to obtain a gleaming white Stratocaster guitar.

The bandmates of Mr. Charlie parted ways at graduation in 1970. Laughner, looking for a larger and more receptive audience, went to San Francisco to pursue his folk rock interests. He returned to Cleveland within a year and began a serious venture into music. He had a few false starts, however.

First, he joined the original and highly respected Cleveland blues/rock band Mr.

Stress. This association proved disappointing to all involved. "He played with us only a few months," Bill "Stress" Miller recalls.

> We had regular nights at the Brick Cottage at the time. Originally there was no cover charge, and the place would be packed. Then the owner decided to charge one dollar admission. I didn't think Pete was as schooled a guitar player, nor into that modern blues/rock style, as some of the guys I'd used in the past. So I was concerned if anyone would pay a dollar to hear him play. I decided to replace him with another guitarist, Chuck Drazdik, who ended up with me for years. Peter had a lot of ambition, though, and was a real self-promoter. He had such intense energy, it was almost contagious. But he wasn't for our band.

Once ousted from Mr. Stress, Laughner continued to play music, briefly forming Blue Drivers with another Stress member, keyboardist Mike Sands. "We played out just a few times, mostly at the Brick Cottage," Sands recalls. "After that band broke up I wanted to continue playing with Peter. He basically told me I was too conservative and not aggressive enough. But we remained friends. He was intelligent, a fast-thinker, very imaginative, and far ahead in recognizing trends. But he was definitely a restless soul."

Between bands, Laughner played solo performances on the folk circuit at places like the Grapes of Wrath (across the street from Chester Avenue's Viking Saloon) while working days at Disc Records. Then, in late 1972, he formed Cinderella Backstreet, a Velvets cover band. Regular Backstreeters included bassist Albert Dennis, guitarist Rick Kallister, drummer Scott Krauss, vocalist Cindy Black, and another female singer (whose name former members don't recall). "I'm not sure how notable it was," Krauss says of the band. "It was more like an ambient thing. We played mostly at the Viking. I remember one time Cindy's whole performance was her just screamin' through every song. The girls sang kinda of off-key, but it didn't make any difference. It was meant to be a more visual thing," referring to their manner of dress and feminine allure.

By August 1973, Cinderella Backstreet was already history. Unhappy with his band's demise, Laughner immediately formed its sister group, Cinderella's Revenge. Members were drummer Eric Ritz and former members of the '60s Poor Girls, Sue Schmidt and Deborah Smith. This band, too, lasted less than a year.

Meanwhile, Laughner found himself gravitating toward another creative outlet—journalism. He started sending articles to two short-lived local publications: *Exit*, and Akron's underground paper *Zeppelin* (where he was first to praise the genius of Bruce Springsteen in the 1973 review "The Wild, the Innocent, and the E-Street Shuffle"). He also had articles published in the *Cleveland Plain Dealer* before becoming a regular contributor to *Creem*, where he became recognized as a respected writer. It was this association that sparked his friendship with Bangs.

Through the years 1974 to 1977, Laughner often traveled to Detroit to see Bangs. The two would also meet and party at New York's Bowery bars. With these trips, Clevelander Laughner brought the growing punk scene back to Cleveland with him by way of fashions, albums, and—especially—attitude. By this time, he was working at Cleveland Heights record store Hideo's Discodrome, which became the center of the underground scene.

On one of his New York trips, Laughner was instrumental in getting Television to play Cleveland's prestigious Piccadilly Penthouse. The show took place in July 1975; and with his local band Rocket from the Tombs opening for Television, that summer event would officially mark a new era in Cleveland rock history—the punk era.

Having played at the Viking Saloon for years, Laughner was well acquainted with doorman/bouncer Crocus Behemoth (né David Thomas), who also served as columnist and music reviewer for *Scene*. Laughner, still doing his solo shows at the Grapes of Wrath that summer of '74, afterward would head to the Viking, where he witnessed the debut performance of Thomas's Rockets. By September, Laughner counted himself in. The band by then included lead guitarist Gene O'Conner and drummer Johnny Madansky (soon to be the Dead Boys' Cheetah Chrome and Johnny Blitz, respectively) and bassist Craig Bell (formerly of Mirrors, who briefly took on the pseudonym Darwin Layne).

The next year, May 5, 1975, found Rocket from the Tombs, with Laughner, playing the Agora. The concert was broadcast live on WMMS. By late that summer, however, the band members' musical tastes were diverging. Both groups broke up, with O'Conner and Madansky forming an all-out punk band (first called Frankenstein, then the Dead Boys) and Thomas and Laughner putting together an art/punk band called Pere Ubu. Throughout the next year, Pere Ubu was the Thursday night house band at the Flats' Pirate's Cove, playing and experimenting with music no one had ever heard before.

Just as punk was making its presence felt strongly in Cleveland, Pere Ubu members wanted Laughner out. His daily intake of alcohol mixed with a variety of drugs, such as dexedrine, methamphetamines, and/or valium, was increasingly causing the promising guitarist to become paranoid and out of control. "It took a long time to work up the courage to ask him to leave," Pere Ubu member Allen Ravenstine wrote in a *Cleveland Edition* article after Laughner's death. "He looked around the room at us for a moment, then packed his guitar case and walked out. He never said anything."

The guitarist moved on to his next musical venture. He drafted bass player Tony Maimone and former Mirrors/Styrene drummer Anton Fier for a new band, Friction. At their debut performance at a trendy Cleveland Heights club, Earth by April, were Pere Ubu members David Thomas and Tom Herman, who then asked Maimone to join their band. He did, and Anton Fier was close behind. Maimone's exit from Friction especially upset its founder. Laughner had been a friend and mentor to the young bassist. It didn't occur to him that both musicians left because they recognized the instability of their leader's endeavors, both musically and personally. But it was apparent to everyone else.

In November 1976, Friction played at Pirate's Cove to a receptive audience. This band included bass player/vocalist Deborah Smith, guitarist/violinist/vocalist Sue Schmidt (later Horning), and drummer Eric Ritz. But once again the collaboration was unsuccessful. "Peter had this incredibly strong drive and spirit and could write interesting songs," Horning recalls. "But after awhile, it became impossible to be a tight band while coping with Laughner and Eric's alcoholism. I mean, Peter's behavior and his playing were very sporadic, and Eric [who later died of liver disease] would often lose his grip on the drumsticks, and they'd go flying every which way. A couple times we all nearly lost our eyesight, they came so close. It was horrible."

Enter Peter and the Wolves. Laughner's last band used several guitarists and drummers and included girlfriend Adele Bertei (guitar/vocals). But a few months later, she kicked him out of his own band, and his health and behavior deteriorated dramatically.

In the last few months of his life, Peter Laughner spent several weeks in the hospital with liver problems. When his doctor told him he would surely die if he continued his destructive habits, he told Lester Bangs he'd reduce his intake to valium and marijuana. Former wife Charlotte Presser often said that Peter had a death wish.

"The thing about Laughner," Girard says, was that "he was not that great a guitarist, technically speaking. With Peter, it was all about feel. He was very impassioned about what he was doing. You couldn't deny him that. He was an artist, just as much as [Lou] Reed. In fact, Reed was his mentor. Unfortunately, Laughner was his own worst enemy."

His most notable contribution was written when Laughner was twenty-one years old. The song "Ain't It Fun" made it to vinyl (through old friends Gene O'Conner [who wrote the music] and John Madansky) on the Dead Boys' *We Have Come for Your Children* LP. The lyrics chillingly became the author's epitaph.

Ain't it fun, when your friends despise what you've become,
Ain't it fun, when you break up every band you ever begun,
Ain't it fun, when you know you're gonna die young.

Peter Laughner was found dead in his bedroom by his mother the morning of June 22, 1977. The official cause was listed as acute pancreatitis. He was twenty-four years old.

Rocket from the Tombs (1974–75)

"We created a monster."

—Jim Girard

This group that sparked two of the earliest and most renowned punk bands, Pere Ubu and the Dead Boys, began as a joke.

It was just another night in the lives of some offbeat musicians (and some *Scene* writers) who called themselves the Great Bow Wah Band. That night, July 2, 1973, history was made at the Viking Saloon. "The first time Dave Thomas ever sang on stage was at the Viking Saloon," recalls Jim Girard, former *Scene* editor and Euclid Beach Band member.

It was to be a promotion for *Scene* [its third-year anniversary]. Mark Kmetzko [*Scene*'s assistant editor] and I decided to get together with that night's house band, Ambleside, and go onstage and do whatever. Just for the fun of it. When I asked Dave beforehand if he could sing, he replied, "Well, I can scat-sing. You know, I can express myself on stage." It was what the jazz guys do, mouthing a melody that an instrument would play, making that sound with your voice.

See, Dave wasn't comfortable singing other people's songs. He even said that at the time. So he hadn't really found his voice, but he knew he wanted to perform on stage. That was his thing. He said, "I'm going to be an impressionistic performer, not your average asshole rock 'n' roll star." He had it all worked out in his head.

So Dave gets up there to sing background vocals to Lou Reed's "Sweet Jane," but instead he was scatting, making these really weird noises and faces. Then Peanuts [future *Scene* writer] comes out with a vacuum cleaner—those kind with the rubber hoses—plugs it into the amp's extension cords and starts vacuuming everyone on stage. It was really crazy. Of course, we were all drunk and having a great time. I think Rich Kabat [*Scene* publisher] almost threw up. He was laughing so hard his stomach hurt.

When it was over, everyone said, "We created a monster," because Dave immediately wanted to do another show. It took a while but we finally convinced the owner of the House of Bud [near Cleveland State University] to book us [the band had already played another show at the Agora in November 1973]. Then David gets the idea to dress up like a tin man for the gig. He wore this tin foil hat like in *Wizard of Oz*, with this blue jean–overall outfit wrapped in foil. The group Bluestone, with members A. J. Robey and Al Retay, was the backup band. The whole evening seemed surreal. But that was it. Not long afterward, David came up to me and said, "Jim, I'm starting my own band, and calling it 'Rocket from the Tombs.' Isn't that a cool name?"

Crocus Behemoth promptly quit *Scene* and became David Thomas, art/rock frontman/vocalist. Members for Thomas's new band, initially, were bass player (now standup comedian) Charlie Weiner, guitarists Glen "Thunderhand" Hach and Chris Cuda, and drummer Tom Foolery (né Clements). Then Thomas formed its most known lineup with guitarist Peter Laughner, bassist Craig Bell, lead guitarist Gene O'Conner, and drummer Johnny Madansky.

Hailed as "Cleveland's first concept band," their influences were obvious. The group played Velvet Underground and Iggy and the Stooges songs, as well as original material, some of which included what became Pere Ubu's debut single, "Thirty Seconds Over Tokyo," with lyrics by Laughner and music by O'Conner.

From its inception, it was clear that this group was from the other side of the musical tracks. The band's debut performance took place, appropriately, at the Viking Saloon on June 16, 1974. Response was basic confusion; much of the crowd had no clue how to react to these new, strange sounds, and most could not decipher the lyrics.

"I went down there to check out their first performance for the 'Making the Scene'

Rocket from the Tombs, 1975. *Left to right:* Gene O'Conner (a.k.a. Cheetah Chrome), Peter Laughner, Johnny Blitz, Craig Bell, and (*seated*) David Thomas (a.k.a. Crocus Bohemoth), seated. *Photo by Fred Toedtman. Courtesy of Craig Bell.*

column," recalls Peanuts. "I went around getting quotes from other musicians who were in the audience. Most wouldn't comment on it because it was just too bizarre." Dragonwyck's drummer, Jack Boessneck, told Peanuts, "God's hand came down from heaven and blessed us because we couldn't hear the vocals."

Another show Rocket fans won't forget took place on Sunday night, December 22, 1974, at the Viking Saloon. It was dubbed the "Special Extermination Night" and featured Rocket from the Tombs, the Electric Eels, and Mirrors.

"I couldn't quite decide what they were going for," Alan Greene recalls. "It was a lot of satire and basic outrageousness. It was when the movie *Earthquake* was out and the trend was 'sense-surround.' So for the big feature that night, David called it 'Dumbsurround,' with PA speakers in the back of the stage, with certain things miked around the room [*sic*]. 'Rocket from the Tombs coming to you in 'Dumbsurround.' It was something to experience."

The group then took their concept to the old WHK Auditorium, where they shared the bill with Akron's the Bizarros and Tin Huey. The concert was sponsored by Cleveland Heights music promoter and Discodrome record store owner John Thompson (a.k.a. Johnny Dromette).

By the summer of 1975, however, members were losing their enthusiasm and camaraderie. O'Conner and Madansky left to form Frankenstein, and Thomas and Laughner joined forces to assemble Pere Ubu.

Short-lived as it was, Rocket from the Tombs is embedded in Cleveland's rock history as the pioneer of alternative bands, which, while giving their audience a lot of laughs, produced several future rock icons.

Pere Ubu (1975–82, 1987–)

It was our turn to take the torch and move rock to the next level.

—David Thomas

The Pere Ubu Rules of Success:
1) Don't ever audition
2) Don't look for someone
3) Choose the first person you hear about
4) Take the first idea you get
5) Put some unique people together. Unique people will play uniquely whether or not they know how to play.
6) Delay centrifugal destruct factors for as long as possible, then push the button
7) Don't Seek Success

The first incarnation of Pere Ubu included David Thomas, Peter Laughner, Rocket from the Tombs' soundman turned guitarist and bassist Tim Wright, guitarist and bass player Tom Herman, drummer Scott Krauss, and saxophonist Allen Ravenstine, who also played what would become a Pere Ubu trademark, an EML synthesizer.

Ravenstine recalls:

We all hung out at the Plaza apartment building [3206 Prospect Avenue]. My parents died when I was in high school so I bought the building with my inheritance. There was a select group of people that came down regularly. It became kind of an "artist colony." Someone had this notion of forming this "concept" band. Meaning that if you took a group of people who had a similar mindset or outlook, put them together with musical instruments, they could create something interesting, and it didn't matter if they could play them or not.

I had heard about David before I met him. Then one day I ran into him in the courtyard of the building and he mentioned this song I'd written called "Terminal Drive." Apparently Pete [Laughner] had told him about it, and we got to talking. That's how I got invited to join.

In the beginning, Wright and Herman alternated playing bass and guitar, until Wright dropped the bass shortly before leaving for New York City. True to the band's formula, members often switched instruments. "Pere Ubu has always been a very logical band. It made its own rules," former member Krauss says. "So it wasn't unusual for any of us to alternate instruments whenever the situation called for it."

Taking the name from the character of Pa Ubu in Alfred Jarry's play, *Ubu Roi,* Thomas thought the title befitting of the music he created—enigmatic, barbaric, dark. Thomas and Laughner initially formed the band solely to put a few of their favorite originals on vinyl. Within weeks the sextet recorded "Thirty Seconds Over Tokyo," with the b-side "Heart of Darkness," releasing it on their own label, Hearthan Records. The song became popular among the underground set, a result of playing it live at the Viking Saloon, Pirate's Cove, and Lakewood's Phantasy Nightclub.

Upon completion of the single, the group decided to stay together and try to get some jobs. Their first gig took place at the Viking Saloon's 1975 New Year's Eve party. Because Ravenstine didn't think he could do live what he could in the studio with his synthesizer, he quit before the debut. Thomas summoned David Taylor as his replacement. Taylor worked at the popular Coventry Road record store Record Revolution and also happened to own an EML synthesizer (a somewhat rare instrument made by a small company in Vernon, Connecticut). Frankenstein opened for them.

"We did a good mix of covers and originals," Krauss says of that night. "I'm sure we did 'White Light, White Heat' [by the Velvet Underground] and 'Pushin' Too Hard' by the Seeds. Then, of course, 'Thirty Seconds Over Tokyo' and 'Heart of Darkness.'"

Although open-minded club owners were few and far between, Pere Ubu found one in Pirate's Cove owner Jim Dowd. It was a "dive bar" frequented by inner-city rabble-rousers and the occasional brave suburbanite. As Krauss recalls,

Nothing was going on in the Flats in the '70s. It was deserted. It was scary. People would say, "Don't go there." Tony [Maimone] was bartending at Pirate's Cove which, on weekends, was a biker bar. One day Tony was telling me his boss was thinking of offering some kind of weekly entertainment to increase business. I said, "Tell him we'll play," because at the time, we'd play anywhere that would have us. So we started playing Wednesday nights, then we convinced Jim to let us play Thursday nights, because it was closer to the weekend. After a while word of mouth brought more bands who started playing there. Devo came up from Akron, followed by Tin Huey, then the Bizarros. That's how things started happening in the Flats.

"We were lucky to get fifty people in there to hear us in the beginning," adds Ravenstine, who by then had rejoined the group. "I remember nights when people were standing on chairs to be up close to the ceiling to get warm because the club wasn't heated."

In April 1976, Pere Ubu was invited to play New York's famous Max's Kansas City. The show was well received and garnered them press coverage in both *Punk* and *New York Rocker* magazines.

From its earliest incarnation, Pere Ubu has been hard to label by the best of critics. The music has been described as obscure, noisy, random, with often inaudible vocals. "Weird, but a good weird," said one reviewer. "An acquired taste," said another. Yet for all its oddities and departures from the norm, Pere Ubu has earned a dedicated following through its decades of existence. And critics everywhere, from the U.K. to their hometown, hail the band as *the* avant-garde (or, as they prefer to call it, avant-garage) band of the underground era. For a band that merely got together to do their own thing outside the realm of the pop genre, their impact on the music scene has been impressive.

Their success has been particularly surprising given their staunch determination to avoid commercialism. Because of that, they've had to look elsewhere to be seen and heard. It was widely understood the music industry rarely acknowledged Cleveland bands, and Pere Ubu was no exception. The group, like their colleagues who managed to break that mold, had to leave town in order to get media attention. Still, that had never been David Thomas's focus. Individualism and freedom of expression was.

"I remember a few times we were dropped [from record companies] because we lacked commercial potential," Krauss says. "I remember one time when a record exec suggested to David that he do something about his lyrics. David stood there looking at the guy, then said, pointing his finger, 'Look, I make art. It's *your* job to sell the product.'"

To many, David Thomas *is* Pere Ubu. Intelligent and well read, Thomas, a 1970 Cleveland Heights High School graduate and son of a college professor, was an early fan of Captain Beefheart (a.k.a. Don Van Vliet). The Beefheart influence is evident in Thomas's often-indecipherable vocals as well as lyrical themes. Both artists ask questions and examine the state of being in their compositions. Both are reserved; both are often misunderstood. But there was no question as to who would lead this band. David Thomas was a natural-born leader.

"In terms of the music, everyone was responsible for writing their own chunk of it," explains Ravenstine. "David wrote the lyrics alone, and we never saw the lyrics; he was very protective over that. He had a very potent veto power in that if he didn't like the music, he'd say, 'I can't write any lyrics to that,' and that'd be it. It was very frustrating. There were pieces of music the group would come up with that we thought were good, but ultimately got scrapped."

The group returned to the studio early in 1976 to record "Final Solution" (b/w "Cloud 149"), again on Hearthan. Before long, Thomas had composed enough material for an album. But first they needed money. According to Krauss,

We started getting these gigs and took them because we needed rent money. For example, we were no band to be playing at a high school dance. But one day our bass player's cousin said his school [Berea High School] didn't have a band for their spring prom, and would we do it? Well it meant $500 so we said sure.

So we're sittin' in the parking lot before the gig, passing the whiskey and smokin' pot, and this old guy comes out and says something like, "Hey, you guys better stop that, and get in there and play your music." Peter looks over at him, and says, "Cool it, Pops." We knew right then there was going to be trouble.

We played the first song, and the crowd just stood there starin' at us. Then Dave gets down and starts doing the alligator. That's when they pulled the power on us, and paid us just get the hell out of there!"

(Details of this event are chronicled brilliantly in a piece written by Allen Ravenstine called "Music Lessons," printed first in the 1991 *Cleveland Edition* and included in *The Penguin Book of Rock & Roll Writing* [New York: Penguin, 1992].)

During the bicentennial summer, Pere Ubu was changing its constitution. Ravenstine was back in. Taylor was out. Wright wanted out. And Laughner's erratic, drug-induced behavior caused his expulsion from the band. Herman remained on guitar, while Tony Maimone took over on bass. Krauss remained on drums. At the suggestion of Wright, Thomas attempted to recruit a proficient local guitarist, Alan Greenblatt (né Greene), who played in Jimmy Ley's Coosa River Band. Although Greenblatt did contribute impressive licks to the next studio recording, "Untitled" (later released on the *Terminal Tower* LP definitive collection), he declined Thomas's offer to join the band. "Untitled" ultimately became the single "Modern Dance" when Pere Ubu recorded it live at Max's Kansas City and changed the title. It also served as the name of their 1978 debut album and their tribute to Peter Laughner, who had died the previous year.

While still the Pirate's Cove house band, the group recorded another single, "Street Wave" b/w "My Dark Ages." That's when Chicago's Mercury A&R man, Cliff Burnstein, came into the picture.

"I think that was directly David's doing," Ravenstine says. "As a writer for *Scene* magazine, he had connections to other writers and record people across the country. Unbeknownst to us, and we actually didn't learn about it until years later, he was sending these people our records."

Whether Burnstein learned of the band through this means or through his habit of regular jaunts to independent record stores searching out alternative discs remains debatable. What is not in dispute is the fact that he liked what he heard and convinced his bosses to form a sister label strictly for such underground sounds. Blank Records resulted, and Pere Ubu was the first to sign.

Now the beneficiaries of a larger record label, Thomas and his bandmates wanted to continue recording in their hometown. The group chose Painesville's Suma Recording (formerly Cleveland Recording), a studio known for its gold and platinum recordings for the James Gang, the Outsiders, Grand Funk Railroad, Terry Knight and the

Pack, the O'Jays, and Wild Cherry, among others. From that moment on, Pere Ubu would record in no other studio, despite some members taking up residence in London and New York.

The Modern Dance was released in February 1978. With Velvet Underground–inspired hypnotic guitar riffs, coarse electronics, animal-sounding vocals, and themes of hopelessness and confusion, the band's gloomy Flats environment was evident in its music. But those who reveled in that theme were delighted with the change from the pop/ bubble-gum/disco sounds that had been dominating the musical mainstream.

After "Disastrodome" concerts at the old WHK Auditorium with the Bizarros and the Suicide Commandos, Pere Ubu made its way through the streets and bars of the city before embarking on an American and European tour to promote its first album. In conjunction with the tour, the single "Data Panik in the Year Zero" was released. Pere Ubu was making its imprint on underground rock. Immediately after touring, the group returned to Suma Recording and emerged with *Dub Housing,* released on Chrysalis Records. The band returned to England with the "Magical Mystery Ubu Tour."

"That was interesting," Krauss recalls. "The record company put an ad in a magazine promoting this tour where the destination to the concert was a mystery. There were about three or four busloads of people, and they drove them out to these caves where we were playing along with Red Crayola. It was the Chislehurst Caves that was used during World War II, so people wouldn't get bombed by the Germans. It was a small room, and we played up on the ledge. I remember it was really cold in there, and Tom wore gloves while playing. But it was a neat gig. I'm sure when all who were there reminisce they say, 'Did we really do that? Were we really there?'" Although the group had a small but dedicated fan base in the United States, Pere Ubu was developing a wide, cultlike following in the U.K.

By 1980, the lineup consisted of Thomas, Maimone, Ravenstine, Mayo Thompson (former Red Crayola guitarist who replaced Tom Herman), and drummer Scott Krauss (who left briefly in December 1977 and was replaced by Anton Fier, who drummed on "Data Panik in the Year Zero"). From 1979 to 1982, albums came in rapid succession. After *Dub Housing* came *New Picnic Time, Art of Walking* (their biggest seller), and *Song of the Bailing Man,* which became the group's final LP before formally disbanding, for a time.

"There were definite problems as far back as '79," Krauss says. "You could say there was a fair amount of friction. I remember when we were recording *New Picnic Time,* we'd drive out to Suma, and David would be standing there burning holes in the grass, just staring at the grass. I think that was very reflective of how the actual sessions went."

Krauss left the band in 1981 (again replaced by Anton Fier), and by the winter of 1981–82 the band was no more. For the next five years, members went on to other projects. Krauss and Maimone formed Home and Garden with bassist Michele Temple and Jim Jones (Electric Eels, Mirrors). Thomas went solo, recorded six albums with various lineups, and labeled his 1987 show "The Flibberty Jib Man," which received good reviews. He frequently toured Europe during those years and moved to London in 1984. He formed David Thomas and the Wooden Birds, which included Allen Ravenstine.

About his solo performances, Thomas has been quoted as saying, "Watching me is a truly unique experience." No one disputes that. His shows are genuine performance art, with dramatic dress (dark Salvation Army trenchcoats and black hat), dramatic lyrics ("the guitar's going to sound like a nuclear destruction"), and dramatic dramatics (continually changing vocal octaves while pacing back and forth across the stage telling stories).

But after a show at Peabody's DownUnder (the former Pirate's Cove) in August 1987, it became clear that Pere Ubu was still a huge part of David Thomas. According to Krauss,

Allen was telling me one day that the president of Rough Trade [Jeff Travis] and Nick Hobbs [Thomas's manager] proposed an offer to release another studio Pere Ubu album. Allen told the guy, "David doesn't want to play rock; he wants to do art." I said to Allen, "Do you know how hard it is to get a recording contract? Here's a guy willing to put up money. This is an ideal situation."

So I wrote Tony, David, and Nick and explained it to them how we should jump at the opportunity. Then Allen heard me talk about it on radio station WERE-AM. He told me later, "When I heard it on the radio, I knew we were getting back together."

So when David & the Wooden Birds came into town to play Peabody's, they asked me to sit in on one gig with drummer Chris Cutler. I was hesitant. We rehearsed one night and it was a lot of fun, so I said okay. And the crowd really dug it. The energy level was high. Suddenly record companies were interested, and David Bates of Phonogram came up with the big plan. We were back.

The newly re-formed Pere Ubu was made up of Thomas, Krauss, Ravenstine, Maimone, Cutler, and Jim Jones. Alternate members in this second incarnation included keyboardist Eric Drew Feldman (formerly of Captain Beefheart), bass player Michele Temple, EML synthesizer player Robert Wheeler, winged eel fingerboardist Garo Yellin, and drummers Scott Benedict and Steve Mehlman. Even Suma engineer and friend Paul Hamann contributed on various recordings.

The hiatus proved to have been just what members needed; the band was on a roll. Their comeback album, *The Tenement Year,* quickly followed by *Cloudland* (hailed as their record with the most commercial appeal), *Worlds in Collision, The Story of My Life,* and *Raygun Suitcase* (Krauss's last participation before leaving the band for good). When Pere Ubu produced *Data Panik in the Year Zero* in 1996, fans and critics alike were excited. The five-CD boxed set, released on Geffen Records, includes the original Hearthan singles along with material from the first five albums and live recordings. It also includes eighteen tracks from the group's early days, including songs of bands Pere Ubu once shared the stage with: the Electric Eels ("Jaguar Ride"), Mirrors ("She Smiled Wild"), and the Numbers Band ("Song"). Old friend and early supporter John Thompson designed the cover. The compilation is considered a collector's item. The album *pennsylvania* was released in 1998 and was followed by the Inertia Tour (which included former MC5 guitarist Wayne Kramer), proving that Pere Ubu is alive and kicking.

In a 1978 *Scene* review of the band's debut LP *Modern Dance,* writer Gary Lupico commented that "musicians look back upon roots, but Pere Ubu *is* roots. Perhaps years from now, maybe even on another planet, beings will be pointing to the five entranced boys from Cleveland as the true innovators."

"We were just doing what we were doing. No one had any knowledge what it meant to anybody," Ravenstine says. "Then, next thing I know, these guys from Paris show up at Pirate's Cove and they're telling us we invented the new wave, and they're taking our pictures for *Life* magazine. A few weeks later, we go from being lucky if we get fifty people to listen to our music, to being whisked away from Heathrow in a limousine to be interviewed by the BBC! And all the while I'm thinking, 'Now where the hell did all this come from??'"

The musical history and longevity of this band makes it a true pioneer (if not patron saint!) of the punk/new wave art form. The group is well respected among fans and critics alike and has also garnered admiration from its own influences, such as former Velvet Underground member John Cale, who has opened for the band. Their broad-based support was evident in 1991, when Pere Ubu was invited to appear on *Late Night with David Letterman.* Mercury Records (their record company at the time) refused to finance the trip to New York, so band members held a fund-raiser, summoning fans and friends for the $2,500 needed for transportation, hotel, rehearsal space, and equipment rental expenses. They raised the money in two short weeks. Among the contributors were Iggy Pop, Lou Reed, REM, the Feelies, Jane's Addiction, the B-52's, and Living Colour, as well as many fans. The band appeared on the popular television show on September 11, 1991.

Pere Ubu's history is one of an enduring group that refused to yield to the rules of the industry as it paved the way for its equally defiant followers.

The Dead Boys (1976–79)

Groups like Pere Ubu and the Dead Boys could only have come from Cleveland. Both groups have publicly acknowledged the rare and charged atmosphere of the time, place, and circumstances that spawned them.

—Jim Jones, member of several Cleveland underground bands

When lead man Stiv Bators, rhythm guitarist Jimmy Zero (né William Wilder), lead guitarist Cheetah Chrome (né Eugene O'Conner), and drummer Johnny Blitz (né John Madansky) decided to take their music east, they hadn't planned on overnight success. After all, with just a few local gigs (mostly at Viking Saloon) and audience indifference (at times even blatant aversion) to their style of music, there was no sign of any future success.

"I'll tell you, we were loathed by most audiences in Cleveland," Zero recalls of those early club gigs. "So when we heard about what was happening in New York with the Ramones, we thought, 'What the hell, let's give it a shot.'" That shot at the punk lifestyle took them to uncharted territories and unexpected places.

It was Joey Ramone's (né Jeffrey Hyman, lead singer of the Ramones) idea for the rebellious musicians to go to New York City. The Ramones had played a few venues in the Cleveland area, including the Agora. But it was a Youngstown gig at the Tomorrow Club (later Youngstown Agora) where the New Yorkers met Stiv and Cheetah. At the time, the two aspiring musicians had just come off a band called Frankenstein and were wondering what to do next.

They decided to check out CBGB, the New York club they'd heard so much about. Bators told friends he felt they'd fit in better because the New York club crowd was into the same kind of music, and "we'd be normal there." The four left Cleveland on July 24, 1976. By the following night, the quartet formerly known as Frankenstein was playing on stage at the famous bar and had adopted a new name, the Dead Boys. Cheetah Chrome (renowned for his trademark leopard-skin spandex pants) remarked that CBGB reminded him of the Viking Saloon in atmosphere and job availability. But while their hometown audience was generally uninterested in them and their music, the crowd in this musty, seminal club accepted and hailed the misfits. Within six weeks these notorious kids from the Midwest managed to change the complete atmosphere at the bar by attracting more punk enthusiasts. And six months later, the Dead Boys were the top punk band in America—after the Ramones, of course.

The Cleveland boys took easily to the Bowery scene. That New York debut had the Dead Boys opening for Television and the Ramones, and the club's owner, Hilly Kristal, took them under his wing and became the band's manager.

"The first thing that struck me about them was how polite they were," Kristal says of the Dead Boys. "It was always, yes sir, no sir. They were nice midwestern kids from Cleveland, quite well behaved. 'Course, that was in the beginning. . . . And musically, I thought they were great. They developed a big sound, more hard rock. Somehow you got the feeling it was huge, just by the way they played. It was fresh. They had real energy and put on a great show. The Dead Boys were something else. They were special."

The Dead Boys became CBGB regulars, along with Blondie, the Ramones, Talking Heads, the Dictators, and the Heartbreakers. They hung out with Sid Vicious and took drugs with Johnny Thunders. They played at CBGB's annual summer festival, which netted them a favorable review in *Variety*, which, in turn, led to an offer to record an album, which led to rock 'n' roll pandemonium. It all came fast and furious.

"We never did catch up with it. Not even to this day!" remarks Chrome, now in his forties. But it all nearly came to an abrupt halt when the group, with swastikas on their shirts and one on Blitz's drum kit, appeared at the Electric Lady, a Jewish-owned recording studio. Genya Ravan, who offered to produce the Dead Boys' first album, was the daughter of Polish refugees and had relatives who died in concentration camps. When she caught sight of the Nazi symbolism, she "freaked." And she wasn't the only one.

"We were bringing in the drums, and first person I see is Peter Frampton," Chrome recalls. "He saw the stickers on Johnny's drums, looked at me, and I growled at him. With horror in his eyes, he ran out the door! You gotta realize back then, all that Nazi stuff, it was just something rebellious to do. Blitz grew up so Nazi-oriented, around E. 44th and Clark, where the headquarters of the American White People's Party was. Plus, there was that *Creem* magazine shot of Keith Richards wearing a swastika. We thought that was cool-lookin'. But, yeah, we understood where she [Ravan] was coming from." Wisely, the group decided to forgo the Nazi symbolism.

Their debut album, *Young, Loud, and Snotty,* was released in the fall of 1977 on Sire Records, a label fast becoming a symbol for this new genre, having signed Talking Heads and the Ramones. With no bass player as yet, the Dead Boys used Bob Clearmountain on the recording, then sent for their Cleveland friend, bassist Jeff Magnum, to join the group. Musically raised on Iggy and the Stooges and the New York Dolls, the band's repertoire also included Alice Cooper material and original tunes. "Sonic Reducer," a song penned by David Thomas (words) and Gene O'Conner (music) in their Rocket days, became their debut single.

The Dead Boys perform at Chippewa Lake Park.
Photo by Bob Ferrell.

The Dead Boys gained publicity as one of the first punk bands to release a recording that got mention in both *Us* and *Punk* magazines. To promote its debut album, the

band went on tour. And its first stop was the Cleveland Agora. Before the show, Bators, Zero, and road manager James Sliman headed to downtown Cleveland's popular Chinese restaurant Chung Wa's to meet Bators's idol, Iggy Pop, for whom the Dead Boys were opening. However, once at the restaurant, conversation between the two singers abruptly ended when an inebriated Stiv Bators passed out in his wonton soup. This story has become Dead Boys legend.

In early 1978, the group headed to Miami to record their second album, *We Have Come for Your Children*. By most accounts, it should have been the band's best effort. It included two cover songs (the Stones's "Tell Me" and Kim Fowley's "Big City"), and they had a big-name musician, Felix Pappalardi of Mountain fame, to produce it. But the Dead Boys hated it.

"He didn't understand what we were trying to accomplish," Chrome says of Pappalardi. "Our music was different from what he was used to. He was just the wrong person to do it, but it wasn't our choice."

At the height of their popularity, the group was hit with its biggest blow. On April 20, 1978, Johnny Blitz was stabbed on a New York street. He had been attacked by five Puerto Rican men during an altercation that originally started with the group's road manager, Michael Sticca. All involved were reportedly inebriated. All were charged with assault. Blitz was stabbed three times in the neck and once in the heart, lungs, and stomach. Police reported that he had been minutes from death upon their arrival. He was on the operating table for more than five hours.

(The horrifying incident came as no surprise to those who witnessed the Dead Boys' lifestyle. With daily injections of a variety of drugs and alcohol, it seemed only a matter of time before excesses would catch up to them. It was obvious that drinking and drugs made for dreadful and destructive Dead Boys.)

A three-day benefit was quickly organized at CBGB where Rick Derringer, the Erasers, and the Criminals all contributed their talents. Former New York Dolls drummer Jerry Nolan joined the other Dead Boys that night.

Bad luck continued to plague the band, however. Immediately following the benefit, Zero went to Max's Kansas City, where a waitress accidentally spilled a drink, a Flaming Bulldog, on him. He was hospitalized with second- and third-degree burns on his face and neck but still managed to play a hometown benefit for Blitz the following week at the Pirate's Cove.

Blitz returned to the fold for their next sold-out performance at the Agora on July 24, 1978. Because he wasn't completely healed, Raven Slaughter drummer Eugene Readon took over on some songs. By now, the group's reputation was national. Borrowing heavily from Iggy Pop in his performances, Bators's onstage exaggerations included self-abuse antics (like hitting his head with a beer bottle) that necessitated the presence of an ambulance at the stage door—just in case. That same year, a photo of the singer (complete with askew smile) appeared in a *Time* magazine article describing the ravages of punk music and its decadent lifestyle. As a result, Bators was deemed the poster boy for everything wrong with his generation. But according to many, it was just an act. "The real genius behind Stiv Bators was he became what the scene called for,"

Raven Slaughter notes. "It was all schtick. If the crowd wanted Iggy Pop he gave them Iggy Pop or Alice Cooper. He would become that persona. But all he really wanted was to be a pop star, not a punk rocker."

By St. Patrick's Day 1979, Chrome and Zero had left the Dead Boys. The remaining members went on to honor commitments with Devo and Pere Ubu for a West Coast tour, but the group had lost its initial energy.

A live album, *Night of the Living Dead Boys,* recorded at CBGB, was released in 1980. Bators went on to form Lords of the New Church in 1982, which released four albums before disbanding in 1986. The Dead Boys then reformed briefly for a reunion tour through the Midwest, giving a much-heralded concert at Lakewood's Phantasy Theater on January 30, 1987. It was to be the group's last concert.

In 1989, Bators moved to Paris. It was supposed to be a new beginning for the Youngstown native who wanted to make it musically on his own. Sadly, he was fatally injured on June 3, 1990. His death came as a surprise, if only for the fact it was so undramatic: the flamboyant showman was hit by a car while walking down the street near his home. True to his nature, he got up and brushed himself off, claiming he was fine. (Some reports claim he was on heroin at the time and that was the reason for his refusal of treatment.) He returned home and later died in his sleep from internal bleeding.

Musicians, both local and national, paid tribute to one of Cleveland's own, gathering for a six-hour benefit concert at the Babylon A Go Go. Among those who played were Dark Carnival (with former Stooges Ron and Scott Asheton) and the Ghetto Dogs (with Cheetah Chrome and former Pagan Mike Metoff). Iggy Pop couldn't make it, but he sent a video of a Bators performance. Messages also poured in from celebrity friends Deborah Harry, Joey Ramone, Johnny Thunders, and Jerry Harrison (Talking Heads).

Through all the craziness, the Dead Boys managed to make their mark in the rock world. Several national bands have covered their songs ("Ain't It Fun" by Guns n' Roses; "Sonic Reducer" by Pearl Jam), and more than a decade after they disbanded, former members still get fan mail. And there is also an L.A.-based Dead Boys tribute band, Moronic Reducer, whose members take on the personae of the original Boys.

Cheetah Chrome, now in Nashville, continues playing music with his self-titled band, while Jimmy Zero has a Cleveland-based graphic design company. On April 9, 1997, Zero and Mirrors bassist Craig Bell were invited to speak at the Rock and Roll of Fame and Museum about the punk scene. Zero told the packed audience, "We were so over the top. We were getting on the cover of magazines before our record was even released." When someone asked him about the decadent lifestyle, he admitted, "It was horrible to watch people disintegrate. These people were my friends [referring to the drug-related deaths of New York Dolls Johnny Thunders and Jerry Nolan], not just names on an album. I don't like the fact they're in the cemetery."

Zero went on to say, "I always thought of us as a bunch of clowns who the spotlight hit for a brief period. Now we're in several books on punk rock and here at the Rock and Roll Hall of Fame!"

(*Opposite*) Stiv Bators backstage at the Music Hall with New York buddy, Blondie's Deborah Harry. *Photo by Janet Macoska.*

The Mirrors/Styrenes (1971–76)

> If you listened to the early Cleveland punk/art rock bands today, like Rocket from the Tombs, the Mirrors, and Electric Eels, you'd be hard-pressed to believe their music is more than twenty years old. Those three bands were light years ahead of their time.
>
> —*CLE* magazine editor Jim Ellis

While many of the garage-rock bands of the '60s and '70s came from Cleveland's East Side, the alternative music bands were emerging from the other side of the river. Formed in 1971 by Lakewood High School students Jamie Klimek (guitar/vocals) and Jim Crook (guitar/vocals), the Mirrors were decidedly left-wing and Velvet Underground/Pink Floyd inspired. Other members included Craig Bell (bass, later replaced by Jim Jones) and Michael Weldon (drums), with Paul Marotta (who occasionally substituted for Bell on bass) joining later (1973) on keyboards. The Velvets' influence was obvious in their repertoire: "Some Kinda Love," "There She Goes Again," and "Foggy Notions"—all Velvets tunes. Another song they included was "Sweet Sister Ray," which was not one of the Velvet Underground's recordings but a live sequel to "Sister Ray." Klimek had the foresight to record the song during their LaCave concert in the spring of 1968. "Let's put it this way," Marotta says. "'Sweet Sister Ray' was basically a forty-minute noise jam. It was one of our favorites, but we sometimes lost our audience on that one!"

In the beginning, the Mirrors was about as underground as a band can get, playing only at friends' homes, a few private parties, and Lakewood YMCA teen dances. "And there was this one bowling banquet we did that was a classic," Bell recalls. "It was down in the basement of this really nice house in Rocky River. We were playing all these Velvets covers for what we thought were these 'older' people when they were probably in the thirties! And they went crazy over us. They thought we were the cat's ass. We had a great time."

Then in 1972, the aspiring musicians' greatest fear was realized. The U.S. Army drafted Bell. Rhythm guitarist Jim Jones stepped in to fill the void.

> I saw Mirrors play for the first time at a dance mixer at St. Joe's/Villa Angela High School in Euclid. I was open-mouth amazed to see my Syd Barrett/Troggs/Velvet Underground hit parade being performed by these West Siders! At the end of the set, as Jamie was packing up, I cornered him, asked him where he'd been all my life and when and where I could catch their next gig. He told me that night was it because their bass player got drafted and Paul Marotta had just come up from Columbus to fill in. Then he asked me if I knew any bass players. I quickly said, "I play bass." Of course I didn't. I was a rhythm guitarist. Then I added, "I know most of the cover tunes you played. I'd love to join your group."
>
> Realizing the trap I'd suddenly set for myself, I added, "One thing, though. Do you have a bass I can use?" I got one, and within two weeks I was "trying out" for

the bass position, which ultimately yielded the recording of "She Smiled Wild." I tell you, it was the Velvets meet the Troggs in Syd Barrett's basement! It became the b/w of the Mirrors' single, released by David Thomas on his Hearthen label [1977].

Secured with an enthusiastic bass player, the Mirrors started playing at CSU hangout Fat Glenn's and had a few gigs at the Viking Saloon and the Clockwork Orange (directly across from the Cleveland's downtown police station).

"The Clockwork Orange was one of the few places that would have us," Marotta recalls. "The owner, Clockwork Eddie, was a great guy and got us playing there weekly. Although we did have to buy a keg of beer for 'Free Beer night.' But we didn't care, we had a regular gig! But then it was sold to an ex-cop, who renamed it the Loose Lounge, and it became a 'cop bar.' So the next time we played, there were these off-duty cops waving guns at us telling us we were too f—— loud. And that was the end of that job!"

The Mirrors continued with their Velvets/Stooges/Troggs covers but also began adding their own material. Most of the originals were penned by Klimek and Crook. Jim Jones, who worked at Record Rendezvous from 1969 to 1984, kept the band on top of the underground sounds of Captain Beefheart, the Stooges, and MC5. "So much more was happening muscially than what was being pumped through the airwaves by most commercial radio stations here," he says. "As chief buyer at the store, I made sure the latest imports, independent releases, local, and classic underground artists were in stock and heavily played during store hours."

In 1974, Bell, now out of the service, returned to the group. "It was always understood that I'd be welcomed back into the band after the army," he says. "Jim did a good job of keeping my seat warm." In the meantime, Jones, Marotta, and Klimek joined drummer Anton Fier (later with Friction/Pere Ubu/Golden Palominos) to form the Poli-Styrene Jass Band (pre-Styrenes), which recorded the single "Drano in Your Veins" (b/w "Circus Highlights"). The Styrenes regularly played the Pirate's Cove until Marotta and company moved to New York on New Year's Eve 1979.

The Mirrors disbanded in 1976, but the Styrenes survived and continue to perform in various formations. Through the late '70s, there were other names for the band, such as the George Money Band and the Styrene Money Band. "I don't know what we were thinking," Marotta says of the name changes. "I guess we were trying to be obscure. And boy, it sure worked! It certainly made it difficult for anyone trying to figure out where and when we were playing next! Then sometime in the mid-'80s, we got this idea we could get more gigs if we reactivated the Mirrors' name. So we played as two different bands: The Styrenes, in which I played keyboards; then we had the Mirrors, where I played bass, Jamie on guitar, and we used different drummers. Then we released *Another Nail in the Coffin,* on the Dutch label Resonance."

The band returned to the North Coast in October 1997 to play at the Euclid Tavern before a European tour. Also in 1997, to the surprise of everyone, including the musicians, Scat Records released a compilation box set, *Those Were Different Times*. It includes unreleased Mirrors/Electric Eels/Styrenes songs from the years 1972–76. The Mirrors selections are "Annie" (written by Bell); "Another Nail in the Coffin"; "How Could I?" and "Hand in my Pocket" (written by Klimek); and "We'll See" (written by Crook).

Paul Marotta's day job is in music as well. He is currently managing director for New World Records, a not-for-profit label that specializes in early American composers, doing approximately thirty titles a year. His company has received a total of seventeen Grammy nominations.

Electric Eels (1972–75)

The Electric Eels was formed when radio fans were listening to songs like John Denver's "Rocky Mountain High," Jim Croce's "You Don't Mess Around with Jim," and Don McLean's "American Pie," and club-goers were hiring nothing but cover bands to promote dancing to the sounds of Top 40.

It's no wonder the Electric Eels didn't take off. It is an understatement to say that this band was, from the beginning, off the beaten path—although they did sometimes play cover material. But that list consisted of TV theme show ditties (*The Patty Duke Show, The Flintstones*), the famous Lawsons' Big O orange juice commercial, and the 1960s Jan and Dean hit "Dead Man's Curve." And they did them all at lightning-fast speed and ear-splitting volume. It could be said that their claim to fame is being the longest-running band with the fewest number of gigs. Nonetheless, the Electric Eels made its mark on Cleveland music history.

"The entire Electric Eels career was exactly five gigs long," Paul Marotta says with a laugh. "No one wanted to hire us. It could be because we didn't play all that well. I always leave that open as a possibility! But then, when bands are just starting out, it takes a while to get their sound together. Plus the fact the equipment was bad, the PA system was bad, and that relates to economics. We'd play gigs with bands like Dragonwyck, who played all the time and had tons of money. So they had nice equipment and sounded really good. But we still felt what we were doing was of some importance."

After unsuccessful attempts to get work at a number of Cleveland clubs, the "eclectic" Electric Eels decided to seek fame and fortune in Columbus. There they managed just two gigs in a two-year period: one was at a college club, Postively 4th Street (later the Moonshine Co-op), just west of Ohio State, and the other was at Mr. Brown's Descent, where the owner pulled the plug on them forty-five minutes into their set.

Heavily influenced by the Fugs and Captain Beefheart, the Electic Eels featured members John Morton (guitar and co-founder), Dave E. McManus (co-founder/vocals/frontman), Brian McMahon (guitar/piano), and Marotta (guitar). An assortment of drummers included Danny Foland and Nick Knox (a.k.a. Stephanoff, later with the Cramps), who came in at the tail end of the formation.

Not only were the group's songs unpopular among club owners, but their early antics didn't endear them to many either. They had a penchant for starting fights wherever they went. Further, it didn't help that a few members flirted with nazism to the point of visiting the American Nazi Party Headquarters (Lorain and 110th Street) wearing shirts bearing a swastika. Their attire also included jackets sometimes covered with safety pins and/or rat traps. Dick Korn, owner of the Viking Saloon, seemed to be the only one willing to take a chance on them.

When they had no luck securing an audience in Columbus, the group returned to Cleveland in 1975, where they promptly broke up. The Electric Eels' music, however, was included in the 1997 compilation box set *Those Were Different Times* to satisfy years of requests. The CD includes Eels' originals such as "Tidal Wave," "Safety Week," "Flapping Jets," and "Wreck and Roll." "There were also a couple of 'polically incorrect' song titles, one which isn't even listed on the package," Marotta adds. "The idea was supposed to be satire, à la Lenny Bruce. It was well thought out, it just was not well understood. Like I said in the liner notes, we thought we were Lenny Bruce. Everybody else saw us as Adolf Hitler!"

Although this group spent more time creating havoc than playing music, they were significant in that their rage captured the mood of the emerging underground punk scene: "The Electric Eels were not, essentially, a rock band," Marotta notes. "It was more an art project with elements of rock music. We didn't have a drummer, just two guitarists and a singer with vocal improvisations." And while the band may have been politically incorrect and users of off-brand humor, they continue to have an underground following. The band members themselves realize they were different in different times. "It was the scariest band I ever heard, let alone played in," Jones remarks. "Art deconstruction with the volume on twelve."

The Pagans (1977–79; re-formed 1982–89)

Formed by brothers Mike (guitar) and Brian Hudson (drums) and Tim Allee (bass), the Pagans was another "different" band. The first lineup included guitarist Denny Carleton, who says of the band's formation:

I used to have these little jam sessions at places like Fottenbottens in downtown Willoughby. My family had known the Hudsons for years, and Mike and Brian used to come to see us play. Brian [now deceased] was a real likable fourteen-year-old kid who played drums, and Mike used to come up and sing. When he started hearing about the punk bands, he told me he wanted to start one up.

People thought it was weird that I was even in the band, because I'm a Christian and basically known from being in more pop-oriented bands like the Choir and the Lost Souls. But I was a musician, and I thought the concept of the Pagans was real interesting. And, actually, I liked the music. I liked the Ramones, and in some ways the Pagans were a lot like the Ramones. They played their songs real fast, doing "Little Black Egg" and "Secret Agent Man" each about a hundred miles an hour. And Mike was such a good songwriter, the Pagans had good original material.

"Denny was the one who taught us all those old covers from his days with his earlier bands," Mike Hudson adds. "And Allee was the other most musical guy in the band. He would tune all our guitars before we went out on stage."

With influences from the Velvet Underground, Iggy and the Stooges, and the Rolling Stones, the quartet began forming their own sound with group-written material. Hudson, then a news journalist at the *Euclid News Journal* (now *Euclid Sun Journal*), was acutely aware of the growing punk/new wave scene. The paper was located across from the Euclid club the Looking Glass (later Insanity, Sensations), and Hudson often wrote unfavorable reviews about the cover bands that played there. "The owner finally asked me what bands he should book," Hudson recalls. "I told him about Pere Ubu, Devo, Rubber City Rebels, Wild Giraffes, and the Dead Boys. It ended up being one of the few clubs to book those groups, other than in the Flats."

The biggest supporter of these bands, however, was a man whose record store had become the home of the wayward and wanton—but those with musical ability. While Carleton admits these prepunk bands were not generally accepted by their peers, they did have a friend in Johnny Dromette. The owner of Hideo's Discodrome opened his doors and pockets to provide a place for his young customers to satisfy their off-the-wall musical interests. Pere Ubu and Devo were first to play in a loft at his record store. In addition, he founded his own label, Drome Records, on which he released records by alternative bands.

"Our first single, 'Six and Change,' was on Wild Giraffes' label, Neck Records, in 1978," Hudson recalls. "Johnny shopped it around to other stores like Record Revolution and Record Rendezvous. And he became our manager."

Dromette had also hosted Discodrome Concerts at the old WHK Auditorium, which became notorious for disorderly conduct. "Those were great, but the last Discodrome concert, which we played at, was kind of scary," Hudson recalls. "The people in the audience threw so many beer bottles on stage, you couldn't move around lest you slip and fall, which we did, and because of the broken glass we became covered with blood. We kept playing, though, until one of the Styrenes' roadies was afraid we'd all get electrocuted and pulled the plug. Which of course, got everyone even more irate. We made it out of there, but barely." Dromette was banned from showcasing any more concerts at the venue.

Another of the Pagans' memorable club dates was opening for the Dead Boys in August 1977 at the Looking Glass. Hudson recalls, "People thought of us as pretty cutting-edge. Then the Dead Boys came in, and suddenly we were the Archies. Things really erupted during their set. People started throwing bottles and smashed the huge looking glass over the bar. The owner of the place shut off the electricity. Then the Dead Boys manager pulled out a pistol and escorted us out. That was the end of that gig."

During the time when local radio stations virtually ignored punk/new wave music (WMMS was called to task many times for refusing to play songs of anything relating to punk-style music), a graffiti war ensued with punk enthusiasts painting "I'm a Mess with 'MMS" over WMMS billboards. Those actions, however, did not help endear the youngsters to radio personnel.

Meanwhile, in 1978, the Pagans released "What's This Shit Called Love?" b/w "Street Where Nobody Lives," and "Dead End America," b/w "Little Black Egg." Their originals, mostly penned by Hudson with music by Allee, played on college radio stations throughout the nation, including University of California, Berkeley. The group went on to play at venues along the East Coast and throughout the Midwest, including New York (CBGB, Max's Kansas City), Detroit (Bookies), and Minneapolis (Uptown, First Avenue, Longhorn).

Carleton left the band in early 1978 and was replaced by Mike Metoff (a.k.a. Tommy Gun). "I was disappointed about where the band was heading," Carleton explains. "They started going too far into that hard-edged punk sound. Plus, I think they thought I was too passive. But I did enjoy the band, with the exception of the punk crowd's habit of throwing beer bottles at you on stage. I wasn't into that at all."

A year later, neither was anyone else. "By the end of '79, the scene was already dying, and Brian was itchin' to get out of Cleveland," Hudson notes. "We played this truly horrible show at the Pirate's Cove, which prompted us to break up afterward, and Brian then left for New York."

In 1981, Hudson and Metoff started Terminal Records to fill the gap left by record labels such as Drome (Dromette had by then moved to Los Angeles). In the midst of recording songs, the two decided to start up the Pagans again. The new formation (ca. 1982) included keyboardist Chas Smith (formerly of the Clocks), bass player Robert Conn, and drummer Bob Richey (later with Les Black and the Amazing Pink Holes). The addition of Smith brought more songwriting talents to the group.

"I had been in the Clocks [with Mike Metoff], which played a lot at the Pop Shop," Smith recalls. "When they broke up, Hudson and Metoff decided to reform the Pagans, and they asked me to join. I became the first and only keyboardist in the Pagans. I also helped write 'Wall of Shame' and other material on the *Pink Album*."

The Pagans' first LP, self-titled, was released in 1983, but it did not fare well. They continued to record, however, releasing *Buried Alive* in 1986, live—*The Godlike Power of the Pagans* in 1987), and *Street Where Nobody Lives,* a rehashed version of *Buried Alive,* in 1989. The compilation *Buried Alive* was their most successful album; it received favorable reviews in *Rolling Stone* and *Spin*.

By 1986, the Pagans had finally won an impressive fan base. "From 1986 to '89, we were playing every big town you can think of in the Northwest," Hudson says, "and were selling out in cities like Washington, D.C., and Philadelphia, and there'd be these young kids mouthing all the words to our songs. Now that was totally cool."

"Things were going real good," Smith notes, "until the night we opened for Stiv Bators's new band, Lords of the New Church, at the Agora. I quit that night, for whatever reason, and Mike Metoff then quit as well. That was the end of the Pagans."

Smith and Metoff went on to form Venus Envy, a band that played throughout the Midwest and released an EP before disbanding. Metoff went on to the Cramps (as Ike Knox) and other bands. After participating in forty various recordings, he quit the music scene. Today he is a printer in Twinsburg. Hudson is "permanently retired" from the music business and works as a city hall reporter for the *Niagara Falls Gazette*.

Smith went on to earn a master's degree in composition from Cleveland State University and now is a "professor of rock and roll" at his alma mater. "I mainly focus on the early period of rock, the '50s and '60s," he says. "Believe it or not, my classes average about 260 students. It's amazing. If someone would've come up to me at the Pop Shop fifteen years ago and said, 'Hey, you'll be teaching this stuff some day,' I'd have laughed in their face!"

The Pagans' music lives on through recordings. In 1996, a 1979 gig at the Pirate's Cove resulted in a posthumous CD, *Pagans/Live at Pirate's Cove*. Another live CD was released in 1998, *Pagans/Live Road Kill 1978–89*. Both recordings feature guitarist Paul Marotta. That same year, Hudson released the EP *Mike Hudson Unmedicated* on Sonic Swirl Records.

Ten years after their last breakup, the Pagans have earned a cult following through the underground music channels. Akron guitarist Marky Ray cites the Pagans as the ultimate band and his major influence. (Ray's resume includes Death of Samantha, Terrible Parade, Death on a Stick, New Salem Witch Hunters, and tours with Nine Inch Nails, Ministry, and the Lyres. He is currently in the Akron-based band 3D.) There are also nationwide tribute bands in the Pagans' honor, keeping their music alive—and loud.

Lucky Pierre (1977–90)

"We were never a punk band, no way," says guitarist Denis DeVito, who wants to make that distinction perfectly clear. "We were melodic, new wavish. But never punk. We got labeled punk because we often played with Pere Ubu on Thursday nights at Pirate's Cove. Plus we opened for national bands like Mink DeVille and the Plasmatics."

Lucky Pierre was formed by rhythm guitarist/songwriter Kevin McMahon, who often gave varied stories on the band's name. "The one I think is probably most accurate," says drummer Dave Zima, "goes back to the '20s. It was a risqué joke about two girls and a guy in bed, and the mailman discovers them and calls the man Lucky Pierre." However the name came about, the quartet that originally also included John Guciardo (lead guitar) and Brian Dempsey (drums) jelled almost immediately.

The group played original compositions penned by McMahon but had a hard time finding venues. "This was pre–new wave, so any band playing originals couldn't get gigs," recalls DeVito, who started on bass but switched to lead guitar with the addition of bassist Tom Lash. "We could only play Hennessy's, Pirate's Cove, and the Phantasy."

Changes in lineup occurred soon after its formation when Guciardo and Dempsey left. Drummer Gary Shay stepped in (replaced by Dave Zima in February 1978) along with Lash, who met the band while he was music director at CSU's college radio station WCSB. McMahon had sent Lash a demo tape, which was played to a receptive audience.

With McMahon's songwriting talents, these West Side new wave enthusiasts wasted no time. In 1977, the group recorded the single "Fans and Cameras," b/w "idlewood," on their own Unadulterated label. The 45 was available at area record stores and quickly sold more than a thousand copies.

"McMahon was a great songwriter. Still is," DeVito notes. "He was a huge Kinks fan and that influenced his writing. He writes beautiful songs. 'Idlewood' was a good example. It had strings and synthesizers. Great tune."

Their second release was "Into My Arms." The b-side of that single, "Match," was recorded live on July 16, 1980, at their sole WMMS Coffeebreak Concert.

"We were one of the few local bands to play a Coffeebreak Concert," DeVito says. "WMMS did not support local bands, especially if you were considered underground. There were some quality records coming out during that time, but 'MMS wouldn't play them. Denny Sanders and Len Goldberg were the only ones who showed interest in local bands. So Denny invited us to play a Coffeebreak. But the host, Matt the Cat, refused to emcee the show because he looked at us as a punk band. Denny hosted it instead."

The group then added keyboardist Tom Miller, broadening the quintet's range. "We were limited with a four-piece," DeVito says. "And when you're playing punk clubs, you got to rock out."

A third release came out in 1981. "stetson," b/w "Once a Child," again boasted original compositions by McMahon. Besides playing in clubs in Chicago and Buffalo, Lucky Pierre's most memorable gig came at Cleveland's Agora, when they opened for another punk band. "We were approached about opening for the Plasmatics," DeVito recalls. "It was a sold-out show so we said, 'Let's do it.' We got to play to a capacity crowd, and it was a great night for us." It wasn't such a great night, however, for the headliner or the club. That was the evening the Plasmatics lead singer Wendy O. Williams was arrested for indecent exposure, and, as a result, the Agora temporarily lost its liquor license (see Chapter 6).

After the group opened for Peter Frampton at the Music Hall in 1982, DeVito left (McMahon replaced him , and Tom Sheridan came in on guitar. Then McMahon moved to San Francisco. Lucky Pierre was on hiatus until its leader returned to Ohio in 1988 and re-formed the group with Lash, Zima, and guitarist Rick Christyson. They also brought in a keyboardist who was making impressive waves along the North Coast, an ambitious young musician who had played in the Innocent, Slam Bam Boo, and Exotic Birds. His name was Trent Reznor.

"Trent was a good friend of McMahon's, so when he went to San Francisco, Reznor went out there with Lash to put some tracks on the next recording we were working on," Zima recalls. "Trent went on tour with us and played for about six months until he got immersed in recording *Pretty Hate Machine*." Reznor began working on his own musical project in 1989 (see Chapter 17). He has continued his friendship with McMahon, later producing his solo project, *Prick*.

This new Lucky Pierre emerged with a five-song EP titled *Communique*. John Guciardo returned to contribute his riffs to the record. The title song later appeared on *Prick*. However, by 1990 Lucky Pierre performed its last formal show in August at the Phantasy Nite Club. McMahon returned to California. When he visits Cleveland, his old bandmates spark a reunion at the Lakewood club. Other notable players through the years included bassist Paul Kompier and guitarist Tom Jares.

Although group members agree that their group could not be labeled with one genre, it was just different enough to warrant the tag "new wave." According to Zima,

> We had a strong English influence. And our songs were more complex. In some ways that worked for us; in the end I think it worked against us. We thrived at being intricate, emotional. With McMahon's unique writing style, each song had these peaks and valleys. Because of that, record companies said we had a "lack of direction." They wanted to pigeonhole us. But we still recorded and played out when we could. For a while we often shared the bill with Wild Giraffes, even though our styles were different. Wild Giraffes were more straight-ahead rock, while we were more melodic. Because of that, our fans were definitely split. For years, our two groups would play Thanksgiving night at Pirate's Cove, and the place would be packed. But I'll never forget how divided the audience was. There'd be the Lucky Pierre people on one side and the Wild Giraffe people on the other. Yet all of us band members were great friends.

Today, in L.A., McMahon continues to record on Nothing Records. Lash went on to System 56, then Hot Tin Roof. DeVito has a new band, Cats on Holiday, with sax and vibrophone player Steve Frieg, who played briefly with Lucky Pierre. Zima, who also played in Hot Tin Roof, works for NASA and prides himself on his massive drum collection.

"I can see us playing again sometime," Zima says. "When we all get together it just seems the natural thing to do." To prove this, Zima, along with Christyson, joined the ranks of DeVito's Cats on Holiday in 2000.

Wild Giraffes (1976–84)

Members of this Lake County–based group were born and raised in Raspberries country. Founders Edgar Reynolds (guitar/songwriter) met Chris King (vocals) when they were classmates at Mentor's Shore Junior High. King was impressed by Reynolds's guitar playing and, by when they were in high school, agreed to be singer for his new band. They added drummer Alan McGinty ("He actually sold his car for a drum set," King notes), bassist Chris Burgess, and guitarist Jeff Iannini.

"The Raspberries were, of course, an influence musically, as well as the fact their success gave area musicians hope," says McGinty, who was also King's next door neighbor. "They played the Beatles and Rolling Stones, and we all liked them. We also liked Cream, and then got into the Sex Pistols and Akron's Rubber City Rebels. That's when we hooked into the punk stuff that was going around. But though our performances were viewed as new wave, our roots were traditional."

How did they arrive at the name? "We were a bunch of knuckleheads at Mentor High School," King says. "We were the misfits. We weren't the jocks, the stoners, the geeks, just kinda in between. Edgar was the talent. So once we decided to form a band, we sat around one day trying to figure out a name. After some time of this, we got to Elephants Gerald (like Ella Fitzgerald), but finally decided on the Wild Giraffes from Kentucky. Then we just shortened it."

During their senior year the group won a Battle of the Bands at Chardon High School. "Four out of the six bands that played there did 'Play That Funky Music (White Boy),'" King recalls. "We were the last band to play and came out looking like the Cleveland Beach Boys with matching outfits, striped shirts, and bell-bottom pants. But we were the only ones to do two original songs, and I think that right there completely surprised the judges. The songs we did ended up being our first single, 'New Era'/ 'Dreams Don't Last.'"

The group took its music from the smooth, power-pop melodies of the Raspberries and the hard-edged, high energy of the Ramones. Their repertoire was broad and included old-time rock hits. "We did Roy Orbison's 'Pretty Woman,' the Beatles' 'I'll Get You,' Willie Dixon's 'Crazy Mixed-up World,' and Elvis's 'Burnin' Love,' which was a hot single for us," McGinty recalls. Whatever songs they played, the crowd could count on some mind-blowing twist. "We did all our songs loud, long, and fast. When we'd finish our set, we all looked like we just walked out of a swimming pool. We had this great synergy together."

Their originals were all penned by Reynolds. The most popular included "A Girl Like You" (his first song, written when he was seventeen), "We'll Never Know," "Love Me," "I Want to Be a Giraffe," and "New Era." This last tune Reynolds wrote about the New Era Burlesque Theater on Prospect Avenue at a time when Mayor Ralph Perk was crusading against pornography during his reelection campaign. (He lost to Dennis Kucinich.)

The single, along with "Love Me," got the East Side band airplay on local college stations, as well as on WMMS. By the end of the 1970s, the Wild Giraffes were known all along the North Coast, playing regular gigs at Lakewood's Hennessy's, the Mistake, Pirate's Cove, Kent's JB's, and Euclid's Looking Glass (often sharing the stage with groups such as Pere Ubu, the Dead Boys, Tin Huey, Hammer Damage, and Styrene Money). The band also opened twice for the Ramones at the Agora.

The second lineup included Reynolds, King, McGinty, bassist Dave Ivan, and guitarist Michael Terrell. Because of its association with early punk bands, the Wild Giraffes was tagged new wave, even being voted "Top New Wave Band" in *Scene*'s 1980 Readers Poll. However, the band members never considered themselves new wave, preferring "original rock" to describe their sound. Either way, it was *Scene* writer Dave Voelker who captured their essence with this telling description: "The drummer hammers out a beat with almost painful intensity, boosted by the throbbing tones of a bass player who looks and moves more like an ape than a human being. Two guitar players trade calculated leads and rhythms that pierce right through the head. A tall blonde guy with boyish looks sings in a classic voice that sounds as if his vocal cords are made of

Turkish Taffee." With those dramatic elements, the Wild Giraffes had no problem drawing an audience.

"During that period, we were pretty hot," McGinty says. "We'd play in front of packed houses where all you'd see looking from the stage was this sea of human bodies. And we were making good money, though we always kept our day jobs."

The group, however, was constantly confused with another Cleveland band, Wild Horses—an understandable mistake, Chris King says, that continues to this day. "We'll spend the rest of our lives saying, 'No, no, that wasn't us. We weren't the 'Funky Poodle' guys. We were the 'Burnin' Love' guys."

The release of the group's debut album, *Right Now,* in 1981, won the Wild Giraffes favorable mention in *Trouser Press* magazine. The article hailed the band's ingenuity, even comparing them to the early Who.

McGinty was first to leave the band, in 1983. He was followed by Terrell, who was replaced by guitarist Bill Elliot, who, in turn, left soon afterward, to be replaced by Thomas Jares. "The late, great Bill Elliot," King recalls with a sigh. "I was sorry when he left. [But] for some reason the chemistry of the band was that Edgar was obviously the writer and had the strongest ideas. And he took more influence from the guitarists. So every couple of years, he'd either get fed up with them or they with him, and we'd end up getting a new guitar player. But every incarnation of the band brought its own uniqueness."

By 1984, band members' interests were going in different directions. In addition, after years of wreaking havoc on his voice, Chris King paralyzed a nerve in his vocal cords. They called it quits while in the midst of recording a second album.

"But it was a great band," King says. "No one ever said we sucked."

Movin' On

As suddenly as it swelled, Cleveland's new wave movement receded by decade's end. The bands that hadn't broken up, such as Pere Ubu, found new life far from their roots in hipper music places like England, New York, and L.A. But the North Coast wasn't finished with the trend yet. The bands and their fans moved south, to Akron, where the scene grew among the industrial sights and sounds of the factories.

Akron's Anarchists

Maybe it is because they were born and raised in a rubber mill town—blue collar all the way. Maybe they felt the only way to escape the same hard-working lives of their parents was through rock and roll. Or maybe they were just bored. Whatever the reasons, musicians in the Akron music scene in the 1970s were bursting at the city's conservative seams. This generation was bound and determined to live a different life. And many succeeded, but they had to get out of town to do it.

Each of these irrepressible young musicians left town a virtual unknown and returned (most only for concerts) a musical hero. Chrissie Hynde went to London and became a Pretender. Devo shook up all of Europe before settling in Los Angeles. The Cramps hit it big in New York. And the Bizarros, Rubber City Rebels, and Hammer Damage all made their marks on the West Coast.

Devo (1973–87)

Was Devo rock, punk, new wave, industrial? Even members themselves don't like to categorize their music, but "avant-garde" is an apt descriptor. This maverick band offered up an art-rock version of Akron-bred pop music that few understood but many appreciated. Two Kent State University art students, Mark Mothersbaugh (vocals/keyboards) and Jerry Casale (bass), knew when they started out they wanted to be different from your average band. They were to be a band with a message.

"The Devo concept was that man is de-evolving through the dehumanizing effect of modern technology," Mothersbaugh has explained many times. True to form, their debut album, released on Virgin Records in 1978, was *Q: Are We Not Men? A: We Are DEVO!* It quickly reached No. 12 on U.K. charts.

Devo emerged as a multimedia musical art show. Original members included Mothersbaugh's and Casale's brothers, both guitarists and both named Bob (Bob I and Bob II, respectively), with yet another Bob, guitarist Bob Lewis, and another brother, drummer Jim Mothersbaugh (replaced by Alan Myers in 1975). Their first live performance was at Kent State's Creative Arts Festival in 1973, where they combined music with graphics. After recording some demos in 1974, Devo surfaced on the club scene.

"There weren't a lot of places for groups like ours to play," says Pere Ubu keyboardist Allen Ravenstine. "Devo played the Bank in Akron a lot, then started coming up to Pirate's Cove. We started switching back and forth, from the Akron club to the Cleveland club."

One unforgettable (hard as they try), disastrous gig, the 1975 Halloween Party at the old WHK building, sponsored by WMMS, made clear that local audiences weren't ready for this unusual band and their music. The conceptual Devo was not welcomed by the pop-oriented crowd, which was turned off by the heavy synthesizer and electronic drums. While playing their own off-brand style of the Stones' "Satisfaction," Devo members were shocked when the crowd began pelting them with beer cans. "And it wasn't even the good stuff,'" members complained. "It was the cheap variety." (According to sources, the crowd was bent on hearing a local version of Led Zeppelin.) Had it been just one year later, however, when new wave had made its presence known on the rock music scene, that very same crowd would surely have cheered and applauded and appreciated them—and bought them all a beer . . . the good stuff, too.

Indeed, by 1976 the scene had changed and the self-described "spud boys" ("*Spud* is a word to describe everyman. In the world of vegetables, the spud is kind of dirty. It comes from the earth. It's lowly, yet it's a staple of everyone's diet. Being a spud is like being a part of the wad, part of mankind's genetic pool," explains Mark Mothersbaugh) suddenly had a cult following that had fans traveling between Cleveland and Akron to hear and watch this theatrical and theoretical band. They released a single, "Mongoloid," b/w "Jocko Homo," on their own Boojie Boy label (the Boojie Boy being somewhat of a mascot), which was later included on the group's debut LP. Until 1977, the group performed regularly at Cleveland venues Pirate's Cove and the Eagle Street Saloon (formerly the Clockwork Orange) and at Akron's the Bank.

From its inception, Devo has been described as quirky, bizarre, and slightly off-kilter. But then, they meant it that way. While playing the club circuit, the group produced a ten-minute film, *The Truth About De-Evolution*. It won a prize at the 1975 Ann Arbor Film Festival. Devo's passion for film ultimately took the group to Los Angeles in 1977. The move would prove pivotal in the group's career.

Their debut LP included songs club-goers were already familiar with, such as "Uncontrollable Urge," "Praying Hands," "Space Junk," and "Sloppy," and the group began hearing their songs on the radio for the first time.

"It was my wife, Susan, who gave the [Devo] tape to Iggy Pop and David Bowie," recalls Tin Huey guitarist Michael Aylward. "They were on their 'New Values' tour, and Susan went right up to them at this club and said, 'You've got to listen to this.' Soon after, they shipped them [Devo] off to Germany."

That European tour brought the Akron band new fans, especially in the United Kingdom. Then they played CBGB in New York, where Bowie introduced the Akronites to former Roxy Music member Brian Eno. After hearing their unique sound, Eno offered to produce the first album, which he released on Virgin Records (a subsidy of Warner Brothers). Devo is considered by many to have been the first industrial band.

Their 1979 album, *Duty Now for the Future* (No. 49 on U.K. charts), earned Devo recognition in the United States as well as a semi-cult following in Japan. *Freedom of Choice* was their next album. And with the help of MTV, they became video stars. The single off that album, "Whip It," was written by Mark Mothersbaugh. The song gave Devo its first U.S. hit when it peaked at No. 14 on *Billboard* (No. 51 on U.K. charts).

"Despite thoughts to the contrary, 'Whip It' was written for Jimmy Carter, who we were fans of," Mothersbaugh has explained. "We felt bad about the bad rap he was getting [on the hostage crisis]. It was our own version of Dale Carnegie, a 'you can do it' anthem. Like when we say, 'When a problem comes along, you must whip it . . . go forward, move ahead, it's not too late to whip it, whip it good.' Yeah, people thought it was sexual. That's probably why it sold so well." Sold well it did, earning the group a gold disc for over a million sales in the United States.

In 1981, there were two releases, *Devo Live* (a mini-album that reached U.S. No. 49) and *New Traditionalists* (U.K. No.50, U.S. No.34). The latter had the band's own rendition of the Lee Dorsey classic "Working in the Coal Mine," which was included in the National Lampoon movie *Heavy Metal*. Their *Oh No! It's Devo!* came out in 1982 with another chart-making song, "The Theme from Doctor Detroit." In the meantime, Devo appeared on *Saturday Night Live* and *Late Night with David Letterman*. By the time

their Warner Brothers effort, *Shout*, was released in 1986, however, the Devo concept was losing its appeal.

Right before Devo disbanded in 1987, David Kendrick was added on drums. In 1988 Devo released *Total Devo* and in 1990 the follow-up, *Smooth Noodle Maps*. Both did well, considering that the band hadn't been on the charts in several years. In 1993 their best-of compilation was released, *Hot Potatoes*.

After ten years in L.A., Mark, Jerry, Bob, and Bob traded in their bright-yellow hazardous waste suits for three-piece business suits. In those suits each found success and ultimately "devolved" into the Hollywood mainstream. Mark Mothersbaugh formed

Devo clad in trademark industrial suits. *Photo by Janet Macoska.*

the company Mutato Muzika. He wrote scores for independent films, TV commercials, and children's shows, including the Emmy-winning *Pee-Wee's Playhouse* and *Beakman's World,* and in 1997 he hooked onto Nickelodeon's *Rugrats* explosion. The weekly series has become an international hit, with a successful self-titled feature film that includes a Mothersbaugh-penned film score. New Yorker Jerry Casale produces music for other bands, as well as the score from the 1989 movie *Animals.*

Despite not having played together for years, Devo was invited to the 1996 Lollapalooza, where they performed six shows on the West Coast. The group was then asked to headline several more the following year, one that included Blossom Music Center.

After all the successes, Mark Mothersbaugh hasn't forgotten the early days. As he told the *Los Angeles Times* in 1997, "I remember playing for twelve people in these tiny clubs in Akron. The reaction was mainly outrage. Guys would rip off our rubber masks and scream 'Play Aerosmith!' To be honest, I kind of miss the really confrontational days."

Tin Huey (1972–79, 1982–83)

When Tin Huey was formed in 1972, founding member and singer/guitarist/keyboardist Harvey Gold didn't want it to be your average rock and roll band. In that he succeeded. The original members, who included sax player/vocalist Ralph Carney (who later played with Tom Waits and the B-52's), guitarist Michael Aylward, bassist Mark Price, and drummer Stuart Austin (a.k.a. Nappy Lemans), didn't fit into any of the categories that existed then. They weren't pop rock, garage rock, or punk rock. A few years later the musical tags caught up to them, and they were finally labeled new wave. But many believe that wasn't right either, as the band veered more toward jazz-oriented art rock, heavily influenced by Robert Wyatt and Soft Machine. Over the years, its music expanded those and other boundaries.

No one remembers exactly how band members came across the name, though Aylward recalls naming it for his brother, Huey. "When Harvey and I were young people, we wrote a song called 'Huey's Made of Tin,' a little song about my brother smashing tin beer cans over his head."

Playing Stooges, Velvet Underground, and Soft Machine covers, the band drew heavily on originals right from the start. As songwriter, Gold found himself another niche. The group released a single, "Breakfast with the Hueys," and an EP, *Puppet Wipes,* both on Clone, the indie label of Akron-based group the Bizarros.

These aspiring musicians liked their music loud. "Mark's [Price] father was a judge, very solid, very respected," Aylward notes. "And we'd be down in the basement practicing and doing all the stuff that we did.... Mark would put the speakers with two-by-fours under them—with just enough air underneath—cranked to capacity. And there'd be Judge Price sitting upstairs, TV volume turned all the way up so he could hear it. Mark's older brother had a band before us, so the poor man had to go through that twice!"

With original music and an offbeat sense of humor, Tin Huey quickly became the darlings of the North Coast college scene. They played at various clubs, including the Bank and JB's. In 1978, former Numbers Band guitarist Chris Butler came into the fold. He recalls:

When I was in the Numbers Band, we'd be playing downstairs and Tin Huey would play up, so I used to go upstairs on break to see them and thought they were wonderful. Plus, I had a fanzine where I did a review of them, and I think that caught Ralph Carney's attention. He later called me and told me Tin Huey needed another writer/musician. He remembered I wrote songs when I was in the Numbers Band. I ended up joining the band. Right after that, I got a call from Robert Christgau [senior editor for *Village Voice*] who said he wanted to come down and hear this Akron sound he'd been hearing so much about. See, when I was in the Numbers Band, I'd sent him some recordings. So all of a sudden, it was like, "Oh shit, what do we do now?" We immediately got together with the Bizarros and Chi Pig, made some posters, and put a show together at JB's. Robert shows up and has a great time. A week or so after that, Robert called and said he had such a good time in Kent he was coming back, this time with A&R person Karin Berg. I hung up and thought, "Now we got to do this all over again! Rehearse, put up posters, get the bands together, etc." So she shows up, enjoys the show. A few days later, Karin calls and says she liked it so well she told her boss, the great R&B promoter Jerry Wexler, and *he* wants to come and see a show. I said, "Oh f——! Not again!" So we beg and plead with [JB's owner] Joe Bujack one more time, get the three PA systems, get opening acts, which I believe were Chi Pig, Rubber City Rebels, and Bizarros. And we put on another show. It was kinda funny seeing these big-business people in this little dive bar in Kent, Ohio.

Tin Huey's steadfast efforts proved worthwhile when Warner Brothers offered them a contract. They opened for Television at New York's Bottom Line the summer of 1978 and then went into the studio to record their debut album. In February 1979, *Contents Dislodged During Shipment* was released. That same year, the Butler-penned "Wait Here, I'll Be Right Back" was included on the *Akron Compilation* anthology released by Stiff Records. Butler recalls those days: "We toured around the country, and let me say it didn't go well. We had a two-record contract and began working on the second album when Warner Brothers called to say they wanted to 'renegotiate our deal.' They told us they'd prefer us *not* to put out another record. So we said, 'Hey, we're just a dumb band from Ohio and a deal's a deal.' They said, 'No, you don't understand. We'll give you $35,000 if you *don't* record.' We said, 'No, a deal's a deal.' They said, 'Okay, we'll give you $40,000.' We said, 'No, that's okay.' They said, '$45,000.' We said 'No.' They said, 'We'll give you $50,000.' We said, 'Well, okay.' We took the money and ran! By then it was clear the band had run its course anyway."

In late 1979, Tin Huey took a hiatus until it re-formed briefly in 1982—minus Butler, plus guitarist/keyboardist/vocalist Ralph E. Boy (Ralph Legnini). Today, founder

Harvey Gold is a successful television producer in New York. Michael Aylward continues various musical ventures in Akron. Chris Butler, now in New Jersey, went on to form the New York–based Waitresses, a band that included Akron natives Patty Donahue (vocals) and Dan Klayman (guitar), with former Television drummer Billy Ficca. The Waitresses' 1981 album, *Wasn't Tomorrow Wonderful,* featured the hit single, "I Know What Boys Like" (*Billboard* No. 41). The song sold more than 50,000 copies, a great number for an independent release. In 1998 the Spice Girls recorded a Waitresses song, "Christmas Wrapping," which was included on the girl group's holiday CD.

Twenty years after the first album, Tin Huey released *Disinformation,* even though the band has not formally re-formed. Another CD is in the works, which will include all previously unreleased recordings from the band's history.

For a group that had no plans for endurance or validity, this rather oddball Kent legend is well remembered and still crazy after all these years. And according to band members, that's not a bad thing.

The Cramps (1975–)

I just think there could be nothing more wonderful than doing what we do, because the records go to everywhere on the planet and if there's great floods and the only thing left is Newfoundland or something like that, I'm sure there are Cramps records there. It's kind of cool.

—Lux Interior, *Scene* (November 1994)

Most fans of this group look at the Cramps as a New York band. And they wouldn't be wrong. The Cramps did indeed become a music entity in the Big Apple, most notably at CBGB, but the group came out of Akron.

"My older brother [Ronald] collected these wild records that only deejays Alan Freed and Mad Daddy were playing," founder/guitarist/vocalist Erick Purkhiser (a.k.a. Lux Interior) has recalled on several occasions.

Young Purkhiser was such an impassioned Ghoulardi fan that he recalls it affecting his early social life. Whereas most guys his age were "cruising chicks" on Friday nights, this Akron-area native sat home transfixed in front of his television screen. "I wanted girls," he admits, "but Ghoulardi was a more powerful drug." (Ghoulardi left such an impression on Purkhiser that his band's 1990 *Stay Sick* album is dedicated to TV's unforgettable Friday night B-movie host from the sixties.)

Like many teens searching for excitement in the late '60s and early '70s, Purkhiser, a 1964 Stow High School graduate, headed for the West Coast in 1968. In 1970, while driving down a Sacramento highway, he picked up a hitchhiker named Christine Wallace (a.k.a. Poison Ivy Rorschach). At that fateful moment, the two began a relationship that would last decades. The duo would wind up back in Purkhiser's hometown, but not for long.

Purkhiser and his California girlfriend found they shared a mutual interest in rockabilly. Their passion for pioneering artists like Carl Perkins, Jerry Lee Lewis, and Elvis led them to form the group whose music they termed "psychobilly" as a result of their somewhat warped versions of '50s and '60s songs like "Surfin' Bird" (The Trashmen) and "Hardworkin' Man" (Captain Beefheart).

The Cramps were deemed the "Addams Family of Rock" for their manner of dress, which included jet-black hair, white skin, and an assortment of clothing that looked to be straight out of Gomez and Morticia's closet. And this was *before* the goth rock genre. The original lineup included Bryan Gregory (guitar) and Ashtabula native Miriam Linna (drums). Other members over the years included drummers Nick Knox (né Nick Stephanoff), Nicky Alexander, Jim Sclavunos, and Harry Drumdini; bassists Candy Del Mar and Slim Chance; and guitarists Kid Congo Powers and hometown buddy Ike Knox (Mike Metoff).

One of their first gigs included sharing the stage with Pere Ubu at a private Fourth of July party in the posh Cleveland lakefront suburb of Bratenahl. The bash ended when Purkhiser fell off the outdoor, hilltop stage and rolled down the hill, bouncing all the way to the beach.

Purkhiser and company saw no future for their style of music here, so they left Ohio. Had they been more patient, they would have been surprised to see an impressive change in the area's music scene. A scant two years later, Akron's underground music would capture international attention.

The Cramps on tour, Paris, 1984. *Left to right:* Ike Knox, Nick Knox, Poison Ivy, and Lux Interior. *Courtesy of Mike Metoff.*

The Cramps took their mischief to New York in 1976. There they shared play dates with the Dead Boys and the Ramones at CBGB. Within months, *Trouser Press* was touting the group as "punk's greatest living rockabilly zombies." By 1980, Purkhiser moved his band to Los Angeles, where they were joined by bassist Slim Chance and ex-Weirdos drummer Nicky Alexander.

According to Purkhiser, their music is all in fun. "I think humor is a lot more powerful than somebody's boring, artistic statement about their feelings. I mean, who cares about that?" he told *Scene* in 1992.

The Cramps continue their musical odyssey, presently based in L.A. Mike Metoff recalls his time with the Cramps: "Sometime in 1983, my cousin Nick Knox called me up from L.A. because they were looking for someone to replace Kid Congo Powers, who had left the group. I had just gotten laid off my job so it was perfect timing. I toured with them throughout North America and Europe under the name Ike Knox. I had been in a lot of bands, but touring with the Cramps . . . well, let's just say it was a pretty crazy time!"

The Cramps' series of recordings appealed to new and old punk rockers alike. After years of being on hiatus, the quirky musicians have once again returned to the studio. Purkhiser, however, maintains a low profile, preferring to keep his private life just that.

Terminal Drive to Punk-Style Rock and Roll

With the development of this new off-brand of rock music, the decade from the mid-1970s to the mid-1980s saw many musical waves. On the heels of punk rock and art rock came new wave, then no-wave. Technically, in the opinions of musicians from those genres, each style of music stands on its own, a separate entity. Yet they all share one common goal: they strive to be different, as Dave Thomas says, "to take rock to the next level." And no matter how the artists choose to bend, shape, exploit, break, experiment, it's all in the name of rock and roll.

Recommended Reading

Heylin, Clinton. *From the Velvets to the Voidoids: A Pre-Punk History for a Post-Punk World.* New York: Penguin Books, 1993

———, ed. *The Penguin Book of Rock and Roll Writing.* New York: Penguin Books, 1992.

Marcus, Greil. *Panthers and Crowd Pleasers: Punk in Pop Music, 1977–92.* New York: Doubleday, 1993.

15 Rock in the Mainstream

The 1970s began with John Lennon declaring "The dream is over." In a sad, ironic twist, that comment foreshadowed the first year of the following decade. The 1980s began with a nightmare.

On December 8, 1980, John Lennon was murdered. At the time he was singing about the media, who continually harassed him, and the American government, who followed his every move because of his highly vocal opposition to the Vietnam War. Yet the irony lay in the true killer. The man who fatally shot Lennon outside his New York apartment building, the Dakota, was neither a newspaper reporter nor an FBI agent. The murderer called himself a fan. So in the end, it was Lennon's ultimate celebrity that claimed his life. The talented visionary would never again contribute to the music genre he helped to create. The death of a Beatle was devastating and unimaginable. Although rock and roll deaths were nothing new, Lennon's was harder to accept on many levels. It wasn't a drug-related death, a suicide, or an unfortunate accident. It was a murder. The world took notice. Its consciousness was raised.

Whether a direct result of the loss of this beloved rock icon or simply the maturation of Baby Boomers, much of the music of the '80s took on political and humanitarian issues, such as the famous 1985 Live Aid concert, USA for Africa, and Farm Aid.

The '80s also saw a shift away from the reckless abandon of punk rock toward nostalgic ballads and catchy pop tunes. Familiar names at the top of the charts were Lionel Ritchie ("All Night Long"), Bryan Adams ("Summer of '69"), John Cougar Mellencamp ("Hurts So Good"), Huey Lewis and the News ("I Want a New Drug"), Culture Club ("Do You Really Want to Hurt Me"), and the J. Geils Band ("Centerfold"). And with his *Born in the USA* LP, Bruce Springsteen became a superstar.

Also in this decade, women rockers came into their own, among them Blondie (featuring Debbie Harry, "One Way or Another"), Joan Jett ("I Love Rock and Roll"), Stevie Nicks ("Bella Donna"), Chrissie Hynde ("Brass in Pocket"), Cyndi Lauper ("Girls Just Wanna Have Fun"), Pat Benatar ("Treat Me Right"), Sheena Easton ("Morning Train"), Sheila E. (Escovedo, "The Glamorous Life"), Madonna ("Like a Virgin"), and the groups the Go-Gos and the Bangles.

But the 1980s' standout contribution to rock music was the music video.

The Dawn of Music Television (Or, Not Everyone Wants Their MTV)

MTV debuted on August 1, 1981, at 12:01 A.M. From that moment on, how we view, and hear, music was forever altered.

The first song played on that TV debut was the Buggles's "Video Killed the Radio Star," an ironic choice for the first play, since, from its inception, an MTV appearance often escalates a group's fame (deservingly or not) and increases sales. This new means of bringing music to the people granted many recording artists another way of promoting their songs. MTV (and its less embellished sister, VH1) also provided new jobs for the hippest among us. Many former deejays became veejays.

In its infancy, this visual phenomenon caught the attention of music lovers everywhere. It took a few years, however—and a series of rather ludicrous videos that turned off many fans—to bring this now-older generation to the sad conclusion that the era of daydreaming and fantasizing to songs on the radio or 8-track or record player was over. This "music aid" was ripping off the treasured gift of imagination music encouraged. Now, instead of recalling what or who was happening in our lives when we hear a particular song, we more often remember the film sequence, the hairdos, the dance moves, the costumes, the theatrics.

Nonetheless, a new industry was born. And, in keeping with its tradition of breaking barriers and pushing limits and influencing people all over the world, rock and roll welcomed music television into "the family."

In Cleveland, the decade looked promising. The old jokes were growing stale; the city was working its way out of default, and the Flats was fast becoming an entertainment mecca. Confidence and "attitude" were making a comeback—as evidenced on t-shirts sporting the slogan "Cleveland—Like It or Leave It."

Musically, however, not much had improved. Although the city still boasted the top radio station in the country, WMMS, musicians still struggled to get gigs and to get their songs played on the radio. The frustration of not being able to secure media access or attention sent many packing to New York or Los Angeles, where some even made "the big time."

Women Find Their Place in Rock

In the 1960s there was Aretha Franklin, Tina Turner, Janis Joplin, and Jefferson Airplane's Grace Slick and girl groups the Supremes, the Shangri-Las, and the Ronettes. The 1970s brought a longer list of female singers and girl groups: Carly Simon, Linda Ronstadt, Diana Ross, Carole King, Helen Reddy, Cher, Bette Midler, Ellen Foley, the Runaways, Fanny, and Girlschool.

Not surprising, the dawn of the eighties found more women—such as Madonna, Pat Benatar, Paula Abdul, and Janet Jackson—becoming rock forces to be reckoned with. And the punk scene provided yet another vehicle for women, such as Patti Smith and Debbie Harry, enabling female rockers to go beyond the safety of pop music. A young Akron singer with just the right voice and style and attitude seized the chance early on.

Chrissie Hynde (b. 1951, Akron)

Nowadays it's interesting because there are tons of girls in bands. It's not even an issue anymore.

—Chrissie Hynde

By age fourteen, Chrissie Hynde knew what she wanted to be when she grew up. Never mind the fact that few women in the mid-1960s made a living as rock and roll singers. All she knew was that the music enchanted her, and she liked the fantasy. As an adolescent she listened to such '60s rock icons as the Rolling Stones, the Yardbirds, the Velvet Underground, R&B singer Jackie Wilson, and Ray Davies's Kinks. But one band in particular left a lasting impression: Mitch Ryder and the Detroit Wheels was the first rock concert she ever attended, and Hynde was in awe.

"Big change in my life that day," she recounted for *Scene* magazine. "First of all, I had never seen a guitar player like that. Jim McCarty. I was absolutely stunned when I saw him. Then they had this fistfight on stage, and it freaked me out. So I stayed after dark to see the second show, and they had the same fistfight. It was staged. Now that's rock and roll."

During these formative rock years, Hynde spent her early years dabbling with a baritone ukulele and singing in a church choir. Then she began teaching herself to play the guitar. It helped, too, that the teenager had a big brother who, in pursuing his own musical interests, paved the way for hers. "I was nearly four years older than Chrissie," said brother Terry, already a member of the Numbers Band then. "I don't know if I influenced her in any one way, but she did come and see the band play pretty often."

After graduating from Akron's Firestone High School in 1968, Hynde attended Kent State University for three years, majoring in fine and professional arts. She sang in Mark Mothersbaugh's band, Saturday Sunday Matinee, before he formed Devo, but she found herself increasingly drawn to something else. She was interested in the growing rock scene in England. It was 1973 when she bought a one-way ticket out of the Rubber City. The twenty-two-year-old got a job as a salesclerk at a punk rock clothing store in London (owned by future Sex Pistols manager Malcolm McLaren) and wrote rock items for Britain's *New Musical Express*. Then, moving to Paris, she joined a band called the Frenchies. She was barely eking out a living, however, and soon became disillusioned with the whole scene. In 1975, Chrissie Hynde went back to Ohio. "I came back to Cleveland to find my roots," she later told *Scene*. "I came back to find someone who had heard of Mitch Ryder and the Detroit Wheels."

Hynde, then twenty-four, took a job as a cocktail waitress at downtown Cleveland's trendy disco club the Last Moving Picture Show. Meanwhile, she hooked up with musician friends Duane Vehr (bass, Mr. Stress Band) and Donny Baker (guitar, E.T. Hooley) and formed the short-lived Jack Rabbit. The band also included drummer Bobby Hinton and guitarist Mike Maudlin. The rock/R&B cover band played mostly at Cleveland Heights' Cellar Door.

"It was Duane who was the real impetus for that band," Baker recalls. "He's the one who got Chrissie to join. One thing I remember distinctly about Chrissie was she always had a sense of where she was going, what she was going to do. She had such drive. And of course, she was an incredible singer—very talented right from the outset. Anyone who hears Chrissie Hynde can never forget her distinct voice."

By 1976, however, she knew her goal was not going to be reached in Ohio. She was ready to give Europe another try. Telling her parents she was returning to England and not coming back until she "made it," Hynde left to seek her fame.

The next four years were busy for Hynde. She took on a variety of day jobs while hanging out with musicians at night. Those friends included members of newly formed punk bands the Sex Pistols, the Clash, and the Damned. Through them she was introduced to guitarist James Honeyman-Scott and bassist Pete Farndon, who joined her in forming their own rock group in 1978. The trio (then unnamed) recorded its first single, the Ray Davies cover "Stop Your Sobbing" (it would reach No. 34 on U.K. charts, No. 65 in the U.S.). Soon afterward, drummer Martin Chambers came on board. The band's name came out of '50s singing sensations the Platters' hit song "The Great Pretender," which Hynde deemed fitting for their group.

In 1978 the Pretenders recorded "Brass in Pocket (I'm Special)," a song penned by Hynde and Honeyman-Scott. It was included on their self-titled debut album. By January 1980 it had become the U.K.'s No. 1 hit. After a mini-tour in the United States, the single topped No. 14 on U.S. charts that May.

The early '80s saw Hynde and her new band playing concerts throughout England. The group's original songs were noticed both on the record charts and in the rock press. The group's maiden album was certified platinum in August 1982. By then the band had released their second album, *Pretenders II,* with the singles "Day After Day" (No. 45 U.K.) and "I Go to Sleep" (No. 7 U.K.). "Back on the Chain Gang," which reached No. 17 in the United Kingdom and No. 5 on U.S. charts, was helped by its inclusion in the soundtrack of the Martin Scorsese movie *King of Comedy*. Chrissie Hynde and the Pretenders were now a worldwide success, and Hynde was quickly labeled one of the most exciting rock vocalists of the decade.

Whereas most female singers up to then projected an image that was either too soft, too hard, too sexy, too demanding, or too accommodating, Hynde appeared to be all of those things, while at the same time none. And she succeeded in breaking barriers that previous decades of rock had built around women. On stage, this midwestern artist is the epitome, and antithesis, of all previous notions of the female rocker—while playing deity to none of them. And though she has denied it in interviews, Hynde is obviously leader of the band. With her songwriting talents and unique stage presence, she not only took the group from obscurity to superstardom but also kept it alive after the drug-induced deaths of Honeyman-Scott (1982) and Farndon (1983). Determined to keep going, she brought in guitarist Robbie McIntosh and bassist Malcolm Foster, who, along with Chambers, released the much-anticipated *Learning to Crawl* LP (No. 11 U.K., No. 5 U.S.). From that came singles "Middle of the Road" (No. 19 U.S.), "Show Me" (No. 28 U.S.), and a song Hynde wrote about her Akron roots, "My City Was Gone." In 1995, she would sing the song with new meaning at the grand-opening concert for the Rock and Roll Hall of Fame and Museum.

And the albums kept coming. *Get Close* (1986; No. 6 U.K., No. 25 U.S.) featured the single "Don't Get Me Wrong," which was a No. 10 hit in both the U.K. and U.S. *Packed* came in 1990 (No. 48 U.S.), followed by *The Last of the Independents* (1994; No. 14 U.K., No. 41 U.S.) with the hit single, "I'll Stand by You" (No. 16 U.S.). Then *The Isle of View* (1995; No. 23 U.K., No. 100 U.S.). And true to form, the band's 1999 album *Viva L'Amore* met with critical acclaim.

The 1990s brought more changes to the group, with new members Billy Bremner (guitar), Dominick Miller (guitar), John McKenzie (bass), Blair Cunningham (drums), and Mitchell Froom (keyboards). By 1994, Hynde and Chambers were joined by guitarist Adam Seymour and bassist Andy Hobson. Throughout the decade, Hynde and company remained very much on the music circuit, touring worldwide and participating in numerous charity events, like the Philadelphia-based 1985 Live Aid concert for famine relief.

When it came time for the Rock and Roll Hall of Fame concert in September 1995, Hynde was the sole Ohio native asked to perform there. Although her name on the roster was welcomed by fans, there came a hailstorm of resentment and anger toward officials who didn't consider other deserving Cleveland artists such as Eric Carmen, the James Gang, the O'Jays, the Raspberries, Tracy Chapman, and Bobby Womack. That aside, Hynde's performance was one of the highlights of the seven-hour concert.

Through her enduring music and dedicated support for causes such as Greenpeace and PETA (People for the Ethical Treatment of Animals), Hynde continues to be an inspiration for women in and outside rock and roll. Further, she is undoubtedly proud of her midwestern roots. "I went around the world," she once told *Scene* writer Mark Holan. "I've seen the world. Cleveland, Akron, northeastern Ohio: Cool."

Rachel Sweet (b. 1963, Akron)

Rachel Sweet is another Akronite who found success in the music industry, as well as in television, movies, and theater. Since she was able to talk, Sweet wasted no time. She made her singing debut at age five at an *Akron Beacon Journal* picnic. When she was nine, she served as her own manager by convincing a bar owner in Florida to grant her an audition, which resulted in her opening for Frankie Valli. She performed in summer stock theater and club shows with Bill Cosby and Mickey Rooney. She ventured into country music as a teen and recorded a few singles. But rock and roll beckoned, and at age sixteen Rachel Sweet was being hailed by critics as the new "new wave princess."

Liam Sternberg, a highly successful music producer from her hometown, as well as a family friend, wrote some compositions for her that helped land a contract with English indie label Stiff Records, which was on board the Akron bandwagon with the signing of Devo and Tin Huey.

The song "Who Does Lisa Like?" brought her notice in New York City and England. Her greatest appeal seemed to lend to the fact her voice was a unique blend of countryish twang with the loud abandon of new wave. Sweet was an admirer of Chrissie Hynde; the music she wrote and sang was strongly influenced by the Pretenders albums.

She dropped out of Akron's Firestone High School (Chrissie Hynde's alma mater) at age sixteen to pursue her singing career; she later took correspondence courses and eventually went on to graduate from Columbia University.

Her 1978 debut album, *Fool Around,* took her on the road as part of the U.K. Stiff Records tour. Because of that connection, Sweet was labeled new wave despite the fact that her music did not exactly fit that genre. In fact, her style has always been hard to pigeonhole, since it varied from soft pop to country to straight-ahead rock. By the time her 1980 album, *Protect the Innocent,* was released, her popularity was well established in England, where she retains a steady fan base. Two more albums on Columbia Records followed, . . . *And Then He Kissed Me* (1981; the single "Everlasting Love," with teen star Rex Smith, made it to U.S. Top 50), and *Blame It on Love* (1982), each showcasing her unique voice and style. *Fool Around: The Best of Rachel Sweet* was released in 1992 on Columbia Records. Although each album contained cover material, it was her originals critics responded to. After taking time off from 1984 to 1988 to finish her degrees in French and English literature at Columbia, she returned to her real love. She sang, performed, and cowrote songs for the John Waters films *Hairspray* (1988) and *Cry Baby* (1990). From there she (like her hometown colleagues, Devo) hooked up with Nickelodeon, singing the theme song for the teen show *Clarissa Explains It All* as well as providing the speaking and singing voice of the cartoon Barbie on the cable Saturday-morning program. She also hosted her own cable show called *The Sweet Life.*

The adventurous and diverse artist then took on acting. In the 1990s, Rachel Sweet played bit parts in the films *All Tied Up, Gypsy,* and *Sing* before going on to theater, where she played the title role in *Theda Bara.* She now focuses on television comedy and has appeared in a variety of shows, including *Night Court, Seinfeld, Hope and Gloria,* and *Dream On.* And during the life of the TV sitcom *The Single Guy,* Sweet served as story editor.

Nina Blackwood

No matter what she does in the rest of her career, Nina Blackwood will forever be remembered as one of the very first MTV veejays.

Born in Springfield, Massachusetts, Nina Blackwood (née Kinckiner) spent her formative years and, more importantly, honed her show business career in Cleveland. She moved to Cleveland's West Side at age seven. There she took acting lessons and participated in plays at the Lakewood Little Theater. Her interest in the arts extended to music when she began taking harp lessons. Ironically, that most classical of instruments is what introduced her to the world of rock and roll. Former Eli Radish bassist Danny Sheridan, who would later become her manager, recalls: "I was on the road a lot with David Allan Coe at the time, so whenever I was in Cleveland, several of us would get together and play, kind of like a jam band. I think this night we were playing at the Viking Saloon. Nina came up to me and asked if she could sit in on the harp. I said, 'Sure,' thinking she meant the mouth harp. Then she walked away. I thought that was strange. But what was stranger was about ten minutes later, she came in with three other people carrying this seven-foot classical harp!"

Since Eli Radish was known for its unique sounds and inventiveness, Blackwood and her massive harp merely added another dimension to its ever-changing repertoire. After that, the Rocky River High School graduate played with Sheridan's various band formations. The bassist showed her how to play by ear and began booking her at local restaurant lounges. With an acting career in mind, she changed her name to Blackwood, began modeling, and won a WMMS-sponsored *Playboy* magazine photo contest. Out of eight semifinalists, the magazine chose four, and this daughter of a former Methodist minister appeared in a 1978 issue of *Playboy*.

By now, the musician-turned-manager and the aspiring actress were sharing a house in the quaint Chagrin Falls. "The conservatives in Chagrin Falls were not pleased," Sheridan recalls. "First, an outlaw rocker, and now a naked woman living in the outskirts of their perfect little town! The Chamber of Commerce nearly cancelled her 'Concert in the Park.' Neighbors clamored to get us to leave town. We did."

Blackwood was ready to pursue her acting aspirations in earnest, so the two moved to L.A. While studying at the famous Lee Strasberg Institute for three years, she played her harp at posh Los Angeles restaurants and hotels, such as the Penthouse Room at the Airport Hyatt. She won her first film role in *Vice Squad,* playing a teenage hooker, and she played a band manager in the pilot for the rock documentary spoof *Spinal Tap.* Just as her acting career was picking up steam, a magazine advertisement for a video disc jockey veered her off course.

With Sheridan urging her on, Blackwood left for New York to audition for a new music/television concept program called MTV. She knew it was the opportunity of a lifetime. And she was right. In 1981, Nina Blackwood became one of the first five veejays in music history. The job looked easy, with just four hours of airtime. But the glorified position demanded long hours behind the scenes researching music news, making personal appearances, conducting celebrity interviews, and doing promotional travel.

The mid-1980s saw her moving on in her career when Sheridan secured for Blackwood her own "Rock Report" on *Entertainment Tonight*, which included covering the MTV video awards. At the same time, she hosted the hit dance show *Solid Gold.* And she counts cohosting the 1985 Live Aid concert among the highlights of her career.

Although they went their separate ways in 1988, Sheridan is once again Blackwood's manager. The musician/actress continues to be recognized on billboards and at vari-

Eighteen-year-old harpist (and later MTV veejay) Nina Blackwood with boyfriend/manager Danny Sheridan of Eli Radish. *Courtesy of Danny Sheridan.*

ous media events. Her infomercial for the CD compilation *Back to the '80s* airs across the country, and her 1999 "Absolutely '80s" syndicated radio show was aired in more than one hundred markets nationwide.

Tracy Chapman (b. 1964, Cleveland)

Tracy Chapman will marry her guitar and live happily ever after.
—Prediction in the 1982 Wooster School yearbook

Tracy Chapman began singing and playing the ukulele at age three. At seven, her mother enrolled her in the Cleveland Music School Settlement, where she learned the guitar and clarinet. At age eleven, she began composing songs on a guitar her mother had finally earned enough money to buy. She wrote her own music but had no hopes of singing them for anyone beyond her family and friends. After all, there weren't many young, poor, black artists in the pages of *Rolling Stone*. So she was content in doing what she loved.

Chapman and her older sister spent their childhoods in an impoverished East Side Cleveland neighborhood; they were raised on values, discipline, love, and culture. "We frequented every museum in the city," her mother recalls in a 1988 *Plain Dealer* article. "She was always exposed to music. It was all over our household. Billie Holiday, Aretha Franklin, Mahalia Jackson, and Joan Armatrading were among our favorites." Her earliest influences were not only these many and varied records; her mother's passion for reading and writing poetry also made a strong impact on Chapman. As a teenager, her musical interests became more diverse, and she romanced various instruments, including the organ and harmonica. But her true love was always the guitar, with which, after a few initial lessons, she taught herself to play with expertise.

At age fifteen, the honor student received a minority-placement scholarship to Wooster, a preparatory school in Danbury, Connecticut. There she began performing her compositions at various school functions. Her style veered toward the acoustic protest songs of the Joan Baez/Joni Mitchell variety but in the tradition of black folk music. Her material often dealt with the homeless, the downtrodden, abuse, and other social ills. It was something everyone, particularly women, could identify with. Struck with her talent, the school chaplain, Reverend Robert Tate, along with some of her classmates, surprised Tracy by banding together and buying her a new guitar to replace the various guitars that were always on loan.

"I was overwhelmed," Chapman says about that cherished moment. "The first thing I said was, 'There's no way I can pay anyone back.' He replied, 'Just keep doing what you do. That's all that you owe them.'" (Later, she reciprocated by thanking Tate in the liner notes of her debut album, which became a multiple-platinum seller.)

After graduating in 1982, she enrolled in Tufts University, majoring in anthropology with a special interest in African studies. During her sophomore year, classmate Brian Koppleman spoke to his father, Charles Koppleman, president of the music publishing house SBK, about her. SBK signed her immediately upon her graduation in 1986. Koppleman was instrumental in securing her a recording contract with Elektra, as well as a manager, Elliot Roberts, whose resume included Joni Mitchell.

Inspired by the music and success of singer Suzanne Vega, whose song of child abuse, "Luka," unexpectedly rose to the top of the charts, Chapman grew more confident. She began recording demos and performing her introspective music at Boston-area coffeehouses as well as at New York's famed Bitter End. In 1987 she recorded her self-titled album, which included the single "Fast Car." The LP was released the following April and was later nominated for the Grammy's Album of the Year (losing out to George Michael's *Faith*). By the summer of 1988, "Fast Car" rose to No. 6 in the U.S. and No. 5 in the U.K. Again, it was nominated for a Record of the Year Grammy, but it lost out to the campy Bobby McFerrin hit song "Don't Worry, Be Happy." Two more Chapman singles made the U.S. charts: "Talkin' about a Revolution" hit No. 75, and "Baby Can I Hold You" peaked at No. 48.

During a time when greed was the theme of the day and much rap music was glorifying hate and crime, Chapman's themes of violence against women, racism, and people's need for each other stood out and helped this singer/songwriter of justice win three Grammy awards for her debut effort. Those honors included Best Pop Vocal Performance, Best Contemporary Folk Recording, and Best New Artist. The latter was no surprise, since critics had been tagging her the most important artist of the year since her debut release. As a young, black, female artist in a white, male-dominated field, Chapman told *Plain Dealer* reporter Michael Norman in a 1992 article, "I think that I provide a perspective in the pop music scene that for the most part isn't provided by anyone else. That's changed to some extent with rap music, but rap music is mostly predominated by black men."

In 1989, Chapman followed up on her initial success with her second LP, *Crossroads*. That album also became a platinum seller, reaching No. 9 on U.S. charts. Meanwhile, the acclaimed singer was busy performing, showing up to sing at notable events such as an AIDS benefit concert in Oakland, California (which also boasted the music of John Fogerty and the Grateful Dead), the 1990 Nelson Mandela tribute concert (Chrissie Hynde also participated), and the 1991 Bill Graham memorial concert. The Cleveland native with a style all her own began appearing on television as well. She performed on the CBS special *Motown 30: What's Goin' On*, on NBC's *Tonight Show with Jay Leno,* and sang "The Times They Are A-Changin'" during the Madison Square Garden celebration for Bob Dylan's thirtieth anniversary in the music business.

While touring and appearing at numerous events, Chapman found time to record her junior effort, *Matters of the Heart,* in 1992. For that she summoned several notable backup musicians, including Bobby Womack. The album reached No. 19 on U.K. charts and No. 53 in the U.S. Her next album came in 1995. *New Beginning* peaked at No. 47 in the U.K., made it to the Top 10 in the U.S., and was nominated as Pop Album of the Year in 1997. The single "Give Me One Reason" also hit the U.S. Top 10 and received four Grammy nominations in 1997: Record, Rock Song of the Year, Best Female Rock Vocal Performance, and Best Song. The song was also nominated for an MTV Video Music Award for Best Female Video.

Her mother, Hazel Chapman, has hinted in previous interviews that perhaps a racially motivated mugging in her hometown when Tracy was fourteen may have had something to do with her determination to fight prejudice through her muse. An acclaimed poet and singer in her own right, the elder Chapman speaks about her daughter's youth and passion for music and human angst: "[Both daughters] understand you can be poor and you don't have to be degenerative. And [Tracy] always thought a lot."

Cleveland Bands and Musicians of the '80s

One word could sum up the state of the early '80s club scene: dismal. Musicians who played original music had little hope of showcasing their songs, and the once-lucrative world of cover bands was drying up. One reason was the sickly economy of the Reagan era, particularly its first few years. Another reason was the new over-twenty-one drinking age (which included 3.2 beer), which severely limited patronage at clubs. Also, the generation that eagerly supported bands throughout the 1970s was now past the bar scene age, having secured stable jobs and started families and taken on new responsibilities. Whereas the phrase coined by this generation, "TGIF" (Thank God It's Friday) once meant time to carouse and party, it now represented the welcoming comforts of weekend home life.

"Things really changed in the '80s, especially in the club scene," notes Wild Horses co-founder/vocalist Bill Buckholtz. "They started cracking down on DUIs [driving under the influence]. They raised the drinking age the same time MTV came into play. So now the choice was go to the bars, see a local group play the Stones, the Who, or whatever, get tanked, and risk getting a DUI. Or you could go to the corner store, buy a six-pack, go home and watch your music on MTV. So what do you think happened?" Despite this gloomy club scene, Cleveland had its share of musical gems in the 1980s. And, as always, diversity was a matter of course. Bands of every make and style ran into the hundreds. Besides the usual cover band scene, there was a variety of music for every taste: country rock, heavy metal, Motown, post-punk, even reggae. And many of these bands were made up of veteran musicians who pursued their musical aspirations while holding down day jobs.

And getting that longed-for recording contract and subsequent radio airplay was every bit as elusive and rigid as it had been in the '60s and '70s, if not more so, since the days of being discovered by a talent scout who just happened to be in the audience were long past. Following is a featured list of the bands that reached the highest ranks on the North Coast in the 1980s. Included in the discussion are groups and artists of the decade whose talent, popularity, and longevity have deemed them noteworthy: Souvenir, Backseat Romance, the Jump, Champion, Human Switchboard, System 56, Slam Bam Boo, Separate Checks (with Laura Ferrell, who later became a TV weather reporter), the Reactions, Walking Clampetts, and the Innocent (with nineteen-year-old Trent Reznor). New wave and post-punk (now called "alternative") were holding strong with Exotic Birds, Death on a Stick, Terrible Parade, the Easter Monkeys (with Jim Jones), Home and Garden (with Pere Ubu's Jones and drummer Scott Krauss), the Clocks (with former Pagan keyboardist Chas Smith), the Revelers, My Dad Is Dead, and Prisonshake. Then there were groups with names like the Bone Heads, Rubbur Heads, and Baloney Heads. (There was also a band that honored its city by naming itself after it—but with a slight spelling change. Clevelend spent much of its decade-long existence traveling throughout the U.S. and Canada, but it was in its hometown that the band broke the Guinness Book of World Records by playing for a straight one hundred hours and thirty minutes—more than four days—in a benefit event to bring media attention to Cleveland in its quest for the Rock and Roll Hall of Fame. See Chapter 19.)

Gone Country: Cleveland's Country Rock Scene

When the Eagles landed on *Billboard* with its self-titled debut album in 1972 after years as Linda Ronstadt's backup band, the California group brought acceptance to rock with country-style leanings. Right on its heels was the southern rock of the Allman Brothers and Lynyrd Skynryd. Still, it took another decade before the music would become mainstream. Leave it to the guy who made disco a sensation—John Travolta, whose 1980 film *Urban Cowboy* introduced country as the newest widespread musical craze. Before the film even left the theaters, clubs were changing their themes to "country." In Cleveland, many bar owners moved out their pool tables and replaced them with mechanical bulls. Some changed their names, including the Painesville Agora, which was renamed the Urban Cowboy. Country line dance lessons were every bit as popular as the disco dances of just a few years before. The once-popular disco club the Dixie Electric Company even featured a weekly "Dixie Country Night." For the first time in music history, country was cool. (And by the 1990s, country rock [or "contemporary country"] would dominate the scene, due in great part to Garth Brooks.)

On the North Coast in the 1980s, there were several notable country rock bands as well as two significant solo country rock artists.

David Allan Coe (b. 1939, Akron)

Orphaned at age nine, "country music's original outlaw," David Allan Coe, made good use of his time in prison, where he spent most of his younger years. There he taught himself guitar and began penning such country pearls as "Penitentiary Blues," "You Never Even Call Me by My Name," "Longhaired Redneck," and, what became the working man's anthem, "Take This Job and Shove It," which made Johnny Paycheck a huge star in 1977.

Another alumnus of LaCave, the Akron native began frequenting the venue when he moved to the Cleveland suburb of Mayfield Heights. Building on country's recurrent theme—"I lost my job, my wife left me, my dog died . . . let's cry in our beer"—Coe personalized it and gave it a highly defiant twist that rebels everywhere embraced.

Coe became well known on the North Coast when he started playing with Eli Radish, considered Cleveland's first true group in the country rock mode, and he continues to boast proudly of his membership during its most formative years (1970–74). "We were the first long-haired country band in Ohio. Playing in that band with [bassist] Danny Sheridan was a real highlight of my life."

He broadened his horizons when he met up with Kris Kristofferson in Nashville and began touring with the singer. By 1974, he had recorded *The Mysterious Rhinestone*

Cowboy, but it was the Steve Goodman cover of "You Never Even Called Me by My Name" that put Coe's name in the Top 10 list of hits in 1975. And like his friend Willie Nelson, Coe has always preferred life on the road. His never-ending tours may have impaired his radio marketability, but they keep him close to his favorite people.

"The other night I talked a lot to my audience and told them what they meant to me," he told *Scene* writer Rex Rutkoski in 1997. "I told them if it wasn't for them I couldn't do what I do. Everything that happens before and after a concert is just one super headache." It's those shows, however, that have made Coe a household name on the festivals and club circuits and that have kept this country music outlaw away from the prisons of his youth.

He had another Top 10 hit in 1983 with "The Ride," followed by "Mona Lisa Lost Her Smile" in 1984, which hit No. 2 on the singles chart. "Long-Haired Redneck" (1976) also charted, and "Darlin' Darlin'" (1985) became his twenty-third studio effort in seventeen years. Albums include *David Allan Coe Rides Again* (1977), *The Family Album* (1978), *Human Emotions* (1979), *I've Got Something to Say* (1980), *Castles in the Sand* (1983*)*, *For the Record: The First 10 Years* (1984), and *Crazy Daddy* (1989). His two biggest hits, however, were other artists' recordings. Tanya Tucker took his country ballad "Would You Lay with Me (in a Field of Stone)" to the No. 1 spot in 1974. (The song was originally written for his brother's wedding.) And "Take This Job and Shove It" gave Johnny Paycheck his first and only No. 1 hit.

For nearly three decades Coe has been content to write about what he knows. Sporting long hair, massive tattoos, black leather, and cowboy hats, he doesn't mind his biker image, though he does take issue when people mistakenly associate him with drinking and drugs. "I've always been a nondrinker and non–drug user," he says. "When people come up to me and say, 'Hey I drank or did drugs with you once,' I tell them, 'Not with me you didn't.'"

Coe continues to crank out recordings despite the nonstop touring. His most recent releases, *David Allen Coe, Live—If That Ain't Country* and *Recommended for Airplay*, mix the old with the new and stay true to the music his fans have come to expect.

"If it wasn't for the music," he told Rutkoski for *Scene*. "I don't think I could have made it through a lot of emotional things I have been through. Music seems to be the pacifier I needed to get me through my life. Some of my music from the earlier days I can't even listen to. . . . I can't sing some of those songs. [But] writing them was like therapy."

Coe's music provided many of his fans with therapy as well. Sheridan, Coe's longtime friend and former producer, fondly recalls their history together: "We still keep in touch, either through Willie's [Nelson] events or phone calls from the bus. But alas, we've moved on to those so-called 'bigger and better things.' Him in Nashville, me in Hollywood. But I'd still love to relive the early days. The buses rolling down some interstate on the way to a new adventure every night, playing and singing hard, as if each note might affect the world forever. David and I always shared a sense of musical destiny—an unspoken certainty that we would succeed, right from the start."

Roger Martin (1950–98)

> Roger always seemed to get up out of the dirt and up on a stage. As they say in the entertainment business, he's got legs.
>
> —James Neff, *Sunday Magazine Plain Dealer* (1980)

Like many country music themes, you don't always get your due until you're dead and gone. Roger Martin would have found that thought amusing. This good-humored self-described hillbilly would have gotten a kick out of some of the stories and articles that circulated upon his 1998 death. Whereas much talk when he was alive focused on his wild excesses, upon his death came a host of testimonials to his entertaining performances, captive presence, and obvious talent—the talent that was always just a note away from big-time fame. He would have laughed his familiar hearty chuckle and boasted, "I told ya so."

Martin did have his share of successes through his years spent singing in honky-tonk bars (several in Nashville) and making various recordings. The country rock phase of the 1980s certainly helped him get jobs. But, unfortunately, it was his extracurricular activities that got him noticed most often—his hard drinking, drug taking, and womanizing ways, the very same themes he sang about.

When his music wasn't making news, Martin made sure his name was. An aspiring musician at twenty-six, with his mind set on stardom, the Cleveland singer wrote his name across an estimated twenty-five overpasses on I-71 on his way to Nashville. He never made it to the state line. Instead of being escorted onto a stage, he was escorted into a jail cell. It was just one example of what he became best known for: being an unrelenting self-promoter.

His enthusiastic self-promotion often tied in to the city he was raised in. "I'm Cleveland 'til I Die" was not just a PR remark but something he proved in everything he did, right to the end. Whatever Cleveland's trials and triumphs, folks would hear or see Roger Martin. He rallied for many of the city's issues, gaining fans along the way. When the Cleveland Indians baseball team was at its peak, he recorded "Tribe Is Alive," which became the soundtrack for a television commercial. When his city temporarily lost its beloved Browns football team, Martin got everybody singing his song "Go to Hell, Modell." And when musicians were complaining about Rock Hall officials excluding hometown talent for the September 1995 opening-day concert, Martin did more than voice his protests; he alerted the media and threatened to perform in front of the stadium gates atop his infamous white limousine (emblazoned with his name and painted piano keys) while the concert was in progress. Of course his plan was halted before one note was strummed, but he did succeed in getting the issue due attention.

Martin was raised in the East Side's Collinwood neighborhood, and he grew up listening to his mother's country music records. He got his first guitar at age thirteen and began teaching himself to play. At age sixteen—and still in the eighth grade—

Martin gave up academics in favor of playing guitar, harmonica, fiddle, and piano. In 1968, he enlisted in the marines at a time when most were doing everything they could to avoid the draft. He didn't last long, however. He witnessed many casualties in the ten weeks he served in Vietnam. Then he was shot in the leg. He wound up in a VA hospital in Maryland for the next two years; there he made the most of the situation by singing and playing Hank Williams songs to other vets. It was his appreciation and compassion for his fellow vets that prompted Martin to found the Vets Helping Vets program for disabled veterans. Martin returned to Cleveland a twice-decorated vet, disabled and with a growing addiction to painkillers.

Upon his return home, he began frequenting the club circuit. One of those clubs, Four Seasons, was owned by WHK deejay Joe Finan. There Martin befriended Cleveland's first shock-jock, Gary Dee, who took the young country singer under his wing and hired him to produce his radio program on WHK. Many folks believed in Martin's eventual recording success—most of all Martin himself. His self-made records, on his own Can-Am label, were played on local jukeboxes and bought up by fans; his first album, *Almost Gone* (1985) did graze the *Billboard* chart, and his second, *Act Naturally* (1989), was a solid local success. But national stardom remained elusive.

Many said he expected too much. Through the '80s he was opening for his heroes—Waylon Jennings, Willie Nelson, Johnny Paycheck, and the Oak Ridge Boys—and those connections only served to fire him up even more. His luck did change, however, when he met respected recording executive Steve Popovich. Like many who watched this colorful character perform, Popovich believed in him, too, and signed

Roger Martin atop his famous limousine with the Cleveland skyline in the background. *Courtesy of John Colak.*

him to Cleveland International Records. In 1995 Martin released *Live: Back from the Dead*, recorded at Cebar's Euclid Tavern on E. 185th Street. The album included songs by Martin's biggest musical influences: Merle Haggard ("Mama Tried") and Dwight Yoakam ("Guitars, Cadillacs, and Hillbilly Music"). It also included his and Popovich's collaboration on "Whatever Happened to Democracy."

Martin kept his name and face in the limelight by doing commercials for Channel 5 television and hosting his own radio shows on two AM stations, WELW 1330 (Willoughby) and WERE 1300 (Cleveland). In June 1997, Martin was asked to sing "The Star-Spangled Banner" at an Indians game at Jacobs Field. Despite constant pain from his ongoing battle from liver disease, he rose to the occasion and, as always, sang with sincerity and all the strength he could muster.

While Martin awaited a liver transplant in April 1998, his musician friends hosted a benefit to cover his hospital expenses. The event was held at the Agora Theater, with fourteen local bands entertaining the estimated three hundred guests. Although the eight-hour benefit concert was deemed a success, Martin died four days later. His funeral procession stretched for miles and included musicians, business executives, and bikers alike, all of whom recounted tales about the consummate musician and devoted Clevelander.

Flatbush (1973–81)

One of the first true country rock bands on the North Coast, Flatbush was a regular at the Viking Saloon, House of Bud, Grapes of Wrath, Bobby McGee's, Pirates Cove, and Kent's Water Street Saloon. Whereas some country rock bands started out as acoustic formations, Flatbush "plugged in" from the beginning. The five-man group concentrated on familiar, danceable, foot-stomping tunes and often had top billing when sharing the stage with their buddies, and rivals, Buckeye Biscuit.

Flatbush was formed by two 1972 graduates of North Olmsted High School. Linn Roath (rhythm guitar) and Joe Dickey (drums) had known each other since junior high and liked the same kind of music, particularly the Eagles and Pure Prairie League. Roath then approached friend Russ Gall to be the vocalist for their new band. Gall and Roath had been in the band Pentecost, which once opened for Badfinger at the Exit (in North Ridgeville). The group's name was the result of a consultation with an amateur fortune-teller.

"Linn's mother was into astrology," Gall recalls. "After consulting the stars, she found the word 'Flatbush' meant music and entertainment, so there it was. Plus, we looked at ourselves as kind of an association, like the Lords of Flatbush, if you will. But that's not how we got the idea. It was in the stars!"

What was also apparently in the stars was this group's unique musical style of combining country sounds with rock influences. The trio was soon joined by bass player Jim Christensen and guitarist Dale Rhome. In 1974 that lineup changed when Christensen and Rhome left and were replaced by Tom Aden (guitar, pedal steel, and banjo) and

Virginia native and Case Western Reserve student Larry Rice (bass and fiddle). They also temporarily added a fiddler named Fred (whose last name has been forgotten over the years) and conga player Lesley Lopez to form what Gall calls their "acid-grass" period, an offshoot of bluegrass.

"The year 1974 was great for us, we were playing all around town," Aden recalls. "We did coffeehouses and all the popular clubs. We played our first Coffeebreak Concert in June that year. We did an All-Star Country Jam at the Agora and opened for Little Feat there, as well. By the end of the year we were named the no. 1 band under the country category in *Scene* magazine."

In 1977, Aden left to manage other bands and was replaced by another North Olmsted alumnus, guitarist Phil Barker. Among the many rock bands that played cover songs by groups like the Allman Brothers and Led Zeppelin, this quintet braved uncharted territory with a repertoire that included country tunes dominated by the likes of Charlie Daniels, the Burrito Brothers, and Pure Prairie League.

Buckeye Biscuit was also making a name for itself along the local circuit. The two bands played many of the same clubs and were often reviewed side by side in local publications, particularly when each released an album at the same time in 1979. By mid-decade, both bands began interjecting more rock into their country style.

"By 1975, the guys wanted to get more into rock and roll," says Gall, who now lives in Austin, Texas. "Lynryd Skynyrd was hugely popular then, so we got into southern rock." With that, the band earned an even larger fan base and was playing club dates five to seven nights a week. Flatbush then began writing and recording original material. The first was the 45 single "Snug as a Bug in a Rug," b/w "Loaded," released on their own Denim Records in 1978. It received airplay on stations WMMS, WGCL, and WZZP. The 1979 single "Baby Love," written for Barker's baby daughter, was also a big request. In 1980, the group released its debut album, *Driver's Dream,* which debuted at No. 23 on the WMMS playlist.

"That's when we started talking with people from Epic Records," Gall says. "They had some openings, but as it turned out, they signed Cheap Trick instead. A lot of guys got discouraged after that, and decided to call it quits. If it had been up to me, I would've stayed with it no matter what. I loved the music and being able to play, travel, and make friends. I was pretty broken up about it."

Flatbush played one last outing at Spanky's West before disbanding in 1981, citing "battle fatigue." Band members scattered to various parts of the world. Roach was last heard to be living in Japan, where his wife plays French horn in the Tokyo symphony. Dickey resides in Atlanta, and Rice is believed to be living in Washington, D.C. Gall is a freelance artist and continues to play music in Austin. Barker and Aden remain in Cleveland.

"I've always wanted to get Flatbush together for at least one reunion," Gall says. "But with everyone scattered all over, it doesn't look good. But who knows? I haven't given up the thought."

Buckeye Biscuit (1974–82)

"Hard-drivin' bluegrass, sweet country sounds" is how Buckeye Biscuit described its music.

"Flatbush and Buckeye Biscuit were the only two local country bands around then, so there were the inevitable comparisons," says founder/guitarist Bruce Michael (a.k.a. Papa Biscuit).

> We called ourselves "the Ugly Sister" to Flatbush, because whenever we played together, they always got first billing. Elbert [Webb Jr., percussionist and lead singer] even wrote a song about it that went in part, "We're a little bit tighter and a lot less used!"
>
> But actually, there was a big difference between the two bands. We didn't want to be a copy band. We did a lot of originals right from the beginning and some obscure songs from well-known artists. That, of course, made us less popular in clubs. Whereas Flatbush was playing all the familiar songs, like Lynyrd Skynyrd's "Freebird," we'd do the more obscure Skynyrd songs, ones people weren't as familiar with.

The group's name came off a bakery truck Michael saw traveling down a Kent street one day. "We thought it was perfect, it sounded like a country-based Ohio band," says Michael, who had, for a time, been a WNCR deejay. "At first, the owner of that business was a bit concerned over our use of his company name. So he sent his daughter to hear us play, and she told him we were really good. So one day I went to see him and gave him one of our T-shirts. In turn, he gave me a batch of cookies. It's a good thing he liked us, because we often heard that the truck drivers for the company were always getting stopped at a light by people saying, 'Hey, you've got a good band there!'"

Buckeye Biscuit did indeed have dedicated fans—and one particularly good friend in Dewey Forward, owner of what became one of the most popular clubs in Cleveland, Peabody's Cafe. When this country rock band was formed in the summer of 1974, it was an acoustic trio with Michael, vocalist/guitarist Ron Franklin, and singer Joel Culp, who played guitar and mandolin. Michael had previously been in a 1960s band called the New Community Singers, who had a regional hit with "Manry and the Sea." (The song was in honor of local hero Robert Manry, who made international headlines in 1965 when he successfully sailed across the Atlantic Ocean in a thirteen-and-a-half-foot sailboat called the *Tinkerbelle*.)

After three years of playing bars such as the Smiling Dog Saloon, Brandywine Tavern, Bojangles, and Kent clubs Mother's Junction and JB's, the group was invited to perform at the grand opening for Peabody's (formerly Cellar Door) in September 1977. This lineup included Michael, who played acoustic guitar, electric guitar, and banjo; Webb on vocals and percussion; Larry Rothstein on bass; and Rod Reisman on drums. Vocalist/bassist/songwriter Ron Jarvis, who joined in 1976, was instrumental in

(*Opposite*) A Buckeye Biscuit poster. *Left to right:* Ron Franklin, Steve Adams, Joel Culp, Bruce (now E. B.) Michael, and Mike Casey. *Photo by Humbert Photography. Courtesy of E. B. Michael.*

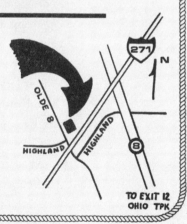

bringing more rock into the group's repertoire. "I had known one of the early drummers, Mike Casey, from my hometown of Orrville," recalls Jarvis. "He joined the band, and soon after, Joel Culp and Ron Franklin left. Buckeye already had several jobs lined up in upstate New York, so that's when Elbert and I were added to the group."

Though the band would go through various incarnations over the years, most Buckeye Biscuit members participated in vocals, thus maintaining the distinct harmonies. The group wasted no time in recording, releasing a four-song EP, *First Batch,* in the summer of 1975.

In addition to possessing musical talent, group members were astute promoters and businessmen. They marketed their own publicity shots, posters, and T-shirts. With Forward's financial backing, the group went into Audio Recording Studio and came out with their 1979 release, *Fresh Candy,* an LP that brought them to the attention of WMMS and WKDD. The lineup then included Michael, Jarvis, Webb, Reisman, and Steve Adams (electric and steel guitar). After five years with the band, Adams left just as the album was completed. Mike Daly replaced him on pedal steel guitar and dobro. Reisman was next to leave, and in came vocalist/guitarist Mike Reid and drummer Jim Yarnell.

The LP was a local success due to the songwriting talents of Jarvis, Webb, and Michael. The Jarvis-penned song "East Cleveland Hotel," played often on WMMS and WMMM 105. Webb's "Will with You" became a WKDD favorite, and Michael's contribution included "Rolling into Wheeling," a truck-driving song that became a West Virginia favorite due to its regular airplay on Wheeling station WWVA.

By 1980, there were more personnel changes. When Yarnell left that year, he was replaced by Dave Ritter, who stayed a little over a year. When he was killed in a car accident in Kent in 1982, Ritter's former bandmates came together for a benefit concert to aid his family. Buckeye Biscuit's final lineup included Michael, Stephe Rousseau (vocals, drums), Jerry Simon (pedal steel guitar), and Dave Parkinson replacing Jarvis on bass.

The popular group played its last show on August 16, 1982. Cause of the demise, according to Michael, was lack of commitment.

"Being in a band is a lot its a marriage, but one with five or six members, which makes it nearly impossible to maintain," Michael says. "I often thought every band should have counselors to help them work through their problems."

Ron Jarvis, however, blames the breakup on the lack of support of their music. "Both Flatbush and Buckeye Biscuit disbanded around the same time, due to finding ourselves on the other side of the fad. Sort of the 'Nehru jacket of music,' as I like to call it. The *Urban Cowboy* phase burned out. Now, of course, this fusion genre has reappeared as 'contemporary country.'"

Members parted on friendly terms, making it possible for reunions. The first one was held the following year, the second one in 1987; both took place at Peabody's Cafe. The 1987 concert became a media event, with promotion on the local *PM Magazine* TV-8 show, with hosts Michael Stanley and Jan Jones.

Today, "core" members continue to make music. Bruce Michael, who now goes by the name EB Michael, plays with Webb in a '50s/'60s classic rock band, the GeezCatz. Since 1992, Jarvis, who also played in reggae bands I-Tal and First Light, formed an "American worldbeat music" band called Macaw. He is also a producer and songwriter who has contributed to recordings by Alex Bevan and local folk hero Pat Dailey. Another former Buckeye Biscuit member, Mike Daly, now plays with Hank Williams Jr.

"Buckeye Biscuit taught me the most about harmony singing," Jarvis concludes. "It also instilled in me an attitude of striving for excellence, of not being happy with a product that is just 'good enough.' I have the utmost respect for the first-rate performers I had the honor to work with in this band."

Deadly Earnest and the Honky Tonk Heroes (1975–83)

Deadly Earnest (né Dennis Earnest) was another talent with Akron roots. After being in several Cleveland bands such as Sheffield Rush and Target (with former Cyrus Erie members Bob and Mike McBride), this Wadsworth native formed his most popular band in 1975. The first lineup included lead singer Earnest (lead guitar/songwriter), bass player Danny Sheridan (replaced by Jay Vecchio when Sheridan became the band's record producer), fiddle player Denny "K.D." Jones (who replaced Darryl Rini), drummer Greg Giancola (a.k.a. GG Greg), and guitarist and mandolin player Joel Culp.

"I began teaching myself guitar at age ten," says Earnest, who also played pedal steel guitar. "My biggest influence was Merle Haggard. Our band had a western/swing influence that ranged from Bob Wills and the Texas Playboys to George Jones. We had a fiddle player early on, Denny Jones, who was 'Mr. Swing-fiddle Extraordinaire,' and a pedal steel player from Nashville, Darryl Rini, who had played with David Allen Coe. That's when we were *really* old country. Later on we became more pop/rock country."

"I knew Darryl Rini back when he went to Shaker Heights High School," recalls Sheridan. "He came back pretty often to jam with us in whatever formation we had at the time. We'd get together as the Buckeye Buckaroos, which was a fictitious name for some of the guys from Eli Radish and other locals. That's when Deadly came in."

Earnest says his nickname was coined by Sheridan. "We'd play five, six nights a week, so we spent a lot of time in bars," Earnest says. "In the mornings, I'd have to go and work my day job at Dick Lorrie Music Studio. Danny and his friend Andy, who worked there, started kidding me that I'd looked half-dead and started calling me 'Deadly.' It also fit in pretty well with my last name."

Earnest's voice defined the band's sound and brought it instant recognition. His vocals were often described as a cross between George Jones and Jerry Jeff Walker. Though their sound was distinctive, the group's style was oftentimes loose. Much of the time band members enjoyed themselves as much as their audience—sometimes too much so. This tendency led to Giancola being named the group's business manager.

"We did really well playing area clubs," Giancola recalls. "We became a corporation, with a corporate I.D. number, an accountant, the whole nine yards. The reason that came about was one night after playing at this bar in Kent, and having ourselves a real good time, I asked Deadly, 'Where's the money?' He said, 'Oh, I forgot.' Well, I can count twenty-dollar bills in any condition. So I went back in, got paid, came out and said, 'From now on, you write the songs; I'll take care of business. We literally shook on it."

Their self-titled debut album on their own Wheeler Recordin' label was released in 1978, with songs penned mostly by Earnest and Culp. The band was soon picked up on the Pacific Arts Records/Warner Brothers label; that record company was a project of Michael Nesmith of the Monkees.

"We were heavy into promotion and had made up these matches with our logo on it," Giancola explains. "Dan Garfinkel [WMMS promotion director] was at a radio convention in Florida. He's having a cocktail with Michael and Katherine Nesmith when he takes out our matches to light a cigarette. Nesmith sees it and says, 'What a cute logo.' It was designed by our bassist, Jay Vecchio. Nesmith starts asking about the band, and Dan tells them about our album and recent Coffeebreak Concert. Then Michael takes the matches back to Carmel, California. Three months later, I'm negotiating a contract with Katherine, who ran the company, and they reissued our first album."

The singles that garnered the most attention were "Wheeler Inn Cafe," "New Mexico," and "Don't Make Me Laugh While I'm Drinking" (penned by Sheridan), which got regular rotation on WMMS. The album was among *Billboard*'s Top Country Picks in October 1979; however, it didn't net enough sales for a second Pacific Arts LP. The band was dropped from the label, and Deadly Earnest and the Honky Tonk Heroes went on the road, spending the next few years touring the country, playing at places like New York's Lone Star Café and the Bottom Line, Tulsa's Cain's Ballroom ("Home of the Bob Wills Band"), and the Columbus Agora. In 1980, the country rock band released their second LP, *Deadly Earnest II,* on their own label. One of the songs, "Rodeo Rider," was written by local favorite Alex Bevan. Once again, this group's effort was chosen as one of *Billboard*'s Top Album Picks in September 1980, and the single "Oklahoma That's a Big OK by Me" was noted among the Top Single Picks.

By then Deadly Earnest consisted of Phil Baron (keyboards), John Daubenspeck (bass), Mike Balas (guitar), and Giancola (drums), with vocalists Robin Stratton (wife of musician Charlie Weiner) and Laurie Domiano (who soon became Earnest's wife). The next lineup, which produced the third album, *The Modern Sounds,* included Earnest, Jones, Bill Watson (upright bass), Daly, Domiano, Stratton, and Greg. That final recording was released in 1982.

"That was the best lineup we ever had," notes Earnest. "But the album took all our own money, and we took a bath on it. It all got to be too much. Plus, when the *Urban Cowboy* scene was over, there were not that many places to play, so I broke the band up. A little later, I moved to Jackson, Wyoming, because we had played there a lot and I'd made friends. But most important, that style of music was still welcomed there." And thanks to Warner Brothers' licensing of the first two albums, Deadly Earnest discovered that his group had a heavy fan base in Holland, Japan, Australia, and Brazil.

Today, Earnest still lives in Wyoming and continues to be involved in music. Along with old friends Denny Jones and Bill Watson, he is planning a new Deadly Earnest release. Out of his home recording studio, he also writes for television, his music having been heard on *Friends* and *Hard Copy,* as well as shows for PBS. Giancola is a booking agent; one of his clients is Charlie Weiner, best remembered in Cleveland for Charlie Weiner and the Weinerland Orchestra. Mike Daly now plays and tours with Hank Williams Jr.

Baron formed a "full-tilt boogie band," Phil Baron and the Bopkats, with former Deadly Earnest guitarist Michael Balas, bassist John Daubenspeck (Jimmy Ley and the Coosa River Band), drummer Mark Hellenberg, and singer Mimi Hart (both from the Athens band Hotcakes). Today the talented keyboardist is back in his hometown of Chicago and plays in two bands: Phil Baron and the Tremblers and Jump City. Both play occasionally at Fat Fish Blue in downtown Cleveland.

R-O-C-K in the U.S.A.

American Noise (1978–83)

American Noise, whose members were already veterans of Cleveland's music scene, formed in late 1978, though the group was then known as 747. What made this band unusual was its *two* keyboard players, something not common in rock and roll bands then. Members included guitarists Craig and Bruce Balzer, bass player Greg Holt (formerly of Pictures), drummer Tommy Rich (later in Donnie Iris and the Cruisers), and keyboardists George Sipl (formerly with Magic/Eric Carmen Band/Breathless), and Jerry Moran (formerly of Dragonwyck).

"That was probably the best of all the bands we were in," admits Bruce Balzer, who also played slide guitar. The statement says a lot when one considers the guitarist's former bands. The Balzer brothers' resume includes December's Children, Ambleside, Circus, and the 1977 band Pictures, with Holt, keyboardist Kevin Raleigh (later with Michael Stanley), and drummer Jim Bonfanti.

American Noise played basic rock and roll at its melodic best. Its new name was derived from a song lead guitarist Craig Balzer wrote while in Circus. "The record company wanted us to change the original band name, 747, because there was another band in Georgia called 707, so they felt it was too close," he recalls. "We settled on the name of one of our songs."

This six-man band took rock and roll seriously. Vowing never to be just another bar band, the group prided itself on original material, rehearsing diligently until it felt ready to record. Several months later, the musicians were on a plane to L.A. to put their music to vinyl for Planet Records (subsidiary of Electra/Asylum) with producer Gary Ladinski, who served as engineer for Cheap Trick's biggest-selling album, *Dream Police.* The 1980 self-titled debut included four singles—"Take It All," "American Noise," "Running Through the Night," and "Anyone with a Heart"—that received regular rotation on local radio stations WGCL and WMMS (which did one better by giving the entire album a regular spin). One of their originals, "Out on the Street" (recorded in Craig Balzer's bedroom, with engineer Rich Reising), was included on the WMMS Buzzard's 1980 compilation album, *Pride of Cleveland.*

Although the group spent much of their time in the studio, concentrating on writing, rehearsing, and recording their material, they did give fans a chance to hear their catchy tunes. The group played a few hometown venues, particularly the Cleveland Agora. But local support, even from radio, proved not enough. American Noise was dropped from its label before releasing its second album. The band persevered. In 1982, this tight, well-orchestrated rock band released a double single on its own label, Criminal Records. "Statutory Sue" (written by Tommy Rich) and the Craig Balzer–penned "Another Girl Like You" did well and, again, got regular rotation on local stations.

By the following year, however, band members were growing weary. "It just was a bad time in the music business," Craig Balzer recalls. "There'd be interest, but record companies were leery of putting money into an unknown band. And we were getting at the age we had to look at the money end, not just the love of it. You almost had to be a lounge act to get a good-paying gig. That wasn't us. It was one of those turnover points."

Today the Balzer brothers spend more time with their ad agency than they do making music, though both admit they can never tear themselves away permanently. "When music is in your blood, it remains a part of who you are," Craig Balzer says. The two hope to one day make more American noise.

Breathless (1978–81)

Like several area bands born in this period, Breathless seemed destined to make it. All the right elements were there.

The band began—and ended—with lead guitarist/vocalist/songwriter Jonah Koslen, who had just come off the early success of the Michael Stanley Band and had earned a following all his own. The name for his new group came easily: "I made up a list of names and liked *Breathless* because there's something hidden in the word that I felt would be good luck. You take out the *r,* the *h,* and one of the *s's,* and you get *Beatles.* The night they played Ed Sullivan was my twelfth birthday, February 9, and I'd just gotten their album as a present. Of course, they had a profound influence on me."

Koslen had already begun writing songs at age thirteen, when he took up the guitar ("mostly self-taught"). His life's work began in earnest while attending Beachwood High School. He formed a band called Picasso with classmate and bass player Bob Benjamin, who later became a member of Breathless. It was during this time Koslen befriended Glenn Schwartz, who taught him some licks of his own. After graduating, Koslen had brief stints in bands such as Jeep (with WMMS music director and deejay Billy Bass as manager) and Snake Eyes (with former Eli Radish members Danny Sheridan and Starr Smith) before joining Michael Stanley in March 1974. By the time Breathless was born, the guitarist had earned the reputation of being a prolific songwriter, penning some of the most popular MSB tunes: "Strike Up the Band," "Nothing's Gonna Change My Mind," and "Ladies' Choice."

Ready to break out with his own band, Koslen left Michael Stanley and formed Breathless in January 1978 with old friend Benjamin, Rodney Psyka (keyboards, percussion, vocals), Susan Lynch (lead vocals, keyboards, synthesizer), and Kevin Kosec (a.k.a. Kevin Valentine, formerly Maxx band drummer and later with Donnie Iris). At the same time, Koslen released a solo album, *Back Tracks,* on his own label, Covert Records. The LP consisted of previously unreleased demos that went back six years. "That collection was just a local release, but I got a lot of good feedback from it," he says. "People still ask me about it today, particularly the song 'Meantime Man.'"

After playing just two gigs at the Painesville Agora, Breathless opened for the Atlanta Rhythm Section ("Imaginary Lover") at Playhouse Square's Palace Theater. That summer saw a change in formation. Lynch had left and was replaced by keyboardist George Sipl, whose resume included Magic, the Eric Carmen Band, and the Euclid Beach Band. Before year's end, Breathless made more changes, bringing in guitarist Alan Greene (formerly of Jimmy Ley and the Coosa Band), and Mark Avsec (former Wild Cherry keyboardist), who replaced Sipl. This lineup headed to Florida to record the band's first LP on EMI/Capitol Records (with John Cougar Mellencamp's producer, Don Gehman). The self-titled Breathless album was released in the summer of 1979. A single from that effort, "Takin' It Back," charted in *Billboard*'s Top 100. It was put in heavy rotation on WMMS (as was "Glued to the Radio" and "Walk Right In") and remains one of its most memorable songs from that debut.

By 1980, Breathless was one of Cleveland's top bands. The dedicated musicians practiced five days a week and constantly worked on new material. The group opened for various artists such as Kenny Loggins, Eddie Money, and Toto. Koslen particularly recalls touring as openers for Kiss: "One thing that stands out about that tour was when we played some places in the South. There were people picketing outside with signs that read, 'Kiss stands for Knights in Satan's Service.' But the concerts went well. We got encores at the end of the sets, despite those few chanting 'KISS, KISS, KISS' all the time!"

The second Breathless album, *Nobody Leaves This Song Alive,* was released in the fall of 1980. Again, it got WMMS support, as "Wild Weekend" was added to their playlist. This effort was decidedly different from the first.

"I liked both albums for very different reasons, " Koslen notes. "The first was very up, light, as in bright. The second album was very dark, exploring darker issues like 'Back of My Mind,' 'Hearts in Hiding,' and 'Crawl in Through the Shadows.' Interestingly enough, in retrospect, it's those songs I've come to enjoy the most."

With the prestigious Belkin-Maduri management and its own veteran musicianship, Breathless was being touted as Cleveland's "next big thing" by fans and critics alike. It didn't happen, however, and by 1981 band members were experiencing frustration, gridlock. "Things were coming to a head," Koslen says of the band's demise. "There were too many stresses between members, and [between] members [and] management.

It all became too much to fight against and, basically, it wore me out. Plus, the lack of national success was disappointing. But I'm proud of what we accomplished. It was a very prolific time for me. I was thrilled with that band. I think the albums still hold up today. But at the time, it was hard to sustain the energy to keep it going every day."

"To this day, I count Breathless as the best band I was ever in, the local cream of the crop," says Alan Greene, who is now fronting his own band, the Alan Greene Band. "There was incredible talent in that band, and we enjoyed an astonishing amount of local support."

In 1982, Koslen formed Jonah Koslen and the Heroes with guitarist/vocalist Danny Powers, bassist/vocalist Eddie Pecchio (brother of MSB's Dan Pecchio), keyboardist/vocalist Dennis Lewin, and drummer Don Krueger (formerly with Magic/Eric Carmen Band). But the band folded in 1984 when Koslen moved to L.A. and emerged himself in various musical projects. Some of those projects reunited him with his old Snake Eyes bandmate Danny Sheridan. The two performed at Farm Aid in 1987 in Lincoln, Nebraska, and when Sheridan produced several episodes for the former hit TV show *Fame,* Koslen wrote one of the songs, "Damaged." He also wrote for "lots of B-movies." He returned to Ohio briefly to join Michael Stanley's Ghost Poets but then moved back permanently in 1997.

In August 1998, Koslen resurrected Breathless for only one night. Along with old bandmate Rodney Psyka, this reunion (of sorts) included bassist Bill March, drummer Don Krueger, guitarist Billy Sullivan, and keyboardist Rich Spina. Held at the Odeon in the Flats, the Breathless concert treated fans to one magical night that took them back to the band's promising era.

Another such reunion, however, is not in Koslen's immediate plans. Presently he keeps busy as a website designer and multimedia producer. He continues to write, mostly, he says, for his children.

The Generators (1980–83)

The Generators was a notable band for reasons other than having inspired the film *Light of Day.* (However, by the time the first page of the movie script was written, the Generators was already history.)

The band actually began as Buzzy and the Buzzards. "Buzzy [Linhart] always thought that would be a cool name for a band," notes vocalist/guitarist/keyboardist/songwriter Mark Addison. The name came to the attention of WMMS, whose logo was of the infamous Buzzard. The radio staff thought it would be a good idea, in terms of promotion, to have this new band play the WMMS-sponsored Coffeebreak Concert.

"I was playing in a band with Gair Linhart when his brother Buzzy asked me about playing this Coffeebreak Concert," recalls bassist Glen "Stutz Bearcat." The band, which included lead guitarist "Neon" Don Buchanan and drummer Frank Musara (later replaced by Jim Fotheringham and then Jimmy Lee), was a hit on that afternoon show at the Agora.

"We developed our own style right away," notes Stutz Bearcat (who declines to use his real name). "Buzzy, who also played the vibraphone, would infuse various tones of jazz, rock, and blues. Buzzy had this unique style and had played vibes on the Hendrix song 'Drifting' on his last album, *Cry of Love*. So we evolved into this jam band, kind of like the Grateful Dead with a little more backbone."

By their next performance, at the Flipside on April 2, 1980, they were calling themselves the Heaters and had added background vocalist/songwriter Kathy Dottore (a.k.a. Eva Dilcue, or Euclid Ave. spelled backward). The group also embarked on an East Coast mini-tour to play venues in New York and New Jersey. Things were going well—until one memorable night at Cleveland's Bobby McGee's.

"Buzzy was a real character," Bearcat says. "If he didn't think the audience was responsive enough, he wouldn't come back out for an encore. The owners would get upset, so we'd go back out without him, and the people liked us just as much. After a few times of this, Buzzy got real mad at us, and this one night, he came back on stage and promptly fired everyone in the band—right in the middle of a song."

Addison became leader of the "new" band and changed both its name and its sound. After putting suggested band names in a hat, the Generators was born. "We did a lot of obscure stuff," Bearcat notes. "We'd do off-the-wall Steely Dan and Al Green songs. We did Elvis Costello's 'Girl Talk,' and this great funky version of 'Take Me to the River,'" before Talking Heads came out with their cover. When Jim Fotteringham replaced Frank on drums, we started doing more original tunes. It became more creative, and we really started kickin' up some dust."

WMMS then held a band contest with a record deal as first prize. The Generators sent in a tape and became one of four finalists. A show to determine the winner was held at the Agora. "By then, we were a real kick-ass, dynamic, powerful, live band," Bearcat says. "We'd been playing six nights a week all around town and had a tight, live musical show. We won and recorded 'Turn on Your TV Set'/'Things Fall Apart' on Buzzard Records."

The Generators sparked a musical following at a time when the club scene was suffering from the changes in the liquor law. They were known for their onstage antics: "Neon Don got his name because he used to light his guitar on fire during a show," Addison recalls. "One particular time, he lit up his guitar on stage at the Euclid Tavern and afterward we gave it to the owners, and that hung above the stage for years." The Generators released "Summertime," b/w "Temporarily Out of Control," in 1980, and its song "I'm a Generator" was included on the WMMS compilation *Pride of Cleveland* (1980).

In 1982, a Hollywood screenwriter paid this band a visit. Bearcat recalls the event.

Paul Schrader was writing a script about a struggling rock band and wanted to get to know a real band to get a perspective. He called and asked Kid Leo if he knew of a band he should check out. Leo told him, "I've got the perfect band for you." So he gives Schrader the number of our manager, David Dubbs.

Now you have to understand, managers get calls like that all the time when you've got a name around town. People always calling saying they'll give you a record deal and stuff like that, which never pans out. And not to be disrespectful, but after a while you don't take any of it seriously because you don't want to get your hopes up.

So we meet up with this guy who no one knows of, who looks like just a young kid. He's quiet and shy, doesn't talk more than ninety seconds at this meeting. Everyone started talking around him, and I was feeling bad for him because no one's paying him much attention. So we get to talking, and I suggest he and I go down to Euclid Tavern, have a few drinks, and listen to this great band, which was the Numbers Band.

Well, we're driving down the road, and knowing he's into movies I start telling him about this cool movie I had just seen with Season Hubley and George C. Scott called *Hard Core*. And in this real quiet voice he says, "Yeah, that's my film." Well, I nearly ran off the road! Then he starts naming a few of the screenplays he'd written—*Taxi Driver, American Gigolo* . . . I was flippin' out! Soon as we got to the Tavern, I called up the guys, and told them what I'd learned and that we really should take him seriously.

For the next ten days, Schrader observed the band on stage and in their homes. But it would be four years before the film would be shot (a third of it was filmed in Cleveland). The film's characters, played by Michael J. Fox and rocker Joan Jett, alternated between high school (filmed at Collinwood High), factory work (filmed at MarshAllan Industries), and weekend gigs at the neighborhood bar (Euclid Tavern) as the Barbusters. By this time, the Generators had long-since split up. Addison was in a band called Nation of One but served as consultant on the film. He also made a cameo appearance, as did Trent Reznor. The two played in the fictional band the Problems. Bearcat was playing bass in the Mr. Stress Blues Band, which was the biggest draw at the Euclid Tavern throughout the 1980s. Often present during filming, he recalls a few memories:

It was funny when the crew found out I was one of the members of the band the movie was based on. They'd looked at me in sure awe. Apparently Schrader had told them a few of our wild band stories, exploits and escapades that, by four years later, must have taken on mythical proportions!

Although the movie wasn't technically about us, there were certain scenes in the film that came directly from our situation. Like the part when the band members are fixing equipment in the garage, and one of the women brings them food. We'd been doing that in Don [Buchanan]'s garage when Schrader was around, and Don's wife brought us some chicken. Another was the part when the band drove to Erie, Pa., for a gig, and the owner screws them out of money. Fox's character gets disgusted, and says, "Yeah, I know the sixties were rough." Well, that came right from us.

Believe me, Schrader had a lot to work with because we were definitely a colorful, alive, and crazy bunch of people.

Interestingly, a song titled "Born in the USA" was first written by Generator Eva Dilcue at Schrader's suggestion. "That was the original title for the movie," Bearcat recalls. "Eva wrote the lyrics, and we collaborated on the music. Later on, he made a deal with Bruce Springsteen to write his own version, and because the Springsteen name would give the film instant credibility and recognition, he went with that one instead." (Springsteen also wrote what ultimately became the title track, "Just Around the Corner from the Light of Day.")

But on New Year's Eve 1982, one of Cleveland's most popular original bands realized it had lost its continuity. One last show at the Rascal House marked the end of the Generators. "We were all going in different directions by then," Addison says. "Plus we had gotten our equipment repossessed as a result of bad management."

Stutz Bearcat, who has been playing in various musical formations since the early 1970s, loves to recall one of his favorite bands. "The Generators had it together. We were one of the biggest bands in Cleveland at the time, had a huge following. We made good money playing original music five, six nights a week. We even had health insurance, which was practically unheard of."

After a few years in Nation of One, Addison moved to Los Angeles in 1990. He presently lives in Austin, Texas, and is guitarist/keyboardist/songwriter/producer in his latest musical projects, the Borrowers and Kitty Gordon. Dilcue went on to form Bunji Jumpers before moving to San Francisco along with drummer Jimmy Lee. In 1989 Bearcat joined guitarist Butch Armstrong and formed the Armstrong Bearcat Band, a musical staple on the local club circuit. Buchanan continues to reside in Cleveland, though he is currently inactive in the music business.

The Action (1977–83)

Guitarist/vocalist/songwriter Michael Purkhiser headed up this Akron-based band. Other members were bassist/vocalist Brent Warren and drummer Brian Shearer (later replaced by Cliff Bryant). The trio knocked out vintage-style rock and roll at clubs such as Kent's JB's, Akron's the Bank and Breakaway, and Cleveland's Agora and was one of the few bands to brave the path of original material in the early 1980s, with Purkhiser penning most of the songs.

"I formed my first band in 1966, the same year I saw the Beatles at the Cleveland Stadium," recalls Purkhiser, a 1972 Stow High School graduate. "Then came Tea, a band I formed in '68. We were probably a bit ahead of our time because we played stuff like Hendrix, and Cream while most of the area bands were still doing Beatles, Stones, and the Who."

Most younger siblings are musically influenced by their older brothers or sisters. In this case, it was the opposite. Erick Purkhiser (who became Lux Interior, founder/vocalist of the Cramps; see Chapter 14) observed what his brother was doing and decided that was something he was interested in. "Initially, of course, Lux was the one buying the records and turned me on to the Beatles," Michael Purkhiser notes. "But I was the first to pick up a guitar and play in a band, directly because of the Beatles. I'll never forget sitting in my room playing 'Please, Please Me' on my record player when I heard John F. Kennedy was shot. That kind of stuff stands out."

When it came time for the Action, it was Brent Warren who got it all started. He placed an ad in *Scene* looking for anyone interested in forming a rock band. "I contacted him," Purkhiser says. "We talked about what kind of band we wanted to put together and our musical influences, which were pretty much the same: Beatles, Raspberries, and Todd Rundgren. We hooked up with Brian and that formation lasted two years. That's when Brian left and Cliff [Bryant] came in on drums."

The first incarnation produced a single in 1978, "Get Back to Me," b/w "Any Day Now," released on the band's own Radiogram Records. The next year, Purkhiser and his bandmates went to New York to stake their claim in rock and roll. There they got gigs at Harrah's, Traxx, and CBGB but declined to make a permanent move there. The group's power pop leanings in the onset of punk and new wave did not interest New York record execs searching out the next Ramones, Blondie, or Talking Heads. "We were getting approached by some record execs, but nothing ever materialized," Purkhiser says.

While holding down day jobs, the Cleveland trio continued to travel the circuit, which included clubs in Boston, Philadelphia, Pittsburgh, Detroit, and San Francisco. They also managed to record another single in 1979, "Radio Music," b/w "Please Oh Please," on Radiogram with Bryant on drums. The song put them on college radio playlists across the nation. At home, the Action began drawing an impressive fan base, opening for acts such as Joan Jett and the Blackhearts and the Romantics. In 1982, the group released its last recording, "She's Got My Heart," b/w "'Til I See You Again." "I felt we were getting successful," Purkhiser says, "but we weren't achieving our goal, which was to get a record deal. Towards the end, we were growing tired of pursuing it with nothing happening."

One night in 1981, the Action played JB's, and the rockabilly cover band called Johnny Clampett and the Walkers (later changed to the Walking Clampetts) opened for them. The bands had a lot in common because of members' shared love for Jerry Lee Lewis, Elvis, Eddie Cochran, and Chuck Berry. The Clampetts would later become one of the bands Purkhiser is most associated with. He joined the group in 1985 and stayed the next five years. When the Walking Clampetts disbanded in 1990, Purkhiser shifted gears and became production engineer for the Akron-based Beatles tribute band 1964. He also has his own business, Purkhiser Electronics, where he builds and designs tube amplifiers and other musical equipment. Presently he plays in an original classic-rock band, 3D, formed in 1997 and made up of guitarist Marky Ray (Death of Samantha, Terrible Parade, New Salem Witch Hunters, Walking Clampetts), bassist Quin Wychanko, and drummer Tom Pace. The group's debut album, a five-song EP entitled *Universal Conquest,* was released in 1998.

The Adults (1979–97)

"I grew up listening to jazz and soul, like Billie Holiday, Sara Vaughan, and Duke Ellington, Miles Davis. And my older sisters were into Motown, so I got a taste of music's diversity early on," says founder/guitarist/songwriter Paul Michael. "I was very aware of how music can set a mood; the feelings, the shivers, the tingles that could make or break my whole day. It is such a powerful force."

And then rock and roll invaded his psyche. "I knew kids a few years older than I, who were very nimble with their fingers on the guitar. They'd put a record on and follow right along. That would just knock me out. So I tried it. I'd be in my basement or my bedroom, and banged, and twanged, and would do these queer riffs. But I was never good at it."

Despite the rough start, Michael found inspiration in a local band.

I saw Raven Slaughter at this annual outdoor summer music festival in Lodi. I rode my bike from Cleveland, about forty miles, with my girlfriend, Crystal Gray. The group had just returned from Florida. I was impressed how professional they were. They had this image, they dressed alike, their name was painted on the drumhead. And their music was unique. They did their own material, which I thought was very cool.

I remember thinking as I watched them, *man, they need another guitar player,* because there were just three of them at the time. I went up to Raven after the show and told him as much. He asked me if I had anyone in mind and I said, "I play guitar." He asked, "Well, how good are you?" I said, "I'm better than you are!" which of course was crazy. But I ended up in the band. That took me out of the basement. I learned about fifty of his songs and stayed about a year. Suddenly I was very driven. I thought if Raven could come up with all these songs and get people to play them, I surely could do that.

His internship served, Michael formed his own band in November 1979. The lead guitarist brought in David Blaze on drums and G. W. Rareshied on bass, and the trio called themselves the Adults. Their debut performance matched them up with one of Cleveland's original heavy-metal bands, Snake Rock, at a movie theater at Broadway and E. 55th Street. Eight months later, the band saw its first lineup change.

"We were just in our infancy when we got a Fourth of July gig at the Mistake [below the Agora]," Michael recalls.

I don't remember the details, but there was a disagreement between myself and the other members. I'd already been doing some rehearsing with Robb Harpy, Raven's drummer, and Karen Jensen, who played bass. I asked them if they were interested in playing the gig. And that was it. The whole sound of the band changed. It got more powerful, more cerebral, more provocative. And Karen sang, so that opened up more avenues. We rehearsed often, and Harpy began contributing ideas as well. We amassed a library of material. It was exactly the direction I wanted to go.

But unbeknownst to us, Karen was a very sick woman. We had played together for months, but she never told us she'd had numerous surgeries, which we later learned were from cancer. Many times we knew she wasn't up to playing but didn't know why. Then, it was like we found out one month, and she died the next. It was real fast.

Meanwhile, my girlfriend, Crystal, had been hanging out at rehearsals and going to the gigs. One rehearsal night Karen was sick, and again we didn't know just how sick. Crystal, not understanding why she wasn't at all enthusiastic, said something like, "I wish I had the talent to sing and play bass. I wouldn't be just sitting there, all bummed out. I'd be jumping around showing my stuff." So Karen says, "Okay, here's the bass. Go for it if you've got so much damn energy." So Crystal picks up the bass, I showed her a few basic notes, and it sounds like a f—— fairy tale, but she just took right to it. None of us could believe it.

"I've always loved music," Gray says. "I was really into Motown when I was younger. And I'm a great dancer, which I think helps me be a better bass player. I've found it's important to have that natural-born rhythm to play an instrument. I had no qualms about playing the bass; I was always real adventurous."

As Karen Jensen's health declined, Gray became a permanent member of the band. At the same time, Marianne Schiebli, who had just acquired a soprano saxophone, joined. The group's music developed into a tight-knit, funky, orchestrated mix of rock and pop tunes.

In the early days, Michael took in shows by area bands Pere Ubu, Devo, the Dead Boys, and the Pagans. The success of those unique, eclectic groups encouraged him to experiment with a variety of sounds—jazz, funk, and pop rock—making it nearly impossible to categorize the Adults. However, because their music was often two minutes in length and usually had a quick beat, critics tagged them "punk," to which Michael vehemently objected.

"That always annoyed me," he admits. "Nothing against punk music, but I felt our music was more cerebral. I put a lot of thought into the arrangements. I was pretty much a tyrant about it."

Throughout the 1980s, the Adults played with the Action, the Generators, the Pony Boys, Lucky Pierre, Wild Giraffes, Hammer Damage, and the Numbers Band. During its tenure, the group opened for national artists Duran Duran, Gang of Four, Joan Jett, Black Flag, Tragically Hip, and Red Hot Chili Peppers. They appeared in local clubs Hennessy's, the Mistake, the Agora, Akron's the Bank, Kent's JB's and Mother's Junction, and Youngstown's Cedars Club.

"That was a remarkable group," Michael says of the lineup that became the longest-running formation. "We sparkled. We played all over. We started going to other cities like Columbus, Cincinnati, Dayton, Detroit, Erie, Buffalo, and Toronto, Canada. Cleveland was a central location so we were never too far away from other major cities. Someone would offer us thirty bucks on a weeknight at one in the morning, and we'd rent a trailer, hook it up to a '68 Cutlass, and go. We'd play anywhere."

"Actually, if you were an original band you had to play outside Cleveland if you wanted to survive financially," Gray adds. "We'd do fifteen gigs on a busy month, and you can't do that all in one place. Then when most of the clubs got their own sound systems, it got easier to move around like that because you didn't have to lug all your own band equipment."

The bandmates' lifestyles allowed for such mobility. While Michael put all his time and energy into the music, Schiebli worked as a hairdresser, and Gray was a bartender, which allowed both to arrange their own hours. Harpy worked various restaurants.

By 1983, the group was ready to put their talents to vinyl. Michael remembers how it all came about:

> This lady who was a fanatic fan of ours told us we should have a record out. I said something like "Well, you should pay for it," and without skipping a beat she replied, "Okay." She was willing to spend the money so it would be right and stand up well against any good recording. We started looking around Cleveland for a producer and couldn't find the right kind of person that knew what we were all about.
>
> So Crystal did some research and found out about the Fifth Floor studio in Cincinnati. People like Roger Troutman, The Gap Band, and Bootsy Collins were recording there. The [studio] was churning out all this cool funk stuff, and put out records that were actually on the charts.

During that time the band was playing the Jockey Club in Covington, Kentucky. Noted R&B producer Gary Platt, accompanied by friend and renowned session guitarist Adrian Belew, came to see the band perform. Belew was well known in the music world for his collaborations with artists such as Frank Zappa, David Bowie, King Crimson, and the Talking Heads. The pair liked what they saw. Platt became producer of the group's debut album, and Belew contributed his guitar licks on the song "Junk Funk."

The album, *Ladies and Gentlemen . . . The Adults,* was released in 1984. The 1,200 copies sold out quickly (and more copies were never made available). But while college radio viewed the album as too polished and "glitzy" for airplay, commercial radio was thumbing its nose at it as an "amateur production." The only local airplay the group got was when urban contemporary station WZAK-FM (which boasted deejay Lynn Tolliver) put "Junk Funk" on its "rhythm roster" (the only white group on it), which guaranteed some time on the airwaves. Ironically, Boston and L.A. stations picked up on the group's songs; but when listeners couldn't find the record in the stores, interest waned.

In addition, Michael notes, there were problems with management. "We got sat on, shelved by our management. There were talks about tours, like with the Simple Minds, but nothing came of it. Meanwhile, we continued to play our regular clubs and to keep our chops up by producing new material. We had put our faith in management but we never got promoted."

Then the club scene began to shift gears, and the Adults chose not to capitalize on the changing times. "There came a whole new generation with the mosh pits, where they all get in a circle and basically hurt each other," Michael explains. "And I had no interest in playing before an audience that expected me to spit water at them and such. That's not what we were into at all. That's not why I write music. I want to see people dance and have fun, so I decided to continue, but on my own terms."

Schiebli left the group in 1985, and Harpy drifted in and out until 1988. Michael and Gray added guitarist/keyboardist John Botten and continued to play, including opening for Nine Inch Nails at the Metropol in Pittsburgh in 1989. The new year brought another release for the band, a cassette called *I Said*. But the buzz was quieting down. The Adults forged on, but in 1995, even mainstay Gray saw no future in it.

I got older and didn't want to go on the road anymore. I remember being on stage one night. I shut my eyes and pretended we had a record contract, traveling on a nice tour bus instead of a beat-up old van, and you know what I thought? That time has passed for me. If it was all offered to me now, I wouldn't want it. The energy and the importance of that was gone for me.

But, oh, how I grieved. I had no idea at the loss I would feel. But looking back, I could say, *my God, I wasted nearly all my twenties and into my thirties, because I was with this band for sixteen years of my life*. On the other hand, I did stuff lots of people only dream about. We were so creative and used different instrumentation. We used various percussion instruments and saxophones, keyboards, even whistles, bells, and tape loops. We were a good band. We didn't fail.

The Adults circa 1996 consisted of Brian Dossa on bass, Tim Caskey on drums, and David Guthrie on sax and keyboards. That lineup produced the last Adults CD, *Playing a Kid's Game*. With material Michael felt was some of their best, the group returned to the road briefly, but the end of the line was near. The year 1997 proved too much for even the Adults' most persevering member.

"For twenty years, it was all I thought about, all I did, all I lived for—every waking moment," Michael says. "I moved into a nice place and am presently in the process of building a recording studio and concentrating on furthering my songwriting. What excited me most about that band was we got to the point where we sounded like a big, big, band. If you closed your eyes and listened you'd think you were hearing nine or twelve people on stage. And we weren't afraid to get creative and experiment."

"I'm Paul Michael's biggest fan," Gray says. "I still think he's one of the most talented, creative composer/songwriters ever. I hope more people discover that. I really loved doing what I did with him for so long."

The Pony Boys (1981–88)

Formed in 1981, the Pony Boys had a love affair with their audience through most of the decade.

"I started putting the Pony Boys together when I returned to Cleveland from San Francisco in the late '70s," recalls founder/vocalist/songwriter Jimmy Armstrong, who studied piano at the Cleveland Music School Settlement in his early teens. "I think we were set apart by our interesting chord progressions and harmony. We did some jazz standards like 'Love for Sale' and 'Witchcraft,' but we souped them up. And our music had a lot of elements of swing and rockabilly, which wasn't big at that time."

Armstrong, who also studied voice at Baldwin-Wallace College, says the Pony Boys' name didn't come, as rumor had it, from the character in S. E. Hinton's *The Outsiders*. "I just thought it was a cool name for a rockabilly band."

"I was getting real tired of the arena rock bands, like Air Supply and Journey, taking over the airwaves," he notes. "I had seen Pearl Harbor and the Explosions, a rockabilly band, at the old Agora. I walked outta there and told my girlfriend, 'I'm putting together a band.' I knew I could do it."

Originally the group consisted of Armstrong, Eric Elliot (on guitar and synthesizer), Greg Shinn (guitar), and Michael Wimberly (drums, later replaced by Michael Acord). Armstrong and Elliot became the McCartney/Lennon songwriting team of the group. Armstrong notes that most of their repertoire focused more on "deep passions" rather than any kind of agenda: "We wrote romantic lyrics."

The inspired quartet began playing local clubs like the Phantasy, Zepher's (Broad Street in Elyria), the Pop Shop, and the Agora, and they soon found themselves opening for national acts like Blondie (at New York's Max's Kansas City), the Ramones (Agora), the Eurythmics (Agora), Michael Bolton (the Front Row), and the most popular rockabilly band at the time, the Stray Cats with Brian Setzer (Agora).

The Cleveland-based group was able to share the stage with diverse musical groups because they prided themselves on their originality that spanned several genres of rock and pop music.

"We got away from rockabilly fairly early on," Elliot notes. "I, myself, was influenced by Todd Rundgren, Jimi Hendrix, and Steely Dan, so I think that all got filtered into our music. Jimmy brought in a bit of a Doors influence. There were some R&B and soul mixed in. We experimented a lot, there was nothing we wouldn't try. That's what made us different. Our sound was not identifiable, though Jimmy's voice certainly was."

The Pony Boys quickly hooked critics. The group with the different sound received acclaim in local publications, such as *Cleveland Magazine* and *Scene*, and national magazines like *Playback* and *Interview*. "We never, ever, got a bad review," Armstrong notes.

There was still more to come. Particularly in the fall of 1987. "The producers of [national TV talent show] *Star Search* were in town to audition local bands," Armstrong recalls. "It took place at Beachwood Studios, and there were literally hundreds and hundreds of local bands, including the Dazz Band, Exotic Birds, and Slam Bam Boo. But for some reason I just knew we would win."

Armstrong's prediction was right on. The Pony Boys played one of its most popular songs, "Orange Flower," and soon the group was headed to Hollywood to tape their segment. "That was a fun time, though I was nervous, of course," Elliot says. "Being on *Star Search* was a big thing back then. We performed 'Don't Love Me in Vain' but lost to a band called the King Pins, though I never heard about them afterward."

In 1986, the band teamed up with Matt Newman and sax player Pete Linzell (of the former national group Trillionaire) to form Buddy World. That group, which focused on old standards by Duke Ellington, Gershwin, and Cole Porter, as well as Latin songs, was well received in New York but nearly ignored in Cleveland. It lasted less than a year.

The last lineup of the Pony Boys included Armstrong, Elliot, Acord, guitarist Jim Demain, bassist Steve "Cal" Goldun, and trumpet player Steve Christenson. "We did a motion picture video and put out an album [*Rondolets and Murder Hymns*]," Armstrong says. "Our music was good, but truthfully, at that point I wasn't into it anymore."

After the Pony Boys disbanded, its members went separate ways. Demain moved to Nashville and is currently an engineer and producer for country music artists. Armstrong and Elliot have remained together and occasionally perform at various Cleveland clubs, such as Marigold's in Cleveland's Tremont section and Club Isabella. The duo is also working on putting another band together called Hippie Cult Leader. "It explores the underbelly of American life," Armstrong says of his new inspiration. "It's more personal. I write about my experiences, including my former abuse of heroin, which is a real monster. Heroin was an awful burden in my life and really did affect my music."

Today, a much healthier Armstong looks at his history with the Pony Boys as a good experience, one that taught him what's really important: "I got so apathetic towards the end [of the band]. I got sick of people in vinyl jackets telling us what we should be doing. I always loved the art part of music, not the business part. I love just playing my music for the music's sake. And fortunately I've been able to make a living at it, despite the inevitable highs and the lows."

Beau Coup (1983–92)

Creating snappy, reflective, or memorable music is not always the hardest thing for a band. Sometimes it's simply coming up with the right band name.

"We tried out all different names," Beau Coup keyboardist/songwriter Dennis Lewin recalls. "We'd already recorded a single, 'Still in My Heart,' which was getting airplay on WGCL. But we hadn't come up with a name we liked. When Dancin' Danny Wright, then host of the local TV show *Rockspot Cleveland* [on WCLQ, Channel 61], invited us to appear on it, we knew we had to come up with something quick. Eddie Marshall from Marshall Ford was with us, and when Danny asked about our name, Eddie said, 'Beau Coup.' So within minutes, Danny looks into the camera and said, 'Ladies and Gentleman, Beau Coup.' And that was it. It was better than anything we'd come up with!"

Everyone who heard this group in action, agreed the name fit. And the story of its genesis seems just as fateful. According to vocalist and frontman Tom Amato,

We didn't set out to be a band; it just happened one night. We were up in the studio above the Agora [Take One, formerly Agency] trying to get some songs together. There were three of us—me, my brother Frank, who just returned from L.A. after being in the rock/funk band with Neil Giraldo called Thrills and Company, and

Eric Messinger [né Singer. Euclid High graduate Singer would later become Kiss's drummer during Peter Kriss's hiatus. Singer also played with Alice Cooper and Black Sabbath.]. We were up there with Hank LoConti Jr., who told us to come downstairs and hear the band that was playing that night, Jonah Koslen and the Heroes. We saw Dennis playing the keyboard and thought, *hey, he's really good.* We knew he was a songwriter, too. So later, he came upstairs and that's when we recorded 'Still in My Heart.' Hank Sr. heard it and said he thought it was the best song recorded there in a long time.

"We also recorded 'Somewhere Out in the Night,'" Lewin adds. "Both those songs ended up on our first album."

Lewin had been playing classical music since kindergarten. His grandfather, a concert pianist from Poland, introduced the classics to him before he was enrolled at age five in the Cleveland Institute of Music. By age twelve, Lewin was studying under Dr. Andrius Kuprevicius, head of the Cleveland Music School Settlement. Before becoming a member of Beau Coup, Lewin was writing jingles and identifiers for WGCL.

After an initial period of alternating members, the lineup stabilized with the dual lead vocals of the Amato brothers, Tom and Frank (who sang with the touring British band Savoy Brown), Lewin, lead guitarist Mike McGill, bass player Bill March (replaced briefly by John Dean), drummer Jimmy Clark, and percussionist Rodney Psyka. Its repertoire of originals had the catchy, pop sound and harmony deemed perfect for Top 40 airplay with the precision of schooled musicians. "Yes playing Tchaikovsky," Lewin once described it. The group spent its first year in the recording studio.

"First we did our own EP of six songs, and that's how we created a buzz," Frank Amato recalls. "We pressed a thousand copies, under the old Agora Records label, because Hank Jr. was managing us. Then we started distributing it to the record stores and radio. WGCL was first to pick up on it. We then hooked up with Carl Maduri from Sweet City Records. Carl was the one who jumped in and got us a deal with Scotti Brothers, which was a division of CBS Records."

That deal ultimately created difficulties for the Cleveland band, but in the meantime, Beau Coup had begun a string of live performances. Tom Amato recalls:

Our first show was opening for Todd Rundgren at Lakeland Community College in 1984. We played a lot at the Agora, opening for Paul Young ["Everytime You Go Away"], John Waite ["Missing You"], Katrina and the Waves ["Walkin' on Sunshine"], and the Bus Boys [*48 Hours* movie soundtrack]. That's also when the 'Parties in the Park' were popular. We played a few of those, with Slade ["Run, Runaway"] and even parody king Weird Al Yankovic.

My personal favorite, though, was when we played a sold-out show with Night Ranger at Public Hall on May 28, 1987—my twenty-eighth birthday. MTV was there with Nina Blackwood, and after playing our last song, "Born and Raised on Rock-n-Roll," we got a standing ovation. I looked out at all the 30,000 lighters that were lit and thought, *Wow, this is the best birthday cake I've ever had!*

Despite their concert success, there were some unexpected hassles. According to Lewin, the group's initial agreement with the CBS's Scotti Brothers subsidiary, Rock and Roll Records, was not being met. Legal entanglements ensued, and it took the band over a year to be released from that contract. By then the musicians had signed with MCA/Camel Records. That, too, was ill-fated. The seven-man band then signed with New York CBS Amherst, a small independent label out of Buffalo. Amherst spanned the music genres with popular artists ranging from '70s hitmakers the Stylistics to the jazz group Spyro Gyra to the elite Doc Severinsen Orchestra. Suddenly, WGCL wasn't the only station giving Beau Coup's songs heavy rotation. One single in particular, "Sweet Rachel," was added to the playlists of more than two hundred radio stations across the country, including ones in Columbus, Phoenix, Salt Lake City, nearby Akron station WBEA-FM, Youngstown's WHOT, and Buffalo's WNYS. The song hit in the fifties in *Billboard*'s Hot 100 in 1987.

The club circuit was also romancing Beau Coup, particularly Spanky's East (Painesville) and West (North Ridgeville) and the Cleveland Agora. Earning a solid fan base, the group, which alternated between five and eight members (including guitarists Steve Schuffert, Billy Sullivan, and drummer Don Krueger), fast became one of the top local headliners. "It was one Agora show that Bon Jovi opened for *us*," Lewin recalls with a laugh. "They'd just come out with the song 'Runaway' and were fairly unknown. The crowd liked them, but were really waiting for us to go on. No one had a clue they would make it so big."

By the time their debut album, *Born and Raised on Rock-n-Roll,* was released in 1987, Beau Coup had caught the attention of Jane Scott.

"To be honest," Lewin says, "as popular as we were, the media shunned us. Yes, the radio stations loved us, but we were getting slammed by some of the local writers. I think maybe because we weren't extreme. We weren't heavy metal, which was really big then. But Jane, she really supported us. She did everything she could to help us. So during that controversy about the *Plain Dealer* wanting to release her because of her age [a mere sixty-eight then], I thought about everything she'd done for us and for all the other local bands. So I sat down at the piano and wrote a song honoring her." One lyric in the song says, "They say you're too old for the new style, but you never mix art and age as one 'cause the older you get, the better you'll shine in the public eye." (That line would prove true when more than two hundred of Jane's fans gave her an eightieth birthday party.)

That song added fuel to the already-burning age issue, and word spread quickly. As a result, Scott got front-page status in the *Wall Street Journal* (see Chapter 10). On January 23, 1988, Beau Coup headlined the Front Row Theater. When it came time to sing "Jane," the group summoned Scott up on the stage and presented her with a dozen roses, much to the crowd's delight. After that, the media left both Scott and Beau Coup alone to do what each did best.

The group made a video to support *Born and Raised on Rock-n-Roll,* but it came too late. By the time it was released, the song had reached its peak and was on its way down in the charts. MTV declined to air it. With record label problems and no MTV sup-

Beau Coup singing "Jane" at the Front Row Theater in 1988. *Photo by James Amato.*

port, that big break remained elusive. Despite the overwhelming fan and radio support, the band couldn't break out nationally, leaving members frustrated and disillusioned by 1990. After an eighteen-month hiatus, the group decided to try again, but within months they disbanded for good.

"I still can't understand why Beau Coup didn't make it as big as they should have," Danny Wright says. "There were a whole lot of people who thought they were going to make it. And with good reason. There was a great mix of talent there, and their songs were really good. Unfortunately, they weren't the only ones to have that happen, though I think Beau Coup deserved it more than most."

Today, former members have gone separate ways. Frank Amato, now a producer and recording engineer, has his own company, Amalon Entertainment. He also continues to sing, mostly jingles for local commercials. Tom Amato is currently a salesman at Classic Chevrolet in Mentor. Bill March is a stockbroker and continues to play in various bands. Lewin is a private piano and music teacher and plays solo; he also hosts his own weekly radio show on WERE-AM, which focuses on Cleveland's eclectic music scene. No matter what its fate, Beau Coup remains one of the most memorable and beloved groups of Cleveland's rock history in the 1980s.

The Dazz Band (1974–88)

Cleveland trivia question: By 1982, what hometown band surpassed all others with a million-selling album and platinum single? Answer: A funky, soulful, horn jammin,' foot-stompin' eight-to-ten-man ensemble called the Dazz Band. The question is tricky because the O'Jays certainly had accomplished that feat in the '60s and Wild Cherry did in the '70s. But the O'Jays were from Canton, and Wild Cherry originally hailed from Steubenville. This Cleveland formation was originally called Bell Telefunk, but because it was too close to Ohio Bell Telephone, the group switched to Kinsman Dazz— "dazz," as in danceable jazz.

"We played regularly at the Kinsman Grille and people thought that's where we got our name," says founder Bobby Harris. "But we really named it in honor of the street where I grew up. Then we dropped the Kinsman and became the Dazz Band."

With singer/saxophonist Harris, the original lineup included Isaac Wiley (drums), Mike Wiley (bass), Kenny Pettus (vocals/percussion), and Michael Calhoun (guitar). They soon added Wayne Preston (alto sax), Ed Myers (trombone), Frank Joseph (keyboards), and Les Thaler (trumpet). The large group formed a unique arrangement of R&B, jazz, soul, pop, and funk, drawing enthusiastic crowds to their live shows. They also brought in Michael Jackson on keyboards.

"I knew Michael Jackson when we both attended Cleveland Heights High School," recalls keyboardist Phil Baron, another early member. "A few years later, in 1976, I replaced him when he left the group. That's when they were still called Kinsman Dazz. I did the audition with them when they got signed to Twentieth Century Fox, but was fired the next day because they rehired Michael Jackson. I couldn't blame them; he really was a bad mamma on the piano."

The group certainly did dazzle its audience, playing its jazz/funk-fusion sounds at various nightclubs around town including the Theatrical Restaurant, Sir Rah House, the Riviera Country Club, and the Agora. Then in 1979, Sennie (Skip) Martin approached Harris and said, "I hear you're looking for a trumpet player. I'm your man." With that, Martin became one of the group's most enduring members.

Along with strong emphasis on the horn section, this band boasted talented songwriters in Harris and Calhoun. Their management was notable as well—Ray Calabrese from Sun Ray Management and record mogul Joe Simone. It was Simone who got the group its first contract in 1978 with Twentieth Century Fox and signed them two years later to Motown Records. The label released "Invitation to Love" in 1980. Included on that release were trombone player Edward Myers III and guitarist Eric Fearman. Keyboardist Steve Cox joined the group in 1981, just as the Dazz Band found its biggest success.

"I was working at Pi Keyboards and Audio in Strongsville when some of the Dazz members came in to buy a keyboard," Cox recalls. "I was demonstrating one, and they liked how I played. At the time, I was in a jazz-fusion band called Merging Traffic, and they'd heard our demo tape. When they realized the connection, I was asked to come in on their next album to program all the sounds for their keyboard player [Kevin

Kendrick]. When he left soon afterward, I replaced him."

The 1981 LP, *Let the Music Play,* was the group's second Motown recording, having previously released two albums on the Twentieth Century Fox label. The group practiced every day, forty hours a week at a rehearsal hall in Highland Heights. In 1982, their third effort on Motown, *Keep It Live,* with the single "Let It Whip," took the group to national status. The Dazz Band had hit it big.

"That was largely due to Joe Simone," Cox notes. "Motown wanted a different song released, and there was a fight about it. They finally agreed to put out 'Let It Whip' as a single but wouldn't put any money behind it. So Joe put up $75,000 of his own money to hire independent promoters, record guys. We did radio and record store tours all along the West Coast, like army troops. And as we worked and worked the record, it started climbing the charts. Then Motown looks at *Billboard* one day and goes, 'Looks like we got a hit.' That's when they started what's called chasing it. They got the credit, but it was really all Joe's doing."

When "Let It Whip" was released, radio stations throughout the country added it to their playlists. As a result, it reached No. 1 on *Billboard* and *Cashbox.*

"That record hit so fast, we jumped right out and went on tour," Cox says. "We were playing major venues and opening for groups like Cameo, Kool and the Gang, the Commodores, and Rick James. The song became *Billboard*'s Soul Song of the Year for 1982." From there it was off to the Grammys.

"We had just completed taping our performance for the *Solid Gold* TV show and went straight to the Shrine Auditorium," Cox recalls. "We'd just gotten to our seats when they called our category in the pre-telecast ceremony. I had a dream the night before that we were going to win it. It was such a memorable night. There were all these great people around us, many whom we admired. There were Michael McDonald, Chaka Khan, Prince . . . and the guys in Toto ["Rosanna"] were sitting in the front row giving us the thumbs up. Later on, David Paich [Toto's keyboardist] told me he voted for us, and that really made my day."

"Let It Whip," written by California natives Reggie Andrews and Leon "Ndugu" Chancler, allowed the Cleveland group to win "Best R&B Performance by a Duo or Group with Vocals" in 1982. Although the Dazz Band went through over twenty different lineups, the members lucky enough to receive the prestigious record award were Harris, Ike and Mike Wiley, Cox, Martin, Fearman, Pettus, and trumpet player and vocalist Pierre DeMudd.

Although the next two releases sold well enough, they failed to come close to the success of their predecessor, and tour offers came to a dead end. The band dropped Motown, citing the fact the label hadn't pushed them enough, and signed with Geffen Records, which produced their final album. By then Martin had left. He was not replaced; rather, Pettus and Keith Harrison took over vocals. After the completion of that release, Cox would leave as well.

"Towards the end, the group put in a bunch of preproduction on the album," Cox explains.

This was to put basic tracks on a computer with the sequencer and samples of all the instruments. There'd be samples of drums, samples of bass. Samples of everything except the vocals and some guitar parts. In other words, they'd take the computer into the studio, push record, and there's the track. All I was left doing was a couple of keyboard overdubs. Same with the bass player.

And in my opinion, the record wasn't good. I told Bobby [Harris], "Hey, this isn't the way we got a Grammy. We got it by the whole band having input. But he was the producer. And personally, I don't think one should produce themselves because you always need an outside ear. You get biased and often can't hear things someone on the outside can hear. I don't believe anyone should produce their own albums—except maybe Prince.

So, the album flopped, as I think it should have. And when there's no album, there's no tour. It all came to a head with me as I was driving in my car on New Year's Eve, 1987. I'm listening to WZAK-FM, and the deejay plays this medley of all of our ballads from the previous Dazz albums—with real strings, with cool, stacked up background vocals, with me and the rest of the band actually playing on the record. I sat in my driveway, still listening, and decided it was never going to be that way again. I went into the house and wrote my resignation.

Keyboardist Bill Stineway replaced Cox, but more changes were to come. The Wiley brothers departed as well and formed American Way. However, tragedy overshadowed their new plans. On January 15, 1988, Mike Wiley, under the influence of alcohol and cocaine, took his own life at age thirty-two. Older brother Ike used the saddest day of his life to publicly caution others on the devastating effects of drugs and alcohol: "I hope other people heed the warning and ask for help before it's too late," he told Jane Scott.

Today, the Dazz tradition lives on, but it is now based in L.A., where Harris and Pettus presently reside. Along with Las Vegas resident Martin, the three former Clevelanders have added more members and continue to tour and record. In 1998, the group released *Dazz Band: Here We Go Again,* as well as a live CD, *Double Exposure,* recorded in 1997 at Seattle's Phoenix Underground. And in early 1999, the reformed Dazz Band played at the Mirage in Moscow. They also wrote a song with George Clinton, "Nothin' but a Jam," which was included on Clinton's album.

Cox also remains in music. The Nashville resident currently plays keyboards for country/pop artist Trisha Yearwood and is featured on her latest album. He admits, however, to a little homesickness: "I'm havin' a wonderful time. I work with excellent musicians and have hung out with Garth Brooks, who's a great guy. But there are things I miss about Cleveland: the Cleveland Orchestra, which I used to go see all the time. The Art Museum, the Indians, and the marinara sauce in those Italian restaurants on Murray Hill."

Reggae Makes the Cleveland Scene

I-Tal (1978–94)

It's music with accent on the upbeat instead of the downbeat. It's Jamaican island music.

—Bob Caruso

Reggae in Cleveland, Ohio? In the late '70s and early '80s, many North Coast music lovers had never heard of this sort of music. But bar owner Dave Valentine got hooked on its beat in the Florida Keys:

I owned the Coach House [now Club Isabella] at the time and used to go to Key West in the winter. That's how I got turned on to reggae. It was 1978, and reggae was all you heard down in the Keys. Bob Marley's second album, *Rastaman Vibrations,* was out then, and I got addicted to it. I got back to Cleveland, and saw an ad in *Rolling Stone* where someone was selling 45s in L.A. I ordered a couple dozen of these reggae records for my jukebox. There were ones by the Meditations, Jimmy Cliff, and Bob Marley. We were the first bar to have a reggae jukebox, I'm sure. It became quite a hit, too. And I started Tuesday's open-mike night.

That marked the beginning of the first known reggae band in Ohio.

"We had just formed the band when we played an open-mike night," notes guitarist/lead singer Dave Smeltz, who wrote and arranged nearly all of I-Tal's original material. "That's when Dave first heard us and became interested because, at the time, no one was playing reggae.

"The name came about when I was reading a *Penthouse* magazine article on Bob Marley, in which there was a dictionary of reggae terms. So I suggested we called the band I-Tal, and George [Gordon] explained what it meant. The language is patois for 'vital' or 'natural.' It is the natural movement of the body when it hears music."

This group boasted two native Jamaicans, Kingston-born George Gordon (percussion, "fancy footwork," and "all-around reggae expert" who knew Bob Marley) and Errol Williams (drums and vocals, later a member of Earth Force), thus giving the band authenticity. Members also included Bob Caruso (congas, percussion), John Wagner (lead guitar), Gair Linhart (keyboards), and Bob Allyn (drums). A few months later, they added the vocal style of Ellie Nore, making it a nine-piece band. Valentine's and Nore's light skin and blonde hair against the coloring of their black bandmates provided a visual contrast that blended perfectly with the kaleidoscopic range of the group's music—music they termed "reggae rock."

"I was always into different music," says Smeltz, whose day job at Record Revolution provided him with a rich education in all the variations of music. "I've collected albums over the years that have long been out of print."

While Valentine, Williams, and Gordon were most influenced by Peter Tosh, Bob Smeltz's wide range of musical interests included Hendrix, James Brown, Long John Baldry, Grateful Dead, and John McLaughlin. Thus it's easy to understand how the group's unique sound emerged. And with his club in the heart of college town (Case Western Reserve University), Valentine had the perfect showcase for this new musical formation. I-Tal debuted there in August 1978.

"From then on, we played every Wednesday and Thursday," says Valentine, who had previously been in the Gair Linhart Blues Band. "That is, until the building's owner booted me out in '79 because she wanted to take it over. I'm still bummed about that!"

I-Tal was one of the first groups to play a WMMS Coffeebreak Concert. They would later perform in the WMMS/Agora lunchtime concert several times and even did one Coffeebreak Concert at Tommy's. The group also played often at Peabody's Cafe and the Euclid Tavern before becoming the Sunday-night house band at the Mistake.

I-Tal in 1979. *Left to right:* Dave Valentine, Dave Smeltz, John Wagner, George Gordon, Gair Linhart, Bob Caruso, and Bob Allyn. *Courtesy of David Valentine.*

Their first release was an EP in 1979. "Rockers" quickly became a local hit and was included on the 1980 WMMS *Pride of Cleveland* LP. Their debut single was released in 1979 (with Linhart's brother, Buzzy, on vocals). The A-side was a Van Morrison cover, Smeltz-arranged "Brown-Eyed Girl," backed with the Linhart-penned "Close to the Wire." Both were, of course, done reggae-style.

"We got great support from the college stations," says Smeltz, a 1973 Shaker Heights High School graduate. "We played often in college towns, like Ohio University [Athens], Ann Arbor, Michigan State [East Lansing], and of course, Kent State [Kent], where we played weekends at Mother's Junction. And Charleston, North Carolina, was like our home away from home. We played a lot at the Old Post Office on Pope Avenue in Hilton Head, too. Those places bring back great memories."

Recordings became few and far between as I-Tal made its way across America and beyond: from Vermont, Maine, and Canada, to Jamaica, Trinidad, and Montego Bay. By 1981, Linhart, Allen, and Wagner were gone. The lineup then included trumpet player Steve Mauer, Mike "Chopper" Wasson on lead guitar, Gino Long on guitar/bass/vocals, drummer Chris Dunmore, and percussionist/vocalist Carlos Jones: "I first heard I-Tal on WMMS during one of their Coffeebreak Concerts. I had just gotten into Bob Marley and couldn't believe there was an actual reggae band in Cleveland. And my brother had a Jamaican friend at work who had told him about I-Tal. So one night we all went to the Coach House to hear them. On their breaks, I went up and talked to Bob Caruso to talk drums and to 'partake of the sacraments.' Of course, I had my congas in the car and asked Dave if I could sit in. It was a very open, laid-back, loose atmosphere. But the music was tight."

After playing steadily for the next six years, members' interests were beginning to splinter. "The band was getting bigger and bigger," Valentine explains. "Dave wanted this big-sounding band, and that certainly made things sound good. But in reality, it's hard to make good money splitting the pay among eight to ten people. That's why you see a lot of three- or four-piece bands now. It's the only way you make decent money. But probably more than that, I didn't want to be on the road anymore." "That was the difference between us," Smeltz adds. "The money didn't mean that much to me. It was the music that was most important."

By 1982, Valentine was out and Ron Jarvis (formerly with Buckeye Biscuit) was in. In 1984, the band split in two. Chopper, Jones, Caruso, and Dunmore formed First Light with Ed Martin (keyboard) and Rod Reisman (drums). I-Tal then was Smeltz, Doc Smith (percussion), Dave Green (drums, later replaced by Keith McFarren), Buddy Hammond (rhythm guitar), Al Morgan (bass, later replaced by Phil Myricks), Tony Moore (saxophone), Wayne Preston (sax, formerly with the Dazz Band) and Dave Lyons (synthesizer, trumpet). With astute soundman Bill Haley, this lineup produced the album *USA* in 1989—a mix of covers and originals.

Valentine returned to I-Tal in 1991 when Smeltz promised him there'd be less touring. Another change united original I-Tal members Valentine, Smeltz, and Wagner and brought in Irene Mraz (vocals/percussion), Chris DeSantis (percussions), Russ Richards (keyboards), and Gus Oswald (drums). The group abandoned long road trips and stayed with their favorite hometown haunts—which included two shows at the newest outdoor summer venue, Nautica in the Flats.

"I've been in many bands, before and since I-Tal," says Richards, whose R&B roots run deep. "But that time with them was my favorite. In the blues bands I played in [such as Colin Dussault] they always wanted me to solo, which was fine. But with I-Tal,

I was just part of the rhythm section, getting into the sounds. And it was so cool to be up there jammin' and look out from the stage and see this sea of neo-hippie, tie-dyed kids swaying to the music, enjoying what you put out. I tell you, it rocked. No matter how I felt when I arrived at a gig, there was this wonderful vibe that'd come over you once you started playing. I'd always leave with a smile on my face."

Throughout its sixteen-year history, this band lived up to its name by producing a natural, flowing sound that people loved to dance to. But by 1994, its beat had slowed down.

"You can't keep playing four, five times a week. You burn yourself out," says Valentine, who now has his own painting company. "You've got to use strategy and not overdo it in certain areas. Then you can make it more of a show, more special. But the money starts driving you."

Smeltz had grown tired as well. In 1994, he gave up his musical therapy for physical therapy. He currently works for a rehabilitation company in Chagrin Falls. Although this pioneering group is no more, it made its legacy in Cleveland rock history thanks to the offbeat passions of founders Dave Smeltz and Dave Valentine. And if he can ever get the guys together again, Smeltz says, he just might consider a reunion.

First Light (1984–98)

Like his bandmates, guitarist/percussionist/vocalist Carlos Jones grew up "feeling the music."

When I was real young, we lived in Virginia. My mom would take us to church, and that music captivated me because it was very rhythmic and spirited. Then because my dad was in the service, we lived overseas in Germany for a few years. All we had was radio, no TV. So I was always listening to music. The first pop album I got ahold of was a Beach Boys record, which I really got into. That is, until 1966 when I traded that Beach Boys album for a Beatles album. "Something's New" had a German version of "I Wanna Hold Your Hand," and others like "Tell Me Why" and "If I Fell." When I heard that album, everything kinda clicked for me. I listened to it constantly.

Soon as we returned to the States, I'd go to a friend's house and play on his drum kit. I tried to play like Ringo. And my brothers and I wanted to grow our hair like the Beatles. 'Course we didn't have the right kind of hair!

Abandoning drum lessons because he "wanted to jam," Jones then discovered Motown in the late 1960s. "Hearing that kind of music, I *really* wanted to jam!" The stage was set when Jones got a drum kit and older brother Keith (a.k.a. Ngoki), heavily influenced by Jimi Hendrix, picked up the guitar. By then the family had taken up residence in Maple Heights, where the brothers got hooked on the soul music emanating from Cleveland's R&B station WJMO and deejay Lynn Tolliver. Once they were out of school, WMMS brought even more musical variety to their lives.

"I got a job after high school at Firestone [tire company] because I was planning on becoming a race-car driver," Jones recalls. "At work, we had 'MMS pumping everyday, 24/7. I'd hear everything from Led Zeppelin to Bob Marley to Elvis Costello—you name it. So my musical tastes were broadening. And I really liked the heavy drums in Santana and Genesis. Then I saw Bob Marley live at Music Hall in July 1978. That changed my world. Right after that, I started growing dreadlocks."

Jones took up the conga drums in his quest for "that sound." And he found a new home in the Coach House, where reggae had just started happening. Jones joined I-Tal in 1981. By the time the group had made a name for itself along the North Coast, several of the band members decided to shift gears. First Light, coined by Jones and guitarist/bassist Mike "Chopper" Wasson, was born.

When first formed, First Light was considered simply an offshoot of I-Tal. But soon the group proved to be distinct. What began as a reggae band grew into a group where tags were meaningless. This six- to nine-piece band mixed reggae with R&B, rock, blues, soca, funk, and rap and sprinkled it with a touch of Latin jazz. "You could call it world-beat music," Jones adds.

However one defines it, the band's funky music was played by a racially diverse group that became a hit on college circuits throughout the Midwest for fourteen years. For most of its existence, First Light boasted the same lineup, beginning with Carlos Jones on percussion and vocals, percussionist Bob Caruso, Chopper on guitar, former Buckeye Biscuit and I-Tal bassist Ron Jarvis, former I-Tal member and trumpet player Steve Mauer, keyboardist Ed Marthey, and drummer Rod Reisman. In 1985, Jarvis left, replaced by bass player Ed Skinner. Chopper then switched from guitar to bass, with Gino Long taking over on guitar. On certain songs, however, the two alternated instruments. Saxophonist and flute player Rob Williams joined the group in 1986 and remained until 1990. Former I-Tal member Chris Dunmore set aside his drums to manage First Light.

At home, First Light drew crowds that often extended out the doors and down the street. And over the course of four days during the 1991 Christmas holiday season, First Light brought in $18,000 for the Empire Club, as reported in *Pollstar* magazine. Much of its years, however, were spent traveling extensively along the East Coast, from Maine to South Carolina.

In 1985, the group started its own label, Thin Ice Records, and recorded a three-song EP, *Musical Uprising*. The title song, as well as "Hold Back Syndrome," was written by Jones, and "Movin' on Down" was penned by Mauer. First Light songs got airplay on college radio in Cleveland, as well as in college towns in Michigan, Indiana, Illinois, Kentucky, New York, and West Virginia. With the 1988 debut CD, *Reggae Meltdown*, all previous notions of this band being strictly reggae were checked at the door. Not only did the release demonstrate the group's melting pot of sounds, it was the first CD release by a local band, and it sold 12,000 copies. In 1992, two more releases were available. Both *Live at the Empire* and *First Light Bootleg* were live cassettes, and they allowed the band to earn enough money to continue recording. In 1996, the group released what became its last CD, *Groove Telepathy*.

In 1984, the "Rock and Reggae" benefit for the Free Clinic was founded, and First Light, along with the band Oroboros, became a musical staple at the annual summer festival. Aggressive promotion was a large part of this group's success. Until the group disbanded in 1998, Dunmore handled all the promoting, budgeting, and marketing for the band.

"Cleveland has always been a nucleus in terms of accessibility," Dunmore says. "New York, Toronto, Boston, Indiana, Chicago, and Nashville are all easy road trips, being just a few hours away. And of course, that means hundreds of great college towns, which has always been good to us."

The group played an average of two hundred dates a year and opened for Living Colour, Taylor Dayne, Steel Pulse, Meat Loaf, and the Clash. Thanks to Dunmore's astute and tireless networking, First Light was invited to the 1993 South by Southwest Music Festival. "That was a *long drive*," Jones says emphatically. "Basically we went there to play for forty minutes at the Mercado Caribe, just to be seen. We spent all our money and didn't make any. But you do it in hopes of possibly getting signed or [to] make some contacts. It was great fun, but we came back very tired and very broke! But it was still a great experience."

Until 1997, the core group had remained the same. Then, after fourteen years in First Light, Carlos Jones wanted to return to his reggae roots: "The group was getting far removed from its original purpose. We were playing much more of the funk rock, and little reggae. There's nothing wrong with that, but it wasn't satisfying me. I wanted to play music that conveyed a message." First Light's last show was on May 30, 1998, at the Odeon.

Jones now heads his own band, Carlos Jones and the P.L.U.S. Band (Peace, Love, and Unity Syndicate), which had actually begun with a 1993 Bob Marley tribute concert at Peabody's Cafe. Presently the group consists of Jones, Caruso, Pete Platten (keyboardist), "The Bush Doctor" (a.k.a. Larry Mazur, percussion/guitar), Roy Isaacs (percussion), drummer Will Douglas (formerly of Oroboros), and bassist Ras Fiya. This reggae group won the 1999 *Scene* Music Award for best reggae/ska band.

"Reggae music brings peace, love and unity among the people who listen to it," Jones says. "It brings together all types of people, and when we play, everyone comes together as one." Amen.

Oroboros (1980–98)

Guitarist/songwriter/vocalist Jim Miller was the nucleus of Oroboros. The 1972 Cathedral Latin graduate explains:

The original concept was to have a band that has some synchronicity and spontaneity in the music. Back in high school—late '60s, early '70s—we were influenced by groups that explored and jammed, like the Grateful Dead, Allman Brothers, and of course, the Beatles and Stones. We learned these groups had influences as well. So when the Allman Brothers did "Statesboro Blues," you had to wonder, who's this guy Blind Will McTell? Or with the Grateful Dead's "Little Red Rooster," you'd ask, who's Willie Dixon? That started me exploring the roots of rock 'n' roll.

Back in high school, if you didn't play sports, which I sucked at, the only other socially accepted thing was playing in a garage band. If you could plug in and play "Gloria" or "Johnny B. Goode," you were an excellent lead guitar player. So I picked up the guitar.

We tried to start the band up in the early '70s and tried different inceptions. But I was traveling a lot in other bands. I was in country bands, blues bands, punk bands . . . so really, I was cutting my teeth.

Finally in 1980, Oroboros was born. "I was in Bellingham, Washington, when I got a call from my best friend and high school buddy, Bill Cogan, who was starting up the band. I was coming back to Cleveland, anyway, for my sister's wedding. Soon as I started playing with them, that was it. I stayed."

The band's original lineup was Miller (guitar/vocals/songwriting), Cogan (guitar, songwriting), Mary Beth Cooper (vocals), her husband, Dave Cooper (trombone), Kevin Kennedy (drums, soon replaced by Rob Luoma), Gary Maxwell (bass), and Rocky Miller (keyboards). Their debut show was at the Flipside on November 18, 1980. Such was the genesis of Oroboros (pronounced *orob-o-ros*), a Greek word that means both change and continuity, represented by a snake swallowing its own tail. Yin and yang. Rock and roll.

The musical circle would bring in faithful fans for a full eighteen years. But it took a while for those fans to catch on. Oroboros, in fear of being typecast as a '60s revival band, soon expanded its repertoire. Original tunes were born out of generations of influences that included blues (Howlin' Wolf, Robert Johnson), rockabilly (Carl Perkins, Chuck Berry, Buddy Holly), folk (Bob Dylan), reggae (Bob Marley), and new wave (Talking Heads), and cover material consisted of those bands, as well as Steve Winwood, Eric Clapton, and Little Feat. Still, the group never strayed from its roots.

"We were pretty much based on the model of the Grateful Dead," Miller says. "We were just young, crazy hippies, and we all lived together in a house on Rushleigh Road in Cleveland Heights. But this was 1980. People, mostly the media, would laugh at us, and say, 'Hey, this isn't the '60s. What are you guys doing?' We were an anomaly. The next generation of that psychedelic revolution thing and we were the only band doing what we were doing along the Midwest. There were some bands on the East and West Coast doing it, like Phish and Blues Traveler, but that wasn't happening around here."

Despite their hippie label—or perhaps because of it—Oroboros found regular gigs at Flipside, Peabody's DownUnder, the Euclid Tavern, and Kent's Mother's Junction. The group saw its first change in lineup when the Coopers left and were replaced by Tony Moore (trumpet/ sax) and Karen Allgire (vocals). But the 1985 departure of Cogan and Rocky Miller almost brought an end to the circle.

"Nothing happened for six months," Miller recalls. "Then I hired [keyboardist] Mike Bradley, and Gary Maxwell and Rob Luoma stayed on. When Gary left later in '86, Dave Downing came in. And on and off and through the years was percussion player Bill Caulley."

With its focus on peace, love, and music, the group attacked many social ills in its original compositions, evident in its 1985 debut album *Different Feeling*. Frequent themes included drug abuse, runaways, and parents' responsibilities to their children. The group attracted the twenty-five-and-under crowd by performing not only in college towns but also at fairs and civic venues for under-agers who didn't have the luxury of hearing bands in bars. The group frequently held shows at the Cleveland Heights Civic Theater and in 1984 co-founded, with First Light, the Rock and Reggae Festival. The annual event has become a summertime ritual, attracting as many as 7,000 music lovers.

"My manager Jeff Bogart and I started that concept," Miller says. "We were good friends with the members of First Light. So we got together with them and said, 'Let's do this arts festival to benefit the Free Clinic.' This was before anyone was doing those kind of festivals. We just thought it would be a good thing to do. We held it at the Meadowood Farms, where it still takes place today."

Another notable festival was the 1994 H.O.R.D.E. Tour at Blossom Music Center, which included the Allman Brothers, Blues Traveler, and Sheryl Crow. "We were playing at Shooters the night before," Miller recalls, "and I invited all of them to come down and jam with us but didn't really think they'd show up. Then boom—the Allman Brothers came up, John Popper and the other Blues Travelers came. So I got to jam with the Allman Brothers, guys I've admired from day one. It was one of the greatest nights ever."

In 1996, thanks to their Web site, Oroboros got invited to a birthday party in Thailand. "At first we thought it was a joke," Miller says. "This guy got ahold of us because they were looking for another band to play this free festival for the King's birthday in Thailand. We did ten dates along these beach resorts. We were the only rock band there and they loved us."

By 1987, Oroboros was a traveling band. It played shows throughout the United States, including Chicago, Ann Arbor, New York City, Boston, and Nantucket, as well as numerous college and ski towns in Colorado. Miller honed his business skills as manager by sending out newsletters and postcards detailing the group's news and schedule.

As a result of weekend shows at the Euclid Tavern, the group released the live album *Psychadeli (Live) at the Euclid Tavern* in 1988. By the early 1990s, Oroboros was a quintet comprised of Miller, Bradley, Luoma, bass player and vocalist Dave Downing, and percussionist Don Safranek. It released a studio CD, *First Circle*, in 1991. One song on the release boasted hometown roots: "The Griffin Song" was about the first boat to set sail along Lake Erie. All of the band's recordings were on their independent label, Oroboros Records. But Miller notes, "It was around that time we got serious about working on getting signed to a major label. We were real close with Electra, but then they signed Phish instead."

Frustrated and succumbing to the usual "burnout syndrome," the band underwent another change in 1993, and this ultimately became Oroboros's final lineup. With founder Miller, the rest of the band included drummer Will Douglas, bassist Scott Swanson, keyboardist/percussionist/guitarist Mike Rotman, and guitarist/vocalist Mike Verbick. That group recorded two more live CDs, *Serpent's Dance* and *Shine,* on their own Maia Records before disbanding in September 1998.

With a rich history that includes opening for the Kinks, Santana, Rusted Root, and members of the Grateful Dead (in the Further Festival), Oroboros's final show took place at Shooters on the Water, on the west bank of the Flats. Miller comments on the reason for the band's breakup:

> Well, first, we got screwed by this producer from this record company, which broke our contract. But that wasn't really it. I found myself working in a democracy. I felt I was doing all the work, yet every decision had to come up for vote, so to speak. Oroboros was a social outlet for people who enjoyed what we were doing, as well as a history lesson. I have always looked at my music as a continual evolution, just like the band name. It was great while it lasted, but it got to where I wasn't having fun anymore. In life, you have to color in the lines all the time. Up on stage, I want to create. I want to have fun.

The circle, however, is unbroken. In October 1998, Miller formed the Jim Miller Band, and the group is currently working on a debut CD. "I'm real happy with this band," says Miller, who also teaches rock history at Cuyahoga Community College. "I've got Gregg Garlock [drums, formerly of the Twist Offs], Brett Miller [bass, formerly of Global 33], Eric Meany [keyboards, backup vocals, formerly of the Janglers]. They're really into what I want to do."

Like Oroboros, this group has become a local favorite. "I carry the old Oroboros crowd with me when we play," he says. "We've always had the best fans in the world. The people who follow us are the most creative, open, and energetic group I've known. They're the ones I want to play for, so they can have a good time and crack out of their eggshell world for a few fun hours. The best part of being a musician is when a fan comes up and says about one of your songs, 'That [song] has gotten me through a rough period in my life.' That, to me, is what it's all about."

LeVert (1982–)

> He never pushed me. He basically said, "I see you're going to try to do this, but I'm not going to give you any special treatment because you're my son. As a matter of fact, you're going to have to work harder than the average guy."
>
> —Gerald Levert on the reaction of his father, O'Jays singer Eddie Levert Sr., when he told him he wanted to get into the music business (*Scene,* February 1999)

LeVert has the music in them. In fact, it's in the bloodline. Members Gerald and Sean Levert's father, Eddie Levert, is the O'Jays cofounder and singer (see Chapter 2). When the O'Jays performed at Leo's Casino, as they did numerous times, the Levert sons were often backstage, soaking up the sights and sounds of R&B in action. During the times their father was away on tour, the young boys would pretend to be O'Jays, using mop handles for microphones while entertaining their friends. "Our mom wouldn't let us play with the real equipment because we just threw stuff around and broke it," Gerald, whose rich baritone vocals have often been compared to his father's, once told Jane Scott.

By 1982, sixteen-year-old Gerald and fourteen-year-old Sean already knew where fate was taking them. Together with friend Marc Gordon, who played keyboards, the three young soul singers began harmonizing and realized there was something in the mix. Dad's famous group wasn't the sole influence, however. These boys grew up on the varied styles of Marvin Gaye, the Isley Brothers, and the funky sounds of Sly and the Family Stone.

LeVert (the capital V makes a better logo) took their talents into the recording studio and emerged with a single, "I'm Still," and a contract with Atlantic Records. The group's 1985 debut album, *I Get Hot,* put LeVert in motion but went largely unnoticed. The following year, they produced their second album, *Bloodline,* from which the single "Pop, Pop, Pop (Goes My Mind)" did significantly better. The record made it to No. 1 on *Billboard's* soul chart in November 1986. Other singles from that release, "Let's Go out Tonight" and "Fascination," grazed the charts as well. The writing of the songs is a group effort, although Gerald is the main songwriter.

"My first goal was always as a writer," Gerald told *Scene* in February 1991. "I wanted to write music for the O'Jays."

After several attempts to produce a song his dad's singing group would accept, Gerald Levert achieved his goal in 1987 when his "Let Me Touch You" became both title and single for that year's O'Jays release. Interestingly, the record was in competition with LeVert's song "My Forever Love" (from *The Big Throwdown* LP), which ultimately rose to No. 2 on the R&B charts that same year.

Along with older brother Eddie Jr. (as road manager) and uncle Reggie Levert (tour manager), the group set out on the road, often opening for the O'Jays. By the time they played the Cleveland area's Front Row Theater on the first tour in 1986, and the prominent Apollo Theater in New York the following year, they captured the interest of a new generation of soul lovers. And the Levert brothers had no trouble finding an accountant and manager. Their cousin, Andy Gibson, who also manages the R&B duo Men at Large, was happy to oblige.

Their music is described as contemporary rhythm and blues with a decisive mix of rap (to appeal to young audiences) and crooning ballads (for their female fans). The combination has made LeVert a constant in the contemporary world of R&B.

LeVert released a third album, *The Big Throwdown,* in 1987. The first single from that LP, "Casanova," put LeVert permanently on the map. It quickly became No. 1 on every major R&B chart and made the pop charts as well, reaching No. 5 on *Billboard's* Hot 100. Another single from that LP, "Sweet Sensation," reached No. 4 on the R&B chart. The sons of a soul legend were a successful entity all their own.

Meanwhile, the group formed a writing and producing team that became Trevel Productions (Levert spelled backward) in 1988. Some of the artists they have worked with include Peaches and Herb, Barry White, Stephanie Mills, former Akronite James Ingram, Anita Baker, Patti LaBelle, Miki Howard, the Rude Boys, and Men at Large. Listening to the wise words of their father about the inner workings of the music business, Gerald and Sean's next step was to start up their own publishing firm, Trycept Music Publishing Company, to safeguard themselves against some of the well-known hazards of the industry.

In March 1988, LeVert was invited to the Grammy awards. "Casanova" was nominated for Best Rhythm & Blues Performance by a Duo or Group with Vocal, but it lost out to Aretha Franklin and George Michael ("I Knew You Were Waiting for Me"). Gerald Levert served as presenter, however, along with Miki Howard. The duo's "That's What Love Is" became a Power Pick/Air Play in *Billboard* and peaked at No. 4 on the R&B chart.

LeVert also released *Just Coolin'* in 1988, whose title track featured rap artist Heavy D. The song went to No. 1 on *Billboard*'s R&B chart, and another single, "Gotta Get the Money," reached No. 4. The "Addicted to You" single not only topped the charts once again but was included in the 1988 movie soundtrack *Coming to America*. In 1990 came *Rope a Dope Style*, which boasted three chart makers. "Baby I'm Ready," went all the way to No. 1, "All Season," hit No. 4, and the title song reached No. 7. The group released *For Real, Tho'* in 1993, just as Gerald Levert's solo career took off. His 1992 album, *Private Line*, peaked at No. 2 on the R&B chart, with successful singles "School Me" (No. 3) and "Can You Handle It" (No. 9). The album obviously pleased fans of both the father and son, as the duo's "Baby Hold on to Me" reached No. 1 by the end of that year.

Then, in 1994, Gerald Levert joined his father for an album simply titled *Father and Son*. And in 1998, his next solo effort, *Love and Consequences*, turned gold and took him on tour with Patti LaBelle. That release includes a cover of Bobby Womack's "That's the Way I Feel About You," and songs with friends Lazy Bone (from Bone Thugs-N-Harmony), Mary J. Blige, and Ken Dawg. Brother Sean also made it on the album with the song, "Point the Finger." "Humble Me" is a duet by another father/son team, Gerald and Lemicah, a third-generation Levert. It was the single "Taking Everything," however, that became the album's strongest effort, peaking at No. 3 on *Billboard*'s R&B charts. In keeping with family tradition, both brothers joined father Eddie to harmonize on the 1998 song "Where Would I Be," from the soundtrack to the film *Down in the Delta*.

Despite Gerald Levert's success as a solo artist, the group that shares his surname continues to produce music. In 1997, LeVert released *The Whole Scenerio*, a twelve-track CD that includes "Mam's House" and "Like Water." That same year, Gerald Levert once again took on a side project, this time with singers Keith Sweat and Johnny Gill, and formed LSG (Levert, Sweat, and Gill), from whom their fans will undoubtedly hear more.

Heavy Metal

Heavy metal's signature sound is believed to have emerged from Link Wray's 1958 "Rumble," with its fuzz-tone guitar distortion, and caught on big with early British rock bands like the Yardbirds ("A Heartful of Soul"), the Who ("I Can See for Miles"), Cream ("Sunshine of Your Love"), and Led Zeppelin ("Whole Lotta Love"). Yet, the name wasn't coined until *Creem* writer Lester Bangs used it in the midseventies, taking the term from passages of William Burroughs's 1959 novel *Naked Lunch*. Before that, the loud, harsh, screeching guitar wails were simply known as the hardest of rock sounds, ultimately perfected by Jimi Hendrix. From there came other influences in the heavy-metal world: Iron Butterfly ("In a Gadda Da Vida"), the Edgar Winter Group ("Frankenstein"), Blue Cheer ("Summertime Blues"), Steppenwolf ("Born to Be Wild," the first song to include the term "heavy metal thunder"), and Deep Purple ("Smoke on the Water"). Perhaps because of the extreme rebelliousness of its sound, the music has always had a heavily male-dominated audience.

The 1970s secured heavy metal's place in music history with the innovative and electric sounds of Black Sabbath (with Ozzy Osbourne), Kiss, AC/DC, Montrose (with lead singer Sammy Hagar), Slade, Ted Nugent (post–Amboy Dukes), and Judas Priest. By the 1980s, this hard-rock music form peaked with big sounds, big shows, and big hair. Groups that dominated the scene include Van Halen (with David Lee Roth), Def Leppard, Guns n' Roses, Mötley Crüe, Megadeth, and Quiet Riot, all of whom aided in mainstreaming this music genre. Soon there were such metal "offspring" as glam metal (Poison, Cinderella, Winger), speed metal (Slayer), thrash metal (Metallica, Motorhead), power metal (Anthrax, Overkill), and European melodic metal (Iron Maiden, Scorpions).

By the mid-1980s, heavy metal dominated the Cleveland music scene with several bands making their mark nationwide thanks to a few attuned college radio disc jockeys in their court. The most prominent of those who put the music first was Bill Peters of WUJC (John Carroll University, now WJCU), whose Friday night "Metal to Metal" show became the radio center of Cleveland's metal scene. In 1983, Peters formed Auburn Records, a label majoring in heavy-metal music, which gave area metal bands a forum for their sound. According to Peters,

When Tim [Stewart, WCSB deejay] was doing his own metal show, we decided to put together a compilation album of the best Cleveland metal bands. We felt it was important to give these groups recognition and exposure. We personally chose the bands and asked them to submit their tapes, and we picked the songs. Other than that, we didn't really know what we were doing; we just kinda winged it. But the album [*Cleveland Metal*] became pretty popular. Tim then decided not to do any more of those projects, but I had a great desire to continue. I had no money, and seven banks turned me down for loans. But I was determined to get something going on my own.

Peters's Auburn Records did get going and soon gained a credible reputation, particularly overseas. The exposure Peters gave these groups brought them an impressive amount of fans that spread to international waters—from Germany to Australia. The label released two compilations, *Cleveland Metal* (1983) and *Heavy Artillery* (1989). Each featured acts from the Greater Cleveland area as well as other cities: Philadelphia (Kraze), Columbus (Deau Volt), Cincinnati (Trigger Zone), and Denver (Titan Force). Peters continues to pump out his favorite music and showcase the bands on his long-running radio show (since 1982) while working for the Cleveland division of WEA (Warner/Electric/Atlantic).

In 1987, heavy metalists thought they found heaven when the nationally syndicated Z-Rock debuted in Cleveland on WCZR 107.3 FM. Playing nothing but heavy-metal music, the station gave great exposure to international, national, and local bands. The Dallas-based Satellite Music Network boasted affiliate stations with the Z-Rock format in fourteen cities, including Chicago, Columbus, and Grand Rapids. Although it filled a void, it did not beat the ratings game and was pulled by every city within two years (in Cleveland it lasted only ten months).

With the death of this viable outlet, it was once again back to college radio for area bands.

While acts like Purgatory, Jagged Edge, Wretch, Black Death (one of the only, if not the only, all-black metal bands in the country), Kidd Wicked, and Priscilla did get their raucous music played on college radio, the music was mostly considered too extreme for commercial airplay. Still, these '80s bands that walked on the wild side with their glitter outfits, platform shoes, flashy shows, and kick-ass attitude drew an intense fan base on the club circuit. By the end of the decade, Bill Peters proclaimed that the rock capital was also the "heavy-metal capital of the world."

Snake Rock (1978–)

This group began in Florida and continues on the West Coast, but its roots are in Cleveland. Cristian Cremona was born and raised in Lakewood. In 1977, he joined the uprooted Daytona Beach band, Raven Slaughter, and changed his name to Snake Rock Slaughter (later shortening it to Snake Rock).

In 1978, the guitarist left Raven Slaughter and moved briefly to Tampa, forming a new band with former Lakewood High School classmate, lead guitarist "Spike" Wray (né Raymond Sipka). The two soon returned to Cleveland. After a few drummers came and went, Tampa native Bert "Crash" Atkins joined in on drums and stayed for nearly a decade. When Spike invited his cousin, bassist Jeff Wray, to join the band, Snake Rock took over on rhythm guitar and shared vocals on most of the band's repertoire. The group's biggest fan, then and now, is Jeff Wray's mother, Betty Beitzel.

"Jeff was just two when he started playing an old guitar of mine that had two or three strings left on it," Beitzel says with a laugh. "When he became serious about it at fifteen, we got him his own guitar and he started taking lessons at DiFiore's Music

Store [on Lorain Avenue]. The other boys would come to practice in Jeff's bedroom, and I tell you, their music would rattle the doorknobs! I remember ironing to 'Smoke on the Water' for a straight hour because they'd play it over and OVER again, until finally I said, 'Enough already!' But I have always liked their music—even then." (Along with husband Luke, Beitzel attended nearly every show, filming them for future reference. Over the years, Beitzel has become the archivist of Snake Rock, saving every article as well as pieces of clothing from the band's glam-rock period. Those came in handy when the rock and roll mom wore one of the outfits—complete with chains and platform shoes—to a Halloween party.)

With the Beatles, Humble Pie, and Kiss as the group's main influences, Snake Rock immediately went into Agency Recording studio to record its first EP, *Animal Captivity*. "It's a terrible record," Snake admits, "We were so young, I think we sound like the Chipmunks. But hey, you gotta start somewhere."

Meanwhile, Snake Rock began its ascent in popularity on the North Coast. "After Raven, we were the first real hard rock band [in Cleveland] that played original music," says the band's namesake. "And I must say, there never would've been a Snake Rock without Raven Slaughter."

At first the group wore the trademark glitter and platform boots and held elaborate stage shows with strobe lights, machine-produced fog, and a fifteen-foot-long snake hanging over the drum set. Soon, the quartet decided less was more and opted for the standard T-shirt-and-jeans garb, though its frontman usually wore a snake vest, and the equipment was covered in snakeskin, in keeping with their name.

They also had a friend in Cleveland Connection club owner Dave Darus, who took them under his wing, became their manager, and began booking the band in his club as well as at Pirate's Cove, the Phantasy, Hennessy's, the Akron Civic Center, the Agora, and the Pop Shop.

"We played with a lot of bands that came through town," Snake Rock recalls. "When we started it wasn't fashionable to be an original band, so we'd open up for a lot of the local copy bands. Then after a few years, we were really popular and started opening up for national groups like Edgar Winter, Molly Hatchet, Humble Pie, Steppenwolf, the Godz, the Guess Who, and Uriah Heep."

In 1982, the group was selected for inclusion on *Playboy* magazine's "Playboy Music Poll" album. After being chosen by WMMS from hundreds of local entries, a blue-ribbon panel of A&R executives picked Snake Rock over eighty international entries. The LP was titled *Street Rock* and included Snake Rock's "Your Hot Love." With the support of WMMS, which put the single on its regular rotation list, this early heavy-metal group was heard throughout northeast Ohio. Their next release, "I Don't Care," b/w "Down and Dirty," won favorable reviews and sold well in the regional market. The next obvious step was to move to L.A.

Manager Dave Darus closed down his Cleveland Connection and accompanied Snake Rock to the West Coast in 1984. The group immediately got gigs at L.A. venues the Whisky A Go Go, the Roxy, the Country Club, FM Station, and Coconut Teaser.

And after three years of constant performing, the former Cleveland musicians got their due when they won station KNAC's "Battle of the Bands" competition in Long Beach. They were voted number one out of the ten best Los Angeles heavy-metal rock bands. As a result, their song "Can't Stay Home Tonight" was the lead track on Chrysalis/Rampage Record's compilation album *Pure Rock*. The event got them noticed, but by then the metal trend on the West Coast was fading fast.

"We were at the tail-end of the metal scene in L.A.," Snake says. "Soon after, people were tired of seeing all the Mötley Crües and Van Halen–type bands. By the time we reached our peak in L.A., record companies were no longer looking for those type bands, and we were skipped over constantly. But what could we do? Change who we were? Do something different just to get a record deal? I mean, we'd been doing it for so many years, there was no way. We'd been doing it longer than nearly all those other bands. So we just kept doing it."

After Atkins left in 1988, the group went through a series of drummers, including David Liston and Jeff Wray's brother, Dave. Then came another huge setback in 1995 when a car accident put both Snake Rock and Jeff Wray in the hospital and out of circulation. Jeff Wray had knee surgery as a result; Snake Rock nearly lost his arm. "I busted my arm in half and had to have it operated on," he says. "And it really messed up my tattoos! But my main concern, of course, was playing again. It took over two years and some heavy-duty physical therapy, but I'm glad to say I'm fully recovered."

In 1999 Snake Rock recorded nearly twenty original songs for consideration by one of the top engineers in rock history. According to Snake,

Roy Cicala [New York studio engineer] happened to walk in one of the studios while a friend was playing a CD of ours. He asked who we were and found out we weren't signed. Then he said, "Well, this guy's got some hits," referring to me, and he said he wanted to meet with us. We went to L.A. and the only thing he wanted from us was a promise that we'd record in his studio [Studio 56].

When you've been dormant for so long, you start losing hope. What's really wild is that after years of pushing ourselves, the doors just opened up without us even trying this time. It's weird, and it's great.

In addition to his music, Snake Rock sells rock and roll autographs and memorabilia. It started back when the aspiring musician began collecting anything relating to the Beatles. He boasts a room in his house solely dedicated to the Fab Four.

Snake Rock and Jeff Wray currently live in Las Vegas, while lead guitarist Mark Ricciardi resides in Los Angeles. A variety of professional drummers record and perform with Snake Rock, including Walter Garces, Tony Ferrante, and Cleveland native Kevin Valentine.

After twenty years, more than 2,000 shows, and numerous disappointments, this hard-rock band retains their Cleveland attitude by not letting time, changes, or setbacks keep them from making music.

Auburn Record artists
invade the streets, 1984.
*Photo by Anastasia
Pantsios. Courtesy of Bill
Peters.*

Breaker (1981–91)

Some of the most notable European heavy-metal bands—Iron Maiden, UFO, and
Scorpions—served as influences for one of Cleveland's foremost metal groups. But
rather than cover their material, Breaker chose to make it on their own original merits.

"We never wanted to do cover material," drummer Mark Klein notes. "We all agreed
we'd rather not play at all than play covers. We liked heavy metal a lot but never got into
the glam image of that period. It wasn't our style. We were just ourselves, playing our
brand of that style of music." The members came together from that mutual interest.

"I first started playing bass back in Maple Heights High School with Mark Klein
[later with Ether Net]," recalls Don Depew, who picked up his first guitar at age fourteen and taught himself to play. "Mark started writing songs right away. As time went
on, we all got into it." Klein's brother, Michael, was brought in on lead guitar, and Ian

Shipley on bass, and Depew then switched from bass to guitar. The group found its niche with the addition of lead vocalist Jim Hamar.

"Finding a decent singer was always a pain," Depew notes. "I mean, you can learn to play guitar, but not everyone has the voice to sing in a band. I had met Hamar earlier but knew him as a guitarist in another band. Then one day, he comes in with a tape that he sang on, and we thought, *Hey, great. He can sing!* Back then there was no real metal scene here. I'd gotten into some punk stuff like Pere Ubu years before and had always liked music that was different. I listened solely to college radio because that's the only place you could hear music like that."

Depew got hooked on heavy metal while working at the Lakeside One Stop. Once the quintet joined forces in 1983, they recorded a single, "Blood Money" (penned by Depew, Shipley, and Hamar), backed with "Afraid of the Dark" (by Mark Klein and Hamar). That same year, two other songs, "10 Seconds In" and "Walking the Wire," were included on the *Cleveland Metal* compilation, first released on Clubside Records by Tim Stewart (WCSB, Cleveland State University) and Bill Peters. The label would later become Auburn Records.

While the new group began working on their own material, fellow musician Snake Rock pulled them from the practice studio and pushed them onto the stage. "I saw their potential early on," he notes. "When I first heard them they were in a practice hall and had never played out. But I thought they were really good. So when club owners [who hired the Snake Rock band] didn't want us having an opening act I'd say, 'You're going to have both bands or we're not going to do it.' I really believed in them."

"When we first got together, we played a lot with Snake Rock," Depew confirms. "That's really how we got our start. Snake would have us open for them and was extremely supportive of us. Because of that, we were able to quickly build a following. Still, I never thought I'd hear a record of ours on 'MMS. But [disc jockey] Denny Sanders liked it ["Blood Money"], and he played it on his show. He also got us on one of the Coffeebreak Concerts. That was great."

By this time, with more metal bands coming out of the woodwork, Breaker found another ally in Peters. The WUJC deejay would become to Breaker what Brian Epstein was to the Beatles. "Bill saw one of our shows and came up to us later and said he really liked our music," Mark Klein recalls. "So we gave him some of our demos and he played them on his radio show. Soon after that, he started Auburn Records."

"I became like an extra musician in the group, not just this record label guy," Peters notes.

A lot of people in the business thought I was too personally involved. At one point, when I was in negotiations with Island Records, Breaker was being considered for a deal, and the A&R person said they'd sign them if we would agree to replace the singer with an Axl Rose type, because Guns n' Roses were really hot then. I said no way. That was one line I never crossed. There was a chemistry there. These guys weren't interchangeable chess pieces.

It was a very frustrating process when you're trying to get to the next step and are constantly coming up against things like that. The band realized my interest in them was what was best for them, not the money.

Breaker was not the gimmicky, flash metal band from L.A. or New York. Their sound was very nontrendy, and in my opinion, the band never wrote a bad song.

The group's European melodic metal sound brought regular listeners to the Cleveland Connection, the Pop Shop, and, later, the Phantasy, the Variety Theater, and the Empire. At the Agora, Breaker opened for the national bands on which they were weaned, such as Nazareth, Metallica, Uriah Heep, and Foghat. The group released its debut album in 1987. *Get Tough* included a rerecorded version of its 1983 single "Blood Money."

"The *Get Tough* album is probably one of the finest produced local releases of any type in Cleveland," Peters says. "It was done at Suma Recording [formerly the Cleveland Recording with local legendary engineer, Ken Hamann] by Ken's son, Paul Hamann, who spent a lot of hours and did an excellent job. The production is incredible." The LP was hailed by critics locally and internationally and sealed Breaker's European connection. Continues Peters,

I was very much in touch with the European market. I was a big fan and purchased a lot of imported records from the new wave of British heavy metal periods, bands like Saxon and Iron Maiden. I started playing all the '80s European metal music on my show because no one could hear these bands anywhere else. I also got into the magazines like *Kerrang!* and *Metal Hammer.*

So of course, after I started the label and putting releases out, I worked these magazines with my product, sending them everything. They got to know my label and really liked it, the quality and professionalism of it. They appreciated the effort I was putting into it, with a low budget and all. So the Europeans began gravitating to Auburn Records and the bands we featured. A writer from *Kerrang!* Howard Johnson, was a big Breaker fan and helped set things in motion for us over there.

Although they enjoyed more recognition in Europe, the quintet remained largely underground. Finally, after over a decade of trying to get their music noticed, time, circumstances, and lack of recognition caused Breaker to fall apart.

"The reason Breaker disbanded was never because of bad feelings, or it not working anymore," Peters notes. "The biggest factors were one of the guys' father got ill and he was devoting a lot of time to him. Then the studio they were working at, Chris Burgess' Beat Farm [Willoughby], closed down. After that, everyone started gravitating away from the band." Depew recalls: "I remember our last show was at the Empire, although we didn't know it then. But things unraveled right afterward."

"The tragedy of it all," Mark Klein says, "was that our second album, which was almost complete at the time we disbanded, was real strong. It was some of the best work we'd ever done."

Ten years after Breaker shattered, the band's music is still very much together. Members discovered their single "Blood Money" was selling for 150 deutsch marks in Germany (approximately seventy-five dollars in American currency). With such encouragement, the group rereleased its debut album in 2000 with added tracks to complete a double CD as well as a six-song EP, *Accept,* both, of course, on Auburn Records. The metal band with original members Depew, Mark and Michael Klein, Hamar, and former member bassist Brook Hodges returned to the stage in May 1999 at the Odeon in the Flats.

"They opened for the Michael Schenker Group that night," Peters says. "He [Schenker, former guitarist in Scorpions and UFO] had always been a longtime idol of the members, especially Michael Klein. I ran into Michael Belkin, and the idea of Breaker opening for them came up. So I pressed up some two-song CD singles and passed them out to the first 300 people at the show as a teaser for the upcoming release. Best of all, the guys got to play with their idol. So it turned out well, and was a good show." Mark Klein notes, "We deliberately didn't play it up because we didn't want it to come across as a big reunion thing. We just wanted to get together and play again and help promote the new release. So we were really pleased to see all these people who came to see us. It was like reliving our glory years."

Klein believes those glory years had a lasting effect.

Looking back, I think Breaker helped build awareness of the scene and of Cleveland. Because we got a lot of recognition from Europe, when people over there hear about a Cleveland band, they take notice now. I think we had at least a little to do with that. Locally, people considered us on the same level of many of the national bands that came through Cleveland. We had a great following. I also believe we opened a lot of doors for other local acts and forced club owners to realize a band didn't have to play strictly covers to bring in a crowd. That whole [metal] scene was fun and very healthy back then. We had our own little community, and often saw the same faces at our shows.

Peters adds:

I put a lot of money into them because I was a fan myself. I looked out for their interest more than any label normally would. The music was the main thing. It was a long-term goal to me, not the short dollar. I took pride in the quality of the product we put out. And those early years were really when I enjoyed it the most. When I did everything myself, on a shoestring budget. We made it happen and it was great. When it got to the point where I started dealing with other labels, you had those outside influences getting in the way of the music, the creativity, the fun. That poisons everything.

But to this day I feel Breaker was the best of all the area metal bands. Its music is timeless, not trendy. That's why there's still tremendous interest in them, particularly in Europe. They bucked the trend back then by being an *original* heavy metal band, and every [local] metal band today, from Mushroomhead to Cryptkicker, owe[s] something to Breaker. They paved the way for these bands.

Shok Paris (1983–89)

This group was also signed and produced by Auburn Records president Bill Peters. Their 1983 *Go for the Throat* LP sold a mere 3,000 copies, but it succeeded in putting Shok Paris on the elite list of Cleveland's most recognized heavy-metal bands.

Members did not all hail from the rock capital. Each came from a different city (Paris wasn't one of them), and they were brought together through a shared love of hard rock music. Its first lineup included Clevelander Ken Erb (lead guitar/background vocals); Maple Heights native Eric Marderwald (guitar/vocals); Marderwald's cousin, Warren native Bill Sabo (drums, later replaced by Jan Roll, then Danny Simmons); New Philadelphian Kel Berkshire (bass/vocals); and Clevelander Buddy McCormick (vocals).

"Buddy only lasted until we recorded the single for the *Cleveland Metal* compilation," says Marderwald, who first played in a band with Breaker's Mark and Michael Klein.

> It was real hard finding just the right singer for our band. We auditioned so many of them, and sometimes it was hilarious. You'd do a phone interview with them and they would sound great, you know, into the same things we were into. Then they would show up . . . .
>
> For example, a guy would be talking about all these vocal styles he had, then sing for us and couldn't carry a tune if his life depended on it. One time we knew we were in trouble when this guy arrives—an hour late—carrying a bag from Peaches Record Store with the two albums that had the songs he was supposed to sing. We thought, *Oh, oh, he doesn't know the words to the songs.* One was Van Halen's "Ain't Talkin' 'Bout Love," and when it was his turn to come in, he didn't. We kept trying it and he kept coming in at the wrong time. And then he lets loose, doing these total Isley Brothers moves, the splits, the spinning around, touching his toes. Then here comes the Rick James stage moves, and we just lost it! We were trying not to laugh, but we were in tears. He clearly wasn't the right one for our band!

Finally the bandmates found Vic Hix (né Hicks) singing in a group at a club in Steubenville, Ohio. They were ready for the next step. The group name, coined by Sabo, meant, according to Sabo, an interesting mix of strong, hard-driving energy with the graciousness of Paris, France. And the title proved fitting of their music. Three songs from their debut album made it to airplay, mostly on college radio. Deejays Bill Peters and Tim Stewart (also the group's manager) played the new group's songs often. The Shok Paris single "Go Down Fighting" appeared on Peters's *Cleveland Metal* compilation LP.

"It was hard getting your songs played on the bigger stations like WMMS," Marderwald says. "But I remember Spaceman Scott played 'Go Down Fighting' a couple of times, which we, of course, were real happy about."

Another single from that first effort, "Caged Tiger," was played by WMMS's top-dog deejays. The group that cited UFO, Scorpions, Judas Priest, and Thin Lizzy as influences, and whose image resembled those bands, soon came to the attention of the L.A.-based I.R.S. (International Record Syndicate).

"We were real proud of the fact that we, a metal band out of Cleveland, got signed to a national record label," Marderwald notes. "None of the other bands could say that at the time. Yet we continually were hard-pressed to get much airplay or regular gigs around town, save for a few clubs." Those clubs mostly included the Pop Shop, Shadows, Variety Theater, and Flash Gordon's, all of which supported early alternative bands. Shok Paris often opened up for national acts such as the Plasmatics, Exciter, Tallus, and Slayer when they played those venues. Through those opportunities, the group built their following.

"I used to see Shok Paris at Flash's, which was one of the best music venues on Lorain Road," recalls heavy-metal fan Craig Bobby. "One thing that makes a band really good—besides good songwriting, of course—is that it has to be able to execute it on stage, put on a good show. Shok Paris was one of those bands that could really pull it off."

In 1986, their debut *Steel and Starlight* was released on Auburn/I.R.S. Records. With this new recording, the group branched out and helped bring more awareness to the emerging Cleveland metal scene. Although Marderwald cites Erb as the main songwriter, the guitarist maintains that the songs were a group effort: "We'd come up with a cool riff or idea. Then usually me and Vic would come up with some lyrics. We all worked well together. The chemistry thing was there."

Upon the release of their debut album, the group hit the road, spreading their metal to other parts of the country. "We went on tour with Savatage, and they were a perfect match for us," Marderwald says. "They had the same style as us, so they were a good band to play with. Then in 1988, the record label put us up in a studio in California to record *Concrete Killers* LP. I remember during that time we were part of what was called a 'charity rock 'n' bowl,' where all the major record labels would rent out a bowling alley and we'd bowl for charity. There were so many celebrities there, guys whose music we really liked—Skid Row, Mötley Crüe, Alice Cooper. That whole period was one of my favorite memories."

The group's second I.R.S. album was to be the one that took them to star status in the metal world. Kevin Beamish, who gained a notable reputation for his work with Jefferson Airplane, REO Speedwagon, and the metal band Saxon, served as producer for that effort.

"Yeah, we had ourselves a good time in L.A.," Erb says, "but it was also, I think, our biggest mistake. I felt it took away a lot from what we originally set out to do. Our first record, all that mattered was the music. The songs were better and from the heart. When we went to L.A., it took our heads out of it. That whole scene affected us, and the album. It seemed real forced. The songs were more contrived. For example, one song I wrote some lyrics to, 'The Heat and the Fire,' was changed by the producer who wanted a more lovey-dovey tune. It just wasn't us."

The song, however, did get radio airplay, and a video was made that was shown on MTV's popular nighttime show *Headbangers' Ball.* "That was real interesting to do," Marderwald says. "They brought people in from out of town, and we shot it right in Cleveland. They came up with some great footage of the Flats area, trying to show the hardcore industrial look of Cleveland. And it fit our sound just great."

Shok Paris received still more national attention when they played a live concert on Z-Rock, and in 1985 their "Marsielles de Sade," b/w "Battle Cry," was included on a *Hit Parader* compilation, *The Wild Bunch,* with artists Lizzy Borden and Grim Reaper. And parts of *Go Down Fighting* and *On Your Feet* were included in the 1987 sci-fi film *The Hidden.*

But it wasn't enough. Malderwald notes,

Z-Rock was very supportive, and the live broadcast we did in Dallas, Texas, was great, and we went on a mini-tour with Lizzy Borden. But I guess we expected more. I remember one of the members from Lizzy Borden telling me they were playing gigs in places like Japan, and we were hoping to cross over to that level. But we felt the [record company] management wasn't doing what they could to get us recognized. For instance, most clubs have a designated night for certain types of music. And we'd come to do these shows in clubs on weeknights and find out we were playing the wrong night for heavy metal. Then we'd go to play a club in another city and find there had been no promotion, no ad in the local papers about us, nothing.

I don't think they knew what to do with us. They weren't that familiar with metal. Plus they were just getting started and had other artists like the Go-Go's and REM before they got big. So the promotions they were doing, we were telling them to do. It was discouraging because you think once you get with an L.A. or New York label, they'll do all that for you.

Then a tour where we were going to open for Black Sabbath fell through. So we weren't selling records because we weren't touring. So they said, "Well, we can't put you out there because you're not selling records." It was a catch-22. Financially we had problems, and everyone got aggravated and discouraged. We started heading off in different directions, and suddenly Shok Paris was a thing of the past.

The group has no intention of reforming or rereleasing their albums. "What's the point? You did it once," Erb says. "I mean, you're not the same person ten years later. You're not coming from the same place psychologically. Sure, technically we could remix the albums and make them better. But everything that goes into making a record, what's happening at the time you're making it, that all adds to it." Malderwald adds: "The thing is, it's hard to find people that, musically, you're really in touch with. Our group was so tight; we got along so well and we were good friends. The whole idea of trying to capture that over again . . . personally, I don't think it can happen."

Manimals (1982–88; 1997–)

Heavy metal as you've never seen it before.

—Breaker bassist Ian Shipley

"I think the most unique aspect of our band was we were able to cross over between heavy metal and punk and attracted fans from both genres. That was quite a feat back in the '80s," says founder/bassist/singer "Larry the Wolf" Cahill.

This heavy-metal/horror band was perhaps the most controversial group during its earliest days. The name was christened by Cahill, and the group played it up by dressing as half-man/half-beast, with claws, fur, and attitude. The Manimals originally formed in Toledo, but the most notable eighties lineup consisted of Wolf, his former North Olmsted classmate Dave Zart (a.k.a. "Dark"), and guitarist "The Wraith."

Cahill's childhood interest in horror films is the backbone of this enigmatic group. "I think I'm predisposed, there's something in my genes," Cahill laughs. "My heroes were Lon Chaney, Boris Karloff, Bela Lugosi. Like Alfred Hitchcock said, 'The fear is in the anticipation, not the payoff or whatever the end result.'"

Born in the Bronx, he moved to Cleveland in his midteens and says he graduated from the University of Transylvania. He was an early admirer of Kiss, particularly bassist Gene Simmons, who also has a passion for horror movies. The formation of the band, however, was happenstance.

"Actually the band started as a result of my interest in selling a comic book idea to a company in Chicago," Cahill recalls. "When I got turned down, I decided to turn the concept into a band and bring it to life by acting it out on stage and do it as a live presentation. We started playing around the Detroit area because that's where I was seeing groups like the Necros and Black Flag play. Plus I was going to the University of Toledo at the time."

As the Manimals began playing gigs in Toledo, they were invited to open for bands such as the Misfits, Government Issue, and Negative Approach. And after making their marks in Detroit, it was on to Cleveland in 1984.

"I think we were the first real hardcore/metal band to play Peabody's," Cahill notes. "They had local bands like Oroboros and national artists like Lone Justice and Belinda Carlisle. Then came us—totally different from any of that. We purposely sought out those venues because we were trying to break these genre barriers. We started having a diverse group of bands open for us, like Spudmonsters, The Guns, and Shadow of Fear. We've always prided ourselves on being very crossover."

The biggest fear for this group was that it would be perceived as a parody rather than a unique and strong rock and roll phenomenon. In forming and developing Cleveland's first horror-rock band, Cahill was exorcizing everyone's childhood demons.

From the start, these musical primates merged heavy metal, punk, and their own unique style into one "horror-core" formation. The group, then and now, is known for pumping high-energy stage theatrics into its repertoire. Upon introduction, the Manimals emerge from cages and slink onto the stage. They growl and hiss and are covered with hair—on their chests, faces, and thigh-high boots. And by all accounts, they rock—hard. A Manimals show is more than music; it explores theatrics reminiscent of the horror movies Larry the Wolf grew up on.

Their shows are always memorable, but one in particular stands out. Many fans recall the show at the Phantasy in 1985 when Larry the Wolf didn't like the actions, or attitude, of one audience member and proceeded to jump off the stage in the middle of a song, chasing the poor fool out of the club before returning to finish the set. (These guys are serious. Each member works out to keep his chiseled body ready to jump on stage at a moment's notice.)

Thrashing out its musical angst at Peabody's DownUnder, the Phantasy, and Shadows (the club that majored in metal), the group attracted hardcore fans at every show. They were a big draw at the Pop Shop, where they were the only band to play both Friday (punk) and Saturday (heavy metal) nights. In fact, the Manimals was the last band to play there (October 20, 1984, with Destructor opening) before the building that included the beloved Agora burned to the ground the following morning.

That same year, the Manimals made a vinyl appearance on an album called *Party or Go Home* on the California-based hardcore label Mystic Records. The group's "Things Under My Bed" was one of the *Forty Bands, Forty Songs, Forty Minutes* sampler LP. In 1986, the trio gathered at Suma Recording studio and emerged with a six-song vinyl EP *Blood Is the Harvest*. The songs, mostly penned by Cahill (including "White Zombie," "Island of Lost Souls," and the title track), were put in heavy rotation on Cleveland's college radio stations. Like many Cleveland bands, the Manimals attracted devotees throughout Europe, particularly in Germany and Italy, as well as in South America. That success came as a direct result of reviews printed in *Maximum Rock and Roll* and *Kick-Ass* magazines.

"We were young and didn't know," Cahill says of their first recording. "It was our first experience [doing an EP], and we did it all in one weekend. But it was well received and has even become something of a collector's item. Dark and I are still real proud of it. I get e-mails from kids telling me they pay forty to fifty bucks for it at these record conventions. I feel bad they're paying that much, and we're not the ones making anything from it. But I'm glad the interest is still there."

"I never really broke it up," he says of his Manimals. "My team just fell apart. It was really difficult finding regular gigs because people stopped going to the clubs. I think part of that was because there weren't enough good bands at that time capturing interest and drawing the crowds. Our shows did very well, but the clubs weren't going to make it solely on us. Our last show was in January 1988 at Diversions on Brookpark Road, and it was one of the best-attended shows we'd ever done."

From 1988 to 1997 the Manimals were in a "long hibernation." Cahill's interest was revived during the 1993 thirty-fifth anniversary "Famous Monsters" convention in Ar-

Larry the Wolf of Manimals. *Courtesy of Larry Cahill.*

lington, Virginia. And it was a call in 1996 from Misfits' bassist/founder Terry Only, inviting Larry the Wolf to make an appearance and sing some songs with the New Jersey band at the Odeon in May 1996, that brought the Manimals out of their lair.

"I was pleasantly surprised how many people remembered the Manimals and asked what happened to us," Cahill says. "I thought, *there's still life in this monster.*"

At the same time, former Manimals drummer Dark, who went on to earn a medical degree from Case Western Reserve University, expressed an interest in getting back with his old bandmate. "We hooked up and started rehearsing Larry's new songs together," Dark says. "And one thing led to another." It led to the Manimals' first outing in ten years at the Cleveland Metal '99 show (at the Odeon in the Flats). The trio, which got a wild reception, included old fan and guitarist Tim Dralle (a.k.a. Count Orlock).

"Tim's the guy I always felt belonged in the band," Cahill says. "He used to come see our shows in the '80s and shares the same interests. So I called him and told him Dark and I were getting back together and would he like to be a part of it? He said sure. Now, with this incarnation, we are a thousand times better than we were previously."

The group went into 609 Recording (Don Depew's Bedford studio) to lay tracks for a new six-song CD, which was available in time for the 1999 release. They truly came back from the dead. This group that was ahead of its time in the 1980s falls right in with today's goth scene, although Larry the Wolf emphasizes it is far removed from that genre:

"I really think people misconstrue the image of horror. I'm influenced by classic horror, not the Freddy Krueger or Jason stuff. That's shocking, but it isn't classic horror. True horror can be psychological. It can also be fun, like "Frankenstein Meets the Wolfman" and "Island of the Lost Souls." Too much of it today is gross and depressing. Some of these groups that call themselves horror are simply out to shock someone. The kids that are into goth, most of them are listening to very depressing music. It's somber. It's downbeat. It doesn't inspire you. All these bands that claim to be horror bands know nothing about horror because if they did, I'd see them at these horror conventions with Christopher Lee, who is a horror icon.

The Manimals' latest release is the full-length CD *Horror-Core*. Larry the Wolf underlines the fact that this regrouping is not to be looked on as a "comeback attempt." "I treat those days [the 1980s] as a prologue to the true Manimals experience in 1999."

Destructor (1984–92; 1998–)

This band had a strong, promising start. But one horrible moment destroyed the group's drive and energy. "Dave's [Iannicca] murder just knocked Destructor right off its feet and ultimately became the beginning of the end," says guitarist Patrick "Rabid" Wolowiecki. "It was so disheartening. There had been such a chemistry there. We were a real family unit."

Bassist Iannicca, at age twenty-three, was killed by an intruder at a private party outside the group's practice hall in the early morning hours of New Year's Day 1988. That action irreparably damaged the most promising Cleveland metal band of the era, which just a year earlier had been enjoying such success.

"I saw Destructor at the Pop Shop in October 1984," recalls Bill Peters. "I didn't know it at the time, but it was the band's first gig. They were louder, thrashier, noisier, faster than any band in Cleveland. Just an absolute wall of noise. Very raw, unrefined. Nobody saw the potential in them, but for some reason I saw it. I liked them, their songs, and most of all, their sense of fun. It was clear they needed work, but the potential was there. And to everyone's amazement, I decided to work with them."

This spirited band was formed by two Euclid High School graduates, Dave "Overkill" Just (guitar, vocals), and Wolowiecki (guitar), who brought in drummer Matt "Flammable" Schindelar and bassist Paul "Warhead" Habat (son of renowned local polka player Eddie Habat). The quartet basked in the heavy sounds of Judas Priest, Bachman-Turner Overdrive, and particularly Kiss. "The minute I saw Kiss at the Richfield Coliseum in January 1978, it was all over," Wolowiecki says. "I thought, now this is it!"

The bandmates were fans of the Manimals and were thrilled to open up for them for their first live show on October 20, 1984. After playing other venues such as Shadows, Cheeter's (later Flash Gordon's), and the Agora, the group went into Suma Recording to lay down tracks for their debut album, *Maximum Destruction*. The music, Dave Just notes, was a group effort. By this time, bassist Dave "Holocaust" Iannicca, another Euclid High alumnus, had joined, replacing Habat. The LP was released on Auburn Records in December 1985.

"This wasn't a technically oriented band so the production may not have been perfect," Peters says of that recording. "But I wanted to translate on record the fun the band projected on stage. The raw energy that was so evident in their live shows. That was our goal. Not to make sure every guitar note was perfect or every drum hit was perfectly in sync. So in focusing on that, we did things such as throwing in an intro I created, where we smashed a TV set in the studio with a sledgehammer. We had these little voices thrown into a song. Things like that, to make you smile a bit. And I think we came off with a good record."

The full-length LP quickly sold more than 5,000 copies and was put on regular rotation on all the local college stations, as well as the nationally syndicated Z-Rock. The songs "Bondage" and "Pounding Evil" were particular fan favorites. Like the other Auburn Records releases, the album got good response in Europe and was picked up by Road Runner Records, which released it in Canada and Japan. "We got phenomenal response in Europe," Wolowiecki says. "We got flooded with fan mail from there. If we would've concentrated our efforts in that direction, I'm sure it would've made a difference. Probably our biggest mistake was not touring Europe at that time."

Instead, they stayed closer to home, playing locally and opening for national acts, including Slayer and Megadeth. Destructor's exuberant performances (including smashing drums and guitars) proved that this band could really rock, complete with the customary chains, leather, and wall of noise that dominated their shows.

"Yeah, they wore all the chains, leather, and spikes," Peters says. "But it was their performances and how they bonded with their audience that really impressed me. This was before the stage diving and mosh pits, but when you saw a Destructor show, the band and crowd were one. There was no line drawn between stage and crowd. The people loved them."

Throughout this active heavy-metal period in Cleveland, Destructor and their comrades remained largely underground for lack of commercial airplay. But this group, while not noted for musical refinement, managed to get its share of gigs—thanks to Bill Peters.

"I had them open up for every national act we could because I wanted people to see their live shows," he says. "One time when Anthrax played Peabody's, they had no stage room. The bass drums were literally halfway sticking off the edge of the stage, into the crowd. But they stole the show. Even under the most aggravating circumstances you sometimes get handed from headlining acts, like no sound check or bad lighting, they would consistently win the crowd over."

The group that few believed in became one of the biggest draws and most entertaining bands on the North Coast, which is why the untimely death of its bass player was even more poignant. Destuctor had big plans for 1988. It had caught the attention of New York–based Island Records and was busy planning out its next album. On New Year's Eve 1987, the excited musicians gleefully hosted a party for friends at their practice hall in Euclid. As the night got underway, an acquaintance of the band arrived with a man no one knew. Peters explains:

> This one guy, who knew the members, was at a bar down the street. When he went to leave, this other guy came with him. He was obviously drunk and became obnoxious. They asked him to leave, several times. Finally he left but stayed out in the parking lot. They were worried he'd damaged their cars or something, so Dave went down [with Wolowiecki] and said, "Hey, we don't want any trouble, please leave." That's when the guy pulled out a ten-inch knife and stabbed him in the heart. Pat and the other guys chased him, tackled him, and held him down until the police came. Dave died soon after, with his fiancée there, who he'd just given a ring to on Christmas Day.
>
> That was so typical of Dave to try to reason with the guy. He was always the peacemaker. People might think that because he was this heavy metal guy, he was this rebellious sort, but he wasn't at all.
>
> Then we had to endure that whole trial. And of course, the defense lawyer was trying to make it look like this metal band called Destructor must have provoked him. So not only was Dave murdered, but they were trying to drag his name through the mud. It was a real tough period—ugly experience.

Iannicca's killer, Robert Bedzyk, received a sentence of fifteen years to life and was denied parole in 1998, largely due to the efforts of his victim's friends and family, who continually write letters to the parole board.

The decision to remain together after the traumatic blow of their bass player's sudden death was not an easy one. Initially, with most of Iannicca's bass licks already recorded, along with other tracks, the group was to release the second album, *Decibel Casualties,* and dedicate it to their fallen friend. Those plans, however, never materialized.

Destructor kicked on but had trouble replacing Iannicca. A series of bassists followed, including Brook Hodges, Jeff Charest, and, in 1990, Habat—just in time for the "Heavy Artillery Show" at the Empire that year. Bassist Tim Greene played from 1991 to 1992. Longtime drummer Matt Schindelar left the band in 1991 to be replaced by Eric Biris. By the following year, it was apparent that the end was near.

"It was just too hard to find someone on Dave's level as far as writer and personality goes," Just says. "The band started out with the four of us and we jelled so well. Maybe it was our fault, but it became a revolving door after awhile, and we just got tired of that."

"As far as we're concerned," Wolowiecki says, "Destructor never really broke up. We were just a victim of circumstances. We really tried to keep going. After Dave's death, we got Brook Hodges from Chicago. He was a great guy and good bass player, but no one was really in the mood to have anyone but Dave there on stage with us. It wasn't Brook's fault, but we were moping around and basically in shock. So he left and joined Breaker."

The early '90s saw the rich and promising heavy-metal scene in Cleveland diminishing. And Peters believe much of that was due to Destructor's tragedy.

When Dave was killed, it not only symbolized the end of Destructor, it marked the end of the Cleveland metal scene. It was definitely a turning point. It took a lot out of me because Dave Iannicca wasn't just a band member, he was my good friend. Losing him kind of zapped me, and I lost my motivation to do anything. It was all a struggle after that. Not only was Destructor's future up in the air, but I was deeply, emotionally, affected. I, of course, wasn't the only one keeping the metal scene together in Cleveland, but I was certainly one of the driving forces. We all were a tight-knit group, like a family. So when I, the coordinator of all this, stopped doing it, there was no direction. Sad to say, the whole scene pretty much collapsed after that.

In 1998, talk about getting back together and a resurgence of European interest brought Destructor back into the limelight. The band reemerged to play the Cleveland Metal '99 show that spring. Later that summer, Destructor participated in the sixth annual "World Series of Metal" held at the Agora. The group released *Maximum Destruction* on CD (on France's Listenable Records label), which includes previously unreleased tracks recorded with Iannicca.

Their band's new bass player, Eric Reineke, they agree, helps bring Destructor back into focus. "We haven't really changed that much," Just says of the band's rebirth. "Our sound is still the same. We still have the same ideas about what we want to do. We're picking up right where we left off."

Alternative Comes to the Fore

Death of Samantha (1983–90; 1992)

Named for the title of a Yoko Ono song, Death of Samantha began with a impromptu gig that got the group's frontman fired from his day job. Drummer Steve-O will never forget it.

It was August 24, 1983. John [Petkovic, guitar/vocals/songwriter] was working at the Parma Heights Ground Round as a busboy, and the restaurant used to have live music, usually acoustic acts. We were just a three-piece then, with David James on bass. This particular night they didn't have an act lined up, and John's boss was out of town. So John tells the interim manager he had a band that could play that night. Well, the guy had no idea and said "okay." So we put up on the marquee, "Playing Tonight Live, Death of Samantha." The guy didn't have a clue.

Now there were always a lot of older people in the restaurant, and we had John Cundiff, with his acoustic guitar, open the show. His music was laid-back, Neil Young–type songs, so he was perfect for that place. Then we got up there and immediately banged out our own version of "I'm Not Your Steppin' Stone" and "Be-Bop-A-Lu-La"—Sex Pistols style.

These people are sitting there with their steaks and lobsters, thinking, *Oh my God, what is this?* So after a couple more songs like that, people started complaining and the manager comes over and politely asked us to tone it down. Well, telling us that was like adding fuel to the fire. We cranked it up more, and the music got louder and rougher. Pretty soon, the guy cuts the power on us. But by then we'd almost completed a whole set, so we were happy. It was our first gig! Suffice it to say, when the big boss got wind of it the next day, John was immediately dismissed. So he suffered for his art.

After that memorable debut performance, Death of Samantha took jobs wherever it could, mostly at the Phantasy, the Pop Shop, the Cleveland Underground, and the Lakefront. The group also played often at JB's. Six months after that first gig, the rebellious trio sought out lead guitarist Doug Gillard, making DOS a quartet—and a punk-glitter one, at that.

"We dressed for the part," Gillard, then twenty-one, recalls. "I was really into the '70s glam look. I'd wear these sort of girlish, stretch-denim, flowery pants, with high Gene Simmons–type platforms and feather boas. Of course, I can't do that anymore, I've lost too much hair!"

"I was more of the class clown," admits Steve-O (né Eierdam), who got the idea for his name from Ringo and also doubles as an Elvis impersonator. (He owns more than two hundred Elvis albums and several Elvis-style outfits.) "I'd come up on stage and do a skit or something before the band went on, to sort of prime the audience. And I was always dressed in something crazy. I had a jumpsuit à la the more bloated version of Elvis, and once I had this big rug coat and wore it all night. I'll tell you, that was torture."

The group was influenced by both international and local musicians. Gillard was a WOBC radio deejay when he joined. Thus, the music he played on his radio show was the music he brought into Death of Samantha: the glam sounds of David Bowie, Roxy Music, and T. Rex. Steve-O brought in the glitter and musical style of Elvis; James idolized James Dean and was a fan of the Dead Kennedys and Cheap Trick; Petkovic was a Velvet Underground enthusiast. The members were all fans of Cleveland rockers Pere Ubu, the late Peter Laughner (they covered his "Sylvia Plath"), and the popular groups of the day, Easter Monkeys and Terrible Parade. Gillard calls their sound "the thinking-man's underground rock."

By 1985, with Petkovic's songwriting skills, the group felt confident enough to begin recording. They produced two singles on the new but short-lived St. Valentine's label. The first one, "Amphetamine," b/w "Simple as That," played on local college radio, as did "Coca Cola and Licorice," b/w "Listen to the Mockingbird." Both immediately sold out the first pressing of a thousand copies. Petkovic paid for a second pressing of the latter single by hocking his guitar. An album was soon to follow on the independent, New York–based Homestead Record label, *Strungout on Jargon* (1986). A twelve-inch EP, *Laughing in the Face of a Dead Man*, was released that same year. To promote their releases, the group hit the road on an East Coast 1986 mini-tour that included Philadelphia (Kennel Club), Boston (T.T. the Bear's), Hoboken, New Jersey (Maxwell's), and New York City (CBGB).

With record distribution both in the States and abroad, and with favorable reviews in *Creem* and *Option* (in which the group was called "The Great White Hope of Cleveland Rock"), the band caught the attention of fans as far away as France, Germany, and Greece. But once again, at home, the group got kicked out of a gig.

"This was New Year's Eve 1985," Gillard recalls. "We were playing the Phantasy and were supposed to shut down at 2:00 A.M. So right in the middle of a song, they pulled the plug on us. We didn't think that was right. I got mad and threw a few beer bottles against the wall. We were banned from the club after that. Well, at least for a while."

In 1987, bassist David James left and was replaced by Dave Swanson, previously of the Reactions. Then DOS released *Where the Women Wear the Glory and the Men Wear the Pants* (1988). *Come All Ye Faithless* was released on Homestead in 1990. The releases were recorded by former Wild Giraffes bassist Chris Burgess at Beat Farm Recording Studio in Willoughby.

Death of Samantha was thrilled when they got to open for Iggy Pop at the Phantasy Theater in 1988. A year later they took off for a West Coast tour that included California clubs Nite Moves (Huntington Beach), Ragi's (Hollywood), Covered Wagon (San Francisco), and the Berkeley Square Marina. A few stops had DOS headlining, with Smashing Pumpkins, Gin Blossoms, and Nirvana—then unknown acts—opening for *them*.

"There was one gig that counts as one of my biggest regrets," Steve-O says. "It was at Green Lime Station in Boston, 1989. Nirvana wasn't even on the bill, but they wanted

Death of Samantha, ca. 1990. *Left to right:* Dave Swanson, John Petkovic, Steve-o, Doug Gillard. *Photo by Steve Wainstead.*

to play, so they opened for us. We met them before the show and got to talking back-stage. Cobain asked for my autograph. Then he brought out their *Bleach* album. He was going to sign it, but I sort of dismissed it. Of course, I feel bad about that now!"

In 1989, bassist/guitarist Marky Ray came in for a brief stint. Ray had played in popular, local underground bands Terrible Parade and Death on a Stick as well as the Boston-based Lyres. By 1990, differences with their record label about promotion brought Death of Samantha to a standstill. The group decided to disband, playing a final show at the Empire with Ray on bass.

Death of Samantha resurfaced briefly in 1992, playing an occasional gig at their old stomping grounds, mostly the Phantasy. During this period, the group's original members were invited to be special guests at a wedding, and for the third time in its illustrious career, the band's antics caused its music to be cut off. This time they had no one to blame but Elizabeth Taylor.

"This guy, who was a big fan of ours, invited us to his wedding at the Ritz-Carlton," Steve-O explains. "Robert Lockwood Jr. played at the reception, and we were just guests. There was me, John, Dave Swanson, and Doug Gillard. Later that night, when Lockwood was finished, we got up and jammed. We did Neil Young's 'Hey, Hey, My My,' and it was about 4:00 A.M. in the morning. Elizabeth Taylor was staying in a suite right above the ballroom because she was making an appearance the next day at the Parmatown Mall to promote her perfume. She complained to management. That was it. We were done."

Death of Samantha fell by the wayside as members' interests went in different directions. The group did reunite once again, in February 1998, at Pat's in the Flats for a going-away party for their friend Steve Wainstead, a prominent figure in the '80s underground scene.

Steve-O ponders why DOS never hit big nationally. "We had two strikes against us," he says. "First, I think we were a little too early. We were just ahead of that underground movement that finally erupted. Then again, that's what also made it so fun. We had our own private clique. The other thing was, truth be told, we were from Cleveland. So there was that stigma throughout the industry that 'nothing is happening there.' On top of that, we were a band from Parma. For those who remember Ghoulardi, it wasn't a town people took too seriously. But being a part of that band was a biggie for me. Everything seemed to click and I was a fan of everyone in the band. I thought it was the best gig in the world."

Today, Steve-O handles advertising for the *Plain Dealer* and is a video enthusiast who has collected vintage film clips of several Cleveland groups in action. Petkovic is a writer for the *Plain Dealer* with his own daily column, "Time Out." In addition, he is founder/songwriter/guitarist for the '90s band Cobra Verde. Gillard had a stint in Cobra Verde and currently plays in Gem and the Dayton-based group Guided by Voices. Swanson, another Cobra Verde alumnus, is presently in New Salem Witch Hunters. He also works a day job at the My Generation music store. Over the years, Marky Ray has worked as a tour manager, production manager, and road technician for various bands nationwide and participated in Lollapalooza '91 and '92. He currently plays guitar in New Salem Witch Hunters and the Akron-based 3D.

New Salem Witch Hunters (1984–)

"I grew up on those old 45s," recalls singer/songwriter Dave Atkins, whose live performances earned him a reputation as one of the wildest rockers in Cleveland.

> I had these three girl cousins who gave me these little Disney records I'd play at 78-speed. And my mom worked as a waitress in Painesville and knew the guy that changed the records in the jukebox. There were records like "Charlie Brown" by the Coasters, "Please Don't Drag That String Around" by Elvis, and one of my favorites, "Western Movie" by the Olympics. That was on the Demon label, and I liked the logo, with the devil head and pitchforks. And the neighbor kids had older brothers who had Beatles and Beach Boys records lying around. First album I went out and bought was *Magical Mystery Tour*. When the "Paul is dead" rumor erupted, I started playing all my Beatles records backwards.
>
> Later, I got into Led Zeppelin, Jefferson Airplane, Mothers of Invention, and Bob Dylan, particularly his "Motorcycle Nightmare" which inspired my first poem.

New Salem Witch Hunters was formed in 1984, though the seed was planted years before, when Atkins and schoolmate Tom Fallon formed a friendship born out of their mutual rock and roll interests.

"I met Tom Fallon in the lunchroom at Shore Junior High School," says Atkins. "I had just gotten the Jimi Hendrix album, *Electric Ladyland,* for my birthday in November 1973, and we started talking about it. We learned we had a lot of the same interests in music, and we were both record collectors."

While attending Mentor High School during 1975–78, the two friends discovered the emerging punk movement and embraced it. Iggy and the Stooges' "Raw Power" and songs by New York Dolls, the Velvet Underground, Patti Smith, and the Sex Pistols gave these East Side music lovers the inspiration for Cleveland's self-described "psychedelic rock band"—punk style.

"As I recall, Dave came up with the name," guitarist Fallon says. "We were into those weird '60s bands like the Thirteenth Floor Elevators. Dave is really into history, so we first called ourselves North Salem Witch Hunters [tied into the Salem Witch trials] after the New Hampshire town that predates Columbus's arrival, known as America's Stonehenge. We came up with New Salem Witch Hunters, which we thought would look cool on a record."

As previous members of local rock groups Frenzy and Revolver, the two set the stage for what would become their best-known band. They knew, however, they needed just the right personalities for what they had in mind.

"Sometime in '84, Fallon and I saw keyboardist Jim Wilson during a Clinical Brain Death Show at the Cleveland Underground in the Flats," Atkins recalls. "We went backstage to meet him. We immediately knew this was the guy we needed 'cause he fell asleep while we were talking to him! The group became me, Fallon, Wilson, our drummer from Revolver, Sam Petrello, and bassist Lair Matic" (later replaced by Jeff Herwick).

The band debuted at the Phantasy Nite Club in September 1985, opening for local groups the Reactions and Death of Samantha. It was there that Atkins and Fallon first met Reactions drummer Dave Swanson, who later played in Death of Samantha and Cobra Verde. In 1991, Swanson began a long association with this band, playing drums, guitar, and, for one show, bass.

In 1986, this group of self-taught musicians released their first single on the new St. Valentine record label. The A-side was "Falling"; the B-side was a Dylan tune, "I Wanna Be Your Lover." Then came a self-titled album, released on Herb Jackson Records (the label of former Wild Giraffes members Chris Burgess and Al McGinty) and recorded in Willoughby's Beat Farm Studio. In most of their earlier compositions, Atkins wrote the words while Fallon created the music. One song, "Fog," was written by Jim Wilson. Many of the songs' themes are dark and thought-provoking. Atkins, a history buff with special interest in man's inhumanity to man, sometimes interjects the atrocities of war and crime into his lyrics. He acts out his anger on stage, which often gives the audience something to talk about the next day.

"I was usually too into playing to notice what Dave was doing," Fallon says. "But I do remember seeing him on fire. He had bought what he thought was a genuine German WWII coat and later found out it might be a fake. So on stage at the Phantasy one night, he ignited it—while still wearing it. He singed his hair, but other than that he came out of it pretty good!"

Another time Atkins, while standing on the bar (as he often does, just before he dives into the audience), hit his head on the moving ceiling fan. Although he cut his head and was bleeding, the show went on. And so did their recordings. "Falling" was played so often on college stations that it was included on Epic's 1987 *America's Best Unsigned Bands, Volume II*. The New Salem Witch Hunters was the only Cleveland band on the compilation. In July 1988, they released another single, "She's Got Wheels," backed with another Dylan song, "Quinn the Eskimo." In 1990, the group released their second album, *Strange Is Truer Than Fiction*. Also in 1990, their songs "Down Draggin' Down," "900,000," and "Unnatural Blonde" were included on the *Hotel Cleveland, Volume II* compilation.

Through the years, the group has maintained a dedicated following with its punk-edged, garage sounds at the Phantasy, Babylon A Go Go, the Grog Shop, Peabody's, Euclid Tavern, and the Agora. They have opened for Johnny Thunders, Salem 66, Screaming Trees, and Chesterfield Kings. With Atkins's stage theatrics, the quintet is a colorful fixture on the local music scene. The current lineup includes Atkins, Fallon, Wilson, Swanson, and Herwick.

The group went on their only tour in 1989, which included Philadelphia, New York, and Cambridge. Along for the ride was bassist Marky Ray, who was fast becoming what he describes as a "rock 'n' roll mercenary," having toured with bands such as the Lyres, Nine Inch Nails, Soundgarden, Ministry, and the Jim Rose Circus. In 1993, the New Salem Witch Hunters released "Dead Man's Girl," b/w "New Curves in School" (the titles from two songs of '60s duo Jan and Dean), on the Pittsburgh label Get Hip Records. Their 1996 release, *Hotsauce and Happenings,* received much airplay (and somehow found its way to Finnish radio). Their most recent CD is *Colonial Root Cellar* (1998).

"The lyrics have always been crazily psychedelic," says Atkins, a mail carrier by day. "To this day nobody really gets what these songs mean. It's just weirdness. But I think the thing that keeps us together is we don't burn ourselves out by playing out often, and we've never done any major touring."

Despite playing out a mere handful of times during the previous year, the New Salem Witch Hunters won for "Best Alternative/Underground Act" in the 1999 *Free Times* awards.

The Age of the Tribute Band

Tribute bands are now common draws in nightclubs. Everywhere around the country there are bands that honor favorite groups by playing their songs and often naming themselves after one of those tunes. The basic difference between cover, or copy, bands and tribute bands is that the former plays a mix of various artists' songs. The latter devote all their time and energy into "becoming" the band of choice. They not only play that group's repertoire, but band members also dress like their idols and mimic their stage acts—right down to strutting on stage like Mick Jagger or swigging pints of Jack Daniels à la Mötley Crüe (although no one usually goes as far as driving a Harley

Davidson on stage like Judas Priest's Rob Halford). For the bands, it has become the perfect vehicle, financially and in terms of longevity. For fans, it is the closest they can get to the real thing. And considering the cost of big-act concert tickets, where the average price is anywhere from $20–$200 (some paid $500-plus to see the Rolling Stones during their 1999 tour), it is undoubtedly a bargain. As a result, club owners readily hire tribute bands.

Throughout the nation, there are tribute nuggets for every taste. In the Cleveland area alone, there are hundreds. Among those that have rocked the North Coast since the trend began in the early 1980s are Substitute (the Who), 1964 (Beatles), Mojo Risin' (Doors), Ozmosis (Ozzy Osbourne), Sugar Magnolia (Grateful Dead), Virtual Halen (Van Halen), Wish You Were Here (Pink Floyd), Morrison Hotel (Doors), Street Survivor (Lynyrd Skynyrd), Powerage (AC/DC), Mersey Beats (Beatles), Battery (Metallica), and British Steel (Judas Priest). There's even a Michael Stanley tribute band, Stagepass. This group formed in 1990 and has earned its own impressive fan base that is as devoted as the originals.

The vocalist/frontman for British Steel, Tim "Ripper" Owens, was so good he ultimately replaced the original heavy-metal band's founder/vocalist Rob Halford. Owens related the story to Jane Scott in 1998. "Two fans videotaped our British Steel band show in Erie, Pa., back in '95. I remember one of them said she'd send it to Judas Priest, but I didn't believe it." Unknown to him, however, the fan happened to be the girlfriend of Judas Priest's drummer, Scott Travis. The fantasy came true when the band's manager got in touch with Owens. After auditioning (just one line from "Victim of Changes"), the Akron native was in. The story was so unusual that the *New York Times* did a feature on the fan that joined the band.

"We had all been musicians for years," keyboardist Jim Powell of Stagepass says of his band's origins. "When we first got together, we hadn't even thought of being a tribute band. But when we began to rehearse, we decided to do a couple of Michael Stanley songs because we all loved the music. We did 'Midwest Midnight' and 'Nothing's Going to Change My Mind.' When we heard Kelly Derrick sing those songs, we were just blown away. We were amazed to hear how much he actually sounded like Michael. So we decided to do more of their songs. And that was it. We became Stagepass." The rest of Stagepass includes guitarist John Nichols, bassist Colin Fitzpatrick, and drummer Kevin Morgan.

"My sister told me about them and how much they sounded like MSB," says devout Michael Stanley fan Kathy Fronckowiak. "But I was skeptical. When I went to see them, I deliberately turned away from the band and just listened, to see how good they really were. And I was shocked. The band not only could play all the songs well, but the lead singer sounded eerily like Michael. And believe me, I would know!"

What does Michael Stanley himself think of a band going around "his town," playing music he and his bandmates worked so hard on through the years? "I think it's great," Stanley says. "I had heard about them, then someone sent me a tape of their music. When I first listened, I tell you, it was freaky. And it's weird. Truthfully I didn't think that [tributes] should happen to you until you're dead!"

The biggest tribute band in Cleveland has to be Moonlight Drive, which honors the Doors. When Clevelander Bill Pettijohn formed Moonlight Drive in March 1981, tribute bands were unheard of. (If one researches the longevity of any nationwide tribute band, it appears Pettijohn's band was possibly the first.)

"I got the idea one night at Tommy's in Rocky River," recalls former Dragonwyck frontman Pettijohn.

It was Thanksgiving Eve 1980, and I was watching the Bowlers [with former members of the Eric Carmen band] perform. Later that night, I jumped on stage at one point and started doing "Light My Fire," and it literally brought the house down. No one could believe I could sound that much like Jim Morrison, least of all me. I surprised *myself!* Everybody was flippin' out. So afterward I went to the bar, got a beer, turned to my friend, Don Krueger, who later ended up drumming for Moonlight Drive, and said, "I'm puttin' together a Doors band."

I called [guitarist] Tommy Brame the next day and said, "Let's do this." I think all the guys were hesitant at first. But I told them it would be something fun to do and probably only last a few months or so. But it really caught on and took us all by surprise.

Moonlight Drive celebrated its eighteenth anniversary in March 1999 at the Flying Machine in Lorain. Although members have come and gone (Pettijohn estimates the list to over thirty), the original lineup was Brame (guitar), Tim Layman (bass), Mark Casterline (keyboards), and Bruce Moore (drums). The group added saxophonist Ray Varga in their quest to put their own slant to the Doors' sound. Other notable members over the years included Don Krueger (Eric Carmen Band, American Noise), Billy Sullivan (Beau Coup, Club Wow), and Michael Cartellone (who went on to Tommy Shaw and Damn Yankees).

After continually selling out the Agora and the Cleveland Connection, Moonlight Drive hit the road. In the years of playing the Lizard King, Pettijohn and his band of musicians have spread their Doors' repertoire from Cleveland to Boston to L.A. and beyond. In December 1981, they played to a sold-out crowd in Chicago's Park West. That same tour, they opened for Grand Funk at L.A.'s Aragon Ballroom. In 1982, they played to 50,000 people at the Chicago Fest, where they opened for E-Street saxophonist Clarence Clemons. From there they went north to Toronto, Ottawa, and Montreal, where another North Coast band, Clevelend, had already established a huge fan base. Pettijohn notes his favorite places to play were in Nova Scotia and Newfoundland.

In its first few months, the members released a four-song EP of Doors tunes. The self-titled release (on Agora Records) included their own creative twists to "Whiskey Bar," "Back Door Man," "Build Me a Woman," and "Gloria." When the band went to Los Angeles and played at the Whisky A Go Go's biggest rival, the Country Club, Pettijohn got noticed by Jim Morrison's sister, Anne Graham, and her husband, Alan. Impressed, the couple helped open doors for the aspiring actor, who had studied theater in college and acted in plays at Lakewood's Beck Center for the Arts.

From that meeting came Pettijohn's film debut, a cameo appearance in the horror movie *Demonville Terror*. And in a case of art imitating life, the frontman portrayed a rock star in the 1983 movie *Strangers in Paradise,* for which he, Brame, and Layman wrote the soundtrack. In 1989, the singer/actor auditioned for the lead in the 1990 Oliver Stone film *The Doors*. As luck would have it, Pettijohn never got the chance. While he waited in the wings for his turn, Val Kilmer accepted the part.

Over the years, Moonlight Drive has opened for the Eagles, Humble Pie, Mountain, and Bruce Springsteen and the E Street Band, among others. Pettijohn has also joined former Doors keyboardist Ray Manzarek and guitarist Robby Krieger on stage a few times, and a friendship was formed that endures today. His notoriety as a Morrison clone and his convincing performances got Pettijohn a gig on the *Jerry Springer Show* in May 1995. "They wanted to do a show about people who make a living as tribute artists and an agent told them about me," Pettijohn recalls. "The producers called and asked if I'd come on, and that's how I got on the show."

The most recent members include Pettijohn and Brame, along with David Holmberg (keyboards) and Al Berdis (drums). Although the band incorporates its own personality and sound into the shows, Moonlight Drive stays true to the Doors' repertoire. This includes lesser-known Doors tunes. Pettijohn says that, in a haunting way, he feels the late singer's presence while on stage. Back when he fronted Dragonwyck (see Chapter 12), the devout Morrison fan made certain the group covered several of his favorite Doors tunes, such as "Break on Through," "Whiskey Bar," and "Light My Fire." But his obsession with the Lizard King goes back even further. "I remember lying in bed at night as a kid, before my voice changed," he says. "And I would pray, 'God, give me a voice like Jim Morrison.' Well, He answered my prayers."

Pettijohn's lengthy musical career has indeed been a blessing. In addition to his stint in Moonlight Drive and his acting opportunities, he is an author as well. Once again like Morrison, Pettijohn kept a journal of poetry. In 1996, the collection became a poetry book, *Deepest Secret Fears: The Gift Given Twice*.

While Moonlight Drive continued on the upswing, Pettijohn formed another tribute band in 1987—this time in honor of the Rolling Stones. For over a decade now, Beggar's Banquet has occupied any free time this consummate performer may have. The group, which debuted the weekend of October 9–10, 1987, includes Moonlight Drive members along with Mike Way (bass), Al Globekar (guitar), and backup singers Katie McLaughlin and Sandy Berdis.

"That band took a little longer to pick up," Pettijohn notes. "I went through several members. Then I got Al Globekar [Circus, Milk], who's a great guitar player. That's when it really took off."

Pettijohn balances the two bands well but admits there is a difference. "I can drink more when I emulate Morrison. For Jagger, I've got to be more on the ball. And either way, I have to stay in shape enough to fit into tight leather pants!"

Besides the club demands, Pettijohn works on various musical projects with musician friends Rich Spina (Love Affair, Gary Lewis and the Playboys) and Billy Sullivan (Beau Coup, Gary Lewis, and the Playboys). The trio acted and wrote music for an independent movie shot entirely in Cleveland—*Rock Robbers,* produced by Richard Lasky and directed by Bruce Patterson (Guerrilla Productions), due for release in 2001. And in celebration of the 1999 return of the Cleveland Browns, Pettijohn the actor participated in a short film called *Revenge of the Dawgs.* The plot focuses on six human dogs who go to Baltimore, kidnap Art Modell, and being him back to "Browns Town" to face Satan for stealing the home team. Only in Cleveland . . .

Notable Solo Artists

Marc Cohn (b. 1959, Cleveland)

Before Marc Cohn received his Grammy award for his chart-topping hit single "Walking in Memphis," this singer/songwriter was yet another talented graduate of Beachwood High School (as was Eric Carmen). After graduating in 1977, Cohn enrolled in Oberlin College as a psychology major. But music soon dominated his interest. He began teaching himself piano and composing his own songs, despite the fact he didn't read music. Although Cohn grew up next door to the legendary Cleveland Orchestra conductor George Szell, he preferred the music of James Taylor, Bob Dylan, the Band, Al Green, and Van Morrison to Beethoven and Mozart.

He joined his first rock group while still in high school, a cover band called Doanbrook Hotel, which ran its course by graduation. Then in 1980 he followed the path of many aspiring musicians and singers and left his hometown for Los Angeles. It was there he was introduced to Jed Leiber, son of legendary songwriter Jerry Leiber, who, along with partner Mike Stoller, was inducted into the Rock and Roll of Fame. He worked on songs with the younger Leiber as well as Andrew Lloyd Webber. After completing his bachelor's degree at UCLA in 1982, Cohn moved to New York City.

In 1985, Cohn formed a fourteen-piece pop/blues band called Supreme Court. The group caught the attention of Carly Simon, who helped them get their most famous gig—as the wedding band for Caroline Kennedy in July 1986. The group disbanded shortly after, but Cohn went on to win a contract with Atlantic Records, which ultimately released his self-titled debut album in 1991. His most famous single from that effort, "Walking in Memphis," became an instant hit, peaking at No. 13 on *Billboard* charts. The song earned Cohn three Grammy nominations in 1992—for Best New Artist, Song of the Year, and Best Pop Vocal Performance, Male. He lost the latter two to the Irving Gordon–penned "Unforgettable" and Michael Bolton's rendition of "When a Man Loves a Woman," respectively. His Best New Artist award was the surprise of the Grammy evening, as he beat out popular newcomers Boyz II Men and C+C Music Factory. That first album displayed Cohn's strength as a songwriter whose muse is often autobiographical. In the song "Ghost Train," he wrote of the death of his mother. His father and his treasured car was the muse for "Silver Thunderbirds." And later, Cohn's broken marriage led to the song, "Lost You in the Canyon."

On the heels of his newfound success came the 1993 *The Rainy Season,* with vocal accompaniments from famous friends. For the title track, he brought in singer Bonnie Raitt (for whom he opened in Australia in 1992). David Crosby and Graham Nash add harmonies to "She's Becoming Gold" and "From the Station." And Los Lobos singer David Hidalgo joins in on "Medicine Man." Five years later Cohn released *Burning the Daze*, which included the single "Already Home."

Neither subsequent album fared as well as the first. But Cohn is determined not to go down in history as just another one-hit wonder. He continues to pen songs of a personal nature and insists it is the art of making music and not fleeting success that will sustain him.

Although he has not been a Cleveland resident for the past two decades, Cohn's hometown ties have always been a part of his music. In 1986, a song he composed for a *Plain Dealer* advertisement, "Heart of the City," was used to bolster Cleveland's campaign to get the Rock Hall built on the North Coast He also contributed his piano talents to Tracy Chapman's second release, *Crossroads*. He returns often to perform at the Odeon, Nautica Stage, and Blossom Music Center. A few months after winning his Grammy, he stood on the revered Blossom stage where he told his audience, "I always wanted to see this place from this side. Fifteen years ago, I was sitting there—way out there on the lawn—watching Crosby, Stills and Nash." That night Marc Cohn opened the show for them.

James Ingram (b. 1952, Akron)

Ingram left his Akron roots for Los Angeles in 1973 as a member of the group Revelation Funk. Like the name suggests, it majored in funky, soulful music reminiscent of artists like Quincy Jones, Ray Charles, and the Coasters. When the group disbanded soon after the move, this R&B performer and pianist made a living as a solo artist at various local clubs.

It was after his meeting with mentor Ray Charles, however, that Ingram's luck turned gold. The legendary singer hired Ingram to write and produce songs for him and play keyboards on his recordings. He also toured with him and contributed on piano to Charles's 1978 version of "I Can See Clearly Now." By 1980, Ingram was active on Dick Clark's oldies package tours, but it was his collaboration with Quincy Jones that nabbed him his first Grammy award. In 1981, Ingram was nominated for Best New Artist but lost to Sheena Easton. He was also nominated for Best Pop Vocal Male Performance for the song "Just Once" (which he sang live on the show). Al Jarreau, however, nabbed that award. But the third time was the charm. The following year, Ingram was chosen as Best R&B Male Vocal Performance for the track "One Hundred Ways," from Quincy's *The Dude* LP. It was one of the few times a studio artist had taken home the coveted statue. The song peaked at No. 14 on the charts and served to bring more musical jobs Ingram's way.

His next project was with Michael Jackson. He co-wrote the song, "P.Y.T. (Pretty Young Thing)," which appears on *Thriller*. It reached No. 10 on U.S. charts and No. 11 in the U.K. Though the song was nominated for Best New Rhythm & Blues Song (songwriter's award), it lost out to another of Jackson's songs, "Billie Jean." The Ingram-penned "Party Animal" also made it for nomination in Best R&B Vocal Male Performance, but once again "Billie Jean" gave Jackson another win.

In 1982, Ingram participated in a duet with singer Patty Austin. Their song "Baby, Come to Me" became a No. 1 song and the "Luke and Laura" theme song for the TV soap opera *General Hospital*. He recorded another duet with Austin, "How Do You Keep the Music Playing?" for the *Best Friends* soundtrack, starring Burt Reynolds and Goldie Hawn. The song reached No. 45 on the U.S. charts. It, too, was nominated for Best Pop Performance by a Duo or Group with Vocal in 1983, but the Police's "Every Breath You Take" took those honors.

In 1984, Ingram was part of Quincy Jones's unforgettable "We Are the World" song for famine relief. That same year he received three more nods for Grammys as a result of his 1983 debut album. The song "It's Your Night" rose to No. 46 and was nominated for Best R&B Vocal Male Performance. But it was a recording with former Doobie Brother Michael McDonald that ultimately brought him the most attention on Grammy night in 1985. The song, with the unusual title of "Yah Mo B There," was nominated for both Best New Rhythm & Blues song (songwriter's award) and Best R&B Performance by a Duo or Group with Vocal. The latter gave Ingram his second Grammy. His third Grammy was not far behind. In 1988, his collaboration with Linda Ronstadt in "Somewhere Out There" (for the Spielberg animated film *An American Tail*) made it to No. 2 on the charts and won a Grammy for Song of the Year. In 1987, he wrote "Better Way" for the film *Beverly Hills Cop II,* and it reached No. 66.

Then came his first solo hit song, "I Don't Have the Heart," from his third LP, *It's Real* (1989). Another hometown colleague, Gerald Levert, helped produce the album, along with Thom Bell. The song went all the way to No. 1 and again earned the singer/songwriter yet another Grammy nomination, for Best Pop Vocal Male Performance, though he lost to Roy Orbison. Other releases include *The Power of Great Music* (1991) and *Always You* (1993). In 1994, Ingram joined Dolly Parton for a duet in "The Day I Fell in Love" from the film *Beethoven II*. He sang with Anita Baker on "When You Love Someone," from the 1995 Billy Crystal film *Forget Paris,* and joined an all-star cast (including Roberta Flack) for the "Colors of Christmas" tour in 1994 and 1995.

College Radio Comes of Age

College radio came to the forefront in the 1980s. The popularity of underground, alternative radio grew as commercial radio became more rigid and predictable. Rather than being slaves to advertising dollars, college stations had the luxury of being supported financially by their institutions. This afforded the program directors and disc jockeys the freedom to play nearly anything they—and the listeners—wanted. Whether diverse selections from obscure rock albums, free-form jazz, classical music, ethnic shows, or the intriguing topics of talk radio, innovative programming was the focus. "Radio roulette," it's been called, and the young deejays get to spin.

In the early days, however, unless you lived near a college station transmitter or happened to pass through town/the neighborhood, chances are that all you heard was static or intermittent waves of clarity as you tried tuning in. Early on, most college stations boasted a paltry 10 watts of power. But by the early 1980s, however, that was no longer a concern, when stations such as Case Western Reserve University's WRUW (91.1), Cleveland State University's WCSB (89.3), John Carroll University's WUJC (88.7, now WJCU), Baldwin-Wallace College's WBWC (88.3), Oberlin College's WOBC (91.5), Kent State University's WKSU (89.7), and the University of Akron's WAUP (88.1) upped their wattage anywhere from 1,000 to 7,500 and, later (for some), to an impressive 50,000.

Run by students and community volunteers who donate their time, these stations are more important than ever. As their larger and richer counterparts opt for stringent computer-generated playlists, this alternative in radio has become the sole outlet for listeners who seek musical diversity.

"Cleveland has long been known for having the most college radio stations in its area, as well as ones that offer the largest range of diversity," notes David Sowd, whose "Radio Free Cleveland" weekly column ran in the *Plain Dealer* from 1987 to 1991, and from 1991 to 1997 in the Sun Newspapers. "From the late '80s to the present, college radio has become the only alternative when it comes to hearing songs from albums, because commercial FM largely consists of a Top 40 or oldies format. For instance, you can hear some Neil Young tunes from his albums on college stations that you'd never hear on commercial radio. There'll always be a growing need for college radio." Sowd, whose name is perhaps most familiar to *Scene* readers for his frank articles and music reviews throughout the '90s, spent time as a college deejay while attending Kent State University in the 1960s.

Longtime college radio fan Nina Morris Mosher, today an East Side realtor, recalls how she got hooked on academic radio. "When I moved from Chicago to Cleveland in 1974, I listened mostly to WMMS. A few years later, a friend introduced me to WCSB and WRUW. What really attracted me to it was there were no commercials. That, plus there was such diversity in the programming. By then, all you seemed to hear on commercial radio was either disco or the same songs over and over again. So I welcomed the alternative it offered. These stations played songs I never heard anywhere else. From then on, I've been a real advocate of college radio and have always contributed to its radiothons."

College radio has also served as a viable outlet for aspiring female deejays, though male voices continued to outnumber women in radio. Phyllis Boehme began a radio career at WRUW in the 1970s that lasted nearly two decades. Though never a Case Western Reserve student, she was familiar with its station since her teen years when she listened to Victor Boc's show. (Boc went on to be one of the first "progressive" deejays on WMMS.) She would take two buses from her Olmsted Falls home to visit him at the station.

"Victor had a different perspective on how to do radio," she recalls. "I think I mimicked him a lot when I first started, until I found my own style. Then one day [engineer] Steve Levitan handed me a study guide to take my FCC license, despite the fact that a female disc jockey was a standing joke when I graduated high school in '68. But I wanted to be a part of it. Radio was always a big part of my life. I had a very rough childhood and adolescence, and radio was my emotional support system. I enjoyed how experimental radio was back then, even on the AM band. Plus, it was all locally programmed, unlike it is today. So you had that intimate connection."

As one of the first and few female college deejays, Boehme served as inspiration to those who came later and brought new awareness to this college campus. Her listeners could count on her to introduce them to the rarest of music material. Soon after her first broadcast in 1972, Boehme became known as "Michigan Mom."

"I was a real fan of a station out of Dearborn, Michigan, WKRN-FM, which introduced me to a lot of the Ann Arbor/Detroit bands. Of course that included the very early MC5 and the Stooges. I was very heavily into that, and once I got the show I played a lot of the more obscure Michigan rock music—from bands like the Rationals, the Underdogs, and Free, all which were hardly known. So the name came from that."

Her weekend program was one of the station's most popular, and she is fondly remembered for her "free-form" leanings and sense of humor. She also introduced listeners to the emerging sounds of the controversial punk and new wave releases and was one of the first deejays to play a Dead Boys tune.

"Then I got into the music coming out of Manchester, England. I fell in love with it and became just 'M. Mom' after that," she says. "This was the early '80s, and I was playing songs from groups like the Buzzcocks, the Fall, and Joy Division. I felt a lot for the underdog. I think if there was a reason for God to put me on the radio [it] was to make people aware of bands like Joy Division."

Case Western Reserve law student Ann Weatherhead was a blues enthusiast's favorite. Her "Annie's Blues Show" first aired in the spring of 1979, and for the next nineteen years she kept blues lovers listening every Monday from 7:30–10:00 P.M., long after she received her law degree in 1981.

"She had a style all her own," Nina Morris Mosher says of Weatherhead. "She was well versed on the blues and always enlightened her listeners. You could rely on her playing songs by Buddy Guy, Muddy Waters, Albert King, B. B. King, the Chicago Blues, which I particularly liked, being that was my hometown. You never knew who you would hear, but you knew it would be something you'd like. And she played local blues, as well, like Robert Lockwood Jr., Mr. Stress, Blue Lunch, and Colin Dussault. I'll never forget the way she'd say 're-quest' with the emphasis on re. And she not only took the requests, she actually played them."

Weatherhead often promoted local artists, earning her much respect and kinship with fellow blues lovers. As such, it was not surprising that her friends and fans hosted a party for her at Wilbert's in the Flats when she retired from radio in May of 1998.

After nearly two decades playing the blues, Weatherhead announced the "thrill is gone" and hung up her headphones. She currently works as a magistrate in domestic relations court.

Many student music lovers who added radio broadcasting to their college curricula used it as a stepping stone to bigger and better things. Former Kent State University student Jeff Gelb began working at WKSU while attaining his telecommunications degree. Today he is the director of information services for *Radio and Records* magazine, and he edited the 1992 book *Shock Rock*. As he recalls,

> I had an hour-and-a-half long Saturday night show called "The World Of Progressive Music." That was back in 1968, so it basically went out on their carrier current to the dormitories. All of my pals would listen to me, and I played the most bizarre music I could find. I was buying everything I could get my hands on, and I kept up with whatever magazines were reporting on it, like *Rolling Stone* and the British music papers like the *New Musical Express*.
>
> The experience was wonderful and helped me understand the logistics of radio. Though, when I got my first professional job at WNCR, I realized how green I was. There were other aspects to consider, such as segueing the songs and commercials. But on the other hand, it was 1971 and neither had a strict format like you have today. I was able to play the songs I liked and turn the audience onto that music.

When WNCR changed formats in 1973, Gelb went to a San Diego station. However, the new trend in using fixed music formats caused him to abandon his radio career in 1977. He has been with *Radio and Records* since then. "The significant thing about the show at Kent was, as far as I know, the first time someone had broken [the station's] classical music format to play anything remotely commercial. 'The World of Progressive Music' was a breakthrough for them and was followed by more programs of that sort. After I left, they began to free up more air time to allow other personalities to do shows like 'Fresh Air.'"

The "Fresh Air" program began with another telecommunications major, John Awarski. "The concept of progressive music at WKSU really started with Jeff Gelb," confirms Awarski, now vice president/general manager at Action Music.

> I'll never forget when he took Stravinsky's "Firebird" and segued it into David Bowie's "Space Oddity." The way he mixed it was so cool, it just flowed perfectly . . . and we all stole the idea! But that's how we opened up our horizons.
>
> When he left, I was asked to put together this show called "Fresh Air" in 1972, and we used the song by Quicksilver Messenger Service as our opening theme. Each night there was a different jock doing his own thing. There was one guy who played primarily Alice Cooper kind of stuff. Another who was into German Rock. One guy, Rusty, would bring in imported albums no one had ever heard of, out of

England and Europe, *months* before you ever heard them on commercial radio. I remember he brought an early copy of the Yes album and then dragged us to Elyria High School to see them play in their gymnasium!

Because we were exposed so early to various groups, we saw many of them before they became well known. In the winter of '72–'73 we went to the Akron Civic Theater to see Pink Floyd. They did *Dark Side of the Moon* before it was released, had the quad systems and all the effects. When they stopped playing, there was total silence. We all just sat there in awe. When people finally realized the song was over, there was this big burst of applause.

It was incredible. We knew we were experiencing something special, and it was because college radio allowed us to be really on top of the music.

Many future disc jockeys, broadcasters, radio engineers, record executives, and musicians spent much of their academic years at the soundboard of their college radio stations. In Cleveland, that list is long among notable personalities. There were, of course, former WCSB students Kid Leo, Jeff Kinzbach, Matt the Cat, and Betty Korvan, who helped take WMMS to national fame. Auburn Records president Bill Peters recalls: "I got interested in college radio by listening to [WUJC's] Mitch Capka's Saturday morning show. It was the only place you could hear heavy metal at that time on a regular basis. I was about twenty and used to call him every week to request songs or just talk to him about the music. Finally he invited me to the station, and I brought some of my own records. He suggested I take the [radio] course, and I've been on ever since." Other media personalities include local TV reporters Ted Henry and Carl Monday, who both honed their communication skills at WKSU.

Guitarist Doug Gillard (Death of Samantha, Cobra Verde, Gem, Guided By Voices) was introduced to alternative music by way of college radio station WOBC (Oberlin College). "I discovered college radio in high school," recalls the Elyria High School graduate. "That's when I learned you didn't have to be an Oberlin student to have a show on their station. So I signed up for an apprentice[ship] and did a show called 'The Burning Theatre' on Sunday mornings from 3:00 to 6:00 in 1984. That summer I also hosted a show on Wednesday and Saturday afternoons."

Gillard went on to be a deejay on WCSB from 1985 to 1991. His program—originally called "Twentieth-Century Groove Angel," then "Groove Angel Unlimited"—showcased area rock bands. From its inception, college radio has provided a clear avenue for musicians, local and otherwise, to be heard and recognized.

By the 1980s, college radio, through its increased wattage and enthusiastic volunteers, earned a respectable and devoted fan base. Its popularity has grown steadily ever since, as rapid changes in radio, brought on by corporate buyouts, have forced listeners to check out what the left end of the radio dial has to offer. College radio has grown up. After some thirty years on the air, it has become a well-honed alternative to commercial radio, its audience larger than ever. Cleveland's longtime reputation as a big radio town extends to this type of programming as well.

"College radio in Cleveland has always been right on top of things," says *Alternative Press* publisher Mike Shea. "It's very influential on what's happening on the Cleveland scene, letting them know what's new, and what's cool. Even the college trade papers acclaim Cleveland as having the best college radio scene in America."

Recommended Reading

Hardy, Phil, and Dave Laing. *Encyclopedia of Rock*. New York: Schirmer Books, 1988.

Pielke, Robert G. *You Say You Want a Revolution: Rock Music in American Culture*. New York: Nelson-Hall, 1986.

Schwartz, Daylle Deanna. *The Real Deal: How to Get Signed to a Record Label from A to Z*. New York: Billboard Books, 1997.

16 Deejays Still Rock in the '80s

Although some of the disc jockeys listed in this chapter actually began their radio careers in the 1970s, their personalities shaped Cleveland-area radio in the 1980s. As typical in the business, various deejays came and went throughout the era. The following include the most notable and best remembered.

"Dancin' Danny" Wright (b. 1950, Kalamazoo, Michigan; WGCL, WNCX, WRQC, WWWE, WKDD, WQMX, WGAR)

"I always thought that [nickname] was a little goofy," Wright says of the moniker that, like it or not, has stuck with him throughout his lengthy radio career. Although Dancin' Danny doesn't exactly recall how he acquired the name, he does remember his habit of jumping around playing air guitar at the many dances he hosted around the country for various radio stations. And in a career that has taken him to more than twenty-one jobs in twenty-four years, it could be used as an metaphor for his employment history.

"I started out at a little station in Everett, Washington," says the Michigan native who graduated from Ron Bailey's School of Broadcasting in Seattle. "From there I went to jobs in San Diego, Sacramento, Oregon, Seattle, and Boston. But when I got to Cleveland, something clicked."

Wright's energetic voice was first heard on Cleveland's WGCL on Valentine's Day 1983. The year before he'd been named *Billboard*'s top disc jockey, and he proved it at his new job. An immediate success, he seemed to connect with his audience and soon topped the afternoon ratings, often beating out Kid Leo at his station's chief competitor, WMMS. He also hosted the short-lived TV show *Rockspot,* which focused on local and national music acts.

"Dancin' Danny was cool," notes Joe Cronauer. "He was one of the first guys I can remember who had his own show with his own theme song. He didn't just talk up the music or the records—he was a little bit of Hollywood right here in Cleveland."

And his career never looked brighter than when he was in Cleveland. Before long, he was being offered a "too-good-to-be-true" radio job in Washington, D.C. He soon found it was just that.

When we beat 'MMS my first year there, it was a big deal. It was written up in both the *Plain Dealer* and *Scene.* And it really kicked off a serious war. They [WMMS management] did everything they could to stop the competition [among FM stations]. At times it got ugly. After all, they weren't used to being second in the ratings. I remain convinced some folks at 'MMS paid to get me out of town because we'd beaten them in '83. Because all of a sudden, I got this out-of-nowhere job offer from this big station in Washington, D.C.

The managers there flew me in, wined and dined both me and my wife, and I was offered double my salary. So naturally, I thought, "This is an opportunity I can't pass up." So I quit 'GCL. But soon as I started the new job, I couldn't do anything right. The program director was constantly on my case, and they kept delaying my contract. Finally I couldn't take it anymore. But before I left, I was told in order for them not to charge me for the moving expenses they'd pay for, I had to sign a noncompete contract that I wouldn't go back to Cleveland. Now what does that tell you?

He took a radio job in Kansas City, but his heart was still in Cleveland. He got his second chance in 1985 when WGCL's new general manager, Kim Colebrook, asked him to return.

"We went to dinner," Wright recalls. "He literally pushed his checkbook towards me and said, 'What'll it take to get you to come back?' I wrote in an outrageous figure and he said, 'Okay.' And that was it." The previous contract was all but forgotten. "I was thrilled to come back. But before my three-year contract was up, the station was sold [changing to WNCX]. The option to keep me wasn't picked up, but they had to let my contract run out. So for my last six months there, I was probably the highest-paid all-night disc jockey in the country!"

The deejay who calls Cleveland his adopted hometown began dancing again. From 1986 to 1988 he worked at Cleveland's WRQC (92-Q, now WZJM "Jammin' 92"). He then hosted an afternoon talk show on WWWE (now WTAM) for a year before moving to Akron's WKDD (1989–91) and WQMX (1991–93). He was fired at the latter because "they didn't think I could do country." He has since proven them wrong.

"I was online one night, browsing through the computer bulletin board, and started chatting with [country music station] WGAR program director Denny Nugent. He asked me to come in and apply, and I was hired right away. That was September 1994, and I've been there ever since."

For two years in a row, 1997 and 1998, Wright was the recipient of the AIR award (Achievement in Radio) for the Best Midday Radio Show. He was also a nominee for the 1999 ACM (American Country Music) Award. In 2000 he was nominated for ACM's Major Market Personality of the Year—and he won.

Wright keeps other interests on the back burner. Over the years he's written several books and screenplays. In the meantime, radio remains Wright's passion.

It's easy to become cynical in this business. This is an industry that can get out of hand with the egos or the lifestyles. There's been many times I looked like the bad guy because I have a low tolerance for that and I'd get fired. But I'm a survivor, and when I'm at a good station with good people, I'll stick around.

On the other hand, there are the perks. I mean, a lot of people live dull work lives. Here, I get to talk to people like Garth Brooks, Clint Black, Reba McIntyre, Wynonna Judd. There are the concert tickets. The times we get to give away money to listeners. And every month we get twelve bottles of beers from microbreweries to endorse, so I get paid to drink beer. This is a great job!

But then, there's still *that name*.

"People think when they meet me I'm going to be this wild 'n' crazy guy, that 'Dancin' Danny' persona. But actually, I'm just a quiet, family guy who likes to mow the lawn. I don't want to have to live up to that hype. I just hope no new owner comes in one day and makes me go back to using 'Dancin' Danny' on the air. I mean, come on. I'm in my late forties. It sounds pretty weird now. I don't want to be an old man and still expected to be that."

Max Heywood (b. 1950; WCUE, WGCL, WZZP, WRQC, WMMS, WMJI)

By the time Max Heywood (né Richard Lee Smith) got his first job in commercial radio, he was already an old hand at the controls. He was just thirteen when he set up his own radio station in his parents' basement.

I built my own transmitter and set up a pirate station with the call letters WKZY 1380—short for crazy. I ran it like a regular radio station. There was a music clock, the records were all color-coded—the whole nine yards. Within two years, I was averaging a 7 share in the Canton market. I actually had other kids working for me, and some went on to radio careers, such as Tom Jeffries [who later worked at WGCL] and Tim Davisson [WGCL, later in sales at Akron's WONE]. During this time I was going to Canton-McKinley High School, same as the O'Jays. Everyone at the school listened to my little bootleg station, so the O'Jays would come down and sing on it. I'm probably one of the first people to get a copy, a reel-to-reel, of their first release, "Lipstick Traces," before it was put out.

By this time, the young Smith was already an astute radio listener. The location of his residence allowed him to tune into a variety of stations, thus educating him on some of the best deejays the 1960s had to offer. His favorites were Cousin Brucie on WABC (New York), Fred Winston on WLS (Chicago), Ron Lundi on WCLF (Chicago), Pete "Mad Daddy" Myers on WHK-AM (Cleveland), and Jack Armstrong on WIXY (Cleveland).

"What really got me into music was when I was five years old, I used to play my father's 78 records when they still released the current product [Top 40] on 78 rpm," Heywood says. "This was before the 45 era. I'd make these little countdowns before the records, for my own amusement. And I'd play all the hits for my babysitters, which kept me busy and kept them entertained! At age nine, I got interested in electronics. My father was an engineer, so I was getting things like tube testers for Christmas presents."

After graduating from high school, he majored in electrical engineering at the University of Akron. At age nineteen, he nailed his first job at Akron station WCUE-FM 1158 (later WKDD), where he supplied the programmers with his extensive music library that ranged from 1948 through the 1960s. He became news director and assistant production manager at Canton station WJAN-TV in 1972, where he worked with Carl Monday, now a local investigating reporter. From there it was onto Youngstown's "hottest" station, WHOT-FM 101. When he got a Cleveland radio job in 1973, Dick "Wildman" Smith took on a new persona.

"When I arrived at G-98, they didn't want me using the same name because Youngstown covered the same area. It was a political thing," he says. "So three minutes before airtime, I hadn't a clue what to call myself. One of the news guys, Greg Anthony, was sitting there with the Bo Donaldson and the Heywoods' LP, and when I told him, frantically, that I didn't have a name, he turned to me and said, 'How 'bout Max Heywood?' And that was it."

Once at Cleveland's popular Top 40 station, Max Heywood became a familiar name, much like his coworkers Tim "The Byrdman" Byrd, Dude Walker, and program director T. J. Lambert. The station, however, was just getting off the ground.

"Back then, we had three-hour shifts and no one had regular hours," he recalls. "I worked 9:00 P.M. to midnight, 6:00–9:00 P.M., and for a short time did overnights. They had no record library per se, so I provided the music there as well."

In 1976, Heywood was asked to join new station WZZP-FM (Zip-106), replacing WXEN-FM. Bob Peyton was once again his program director, and the deejay was promoted to assistant program director and music director. Although this new energetic station boasted a popular mix of Top 40 songs by '70s artists Hall and Oates, Abba, K. C. and the Sunshine Band, and Bob Seger, heavy competition forced it off the airwaves in 1979. In the interim, Heywood served, off and on, as chief engineer for Canton country station WNYN 900 AM from 1972 to 1987, working for nationally known radio voice

Don Keyes. Heywood also started his own company, Heywood Formatics and Syndications, in 1975, which provides preprogrammed music—along with his unmistakable voice—at clubs throughout the area. He began by making tapes for clubs around his hometown, and the concept caught on, particularly as disco forged ahead.

"I was doing this in the nightclubs long before the broadcast business started [radio using prerecorded music and voiceovers]," he says.

By 1982, Heywood was back at WGCL. There he worked with notable personalities Dancin' Danny Wright, Jim King, and "Uncle Vic." He remained there until 1986, when the station changed owners and call letters (WNCX).

"The highlight there was, of course, when we beat WMMS in the ratings," he says. "We really smoked them, and they weren't happy because no other station had been able to do that for years. I firmly believe that's what caused 'MMS to suddenly start playing more of the contemporary hits like Michael Jackson's 'Billie Jean' and Prince's '1999.' That was an interesting time in radio."

His next stop was WRQC-FM (92-Q), the station that caused a real buzz in 1986 in its campaign to get the Rock Hall built in Cleveland (see Chapter 19).

"I had been broadcasting from the Rascal House [near Cleveland State] since my original G-98 days," he says. "It was the area's first all-video nightclub. We played videos and music from 8 in the morning 'til 3 A.M. We had real broadcasting equipment, and channels 3, 5, and 8 used our Sony 5850s for some of their news footage.

WRQC, whose ratings were never on par with rivals WMMS and WGCL, showed a marked increase in Heywood's time slot. In fact, it was the first time the station had ever beaten WGCL. In 1987, he left. The next thing listeners knew, that voice was being heard on the station he was often in direct competition with—WMMS.

"When I first arrived, the old staffers there couldn't believe this G-98 guy got a job at 'MMS! The program director was from L.A., so he wasn't aware of the history [between the two stations]. But it turned out fine because I never took it personally. Within weeks, they all forgot about it and was glad I was there because I helped get the ratings back up."

Heywood remained at WMMS from 1988 until 1991. Over the next few years, he took time off from the airwaves and worked behind the scenes as a radio consultant. Since 1995, Max Heywood has worked as a part-time disc jockey, backup music director, and music programmer at oldies station WMJI-FM.

"It works out good because I don't have to be there everyday," he says. "I come in as needed, and it gives me time to pursue other things."

Those other things include owning an advertising agency and keeping the music alive with his longstanding Heywood Formatics and Syndication.

TR (b. 1952, Cleveland; WMMM, WMMS, WKDD, WMVX)

Call Tom Rezny (TR) a radio survivor. He's one of the few deejays in town to have maintained a steady radio job since 1975. During that time, he was off the air just one month.

"That was when OmniAmerica took over WMMS in 1994," he says. "There were a lot of people let go, including myself. I wasn't sure what I was going to do next." Fortunately he had a friend in longtime radio engineer (now WKDD program director) Chuck Collins, who helped secure him a radio job—for the second time.

But back in 1974, as a student at Bowling Green State University, Rezny didn't have a radio career at the top of his list. The nineteen-year-old physics and chemistry major decided to earn some credits working at his college radio station.

"I got into college radio [WFAL] in my junior year because it looked like fun," recalls the Bedford High School graduate. "I grew up listening to all the AM stations, especially WKYC with Martin and Howard. Then, of course, FM. But becoming a deejay never entered my mind. Once I started doing it, however, I fell in love with it. And there went physics and chemistry."

In 1975, WWWE engineer Chuck Collins told Rezny's brother Ed about a new FM rock station starting in Cleveland, WMMM 105. He in turn told his sibling. The aspiring disc jockey sent Operations Director Eric Stevens a tape. Within weeks TR was on the air.

After debuting on the 7:00 P.M.–midnight shift for the first year, Rezny switched to middays (10:00 A.M. to 2:00 P.M.), which he found were the perfect hours. "You don't have to get up early and you're off in time to go out at night," he says. He also had good mentorship there, working with Stevens (KYW, WIXY) and former WNCR disc jockey David Spero. The station that touted itself as the "Home of Continuous Music" became a serious rival for WMMS by the late 1970s.

For the next seven years Rezny enjoyed every aspect of the business. The energy and drive M-105 produced in its attempt to vie with WMMS kept the novice deejay on his feet—in more ways than one.

"We did a lot of charity work, and I remember one benefit for the American Cancer Society where I roller skated from Akron to Cleveland with a skating club. It was a full-day affair, from eight in the morning until six in the evening. I had worn the wheels down by the time I finished. But it was a good time."

In June 1982, WMMM changed formats, call letters (WMJI), and deejays. Soon after, TR's soft, professional voice was being heard on the very station he had spent years competing against, WMMS.

"I started there doing fill-ins and working part-time," he notes. "Then Betty Korvan left in 1984, and I took over her evening spot [10:00 P.M.–2:00 A.M.]."

For Rezny it was good timing. The deejay had arrived at Cleveland's premier rock station just as it was enjoying its biggest ratings ever due to its controversial switch from its long-held AOR format to CHR. There, Rezny worked with some of the great Cleveland rock jocks, such as Kid Leo, Denny Sanders, BLF Bash, and Jeff Kinzbach.

After five years, TR's job switched from air personality to WMMS production director. His job seemed steady until WMMS was suddenly sold to OmniAmerica in 1994. And just as quickly, Rezny found himself without a job. Once again, his friend Collins helped him out. Rezny was hired at Akron rock station WKDD, where he started as evening deejay. A few months later he became production director, a job in which he remained until 1997. Rezny was surprised when he was summoned back to Cleveland.

"The former 'MMS promotion director, Jim Ochavic [currently WMVX promotion director] called me when Randy James took over 'Mix-106,'" he recalls. "I liked Akron, but I was thrilled to come back to Cleveland."

Rezny joined Cleveland's newest radio station in January 1998. Although he started as a deejay, he was soon promoted to production manager. With its current format of "greatest hits of the '80s, '90s, and '70s," WMVX, "Mix 106," has brought a new concept to Cleveland airwaves. The station focuses heavily on preproduced music and IDs, with limited on-air personalities. But TR insists radio is still fascinating, and with over twenty years in the field, he looks forward to staying with it. Unless of course, he gets an overwhelming desire to pursue his interest in physics and chemistry. That prospect, he agrees, seems doubtful.

"Spaceman Scott" (b. Scott Hughes, 1960, New York; WMMS, WNCX, WRQK, WMMS)

Although he grew up in Strongsville in the 1960s, Scott Hughes didn't listen much to Cleveland's top AM rock radio stations. His favorite came out of Detroit. "I was a CKLW freak," he admits. Moreover, he hadn't a clue he'd end up on Cleveland radio airwaves—at least not as part of the crew. Blame it all on WMMS's morning duo, Jeff and Flash.

"I was one of those guys who'd call them up every morning and harass them," Hughes says. "I was about nineteen, working at a Tow Motor Company in Strongsville, and it was like a goal of mine to see how many times they'd put me on the air. So sometimes I'd disguise my voice. I think Jeff liked me calling in because I was always so upbeat. He started calling me 'Wild Man.' Then I started calling up Leo, Denny, and Bash. They all got to know who I was!"

Then in 1982, Hughes got laid off from his job. Contemplating his next move, the "phone harasser" went for the obvious.

"I called up Jeff and asked him if he thought I had a chance in radio," he says. "He referred me to the Ohio Broadcasting School. Ten weeks into the twenty-week course, I started calling Jeff about a job. He kept hanging up on me. I pursued him relentlessly until he said, 'Okay, come on in.' I became Jeff's gofer. This was before we had 'Metro Traffic,' so I used to steal the traffic reports from WERE by listening to it in another room, then give it to Jeff to read on the air. From there I started doing promotions and other things for the Buzzard Morning Zoo. I never did finish the course. So really, it was Jeff who gave me my break. I probably wouldn't have gotten anywhere without his help."

The fan became an employee. And with WMMS's penchant for nicknames, Hughes's tag came easily. "I was young yet, so I did a lot of partying. When I'd come into the station in the mornings, Jeff would say, 'Man, you look spaced-out. So I became Spaceman Scott.'"

He started his new radio job in May 1983. But although he was excited to work at this renowned station, Hughes was surprised to learn there wasn't the good-time, free-spirited camaraderie group always exhibited on the air.

"When I got here, I found it was a whole other ball game," he recalls. "Everybody was making big money. Everybody had an agent. Those party years were pretty much over, and everyone was going in different directions. I always assumed everyone loved one another at 'MMS. In reality, no one talked to one another much, and there was some backstabbing. At first it was very disillusioning. But I forgot about it after a while because I got along with everyone and was busy working with Denny and Leo, who taught me so much about the business. John [Gorman] was a huge influence on me as well. I'll always be grateful they all took that time to work with me."

Hughes came in just as the station was experiencing one of its many controversies.

"That's when they switched over to the CHR format," he says. "And for whatever it's worth, that's when the ratings started skyrocketing. We had the largest ratings ever. But internally, things weren't good."

When nearly half of the WMMS crew left to join newcomer WNCX in September 1986, Hughes was among them. He was hired for the 6:00–10:00 P.M. shift, but four months later, management changes left him unemployed. After six months "of playing golf," he was offered a job at Canton station WRQK-FM 106.9, where he worked the morning shift (6:00–10:00 A.M.). Then John Gorman found him a job at Tom's River, New Jersey, station WJRZ before summoning him back to WRQK as program director in 1989. The Cleveland deejay came full circle when he returned to WMMS in October 1992.

"My wife was Milt Maltz's secretary at Malrite," Hughes explains. "So she helped me get back in, on a part-time basis. This despite the fact that Michael Luczak [program director] was running it then, and he didn't wanted anything to do with 'Gorman's people.'"

When John Gorman returned to the helm in 1994, Hughes took over the afternoon-drive shift. When Nationwide bought WMMS in 1996, Gorman left, while Hughes stayed. The disc jockey also got a promotion. He was named music director and assistant program director. He remained at the station as assistant PD for its new owners, Jacor of Cleveland. He says it's important, particularly in the industry today, for aspiring deejays to learn the ropes in order to stay employed.

"The best thing one can do, besides learning the broadcasting side, is learn to do sales and promotions. Be diversified. It's the only way you can last anymore in this business."

Sales knowledge came in handy when Spaceman was let go at WMMS in the fall of 1999. He is now part of a unique concept, Groovy Candies. The company that makes the goodies, Sugar Memories, is Cleveland based and markets by-gone candies of the 1960s, such as Jujubes, Fizzies, Skybars, and Zagnuts. On his radio days, he says, "I hope radio goes back to local ownership one day—but Jesus will probably walk on the earth again before that happens."

Bill Louis (b. 1957, Cleveland; WNCX)

When Cleveland radio fans think of Bill Louis, they think of music knowledge. Louis has indeed taken former Norm N. Nite's place in educating hometown listeners on the subject of rock and roll. "He's a walking rock encyclopedia," coworker Paula Balish says of Louis. "Bill is the consummate disc jockey who really has the passion for what he does. He knows his stuff."

The Cleveland native who grew up in the Old Brooklyn neighborhood paid his dues working in radio stations far and beyond his hometown before settling in at WNCX in 1987.

After graduating from Parma's Padua High School in 1975, Louis started working for his brother-in-law at a construction company. Although he was told he'd have a job for life, Louis wasn't sure that's how he wanted to spend it. One "snow day," while sitting around with his buddies "playing rummy, drinking beer, and watching those ridiculous prize movies," a TV advertisement gave him his answer.

"There were two commercials that ran regularly," he recalls. "One was for a law school, the other was for Ohio School of Broadcasting Technique. I figured I'd make a better disc jockey than a lawyer."

Eight months of training later, in 1979, Louis was on his way to New York for his first radio job, at Geneva station WECQ. It was the beginning of several years away from his hometown.

"I'll never forget driving east, down I-90," he recalls. "And seeing Cleveland disappear in the background—away from family and everything I knew. Never had I felt such a sense of isolation, of being totally on my own." He also quickly learned of the instability of the profession he'd chosen. For the next few years, he had stints at stations WOND (Atlantic City, New Jersey), WVBS (Wilmington, North Carolina), WMJY (Long Branch, New Jersey), KSMG (San Antonio, Texas), WSHE, and WMXJ (both Miami, Florida).

"My program director at the Miami station, ironically, was another former Clevelander, Charlie Kendall, who was at WMMS in the early '70s," Louis recalls. "It was great working with him, and he taught me a lot. We had a good time both in and out of the station."

On September 25, 1987, deejay Bill Louis finally made it onto the Cleveland airwaves. Taking veteran radioman Ted Alexander's place on middays at WNCX, Louis quickly gained a fan base through his enthusiasm, friendly manner, and rock 'n' roll data. When former program director Bob Neumann left the station for WMMS in

Left to right: Southside Johnny with guitarist Bobby Bandiera and Bill Louis in 1991. *Courtesy of Bill Louis.*

1996, it was no surprise Louis was chosen to take his place. He now pulls double-duty as he continues his weekday show from 11:00 A.M.–3:00 P.M. His noontime "Classic Cafe" request show is among the few staples in radio today.

One thing that endears him to his listeners is that Louis is a native Clevelander who knows and appreciates the city. His memories of growing up with rock on the North Coast are numerous.

His favorite rock artists include David Bowie, Bob Seger, Yes, and Bruce Springsteen. "I saw Springsteen back in 1974 at the Akron Civic Theater," he recalls. "Back then, you didn't think in terms of 'commercial viability'; you just thought, 'This guy's a genius.' This was before the coliseums and big halls. So you got that intimate feeling, like he was playing just for you in your living room. He didn't dazzle you with special effects or laser lights; he dazzled you just by playing the music—the whole band exploding, on time, flat out into the song. It was amazing."

In the 1970s, Louis frequented "any dive bar I could get into with a fake ID." When he came of age, he spent his free time at the Agora, Pirate's Cove, Mad Hatter, Smiling Dog Saloon, the Library, and the Viking Saloon.

"I liked so many of the local bands, but my favorites were probably Flatbush, which played often at the Pirate's Cove, and Fayrewether, which played a lot at the Agora.

"Then there was the World Series of Rock at the old stadium," he adds. "There were so many, but you'd have to mention the Rolling Stones, J. Geils Band concert in '75. And Santana, Crosby, Stills and Nash, the Band, Jesse Colin Young in August of 1974. What a time that was."

Louis's love of rock history formed early. Growing up he listened to all the hits of the era on AM rock/pop stations like Windsor/Detroit's CKLW (with future Cleveland deejay Larry Morrow) and the closer-to-home KYW and WIXY.

"I remember all those jocks back then," he says. "I particularly liked Mike Reineri, Lou 'King' Kirby, Jack Armstrong, and, of course, Billy Bass."

His first concert was the Monkees on January 15, 1967, at Public Hall. "I know the date because my stepdaughter recently gave me a replica of a Monkees tour shirt from that and on the back it listed Cleveland, Ohio, with the date on it. No, my memory isn't *that* good."

His listeners would disagree with that statement. Louis has earned the reputation as a well-versed rock and roll professor. It comes from being a voracious reader who, because of his personal interest in the subject, retains the information.

"I like books that are dedicated to specific artists, or time periods, that give more input," he says. "There are a few magazines I particularly like, such as the British publication *Mojo*, which is fascinating. There's also a technical magazine called *Mix* that has features on recording instruments, microphones, and such. You can get some remarkable information from that."

Because of the knowledge he's acquired over the years, when rock buffs have a trivia question, they know who to call.

"I'm always getting phone calls from people settling bets, or even ones who need an answer to a question for another station's contest," he says. "When someone calls asking me something about the Turtles, I know it's for an oldies station contest.

"It's real flattering that people view me as this expert. But I try hard not to come across as a know-it-all. It's something I'm not comfortable with because there's always someone out there who is a bigger fan, who knows more about a band or musician than I ever will."

The research comes in handy, however, when Louis interviews the assortment of personalities who visit him on his radio show. Anyone who's anybody in the rock world in town for a concert takes time to talk with one of the few remaining deejays who does live interviews.

"One of the challenges of interviewing these people is not to ask them the same questions everyone else does," he says. "Of course, you have to ask a few that are generic in nature, but about a third of the way into the conversation, I'll ask something that really puts them back on their heels. It makes for a more interesting interview for everyone. Plus, you establish a certain credibility with them."

Credibility is the key word, and something Louis doesn't take lightly. After all, it's not easy being considered in the same category as Norm N. Nite.

Dia Stein (b. 1959, Albany; WMMS)

"When I first arrived at WMMS in 1980, all I kept hearing was war stories about when Billy Bass and Martin Perlich were there. I finally said, 'Enough already.' Obviously it was an important part of the emergence of the station. Yet I feel the time I was there was every bit as creative and fun."

Although Dia's most important job was behind the scenes, her on-air personality and enthusiasm for the music struck a note with listeners. She credits, however, not her own talent for her success, but the women who preceded her.

"There were several women disc jockeys I admired," she says. "There was Karen Sevilli in Detroit, Mary Turner in L.A., Carol Miller in New York, and Betty Korvan in Cleveland. Especially Betty. If there wasn't a Betty Korvan, there wouldn't be a Dia Stein. She was very good at what she did, and terrific to learn from. But I do have to say that my true mentor was Allison Steele on WNEW [New York]. She was the first woman to have any real variety on the air. Strangely enough, when I left Cleveland to go to New York, I got a job at K-Rock, and who should be working there but Allison Steele. So for the next few years, I worked closely with her. She was an amazing woman and we became very close. In fact, I gave her eulogy when she died of cancer in 1996."

While listening to the voices of those pioneering women of radio, Stein began journalism studies at Syracuse University. At a colleague's suggestion, she tried her hand at college radio, where she ultimately became program director. Her eventual ties to Cleveland and WMMS emerged in 1980 on a boat. Not on Lake Erie, but on the Gulf of Mexico.

"I was working at this Tampa station called 98-Rock [WQXM-FM]," she recalls. And I was friends with Henry Paul, the guitarist from the Outlaws ["High Tide, Green Grass" and "Riders in the Sky"]. The Outlaws was to Tampa Bay what Michael Stanley is to Cleveland. So one day Henry calls me up and tells me the group had been hired to open the new Tampa Agora. He said there was a boat party that night, and would I like to go?

So I get on this boat and there's Kid Leo. I was completely thunderstruck because I had just sent him a fan letter a few months before that. See, I was a huge 'MMS fan ever since I heard Bruce Springsteen play the Agora in 1978, which was broadcast over a dozen or more cities, including WNEW, where I heard it. I'll always remember the part when Kid Leo said he was going to meet God, referring to Springsteen, and hearing all those great Kid Leo quotes.

So in the letter I wrote to Leo, I mentioned Steve Dahl, who was a very popular disc jockey in Chicago at The Loop [station WLUP]. He had pulled this stunt where he burned all the disco records in Kinzie Park [accompanied by former Cleveland deejay Bill Stallings]. This was at the height of the "disco sucks" era, so people all over the country were talking about how Steve was the best deejay and The Loop was the best station in the country. Because I was such an 'MMS fan, I told Kid Leo in the letter that, to me, the comparison of The Loop to 'MMS was like comparing

WMMS deejay Dia Stein with "Diamond Dave" David Lee Roth (*left*) and Kid Leo, 1987. *Photo by Brian Chalmers.*

a '74 Fender Stratocaster to a '57 Les Paul. They're both great guitars, but you'd rather have the Les Paul. Then I added, "and I think you're the Les Paul of radio." So I asked Leo that night if he remembered getting a letter like that, and he said, "*You* wrote that letter?" We connected right away, and after finding out I was a deejay, he asked me if I'd like to work at 'MMS. Mind you, I'd just gotten a job offer to work at—you got it—The Loop, which, of course, was a great opportunity. So I thought about it, for a day, then went with my heart.

Stein began her decade at the station working weekends and filling in for vacationing deejays. Her on-air hours rotated often through the years, but her most permanent assignment was in the production room working on what became the classic WMMS commercials, the station's "Backstage Pass" shows, and various promotional ideas. She recalls that creative time:

We were always bouncing ideas around. There'd be me and Tom O'Brian, a great production director, in the production studio. And John Gorman's office was next door. So we'd all gather in John's office and be hanging upside down on the couches, reading magazines, and chatting until someone came up with an idea. Then we'd venture into the production studio and whip up something that was incredibly funny, or incredibly stupid, or just really bad. But whatever we came up with, it always worked. Like the Buzzard Christmas Carol, or the Camp Buzzard, which was really creative. That's when Leo came to me and said, "It's Labor Day weekend and we don't have any money. What are you going to come up with?" So we thought, well, we have some great tapes in the archives, what can we do with them? So we brought out all the jocks up on the roof of the Statler Office building, miked them on the roof, and pretended we were having a concert at "Camp Buzzard." We gave listeners directions that led to nowhere and phone numbers that didn't go anywhere; the jocks would talk to each other, and you could hear the wind and the cars in the background, which made it sound so real. And the concerts were mixed in the background. Then Matt would throw it to TR, and TR would throw it back to Boom, and Boom would throw it to Bash, and Leo would be on the stage. We had made the whole thing up. But it sounded great.

Another program of note was her Sunday night show, "Backstage Pass," in which she interviewed various artists who came into town.

"I was lucky to be there when I was," she says of her WMMS days. "It was such an intense time. The strange thing about it was we were all so different in personality. We were these very different people thrown into this one radio station. But it was a perfect fit because where I may have lacked, somebody else filled in. And we were at the same point in our lives where we were all discovering the same things at the same time, and falling in and out of love with each other. We were a tight-knit group. It was family, and it was fighting, and it was incredibly creative."

Then things began changing rapidly at the groundbreaking station, along with the music of the 1980s. As a result, the disc jockeys were enjoying less and less freedom and facing more and more corporate demands.

"As all great things do, it began falling apart," Stein says. "It got weird at the end; everyone was splitting in half. My allegiance was with Kid Leo. So when he left [December 1988], I didn't stay long afterward."

The past decade in New York has been good for one of WMMS's favorite female voices. And like the fluke that caused her to move to Cleveland, another fateful inception whisked her to New York.

It was when Paul McCartney's *Flowers in the Dirt* LP was released. Capitol Records was flying disc jockeys from different cities to New York to hear McCartney do a press conference. Then, if you were lucky, you got a ticket to see him do a private concert at the Lyceum Theater.

Janet Macoska and I were sitting in my hotel room before the press conference discussing what we were going to do next. That's when I get a phone call from the producer saying the guy that was supposed to host it had food poisoning [coincidentally, he was former 'MMS alumnus Charlie Kendall]. So he asks me if I would host the press conference—like, now. I had no time to be nervous. I ran across the street, shook hands with Paul McCartney, who was expecting a man, so right away he knew something was amiss. But he winked at me and reached over, squeezed my knee and smiled as if to say, everything will be okay.

The last-minute stint resulted in a longstanding friendship between Stein and Paul and Linda McCartney, as well as a new job. Demonstrating that she could think quickly on her feet, Westwood One hired her as program editor for on-air personalities. She began hosting coast-to-coast broadcasts and working with morning shows at over 200 network affiliates. In 1996, she was promoted to director of programming for a Westwood One young adult network, "The Source." Ironically, this has kept her in touch with her Cleveland friends, as her affiliates include WMMS and WMJI.

Ruby Cheeks (b. 1956, Province, R.I.; WMMS, WNCX, WWWE)

The daughter of a Cleveland native, Ruby Cheeks spent her summers on Ohio's North Coast. "I stayed often at my grandmother's at E. 111 and Buckeye Road in Cleveland," she says. "So I well remember listening to all those great radio stations. There were the AM stations, WIXY 1260 and WHK. Throughout my teen years I listened to WNCR, WMMS, and M-105."

Cheeks didn't become a permanent Cleveland resident until 1984, when she was hired at WMMS after a series of radio jobs. Her journey into broadcasting began as a college dare in 1976.

"I was on the beach in Fort Lauderdale," she explains. "My girlfriend and I were lying there listening to the radio when we heard an advertisement for a broadcasting school. My friend said, 'I dare you to go for that.' I looked at her and replied, 'Yeah, okay.'"

The college English major enrolled at the Brown Institute for Radio and Television Broadcasting. She didn't have to travel far; the Minneapolis-based institution had a satellite school in Fort Lauderdale. From there, it was on to radio jobs in New England (WPJB 105), West Palm (WNGS 92, WIZD 99), Jupiter, Florida (WCEZ 97), and back to Fort Lauderdale (K-102). It was when she was at WPBJ that a colleague nicknamed her Ruby Cheeks— for obvious reasons.

When she first arrived in Cleveland, it was for a position as promotion manager for A&M Records. Six months later, John Gorman approached her about adding a female voice to Jeff & Flash's "Morning Zoo."

"The timing was right, on both sides," she says. "And the chemistry was right. Soon as I came on with Jeff & Flash, we kicked . . . ."

Cheeks tells it like it was. The morning ratings for WMMS climbed considerably once she joined the "Zoo Crew," and according to the ratings period for the winter of 1986, the morning team was boasting a 18.6 share—figures that astounded radio executives (the average at that time was closer to 6). The job was close enough to perfect for the feisty deejay. Her natural assertiveness (sometimes construed as aggressiveness) was not only allowed, it was encouraged. She freely voiced her opinion on current events, which became a staple of the show. In doing so, she won over many fans, both male and female. "I loved that period," she says.

Every day was a new adventure. I really think we were the predecessors to Howard Stern. We were doing a lot of talk, especially on the issues of the day. In retrospect, I have to pinch myself because it now seems so surreal. Right from the start, people knew who I was on the street. In six months, I had that town by its ear. It was amazing.

I may be a tad arrogant in saying this but I'll say it anyway, since I've never been one to mince words. I think had we left the station intact, that is Jeff, Flash, me, and Boom [Len Goldberg] been allowed to continue as we were, the Howard Stern Show would never have gained the status in Cleveland that it has. But by then, the whole Buzzard thing had been dismantled, and it was prime for the picking.

So what did happen? With three years as a winning part of WMMS's largest ratings period, Ruby Cheeks was the talk of Buzzard town. This became evident at the 1986 Riverfest, when she was swamped with people shouting her name in chanting tones. Cheeks was also named one of *Cleveland Magazine*'s Most Interesting People of 1986. Her greatest appeal seemed to stem from controversy, having earned a reputation that alternated between energetic and spontaneous with a quick wit, to hard-edged and tough. Then again, as she would later discover, that old cliché was true. You had to be tough to live in Cleveland. That's where Ruby Cheeks spent some of the most difficult years of her career. When the WMMS diva was switched to evening shift (6:00–10:00 P.M.), it was touted in the papers as a promotion, a chance for her own prime-time show, and something Cheeks had always said she wanted. However, behind the scenes was a different story. Hovering over her like a real-life buzzard was the rumor that her connection with her audience had produced so much attention it often surpassed that of her co-workers, Jeff and Flash.

"We were all doing great morning radio together," she later told *Plain Dealer* reporter Roberto Santiago. "But they couldn't stand that I was getting more popular than they were."

She proceeded to recount the fateful day when she walked into the WMMS studios and overheard a conversation between Jeff and Flash about her "new replacement."

"I didn't want to leave. It wasn't my decision to leave," Cheeks notes. "They replaced me with that Roberta somebody, and how long did she last, about a heartbeat? After that, there was never the success, nor the ratings, nor the loyalty."

Her ever-present fortitude, however, helped her bounce back as she won over her evening audience with regular spots like "Ruby Tuesday" and "Ruby's Jewel of the Night." Then Kid Leo departed for New York City, and Cheeks was given his 2:00– 6:00 P.M. shift. By October 1989, however, the captivating deejay was ready to move on.

"I was tired of the craziness going on at the station," she says. "I'd gone through too many program directors, too many general managers. That station had been solid for so long. Decades. Then suddenly, there was all this turmoil. And it has continued to get worse because they get clueless people in there that don't understand what that station is all about. As long as they bring people into the station who don't have a clue to its heritage and its roots, it'll continue to wallow. You need to have your finger on the pulse of what's going on. Have some knowledge of its background. And most of all, have some respect for it."

When she decided to leave WMMS, she left Cleveland as well. She accepted a job at WAAF-FM in Worcester, Massachusetts. But she wasn't happy. By June 1991, Ruby Cheeks was back in town.

"I wanted to go back to 'MMS," she notes. "But when I said, 'Hey, put me back on with Jeff & Flash, let's burn these phones up.' I was told by management, 'What's the entertainment value in that?' They wouldn't do it. So I went across the street. Norman Wain hired me to do the seven to midnight shift on WNCX. Later I took over the shift directly after the Howard Stern Morning Show."

But not for long. Citing her dismay with the way the station was being run, Cheeks left in February 1994. A few months later, she shifted gears and signed with AM station WWWE 1100, with an all-talk format.

"I was real excited about doing it. I love talk radio. It gives me a chance to vent. It's my catharsis," Cheeks says with a laugh. She was given her own Saturday morning talk show. It seemed to be right up her alley, given her passion for hot topics. One topic, however, made undue headlines.

In March 1996, the *Plain Dealer* reported that Cheeks was resigning from the station. The heat was on when the article noted she was leaving due to complaints that she allowed callers on her live show to speculate about a then-unsolved murder in Cleveland. Although the headline, "Radio Personality Quits in Wake of Controversy," was retracted the next day, the damage was done. "I should have sued the [expletive]," she says of the newspaper. "I quit because of another job offer, not for anything talked about on the show. I was only following orders in the building. I was an Indian, not a chief, in terms of program content. But I became the scapegoat."

Despite the unhappy memories, Cheeks, now residing in Philadelphia, confirms that her fondest times rest in Cleveland and her first North Coast radio job.

The great thing about 'MMS was, it wasn't just a radio station. It was a lifestyle. It was so influential in people's lives, whether you worked there, or as a listener. That station really motivated people; it was in-your-face. I've been in this business over twenty-three years and have never seen anything that duplicated it or remotely replicate it—before or since.

They laugh at me here in Philly and say, "Cleveland?" Like, what's so great about Cleveland? But they don't understand. They weren't there, they didn't work there. They have no baseline for comparison. I tell them how the audience in Cleveland was so educated on the music. They knew their rock history. They knew what an Arbitron was. There was so much inside information that was disseminated through 'MMS to the public that, in normal situations, the public wouldn't have been able to grasp. But because the audience was so astute, they understood.

During that entire time, you lived, breathed, and died 'MMS. Nothing will ever be like that again.

But Cheeks prevailed, even after the WWWE nightmare. Although she says she would like to return to Cleveland radio some day, she is currently at rock station WYSP-FM 94. There she focuses on sales and marketing, while keeping her on-air post doing fill-ins and weekend programming.

Maria Farina (b. 1964, Pittsburgh; WMMS, WPHR, WENZ, WMVX)

After ten years, four stations, and twelve different program directors, Maria Farina was ready to "shut" the revolving door of her radio career. That is, until she was offered a job she couldn't refuse.

"I was really ready to quit radio when I got a call from WMVX program director Randy James, and he asked me to send in a tape," Farina said in 1997. "The hours were good, and the money I couldn't pass up. So here I am. Yes, radio has changed a lot in the years I've been in it. But although the role of the deejay is certainly diminished, I think the listeners will always demand that personal touch."

Growing up in Pittsburgh, Farina listened to FM stations WAMO and WDVE. "I especially loved 'DVE. It was hard rock and just a great station. That's when I started really getting into radio. I'll never forget being in the car and talking up to the exact moment Fleetwood Mac started singing, and my dad saying, 'Hey, you're pretty good at that.'"

Still, as a journalism major at Ohio University, Farina was planning to be a foreign correspondent. "I went into college radio [WOUB Athens] figuring I'd end up in television. But everyone was telling me what a great voice I had, why don't I stay in radio? I thought, well, I've always loved music. I come from a very musical family. Why not?"

After graduating in 1986, she shopped around, sending her resumé to "every radio station from Pittsburgh to Cleveland." "I had heard of WMMS through a guy I'd been dating all through college. He loved the Buzzard. Everything was the Buzzard—stickers, shirts, etc. But first I got a call from Danny Wright at WGCL and was considering that. Then the next day I got a call from John Gorman. Naturally, I figured this is where I have to go. I'll never forget driving up to Cleveland with my parents. My dad, the ever-proud parent, was telling these people at a rest stop, 'You know she's going to work at WMMS.' And they seemed genuinely impressed, saying, 'MMS? Wow.'"

Beginning her first radio job at such an established station, the twenty-two year old had no idea what she was getting into.

I think some people resented me because I was so green. I was totally naive. I didn't know the relationship everyone had with one another. I wasn't immediately accepted. That took awhile. But I had a great mentor in Dia Stein. She taught me how to script my breaks in a way that sounded natural. She told me to keep a picture of someone I really liked by my playlist and talk as if directly to that person, rather than thinking of the whole listening audience. Dia used a photo of Bruce Springsteen for that. I alternated between my boyfriend and my dog. It worked great. People have often said to me, "It sounds like you are talking just to me!"

Dia was a wonderful example for me. She was the epitome of class and preparedness, and had a beautiful voice. I just thought she was it.

In September 1986, John Gorman left for WNCX, taking much of the staff with him. "That's when we started going through a number of people and program directors, and changing the music. Like, who would have ever dreamed we'd be hearing Whitney Houston or Michael Jackson coming out of 'MMS? The station's popularity was plummeting. By the time I left in '89, it was pretty much done."

The 1989 summer Arbitron ratings substantiate that fact. The station that, just a few years before, had boasted higher ratings than its two competitors combined fell behind "adult contemporary" stations WMJI-FM and WLTF-FM. The '90s would not be any better for WMMS.

Farina became the fourth disc jockey to leave the station within a year. She felt bad enough, but her peers' reactions were worse. "Anytime anyone left 'MMS, they'd hate you. It was like an Italian family: 'How can you do this to us?' 'You're leaving the family, what are you doing? How can you be so ungrateful?' Of course, it eventually settled down. But at the time it was terrible. And the irony was that it really *was* like a family to me. I did become close to them, liked TR and Matt the Cat. It was nice to be in a workplace where everyone looked out for each other. But if you left, they felt betrayed."

Although she resigned with no prospects lined up, Farina had no trouble securing one. She was soon offered the coveted morning position at Top 40 station WPHR-FM ("Power 108," later WENZ and Z-107.9). Her first partner was Jim Bosh, later replaced by John Landecker. She moved to nights, then to middays before the station, without warning, changed its call letters and format in 1993. She recalls:

I'll never forget driving into work that day. I was listening to the station and they were playing "It's the End of the World As We Know it" by REM. I thought, oh, I like this song. Then they played it again, and I thought, that's weird, maybe someone made a mistake. Then, they played it *again*, and I thought, oh, my God, I'm getting fired today.

There's always rumors going around when a station is about to change, but you never know the validity of those rumors. This one turned out to be true. So I get into work and was immediately sent to [program director] Lyndon Abel's office. He told me they were firing everyone except me and Rick Michaels. I was so happy and relieved, I literally jumped up and hugged him.

The new station, WENZ ("The End," now Z-107.9), became one of Cleveland's top radio stations and one of few to push local talent with the Sunday night program, "Inner Sanctum." The 7:00–9:00 P.M. show with host Johan, the Agora promoter, gave bands and artists a place to showcase their music at a time when WMMS had long abandoned giving them airplay.

Farina says her days at WENZ were the happiest of her career. The good times ended, however, in September 1996, when yet another management change caused her to lose her position at the modern music station. She then took her voice tape and began freelancing for radio and television commercials as well as on and off-camera industrials (stations for IDs and commercials). In January 1997, Farina found a new radio home at Cleveland's newest success story, WMVX ("Mix-106.5"). The station is one of the first to put disc jockeys in the background, with its "more music, less talk" motto. But when that station was sold, Farina survived moved on to do the morning show on 104.1 with former WMMS jockey Danny Czekalinski.

"My one biggest regret was that I didn't pursue a career in television," Farina says. "If they do end up phasing out the deejays, I may just have to go for that."

17 The '90s Go to Extremes

Rock and roll '90s style was a colorful potpourri of novice and veteran musicians alike. The music became diverse and, in many cases, extreme. While the multiplying subgenres left some to doubt the health of rock and roll, and despite the rumors that "rock is dead" reverberating through the media during the decade, the first few years of the 1990s saw new takes on rock music that reinvigorated the industry—at least for a while.

In its debut years, it looked like grunge rock would be the craze of the nineties. This new style came fast and strong and, refreshingly, not out of New York or Los Angeles, but Seattle. A band called Nirvana produced a powerful new sound with its debut single "Smells Like Teen Spirit" (1992). The group was fronted by Kurt Cobain, who became a cult hero and rock icon, largely due to his suicide in 1994. "Seattle-born grunge" burst onto the music scene with fierce intensity. Along with Nirvana came Pearl Jam, Soundgarden, Alice in Chains, Hole, and Screaming Trees. Generation X basked in the dark, hard-edged, and often violent sounds of grunge, rap, and goth. But like punk rock before it, the popularity of grunge was short-lived.

Included among the many subgenres of rock are indie rock, death metal, hardcore, industrial, thrash, rap/hip-hop, funk, goth, technopop, ska, postpunk, and avant-garde/experimental. But in a seemingly desperate attempt to hang on to their roots, R&B, rockabilly, and even swing enjoyed resurgences in the '90s.

In the lakefront city that would officially be crowned "the Rock and Roll Capital" in September 1995, the local club scene experienced both highs and lows. By decade's end, however, things were looking up. An eclectic range of musicians played steadily at hundreds of venues throughout the Greater Cleveland area, and the best ones were getting recognition for their efforts via the first annual *Cleveland Free Times* Music Awards and the *Scene* Music Awards, both in 1999. Interestingly, the two magazines' winners were often different, further proof of Cleveland's diverse musical taste: *Free Times* winners were Mr. Tibbs for best funk act, Sax-O-Tromba for best ska/reggae, Jahi for hip-hop/rap, Al's Fast Freight for country/Americana, and the Conservatives for best punk/hardcore; *Scene* readers chose Bone Thugs-N-Harmony for best hip-hop, the Twist Offs for funk, Carlos Jones and the P.L.U.S. Band for reggae, the Cowslingers for best country act, and Hostile Omish in the punk/hardcore category. Despite this mélange, the polls showed some steadfast favorites. Bluesman Robert Lockwood Jr., folk singer Anne E. DeChant, and rock bands Rosavelt and Mushroomhead took honors from both the *Free Times* and *Scene*.

And young rock groups such as Curmudgeon (an impressive trio with two members fresh out of high school) listened to former Cleveland underground artists Rocket from the Tombs, the Dead Boys, Electric Eels, Mirrors, and Peter Laughner to learn their craft and make their own brand of punk. Clearly, this next generation born and raised in the rock capital seems determined to continue the rich and diverse tradition that has come to be expected of the Cleveland music scene.

But while most active North Coast bands may not have landed on the cover of the *Rolling Stone* or had songs listed in *Billboard*, they have been instrumental in keeping live music thriving.

Groups and Artists of the '90s

Choosing the bands to profile in this history is not easy. If the criteria could be defined as to which ones do their best in pleasing their audience over the years, both in musical ability and sheer entertainment, this book would never see completion. Looking back over the decade, there are numerous bands of note, as the '90s saw its share of diverse rockers. Some made their names more outside of Cleveland than in. Others, for various reasons, keep their fan-base fires burning at home. Either case, as always, the number of bands and musicians runs into the hundreds: the Waynes (pop rock), Moko Bovo (blues), the Simpletons (pop rock), State of Being (industrial), Prisonshake (alternative), Filter (industrial), Lestat (techno-pop), the Cowslingers (rockabilly, or "cowpunk"), Al's Fast Freight (alternative country), Slack Jaw (post punk/power pop), Ether-Net (British-style rock), the Revelers (indie rock), Coltrane Wreck (alternative), Cows in the Graveyard (avant-garde/experimental), Third Wish (folk rock), Deaf Children at Play (grunge), Quazi Modo (classic rock), Stacie Collins (country), Speaker/Cranker (post punk), Qwasi Qwa (pop rock), Gem (indie rock), Cryptkicker (death metal), Craw (indie rock), the Chargers (garage punk), 3D (pop rock), and solo artists Jahi (rap/hip-hop) and Bill Fox (pop singer/songwriter). There were female-dominated bands such as the Vivians, the Librarians, and the Heathers. And with notable musicians like veteran guitarists Jimmy Black, Greg Nelson, and Ted Riser, and newcomers such as Mike Farley, Tony Lang, Stacie Collins, and Thomas Reed Smith, the North Coast continues to offer a wide range of musical options on any given night.

Alternative Rules

As rock steered away from the mainstream and subgenres split like branches on a tree, "alternative" became the catchphrase for any music that couldn't be confined to any one category.

As rock and roll music continues to grow and expand, the term "alternative" safely labels groups that choose the independent route of musical styles.

Cleveland has always had and will continue its historic musical conglomerations of the alternative nature. Some of the '90s bands were fueled by young, aspiring talents, while others had roots that stemmed far back to the past. Each brought—and many continue to bring—people together to share one common goal: to rock.

Sons of Elvis (1990–97)

Back in 1995, the rock/pop band with the hardcore/alternative twist was being heralded as Cleveland's next big thing with its promising debut CD and single "Formaldehyde." The lineup, which never changed in its seven-year history, consisted of guitarist Tim Parnin, bassist Dave Hill, drummer Pat Casa, and lead vocalist/lyricist John Borland. Dreams of pink Cadillacs, pretty girls, and mansions on a hill, however, were never these guys' motive.

"We were four close friends who just liked to play music together," Parnin says. "It was more about playing good music with your friends than purposely trying to put together some 'awesome' band, looking for members in a rock paper." But how did these four musicians who look nothing like Elvis Presley get their band name?

"The group's name came from this support group Pat [Casa] had formed back in grade school," Hill explains. "He was kind of heavyset and the kids would make fun of him. So he got all the other fat kids together and they called themselves the 'Sons of Elvis.' Later he slimmed down and got kicked out of the group."

Perhaps out of revenge, Casa decided to use the name when his college roommates formed their rock band. Hill, Parnin, and Casa had graduated from St. Ignatius in 1987, and all chose to go to New York's Fordham University, where they hooked up with Borland. It began as a diversion from their studies, but soon the Sons of Elvis were spending many a night playing music at nearby clubs. After honing their repertoire, the quartet, which cites Led Zeppelin and Cheap Trick as influences, began getting gigs at several New York bars such as CBGB, Irving Plaza, Maxwell's, Woody's, Pyramid, and the China Club. They fast developed their own sound.

"Initially, we started off with more of a college full-chord sound," Parnin says, "then evolved into more riff-oriented, groove-oriented music with a lot of vocal melody on top. It became more aggressive as time went on."

"I think Pat defined our sound," Hill adds. "He had this wild drumming style, kind of like a funky version of Keith Moon. When we were playing the New York clubs, record-label guys began showing up, then pretty soon the A&R guys showed because they'd heard about our live shows, which were pretty energetic. We were intense."

After being approached by several labels, the band was signed to the independent American Empire Records in 1993. When the company went bankrupt three months later, the national label, Priority Records, picked up their contract. The label was owned by Joe Grillo, former Atlantic Records marketing vice-president who had promoted Stone Temple Pilots, Tori Amos, and others. Things looked promising.

"I think there is truth to the fact it's harder to get a record deal in a city outside L.A. or New York," Parnin notes. "Like in New York, all the big labels are based there. That's the reality. There's just more people in the industry who can walk a couple blocks to see you perform, instead of hopping on a plane to go to Cleveland. The odds are better."

The band's debut CD, *Glodean,* spawned the popular song "Formaldehyde," which was often heard on WMMS and the Sunday night WENZ program "Inner Sanctum," which showcased the local music scene. "WMMS played that song so much it became almost annoying," Parnin laughs. "It was on all the time, and they played it continuously for the next three years."

The album, which they say was named after Barry White's wife as both a tribute to the throaty singer and because "we thought her name was cool," sold 70,000 copies, and "Formaldehyde" became one of WMMS's Top 10 singles of the year. But the group's music wasn't just a hit in its hometown. During the years from 1993 to 1994, Sons of Elvis traveled across the country playing radio festivals in New Orleans, Phoenix, Philadelphia, and New York (most notably the College Music Journal festival), all the while enjoying radio airplay in those and other cities. By 1995 the native Clevelanders returned home. Borland remained in New York and would travel to Cleveland for various gigs at the Phantasy, the Grog Shop, Peabody's DownUnder, the Odeon, and the Agora.

"We refused to consider getting a new member [to replace Borland]," Hill says. "We always hated when bands did that. So we continued to get together to rehearse and write new songs."

Despite their perseverance, the group's contract was broken when the label switched its genre to strictly rap music in 1996. "But we kept playing, " Parnin says. "Being signed was never a factor in our playing music."

Then while working on a new release, tragedy struck. "John got into this real bad car accident," Hill says. "So we were in sort of a hiatus until he got better. Again, we didn't want to replace him. But it took a long time for him to recover. By then, we passed on a [new] record deal and things pretty much dissolved themselves."

The Sons of Elvis accepted reality and eventually went on to other musical collaborations. Today, Hill and Parnin are both members of Uptown Sinclair. Hill also plays in Cobra Verde. In addition, Hill composed the theme for HBO's *Reverb,* a weekly one-hour live rock show. Parnin is also guitarist in VUA (Vanduls Ugenst Alidarecy) with former Faith No More singer Chuck Mosley. Casa runs his family business, and Borland is an English teacher on Long Island.

Spudmonsters (1988–98)

What's a spudmonster? "A couch potato that has mutated even further," explains Devo fan and original Spudmonster singer Roger Warmuth (a.k.a. Joe Gizmo).

Contrary to the mental picture the definition presents, this hardcore/thrash/punk/

metal band was nothing near frightening. This quintet, initially called Joe Gizmo and the Spudmonsters, was more into having a good time.

The Spudmonsters evolved when guitarist and Lakewood record store owner Chris Andrews (of Chris' Warped Records) formed the band with Warmuth (later replaced by John Keener, then Don Foose), Alex Strouhal (guitar), Rick Keihl (drums), and Ian Shipley (former bassist in the heavy metal band, Breaker; later replaced with Joe Kilcoyne, then Steve Swanson). Their favorite hometown haunts were the Empire, Phantasy, Peabody's DownUnder, and Flash's.

"I knew Chris Andrews from Warped Records," recalls Warmuth, a 1978 Lakewood High graduate. "We just got together, basically, to have fun with it. I was surprised when the group hit big in Germany."

With fun their primary purpose, the group became renowned for stage performances that included the singer, dressed as a mad scientist, throwing out bags filled with confetti, pizza boxes, and, well, garbage.

"'Garbage day' was mostly written by Ian," says Warmuth of their popular song. "Living in Lakewood, I couldn't relate to garbage day because they came in the yard to pick up the garbage. But everyone else I knew would complain, 'yeah, gotta take the garbage out.' I've moved since then and have a real long driveway, so now I'm like, 'Oh no, it's garbage day!'"

The song was later included on the group's debut album. The Spudmonsters' stage antics also included distributing mass quantities of beer. One night, in particular, that came in handy.

"We were always moving around on stage," Warmuth recalls. "The bass player and I were running around, and we were goin' at each other and I collided with the corner of the bass, right on the forehead above my left eye. We had the cooler full of beer right there, so I immediately grabbed a bunch of ice. It felt good, but then it looked like I was bleeding worse as the ice started melting and I was dripping red!

"But as they say, the show must go on, and it did. But I have a scar there to forever remember it by."

Frontman/vocalist/songwriter Don Foose joined the band in 1990 just as the group got its first break. The signing of the Spudmonsters to Germany's Massacre Records in 1990 sparked several European tours and ultimately produced three releases. Those included *Stop the Madness* (1993), *No Guarantees* (1995), and the 1997 CD *Moment of Truth* (on Massacre Records in the U.K., Century Media Records in the U.S.).

"Joe [Kilcoyne] had left our band to join another band who signed with Massacre," Foose explains. "He gave them a demo of ours and they liked it. After that first record was released, they invited us to Europe to open for Biohazard, which was a big hardcore band at the time. We played in front of about 1,300 people a night. It was great."

The band, critics agree, cannot be pigeonholed into a specific genre.

"When the group first formed in 1988, the group was considered a punk crossover," says Foose, a 1985 Brunswick High School graduate. "I used to see the Spudmonsters live at the Phantasy and always liked their music. Then when I read in *Scene*

Spudmonsters Don Foose (*left*) and Scott Roberts jump into action at the Agora, May 1997. *Courtesy of Don Foose.*

they were looking for singers, and I auditioned. So after Scott Roberts [guitarist] and I joined the band, it took on a more hardcore influence. I was into the more straight-edged music like the Guerilla Biscuits, Youth of Today, and Judge."

Just what is hardcore? "The songs are usually two minutes or less, and straight to the point," Foose explains. "You won't hear guitar solos. These songs usually are about life, things that depict deep meaning, with sort of tribal beats to it." Foose, a Hare Krishna, says his lyrics took on a more serious side than those of previous Spudmonsters.

"Their first singer, Roger, wrote songs with humorous elements. For instance, he wrote a song called 'Beer Rules,' which was basically about . . . beer. It was always a crowd favorite. He was more into the fun and good times. And he was the best at that, a real good songwriter. But I just had a different style. I wrote lyrics with deep, thought-provoking themes like suicide, isolation, and dealing with life's struggles . . . self-realization. I thought it was interesting how we fused the two together."

Each member contributed his talents to their originals, with Foose writing most of the lyrics. In 1990, their song "I'm Not Guilty" was included on Auburn Records' *Heavy*

Artillery compilation, which featured twenty area metal bands. The Spudmonster single received heavy airplay on college stations and spent some time on WMMS's and WENZ's regular rotation list, and a video promoting "Garbage Day" was played on MTV. The group continued to include favorite cover songs, such as Motorhead's "Ace of Spades," Bad Brains' "Right Brigade," and Cro-Mags' "Malfunction," in their live shows.

The hometown crowds were eating them up, but the Spudmonsters had little time to play Cleveland clubs in their quest for international fame. Aside from traveling across the U.S., their European jaunts often took them on ten-week tours that included England, France, Germany, Poland, and Belgium. From 1990 until 1995, the group counted seven full-length European and three full-length U.S. tours.

The frequent traveling, and particularly the business aspect, began taking its toll by 1996. That's when Andrews, by then an entrepreneur, gave up rock and roll for his growing chain of record/video/nostalgia stores. The final lineup became Foose, Steve Swanson (bass), Scott Roberts (guitar), Eric Klinger (guitar), and Eric Mathews (drums). The latter two members went on to play in the up-and-coming national band, Pro-Pain.

The group's last years were good to the mutating spuds. The reenergized band continued its frenetic lifestyle. The third album was selling well and the tours were successful for a while. But the musicians hadn't anticipated a change in music trends. The hardcore scene, especially in Europe, began drying up, according to the group. That, in conjunction with the rigors of being on the road, finally wore them down.

"I practice Eastern philosophy, and the pace was wearing me physically and mentally," Foose notes. "Plus, we were getting ripped off from the promoters. I think we got to the point where we got about as big as we were going to get."

Their final concert took place at the Odeon on January 17, 1998. The Spudmonsters came full circle when original frontman Roger Warmuth joined the group on stage that night, playing to a sold-out crowd.

Don Foose now fronts Run Devil Run. The group includes Mike Ski (former bassist in Brothers Keepers), Richie Ferjanic (drums), and Kevin Roberts (guitar). In May 1999, the group was part of the much-heralded Dynamo Festival in Eindhoven, Holland. Sharing the same bill as Metallica, it was the first Cleveland band ever to play the three-day festival, which attracts up to 80,000 music lovers.

Cobra Verde (1994–)

Death of Samantha founder/guitarist/songwriter and *Plain Dealer* entertainment columnist John Petkovic wants it known that there is a difference between present-day Cobra Verde and its original incarnation: "In terms of getting together to practice on a regular basis, doing extensive touring, or recording as a designated group, [the early] version of Cobra Verde was not a band."

Nonetheless, from the beginning, this musical project is considered an impressive collaboration of noted and skilled music makers. And true, it was never meant to be a performing band in the first place. The friends merely got together to record some songs at former Breaker bassist/guitarist Don Depew's recording studio, where many Cleveland musicians record. Then Robert Griffin from Scat Records (then Cleveland-based, now in St. Louis) approached Petkovic about making a record for his label. Petkovic, in turn, contacted his ex-DOS bandmates Doug Gillard, Dave Swanson, and Don Depew.

Once the group laid down tracks that ultimately led to the 1994 full-length CD *Viva La Muerte*, Petkovic realized it was time for a band name. A film buff, the guitarist/songwriter adopted the name from German director Werner Herzog's movie of the same title. They then took their music out of the studio and played their first show in July 1994 at the famed Agora.

How would they characterize their sound? "A garage-band version of Roxy Music with a blue-collar Cleveland twist to it," is how Swanson describes it.

By year's end, *Viva La Muerte* was named one of the top indie records in *Rolling Stone*. Although a rare event, Cobra Verde played a few out-of-town gigs, including shows in Chicago and New York City for the Scat Records' "Insects of Rock" tour. Since then, the band has treated its fans to an occasional show at the Grog Shop, Euclid Tavern, and the Odeon.

During the next few years they produced a six-song EP, *Vintage Crime,* and a few singles. In 1997, the group released the CD *Egomania (Love Songs)* on Scat, which was recognized in CMJ's college radio charts. Meanwhile, the Cleveland musicians hooked up with another band they met on the Insects of Rock tour, Dayton group Guided by Voices, headed by Robert Pollard. Cobra Verde participated on GBV's 1997 CD, *Mag Earwhig,* critically acclaimed in *Rolling Stone, Billboard,* and *Entertainment Weekly.* A U.S. tour with both bands followed. But although the concert tour itself was successful, it ultimately caused a rift among band members.

"I left after the Guided by Voices tour in December '97," Swanson notes. "Early the next year, Bob [Pollard] called Doug and asked if he wanted to remain in GBV. Doug said okay. That, in turn, created tension between John, Don, and Doug."

A few months later, Depew left as well, but Petkovic's inspiration lives on. He has since recruited other notable musicians, including drummer Mark Klein (formerly of Breaker, and currently in Ether Net), bassist Dave Hill (formerly of Sons of Elvis), guitarist Frank Vazzano (also plays in Quazi Modo, and keyboardist Chas Smith (formerly of the Clocks and the Pagans). Petkovic and Smith also play in a band called Einstein's Secret Orchestra.

Cobra Verde released *Nightlife* in the fall of 1999. The fourteen-song CD consists of previously recorded material from some of those early studio gatherings and, in Petkovic's words, features "tons of overdubbed synths, guitars, and sounds mixed together." Various musicians took part in the recordings, including sax player and former Akronite Ralph Carney, whose history includes Tin Huey. Appearances on the September 1999 cover of *CMJ Monthly* and at that year's CMJ (*College Music Journal*) festival held at New York's CBGB's, and reviews in *Interview* and *Playboy* will undoubtedly get their name and music noticed. With the European fan base earned by Death of

Samantha, Cobra Verde has gained an impressive amount of interest in England, France, and Germany. Consequently, Cobra Verde may just stand the test of time—despite its less-than-ideal proximity.

"The problem with [producing music in] Cleveland," Petkovic says, "is that it's on the outskirts of the larger markets like New York, Chicago, Boston, Seattle, LA, and San Francisco. It's in its own world, a vacuum, per se. So it's harder to get the good stuff marketed at large. On the other hand, it allows you to do your own thing and develop your own sensibilities."

Hostile Omish (1987–)

If the title doesn't clue you in on the style of this band, their manner of dress gives it away every time. Donning Amish-style suspenders, wide-brimmed hats, and impish grins, this "comedic post-grunge-metal-barncore" group's beginning was a smash hit. Literally.

"I was driving along out in Middlefield," recalls singer Lenny ("Lank") Laska, one of the original members. "The speed limit out there is fifty miles an hour. I was coming up over a hill and when I came back down the hill, all of a sudden there was this Amish buggy. I had no time to react and ran smack into the back of it. The car went right through the buggy but surprisingly no one got hurt, not even the horse. But immediately the guy jumps out and starts screamin' and yellin' at me and being real hostile.

"Now we had just put the band together, and when I related the incident to the guys, we came up with the perfect name: Hostile Omish."

The group's fascination with the Amish prompted frequent trips to the small country towns of Middlefield, Orrwell, and Mesopotomia in Ohio's "Amish Country" in order to accurately fake authenticity.

Of course, none of the band members are Amish. They all live in the very modern Cleveland suburb of Oakwood Village (just outside the Solon/Bedford area). Had their family roots actually stemmed in Amish Country, this punk quartet, which sings of fascism ("Quilted in Fascism"), lesbianism ("Vagitarian"), and body functions ("We Throw Poop"), would have been shunned long ago—or perhaps deliberately run over by a wayward buggy. They've been called rude, crude, and lewd. They take it as a compliment.

Three members are brothers. The Hostile Omish are lead vocalist and guitarist Bob Schwind Jr. (known as Filth), bass guitarist Dave Schwind (who goes by the handle "Davey Do Right Don't Do Me Dirty"), and drummer Joe Schwind (a.k.a. Skwid). Cousin Lenny remained with the band until 1993, and Jason Kosar (Flankel) originally served as "butter-churner" from 1990 until 1993, when he was promoted to rhythm guitarist. He remains a permanent fixture in the band. Other members through the years include singers David Lasky (a.k.a. Dave Revolution), who sang with the band from 1993–94, and Lester Sexton (a.k.a. Rhubarb) from 1995–96.

It was through brother Joe that the band materialized. Back in 1985, he was drummer in a death metal band called Synastryche.

"My band needed an opening act for this one gig," Skwid says of the group's genesis. "So I told my brothers they had three months to learn to play instruments and make up a few stupid songs so they could open for us. At first they sucked. Some weeks later, I quit the other band and joined them, and we worked on it. We developed our own style."

Their style is not to be missed in their live shows. This unruly pack of barnstormers boasts two full-time butter-churners. At first it was "Zed" and "Lard" (Brian Strazek and Tony Lanasa, respectively) followed by Dave Michalik (a.k.a. Fenis) and Paul Doxey (a.k.a. Otterbine). Rumors that they traded cows and chickens for their musical instruments have been wildly exaggerated. When not making music, the brothers make windows and doors.

Their influences are not surprising, yet each one claims to like a different style of music. Dave Schwind listens to '50s music, while Jason is a "Deadhead." Bob Schwind gravitates toward punk and listens to the Dead Kennedys, Dead Milkmen, the Dead Boys, and the Ramones. "I first met Joe when he was still in Synastryche," recalls promoter Jim Clevo. "Joe told me about him and his brothers forming this new band, and he dragged me over to his house. It was late at night, so my first encounter with the Schwind brothers was in their pajamas in their living room. They were just kids then and, yes, [their premise] seemed strange and stupid, but I immediately recognized the entertainment value, and talent, as did those who saw them perform live. They eventually went from being a teenage thrash-metal joke band to a *serious* thrash-metal band."

In 1987, the young group entered a Battle of the Bands at Flash's in Lorain. They got into the finals but lost by one vote. With their over-the-top and politically incorrect

The Hostile Omish.
Courtesy of Joe Schwind.

themes (as well as their habit of leaving a pile of destruction on stage that left club owners fuming), Hostile Omish was the most banned band in northeast Ohio. It took another three years for the group to tame down enough to start getting hired again. They have since built a cultlike following thanks to gigs at Peabody's DownUnder, the Phantasy, Trilogy in the Flats, and the Euclid Tavern. In 1990, college radio station WUJC sponsored them at the Undercurrents Music Festival, in which they participated for the next three years. The group's music was included in several music compilation CDs, including *U.S. Rocker Audio Magazine 1 and 2, Distant Thunder* (Underground Expressy/Heavy Metal Demolition), *Hit 'Em Hard* (CMG, Cleveland Music Group), and *Northcoast Blend* (NORML).

The biggest attraction of this offbeat band is its sense of humor, raw as it is. While some contemporary groups such as Marilyn Manson release their angst with lyrics of hate, abuse, and violence, Hostile Omish uses these themes as fodder for play, rather than in-your-face executions. In that respect, this post-punk group, for many, is a lot easier to take. Brother Joe writes most of the lyrics while the other members kick in the music—music that's lightning fast with a beat even newcomers can't resist bouncing their heads to. The Schwind brothers also have the approval of Mom, who is usually present at shows, and with whom they still live.

"When they were babies, I used to play the radio at night to help them sleep," Joyce Schwind says. "Music has always been in the family. My father was a drummer, my uncle played accordion and the saxophone. But the kids never took lessons. They all just started messing around with the instruments as teenagers."

The boys also grew up watching Nickelodeon, so it is only natural that they often incorporate old TV theme songs into their performances. With a collection of eighty original songs, their set list is different every time. But each of their live shows promises to be entertaining—if not everyone's bale of hay. In 1999, the group was hired to play the WEA (Warner-Electra-Atlantic Records) festival in North Carolina, in which they were assigned opening night. At the 1999 South by Southwest Music Conference, Hostile Omish was such a hit at Maggie May's that an audience member approached them after their show to hire the group to play at a family barbeque the next day.

Their recordings include CDs on their own Punge label. Their debut CD, *Broken Buggy,* was released in 1990. In 1992 came *Caution—This Buggy Makes Wide Right Churns. Quilted in Fascism* was released in 1994 and *Barncore* in 1996. An EP was released in 1998, *Fuel-Injected Love Shammy,* and was later included on their 1999 CD *One Horse Power.* A double CD, *Olde Order of Omish,* was released in 2000.

Hostile Omish won a 1999 *Scene* award for Best Punk Band and performed at the subsequent show at the Agora. When the announcer bounded on stage to introduce them, he said, with thick irony, "And now for the 'comforting' sounds of Hostile Omish." The group then went straight into a jock-inspired song, "The Bedford High School Marching Band."

Take your girlfriends by the hand
Kick your ass and start to slam

Eat some cheese and eat some spam
With the Bedford High School marching band.

As critic David Martin wrote in a *Scene* review on the band, "Hard to take seriously? Yes. Crude as all get out? Oh, yeah. Fun to listen to? And how."

From Alternative to Industrial to Goth

Many mainstream rock and roll lovers consider the 1970s punk movement as music from the dark side. Yet Trent Reznor's Nine Inch Nails as well as Marilyn Manson—whose influences were Alice Cooper, Kiss, and the Dead Boys—make those once-pioneering artists of shock rock look as saccharine as Frankie Avalon and Annette Funicello.

Trent Reznor and Nine Inch Nails (1989–)

Nine Inch Nails, for all intents and purposes, consists of one member: Trent Reznor.

Like Cleveland legend, Joe Walsh, Reznor was neither born nor raised in the Cleveland area. Michael Trent Reznor was born May 17, 1965, in Mercer, Pennsylvania. Yet, also like Walsh, this '90s visionary was living in Cleveland when he honed his musical skills. He was also a member of several notable Cleveland bands, such as the Innocent, Exotic Birds, Slam Bam Boo, and Lucky Pierre. In addition, his manager, John A. Malm Jr., is a Cleveland native as well as partner in their record label, Nothing Records. Thus, Trent Reznor and Nine Inch Nails qualify for inclusion in Cleveland's rock history.

After moving to the North Coast in 1985, the twenty-year-old keyboardist first joined the Innocent (replacing Gary Jones) with renowned Cleveland musicians Alan Greene, Rodney Psyka, and Kevin Valentine. Prior to Reznor becoming a member, the group signed with Red Records, a Chicago-based label known for its 1984 platinum-selling single, Chicago Bears' "Superbowl Shuffle." After recording its first and only album, *Livin' on the Streets,* the Innocents hired Reznor just in time for him to get his photo taken for the record cover, despite not having participated on the LP.

"After we learned Gary was leaving the band, we went to check out this group from Erie, Pa., called the Urge one night at Spanky's East in Painesville," guitarist Greene recalls. "We were immediately struck by this kid on keyboards whose name we later learned was Trent Reznor. He looked really good on stage, played to the audience, and it was obvious he wanted to appear a certain way. I remember his keyboard was on this swivel, pivoting stand so he could play in towards the band, then at a moment's notice, swivel back towards the audience. He was very visual."

Soon after, the impressive keyboardist joined the Innocent and played with them for several gigs around town—until he grew bored. The band's rather pop sensibility was too light and commercial for Reznor, and after a year he dropped out. He has since tried to hide his history with that band.

"At first, he seemed enthused and excited about being in our band," Greene says. "But during this time he got his first exposure to some pretty jive record people. Yet, young as he was, I could see Trent saw right through them.

"I'm sure he underplays that period because our band was a pretty commercial venture. Not at all what he later became known for. We were mainstream rock, not cutting-edge. Musically, it had integrity, and it was good stuff. But it was groomed to fit into that marketplace. Though he may prefer not to acknowledge it today, in all honesty, that experience probably helped him learn the business and grow into what he eventually became."

While working at Pi Keyboards, Reznor, who was classically trained on piano beginning at age five, joined the Exotic Birds with singer/guitarist/percussionist Andy Kubiszewski. The group was managed by John Malm, an avid supporter of local bands. Exotic Birds produced an EP, *L'Oiseau,* before breaking up in 1987. (They would later re-form without Reznor). The soon-to-be-famous keyboardist also did a stint with Slam Bam Boo, a Top 40 synth-pop cover band. It was while in Slam Bam Boo that Reznor got a cameo in the movie *Light of Day.* The group, named "the Problems" in the film, managed to perform half a song before focus shifted back to the real stars of the movie, Michael J. Fox and Joan Jett. He also participated in the Slam Bam Boo single, "White Lies" b/w "Cry Like a Baby," before departing.

Reznor joined Lucky Pierre in 1988, at the urging of friend and group founder Kevin McMahon. Reznor toured with the group and contributed his keyboard talents to the band's EP, *Communique.* Yet there remained a hole in his soul. He was fast becoming disillusioned with the direction the rock scene was going.

"It seems to me rock has become very homogenized, so incredibly safe and politically correct for the most part, and whatever danger might have existed at its inception has been packaged, labeled, marketed and sold as product," Reznor told *Circus* magazine in 1994. If Reznor's ultimate goal was to avoid that reality, he succeeded beyond expectations. His music is neither homogenized nor politically correct. It is somber and so filled with life-questioning angst that Nine Inch Nails' music is often referred to as "doom and gloom rock." It's stark, blatantly honest, searching quality is what adolescents identify with. For that, Reznor has earned a Grammy award, owns a mansion in New Orleans, and has produced soundtracks for Hollywood films.

It all began simply with his waking up one day and realizing he wanted to do more with his life. In an interview with *Spin* magazine, Reznor explained how he was getting tired of playing keyboards in other people's bands and on other bands' recordings.

"I said to myself, 'You're twenty-fucking-three years old, what the fuck are you doing?' I was getting high a lot. I was turning into what I'd never wanted to be. So I made a pact with myself." That pact included abandoning drugs for making music. While still working at Pi, Reznor befriended Bart Koster, owner of Right Track Recording Studio (later Midtown Recording).

"Trent was a meticulous person, and I saw the drive and intensity in him right from the start," recalls Koster. "He put his whole into whatever he was doing. He'd been coming around for some time, and at one point he approached me about working on some demos in the studio. He seemed genuinely earnest, so we worked out a deal. He would do various jobs, which included engineering, and in turn, he could work on his music when the studio was closed. I didn't mind; it didn't cost me anything. I was glad to do it because I knew he was going to amount to something. He was so driven."

"I was working as an engineer at Right Track from 10:00 A.M. to sometimes 10:00 P.M.," recalls Grammy-winning Dazz Band keyboardist Steve Cox. "I remember Trent would come in at the end of the business day and start doing his own thing about the time I was leaving. And on many mornings, he'd still be there when I came in the next morning, working on what became *Pretty Hate Machine*. He worked very hard on that project. He had a great vision for what he wanted to do. When he was finally finished with it, he played it for me in the studio. I looked at him and said, 'Mark my words, brother, you're going to be a star.' When he won the Grammy [in 1993 for the single "Wish"], I sent him a note that said, 'Congratulations from one Grammy award winner to another. . . . I told ya so.'"

The self-described "computer dweeb" is a self-made man. He could have gone the way of many aspiring musicians, content to play local clubs while holding down a day job. Though not necessarily wanting to be the superstar he became (he prefers privacy), he chose to go to the extreme, producing computer-generated sounds no one else was making. And it quickly found an audience. His debut LP, *Pretty Hate Machine* (TVT Records), emphasized electronic music with an industrial sound, and it captured a generation that was fast becoming bored with mainstream pop rock. "Head Like a Hole" was its first single, and the video was put on regular rotation on MTV.

This proved to be a problem, however, when Reznor set out to play his new music live. He now had to form a real band and somehow manage to duplicate that music outside the studio. For that he summoned guitarist Richard Patrick (who would go on to found Filter in 1994), drummer Chris Vrenna (previously with Exotic Birds), and keyboardist Nick Rushe, all of whom worked doggedly with Reznor to recreate the sound for the live stage. The ever-creative Reznor managed to combine live musicians with prerecorded tape loops. Meanwhile, another single from the debut, "Down in It," hit No. 16 on *Billboard* (then an unusual occurrence for an independent label). The newly formed Nine Inch Nails honed its act at the CMJ Marathon in New York, then returned for a December 29, 1989, play date at the Phantasy Nite Club. The following night it was on to Pittsburgh's Metropol, where Cleveland band the Adults opened for them. From there came a series of club dates to promote the new release, as well as an appearance at New York's Academy Theater for the 1990 New Music Seminar.

Over the next few years, Nine Inch Nails, with Reznor as frontman, would include keyboardists Lee Mars, James Woolley, and Charlie Clouser, guitarists Robin Finck, bassist Danny Lohner, and drummer Jeff Ward. Noted session guitarist Adrian Belew and former Exotic Birds leader Andy Kubiszewski also participated in recordings.

Trent Reznor (*right*) with concert promoter Jim Clevo at the Phantasy Nite Club, May 1990.

By 1991, there was no looking back for Trent Reznor, as he left Cleveland for good. Touted as one of modern rock's most important voices, Reznor has been placed in the same category as Nirvana's Kurt Cobain and Pearl Jam's Eddie Vedder. A Ministry and Skinny Puppy fan, Reznor toured with both groups, and Nine Inch Nails was included on the first Lollapalooza tour in 1991, in which he is noted for stealing the thunder from headlining act Jane's Addiction.

As a result of intense touring, the debut album, a critical and commercial success, was certified gold in 1992. By then, Reznor and John Malm cofounded Nothing Records, with Tony Ciulla as president. Ciulla is formerly the co-owner of the now-defunct Empire club, and former marketing director for Blossom Music Center. Other bands signed to the Nothing label include Prick, Marilyn Manson, and British groups Pop Will Eat Itself and Coil.

The years of touring were good for record sales, but it was Reznor's presence at Woodstock '94 that left NIN's indelible imprint on rock's history. There Reznor solidi-fied his presence by giving a performance stark in both sound and appearance. The picture of his mud-splattered body on center stage was printed in publications through-out the world. From that moment on, Trent Reznor was a superstar—whether he liked it or not.

His follow-up releases include the EPs *Broken* (certified platinum in 1992) and *Fixed* (1992) and the fourteen-song CD *The Downward Spiral*. That 1994 release debuted at No. 2 on *Billboard*'s album chart—despite the ensuing controversy over its repetitious, angry theme and crude language, and also for being recorded at the L.A. house where the 1969 Manson killings took place. The song titles "Piggy" and "March of the Pigs" seemed direct references to that event, though Reznor denies having done it purposely. In previous interviews, Reznor says he was unaware of the history of the house he was renting until after moving there. "I don't want to be looked at as the guy who supports serial-killer bullshit," he said in a 1997 interview with *Rolling Stone*. Accusations aside, *The Downward Spiral* sold swiftly and was ultimately certified multiplatinum. *Further Down the Spiral* came next in 1995. That same year, Reznor took home another Grammy for Best Metal Performance for "Happiness Is Slavery." After that, the musician delved into film scores. He provided the movie soundtrack for Oliver Stone's *Natural Born Killers* and David Lynch's *Lost Highway*.

It took nearly five years, but the return of Nine Inch Nails, with the galvanizing 1999 release of *The Fragile,* brought critical raves despite an eighteen-month delay in its release.

Trent Reznor admits that his music is dark. He acknowledges his demons, exorcized through his intense lyrics and stark musical sound by way of technology. It is all there: the anger, the rebellion, the harsh realities, and innumerable (and often unanswerable) questions. All this and his technological genius have made this onetime Clevelander a music phenomenon.

Marilyn Manson (1993–)

He's feared, idolized, loathed, and adored. Like him or not, this shock rocker has become the king of rock's dark side. Taking his stage name from '60s icons Marilyn Monroe and Charles Manson, Brian Warner was determined to make himself known.

In the past, Alice Cooper, Ozzy Osbourne, and Kiss represented what every parent warned his or her kids about. Shock rock then meant stage theatrics, with guillotines, fake blood, and the occasional boa constrictor. Actions such as chopping off mannequin heads and biting bats were meant to thrill adventurous teens and terrify concerned parents. In hindsight, that was nothing.

The '90s version of shock/gothic rock (largely initiated by British bands Joy Division and Bauhaus) came complete with ear-splitting music that screeched disruptive themes of violence, sex, and Satanism. Yet this dark side of rock fast became the newest trend in music and fashion—perfect timing for this Canton native who always had an interest in horror fantasy and over-the-top theatrics. Beginning with the 1994 debut album *Portrait of an American Family* (produced by Nothing label's Trent Reznor), Marilyn Manson typifies the consummate meaning of "every parent's nightmare." But then, that's precisely what Warner is going for. His vision is not that of an accomplished musician but rather of a rock and roll superstar.

It began in Fort Lauderdale, Florida (where his family moved in 1990), miles away from the suburban atmosphere that spawned him. This complex and controversial figure began life as the only son of a furniture salesman and a nurse in Canton, Ohio. Born January 5, 1969, Warner attended Heritage Christian School, which he later said was a reason for his resentful attitude toward organized religion. The boy (whose mother claims has a 170 IQ) left there in tenth grade to finish his education at GlenOak High School. In 1993 he formed his first band, Marilyn Manson and the Spooky Kids in Miami. All band members adopted the first names of a movie star with the surname of a serial killer. Besides Manson, there were keyboardist Madonna Wayne Gacy, guitarist and bassist Twiggy Ramirez, guitarist Daisy Berkowitz (later replaced by John 5), and drummer Ginger Fish.

Within a year, Marilyn Manson dropped the "Spooky Kids" and became the first to sign with Trent Reznor's Nothing record label. From that came the group's debut album, quickly followed by the EP *Smells Like Children,* which brought the band due notice with the single "Sweet Dreams (Are Made of This)," a cover of Eurythmics' hit song. A much-publicized tour with Nine Inch Nails sealed Marilyn Manson's notoriety. On the heels of that came the 1996 release of *Anti-Christ Superstar,* which debuted at No. 3 on *Billboard*'s album charts and sold more than a million copies. There were interviews with *Rolling Stone, Spin,* and *Alternative Press,* and the Manson name alone was guaranteed to ignite a range of emotions.

His "performance art" productions, extreme in every dark sense, are deemed offensive to the average woman, God-fearing Christian, and animal lover. His stage persona demands attention with such antics as ripping out pages from the Bible, simulating sex acts, and wiping his derriere with the American flag. Frank Sinatra he is not. But his mostly white middle-class teen fans embrace it. While many cannot understand what attracts young people to this lifestyle, others see it as simply another means of youthful rebellious expression.

"Marilyn Manson represents the sign of the times," notes *Alternative Press* publisher Mike Shea. "Kids need something to feel independent from the rest of the world, to attach themselves onto something that fulfills that rebel side of themselves. The trick for him will be if he can adapt to the next sign of the times. It'll be interesting to see if [Manson] can stay on top."

Interesting is the key word. By the time *Mechanical Animals* was released in 1998, he was ready to reinvent himself for fear of becoming all too predictable. Both the music and the artist suddenly showed a slight deviation from the Manson of the past. He went from goth-king to glam-queen or, as one could say, from Alice Cooper to early David Bowie. Again, fans raved and records sold, but the ultimate question seems to be how long, or far, this embodiment of horror can take his alternative image. His elaborate shows and cutting-edge material, which initially brought acclaim for its ingenuity, may now, critics hint, be edging closer to extinction.

When the time does come and his Manson days are over, it seems unlikely Brian Warner will be satisfied to trade in his ripped fishnets, leather G-strings, and thigh-high platform boots for a three-piece suit and nine-to-five job in his hometown. Yet there are many who indeed hope he will disappear into the obscurity of suburban life. Those who despise what Manson exemplifies see him as no less than Satan himself and everything that is wrong with the world today. His demonic persona backfired in the wake of the 1999 Columbine High School shootings in Littleton, Colorado. Just days after the April incident, Manson and his goth cohorts were scheduled to perform in nearby Denver, but the concert was abruptly canceled. For months after the horrific event, the media pointed fingers at Manson's music, stage performances, and emphasis on hate as having a profoundly negative influence on today's youth.

Many young musicians, however, agree that music, no matter how morose or in-your-face, does not propel a person to go on a killing rampage. Nineteen-year-old Derek Deprator, of the Cleveland band Curmudgeon, though not a Manson enthusiast (his group wrote a song called "Marilyn Manson Is a Dork"), defends the purpose of all variations of music: "We do songs of teenage rage. We've worn all-black clothes and painted our nails red. That doesn't mean we're out to kill people. I was an outcast in school myself, so I turned to music to deal with my angst. And it is hard rock music that actually saved me, literally. It provided an outlet for my anger, and/or confusion. I swear I wouldn't be here without it."

This may be how Manson feels. But as long as his "I love hate, I hate love" theme songs continue, he will be up against criticism and spark controversy. He will most likely be remembered for his coarse lyrics and eccentric stage presence rather than for any of the music he has created.

Mushroomhead (1993–)

In keeping with the industrial/shock-rock tradition of Nine Inch Nails and Marilyn Manson, this nine-member group (two of whom are strictly dancers) is yet another "out of the ordinary" ensemble.

The group's live theatrical shows consist of thrashing metal/punk/industrial music executed by costumed individuals who take the word "performance" to the extreme. On stage, the masked artists take on new names, new faces, new shock—such as the S&M act performed by the group's only female, Roxy, and her accomplice, Bronson. Mushroomhead members are bound to offend someone, and they thrive on it.

Drummer Skinny (a.k.a. Steve Felton) says it's all hype. "Our shows are not as wild and lurid as the press makes out. Sure they are chaotic, definitely different from the norm. But I wouldn't compare us to Marilyn Manson. Personally I can't relate to that because I don't listen to him."

The media hype, coupled with their elaborate performances, has produced impressive sales for not only their releases (which include a multimedia CD) but also Mushroomhead T-shirts, calendars, posters, and mousepads. Aside from obvious marketing skills, this nine-piece band is musically strong. The group boasts members of previous bands Purgatory (singer Jeff Hatrix), Hatrix (Hatrix and Steve Felton), Mystik (guitarist J. J. Sekula and former Spudmonster bassist Joe Kilcoyne), and Unified Culture (singer Jason Popson and Sekula). However, few realize who's who as Mushroomhead members only go by their stage names, even on the albums.

The 1999 lineup consisted of Dinner (Rich Moore, guitar), Pig Benis (Jack Kilcoyne, who replaced brother Joe, bass), Skinny (Steve Felton, drums and samples), Jeffrey

Nothing (Jeff Hatrix, vocals/songwriter), J. Mann (Jason Popson, vocals/songwriter), Shmotz (Tom Schmitz, keyboards) J. J. Righteous (J. J. Sekula, guitar) and the aforementioned Roxy and Bronson.

As far as influences go, members agree each of them listened to a variety of music ("from Megadeth to Floyd"), and the conglomeration produced their kaleidoscope of sound. "Mr. Bungle comes to mind," Skinny says, "but we're not like them. We developed our own style early on."

The first Mushroomhead show took place at Flash's in Lorain in October 1993. On the heels of that performance, the group opened for the Virginia-based band GWAR at the Agora. That's when they honed their self-described "mind-expanding psycho-metal" sound.

Since then, this masquerade has become the talk of the town. The group, whose band name simply "came up," began playing clubs like the Grog Shop, Lorain's Flying Machine, Peabody's DownUnder, and the Phantasy Nite Club. In June 1995, Mushroomhead released 1,000 copies of its self-titled debut CD on its own Mushroomhead Records, which sold out almost immediately.

"We had been friends with the owner of Mars studio in Streetsboro," Skinny says. "Bill Korecky was really instrumental in getting that first effort off the ground for us. He is probably the biggest reason it exists."

Immmediately, college radio picked up on the Mushroomhead sound and put its songs ("In Different," "Too Much Nothing," "43," and "Elevation") in heavy rotation. Thus began its zealot appeal. By 1996, the group was selling out every venue it played. Its Halloween shows are probably the most renowned, which repeatedly fill the 1,800-capacity seating in the Agora Theater. It is now an annual event. "I've had the opportunity to watch this band mature and develop," says record promoter Jim Clevo, an early advocate of the band. "From their *Superbuick* release sellout at the Odeon in September '96 to their Thanksgiving show in '97, they've developed into a powerful local force with a fan base unlike anything anyone has seen before [in Cleveland]. They've cultivated into real musicians and performers based on something more than just shock value. The sold-out Halloween shows of '98 and '99 have really proved they are the greatest and most successful independent Cleveland band, and will stand alongside the likes of Pere Ubu, Michael Stanley, and Robert Lockwood Jr. as one of the legendary names in Cleveland music history—whether the local critics want to acknowledge that or not."

Beginning in 1996, the group began participating in several CMJ Marathons and other out-of-town music conventions, acquiring diehard fans along the way. But the controversy continues. In the spring of 1999, Mushroomhead was asked to perform at a benefit for high school radio station, WSTB. They agreed, but the city's mayor didn't.

"The school board wanted to have it," Jeff Matrix says, " but the mayor and the police chief said they didn't have adequate people on the force to protect the city."

When it was announced the group would be unable to perform, students protested vehemently. With the involvement of the ACLU, the result was a change in the city charter amendment, thus allowing them to play. However, a few days before their scheduled concert the Columbine killings made international news, and city officials promptly cancelled the Mushroomhead concert.

But their popularity lives on. That same spring, the group won the *Cleveland Free Times* Award for best metal act and best live show, and the *Scene* People's Choice Award for hard rock band of the year, as well as best overall band. In the fall of 1999, the group released its third full-length CD, *M3*. "When we were in the early bands, we'd do everything people told us we should do," Hatrix says. "But with Mushroomhead we loosened the boundaries; we decided to just have fun and do something people will remember. There's no formula for success, and as far as genres go, we're all over the map. But it's working out better than we ever expected."

It is clear that Mushroomhead isn't just for Halloween anymore.

On a Lighter Note . . .

Jehova Waitresses (1989–97)

This band headed up the resurgence of folk rock in 1990s Cleveland. With the focus on vocals and acoustic guitar, the group soon added one interesting commodity—the violin. After admiring John Mellencamp's usage of the string instrument in his band, the group's founder/singer/guitarist/songwriter Linda K. Roy brought in violinist Kristine Kochilla. Other members included Roy's husband, Kevin Christopher Roy (guitar/songwriter), Jeff Harmon (drums), and Philip Neel (bass). The addition of the violin gave this quintet the edge needed to separate it from the pack of mainstream pop and underground alternative bands. The group also had a unique asset—its name, which ultimately was deemed "Best Band Name" in the 1996 year-end issue of *Entertainment Weekly*. The seed for the unusual and perhaps controversial moniker had been planted long before the Cleveland group's formation.

"When Linda was in high school in New York," recalls Harmon, who was with the band from beginning to end, "She and some friends went to Denny's and had this waitress who was very persistent and kept bothering them and coming back to their table. She reminded them of the Jehovah Witness people who come to your door and you can't get rid of them. So they tagged her the Jehovah Waitress. Linda remembered that when we started the band."

The group formed when Linda Kachler placed an ad in *Scene* magazine. Musician and architect Kevin Roy responded. Before long, the two were making music together (they later married). The quintet started playing locally at the Phantasy Nite Club, Symposium, Peabody's Café, and the Grog Shop. In addition, they performed at various music festivals and record conventions. And rather than sing the usual topics of sex, drugs, and rock 'n' roll, Jehova Waitresses explored such themes as Alzheimer's disease ("Hey, Bill"), the dehumanizing effects of life in the city ("Sidewalk's Path"), and the trials and tribulations of a Catholic education ("Days of Obligation").

The band took advantage of the early interest in them by self-releasing a six-song debut, *Hard Up for Innocence,* in 1990. The CD sold a mere 600 copies, but the rave reviews were encouraging. The following year, Alan Grandy came in on bass, and when the band needed a new violinist, Grandy suggested Janice Fields, a classically trained pianist who worked with him at Tommy's Restaurant on Coventry Road. Grandy had been the lead singer/guitarist for longtime '80s band Terrible Parade. But it was in the late '70s that Grandy first attached himself to the Cleveland music scene.

"I was the 'dorm folkie' when I put my first rock band together at Ohio University," he says. "Growing up with my parents' big-band music mixed in with my favorites, the Beatles and Black Sabbath, I always appreciated diversity in music. And when punk came, I hooked right into it. All my friends were from Cleveland and they knew the guys in Pere Ubu and Devo. We'd go to a club like Pirate's Cove and see Pere Ubu play, then the next day go to Hideo's Discodrome record store and there would be Dave Thomas [Pere Ubu singer] working there. That's how it was. There was that immediacy to the whole scene that was great."

With his potpourri of musical interests, Grandy put yet another edge to the Jehova Waitresses' repertoire. He began contributing to the songwriting, and in the summer of 1992, the group recorded *Shake Your Buddha* at Willoughby's Beat Farm Studios, where many local artists recorded until its demise later that year. The CD was released that November on Grandy's own Sounds of the Sea record label. Other releases on his label included the compilation CD, *They Showered Us with Beads and Flowers* (1991), which showcased Cleveland's growing folk/acoustic groups such as Odd Girl Out and the Waynes.

"I was more the business guy of the group because I was more objective," Grandy says. "I did nearly all the bookings for the band. And with the label, I was able to call people and say, 'Hi, this is Alan Grandy for Sounds of the Sea Records, and there's a band on my label, Jehova Waitresses,' and after waiting for the laughter to stop, I'd say, 'They have a new record out which got great press' and so on."

The group spent the rest of 1992 and part of 1993 on the road and, as a result, sold out its first pressing of 1,000 copies. The group's songs were included on several compilations, including another Sound of the Sea record, *Field Day*, and the 1990 CMJ compilation CD. Constant comparisons to the '90s band 10,000 Maniacs only helped the group secure more jobs.

"We were constantly coming up with new material," Grandy says, "and were anxious to get as many gigs as we could, especially out of town. Chris Porter, whose label, 'Presto!' had released Terrible Parade's *Where Were You . . . When the Lights Went Out* CD, booked us at the Boston clubs he ran, such as Bunratty's and the Middle East. We'd go on the road for weeks at a time playing the Beat Kitchen and Schuba's in Chicago, Brownie's in New York, and the T-Bird in Asbury, New Jersey. Then we'd come back and play our regular clubs and get a real nice homecoming."

The group then played the 1993 South by Southwest music conference, for which they received numerous reviews heralding their efforts. By then, Jehova Waitresses was a mainstay at Cleveland's own Undercurrents Festival. Radio airplay, however, was restricted to mostly college broadcasting, although lower-watt commercial station WENZ put the band's songs in regular rotation. The 1994 *Perfect Impossible* CD became the group's third and final release.

"The [Cleveland-based] Revelers had just gotten back from recording with a fellow named Kramer who ran his own label, Shimmy Disc, in New York. After talking to [the producer], he suggested we record an LP [with him]. We were ready, we were prepared, and we rehearsed like the dickens. Then we went and recorded it in three days. Engineer Steve Watson was really the hero of the sessions. He got the performances out of us. We worked three seventeen-hour days, then Kramer came in to mix the entire record in one day."

The group accepted an offer to use Kramer's nationally distributed independent label and released the CD on Shimmy Disc Records, which ultimately sold 2,000 copies. By early 1995, Fields left and was replaced by Ed Caner. Soon after, Grandy left and the group brought in bassist Paul Lewis. When Caner departed that same year, Jehova Waitresses remained a quartet until it disbanded in 1997. The reason? A typical case of members veering off in different directions.

"We never formally broke up," Harmon says. "Kevin and Linda moved to New Jersey for work. That's when me and the bass player [Paul Lewis] formed Superkreme."

Harmon went on to do stints in the Throckmorton (with Caner), the Waynes, and with bluesman Colin Dussault before joining Superkreme, which included guitarist Matt Sobol (formerly with the Waynes). Alan Grandy went on to a busy solo career and in 1997 released his first solo project, *Crown O' Stars,* on his indie label. The following year, he produced local artist Pepper Action's debut CD.

Odd Girl Out (1990–95)

In the same folk-rock vein as Jehova Waitresses, this band, founded by lead singer/ songwriter Anne E. DeChant, lead guitarist/singer/songwriter Victoria Fliegel, and rhythm guitarist Alexis Antes, was constantly being compared with the nationally known Indigo Girls. Was that a bad thing?

"Actually, no," says DeChant, whose band did perform the Indigo's song, "Closer to Fine." "Although I think, at first, it was just because ours was also a female-dominated band that played acoustic instruments. But I think it was a fair comparison, considering our philosophical song lyrics, the harmonies, and the mixture of our voices. Plus, I think the comparison was flattering."

The band name was initiated by Fliegel's friend, who once mentioned it would be a good name for a female band. The trio agreed. After all, there were few female-dominated bands in Cleveland, or ones that explored serious topics in their music. DeChant's bachelor's degree in philosophy undoubtedly affected her songwriting, which focused on human relationships. Odd Girl Out's music took on controversial issues such as teenage pregnancy, spousal abuse, and the war's effect on Vietnam veterans. Their songs touched a chord with their rapidly accruing fans, who could identify with the topics.

Growing up in Avon Lake, DeChant was raised on church music she heard in her Catholic grade school, in addition to John Denver, Olivia Newton John, and Nat King

Cole tunes her parents liked. She began playing acoustic guitar at age ten and was encouraged by her teachers to join the choir. She participated in school choirs until high school, when the "girl with the beautiful voice" opted for athletics instead.

DeChant first teamed up with Fliegel in 1989 when they discovered their mutual interest in folk music. A few coffeehouse shows later, however, they went their separate ways. DeChant then spent some time singing backup with Craig Robinson at the Barking Spider Saloon near Case Western Reserve University. In 1990, she decided she wanted to front her own band.

"Our first show was at the Allen Theater. It was just me, my friend Alexis [Antes], and her mother Bobbie Antes [a.k.a. Mama Cass]. But Bobbie wasn't able to make the time commitment needed for a group. So I called Victoria."

A year later, the women added drummer Brian Bretton and started securing club dates at the Symposium, the Empire, Peabody's Cafe, the Phantasy, and JB's. Bass player Chris deHaas joined soon after.

"They [Bretton and deHaas] were very sensitive musicians," DeChant notes. "They were careful not to tread on what we'd already established. We were very lucky to find members who respected that."

Odd Girl Out fan deHaas, who had previously played in rock and polka bands, knew he wanted to be a part of this folk-rock group.

"A friend of mine told me the group was looking for a bass player," he recalls. "They were playing at WRUW's Studio Rama concert, which was broadcast live, so I taped their set at home. I learned all the songs and made a demo tape with me playing bass to them. I then went to where they were playing next and gave Brian the tape. He called a few days later and that was it. I loved their songs and was impressed with them because they had interesting, intelligent lyrics, and catchy, three-part harmonies. It was about as heavy as you can get with acoustic guitars. A real nice folk-rock sound."

That sound had already been given some airplay on WMMS.

"What really thrust us into the limelight," DeChant says, "was when one of our songs, 'Leavin'' from a four-song cassette, was included on the 1991 WMMS *Northcoast Buzzard Tracks, Vol. I* compilation CD. For some reason, [that song] really caught on and got a lot of attention."

Besides playing dates in college towns such as Ann Arbor, Bowling Green, Slippery Rock, and Oxford, Odd Girl Out romanced the Cleveland music scene. Throughout the mid '90s, the group was seemingly everywhere on the North Coast. They appeared at Undercurrents '92 and '93, and played outdoor venues including Edgewater Park, the Cleveland Stadium, and Blossom Music Center.

"That was very exciting," DeChant says of their Blossom debut. "I kept recalling how, just a few years before, I was there watching the Michael Stanley Band, and here we were on the same stage."

Then came a 1993 performance at the esteemed Front Row Theater, in which the quintet opened for British singer Joan Armatrading. When they performed at Euclid's Shore Cultural Center, they recorded it for their *Odd Girl Out: Live in Concert* CD. It did well regionally but failed to graze any charts. Yet during its five-year history, Odd Girl

Out became the darlings of the local media. The group was well liked and consistently received good reviews in the *Plain Dealer, Cleveland Magazine,* and *Scene.* But by 1995, members were ready to move on.

"We all sang and the others began writing as well," she says of her first band's breakup. "As time went on, I began to see my original perception was getting lost because I still wanted to front a band and that was no longer the focus. Although OGO was working, it started not to work. I think we got lazy. I noticed we had the same set list all the time. For me it became nonproductive. It was a difficult thing [to disband], but it wasn't a bad thing. It just reached a point where I realized who I was as a performer. And I wanted to write more, add the electric guitar to some songs, basically have more control."

She formed a self-titled band and, in 1997, released a CD, *Effort of the Spin,* with guitarist Frank Romano, bassist Mike Crow, drummer Rich Carpenter, and keyboardist Jon Denney. Presently she has a new lineup with Victoria Fleigel on lead guitar and backup vocals, drummer Amy Good, and bassist John Weiler. This band won the *Scene* Music Award for Best Folk/Acoustic Act, and the *Free Times* Award for Best Vocalist, as well as Best Folk/Americana Act in 1999. The group was also the only regional band to be invited to play the 1999 Lilith Fair at Blossom Music Center. As she has for the past decade, DeChant continues to work days, teaching preschoolers at an area daycare center.

Today, Alexis Antes is concentrating on a solo career and was nominated by *Scene* for best Folk/Americana act in the 1999 Music Awards. Brian Bretton is co-owner of a restaurant and plays in a band called One-Eyed Jack. Chris deHaas, who has just started his own Internet company, continues with his music as well. He's currently playing in a church group and plans to build a home recording studio and perhaps put his own band together in the next few years.

They Call Them the Rappers

Like the "doo-wop" vocals of the 1950s and 1960s, rap music began on the urban streets and soon ventured into the school hallways. The roots of rap grew from the fast-talking disc jockeys who used this style to make radio listening a more entertaining event. Although the technique is considered a black cultural movement, one of the first deejays to pioneer this "rapid rhyming" technique was none other than Pete "Mad Daddy" Myers, though he did it without music. He then took that form to New York airwaves, where he earned thousands of dedicated fans, both black and white. However, by the time the trend went mainstream, Mad Daddy was all but forgotten. In 1970, Jamaican-born Bronx deejay Kool Herc (né Clive Campbell) took that rappin' style and put it to the music he was playing. Then he developed the art of using two turntables to create sound effects that sealed the phenomenon. The heavy disco pulse of the 1970s brought the movement up from the underground and helped usher in this rhythm-oriented style. The rhythm and rhyme patterns of rap blended perfectly with the physical acts of the urban street craze of break-dancing and double-dutch jump-roping. "Rapper's Delight," the 1979 song by the Sugarhill Gang, is considered to be the first official rap record. It made it to the Top 40 chart and secured the music genre into cultural history. Soon after, New York deejay Grandmaster Flash (né Joseph Saddler) termed the music and lifestyle "hip-hop."

It wasn't until the '80s, however, that rap became a true entity, thanks to such black rappers as Run-DMC, Public Enemy, and the Fat Boys and white rappers the Beastie Boys and Vanilla Ice. In 1988, singer/actor Will Smith (a.k.a. Fresh Prince) and DJ Jazzy Jeff were the first to get a Grammy for Best Rap Performance for their song "Parents Just Don't Understand." Since then, rap music has become the most significant subgenre of rock music. In 1998 and 1999, there were more Grammy awards given to rap, and rappers, than to any other style of music.

Once again, Cleveland was not to be left out of this latest trend. In 1986, the city hosted its first Rap Music Awards, held on May 25 at the Music Hall. Among those who performed and/or presented awards were the Fat Boys, the Jets, Kurtis Blow, and Cleveland's own Dazz Band. It was also noted in the *Plain Dealer* during that time that longtime WZAK disc jockey Lynn Tolliver and WDMT's "Dean Dean" Rufus were playing more rap music on their stations than any other deejays in the country, according to one record executive.

It wouldn't be long before one of the most successful rap groups in the '90s would be unearthed on the North Coast.

Bone Thugs-N-Harmony (1992–)

The names Bizzy Bone, Krayzie Bone, Layzie Bone, Wish Bone, and Flesh-N-Bone mean a lot in the world of rap. And for this group of self-described ghetto boys, their rapid accession into the big time has given new meaning to the phrase "overnight success." They came, they rapped, they beat the odds.

It all started when friends from Cleveland's tough neighborhood of E. 99th and St. Clair Avenue found they could sing in perfect harmony. That was back at Franklin D. Roosevelt Junior High School, where they used to rap in the hallways between classes. They honed their unique style by participating in area talent shows, where they consistently beat out their competitors. After graduating from Lincoln West High School, they learned about the inner workings of a recording studio with record store owner Kermit Henderson. Originally they (except Flesh-N-Bone) called themselves B.O.N.E. Enterpri$e and began writing their own songs. In 1993, the group recorded an album, *Faces of Death,* on Henderson's indie label, Stoney Burke.

From there, Anthony Henderson (Krayzie Bone), Bryon McCane (Bizzy Bone), Charles Shruggs (Wish Bone), Steve Howse (Layzie Bone), and Stan Howse (Flesh-N-Bone) took a Greyhound bus to L.A., determined to capture the attention of their rap hero, Eazy-E, founder of the successful gangsta rap group, NWA, and Ruthless/Relativity Records. And they did, though it was via the phone lines, not in person. But when they rapped their tunes over the receiver, Eazy-E was impressed. He invited them to his Cleveland concert, so it was back to the North Coast for a backstage audition.

"They do rap and harmony and everything else," the late Eazy-E told *Plain Dealer* reporter Sheila Simmons. "They had a rap style that was different."

That difference bought the low-budget rappers a free ticket to L.A. With backing from producer Eazy-E, the quintet was brought into his studio to record an EP, *Creepin' On Ah, Come Up,* in 1994. Hardly a catchy title, but the songs were snappy enough for rap enthusiasts to quickly snatch up three million copies, earning Cleveland's first rap group a gold record. Within months, sales rose first to multiplatinum status and eventually to quadruple. The overwhelming success was followed by the 1995 debut album, *E. 1999 Eternal,* which not only gave the singers another multiplatinum hit but also knocked Michael Jackson's *HIStory* off the top position on the pop album charts. Forget the cover of the *Rolling Stone*: these rappers got on the cover of the *Source* magazine, the bible of the rap/hip-hop world, and earned a Soul Train award nomination for best rap group. The homeboys had made good.

And like fellow Clevelanders before them, Pere Ubu and the Dead Boys, their music grew out of the city's industrial, hardcore setting. With distinct harmonies coupled with poetic rhymes and life-and-death themes, it became obvious these street-style rappers would know the same success. Their mission statement, however, is contradictory. Each member writes his own part, so every song is diverse and innovative. Consequently, one focuses on murder, another on jealousy. One threatens an enemy, while another cries out for justice. Still another recounts the loss of a baby son. The origins of the group name is no more self-explanatory. "B-O-N-E" is said to mean either "Budded out Niggas Everyday," "Brewed out Niggas Everyday," or "Brother on Normal Elimination." You decide.

Although the definition of "Thugs" is more obvious, members say it also means "Trues Humbly United Gatherin' Souls"—in other words, they say, a peacemaker who can nevertheless hustle. Well, at least the harmony part is clear. And those voices are distinctive. Krayzie has a resonant quality in his voice. Bizzy's fast-talking jive and high pitch make listeners stand up and take notice. Layzie's voice is almost like his name, smooth and slower-paced. Wish Bone's voice is deep and forceful. And Flesh-N-Bone, an "unofficial" member because his name was left out of the record contract, has a voice reminiscent of the old style of rhythm and blues.

After the single "Thuggish Ruggish Bone" hit No. 19 on the Top Rap singles chart, the group returned home to make their first video for that record. Filming in their old neighborhood made perfect sense, as the song is autobiographical. The twenty year olds wanted to capture the everyday street life that ultimately influenced their lyrics. The video broke a record for the most requests on the Box, a by-request video channel. The group launched its own record label, Mo Thugs Records, with the release of *Mo Thugs Family Scriptures* in the fall of 1996. All this before their first major national tour, the Budweiser Superfest. That tour brought the boys back to their hometown in August 1997 to play a jam-packed Gund Arena, along with Mary J. Blige, Aaliyah, Dru Hill, and Ginuwine.

By the time Bone Thugs-N-Harmony released its sophomore effort, *The Art of War,* in 1997, the group had already won a Grammy award for Best Rap Group Performance for "Tha Crossroads," the single that, amazingly, entered *Billboard*'s Hot 100 Singles charts at No. 2 and moved up to No. 1 the following week. That made the record the highest-debuting single since the Beatles's "Can't Buy Me Love." In addition, the song's video, a tribute to departed loved ones, was nominated in four categories for the MTV Video Music Awards. Not bad for some "regular dudes" from the poor side of town. The only damper on their success was in March 1999, when the group learned that Eazy-E, their mentor/manager, had died from AIDS. That's when they also discovered, in the ensuing paperwork, that Flesh-N-Bone was not a contractual member of the rap group.

Perhaps because of the contract omission, Flesh-N-Bone was first to take advantage of the group's new label and released his first solo effort, *T.H.U.G.S.: Trues Humbly United Gatherin' Souls,* on Mo Thugs Records with distribution through New York's Def Jam Music Group. The CD debuted at No. 8 on *Billboard*'s R&B chart and No. 23 on the pop chart. Before he began serving an eleven-year prison term for parole violation and possession of a semi-automatic weapon, he managed to release *Fifth Dog Let Loose.*

Bizzy, often said to be the most popular Bone, was next to release a solo full-length CD in 1998, the first to combine both Mo Thugs and Ruthless/Relativity labels. *Heaven'z Movie* debuted at an impressive No. 3 on *Billboard*'s charts, and in a *Rolling Stone* review, writer James Hunter called Bizzy "one of hip-hops jazziest cats." Bizzy Bone also lent his vocals to Sean "Puff Daddy" Combs's song "Angels with Dirty Faces."

Critics and fans also liked Krayzie Bone's ambitious 1999 double album, *Thug Mentality,* on Relativity Records. He was joined on several cuts by musical friends Mariah Carey and Snoop Doggy Dogg. At the same time, Krayzie began his own label, Thugline Records, to which he signed several artists.

These busy Bones have used their personal hardships as launching pads to success. And whether with their solo projects or together, Bone Thugs-N-Harmony continue to provide their fans with music they can relate—and rap—to. The group came together again in 2000 to produce *Resurrection.*

Akron/Kent Scene

Since the 1970s these two cities south of Cleveland have been boasting some great musical talents. Nineties standouts include Kent bands Fuzzhead and Indian Rope Burn and Akron's Hilo, Zero Parade, and Spawn. The bands profiled below became fan favorites.

Dink (1990–2000)

Add this band to the roster of those who experienced both the thrill of major-label status and the agony of record-label reality. The leader of this band was founder/songwriter/guitar programmer Sean Carlin.

"Actually I didn't pick up the guitar until after forming the band. I always played piano," Carlin says. "I started going into the Kent bars, under age, of course, and saw cool bands like Tin Huey, Chi Pig, the Numbers Band, and this band called Baby Sirloin. After high school, I worked at Pi Keyboards with a lot of notable musicians like Trent Reznor, Frank Vale [Exotic Birds], and Steve Cox [Dazz Band]. I was a gear junkie, so I had to work at a music store to support my habit! Then I started playing in a lot of funk and jazz bands until I got turned on to electronic stuff and got into Depeche Mode, Ministry, Skinny Puppy, and that whole Chicago Wax Trax thing."

Carlin and friends Rob Lightbody (slide guitar/vocalist/lyricist) and Jer Herring (guitarist/vocalist/lyricist) decided to form a rock band. Soon they met up with bass player Jeff Finn and Dutch drummer Jan Eddy ("Ed") Van der Kuil.

"Ed had played with the Numbers Band in Europe," Carlin says. "He had come to Kent on vacation to see Bob and Jack [Kidney] back in '90. Ed really liked it in Kent. So we were doing our first session at Electro-Sound at the time and invited him to stop by. From then on Ed was a Kent guy. He'd come with us to the Town Tavern on Franklin Street [now Mugs], which was the coolest bar in Kent. You'd see every kind of person there imaginable—cross-dresser, junkie, musician, art dude . . . . It was quite a scene back then. Ultimately Ed became our most famous member: that Euro-guy in Dink."

Lightbody coined the band name, and members say the meaning can be disparate. Their music, however, is distinctive: an industrial base fueled by computers and featuring heavy drumming and shrieking guitars. The group generated that sound in Carlin's home studio and, in the rich Kent tradition, practiced at the renowned Kent studio the Coop, once the practice hall for the James Gang, Glass Harp, and Devo. Dink created a buzz during its 1993 European tour, which included the Metropolis Festival in Rotterdam, Holland. Once setting foot back in America, the quintet emerged at that year's CMJ Showcase in New York, then returned home to Kent's JB's, Akron's Daily Double, and Cleveland's Phantasy Nite Club, Flash's, and the Grog Shop. Meanwhile, Dink's demo song, "Green Mind," was getting airplay on Cleveland station WENZ, "the End." It was the second song played on the station's then-new "Inner Sanctum," a Sunday night program featuring local artists.

"The End, bless them and curse them, started playing it," Carlin says. "In the meantime, we had gone to do the Dutch tour and when we got back, someone from the station called us and said, 'You guys oughta get down here. Your song is getting a ton of requests.' Then we started getting approached by all these record companies—Atlantic, Warner Brothers, Island Records . . . . We sent demos to independent labels Third Mind, Road Runner, and Blue Grape in New York, who all promptly threw it in the garbage. But at Blue Grape, this assistant walked past the waste basket, was captured by the cover, retrieved it, took it home, played it, and liked it."

But it wasn't until the group performed at Cleveland's Undercurrents (a North Coast version of the South by Southwest convention), that Dink got due notice.

"Steve Popovich helped us out on that end," Carlin notes. "He talked to these people he knew at Capitol about us. So when we played Undercurrents '94, this guy came up to me and says, 'I'm lookin' for someone from Dink.' First I asked, 'Do they owe you money??'

"It was Patrick Clifford from Capitol, who had bought our demo in My Generation music store in Westlake. When he saw us play live, I guess that sealed the deal."

From there it was on to L.A. to meet with Gary Gersch, then-president of Capitol Records. "We took the two tapes we'd made for the cassettes we'd been selling and hired Dave 'Rave' Ogilvie from Skinny Puppy and some guys from KMFDM, who helped remix it. We stayed in Hollywood a few weeks and felt like celebrities, traveling around in a limo and staying at the legendary Roosevelt Hotel. On the side of the Capitol building there's this 20-foot-by-20-foot poster of the bands they represent, and there we were—next to the Beatles and the Beastie Boys."

Their 1994 self-titled full-length debut was a collection of their previous two-song EPs and new material. Three songs from that release, "Angels," "Get on It," and a remixed, guitar-driven "Green Mind," made it to *Billboard*'s dance chart hits. The latter song included parts of a commercial by Cleveland's famous used-car dealer Bob Serpentini. Portions of the song's video landed on MTV's *Beavis and Butthead*. The CD sold in excess of 100,000 copies.

"Cleveland wasn't even our biggest market," Carlin says, adding that Dink also played shows at the Odeon, Agora, and Nautica in the Flats. "We sold a lot of records in Chicago, Dallas, Miami, San Francisco, Salt Lake City, and New York City."

To promote their new release, Dink went on a six-month tour with Pop Will Eat Itself, Compulsion, Lords of Acid, and the German industrial-rock band KMFDM. The group released an EP, *Blame It on Tito,* in 1996, but another full-length CD wasn't in the cards. The Kent band was dropped from Capitol Records in spring of 1998.

"We're the poster boys of everything that can go wrong with a major label deal," Carlin says. "There's no book of 'Rock 101' which you can study to keep from getting ripped off. I mean, there was a lot of money being tossed about, and we saw little of it."

Their industrial tag genre began to wear on the members. "When we were recording our first record," Carlin says, "they [record execs] were saying to us 'dance music doesn't sell.' Yet we'd had incredible success internationally with 'Green Mind,' which was quite danceable. Then we made a straight rock record. And that's when electronic music was catching up to us, and they were like, 'you gotta make a dance record 'cause dance music sells.' First we were ahead of our time, then we were behind the times. Then again, you always want to buck the system, ya know?"

The downward slide began to escalate when the group's new manager suggested they let Lightbody go. The group agreed. Dink was now a four-piece band.

"Sure, I felt bad," Carlin says. "Rob and I went from being the best of friends to being the worst of enemies. I mean, there were reasons why we did it, but it came down to the simple decision of what was the best for the four [members] in lieu of the saving of the one. Bottom line is, it is a business, and unfortunately, it can be ugly. We had several management companies, and in hindsight I agree we made some bad business calls. Nevertheless, that move was definitely the beginning of the end."

Things culminated during a scheduled headlining appearance at WENZ's annual

"End Fest" at Blossom Music Center. Dink was there but never went on stage. The band, so close to hitting the big time, had hit rock bottom.

"Ed had returned from Europe and quit, but said he'd do the show," Carlin says. "Then our show time got changed and he got fed up. We all had just about enough by this point. What had once been an awesome thing was now like beating a dead horse."

That was nothing compared to the beating the band received the next day on live radio. As Sean tells it,

> The next morning on the End, boy, they just massacred us. Soon as I awoke, my mother and some friends called saying, "Whatever you do, don't turn on the radio. They are blasting you all over the place." So of course I turned on the radio in time to hear [deejay] Howie Greene say, "I'm going to crucify this band; their career is over." Then he goes for the throat by telling listeners there was this one kid crying at the show because he couldn't see his favorite band, Dink. That was it, I called him on the phone and said, "Howie, this is Sean from Dink," and he started in on me, just going on and on. I finally said, "Man, who do you think we are—the Beatles?" And he hung up on me.
>
> Not long after that, Howie got fired and the station got sold. So they got theirs. And actually we ended up using parts of that for a song we call "Howie Greene Mind."

When Herring left the band soon after, Dink appeared to be dead. Yet, despite a lawsuit under way over who is legally entitled to the band name (coined by Lightbody), a new Dink has reformed with Carlin, Lila Waltrip (bass/vocals), frontman Billy Farkas (guitar/vocals), and former TwistOffs drummer Eric Baltrinic. "We've moved on," Carlin said. "We're not a cover band of the old lineup, but rather an extension of it." Sadly, this new formation didn't survive and called it quits in 2000.

TwistOffs (1984–)

"I was born and bred in Kent, Ohio," says guitarist/vocalist Erik Walter, who started playing the guitar in third grade. "We played our first gig appropriately at JB's, way before we were legal. That was back in '84, when [guitarist] Phil Adamek and I were just fifteen."

Walter began his music career playing folk guitar with the nuns at St. Patrick's grade school before gravitating toward the Who, the Rolling Stones, the Kinks, then to new wave groups like the Clash and Buzzcocks. He may have missed the glory days of Kent's music scene when the James Gang, Glass Harp, and the Numbers Band attracted record execs to JB's, but the bar was still the place to go.

"John Teagle from the Walking Clampetts was managing JB's at the time, and Phil knew his girlfriend from working at the same Denny's as she did," Walter recalls. "No one had a driver's license, so we'd ride our bikes down to the bar, hide them behind the auto parts store, and go in. John made us promise not to drink in there, and we'd see [local] bands like the Offbeats, Raggedbags, and Infidels. After awhile John started pushing us to get together and do a show there. So when we were fifteen we took him up on it and opened for the Diffi-cult."

The initial formation consisted of Walter, Adamek, Greg Schiedlowski (vocals/sax), and then-eighth grader Scott Jaykel (drums). It lasted one show. "Scott's parents weren't hot about him playing in a bar," Walter says. "We went through several members until 1989 when we got a more stable lineup."

That lineup included frontman Walter, Kevin Zelina (bass), Louis Giffels (drums), Brian Fricky (trumpet), Allen Mothersbaugh (trombone), Mike Fasig (saxophone), and guitarist Patrick Drouin Wilbraham (who goes by Pat Drouin). The Mentor-native guitarist was already a veteran of the local music scene when he was "slapped silly" by the group's frontman.

"They needed a new guitarist, and Erik had heard about me," Drouin recalls. "So Louis Giffels took me to Mother's Junction where they were playing. Upon introduction, Erik stands up and with the palm of his hand, just slaps me upside the forehead—Thonk! I proceeded to jump on him and wrestled him down. We got up and he goes, 'Yep, this guy will do.' I guess it was some sort of test. Had I been a wuss, maybe I wouldn't have gotten the gig."

Drouin notes he got interested in playing the guitar in part because of his "neighborhood hero" Choir/Raspberries guitarist Wally Bryson, who lived down the street from him. After high school, Drouin played in area cover bands before joining original band the Bomb (with Hammer Damage drummer Mike Hammer and frontman/guitarist Chuck DeFrancis).

"First time I played with them I totally sucked," admits Allen Mothersbaugh. "I didn't know any of their songs and ruined about $300 worth of percussion equipment from beating the hell out of it. But I was thrilled to be there." Not surprisingly, Mothersbaugh's greatest musical influence was Devo. "Not just because Bob and Mark are my cousins," he notes. "But I saw their farewell show at the Akron Civic Theater in '79, right before they went to California. At one point, Bob came running down the aisle and stood on our chairs playing the guitar. I thought that was way cool. I loved their music but never thought about being in a rock 'n' roll band until then. After that I was blatantly inspired."

The Twist Offs gave credence to that inspiration as the group came into their own by the early 1990s, sharpening their musical skills at JB's and Mother's Junction in Kent and the Daily Double in Akron. The band recorded two EPs, *Testing Testing* (1985), *Looking for Bugs* (1987), and a two-song 45 in 1990 before producing its first full-length CD, *Make Me Laugh*, in 1991. A single from that effort, "Win or Lose," was featured on the WMMS *Buzzard Track 1991* compilation CD. The tune was on the station's playlist and soon put in heavy rotation. It also was played on WENZ-FM 107.9.

"We've always had a tough time describing our music," Walter notes. "All the members are into different stuff and from different backgrounds. We'd come up with all kinds of genres for our sound, like World Beat, ska, alterna-speed-polka, Spanish marching-band acid rock, Afri-country skankabilly . . . . I'm starting to scale it down to just 'rock.'"

"Rock" would certainly describe their live shows, which are known to be energetic, frenetic, and always eclectic. The Kent band made its way up the North Coast to play at the Cleveland Underground, Symposium, Euclid Tavern, Peabody's, and the Phantasy. The TwistOffs had good company when they were invited to play a notable concert at the Flats' Nautica in July 1991. They shared the bill with I-Tal, Frankie Starr and the Chill Factor, and bands they'd later play with at the annual Rock 'n' Reggae Festivals—First Light and Oroboros. The group was also a mainstay at the annual local Undercurrents shows and has participated in the national South by Southwest Music and Media Conference held yearly in Austin, Texas. Over the past decade they have done over 1,500 shows across the country, in cities such as Denver, Boulder, Salt Lake City, San Francisco, Los Angeles, San Diego, Seattle, Albuquerque, Boston, New York, and Austin as well as in Canada.

"We played the Wetlands, the Lion's Den, and Coney Island High in New York," Mothersbaugh says. "We'd park our bus on the street and get littered with tickets. But nobody could tow it. Besides, they've got more to worry about than a bunch of hillbillies from Ohio."

"We've must have driven our converted school bus a total of a quarter-million miles and spent more time in it than an average aggravated-manslaughter conviction," Walter adds.

After seeing a TwistOffs show, Aris Nisman, CEO of the Virginia-based Degy Management, offered to represent the band. He told the members theirs was the "most exciting and boisterous live show I've ever seen."

Drouin modestly agrees. "Our live shows have always been our calling card, " he says. "And what drew me to the band is the diversity of Erik's songwriting and the fact we all embellish it with our own particular styles, creating a very eclectic mix."

As the buzz began circulating about "the world's favorite party band," the septet continued releasing music. The 1994 live CD, *Live in Ohio* (*live* as "rhymes with sieve, instead of jive"), recorded at Peabody's DownUnder, was followed two years later by the studio release, *Cup of Fish*. In 1998 came *Big Sounds from the Township,* which featured noted producer/former Sire Records founder Richard Gottehrer (Blondie, the Go-Go's) and was mixed by Jeffrey Lesser (Sting, Lou Reed, Sinead O'Connor). Members on that release include bassist Dustin Elliot, drummer Gregg Garlock, and sax player Andy Stephan. Their songs have been featured on MTV's *Real World*, ESPN's *X-Games,* and *Peewee's Playhouse.*

Over the years, the band has opened for national acts such as the legendary Bo Diddley, UB40, the Offspring, Rusted Root, Fishbone, Spin Doctors, and Dread Zeppelin. After being named the best dance band in *Scene* Readers' Poll in 1993 and 1994, the TwistOffs won a 1999 *Scene* Music Award for best funk group.

Although the group's formation remained fairly stable throughout the decade, they did experience some internal changes. In 1997, Dustin Elliot (who replaced trumpet/bass player Dave Connolly) was replaced by Walter's younger brother, Kevin, while drummer and percussionist Eric Baltrinic replaced Gregg Garlock (who went on to the Jim Miller Band). In December 1998, Mothersbaugh left to concentrate on solo work. Then Ian Early (who later played in Cherry Poppin' Daddys) was replaced by saxman Mark Meilander. In the summer of 1999, the group lost its drummer, Eric Baltrinic, to a reformed Dink.

"We spent a lot of years going through a string of painful drummer experiences," Walter says. "Finally in March 2000 we found Peter Heroux, who's a longtime school pal of Kevin's."

The Twist Offs' latest lineup includes the Walters brothers, Heroux, Drouin, Fricky, and Meilander. The group is planning a new release for 2001. Says Walter, "We're kickin' and screamin' into the next millennium."

Macy Gray

In early 1999, not many people were familiar with the name Macy Gray. But what a difference a year makes. By the beginning of 2000, this Canton native was one of the music world's "newest sensations." That wasn't in the plans when the R&B singer/songwriter was majoring in screenwriting at the University of Southern California.

"It was a gradual thing, not something I really thought about," Gray says. "While in college, I was hanging out with a lot of musicians and started playing clubs in L.A." Those clubs included the Whisky A Go Go, the Mint, and the Dragon Fly. It was at those venues that she began to attract an audience, as well as friends in the music business. One man had a studio and asked the screenwriting major to write some material for his songs. That, Gray says, is when things began to click. Word got out and more musicians came her way in search of her talent. Soon, she was urged to record a record and signed with Atlantic Records. She completed an album for the company but, unfortunately, the record deal fell through when in-house changes occurred. However, in the interim, a record exec from Epic got ahold of the recording, liked what he heard, and offered her a contract in April 1998. The former Natalie McIntyre (who "stole" her new name, Macy Gray, from someone she knew in Canton) made her CD debut that year, and in the fall of 1999 *On How Life Is,* produced by Andrew Slater (who also produced the Wallflowers and Fiona Apple) was released. It quickly sold more than 300,000 copies. Gray soon embarked on a tour that included the U.S., Europe, and Asia.

The singer's popularity is due in part to an unusually rich, haunting voice that reminds older fans of classic blues artist Billie Holiday. Her younger fans are intrigued by her fresh, soulful voice, identifiable song themes, and a commanding presence, emphasized by a truly original sense of fashion.

This shy girl never dreamed she'd grow up to be "a helium-voiced soul diva," as one *New York Times* reviewer described her. Although she didn't come from a musical family, Gray says she listened to and admired Aretha Franklin, Marvin Gaye, James Brown, Stevie Wonder, and Prince. The second member in a family of five children, and daughter of a barber and a schoolteacher, she was "not much of a talker," according to her mother, Laura McIntyre. Gray, a 1986 Canton South High graduate, adds that she's always been better at writing her feelings and thoughts on paper than expressing them verbally. In retrospect, it seems natural that she would gravitate toward a songwriting career.

Macy Gray is still quiet, reserving her thoughts for her lyrics, which reveal a deep thinker who has had her share of life's challenges. Her bestselling "I Try" and "Still" focus on love—the good and the bad. Her "Do Something" addresses the common adolescent question of where one is going in life.

The year 2000 was a busy one for Macy Gray. In January, this mother of three was nominated for two Grammys: Best New Artist and Best R&B Female Vocal Performer. In March she was named Best International Newcomer and Best International Female Solo Artist at the 2000 Brit Awards. And in July, she was the opening act for Carlos Santana on his North American tour. In September, she was named Best New Artist by the MTV Video Music Awards for her "I Try" video. At this writing, Macy Gray is working on her sophomore effort, a release her many fans anxiously await.

That Old-Time Rock and Roll

The '90s were the decade of musical comebacks. The Eagles reunited. Led Zeppelin's Jimmy Page and Robert Plant joined forces on tour, as did Grand Funk Railroad, Jefferson Airplane, Canned Heat, Black Sabbath, J. Geils, Bad Company, Cheap Trick, Journey, Foreigner, and a host of seasoned musicians who struck out on their own or formed new bands. Even the late-1970s one-hit wonders, the Knack (who could forget "My Sharona"), returned with a new release. Then there are the aging Stones, who never quit rolling.

Here on the North Coast, much of that tradition holds true as well. On any given night, music lovers can see and hear veteran musicians and bands such as Glenn Schwartz (with brother Gene and/or Robert Lockwood Jr.), Mr. Stress Blues Band, Sittin' Ducks (with former Choir mates Dan Klawon, Ken Margolis, and Wally Bryson), the Numbers Band, the Jim Miller Band (formerly of Oroboros), Carlos Jones and the P.L.U.S. Band (formerly in First Light), MaCaw (with former Buckeye Biscuit's Ron Jarvis), Frankie Starr, and others.

These venerable musicians have reformed, rejuvenated, and reinvented themselves in various ways to continue their musical journeys. And they use their decades of experience to keep the rock and roll capital alive and jamming.

The Armstrong Bearcat Band (1989–)

Armstrong Bearcat has been a customary fixture on the local music scene for the past decade. The trio consists of well-respected musicians who have managed an unusual feat—staying together. The usual question is how. The answer seems simple.

"It's easy money!" Glen "Stutz Bearcat" says with a laugh. "Of course, you have to have camaraderie and a good sense of humor. Butch [Armstrong] and I complement each other real well. Things I like doing, he doesn't, and vice versa. We're like a husband and wife. Knowing I'm absent-minded, he'll take home my guitars at night because he's afraid I might forget them! We look out for one another."

And both were born and raised on rock 'n' roll. Like Armstrong, Stutz Bearcat, who took lessons at the Cleveland Music School Settlement, was among the thousands of kids begging his parents for a guitar after seeing the Beatles on TV.

"I saw all those girls yelling and screaming over them and thought, 'Hey, that's not a bad way to make a living! My parents got me this twenty-dollar Baron guitar. But I had a hard time with it. I couldn't understand why I couldn't play it until I figured out the strings were like an inch off the fingerboard! Later on, a couple of strings broke and all that was left was the three lower strings. I found I could depress one string one at a time. So I started playing the bass parts to my records, and that's how I became a bass player!"

After playing in the Generators, Bearcat toured with British band Savoy Brown before joining the Mr. Stress Blues Band in 1985. The bassist remained with the group until 1988. He first got together with Armstrong while playing some well-remembered jam nights at the Euclid Tavern.

"There was me, Alan Greene, Don Buchanan [guitar], and Tommy Rich [drums]," he recalls. "We called ourselves the Stress Eliminators. When Don left, Butch came in. Once he started playing with us, it became Butch and the Ramrods to let everyone know he was in our band! That became our Sunday night gig for the next two years."

Meanwhile, Bearcat was asked to play bass with an upcoming young blues guitarist named Frankie Starr. The collaboration lasted less than six months.

"In March of '89, Living Colour was in town for a concert at the Phantasy Theater, but their opening act went to Buffalo by mistake," he recalls. "So Weisel Strictnine from Belkin called Frankie Starr to open for them, but he turned it down. Weisel then called me. I contacted Kenny Ruscitto [former Stress drummer] and Butch, and we said, 'Sure, we'll do it.' When Frankie's manager found out. She was so mad. She swore at me up and down and kicked me out of the band. But that was okay because after that show, we started getting a lot of calls to play, so Butch and I formed Armstrong Bearcat."

Butch Armstrong (a.k.a. Joey San Filippo) began playing guitar at age eleven. His cousin, Tommy San Filippo, was known in the area as a member of local bands the New Continentals and Grapevine. His younger brother, Vito, was also a noted bassist whose resume includes touring with the O'Jays, Tower of Power, Joe Cocker, Bob Dylan, and Billy Idol, among others. Growing up on the North Coast, Armstrong had observed all the great local guitarists like Glenn Schwartz, Joe Walsh, and Wally Bryson before joining his first road band, Rastus. Through the early 1980s, he was in Goodfoot. He became Butch Armstrong after getting a short haircut (when all his peers had long hair) and wearing an army coat and hat, which sparked nicknames like General Butch, George Armstrong Custard, and General Butch Armstrong, then to the name everyone knows today. The butch haircut soon gave way to a complete shave, and today his Yul Brenner look and long, dark beard have become part of this guitarist's persona. Armstrong says he missed his biggest break during a brief stay in L.A. in the late '70s.

Noted guitarist Butch Armstrong (*right*) jams with Humble Pie drummer Jerry Shirley and former Pie member Peter Frampton at Willoughby's Saraha Club in September 1990. *Photo by Brian Chalmers.*

Through the years, I've played in bands from all the trends—the Beatles trip, the soul trip, the disco trip, the Top 40 trip. And if I could give any advice to aspiring musicians, it would be to learn how to sing. That's how I missed my best opportunity—to join the band Chicago—because I couldn't sing. I was asked to attend their rehearsal in L.A. They asked me to play "Saturday in the Park" and "25 or 6 to 4," then a few more after that. They seemed very impressed with my guitar playing. Then they asked me to sing. When I didn't, I could tell they were disappointed. Still, I was asked back for a second audition. But they ended up hiring someone who was starring in the musical *Hair*.

That taught me a great lesson. After that, I forced myself to learn how to breathe right, and I would sit in a room and just practice changing and honing my voice. I learned my body is its own instrument, and one can learn to play it like any other instrument.

Armstrong now sings on most of the songs performed by this trio, which includes drummer Billy Coakley. For over a decade, the band has performed at clubs throughout the North Coast. Although Armstrong and Bearcat have remained together, they've gone through their share of drummers. The list includes Ruscitto, Frank Embresia,

Tommy Rich, Akronite Duane Jackson, and Mike Miheli. Coakley has been with the band since 1995.

"It's hard to classify us because we do a lot of varied material," Bearcat says. "I suppose you could call us a blues/rock/funk band. But then, some blues people don't like us because we're not blues purists. We'll play some old bluesy stuff, along with John Lee Hooker and the Isley Brothers, but funkify it and put it in a three-piece format. We also write original songs with heavy rock/funk jam tones. Plus, we'll play any gig that will have us. For example, one weekend we did an opening show for Commander Cody. The next night we did a wedding. The next, a roadhouse in Chippewa Lake. We still play four to six nights a week. We're musicians. We play whatever the situation calls for."

The Alan Greene Band (1998–)

Although this particular group does not have a long history (yet), its members certainly do. This power trio consists of bass player John "Slap" Daubenspeck, whose resume includes Jimmy Ley and the Coosa River Band, Deadly Earnest and the Honky Tonk Heroes, and Phil Baron and the Bopkats. Drummer Michael Miheli has been in previous bands including Armstrong Bearcat, while guitarist Alan Greene's name rings a bell with thousands of Cleveland music lovers.

Greene (né Alan Greenblatt) has played lead guitar in some of the best Cleveland rock formations. Active in the local music scene since the late 1960s, Greene is considered one of the top guitarists in Cleveland, right alongside Robert Lockwood Jr., Glenn Schwartz, Wally Bryson, Butch Armstrong, and Jim Jones (Pere Ubu, Easter Monkeys). Some of the more notable bands Greene has added his riffs to are Jimmy Ley and the Coosa River Band, Pere Ubu, Breathless (with Jonah Koslen), the Innocent (with aspiring keyboardist Trent Reznor), Mr. Stress Blues Band, Donnie Iris, Cellarful of Noise (with Wild Cherry keyboardist Mark Avsec), and the reformed Humble Pie (with original drummer Jerry Shirley). Early stints in '60s bands GangGreen, Hessler Court, Orville Normal, and Bazooom can also be added to his impressive resumé.

Like most of his musical colleagues, Greene decided to learn guitar during Beatlemania. He had been playing the trumpet for ten years under the direction of Cleveland Orchestra musician Warren Burkhart. Greene admits to having a deep passion for rock and roll while maintaining a strong appreciation for the "aggressive side of blues."

"I stole from the best," he says laughing,

Eric Clapton, Jeff Beck, Jimmy Page, Hendrix, and Glenn Schwartz. In fact, I'll never forget one night my wife and I stumbled into the Mistake, and though I knew of Glenn, I didn't know him to see him. So he was up there jammin' and every now and then, something caught my ear and I said to my wife, "Boy, you know, it almost sounds like this guy has been listening to some of my riffs." Of course it was very presumptuous of me, but we'd been playing so long at that club I thought, well, maybe this guy has seen us a lot, and musicians inevitably pick up what they listen to. Then as we were leaving, I heard people saying "Glenn Schwartz, Glenn Schwartz," and I finally realized who this guy was. So we immediately went back and sat down. And I thought, here I am thinking this guy was borrowing from me when it was totally the opposite. I was hearing my own playing that Glenn inspired *me* with—that attitude, that style of playing. It certainly was very humbling.

By the early 1980s, Greene was as well known on the local circuit as Schwartz. During that time Mr. Stress, then enjoying the height of popularity as house band at the Euclid Tavern, was looking for a good guitar player. Greene came first to mind.

"I'd known of Alan from his days with Jimmy Ley," Bill "Mr. Stress" Miller says. "I always appreciated his talent and was happy to have him. We got along famously, and he was with me before and after the Innocent. Out of all the guitarists we've had, he was one of the best."

In 1991, Greene got together with Jerry Shirley, drummer for Humble Pie ("I Don't Need No Doctor," "30 Days in the Hole"). "I had seen Jerry play several times at the Sahara Club in Willoughby Hills," Greene recalls. "So on a whim one night, I put myself in the position to jam with him on stage. I wanted him to hear me play, and simultaneously, he and I just started grinning at one another. We connected. He seemed to respect where I was coming from. We had come from the same generation, the same roots. I was speaking his language, and he liked what I did. So when his lead guitarist, Wally Stocker [formerly of the Babys], left the band, he called me up and asked me to play a string of dates on the East Coast. I've played with them ever since and their schedule is such that I can do both bands."

"He was the perfect guitar player for Humble Pie," Shirley notes. "We gave him a tape, he learned it, and, having never rehearsed with the band, played with us for the first time in Pittsburgh and he never missed a note. He was great."

Greene can also boast songwriting credits for a song Carlos Santana recorded. "Mark Avsec and I had written a song called 'Too Much Love.' Mason Ruffner, an excellent guitarist/writer/singer, heard a demo of it and suggested the song to Carlos. The lyrics, however, were a bit too cynical for him, so Mason altered the words a bit and changed the title to 'Angel Love.' Carlos did record it, though it didn't get on an album, and I got to hear him play it at a Blossom concert. That was a terrific feeling."

Greene also coproduced the cable TV program *Cleveland Rocks*. Although the show was short-lived, the opportunity enabled him to interview some of his personal heroes, such as B. B. King, Stevie Ray and Jimmy Vaughan, and Albert Collins. During 1996–97 he had a notable power trio called MPG with former James Gang bassist Dale Peters and drummer Michael Miheli.

After more than two decades of being in other people's bands, and while Humble Pie dotted the country from coast to coast with periodic shows, Greene decided it was perhaps time for his own group.

"I've always liked being the side guy," he says. "I always saw myself in that role. You get to play without having to make all the decisions, carry out the burdens or deal with the hassles. But as one gets older, you start seeing things from different vantage points.

You become less satisfied with some of the decisions that are made for you and you want more control of your own destiny."

Fate brought in an old friend from his Jimmy Ley days. "I ran into Alan again when Jay Allen, the drummer from Jimmy Ley and the Coosa River Band, was in town," Daubenspeck recalls. "Every time Jay comes back he wants to get together for a jam session. So he calls me, anonymously, and leaves a message to be at the Moss Point Tavern with my equipment, ready to play. I expected it to be just another pickup job. I walk in and Jay and Alan are sitting there, grins on their faces. So we played a bit together and afterward, Mike Miheli, who owns the bar, suggested we get together to do some gigs around town."

On January 31, 1998, Greene, for the first time, was leader of the band. The group's debut at Danny Boy Tavern filled the room with longtime fans and won over new ones with its vast repertoire, which includes covers of Fabulous Thunderbirds, Van Halen, Johnny Winters, Albert Collins, and Guitar Slim. With their individual, broad backgrounds, the trio manages to introduce a diverse selection of original material as well. This new formation gives Greene and longtime music buddy Daubenspeck a renewed sense of satisfaction.

"Originally it was going to be something to do once or twice a month just to pick up some extra money," Daubenspeck laughs. "But right from the start we've been working three nights a week. And we're at the point in our careers where we can pretty much play what we like. Our music runs the gamut. A lot of guys get locked into just one style. My influences span from Hank Williams, Sr., to Ozzy Osbourne! I can play country, rock, blues . . . . To me it's all part of being a well-versed musician." He adds, "Our original stuff is a collaboration. It's becoming very [Joe] Santriani-esque, stick it in your face. And nothing makes me and Mike happier than just giving Alan solid backing and turning him loose to do his thing."

The Alan Greene Band released a live CD in 1998, recorded at Wilbert's Bar and Grille. The group is planning more releases.

The Burnt River Band (1976–)

As one might guess by the name, this bar band was conceived when Cleveland was at the height of bad press (a five-minute fire caused by petroleum-soaked timber caught under a bridge over the Cuyahoga River produced a media flame burner of its own in 1969). Although best known as a "biker band," this band's blues/rock, ZZ Top–style music can not be underplayed. In fact, with all the hundreds of bar bands out of the North Coast, the Burnt River Band stands alone.

"I grew up listening to a lot of Muddy Waters, Hound Dog Taylor, Howlin' Wolf. Then later, I got into Johnny Winter and Paul Butterfield," founder/harp player/guitarist/vocalist Stanley Nicholas says of his influences. "The original band was with Dan Young on guitar, John Lewandowski on drums, and Clyde Deubl on bass. Although we've often changed members, the Burnt River Band has played nonstop for over twenty years."

Their first gig was, appropriately enough, on the biggest party night of the year: New Year's Eve 1976. Since then, this pack of born-to-be-wild musicians has shared the stage with notable rockers such as Johnny and Edgar Winter, Steppenwolf, Marshall Tucker Band, Doobie Brothers, Lynyrd Skynyrd, Stray Cats, David Crosby, Mitch Ryder, and country artists Johnny Paycheck, David Allen Coe and Cleveland's own Roger Martin. With humble beginnings in neighborhood bars, Burnt River's music and reputation soon spanned the country.

"What really made our name known was the Harley Rendezvous, the motorcycle rally in Saratoga, New York. There were 9,000 people there to hear us, so it was really a shot in the arm," Nicholas says.

That exposure brought them gigs on every coast: Toronto, San Francisco, Boston, and Fort Lauderdale. In 1984, the Harley enthusiasts were invited to play at the annual H-D Motorcycle Rally and Races event in Sturgis, South Dakota. Since then, they've become the house band at the Buffalo Chip concert every year. They also play yearly at the American Motorcycle Jamboree in Cobleskill, New York, and are a regular sight at the annual Bike Week in Daytona, Florida.

And like every band, changing members have been a constant.

"There are two which I refer to as 'honorary members' because I can usually rely on them when I need them," says Nicholas (who works at the Ford Motor Engine Plant by day). "They are Bob Bene on bass and Don Shilling on drums. Our current band, however, has been the most stable, and I think will be with me a long time. They include Dan 'Shotgun' Kriah on bass, K.C. Woods on guitar, and Joe Chot on drums."

The band does many cover songs, such as "Key to the Highway," "Every Day I Have the Blues," "Flip, Flop, and Fly," "Messin' with the Kid," and "Midnight Special." But they also have a list of originals, all penned by Nicholas. Their first album, *Burnt River—Live at Carlton Harley-Davidson,* was recorded in 1982, and their latest, *Boogie with the River* (produced by Roger Martin), was released in 1995.

The Burnt River Band proves that you can keep your day job and still play your music. . . . And it doesn't hurt to have thousands of music-lovin' biker fans.

18 The Prominent Deejays of the '90s

The following is a list of the remaining (and a few former) disc jockeys whose voices continue to spark interest in the music, while their personalities allow listeners to still believe in yesterday.

Brian and Joe (Brian Fowler and Joseph Cronauer; WONE, WENZ, WMMS, WMVX)

When it comes to these two Cleveland disc jockeys, you can't talk about one without the other. After all, since early in their radio careers, it's always been Brian and Joe. And their personal history is full of coincidences.

Both were born in 1963. Both grew up in Parma, and although they attended different high schools (Brian, Valley Forge; Joe, Normandy), both took vocational broadcasting classes (Brian, radio; Joe, television), which was how they met and began their enduring friendship. When it came time for college, both happened to enroll in Ohio University, majored in telecommunications, and graduated the same year, 1985.

The similarities don't stop there. Both their mothers are named Jean, their fathers are Joe. Although their wives have different names, the women are best friends as well.

Brian was Joe's best man and Joe was Brian's. When Joe and his wife had their first of four children (so far), Brian and his wife were the chosen godparents (both are Catholic as well). When Brian's son came along in 1995, the choice of godparents was a given.

In 1985, Joe moved to Nashville for a job as production director (and eventually program director) for Christian station WWGM. Brian, in turn, went to Lancaster, Pennsylvania, for a job at WLAN. Later that year, Brian was summoned to Akron for a job at WONE-FM, quickly moving from weekend deejay to host of a morning show. The AOR station's biggest competitor was WKDD (formerly WCUE), and Brian convinced his program director, Brian Taylor, that he could beat them in the ratings if he had his hometown buddy with him. During their college days, Brian and Joe had done comedy acts on "open-mike night" at both Akron's Hilarities and the Cleveland Comedy Club. The two were thrilled to be teamed up for "The Brian and Joe Radio Show," which debuted on February 29, 1988. The comedic duo soon attracted a strong fan base in morning radio (after years of camaraderie, they had their timing down pat). Within months, Brian and Joe had secured their ratings (number one in the key demographics, ages 18–34) against the competition: the John Lanigan Show, the morning show at WKDD, and even WMMS's "Buzzard Morning Zoo." In September 1990, the company sold the Akron station, moving Brian and Joe to Denver station KAZY. But things were different there, with a general manager who didn't see things the same. A year later, it was back to Ohio, where the deejays worked at Dayton station WAZU ("the Big Wazoo").

In July 1992, the duo found themselves back in Cleveland after taking a job at WENZ ("The End")—thanks to station manager Mark Hyden, who remembered their impressive WONE days. "Brian and Joe" not only copped the coveted morning slot, they arrived at an alternative rock radio station brimming with contemporary, innovative programming. The deejays promoted their own fan club, which they termed the "Brian and Joe Personal Friend Tour." Card-carrying members, whose ranks quickly rose to 10,000, had their own "impersonal" number. While playing the favorite music of Generation Xers, Brian and Joe were given the freedom to do what they did best. Life was good, and it was about to get better.

"When we were at WENZ," Joe says, "We were doing as good as you can, considering the frequency and the actual signal. We were getting noticed, no doubt about it."

"And unbeknownst to us," adds Brian, "WMMS was getting ready to change formats. I think 'MMS knew they had to blow 'the End' completely out of the water, so they wanted to bring us on before making the switch. But we were under contract, we couldn't legally leave. What was neat about that deal was 'MMS literally stole us. Once we agreed on terms, they told us to walk out of the contract, and we'd be covered legally. Our agent and his law firm looked at it up and down to make sure. So we did it because we wanted that chance—to be a part of what they were promoting as WMMS—the Next Generation."

While the stations were negotiating, a June 3, 1994, *Plain Dealer* article announced that WENZ was not renewing the deejays' contract. That same edition ran a picture on another page of the new "Morning Zoo" duo (replacing Jeff and Flash) with bags over their heads, supposedly to tease the audience. However, the two wore T-shirts with a "B" and "J" clearly visible, making the secret no big surprise. The two escaped a "noncompete" contract and became the morning crew for a new generation of Buzzard listeners. They couldn't believe their luck.

"It wasn't just that we were a part of WMMS," Joe notes. "It was the fact we were meeting and working with people everyone grew up listening to—the legends of Cleveland radio. Now that was awesome."

By now, Brian and Joe were capturing attention wherever they went. They attribute their success to combining the best things about the Cleveland disc jockeys they were weaned on, then adding their own individual twists.

"I liked several deejays, each for different reasons," Brian says of his influences. "Jeff Kinzbach had this great low voice, perfect for radio. I liked the humor of Danny Wright. 'Uncle Vic' was funny, too. John Lanigan was, and still is, a terrific talk-show host. And there was Ray Marshall on WWWE-AM 1100, who always pronounced his Ws just perfect. Even today, if I hear a deejay enunciate his Ws wrong, it bugs me!

"But I never really had hopes of working at any Cleveland station. I just wanted to be in radio, doing exactly what I'm doing now. And make good money at it, of course!"

"I was actually a big G-98 fan growing up," Joe recalls.

So I liked all those deejays. But I felt forced to tune into WMMS because the peer pressure in school was unbelievable. You had to know what was going on at 'MMS or you were considered a dork!

Growing up in Cleveland when we did, you never knew what bad radio was, or TV for that matter. You became so conditioned. It wasn't until I left Cleveland and started hearing a lot of bad markets that I realized how good we had it.

My main goal has always been to entertain in one form or another. And radio is an awesome form to do it in. It's a different stage you go to every day. I feel so fortunate that we've been able to make our mark in our hometown and be successful in such a competitive field.

One interesting note is that until he was working in Nashville, Joe had no idea he had a cousin who had also been a deejay—in Vietnam. Adrian Cronauer's life was chronicled in the 1987 movie, *Good Morning, Vietnam,* starring Robin Williams. He recalls:

I'll never forget one evening I was watching *Entertainment Tonight.* And there was Robin Williams on the set of his new movie. I happened to notice his uniform and saw the name *Cronauer* on it, and shouted, "Hey, that's my name!" So I called the *ET* people and asked for information about the movie, and found out the script was based on Adrian Cronauer. I called my parents, and my mother turned into Alex Haley. After some research we found out that yes, he's my dad's second cousin from Pennsylvania. We hooked up with him soon after that, and I called him, and when we got our Akron show we had him on the air. It was great. We hit it off right away and now we're one big happy family. He and his wife, Jean, came to my wedding. He's a lawyer now, and ironically, his wife works for a radio station in Washington D.C.

The Cleveland Cronauer and his partner, Joe Fowler, got national attention as well when they became the first disc jockeys to broadcast from the Rock and Roll Hall of Fame. On August 24, 1995, one week before the hall's opening, Brian and Joe aired their morning-drive show from its state-of-the-art radio studio. Other local AM and FM stations got their turn as well, and since then, radio stations from all over the world have broadcast shows from the Rock Hall.

The next few years for Brian and Joe would be filled with revolving-door station owners, format changes, and time slots. One morning in April 1996, while the deejays were preparing to leave for L.A. to appear in the "Drew-Stock" segment of *The Drew Carey Show* (the only deejays invited to appear with rockers Little Richard, Joe Walsh, former Browns quarterback Bernie Kosar, and actor and Cleveland native Martin Mull), they were told the station was going in "a different direction in the morning format." The different direction was an ill-fated decision to bring in a female rival for WNCX's Howard Stern, Liz Wilde.

"We thought, this is it. There was nowhere else to go in Cleveland; morning radio was locked out," Joe says. "But when we left mornings, the ratings began a downward spiral. When Liz came on board, [the station] started losing a lot of money because clients started pulling out. Some of them, like McDonalds, simply refused to be on with her. The station realized that in order to maintain the same client pull and not lose any money, they put us in afternoon-drive and moved the clients to that time period."

Their new hours gave them the opportunity to interview some of their favorite rock groups. "Rock 'n' rollers just don't do mornings," Joe says. "So afternoons allowed us to have a lot of them on our show. It was great meeting Jon Anderson and Steve Howe of Yes. I used to play those Yes albums so many times on those old turntables [that] the needles and the arms would totally wear out."

"Both Kiss and Aerosmith were the best," Brian adds. "They came in and actually did the show with us. They had their own mikes and worked the control board. We usually get the guests for twenty minutes. These guys were there an hour and a half. They were having so much fun, we couldn't get them out of there! It was a really great time."

When the format changed once again in the fall of 1998, time had run out for Brian and Joe's WMMS years. The renowned deejays were offered another morning show on new station WMVX-FM 106.5. And "Brian and Joe's Morning Radio Show" is still alive and well.

"Our careers have been amazing," Brian says.

And we've done some pretty crazy things. When we were at 'ENZ, I lost a bet with Joe and had to run naked down Euclid Avenue. Then, at 'MMS, Joe lost a bet with me and had to run naked down Huron Road. Another time at 'MMS, we bet the

Browns against the Steelers in the 1994 Playoffs, lost, and had to jump into Lake Erie with a water temp of thirty-seven degrees.

We've been together so long and been through so much. We've seen people put together for a radio show and it doesn't work. All the parts have to fit. There has to be that chemistry. Ours is built in. We've got all those similarities and maintain a respect for one another. [Our friendship] is not an act. People know what they get on the air is what they're going to get off the air.

"We've been very blessed," adds Joe. "One thing Brian and I have a very strong commitment to is our faith, which has certainly seen us through all the changes. We're grateful to God, not just for the opportunity, but the longevity we've enjoyed in Cleveland radio."

Although predicting their future in broadcasting could be likened to forecasting Cleveland weather, this unique radio pair, as well as their listeners, hope the two will remain a team.

"We've persevered through so many managers and owners," Brian says. "We've been on WENZ mornings, WMMS mornings, 'MMS afternoons, and now Mix-106 mornings."

WMMS deejays Brian and Joe lose a bet and prepare to endure the chilly waters of Lake Erie, 1995. *Photo by Brian Chalmers.*

"Plus, we're from Parma," Joe interjects. "You know, everybody in Cleveland makes fun of Parma, and everyone around the country makes fun of Cleveland—or used to. So we are literally at the *bottom* of the comedy totem pole. We're used to that and we can take it. But we can also give it back! So after all the changes in radio and being able to take some ribbing, we're survivors. 'Brian and Joe' are still here, and planning on being around for a long time to come." Radio willing.

Jerry Shirley (WNCX)

How the drummer for British band Humble Pie ever ended up in Cleveland is a story in itself. But then there are the events that led him to become a Cleveland disc jockey. But perhaps most surprising to some is the fact this rock and roller remains on the North Coast willingly.

A lot happened before Shirley became a Clevelander. Born and raised in London, he began his drumming days when he was just a boy. His parents lived above a pub that had a drum kit in the corner, which his father allowed him to "fool around with" when the bar was closed. By the time Jeremy Duncan Tipson Shirley was nine, his talent for keeping a beat was evident. And he couldn't have had better influences: His dad was a drummer in a swing band, and he grew up listening to "the old swing drummers like Gene Krupa, Buddy Rich, and Sonny Payne from Count Basie's Orchestra. Then, when rock 'n' roll started kickin' in big time, I was a huge fan of Keith Moon, Mitch Mitchell, and Charlie Watts. My biggest American influence was Al Jackson from Booker T. and the MG's."

By the time Shirley had reached his teens in the mid-1960s, he was in his brother's rock band, Apostolic Intervention, which shared the same manager as the Rolling Stones, Andrew Loog Oldham. They also shared the same record label with the Small Faces, which boasted a young singer/guitarist named Steve Marriott. Shirley befriended Marriott when the guitarist and Small Faces bassist Ronnie Lane wrote a song for Shirley's band, which Marriott ultimately produced. Then Shirley was introduced to Peter Frampton, and the rest is rock history. Marriott, Frampton, Shirley, and former Spooky Tooth bass player Greg Ridley formed Humble Pie in 1969. Shirley had just celebrated his seventeenth birthday.

The group began making waves that spread all the way to American shores. Their U.S. concert debut included a whirlwind six-week tour in places such as New York, Boston, Philadelphia, Washington, D.C., Detroit, Chicago, Grand Rapids, and Cleveland. Shirley recalls his visit to the North Coast:

I still remember that first Cleveland concert. We opened up for the Moody Blues at the Allen Theater, I believe. I remember, even then, being impressed by the enthusiasm of the audience. What a musician judges an audience by is their reaction to you. The louder they are, the more they participate, the more you get into it, and the more exciting the show is. Typically, back then there were a few select places musicians felt had the best audiences. They were Chicago, Detroit, Atlanta, anywhere in Texas, and in amongst all that, Cleveland shone. They were probably the loudest of 'em all! I don't know, maybe there's something in the water. But you knew when you came to Cleveland the place would be alive.

Shirley had such fond memories of the North Coast city that, two decades later, after meeting his future wife at the Sahara Club in Willoughby Hills, he opted to make it his home and put the once-defunct Humble Pie back together. What he never expected, however, was becoming host of his own radio show. But when the offer came, he was glad to oblige.

Things were looking good for Jerry Shirley in 1989.

"I had just reformed the band," he recalls, "and we were getting ready to play the Agora [which was recorded for a live album to benefit the upcoming Rock Hall]. As part of the promotion I was invited to WNCX for an interview with Bill Louis on his 'Classic Cafe.' It went real well, and apparently Bill told his program director what a good time we'd had on and off the air and I guess one thing led to another."

Shirley was given a Saturday morning show on WNCX highlighting the best of British rock. "The British Bunch" was a welcome change of pace for listeners, and with his inside knowledge and thick Cockney accent, the rock and roll drummer fast became a rock radio star. When the first ratings book showed Shirley with the highest numbers in that time period, no one was more surprised than he. Then program director Doug Podell gave Shirley his own morning show, "Mad Dogs and Englishmen." To give the show an initial boost, his first on-air guest was old bandmate Peter Frampton. And unlike its competitors, the show's format was loose, harkening back to '70s progressive radio, and, thanks to its host, the only radio program that promoted local music. For that he was reprimanded.

"At first when I'd done such a thing, that is, played a demo tape by Armstrong Bearcat, which I loved, the programmers had a cow. They said you just don't go on prime time radio with a local band without permission. But the listeners, in turn, loved it. And as a result, I was then able to promote these local bands on the air. I was very glad of it because Cleveland has some of the best players, musicians, to rival any other market. And that's no lie."

He notes his favorites as Mr. Stress Blues Band, Frankie Starr and the Chill Factor, Robert Lockwood Jr., Ted Riser's Band, the Numbers Band, and Armstrong Bearcat.

The good-humored radioman also liked to recount on air his days when his band was on top, with big houses, big cars, and playing big concerts. One particular story he enjoyed telling listeners was when Humble Pie played the Akron Rubber Bowl in 1972.

"Black Sabbath was headlining," he recalls. "We had been on a hot streak then, so there'd been a bit of noise about the Pie being the *second* band on the bill. So we went out and gave quite a ballsy performance. Then, as we were leaving, our chartered Lear Jet flew right over the stadium and interrupted the planned fireworks show. I think it put a bit of the wind out of their [Black Sabbath's] sails.

"I'd tell all kinds of stories like that. And I'd have listeners call up and sing a song along with me. It was a good gig."

While Shirley was enjoying his success as both a disc jockey and active musician with the reformed Humble Pie, he decided to take advantage of his status and do the charity work he'd always thought about.

My family has a long history of involvement with the Salvation Army. So I grew up aware of the benefits of charity organizations. My father, especially, always worked with charities for children in need.

So when I got into radio, I decided to use the airwaves for as much charity as I could muster. Though by no means was I the only one involved. I was sort of the flag waver. There was a tremendous amount of effort from many individuals in and out of the industry. During this time I found out Cleveland was known to donate the most to charity, per capita basis, than any other city in America. So one day on my morning show, I announced my idea for getting a celebrity guitar to auction off for Camp Cheerful for Handicapped Children, an organization similar to those my father was involved with in England.

Within minutes, Shirley had his guitar when Brady Bulger, president of American Music Brokers and Brady-Wayne Productions, heard Jerry's announcement on the radio and offered to donate an acoustic Gibson J-200 with mother-of-pearl inlay, a rosewood neck, and lustrous ebony finish, valued at $2,200. The first celebrity to sign it was none other than Bob Dylan when he was in Cleveland for a concert.

"Once Bob Dylan signed it, it was a no brainer," Shirley says. "Everyone I took it to figured, well, if Dylan signed it, we'll sign it, too. I then went to England and got Paul McCartney, George Harrison, David Gilmour [Pink Floyd], Pete Townshend, and Ron Wood to sign it. Then David Spero [Joe Walsh's manager] took it to Los Angeles and got signatures from Walsh, Peter Frampton, David Crosby, and Graham Nash. Then came autographs from B. B. King, Robert Cray, Buddy Guy, Gregg Allman, Steve Miller, Steve Winwood, and the Grateful Dead's Jerry Garcia and Bob Weir. It kept snowballing to the point we realized we needed two guitars."

That came easy. Greg Markovich of G. G. Marko Company donated a cherry sunburst Gibson Hummingbird worth $1,800. After David Bowie, John Mellencamp, Stevie Nicks, Don Henley, Todd Rundgren, and members of Van Halen, ZZ Top, and Lynyrd Skynyrd, among others, signed it, the "Star Guitar" was raffled off during a concert at the Agora in February 1992 —eighteen months after Shirley originated the idea. The project netted approximately $12,000 for the charity. The J-200 is currently in the possession of Camp Cheerful, waiting for its value to increase before being auctioned.

"No sooner had we completed the project," Shirley notes, "the bottom fell out of the collectibles market for a few years. So I told them to hang on to it."

In 1992, Shirley was relegated to overnights when WNCX brought in the Howard Stern Show. The midnight to 7:00 A.M. shift was horrific, he says, and took a toll on him physically and mentally. But by the end of 1996, he would experience something far

Jerry Shirley salutes celebrities who signed his star guitar. *Photo by Jeff Bishop.*

more detrimental, which stemmed from an event that abruptly ended his radio career. Ironically, it resulted from a charity project.

"The idea for '30 Days in the Hole' came about through then-program director Doug Podell. He recalled a similar charity drive in Detroit where he used to work, whereby he got someone to live in a trailer during the holiday season up until the time [a semi-truck] got filled with food. So he had the idea; I had the charity, which was the Salvation Army. The premise of it was I'd stay in the trailer for thirty days or until we achieved this goal. It was my idea to fast the whole time, taking in nothing but water and broth, and I did it. The first year, 1991, we reached the maximum weight of 40,000 pounds [in canned goods] in five days but stayed and filled another two-and-a-half truckloads [forty-eight-foot trailers], and it went from there."

The drive was so successful every year that on December 11, 1995, Mayor Michael White proclaimed it "Jerry Shirley Day" in Cleveland for his helping collect more than 300,000 pounds of food and more than $40,000 in cash over the five-year period.

Yet by the following year, Shirley would be renowned for something quite different. It was an ugly incident in his otherwise scandal-free career. And it is a story recounted many times in the press. One week into the 1996 holiday charity drive, Shirley was holed up in his trailer one night when he was visited by two female "exotic dancers." The incident left Shirley passed out on his bed and a reported $600 missing from the cash donation box.

"It was my fault as far as I let my guard down," Shirley explains. "Like an idiot, I chose to take a drink after two-and-a-half years of sobriety. I'd also been on strong medication for my back, so the combination, of course, took me out. I don't remember any of it. The two ladies took total advantage of the situation. And of course, the press, at first, made it look like I had stolen the money. Fortunately, the authorities found the ladies who had indeed taken it. [But] I paid the price, for sure."

The price was his being fired from WNCX and having no one, not his co-workers, not the Salvation Army, stand by him. And while a set of his drumsticks sat mounted on a wall with those of his colleagues in the nearby Rock and Roll Hall of Fame, Shirley was out of a job, his reputation tarnished, and his marriage crumbling. Although he was not charged in the theft, he was charged with possessing too many prescription drugs than were allowed by law. He ultimately accepted a plea bargain, but it didn't end there. Because his drug charge was a felony, thus a deportable charge, he faced the threat of deportation.

After participating in a recovery program, and because of Shirley's overall contribution to the community through his charity efforts, the rock celebrity was vindicated in October 1999. Today, he remains in the Cleveland area, works as a carpenter, and has managed to keep Humble Pie alive with occasional out-of-town gigs.

"From the very start of my working with him," concludes Humble Pie guitarist Alan Greene,

we've always shared a mutual respect. In part, because we come from the same rock 'n' roll roots. His old-school musical knowledge was what I was influenced by. It was the real thing to me. And that profound knowledge and experience shows through. For example, in the recording studio, he knows exactly what will work. He has that innate ability to map things out and to know what fits. And though his success level is far and away greater than mine, and he has many notable friends all over the world, he has always treated me very well and fairly.

In my opinion, the original Humble Pie produced some of the best music of that era. And for me to have the opportunity to be a part of that, to be affiliated with that . . . it's an honor. When you go into the history of Jerry, you realize the people he grew up alongside of are today's top names [in rock]. Everywhere we go on tour, there's established musicians of stature, saying, "Hey, buddy how're ya doin'?" I have a lot of respect for him and his history.

Dewey "the Dew-Master" Stevens (WNCX)

In the radio business, one's longevity and success often depends on the luck of the draw. Dewey Stevens's (né Dewey Roach) entry into radio and subsequent survival began with a flip of a coin.

"WNCX had just started," recalls Stevens, who had enrolled in Connecticut Broadcasting School after getting laid off from his job at Ford Motor Company. "Denny Sanders [who was instrumental in getting the new station off the ground] came to the school as a guest speaker while I was there. Steve Church and Bernie Kendall were our main instructors. At the end of class, Bernie calls three of us over and says, 'You know, there's a position open [at WNCX] for a board operator.' Then they said, 'Well, we really only need one of you. All of you are good on the boards, so the only diplomatic thing is to toss a coin and the odd man gets the job. They got heads, I got tails. Guess who got the job?"

Stevens worked nights for a few weeks until new owners came in with program director Harry Lyles in March 1987. According to Stevens,

> He [Lyles] sent a memo to everyone which said, "I don't care who you are or what you do at the station, I want to interview everyone." So I thought, well, I'm done.
>
> Now Harry was a pretty intimidating guy. So it's ten in the morning and I'm sitting in his office, waiting to get bounced. He says, "We're not having any more board ops at the station." I said, "Okay, well, nice meeting you." Then he says, "Tell me about yourself." I mean, he wanted to know everything. After about an hour and a half, he says, "I like your voice. I think I might be able to use you. I'm going to put you on the air, give you a trial." I couldn't believe it.
>
> He tells me I'll be starting that night at 2:00 A.M. Well, of course I was too excited to sleep that whole day. So I'm passing time watching Johnny Carson and I doze off. When I wake up it's a quarter to two. I jump in my car, drive 'bout a hundred miles an hour and get there just as Nancy Alden's [formerly at Akron's WKDD] getting off her shift. She was the nicest person. She told me not to be nervous and said if I had any problems to call her because she lived just ten minutes away. But I guess I did all right because the next day Harry says, "You've got potential. I think I can make you a star." He hired me for the Sunday overnight shift, midnight to 6:00 A.M. So I was the envy of my broadcasting class because I had a radio job before I even graduated.

Luck may have opened the doors for "The Dew-Master," but it was his deep, clear voice, smooth delivery, and natural on-air personality that has kept his ratings high and his name on the list of WNCX's most familiar deejays. Not wanting to use his surname, Stevens pondered several ideas before Lyles suggested the name of a now-defunct wine cooler called Dewey Stevens.

"Growing up I always listened to Matt the Cat on 'MMS," says Stevens, a 1977 Lincoln West graduate. "Once I got on the radio, people said I sound like him, which I take as a great compliment. One of the biggest thrills I've had at the station was when we beat 'MMS in the ratings for the first time in '89. It was an exciting time because we were a small-budget station, and everyone there was a hometown jock and we promoted that. We got something like a 7-share, and 'MMS was down further than that, which was significant considering their past 11–12 shares. That's when I really felt I was part of a team."

The board-op-turned-deejay was happy in his new role. From 1987–91, Stevens was on the air at various times in the evening, six nights a week. He also had to learn how to deliver outside the studio when it came to emceeing concerts.

"The first band I ever introduced on stage was Ten Years After, at the State Theater, which holds something like 2,000 people. I was still new to the business and was real nervous. Brett Summers told me, 'Go out there and before you even say your name, get them to cheer about something, anything. Say something like, who likes rock 'n' roll? And they'll cheer. After that, say your name, and they'll cheer. You'll feel good, and anything you say after that they'll cheer.' He was right. It was great to stand there and no matter what I said, the audience cheered. Now when new deejays ask me how to get over stage fright I tell them what Brett told me. It works every time."

Meanwhile, in 1990, Stevens took on an assistant director's job at his old broadcasting school. The following year, the tired disc jockey gladly accepted an offer to do weekend shifts at the station.

"The school then gave me a raise and offered me a director's job at their new school in Chicago," he says. "I was there six months but didn't like it. When I came back home, Doug Podell was the new program director at 'NCX. So I called him, and in a week I had my job back. It was for the same weekend shift, and I was really glad to be back."

Then in 1997, Stevens got an offer he almost couldn't refuse. Former WNCX program director, Bob Neumann, who had left to become WMMS's program director, called Stevens to say he was willing to pay him more than his current wages if the longtime deejay switched stations.

"That was a tough decision," Stevens says.

I thought, wow, WMMS. It was like a dream come true. And I thought, well, maybe it is time for a change. But then I had to make the most dreaded phone call of my life. I had to call Bill Louis and tell him I was leaving.

He was upset, of course. I told him, "Bill, this is WMMS, the station we all grew up with." He said, "But it's not really the same station." Which was true. So it made me think. Then he told me not to do anything until Walt Tiburski [WNCX general manager] returned from out of town. A few days later, Bill calls me and offers me the same money to stay. Because I was never unhappy there, I did. It was the right decision.

One thing about WNCX that makes it stand apart from the other stations is all the jocks are hometown, like 'MMS used to be. Even the general manager, Walt, is a native Clevelander. I really think that means something to the audience, and it shows in our consistent ratings.

What's really fun about this job is turning people on to the music. I remember back in '89, I got a call from this seventeen-year-old kid after I played "Cloud Nine" from George Harrison's album. He asked me who this George Harrison guy was— no kidding. I told him he used to be in a band called the Beatles. About three weeks later, he calls back and says, "Hey, Dewey, I bought that George Harrison album.

Then I went out and bought all the Beatles CDs, too. I love 'em, they're the greatest thing." I felt like I expanded his musical horizons a bit.

I've been at 'NCX longer than anyone, not counting the six-month hiatus. I've seen six or seven ownership changes, numerous program directors come and go. If it ended tomorrow, I'd have no regrets. It's been a nice ride.

In September 2000, Dewey was on hiatus once again due to his work schedule. However, he hosts a syndicated sports show, "Mark Lawrence: Against the Spread," which airs in thirty-seven cities.

Rocco "the Rock Dog" (WMMS, WENZ)

It was an old FM converter he used in his car that perked up the listening ears for the future "Rock Dog."

"I could pick up the cool Cleveland stations like G-98, M-105, and 'MMS," recalls Rocco (né Rick Bennett), who grew up listening to Detroit's CKLW-AM and Akron's WHLO-AM. "That's when I started seriously thinking about getting into radio."

After graduating from Cuyahoga Falls High School, the son of a marine did a two-year stint in the air force before returning home. There he enrolled in the University of Akron, where he pursued his love of radio, majoring in communications. He also started hanging around deejay friend John Griffin, who worked at then-AOR station WCUE-FM (now WKDD). Bennett soon dropped out of college to attend the WIXY School of Broadcasting.

"Cleveland was a hotbed then," he says. "And you had all these great deejays coming into that school to share what they knew. So you were getting taught by the best, who worked at the best stations at the time."

As a result, Bennett got a job immediately upon graduating in 1977. He began working middays at station WOMP-FM in Belair, Ohio. From there he traveled to rock stations in Charlottesville, Virginia (WWWV-FM), Hartford, Connecticut (WHCN-FM, the Walrus), and Orlando, Florida, where at WDIZ-FM, "I was there for about a cup of coffee."

The Akron native then got homesick and moved his young family back to the North Coast in 1983. He was hired as an engineer to build a brand new radio station in Cleveland, public radio station WCPN.

"That was way cool," he says. "It was the first time public broadcasting went on the air here. My chief engineer and I won an OAB award [Ohio Association of Broadcasters] for technical excellence for that. It was exciting being there in the beginning, and that experience set me up for the rest of my career. Since then, I've built or rebuilt five stations in this market."

In 1984, engineering positions opened up at Cleveland's WGCL-FM and WERE-AM. But he still harbored a desire to be a jock.

"I had those years of AOR experience, but to be on the air in Cleveland was tough. You couldn't break in. I sent tapes to 'MMS but didn't hear from them. That's where I wanted to work 'cause that's the station that gave me the desire in the first place."

Ultimately he applied for yet another engineering job at his favorite rock station and began working part-time, "just to get my foot in the door."

"I kept stickin' my face in Kid Leo's so he knew who I was," he says. "I always volunteered whenever they needed a spare voice for a commercial or announcements. Jimmy Octavic gave Leo one of my tapes he found in a drawer somewhere and said, 'Hey look, the engineer kid thinks he's a deejay.' Well, Leo listened and liked it. He put me on weekends in 1986."

His style, reminiscent of one of the most popular comedians in the '80s, the late Sam Kinison, was embraced by 'MMS listeners. But "Rock Bennett" felt he needed a punchier name.

Of all people, it was Browns' defensive cornerback Hanford Dixon who came up with one. "Hanford used to come on the air on Monday mornings with Jeff and Flash and talk about the Sunday game," Bennett recalls. "That's when they just started calling them the Dawgs. So one day he signed a poster for me that said, 'To Rocco, the Rock Dog.' So I was actually dubbed 'the Dog' by the Top Dawg!"

When Leo left in December 1988, Rocco was first to replace him. Then Ruby Cheeks vied for the prime air spot, and Bennett was bumped back to engineering, with airtime on weekends. When Michael Luczak came on board as program director in 1989, "Gonzo Radio" was born. According to Rocco,

Michael wanted a night program that was balls-to-the-wall. He let me have the freedom to just do whatever I wanted from seven to midnight. I played Guns n' Roses, Judas Priest, AC/DC, Aerosmith. At ten we did "Led for the Head," a half-hour of Led Zeppelin. I did "The Manly-Man" feature, a spoof on male-chauvinist pigs, saying the worst things about women. Both sexes loved it 'cause it was actually making fun of political correctness.

Probably the most important thing I did on that show was I had a lot of local bands come on. I'd bring in ZaZa, First Light, Kidd Wicked, Big Machine, bands like that. Gonzo gave local bands a voice, and I'm proud of that.

The show was just different enough to catch evening listeners' attention. Soon it went from ninth to first place in the market ratings. The Rock Dog's boost in popularity extended to a Saturday television show on Channel 19, *Gonzo Radio: The Buzzard B-Movies.*

Things changed, however, in 1992. The station moved to the bigger, better Tower City complex, with Bennett as chief engineer/project manager. The job forced him off radio as he readied Malrite Corporate Headquarters and stations WMMS and WHK for their upgrade. A year later he was back on the air, on afternoon drive with Mike Olszewski, which garnered them the No. 1 spot in their target demographic, ages eighteen to thirty-four. By 1994, ownership changes gave way to unemployment. That is, until WNCX's Doug Podell came calling. Bennett was hired as a part-time deejay on middays until a better offer came his way. "I really wanted to do mornings," Bennett says. "Plus, I needed a full-time gig. So when WENZ [FM 107.9] offered both to me, it was a no-brainer."

After some false starts, he hooked up with a partner, thus the beginning of "Rocco and Tobin in the Morning" show, which lasted two years. In 1995, Bennett was promoted to program director, where he remained until the alternative rock station was sold to Clear Channel. Bennett was moved from mornings to afternoons and was ultimately released when the station was once again sold in May 1999.

"'The End' was a great radio station," he says. "When it died, that was a tremendous loss to Cleveland radio."

Bennett is currently chief engineer for WENZ and WERE, continuing to ensure listeners hear their favorite stations loud and clear. Yet he misses being on the airwaves.

"I lament the actual art of being a deejay," he adds. "The creative ability of mixing music and creating songs—that's all gone, along the passion that kept burning in me while I was on the air. Radios are jukeboxes now. The art is dead. There are no more 'shows,' there's 'shifts.' We really need to get back to freeform radio that now only exists in AM, the low-power FM, and the Internet. But whatever we're experiencing now will soon be obsolete anyway because here comes digital radio—another revolution in progress."

Paula Balish (WNCX)

Paula Balish grew up on radio. "My father was always coming home with radios for me," says the nighttime deejay at WNCX. "There used to be this guy they called the trunk man who'd come by their work site, and my dad would always buy me a radio. I'll never forget the very first one he gave me. It was this neat little nine-volt GE transistor when I was six years old."

As a teenager, Balish graduated to stereo systems and spent the majority of her time playing albums she heard on Cleveland FM radio stations such as WNCR, WWWM 105, and WMMS. She collected albums of her favorite groups like the Band, the Allman Brothers, and the first man she remembers having a major crush on, Bruce Springsteen.

"I was fifteen and always calling up Betty Korvan [WMMS], begging her to play anything by Bruce," she recalls. "Betty was great to chat with late at night. And she was probably the first to make me feel like maybe that's what I wanted to be when I grew up."

After graduating from Mentor High School in 1980, Balish moved to Florida and enrolled in the Connecticut School of Broadcasting. She began her radio career in Riviera Beach, Florida, at WNJY-FM, a big-band station.

"Working there actually gave me an appreciation for 'the music of your life,'" she says, "even today I have a preset button in my car radio set to WRMR 850-AM" [which boasts venerable disc jockey Bill Randle; see Chapter 1].

After the '40s station, she found herself at WPSL-AM in Port St. Lucie, playing '50s music, or "Gold Classic." But her dream was to work at a rock station. When Balish returned home in 1988, she got her wish. After sending in a tape, she was hired at WNCX, a two-year-old station with lots of potential and exciting coworkers. During her first stint there, Balish worked with, among others, Bill Louis, Brett Summers, Rick Rydell, Ruby Cheeks, and Dewey Stevens.

"Female jocks have a problem sometimes, often coming off sounding too rough or too sexy," Stevens says. "Paula has found that happy medium. Plus she's very much herself on the radio and that makes a good deejay. The audience knows she's being sincere."

But her first experience at a major rock station was overshadowed by her sincere expectations.

"I learned a lot there, but it wasn't like I thought it would be," she notes. "I anticipated being really busy doing promos and having fun opportunities. I was on the overnight shift, which was a much less listened-to time period.

"But Rick Rydell was doing mornings then, and I'd stay after my shift and help him out, something like a gofer. He shared a lot with me and told me to just be myself on the radio, and to trust my instincts. Rick was like my big radio hero, just great at what he did. He's doing radio in Alaska now, but I always remember his advice."

In 1992, a change in program directors found the energetic female disc jockey suddenly out of a job. But not for long. For the next three years, Balish worked at Youngstown rock station WNCD 106, "the Wolf." She began on the six-to-midnight shift and later promoted to afternoon-drive time (2:00 to 6:00 P.M.). Then in the spring of 1995, Balish heard WNCX was looking for someone to replace the departing Lisa Dillion.

"I sent a tape to the new PD, Bob Neumann, who had replaced Doug Podell," she says. "He called me and I came back. To this day, I remain loyal to Bill Louis because I think he put in a good word for me and helped me get my job back at 'NCX. I've been grateful ever since because I love my job now. And I was so happy when Bill was promoted to program director [fall 1996], after going through about four of them. Bill was the obvious choice because he'd always been interim PD, so it just made sense."

She was given the 7:00 P.M. to midnight shift, opposite WMMS newcomer Jennifer Wylde, who had worked with Balish at the Youngstown station.

"My boss there [at WNCD] was a jerk," Wylde recalls. "He used to yell at me a lot and give me a hard time. I remember Paula saying to me, 'Hey don't listen to him, you're great.' She helped me gain more confidence in myself. It's funny we ended up in competition with each other, but we were always friends."

Through her career as a Cleveland disc jockey, Balish has seen many a concert and has had the opportunity to interview her favorite rockers.

"In terms of my favorite interview, though, I'm hard-pressed to single one out," she says. "There are certain people who make you feel at ease and give better interviews. I enjoyed talking to Meat Loaf, the group Little Feat, and John Fogerty. Although with Fogerty I was so awed by him because he's such a legend, I kept thinking, *What am I doing talking to this guy?*

"Then there are those like George Thorogood, who it took a while to warm up. But then I couldn't get him to shut up! But it's not hard doing interviews, I figure the stuff I want to know, listeners want to know too."

Contrary to popular belief, disc jockeys don't always get the best seats for concerts. So when they do, they can be as excited as the next guy, or girl.

"When I was working at 'NCD," Balish recalls. "Cornell Bogdan [deejay and salesman], who is still a good friend of mine, knew I loved Keith Richards. So when Keith came to the Pittsburgh Civic Arena for a solo concert, Cornell got me fourth row seats! I was ecstatic. I remember watching Keith, right there in front of me, cigarette dangling, and I just started crying! I was just so happy seeing Keith Richards 'cause he was always my favorite Stone."

With all the changes radio has seen over the past decade, Balish counts her blessings that she continues at WNCX, along with her favorite coworkers Michael Stanley, Dewey Stevens, and Louis.

Lisa Dillion (WMMS, WHK-AM, WNCX, WZJM)

Although Lisa Dillion was born and raised on the extreme east side of Cleveland (fifteen miles west of the Pennsylvania line), she paid her radio dues in California.

"I was a prelaw student at Marquette University [Milwaukee], when a job opening at the campus radio station caught my attention," she says. "I needed to get a work-study job and thought, 'This sounds interesting.' I had done some acting growing up, and radio is a form of acting. My mother had been encouraging me to get into that. But I also wanted to be a lawyer. I wanted to help the legal system because there are so many injustices."

Her college radio experience lasted one semester, when she and her parents moved to Southern California. After enrolling in California State in 1980, an advertisement led her to the Academy of Radio Broadcasting in Huntington Beach. Six weeks into the course, she had a radio career.

"I was offered a job at KFXM-FM in San Bernadino, where they put me on the morning show," she says. "I was nineteen years old and had no idea what I had— market number 26 and the highest-paying shift. Most deejays don't just up and get a morning show their first time out. I just thought, 'Hey, this is really fun.'"

From there, Dillion was all over the radio road. She honed her talents at West Coast stations KWRM-AM (Corona), KCAL-FM (Redlands), KEZY-AM-FM (Anaheim), and KGGI-FM (Riverside), working various shifts. In 1986, another morning program took her to Detroit and FM station WHYT (Power 96). After a few months, it was obvious she and her partner lacked the necessary chemistry. She began considering other options.

All at the same time, I had job offers at stations in Kansas City, Miami, San Francisco, and Cleveland's WMMS. And that was the station I really wanted, but they were dragging their feet. In the meantime, I was putting the other stations off until I heard the word from 'MMS. Finally I pushed and got an interview and audition, and the program director at the time, Jeff McCartney, hired me. That was in 1988.

I got the morning shift with Jeff and Flash. That was when they began changing the format to a more rock Top 40, dropping much of the classic artists for pop. When Kid Leo left, I was in the midst of a divorce and was planning to return to California to get away from everything. When I told the general manager I was quitting, he said, "You can't do that, we're putting you in afternoon drive." I tell you, my knees buckled. They offered me a great raise and talked me into staying. That was a wonderful thing for me. I did afternoon drive with Mike Olszewski, who is wonderful, and we beat the ratings record for that time slot. I was really happy.

The happiness was short-lived. By 1993, WMMS was in the throes of numerous changes in ownership, general managers, and program directors. The corporate pendulum had begun swinging with increased speed in the late '80s and would continue with frustrating consistency through the next decade. The change under Shamrock Corporation involved releasing WMMS mainstays, such as disc jockey Matt the Cat and Len Goldberg, and moving Dillion to middays with a cut in pay. She was no longer happy. But she did it.

In 1994 Nationwide took over, releasing nearly all the deejays. Dillion, wanting to stay in Cleveland, took a job at WHK-AM, where she hosted her own talk show, "Lookin' Good," focusing on beauty, health, and fitness. But it didn't pay the bills. She knew what she had to do next.

I had to call and ask WNCX program director, Doug Podell, who I had previously beat in the ratings book, for a job. He wasn't returning my calls. I'm thinking, *This guy must hate me. What can I do to get his attention?* I was getting desperate for work. So I went to a shoe store, bought a pair of shoes with really high heels. Took one shoe, threw it away, put the other in a box with a note that read, "I'll do anything to get my foot in the door."

I wrapped it and had it delivered to Doug. I didn't think much of the fact I'd used an old WMMS mailing label on it, and when it arrived, he thought it was a bomb or something. He even had the security guard take it outside and examine it before opening it. That's when I finally get a call. And first thing out of Doug's mouth was, "You are out of your mind. What were you thinking?" I said, "I was just trying to get your attention." He said, "Well, you got my attention, you can come work for me."

She began there in August 1994 on the midday shift but was soon switched to 7:00 P.M. to midnight. When a high-paying job offer at Washington, D.C., station WBIG came in March 1995, Dillion couldn't refuse. But the stint was ill fated. She returned to Cleveland but left again in August 1995, when she moved to Detroit station WCXX-

FM. She served as news director on the "JJ and the Morning Crew" show for two years before being replaced by a former disc jockey. She shifted gears when hired for a classical station, WQRS-FM, changing her name to Lia Damato to differentiate from her rock deejay status.

A few more changes ultimately brought her right back to Cleveland. In October 1999, Dillion, now Lisa D., was once again teamed up with Mike Olszewski to hold down the morning shift on "Jammin' Oldies" station WZJM 92.3.

"But the highlight of my entire career was working at WMMS," she adds. "I did cruises with Jeff and Flash, trips to Jamaica and Florida, and did voice-overs for TV. There were some phenomenal disc jockeys there, they had guts. Kid Leo just took the bull by the horns and said, 'I'm going to do it my way, and I'm going to play this record, and turn the world onto something different.' I'm proud to have worked at such a legendary station."

Jennifer Wylde (WMMS)

"I know it sounds like a cliché, and a little too cheesy, but I really did grow up on 'MMS," Jennifer Wylde says. "I listened to Kid Leo every day after school and used to call and harass him by constantly requesting songs. If he didn't play them, I'd call him back and say, 'Hey, this is Jennifer, when ya gonna play my song?' I thought later he must've hated that, but when I met him at the opening gala for the Rock and Roll Hall of Fame, he remembered me and was real cool about it."

Her initial tie with Cleveland's venerable rock station was through her older sibling.

"My brother, David, had interned at WMMS," she recalls. "He used to get these free concert tickets, and when I was in fourth grade, I got to go to my first rock concert. It was at the Richfield Coliseum to see UFO and Cheap Trick. Then the next year I got to see Bruce Springsteen there. Now that was the height of my young life!

"Throughout my teens, I was a real rock 'n' roller, and 'MMS was my station. I used to make fun of my friends who'd listened to the Top 40 stations like G-98 or M-105, which I called the 'MMS wannabe station."

A 1988 graduate of Beachwood High School, Wylde hadn't given any thought to becoming a disc jockey. That is, until she went to the University of Minnesota.

"When I moved to Minneapolis," she says, "my brother knew someone at station WLOL and told me to talk to him about a job. I started out there doing call-out research in the evenings, which I hated. I didn't want to work there 'cause it was Top 40 and I wanted to work at a rock station. So I'd blow off my job and hang out in the studio with the night jock, Allen Kable. He started putting me on the air and thought I was witty and had a good radio voice. Pretty soon it was, like, forget college."

Wylde traded academics for radio broadcasting school. She accepted a menial job hanging banners and doing various promotional duties at Minneapolis's "cool rock station," KQRS-FM. Program director Dave Hamilton took the young intern under his wing and offered her a spot on their sister station in Duluth, Minnesota.

"He said, 'I can't put you on the air here because you have no experience. But if you're willing to drive three-and-a-half hours in the middle of winter, in subzero temperatures, to do weekend overnights, I can get you that.' It sounds crazy, but I wanted to be on the radio so much I jumped for it. It gave me my shot."

After paying her dues, the now-homesick deejay put together an air-check tape and began shopping it to stations closer to her hometown. What happened next is a familiar story.

This Canton station program director, Lisa Rodman, literally found my tape at the bottom of the barrel. She listened to it and, though she realized I was a novice, decided to give me a try. What was great about that was the consultant for that station was none other than former WMMS program director John Gorman! So about seven months later, in 1993, Gorman took over 'MMS again, and took me with him.

I really have to give credit to John Gorman. He hired me with little experience and gave me my own show on the evening shift. It was unbelievable. But I thought I was going to get canned my first night. You couldn't even hear me because my mike was down too low, and the music was up too high. One of the record promoters, Dave Watson, who was my brother's friend, called me to tell me my levels were really off. I could've died. Here I was—my big debut on WMMS, all my friends and family were listening, and it was a disaster.

First-day jitters aside, Wylde's ratings began to steadily rise until her 7:00 P.M. to midnight show was the most-listened-to show by 1994. That same year, WMMS was sold to Nationwide, and soon WNCX's program director left there to take WMMS in a different direction. Wylde was one of the few disc jockeys kept on. But in 1997, personal upsets forced Wylde to take a leave of absence, and the disc jockey moved to Florida.

"And I never went back," she says. "I ended up getting a job at West Palm Beach station WPBZ, and made a new life for myself. But I do regret not having a last show on 'MMS, because I truly loved it there."

Wylde now works for Capstar Chancellor Broadcasting, a syndicated company that pre-records radio programs for various markets—a sign of the times in radio broadcasting.

I tape shows for various formats, like country, jammin' oldies, and classic rock stations around the country. My show airs in Savannah, Georgia; Greenville and Columbia, South Carolina; Birmingham, Alabama; Fort Pierce and Jacksonville, Florida. I go into a studio and record a show that is broadcast in other markets. Companies have started that because it's hard to find good air talent. For instance, you're not going to get a Spaceman Scott or a Paula Balish in Alabama or Savannah, Georgia. So they get someone outside the market and air their show. Overall, it's better for the medium. I do a whole show just like any other show. I have to entertain. I talk about current events, or what's happening with celebrities, but then you also have to know what's happening in that particular town, upcoming appearances and such.

I can remember people saying, "Jennifer Wylde is great at nights playing rock 'n' roll, and that's *it*." But I've proved everybody wrong. Of course live radio is where my heart is. But right now this job has proven that I can do all kinds of radio formats, and that'll help me down the road, I believe. It's serving a purpose. But I don't think this will take over live radio. I think listeners want to know someone local is behind the mike, at the very least in the mornings. I'm still very much an advocate for live radio and hope to return to it someday.

When the Music's Over

By 1999, radio, in many people's opinions, had lost its groove. It is a private party given by huge conglomerates run by lawyers and tended to by market researchers, consultants, and focus groups. Fewer music enthusiasts aspire to be disc jockeys today. And still fewer are even needed. As several radio veterans have pointed out, perhaps someone gutsy enough to risk a change will come along, and people will once again be rushing for the radio dial so as to not miss one utterance from a unique character, like they once did for Alan Freed's "Moondog Show" or the weird Mad Daddy or the eclectic Martin Perlich. Like the nights music lovers fell asleep listening to the ultrahip Billy Bass. Or rushed to catch a sports personality talking touchdowns with Kid Leo. Or got their Friday after-work fix of a ranting "Get Down" episode with Murray Saul. Those radio days—when the deejay was in control—caught listeners off-guard and in tune. Those were days when surprises and fun were a radio guarantee.

Recommended Reading

Clevo, Jim, and Eric Olsen. *Networking in the Music Industry*. New York: Rockpress Publishing, 1993.

Fein, Art. *Rhino Presents The Greatest Rock and Roll Stories*. New York: General Publishing Group, 1996.

Huxley, Martin. *Nine Inch Nails: Self-Destruct*. New York: St. Martin's Press, 1997.

Ward, Ed, Geoffrey Stokes, and Ken Tucker. *Rock of Ages: The History of Rock 'n' Roll*. City: Summit Books, 1986.

Part 5
Rock 'n' Roll Is Here to Stay

19 The Rock and Roll Hall of Fame and Museum

Belief at the beginning of a doubtful undertaking is the one thing that will assure its successful outcome.

—William James

This bit of wisdom could have been the theme for Clevelanders' unrelenting drive to get the Rock and Roll Hall of Fame and Museum built in their city. No matter what's been said, or what jokes have been made about this city through the decades, one irrefutable fact remains: Clevelanders are believers. And it is precisely that trait that has made them such zealous fans, be it of baseball, football, or rock music.

Most Cleveland fans, who have experienced painful losses over the years with both the Indians and the Browns, seem to respond to disappointments by taking on the philosophy of that old 1940s song, "Accentuate the positive / eliminate the negative." That attitude was going to be needed in heavy doses beginning in 1985.

All Clevelanders needed to hear was that there was the remote possibility that a rock and roll hall of fame and museum could be built in their own backyard. All it took was a national newspaper like *USA Today* to test their enthusiasm when it produced a poll asking about the appropriate place for a rock hall. All it took was the tenacity that makes this city's die-hard fans so true-blue . . . and ten long, agonizing years of working and waiting and hoping and believing.

Why Cleveland?

To the average person who has never experienced rock and roll on the North Coast, that question is worth asking. What has Cleveland offered rock music? Most acknowledge phrase-coiner Alan Freed, but others want more evidence of merit. After all, Memphis had Elvis. San Francisco had the 1960s hippie movement. Philadelphia had the "Philly Sound" and Dick Clark. Nashville had the Grand Ole Opry. And New York has everything else, namely the money and the clout. But what would soon become apparent during Cleveland's quest for the Rock Hall was that Cleveland ultimately had something no one could take away: heart. And with that Clevelanders raised the money. With that they earned the Rock Hall. With that they convinced the nonbelievers that the heart of rock and roll really is in Cleveland.

That Alan Freed gave this music phenomenon a name is merely the beginning. Since every page in this book sufficiently answers the question in full, this chapter chronicles the long and winding road that finally led it back to where it all began in the first place: to Freed and the Moondog Coronation Ball.

Countdown to the Rock Hall

It's time for us to think about preserving [rock and roll's] history.
—Jann Wenner, *Rolling Stone* founder/editor

Remember, WMMS was the number one rock station in the nation, and Cleveland was the number one rock market, selling more records per capita than any other city.
—Kid Leo, Cleveland deejay

"I first heard of the whole idea when I got a call, back in 1983, from Lesley Gore ["It's My Party"]," Norm N. Nite says. "She told me, 'Listen, there's some people who are talking about putting together a Rock and Roll Hall of Fame. We're having a meeting and we would like you to attend.' The first meeting there was Suzan [Evans], someone from *Billboard* magazine, and a few others. Everyone had all these great ideas, and sometime later we had another meeting. But I was getting the impression that nothing was going to happen because there was no one who seemed to be a mover and a shaker. I was ready to give up on attending any more meetings. Then in the summer of '84, Suzan Evans called to tell me a whole new group of people had come on board, and things started to take shape."

Thus, the Rock and Roll Hall of Fame Foundation was established in New York City by Atlantic Records cochairman Ahmet Ertegun and lawyer Suzan Evans (who would soon give up law for rock and roll). The duo quickly summoned *Rolling Stone* founder Jann Wenner; record executives Seymore Stein (Sire Records), Noreen Woods (Atlantic), Bob Krasnow (MCA); and entertainment lawyer Allen Grubman. The idea became a reality on August 5, 1985, when a board of twenty-one members, including Nite, was assigned the arduous task of "building" a hall of fame and museum to honor rock and roll's greatest contributors and influences.

But the idea wasn't new, it seems. Agora owner Hank LoConti had thought of it years before.

In 1978, I took my partner down to the West Side of the Flats and said, "This is where entertainment is going to boom." He said, "You're crazy. All you have here are some biker bars and D'Poos." Then I showed him the Powerhouse and began plans to move the Agora into there, along with a rock and roll hall of fame. It was a huge building, and there was plenty of parking. Ultimately there were two reasons why I didn't do it: the river, and the structure of the building made it extremely expensive. Even then, I think I may have done it, except the access was bad. It wasn't easy to find or get to. And at that time, it was not a good area. If some kid made a wrong turn down there, well . . . I didn't want to be responsible for all of suburbia. So I didn't do it.

LoConti explored several more options in the same area. Each one fell through. San Francisco rock promoter Bill Graham had also given thought to forming his own rock pantheon. He kept the concept on the back burner until, ultimately, his city was in line with eighteen others to become rock's official home.

Meanwhile, back in Cleveland, the executive vice president of the Greater Cleveland Growth Association, K. Michael Benz, having heard about the hall of fame idea, had already started getting Cleveland involved, summoning the help of his civic comrades, WMMS, and other rock radio stations.

"It was in April of '84 when I got this call from George Dibria saying he'd like me to meet with his friend, Michael Benz," LoConti recalls. "Michael says to me, 'You know, they're building a rock and roll hall of fame in New York. Do you think there's a chance of it being built in Cleveland?' I said, 'Yeah, about one in a million.' Then I said, 'There's only one guy that's on the inside who could even get their ear, and that's Norm N. Nite."

Nite recalls,

In May of '85 I was approached by Hank LoConti to attend a meeting being held at the Growth Association. There was Michael Benz, his boss, Jules Belkin, and Bill Smith from WMMS. That's when they asked me to intercede on behalf of Cleveland. When I returned to New York, I had a meeting with Ahmet and asked him what he thought about the hall of fame being in Cleveland. He said, "No, it's going to be in New York." Now if I had gotten up, shook his hand, thanked him for his time, and walked out the door, what happens to this history? I stayed and told him all the reasons why he should consider Cleveland. And I must have hit the right buttons, because he said, "Tell your people they can come to the meeting in July."

By then, word of New York's plan was spreading through the industry fast. Benz, Governor Richard Celeste, and Cleveland mayor George Voinovich high-tailed it to the Big Apple that summer to represent the city. Among those who joined them were Cleveland Chamber of Commerce president William Bryant, New Cleveland Campaign executive director George Miller, and WMMS executive Carl Hirsch.

"Usually the meetings ran about two hours," Nite says. "I knew they needed at least forty minutes. Ahmet was going to have them give their presentation at the end of our meeting, which amounted to about ten minutes. I, in turn, suggested they go first to "get it over with." Because if they had gone last, everyone would have been tired and wanting to go home. They wouldn't have been receptive, and all the time and effort they'd spent on it would have gone right down the drain."

The Cleveland team showed the New York group just how serious they were. A video highlighting the city's vintage rock roots was shown (narrated by Ernie Anderson, a.k.a. Ghoulardi) along with a portfolio of press clippings and other features. By the end of the presentation, one of the committee members passed a message to Suzan Evans that read, "Pack your bags, we're going to Cleveland." And so began the long, strange trip.

There were several reasons why Cleveland wanted the Rock Hall so badly. City officials saw it as an economic boon, with the possibility of making Cleveland a more desirable tourist destination. It also fit in perfectly with the city's ongoing revitalization, what some were even calling its renaissance. In short, they saw the money. The governor, not necessarily an advocate of the music itself, saw the prestige. And the fans, the tried-and-true rock and roll lovers, saw it as a long-overdue declaration that Cleveland really was the rock capital of the world.

Not only did city officials take off running with the idea, but Cleveland radio stations immediately began rallying for the cause. To create a buzz, a petition drive was quickly mounted, and in less than a month 660,000 signatures backing Cleveland were obtained. People of every generation throughout northeast Ohio, not just rock enthusiasts, knew what an asset this would be for their city. Kid Leo, ever the Cleveland supporter, did one better by summoning music celebrities to write letters of endorsement. They did. And in droves. Among those who answered the disc jockey's rock call were the Kinks, Rod Stewart, Pete Townshend, Bruce Springsteen, Neil Young, the Beach Boys, Tina Turner, the Everly Brothers, Daryl Hall and John Oates, Pat Benatar, Michael Jackson, Sting, Cyndi Lauper, Glenn Frey, and even Dick Clark. All emphatically supported the Rock Hall being built in Cleveland. Many cited the same reasons:

- Alan Freed gave rock and roll its name.
- Cleveland radio stations have long been recognized for their trend-setting programming.
- The very first rock concert was held in Cleveland.
- Cleveland is known for breaking more groups and artists than any other city.
- Its musical venues offer fans of live music the opportunity to attend hundreds of area concerts in record numbers.

- Cleveland had always been a springboard for new talent within the industry, by way of support and exposure.

And most of those letters ended with, "Cleveland has worked long and hard to support rock 'n' roll. It's only right they play host to the Rock and Roll Hall of Fame."

What really got the committee's attention was the whirlwind, five-hour trip Cleveland hosted for New York's rock hierarchy in September 1985. Tripping down the avenue in a Lolly-the-Trolley tour bus, Ahmet Ertegun and company were treated to a personal tour of eighteen possible sites for the Rock Hall, including ones with a rich musical heritage (such as the site of the former Arena). At the suggestion of Congresswoman Mary Rose Oakar, the bus turned onto Prospect Avenue—to the horror of other Clevelanders on board (after all, Prospect had seedy adult bookstores, hookers, boarded-up buildings, and homeless people). But Prospect was the address of Record Rendezvous, which is as much a part of this city's rock history as the Moondogger himself. That fateful turn became a definitive moment for Cleveland. Upon seeing the renowned record store, Ertegun stopped the bus, got off, and proceeded into the old building. The founder of Atlantic Records spent time chatting with the young people there about rock and roll and even bought some records for his own collection. By the end of that stop, he was open to the notion that Cleveland was, perhaps, the right place for the Rock Hall after all, even going so far as to sign a pro-Cleveland petition before walking out the door.

But as word spread, other cities got in on the action, with Memphis, San Francisco, Los Angeles, and others joining the race. For Cleveland, still stinging from decades-long economic tough times, there was the question of money. Despite not having worked out a fund-raising strategy, an eager, and competitive, Cleveland bid $26 million, when the estimated cost was $20 million. The thinking was to first win the bid; they'd worry about the money later.

As Cleveland movers and shakers staunchly pushed, prodded, and prayed, other cities in the running began dropping off the list. Then, in January 1986, in response to all the hoopla surrounding the issue, New York–based *USA Today* decided to see what readers thought. On January 20 the paper asked people from around the country to call and vote for the city most deserving of the Rock Hall. The reaction was overwhelming; it was the largest response ever produced by an American newspaper phone-in poll. Equally amazing was the result. The first tally showed Cleveland in the lead with 48,728; Memphis with 2,282; San Francisco, 1,683; New York, 1,145; New Orleans, 1,069; Nashville, 773; Chicago, 579; and Philadelphia, 482. The outcome was so one-sided that *USA Today,* in an unprecedented action, added an extension of fifteen hours to allow other cities a chance to catch up. This fueled talk of unfair practice.

"I don't think the extension was right," Denny Sanders told the *Plain Dealer*. "It's like a football game with a minute to go in the last quarter, 32 to 6. Then someone runs out on the field and says, 'Let's extend the game to give the losing team more of a chance.'"

"We'll just have to bury them again," Benz said. People returned to the phone lines and, once again, Cleveland came out ahead. Big time. With the encouragement of local radio stations, 110,315 people called in voting for Cleveland. Second place was Memphis, although the gap was wide, with a total of 7,268. (Ohio Bell was happy, too. The cost of the 900 number added up to some $55,000.)

That March, while city officials and fans patiently awaited a decision from New York, other events were developing. Soon after the *USA Today* poll, Eric Carmen and his lawyer brother, Fred (then mayor of Mayfield Heights), decided to write a song celebrating their city's national radio influence, a song honoring the diversity of Cleveland rockers, a song telling the world (and New Yorkers in particular) that Cleveland is where rock and roll was born and nurtured. The song was called "The Rock Stops Here." Once the idea was set in motion, the Carmen brothers formed their own record company, recorded the song, acquired sponsors, formed a distribution network, got it mastered and pressed, arranged the artwork, and designed the sleeve—all in two weeks' time. Summoning several musician friends, the two succeeded in making a record that had all the energy and beat of a true rock 'n' roll classic.

"I had done studio work with Eric several times, including the 'Hungry Eyes' soundtrack," says Cleveland native, guitarist Darris Atkins, whose musical resume includes Rastus, Satta, the Tower City Cools, and Nation of One. "Eric put together this power session, and it was like a whirlwind. It all came together really fast."

On March 7, Carmen presented Mayor Voinovich with the hot-off-the-press single at a press conference, an event that was broadcast repeatedly on network news throughout the day. In addition, the group of musicians that included former Beau Coup keyboardist Dennis Lewin and drummer Don Krueger produced a video featuring archive clips of Chuck Berry, Jerry Lee Lewis, and Elvis mixed with various Cleveland landmarks.

It wasn't the only song written supporting Cleveland. Longtime disc jockey and WZAK program director Lynn Tolliver Jr. wrote and produced "Where Rock Began to Roll." He had a little help from his friends on this one. Former Dazz members Skip Martin, Ike Wiley, and Eric Fearman donated their talents to arranging and composing the music. The song debuted on Tolliver's radio program on March 6 and was an instant hit with listeners.

But guitarist/piano player/backup musician Dennis Chandler was ahead of them all. Back in 1984 he had written "Can You Feel It (That Rock 'n' Roll)" as a tribute to the Cleveland rock scene, and his band, the Stratophonics, first played it during the group's tenure as WHK's house band. The song was used often for the many events that took place during the 1986 campaign drive.

Moondog Madness

The town was now abuzz. An idea was forged for a Rock and Roll Hall of Fame Day, with parties throughout the greater Cleveland area in commemoration of the thirty-fourth anniversary of the Moondog Coronation Ball. On March 21, 1986, the Moondog Coronation Ball II got under way at the Tower City Central Skylight Concourse. The committee members pulled out all the stops when it was announced that none other than Chuck Berry had agreed to headline. With Eric Carmen and the Innocent added to the bill, the show was an instant sell-out. But unlike the preempted one three decades before, this concert played out in its entirety and was a rousing success. The party didn't stop there. "The Rock 'n' Roll Birthday Bash" at the Palace Theater featured Norm N. Nite spinning records, along with Chubby Checker, Eric Carmen, and local celebrities. Checker also made a late-night appearance at Maxwell's (W. St. Clair). Peabody's DownUnder played host to ten local bands, and '50s-style sock hops entertained supporters and celebrants at Spanky's (both North Ridgeville and Painesville locations) and Brooklyn High School.

Rock radio stations were jumping as well. WMMS sponsored rock parties at the Akron Agora, the Mining Company, and Monk-E-Bizness, which showed the film *Go Johnny Go* at the Hanna Theater. WGCL had Moondog birthday bashes at the Rascal House, Flash Gordon's, the Beach Club, and Utopia. Urban contemporary station WZAK had James Brown lookalike contests. WMJI offered "Magic Night Out at the Roxy Bar and Grille." Governor Richard Celeste arrived at the opening ceremonies on

Governor Richard Celeste and Congresswoman Mary Rose Oakar, among others, celebrate Cleveland's bid for the Rock Hall, 1986. *WMMS Archives.*

Public Square wearing a "The Rock Stops Here" jersey. The local band, Wild Horses, was there to play to the crowd, but temperatures stopped them cold. "It was so impressive to see thousands of people gathered on the square on a March night in Cleveland," recalls guitarist Steve Jochum. "But it was really, really cold. We played about three or four songs and my fingers couldn't move anymore. We had to quit. Still, that was probably my favorite gig of all!"

At the ceremony, Celeste unveiled a bronze plaque honoring Alan Freed, which was later placed on the site of the former WJW studios in Playhouse Square. The official celebration ended with fireworks in the Flats, courtesy of WMMS. An estimated 50,000 people filled downtown Cleveland for the festivities.

"There was a great turnout, and it was a fun night," recalls Innocent guitarist Alan Greene. "We tried treating it just like another gig, playing songs from our recent album. But there was all this energy. I do remember, though, it [the concourse] wasn't the best place for a concert. It had the acoustics of an airplane hangar. The place had huge walls and ceilings, like an echo chamber. Thunderous kind of environment. But no one seemed to care. For me, it was exciting and thrilling to be on the same bill as Chuck Berry. And despite all the other events going around town, this was thecrown jewel."

Those who couldn't make any of the shindigs were still invited to take part. At 7:58 P.M., two minutes before Cleveland's most memorable party since Bruce Springsteen's 1978 Agora/WMMS concert (see Chapter 6), nine radio stations and five television stations simultaneously played the Bill Haley song "Rock Around the Clock." This night made national news, and once again, as planned, all eyes were on Cleveland.

But to the disbelief of many, the *Chicago Tribune* reported on April 6 that Los Angeles had been selected as the site for the Rock Hall. Breaths were held—until the next day, when it was reported the *Chicago Tribune* had been wrong.

And the Band Played On

In April, the rock group named in honor of their city showed up to play at the Rascal House and stayed for four days straight. Clevelend, consisting of lead singer Polly Zaremba, Peter Zaremba (vocals/trombone), Michael Zaremba (bass), Roger Reddy (keyboards), John Burkett (guitar), and Rich Chillemi (drums), held a marathon concert, sponsored by rock station WRQC-FM (92-Q), that began at 2:00 P.M. Monday, April 7, and ended at 6:30 P.M. Friday, April 11. They played one hundred hours and thirty minutes of continuous live rock and roll. In this astonishing and record-breaking effort to support the Rock Hall in Cleveland, the group made it into the *Guinness Book of World Records* as the longest continuously playing band in history.

The idea was the brainchild of WRQC general manager Zemira Jones. Fearing that other local stations might beat him to it, he kept his idea, and plans, quiet—not even discussing it with the band or club owner until five days before it was executed. Explaining his event, he told *Scene,* "We needed a promotion that represents the entire city of Cleveland, what it embodies in rock 'n' roll, and that has nothing to do with money. But [it] has everything to do with music, the talent of the artists, and the people that appreciate it, and the sweat they put into it over these many years to make rock and roll what it is."

"We were approached about the idea by WRQC program director Tracy Benson," recalls band member Polly Zaremba.

We thought they [WRQC staff] were crazy! We never thought we could pull it off and we weren't even sure how to go about it. But after discussing it further, we decided to go for it.

We were all trained musicians, so we simply began with our regular sets, then started ad libbing, playing a lot of blues. The important thing was to keep playing no matter what. We did thirty-three straight hours, then had an hour and a half off. But we couldn't sleep; we were too hyped-up. We were monitored by Guinness and weren't allowed to leave the stage area. There was a port-a-potty in the back, and even then, we had to carry a tambourine or something musical with us. The Rascal House was open to the public twenty-four hours a day that whole time, so we were always on display. People would pour in at all hours. Phil Collins was in town during that time and he came to see us. Plus, there were over 150 local musicians who came by to support us. Many of them jammed with us after their own gigs, to keep us motivated. I swear we couldn't have gotten through it without them.

The band saved up their hourly five-minute breaks in order to allow for two or three hours for sleep. However, they only managed a total of four and a half hours during the entire five-day stretch. After three days of continuous playing, band members began to hallucinate. Guitarist Ben Curlutu called it quits. No one could blame him. Zaremba and her bandmates have dim recollections of the last few days. "They were pretty out of it after awhile," group manager Ken Dudek recalls. "They made me stay up with them, but I managed to sneak out once in a while for a nap. It was real exciting towards the end, though. Right before the countdown, in comes Governor Celeste and Mayor Voinovich. There were 167 radio stations carrying it [the countdown] live. The AP and UP wire services were covering it. And it was shown on MTV, live across the country. Afterward, we got responses from people in Europe who heard it, and a good friend of ours, who didn't know we were doing it, heard it on his car radio on an L.A. freeway and literally drove off the road!"

With worldwide coverage, the steadfast efforts of this persevering band became instrumental in helping convince the New York board to concede to having the Rock Hall built in Cleveland. The group was given a plaque and a letter by the mayor and governor, deeming its contribution the single most-impressive event the city had staged in its efforts to obtain the Rock Hall.

The Rock Stops Here

On May 5, citing, "Clevelanders' incredible community enthusiasm and professionalism," Rock Hall board chairman Ahmet Ertegun declared the city as truly the rock and roll capital of the world and now the official home of the Rock and Roll Hall of Fame.

On the grounds of the Burke Lakefront Airport, the announcement was received by the hundreds in attendance who had worked so doggedly to snag the coveted Hall. With "Cleveland Rocks" playing in the background, local TV and radio interrupting regular schedules for live broadcasts, and the Indians winning its sold-out game on a sunny day in the Municipal Stadium, all was right in the world for Clevelanders.

In November, local singer/songwriter Marc Cohn agreed to offer his single "Heart of the City" (previously used as a *Plain Dealer* advertisement jingle) to be sold as a fund-raiser for the Rock Hall. With Rock Hall costs rapidly accumulating, it was soon clear that much more would be required. Meanwhile, talks on a proposed site for the building were put on the table until January 1987.

Just as all the celebrating began dying down that winter, much of the work was just beginning. Throughout the next year, board members and Cleveland and New York's political and music executives discussed site locations, debated over which city should play host to the annual induction, and watched helplessly as overall costs that began at $20 million escalated to a total that shocked everyone. Months turned into years.

1987

First on the agenda in January was settling the matters of where to build the Hall, who would design it, and who would build it. Also, where would the money come from?

After officials considered spots in the Flats, the former site of the Cleveland Arena, Playhouse Square, Central Market, and the Lakefront, Tower City seemed to best fit the bill, in terms of both finances and accessibility.

When the New York board returned to Cleveland for a final assessment, funding was discussed, and money became the root of what would be a long-strained relationship. The partnership between the two boards showed tension early on. The corporate funds that earlier seemed so easy to obtain were only trickling in and were far less than originally anticipated. Companies were reluctant to donate huge amounts to a project that still had many question marks attached to it. New Yorkers' impatience and Clevelanders' frustration succeeded only in stalling negotiations. Meanwhile, estimated costs rose to $25 million.

In February, the Cleveland Foundation came through by setting aside $350,000 of the $4.2 million in grants it approved for predevelopment for the proposed Rock Hall. This is when Clevelanders first heard the name I. M. Pei, who would soon be hired as the project's architect. Other Pei designs include Washington's National Gallery of Arts East Building, Boston's JFK Library, and the expansion of the Louvre Museum in France. Though not schooled in rock and roll, Pei received a crash course in rock history from Jann Wenner. He proved to be a quick study.

In June, the Cleveland Founders Club (a grass-roots campaign) launched a drive to obtain 100,000 contributors. The club managed to yield a scant 7,000 supporters. Rumblings about whether Cleveland would ultimately lose the Rock Hall began. The annual "Party in the Park," sponsored by the Cleveland Growth Association, moved from the park to the proposed Rock Hall site on Huron Road. Fan favorites Donnie Iris and the Cruisers donated their time and energy to the free event, and all proceeds went to the Rock Hall's Founders Club.

On December 3, in Manhattan, Pei unveiled the model of the Rock and Roll Hall of Fame and Museum. Head of development J. Richard Kelso described the distinctive building as "gorgeous" (officials are mum on the description). And as Pei enthusiastically promised a building that would represent the "energy, openness, and youth that is rock 'n' roll," the estimated cost jumped to $40 million.

"Now the hard work begins," Ertegun said, not realizing just how prophetic those words would become.

1988

The third Rock and Roll Hall of Fame ceremony was held in New York's Waldorf Astoria Hotel. The already-hot issue on Cleveland hosting future inductions was fueled further when Ertegun was quoted as saying the ceremonies would never take place in Cleveland because "this is where the record industry is." As the building's design was made public, and praised, tension between New York and Cleveland escalated.

In March, money was once again the key issue. Milton Maltz, on behalf of Malrite Corporation and WMMS, made a $250,000 contribution. The company was one of the first corporations to make a donation, and they hoped that others would follow the lead. Few did.

Mayor Voinovich was told that if the Cleveland-based portion of the board could not raise the $13.5 million soon—half of the $28 million required before the New York–based foundation kicked in any financial contribution—the city might not get the Rock Hall after all.

The city raised the money by September, largely due to pledges from local business leaders such as Higbee Company chairman Robert Broadbent and the CEOs of BP America, East Ohio Gas, and U.S. Nestle.

In October, Larry R. Thompson, a native of Vandalia, Ohio, was appointed Rock Hall director. The lawyer, previously the special assistant to Ohio State University president Edward Jennings, was credited with obtaining the obligatory financial commitments. He promised that the museum would be a celebration of the "roots and roll of rock music." Meanwhile, groundbreaking for the Rock Hall was delayed until fall of 1990, as the estimated cost rose to $48 million.

1989

With Cleveland still $33 million short of its goal, the noose was tightening. It was up to the new director of development, John Zoilo, an economics graduate of Marquette University, to meet the challenge. Indeed, in an interview with *Plain Dealer* reporter Debbie Snook, Zoilo cited the challenge of getting funds for the Rock Hall as one of the main reasons he accepted the job. As director of the grass-roots campaign for the Statue of Liberty foundation from 1984–87, Zoilo was instrumental in raising $30 million. And having worked for a Washington, D.C., sports marketing firm, he had experience securing sponsors. If a challenge was what he was looking for, he had come to the right place.

To Clevelanders, it appeared that New York was waiting in the wings to erect more hurdles with every leap the city made. This time, the board demanded that Cleveland cough up $40 million in six months or lose the Rock Hall. Mayor Voinovich surprised them with an ultimatum of his own. "We had jumped through all the hoops, done everything we promised, and they were still screwing around," he later told *Cleveland Magazine*. "We were years into this thing and we didn't have a piece of paper yet."

On May 23, 1989, the Cleveland mayor made the New York–based Rock and Roll Hall of Fame Foundation sign a formal joint operating agreement. Part of the agreement stated that Voinovich must raise the money in the allotted time, and, in turn, the New York board was to stop threatening to take the Hall away from Cleveland.

Two months before deadline, the Ohio General Assembly approved another $1 million (added to the $4 million allotted three years before) for construction, and Cuyahoga County okayed a $5 million bond issue. As the countdown continued, Norm N. Nite promised to donate to the Rock Hall fund 50 percent of his royalties from his book *Rock On Almanac*. Richard and David H. Jacobs came through as well with an "undisclosed amount." Ian Hunter and former Mott the Hoople bandmate Mick Ronson became the first to give a benefit concert (at Music Hall) with all proceeds going to the Rock Hall.

Frustrations continued, however, with the latest snag. "Look elsewhere" was the message from Jack Kemp, chief of Housing and Urban Development (HUD), who rejected Cleveland's request for a $6.9 million urban grant for Urban Development Action Growth (UDAG). The grant would have been used for construction funds.

To add insult to injury, the only glory Cleveland had at this point was stripped away with one article. On October 24, Cleveland was to officially announce the 1990 class of inductees during a live press conference from the Palace Theater. Just hours before the noon ceremony, *USA Today* and other New York newspapers published the entire list. The information was to have been secured under lock and key until the formal announcement. The New York leak was viewed by many Clevelanders—particularly Norm N. Nite—as a deliberate slap to Cleveland.

By November, time had run out. Cleveland made it—one day before the deadline. Hope was restored as the city reached its $40 million interim goal. It had been no small task. With $25 million from the city, county, and state; $10 million from local businesses;

and $1 million from individual donors, the final $4 million was raised in that last month, thanks to Robert Broadbent, who personally acquired it through his corporate connections. A national fund-raising campaign was the next step. The Ford Motor Company came through with a $250,000 contribution to the hall.

1990

In January, newly elected governor George Voinovich moved to Columbus, Michael White became the mayor of Cleveland, and the highly anticipated Tower City opened to grand applause.

Meanwhile, back at the Rock Hall, ten Ohioans were named to the board of directors, though none had a rock and roll background. Among them were Mayor White; former governor Celeste; Sandra Austin, senior vice president of University Hospitals; Richard Pogue, managing partner at the law firm of Jones Day Reavis and Pogue; and Albert B. Ratner, chairman and chief executive officer of Forest City Enterprises. The board also appointed Stouffer Hotel Company president William N. Hulett as rock hall cochairman, replacing Broadbent.

With the completion of Tower City, New York board members changed their minds about the Rock Hall's proposed residence. According to a *Plain Dealer* article, the decision to move the site location was directly related to competition with the Record Town store in Tower City, since the Rock Hall plans included a record retail store of its own. The board denied the report, citing that the prospective space was too restrictive for future expansion.

It was back to the drawing board. Plans for the Tower City location were officially dropped, and Pei and the New York group returned to Cleveland to consider other possible sites.

By December it was official. The new site for the Rock Hall was to be on the newly revamped North Coast Harbor. More good news came when the museum acquired its first piece of rock memorabilia: the original handwritten lyrics to one of Jimi Hendrix's most popular songs, "Purple Haze." The reported price was $17,600.

1991

A January news conference introduced exhibit designers Bruce and Susan Burdick of San Francisco, who revealed interior plans for the Rock Hall. But in March a troubled Cleveland school board scoffed at a proposal to give $18 million in city tax money to the Rock Hall. The bargaining wasn't over.

In a May issue of *Scene,* editor Mark Holan put in bold headlines what everyone was thinking: "Five Years and Nothing to Show for It." The editorial expressed the mounting frustrations that gripped both boards (and had been doing so for years) and that had begun affecting Cleveland rock fans. A week later, newly appointed curator Bruce

Harrah-Conforth defended the "long-time coming" for *Scene:* "We're building some-thing that has never been done before. A first-class, world-class museum dedicated to rock and roll. What we're talking about is building something that is unique in the world. It took *15* years to build the Kennedy Center. People don't think about that."

Most people agree that the choice of Harrah-Conforth as director of Curatorial and Educational Affairs was a good one. Unlike most of the politicians and business-people that comprised the board, Conforth had a rich rock and roll background. After completing his doctoral dissertation ("Traditionalizing Rock and Roll: Haight-Asbury 1965–68") at Indiana University, the former rock guitarist taught rock history there, including such courses as "Born in the USA: American History and Popular Culture," "The Literature of Rock and Roll," and "Hippies and Punks: American Cultural Movement."

In September Pei returned to present his modified museum for the new harbor-front location. Although there was talk of it resembling his other notable buildings, including the Louvre addition and the Kennedy Library buildings, it was widely ac-cepted as an appropriate design to enshrine rock and roll.

Meanwhile, construction costs rose to $60 million, and groundbreaking was again pushed back—this time to the fall of 1992. In October, local architect Robert P. Madi-son International, Inc., was hired. And more memorabilia was all the while being col-lected—this time Janis Joplin–related items were donated by her fellow rockers Big Brother and the Holding Company.

The year ended in a commitment—finally. In December, designer I. M. Pei signed a $5.35 million contract.

1992

The early part of the year seemed to set the tone for the rest of 1992. In January, the lack of needed corporate sponsorship was attributed to the "horrible" economy. In February, it was announced that the groundbreaking would be delayed until the sum-mer of 1993. Then project director Larry R. Thompson announced his resignation. Mayor White suggested that Thompson was frustrated at the continual delays in groundbreaking. Few could blame him. K. Michael Benz took Thompson's place, re-marking, "I really need all the help I can get. If any of you have money, we'll be glad to accept it."

In March, Cleveland lawyer Howard Krantz donated his extensive Elvis Presley collection to the Museum. Commenting that it was his "civic obligation" to Cleveland, Krantz handed over Presley's karate jacket, a blue suede coat, autographed records, a likeness of the RCA Records mascot (the dog, "Nipper"), and other notable items.

On June 25, the Rock Hall showed off its 150 acquisitions in a public exhibition at the Cleveland Western Reserve Historical Society. The "Are You Experienced" exhibit, honoring Jimi Hendrix, was included. Former bass player for the Jimi Hendrix Experience, Noel Redding, attended the opening, which showcased, among other articles, a brown suede and leather jacket worn by Hendrix.

Roger Loecy, owner of Shooters Live, the Flats' newest club, and Shooters on the Water restaurant, donated $25,000 to the Rock Hall in September. Total fund acquisition was at that point $44 million in cash and pledges. The Cleveland board, however, was still desperately seeking sponsors while awaiting a $5–10 million state capital improvement endowment. The price tag read $84 million to build what was then being labeled as the "Phantom Temple of Rock."

In October it happened again: a leak of the 1993 inductee lists was printed in *USA Today*, stealing the annual "privilege" from Cleveland. Benz canceled the announcement ceremony. It was also decided that the Rock Hall's induction dinner would be held outside of New York for the first time—in Los Angeles, not Cleveland.

In November, just as it seemed Cleveland had nowhere else to go for funds, Port Authority board member Dennis Lafferty suggested that although the Cleveland–Cuyahoga County Port Authority had never issued bonds, it certainly could, if tapped. Although details were complicated, the New York board unanimously approved it. In the meantime, the New York board voted to add $5 million to the Rock Hall coffer.

1993

The Port Authority approved financing agreement for the Rock Hall. As the Hall's "landlord," it would issue $38 million in bonds and would oversee construction and installation of equipment.

In March one cherished item on the way to the Rock Hall was lost. A gold record from the first pressing of the 1973 soundtrack of *Jesus Christ Superstar* was last seen in the trunk of a cab taking the actors Ted Neeley and Carl Anderson to a press conference in the offices of the Rock Hall in the Terminal Tower building. The two were in town to appear in the stage version of the musical playing at the Palace Theater in Playhouse Square. The record, to be used as a stand-in for the official gold disc, was borrowed from MCA Records and was to be donated to the Rock Hall. The missing record got front-page notice. When a cabbie returned the record a week later, the item was printed at the bottom corner of section B, near the obituaries.

On April 1, it was announced in the *Plain Dealer* that Paul McCartney would headline a major concert for the formal groundbreaking in July. Other acts approached included Billy Joel, Bruce Springsteen, and Paul Simon, but details were sketchy. A few days later, the McCartney rumor was scaled back to a cameo appearance. The proposed concert was scheduled for June 7 at the Cleveland State University Convocation Center. Weeks later, however, none of the delegated acts had agreed to perform, and the concert was promptly canceled.

In June, ground finally broke at North Coast Harbor. The ceremony was attended by Chuck Berry, Billy Joel, Pete Townshend, Sam Moore (of Sam and Dave), Ruth

Brown, and Dave Pirner (Soul Asylum), as well as Ertegun, Mayor White, Governor Voinovich, Pei, and Wenner. A crowd of more than 6,000 fans watched as Joel and Townshend played air guitar with their shovels before loosening the first layer of dirt. The Rolling Stones' "Satisfaction" played in the background.

In August, Benz stepped down and Shaker Heights native Dennis Barrie became director. Aside from his Midwest directorship for the Smithsonian Institution's Archives of American Art from 1972–83, Barrie, with a Ph.D. in American cultural history, is best known for his ten years as director of Cincinnati's Contemporary Arts Center. In 1990 he received national prominence when he was indicted on obscenity charges for allowing the controversial exhibit of Robert Mapplethorpe's photographs to be presented there. He was later acquitted. With the free expression always associated with rock and roll, Barrie's act of liberalism well-suited him for the Rock Hall job, and he also proved to be a valuable asset in organizing artifact collections.

In December there was another change in direction. Cleveland native James Henke, vice president of product development at Elektra Entertainment, was appointed chief curator, replacing Harrah-Conforth. Henke grew up in the Lakewood area, where his first writing experience was for Cleveland's short-lived underground newspaper *Great Swamp Erie da da Boom*. In 1976, he graduated with a B.A. in journalism from Ohio Wesleyan University. After a year as copyeditor at the *Plain Dealer,* he moved to New York to become a copyeditor for *Rolling Stone.* He rose up the ranks there to become music editor, a position he left at the end of 1992. In the meantime, he co-edited two anthologies of rock history, *The Rolling Stone Illustrated History of Rock and Roll* (3rd ed.) and *The Rolling Stone Album Guide* (New York: Random House, 1992). He also authored *Human Rights Now!* in support of Amnesty International's Universal Declaration of Human Rights. And, like many rock and roll enthusiasts, Henke was in a rock band in high school. (It appears he was ahead of his time. The group's name was Nirvana.)

Henke immediately got to work, acquiring Sun Records Sam Phillips's impressive collection of historic memorabilia, including Elvis's piano, on which he pounded out his first songs. This was no easy task; it took the curator eight trips to Memphis to convince Phillips to donate the artifacts. But now that ground had been broken, more merchandise was turning up and being offered, which gave insiders hope that there would be something for fans to actually see upon museum visits. In addition, Barrie put on the pressure to include interactive and audiovisual exhibits.

By March 1994 the Rock Hall had 100,000 items in its possession and was actively searching for more. Three key people were assigned the daunting task of acquiring more artifacts in time for the Hall's opening on Labor Day weekend 1995. Music journalist David McGee, based in Nashville, was to focus on the Memphis, Nashville, and Muscle Shoals, Alabama, area. Former *Rolling Stone* writer Michael Goldberg was to concentrate on the West Coast, including the Bay area, Los Angeles, and Seattle. Chosen as consultant to the collection in the blues and roots archives was Robert Santelli, who taught courses on popular music at Rutgers University; authored books on pop, rock, and blues; was music critic for the *Asbury Park Press;* and wrote freelance for the *New York Times, Modern Drummer, Guitar Player,* and *Rolling Stone.* Santelli, who eventually moved to Cleveland and became the Rock Hall's director of education, produced an array of high-profile educational programs for the public, including the successful "American Music Masters" series, an annual week-long event during which the Rock Hall honors an American music pioneer with a lecture program and all-star tribute concert.

1994

On July 28, 1994, the final fifteen-foot steel beam, signed by construction workers and fans, was lowered into place on the Rock Hall on the corner of E. 9th Street and Erieview Avenue. It was worthy of celebrating. The "Topping-off" ceremony brought more than 5,000 rock music lovers to the downtown site. On hand were Kid Leo, who served as master of ceremonies, and an all-star band of twenty Cleveland musicians: Bobby Womack, Wally Bryson (the Raspberries), Jim Bonfanti (the Raspberries), Michael Stanley, Michael Calhoun (Dazz Band), Sonny Geraci (the Outsiders), Kenny Margolis (the Choir), Dale Peters (the James Gang), Rich Spina (Love Affair), Joe Vitale (Barnstorm, Crosby, Stills and Nash), vocalist Sasha (Michael Stanley Band, the Ghostpoets), and Gary Lewis (the Playboys). Organizers for the event included John Awarski (Action Talent), who served as band coordinator; Bryson, music coordinator; Kevin Dugan (former Agora roadie, presently personal technician for Van Halen guitarist Michael Anthony), stage manager; and Buddy Maver (drummer for Rainbow Canyon, among others), assistant musical coordinator.

As the party got under way, the sky darkened dramatically, and lightning danced out over the lake. Wally Bryson, whose rebellious rock roots run deep, defied the approaching weather and led his musical comrades in their own rendition of the Beatles' "Rain." It was rock and roll at its best. And the musical force seemed to sway even Mother Nature. The dark clouds moved on and the sky brightened. The next song could well have been "Good Day Sunshine."

The rest of the day was warmed not just by the sun but by the pride evident on participants' beaming faces. There were the obligatory speeches and introductions by the usual group of dignitaries—Governor Voinovich, Jann Wenner, Ahmet Ertegun, Richard Celeste, I. M. Pei. But the real surprise was the presence of Jerry Lee Lewis, who banged out "Whole Lotta Shakin'" and "Great Balls of Fire." He told the audience, "It's a great honor to play here. Cleveland is my favorite city in the rock 'n' roll industry."

In a frank interview with *Plain Dealer* reporter Michael Norman, Jann Wenner declared that the New York and Cleveland rock rift was over: "All that stuff about infighting between New York and Cleveland is in the past. We have made some great friends in Cleveland and we are working now as a team." Admitting that the people in New York were not initially sold on the Rock Hall being in Cleveland, he added, "In retrospect, one of the smartest things we did was go to Cleveland. The people there wanted and needed this project and worked enthusiastically to make it happen. I don't know if any other city could have pulled it off."

On October 14, Yoko Ono presented the Rock Hall with many of John Lennon's personal belongings, including childhood mementos, several handwritten lyrics of songs from both his Beatles days and his solo career, the black Rickenbacker 325 electric guitar he used during the 1965 concert at New York's Shea Stadium, the lime-green uniform Lennon wore on the cover of *Sgt. Pepper's Lonely Hearts Club Band,* his wire-rimmed glasses, and, perhaps most notable of all, the collarless jacket he wore in the early Beatles days. Henke called the artifacts "the centerpiece" of the Hall's collection and believed Ono's generous contribution would encourage more artists to donate.

September 1, 1995—BLAST OFF!

Ten years—and $92 million—later, the struggle was finally over. And for one glorious Labor Day weekend, there were no naysayers, no bad blood, no delays. Only celebrating. The Rock and Roll Hall of Fame and Museum was ready to open its doors.

The party began early. There was live coverage on NBC's *Today* show (camped out on the second floor of the Rock Hall), *CBS This Morning* (on the third floor), and ABC's *Good Morning America* (broadcasing from the main exhibit floor). Little Richard was there, as well, and he closed *GMA* with "Good Golly, Miss Molly," a song once banned from radio airplay.

The impressive 150,000-square-foot structure, boasting a triangular glass tent (which reflected the water of Lake Erie) and a 165-foot aluminum tower, was scheduled to open to the public at precisely 10:00 A.M. on Saturday, September 2, 1995. For the first time in nine years, no one seemed to be counting costs as sidewalk vendors stood on every block of the city and more than 10,000 people bought up anything related to this much-anticipated day. Everyone was reveling in rock and roll. (Even hotel employees greeted guests dressed up as their favorite rockers, such as Little Richard, Elvis, and Elton John.)

On Friday, at 11:30 A.M., the "Rockin' in the Streets" parade moved down E. 9th Street with 1,100 participants shaking, rattling, and rolling (and the parachuting "Flying Elvises" soaring overhead) down to the Rock Hall. Divided into groups representing each era of rock music, the procession began with the 1950s, featuring women in "spinning record" skirts and hats and Maybellene, the car that inspired the Chuck Berry song. The series of rock continued through the 1960s with the Beatles (represented by four Volkswagen Beetles complete with John, Paul, George, and Ringo license plates), the Doors (people carrying real doors in various colors), and the "virtual" Rolling Stones (fiberglass-sculpted balls, complete with faces, rolling down the avenue). From there, it was on to the glitz and glitter of the disco'd 1970s, dancing skeletal forms honoring the Grateful Dead, and theme-oriented floats that included Tommy, the Who's Pinball Wizard, a camera and TV representing MTV, and Tina Turner's legs. Toward the end came high-flying, fifteen-foot papier-maché puppets of Elvis and Madonna. The Material Girl likeness made its way through the crowd with bullet-point, twirling pasties attached to her favorite asset. Perfect!

(*Opposite*) Cleveland celebrates the opening of the Rock and Roll Hall of Fame and Museum, September 1, 1995. *Plain Dealer.*

The parade came to a halt in front of Key Plaza, where the opening ceremonies would begin. In true rock 'n' roll fashion, the ribbon-cutting ceremony kicked off with the Jimi Hendrix guitar-wrenching 1969 rendition of the "Star Spangled Banner." The huge crowd stood respectfully silent as the music blasted through the public-address system, with roaring jets from the Cleveland National Air Show flying across the sky just as the last note was being strummed. The sight of all the three-piece-suits with hands over hearts listening to the ear-splitting, psychedelic Woodstock recording had Boomers in the audience envisioning Jimi looking down upon this peculiar, and highly ironic, sight with a smirk on his face. That thought alone did Cleveland rockers good.

On stage sat all the dignitaries that made this day a reality: Ahmet Ertegun, Governor Voinovich, Mayor White, Little Richard, and Yoko Ono. Voinovich stood at the podium among the group of hundreds of thousands and proclaimed, "We did it, Cleveland!" Indeed. With the emotional commitment demonstrated by Clevelanders by way of Alan Freed's passion, Leo Mintz's clarity, Hank LoConti's vision, and Norm N. Nite's commitment and drive, this dream had come true for all who love to rock and roll music.

The bad news on the day of much-deserved celebration was that some of those who helped make it happen were left out in the cold.

"We had pushed and pushed to get the Rock Hall built in Cleveland," recalls former WMMS disc jockey Jeff Kinzbach, who like several of the Hall's greatest advocates, didn't get an invitation to its grand opening. "Then when it finally came to pass, the Rock Hall officials never acknowledged Flash and myself, which was very disappointing. But Hank LoConti was great. He called us up and said, 'Hey, you guys are going with me to the Rock and Roll Hall of Fame ceremonies as my guest.' Both of us were so gratified he did that for us."

The slight to many of those who labored hard to get the Rock Hall built in Cleveland—in fact, built at all—later gave way to bad public relations and hard feelings. In her "On the Rocks" column on this topic, Sun Newspapers reporter Joanne Drauss Klein said, "Problem is, all of the true cheerleaders—the ones who had the Rock and Roll Hall of Fame imprinted on their hearts, not just on their paychecks—have been drained of their passion. They've been slighted and minimized and insulted and forgotten by people whose jobs they essentially helped create."

When it came to planning the weekend's activities, it was clear New York was still running the show. Janet Macoska was disappointed to learn she would not be allowed access to photograph the grand-opening ceremonies. This Cleveland-based photographer has shot nearly every rock star from the early 1970s on (see Chapter 9).

I applied for credentials to cover it. I don't recall exactly what the problem was, but what it came down to was there was no way I was going to be able to cover it. The Associated Press, a couple of New York photographers, and the *Plain Dealer* ultimately got access. The arrangement was for the other photographers to be put in the back on bleachers behind the stage, and it wasn't what I wanted to do. But as it turns out, I got a ticket to sit in the plaza area through a friend. So we went to the ceremony like regular people and I took this snapping camera, a little point-and-shoot thing, and I got better pictures than those photographers who were stuck in the bleachers in the back. And I was happy to cover it that way—to actually be there just as a music fan.

Those photos were later published by *Cleveland* magazine and *Goldmine*. And although she had a ticket for the Rock and Roll Hall of Fame and Museum concert, Macoska boycotted it, feeling that many in the Cleveland media were not treated properly. She wasn't alone in that assessment.

Cleveland musicians were also left out when it came to the Saturday night concert. Although there are internationally known acts from the North Coast, only one—Chrissie Hynde of the Pretenders—was invited to play to the hometown crowd at the Municipal Stadium, where so much rock history had been made. The omission did not go over well among Clevelanders. Many voiced their opinion to the media, and country artist Roger Martin took it a step further by announcing he would give a free concert outside the stadium for fans. Officials made sure Martin would not follow through. Many music fans, however, agreed that these musicians had a legitimate complaint.

"We all worked to get the Rock and Roll Hall of Fame built here," said Sonny Geraci. "Plus there's a lot of talent that comes from this city. It sure would've been nice, and appropriate, for them to have some hometown bands playing on that bill. I tell ya', we would've torn that damn stadium apart!"

Nonetheless, the sixty-five-year-old stadium rumbled with nonstop rock and roll music. Along with 2,000 international journalists reporting on the events, and some 60,000 rock fans (who paid anywhere from $30 to $540 a ticket), a roster of nearly thirty all-star acts strutted their stuff Saturday night for a concert as historic as Woodstock (the first one). Broadcast live on HBO (pay-per-view), with Len "Boom Boom" Goldberg and Kid Leo hosting the event, the show began at 7:30 P.M. and didn't skip a beat until Chuck Berry and Bruce Springsteen played the last note at 2:15 A.M. Sunday morning.

Inside the jam-packed stadium there was no such thing as a generation gap, as entertainers shared the stage with their musical offspring and played to the delight of rock connoisseurs from ages eight to eighty. The younger set was there to see Soul Asylum, Melissa Etheridge, Natalie Merchant, Sheryl Crow, and former Guns n' Roses guitarist Slash. The more seasoned Boomers came to see and hear Chuck Berry, Jerry Lee Lewis, James Brown, Aretha Franklin, Booker T and the MG's, Al Green, Johnny Cash, Sam Moore, Jackson Browne, Iggy Pop, Lou Reed, and John Fogerty. Then there were everyone's favorites: John Mellencamp, the Kinks, the Allman Brothers, the Pretenders, George Clinton and the P-Funk Allstars, Ann and Nancy Wilson (Heart), Bon Jovi, and Bruce Springsteen and the E Street Band. Surprises of the night were Bob Dylan, Eric Burdon (the Animals), Bruce Hornsby, and Robbie Robertson (the Band). All sang tributes to their personal influences.

While Springsteen was singing "Darkness on the Edge of Town," one ambitious female fan squeezed through security and jumped on stage to hug and kiss the New Jersey rocker. He simply laughed. And before guards snatched her away, he smiled and said, "Hey, that's rock 'n' roll." Indeed.

January 24, 1997: The "My Town" Exhibit

Taking the name of Michael Stanley's 1983 hit song "My Town," this long-awaited exhibition served as further answer to the question "Why is the Rock Hall in Cleveland?" Jim Henke (museum curator) and Erin Hogan (curatorial coordinator) gathered and arranged historic mementos relating to Cleveland rock history and exhibited them in a glass case on the museum's second floor.

The collection of artifacts told the story. There were photographs of Alan Freed at the mike; Leo Mintz in front of his legendary Record Rendezvous; an original poster from the Moondog Coronation Ball; sheet music from the Poni-Tails' 1958 hit "Born Too Late," alongside the ponytail hairpiece worn by member LaVerne Novak; a choirboy shirt worn by Choir drummer Jim Bonfanti; the first *Scene* and the debut *Alternative Press;* and signs from the old Agora and LaCave. There were drumheads, album and singles covers, written lyrics, and stage costumes from bands ranging from Bocky and the Visions, Tom King and the Starfires (and later the Outsiders), the Grasshoppers, and Baskerville Hounds to the Choir, the James Gang, and Damnation of Adam Blessing. There was the original 1966 contract between the Belkin brothers and the Four Freshmen at Music Hall, which was the start of Belkin Productions. Clothing also lit up memories, with the yellow industrial suit and red energy-dome worn by Devo member Mark Mothersbaugh hanging auspiciously near the end of the showcase. Walt Williams of the O'Jays had his bright-orange sequined jacket hanging alongside publicity photos of the Canton-boys-made-good.

Perhaps most important, however, were the guitars. There was Wally Bryson's signature Gibson Flying V, Joe Walsh's 1959 Gibson Les Paul, Phil Keaggy's 1971 Gibson Les Paul, and Michael Stanley's 1958 Gibson Les Paul.

Along another wall was a photo display highlighting the many notable stars who were fixtures at Leo's Casino, including the Temptations, Aretha Franklin, Smokey Robinson, James Brown, and the Supremes. Next to that was a pictorial tribute in honor of Jane Scott, with photos of her with some of rock and roll's best: the Beatles, the Who, Bruce Springsteen, Alice Cooper, and Sting.

Many of Cleveland's stars were on hand for the exhibit's opening, including Wally Bryson, Jimmy Fox, and members of the Poni-Tails and the O'Jays. One visitor from Seattle remarked that the exhibit "explained a lot" in terms of the rich history that gave Cleveland an edge when it came to becoming the official home of rock and roll.

Although the exhibit was too short lived, lasting less than a year, there are continual efforts being made to honor Cleveland's rock history. In 1998 the Rock Hall began what will be an ongoing program designating various sites as historic rock and roll landmarks.

In conjunction with these events, Jim Henke says the Rock Hall is in the process of planning a permanent display devoted to the history of the Cleveland rock scene.

May 7, 1997: Cleveland Hosts the Inductions—Finally

It was about time. The previous eleven years had been filled with disappointment and irritation that, despite the fact that Cleveland was the official home to the Rock Hall, the city hadn't hosted one induction ceremony. Finally it was going to get its due. Once again, the spotlight was on Cleveland. And the city reveled in it.

The 1997 inductees included the Bee Gees, the Jackson 5, Parliament Funkadelic, the Young Rascals, Joni Mitchell, Buffalo Springfield, and Crosby, Stills and Nash (Steven Stills became the first person to be inducted twice in the same night for his musical contributions in both Buffalo Springfield and CS&N). The night began with a lively seven-minute funk-filled set by George Clinton and the rest of Parliament-Funkadelic. The annual end-of-the-night jam session had everyone rockin' to the Bee Gees, the Rascals, Parliament-Funkadelic, and CS&N, along with presenters Tom Petty, James Taylor, and Emmylou Harris. In between were highlights, such as the onstage reunion of all five Jackson brothers, who were inducted by friend and Motown labelmate Diana Ross.

The Sunday before, May 4, had marked the twenty-seventh anniversary of the Kent State shootings. Crosby, Stills and Nash did not forget. The trio played a low-key concert in observation of that historic day. Their song "Ohio," written by sometime-member Neil Young in anger over the senseless Kent State killings, put the commemoration into perspective. (Young did not attend. He had previously voiced his opinion that too many musicians, and not always the most deserving, are inducted into the hall.) And later that evening, in true CS&N form, the down-to-earth music men gave a private, sold-out, two-hour performance at the Agora for their greatest commodity: their longstanding fans. Tickets were a reasonable $25, with six hundred of them given away by local radio and television stations. In thanking the rock devotees for their support over the years, Graham Nash added that this night belonged to those who "can't get in over there," referring to the star-studded induction ceremony and party.

"We have a lot of fans here who wanted to see us be inducted," David Crosby explained to Michael Norman. "We thought we would do a show just for them. We knew if we played here, we'd have a ball." They did. And so did the 1,800 who were there to witness the less-profiled historic event.

"They did all their best songs, and sounded great," Hank LoConti Jr. said of the CS&N performance. "It was so profound. Without being melodramatic, they, along with their manager, Gerry Tolman, are one of the few humanitarians left in this business."

Of course, the evening didn't go off without a hitch—or two. On the eve of this long-awaited event, the chief executive officer of the Rock Hall, William N. Hulett, announced his resignation, though he said he would remain a member of the Rock Hall's executive committee. In addition, most of the Cleveland media were sequestered in a press room to cover the inductions via monitors—far away from the live action. "We might have well been home watching it in our living rooms," commented one reporter.

And although there were no inductees announced for Cleveland artists or influences, the evening still brought a feeling of honor among some. Hank LoConti Jr. recalls: "I went to the induction ceremonies with my father. He wasn't planning on going, but he missed his flight to Russia. So at the last minute, we went. It was great to see so many celebrities coming up to my dad and thanking him for giving them a place to play their music, and getting the hall of fame off the ground in Cleveland. They know he, along with Norm N. Nite, had a lot to do with the initial workings of the Rock Hall. My proudest moment was being able to go there with my dad and seeing him get acknowledged like that."

Former Agora promo man Johan recounts his favorite memory of the event.

I'll never forget being at work the next morning after the inductions. Steve Popovich comes into my office [located below Cleveland International Records] and says, "Hey, I'm going to have breakfast with Miami Steve [Bruce Springsteen's E Street guitarist]. Would you like to come?" He knew I was a big fan and would love to meet him. I said sure.

So we go down to the Renaissance Hotel and as we're pulling up in front, there's two limos parked in front of the door, and who's getting into the limo? The Jacksons. So Steve pulls his car up next to it, and just as the last Jackson is getting in, he rolls down his window and yells out, "Hey, Tito, it's Popovich." Well, Tito hears the name, turns around, spots Popovich, and says, "Oh my God!" He then sticks his head back in the limo and yells, "Hey, guys, it's Popovich." [Steve Popovich, was the A&R man for Epic when he signed the Jacksons to that label, and he was ultimately responsible for the release of Michael Jackson's *Thriller*.]

Now, right in the middle of the street, the Jacksons (minus Michael) pile out of the limo, one by one, and come over to talk to Steve. They hadn't seen him in ten years, so it was quite a reunion. They all stood talking while other cars had to go around us. Before long, there's a crowd forming, and people started wondering who *I* was!

So I got to shake all their hands, and I tell you, I was in awe. As if that wasn't enough, we parked, went in to have breakfast with Miami, and here comes the Young Rascals to join us. Then Ricky Skaggs comes over. I mean, everyone who was anyone in town for the inductions was coming up to Steve. He was the celebrity, and it was great simply being a bystander to all this.

When asked when, or if, Cleveland will host another induction, Henke says, "There will certainly be more inductions here; we just don't know when at this time. What many people don't realize is that this is a museum. The actual Hall of Fame is in New York. Plus, the record industry is in New York and Los Angeles, so it's easier for the inductees to attend the ceremony. There are plans to continue rotating the inductions between L.A., New York, Cleveland, and eventually on an international basis. There's also talk of having inductions held right at the Rock Hall. It's all a work in progress."

20 Personal Reminiscences of Musicians, Fans, and Friends

Of the hundreds of people interviewed for this book, many had fond memories of their experiences related to the music. Be they the performers themselves, the fans who saw a particularly unforgettable concert, or friends who were close to the people who made the music, when asked for memorable stories, these music lovers had no problem producing them.

Not all relate directly to the North Coast, yet each anecdote proves that anything connected to the music can be shared and enjoyed by all. That in itself is testimony to what this book is all about.

Some of the stories and memories are humorous, others reflective, all entertaining. The following are the best of the best of these memories.

Musicians

Bobby Womack

I'll never forget when Sam Cooke gave me and my brothers money to get us a brand new station wagon to drive to Los Angeles. And me, being somewhat of a rascal, told my brothers, "Hey, man, let's get a used car instead and keep the rest of the money." So I go to this used car lot and first thing I see is this big ol' green Cadillac. I was always impressed with anyone with a Cadillac. So, of course, I bought it and first thing I did was drive it to my old high school at East Tech. I pull up in the parking lot and blew the horn as loud as I could until everyone was lookin' out that window—including my old teacher, Mr. Washington, who used to whack me on the head saying I'd never amount to anything. I yelled out, "Hey, Mr. Washington, remember me? You told me I was going to be a janitor! And all the kids were looking out and screamin,' "Go Womack, go!" Everyone was going crazy. I wanted to show them all that I was becoming what I told them I would. Trouble is, when I went to leave, the car wouldn't start. Well, I started praying a sermon like you never heard before: *Oh God, not now. You can do anything to me later, take my life around the block. But please, please, let me drive this car off this parking lot!*

All of a sudden, it started up. Boy, I *flew* outta that lot! And that's the car we drove to L.A. in, with our names across the side of the car. 'Course, it broke down all the way, from Youngstown on. There was a hole in the gas tank, the headlights went out one night, and one day we're driving along, it started rainin.' I turn on the wipers and the damn things flew across the highway! It took us about two weeks to get there, and meanwhile Sam was gettin' real nervous: "Where are those damn kids?" Finally, there we were, pushin' that green monstrosity down Hollywood Boulevard But Sam was such a great guy, he never said nothin' about the rest of the money! And I'll tell you this. Those were some of the best days of my life.

Walt Williams on the "Mighty" O'Jays

Probably one of the funniest, and most embarrassing, things that happened to us occurred on stage in Houston. It was a show we did where, during the song, "Traveling at the Speed of Thought," we'd come out on stage wearing these big capes with pleated wings so when we raised our arms, it looked like a full wing. There was always a dry ice fog for us to make our entrance. And this time they loaded the stage with this thick, immense fog. So now it was time for us to come out, one at a time. So here we go. Unfortunately, none of us saw the cable running along the floor in front of the path where we came out. Sammy came out first, tripped over the cable, and fell. Then Eddie came out, stumbled over Sammy, and fell. Then it was my turn. I stumbled over Eddie, I fell. We missed all of our cues as we were stumbling around in the fog. People backstage were in tears they were laughing so hard. The audience picked up on it and they started laughing, too. Here, everybody had been waiting to see the "Mighty O'Jays" and there we were on stage—flat on our backs! Yeah, we were traveling at the speed of thought, all right! But we sure gave the crowd their money's worth that night!

Ian Hunter (Mott the Hoople)

The first time I came over to the States was in 1972. Mott the Hoople was doing a club tour, which included the Cleveland Agora. At the time we didn't mean nothing in New York or L.A.— that came about a year later. It was the same with Bowie. So we really needed to fill up a club. Cleveland was already hip to us, but we were astonished to find we'd sold out the Agora. The crowd was great and really into our music. After that we always knew [that] when you got to Cleveland, it was a party. So when I started seeing these comedians on TV with all these jokes on Cleveland, I really couldn't understand it. To us, Cleveland was the hippest place in the world, they discovered us!

So one night, I was in New York and started writing this song, which became "Cleveland Rocks." There's been rumors for years that I originally titled it "England Rocks," but that's not true. I originally wrote it with Cleveland in mind. But right after that, we went on a tour in England, so I changed it to accommodate the tour. Then it was recorded as "England Rocks." Later, of course, it became whatever city we happened to be playing. But it's important to me people know that it was meant for Cleveland. And I think it's great that Drew Carey is using it, though I suspect Clevelanders are getting bloody tired of hearing that song by now!

Southside Johnny

Cleveland holds many great memories for me. I remember the first time we played Blossom. They told us the place held some 18,000 people, 5,000 in the pavilion. So this was big time for us. And I was a little worried about attracting that many people. I thought, well, if we get 4,000 people, I'll be happy. Then it started raining that day and I was really sweatin' it. I was standing on the stage in the afternoon when I started seeing people coming. And they kept coming, and coming, with blankets and coolers. It was an amazing moment for me. Then the rain stopped and we ended up playing before 20,000 people!

But what I most remember about Cleveland is playing that first night at the Agora. The feeling of walking on stage outside the little area you've already conquered [Asbury Park] and being so accepted and enthusiastically received was amazing. I'm sure it helped us play well. It was unforgettable. And I'm just as sure had we gone on and sucked, they'd have walked out the door. Clevelanders don't cut you any slack when it comes to their music.

From that moment on, Cleveland became our home away from home. It also became legendary throughout the industry that when you play in Cleveland, you get the real rock 'n' roll audience. I've talked to guys from England and they all agree. Cleveland just has that little magic where you can go and just be a rock 'n' roll band. You don't have to be a sex symbol or rock icon. You can just go and sweat and play, and the audience sweats and sings along with you. And *that* is why you get into the business in the first place. Cleveland brings that out in almost every band. Maybe it just comes down to attitude.

But as far as the business itself goes, the one thing that is bothersome to me is these rich, famous rock and rollers have all these layers between them and their fans. It's still odd to me rockers have that, and it just seems so wrong. Me, I like to be allowed to cut loose, that I don't have to mind my manners. And Cleveland audiences allow that.

(This performer regularly has more than fifty of his fans joining him on stage by the end of a concert.)

Steve Cox (keyboardist, Dazz Band)

I'll never forget back in high school writing a fan letter to Robert Lamm, the keyboardist with Chicago. I was a big fan of his, and it thrilled me that he wrote back. In his letter, he encouraged me to continue in my music. Well, the night before the Grammys, they had a party for all the nominees. Chicago was there, and I got to meet Robert in person, and told him about the letter.

We stayed in touch after that, and when they played Blossom, he got me a guest pass. The next day, he did a radio interview and was asked what advice he'd give to musicians today. He said, "You know, ten years ago, I gave advice to a kid in high school who was just learning how to play, and told him not to ever quit. And a couple months ago he won a Grammy." Hearing that made me real proud.

Danny Sheridan (Eli Radish)

When I was in Eli Radish, I had this chicken that stayed with us on stage. She was kind of like our mascot. Her name was Morphine the Wonder Chicken. I trained her to come when I called her, and she'd follow me around on stage. We took her on the road with us when we went on tours. One show was when we opened for the Who—I think it was in Chicago. In the press the day after the concert, the Who got two paragraphs, our chicken got three. We thought it was pretty funny, the Who getting upstaged by a chicken! We also brought her along with us on the Doors tour. When Jim Morrison first saw her, I think he thought he was hallucinating!

Donnie Iris (the Jaggerz, Donnie Iris and the Cruisers)

I started playing in the mid-'60s with the Jaggerz, opening for some of the biggest groups of the time, like the Beach Boys and the Supremes. At that time we had a No. 1 hit record called "The Rapper." So by the time Donnie Iris and the Cruisers started playing Cleveland, we'd played a lot of places and with a lot of different groups. But honestly, Cleveland has always been one of my favorites, and we got great air play there. I especially enjoyed those concerts we did with the Michael Stanley Band at Blossom and the Richfield Coliseum back in the mid-'80s. Those were great shows because oftentimes after Michael's show, I'd come out on stage and jam with them and we'd all just have a ball. There was a lot of camaraderie there. As a result, Michael's band and mine became great friends. And the audience was always terrific, even when the weather wasn't. I remember one show we headlined at Blossom. It was one of those cold, nasty Cleveland rains in early June. I was standing looking out over the lawn before the show and seeing the crowd with their blankets, and they were sliding down that hill, havin' a blast in the miserable rain. Not minding it at all.

And I'll never forget the old Cleveland Agora. I really miss playing there [on East 24th Street]. The place was always packed. The first time we played there was when "Ah, Leah" came out, and we were doing clubs all over the country . . . but the Agora stands out. It had a real electric atmosphere.

I've made a lot of good friends, too, in Cleveland. Mark Avsec in particular. I met him when he was in Wild Cherry and we were both recording in the same studio, Jerree's, up in my neck of the woods near Pittsburgh [Beaver Creek]. We roomed together on the road with Wild Cherry. It was then that a couple of the guys from the group were leaving, and Mark asked me if I was interested in joining as the band's guitarist/background singer. Soon after, Mark and I decided to form Donnie Iris and the Cruisers. Bottom line? Cleveland is just one great rock 'n' roll town.

Dan Klawon (guitarist of several bands, most notably the Choir)

I first met Joe Walsh when I became friends with guys in the Akron/Kent band called the Turn Keys. He didn't sing in those days, just played great guitar. When we formed the Power Trio together, Dave Burke and I didn't sing either, so that's when Joe started singing lead. Later Jim [Fox] asked me after Joe left if I was interested in joining the James Gang, but I was still kind of mad he stole Joe from the Power Trio, so I said no.

I'd love to get together with Joe again, but it's too hard, too many people to go through. When you find out all the people who try to get to him when he's in town . . . I just don't try anymore. The last time I talked to him he was with the Eagles and I was in L.A. He gave me tickets to see their concert at the Coliseum. He told me to meet him backstage after the show. So I made the attempt, but of course there were these big husky guys standing there. I told them I was an old friend of Joe's and that he told me to meet him there. They said, "Yeah, right." So I went around the outside of the Coliseum to see if they were packing up. I see these long-haired guys walking around, and one of them is wearing an Eagles shirt. So I thought, all right, my kind of people. I walked up and told the guy if he sees Joe to tell him Dan Klawon is out here waiting for him. The guy looks at me and says, "Dan Klawon? I know you!" Turns out it was Glenn Frey. He knew me right away, but I didn't remember him at first. You see, when I was still in high school, I'd skip my Friday classes and hitchhike to Ann Arbor and Detroit, which had a killer rock scene then. Sometimes Joe went with me. I saw groups like the Who and Procol Harum in these neat little clubs there. Everybody used to go and party at this one house, and I'd see both Glenn Frey and Bob Seger there quite a lot. I met Seger on the eve of his "Heavy Music" coming out. I was over at his mother's house and he played it for us. Then of course, Seger, Glenn, and Joe all hit the big time. After that, that was it. I never saw those guys again.

Dan Pecchio (Glass Harp, Michael Stanley Band, others)

Probably the one thing that stands out most from those years of playing in the Michael Stanley Band was when we played with Cheap Trick at the Richfield Coliseum in 1979. As soon as we finished, we went backstage and were standing around when I looked out at the audience and saw the standing ovation, with all the lighters lit up throughout the whole place. Now we had just come back from being on the road, and [drummer] Tommy, I have to say, had a bad habit of complaining. He'd complain when we were home that, "Oh we gotta do this video today," and once we'd be on the road, he'd complain about not being home. We were young and didn't realize what we had. So when I saw this awesome sight, I went over to Tom, who was talking and not paying much attention. I grabbed him and said, "Hey, Tom, just stand here a minute. Don't say a thing; just look out at that." So there we were, standing there, gazing at the lights and hearing the chants. I had my arm around him and said, "Tommy, enjoy this moment. We may never experience anything like this again, I mean, who knows?" When such an encompassing moment like that happens to you, you have to stop and acknowledge it.

Tommy Dobeck (Circus, Michael Stanley Band)

I remember that night Dan Pecchio refers to very well. We'd just come off the road opening for other bands that, at the end of the night, had lighters lit for them. We'd play that first hour, then a group like the Eagles would come on. We were the warm-up act, where everyone came in just as we were finishing our set. So later we'd sit around and watch the shows, and we'd see the whole coliseum-sized venue or stadium with the lighters up.

So that night, I was so beat after the show I just wanted to go backstage and catch my breath. I had the towel over my face, just tired. I was in my early twenties, so I guess I was too young to appreciate it or think of it in terms that I do now. But I'm really grateful to Dan for doing that because now I have that great memory.

Butch Armstrong (guitarist)

I was a big James Gang fan because of Glenn Schwartz, who was the lead guitarist at the time. I was bummed out when he left the group. I didn't think anyone could take his place. So the first time I saw Joe Walsh at the Chesterland Hullabaloo, my friends and I didn't stay. The next day in school, I heard all about how great he was. I was fifteen when *Yer Album* came out and I learned every riff Joe played on every song. I finally got to meet him one night in '69, when James Gang was playing at Boston Mills Ski Lodge. During the break, I got the nerve to go up and talk to him, and told him what an inspiration he was to me. I asked him questions about the guitar he used, an old Gibson Les Paul Gold Top. He was really nice and began giving me helpful hints on how to set up a Les Paul, like modifying frets, pickups and bridge saddles. Then to my astonishment, he let me play it! It played every bit as I expected. I promised myself at that moment that I, too, would help kids learn to play.

Years later, Joe was in town for a James Gang reunion at Peabody's DownUnder. My friend Eddie Marshall called me to say Joe was in need of some equipment. So I brought it down for him. After the show, I gave Joe my Coricidin bottle. I knew he used them for playing slide guitar, and you can't get ones made of glass anymore; they're all plastic. He was really appreciative. Then I showed him the Epiphone guitar Joe had given Glenn Schwartz, who later passed it on to me.

But I'm sure Joe hasn't a clue I was that kid he let play his guitar at Boston Mills thirty years ago. But that's one thing I'll never forget. And nowadays when I'm playing these jam sessions and a young kid comes up to me, inspiration in his eyes, I take off my guitar and say, "Here, kid, play it." And I think of Joe Walsh.

Fans

Concert-goers Dennis Fedorko, Laura Pistillo (née Spahlinger), and Mark Fulmer

There is one concert above all others that remains etched in our minds. It was in the fall of 1969 at Public Hall. There was much buzz going around about Led Zeppelin coming to town. They had just come out with their debut album, and everyone was anxious to see them live. Not only that, but Grand Funk was the opening act.

There were about three or four of us couples, all crammed into one car as we headed towards downtown. The concert was general admission, so we got there early enough to get ninth row. Grand Funk Railroad came on and just blew everyone away. They just rocked. So by the time Led Zeppelin started their set, everybody was really pumped.

Soon as they got on stage, they started into the songs from their debut album. But something didn't seem right. And with each song they played, Robert Plant started leaning more and more into Jimmy Page for physical support. It was pretty clear they'd been doing a whole lot of partying backstage. By the time they were into the fourth or fifth song, someone brought out a chair for Plant so he wouldn't fall over! One of our friends [the late Bruce Harrington], started booing because they were really playing bad, and pretty soon people started calling for Grand Funk to come back. So Zeppelin did a few more numbers, then Grand Funk returned for another set. They gave such a memorable performance, and to the delight of the female audience, Mark Farner took his shirt off in the middle of a song!

The point of the story is it just proves that, in Cleveland, it didn't matter who you were. You better give a good performance because the audience will call you on it.

Paul Michael (the Adults) on being a fan

Back in the '70s, it used to be a big thing to see if you could sneak into a big concert for free, to see how creative you could be. I knew people whose sole goal in life was to get into a concert for free. They'd go so far as keeping a tally sheet on who they saw and how they got in. I knew kids who got into the Allen Theater because they knew how to get into the heating ducts, things like that. Those days are surely gone; there's no way you can do that now. I only managed it a few times. I saw Led Zeppelin that way. I crawled through a broken window at the Richfield Coliseum. But the most memorable time was when Crystal [Adults' bass player] and I scaled a fire hose up the wall of the Public Hall building to see the Tubes. This was back in '77 or '78. Then, a few years later, we opened up for the Tubes at the Agora. And at first the crowd was quite hostile. They didn't want to hear us; they wanted the Tubes. So after the first song we played, I related the story to them of how we got ourselves into a Tubes concert for free and how cool it was that we were now opening for them. That blew them away, and from that moment on, we totally won them over. It ended up being one of our best shows.

Jeanne Coleman (who has seen Springsteen live more than thirty-eight times)

My life changed somehow on August 9, 1978. That's a heady statement, but it was the first time I saw Bruce Springsteen live.

It was at the Agora Ballroom. Capacity: nine hundred. Nine hundred of the luckiest people in the city. WMMS, celebrating its tenth anniversary, held a mail-in contest for free tickets to see Bruce Springsteen and the E Street Band. I sent in five entries,

Bruce Springsteen and Clarence Clemons, having as much fun as their fans at the 1978 WMMS/Agora concert. *Photo by Bob Ferrell.*

with five different addresses of family and friends. And I won it! I invited my sister, Gerri, to go with me. Walking into the Agora was entertainment in itself. Posters, displays, and photographs of all the great rock artists. A colorful Who's Who of rock legends.

The host, Kid Leo, an avid Bruce fan himself, could hardly contain *his* excitement as he announced, "Round for round, pound for pound, there ain't no finer band around . . . Bruce Springsteen and the E Street Band!!!" As amazing as it sounds, it seemed Bruce was as elated to be with *us* as we were with him. We saw men hugging men, women being hugged and lifted in the air as the excitement swept through the crowd.

Charisma? Bruce held the patent on it. I've never seen anything like it before or since. He took us all on a emotional high that night—the rebellion of "Growing Up," the uncertainty and desperation in "Backstreets" and "Born to Run," the passion in "Jungleland," and the warm memories of my yearly family vacations brought on by "4th of July, Asbury Park." He somehow found a direct line to your soul because his stories come from the heart.

As the night drew to a close, the magic coming to an end, it was as if we had all been guests at his private party. After several encores, the lights went on, but half the audience, the stubborn ones, the *lucky* ones, refused to leave. We stood there, drenched, strained vocal cords, crying out for more . . . and he came back! Bruce went into a rousing rendition of "Twist and Shout," bringing me full circle musically—from that day to another magical day when this ten-year-old girl's dream was realized as she sat in the Cleveland stadium watching the Beatles perform right before her eyes.

I headed home, feeling cleansed and somehow changed by the sheer passion that raged inside the Agora that night.

Jim Kluter (one of "the Cleveland Boys," along with Joe Juhasz and John Kusznier)

Joey Juhasz and I were lookin' for something to do Fourth of July weekend 1976. Springsteen's *Born to Run* had just come out. But we'd been fans since his first album, *Greetings from Asbury Park*. So we got it in our heads to go to Asbury Park and see if we could find him. And we did. At the Stone Pony. And somehow, we found out he was playing softball that Sunday afternoon against a rock magazine, *Crawdaddy*. Their team was called the E-Street Kings, and of course it included Miami Steve and other friends.

The Cleveland Boys with Bruce Springsteen, 1976. *Left to right:* unidentified friend, Jim Kluter, Don Tallon, Bruce Springsteen, and Joe Juhasz. *Courtesy of Jim Kluter.*

So we go up to where they're playing and talked briefly to Bruce and told him we were from Cleveland. Then, while we sat up in the bleachers, the E-Street Kings realized they didn't have enough players. Bruce points up to us and says, "How 'bout those Cleveland boys?" (And we've been called that ever since.) We played—and won—a double-header, and Bruce later asked if we wanted to stay at his place that night. He was renting this old house with hardly any furniture in it. He put us in the band room, and I remember lying in there that night, right next to his guitar and seeing some papers with half-written songs on them. I think now, *what a place that was to be!* So over the years, we'd fly all over to where he was playing, and he'd give us backstage passes and seats in the first five rows. It got to be a joke. He'd see us and go, "Oh, there's those Cleveland Boys again!" Sometime in the late '70s we took a month off and toured in his bus, up and down the California coast, from San Francisco to L.A. We'd stay at the hotels with him, 'course, they were the Motel 6s and the Days Inn. Not the Ritz-Carlton!

But of course, when *Born in the USA* came out, there were more and more layers as far as security. But we'd still get to see him occasionally. During his last tour in 1999, we saw him in Cleveland, and stayed in Chicago for a week to see all three shows and saw him backstage. And we realize that's really something because, at this point, he doesn't have to give us the time of day. But that's the kind of guy he is. When you talk to him, even after all this time as a rock star, he's a just regular guy. He still has that knack for making you feel like you're one of his best friends. But it's funny to look back and think, *wow, we really kinda grew up with him. How'd we do that?*

Friends of Rock 'n' Roll

Peanuts (former *Scene* writer and publicist)

It was 1972 when David Bowie first came to town to play Music Hall. He wasn't that well known yet, only to those who listened to 'MMS. So after his show, Bowie loads up the limo and heads to the Agora, not realizing it's full of college kids. So he's walking around and everyone's looking at him with his orange hair, green jumpsuit, and cape and saying, "Hey, look at the faggot!" Finally he gets so aggravated he goes back to the limo and asks the driver where can he go to see a good band. So the driver takes him to Hennessy's in Lakewood. Labrynth was playing, so as their manager, I was there. It was one in the morning, and this black guy in a suit with a Jamaican accent, Bowie's body-guard, walks in and asks the doorman, Leo Cronin, if he could bring David Bowie in there. He said, "Yeah, sure." Few minutes later, up pulls the limo and in walks Bowie in all his colorful glory. Word spread fast and someone tells me, "Hey, David Bowie's here." Of course, I don't believe him and I ask Leo. He says, "Yeah, he's at the pinball machine." I go there and, sure enough, there he is. Well, the guitarist, Jim McCartney, sees him and tells the band, who hasn't seen him yet, to do their Bowie medley with the songs "Moonage Daydream," and "Suffragette City." Well, I about shit, thinking, *I'm gonna kill these guys.* By now the rest of the guys in the band notice him, and they're lookin' at McCartney not believing he had them play these songs with the "man" right in front of them. But next thing we know, Bowie's buying shots for the band, and drinks all around. He was fascinated with the guitarist, Carl Wesley, and afterward said to him, "Great solo." Then he invites the waitress and her sister and another girl to breakfast. They all hop in the limo and go to what was then Cleveland Café, now Perkins. When he gets ready to leave he tells "Father Fred" Bills [bar owner], "I had a great time tonight. Hennessy's is truly the home of the stars." And that's how Hennessy's got the nickname, "Home of the Stars."

A week later, Father Fred gets a package from New York, and it's an autographed picture of Bowie. That photo hung over the bar until '76 when the bar changed hands. It was still there on loan until it changed hands again. No one knows what happened to the picture after that. Father Fred never got it back. But anyone there that night Bowie came in will ever forget it.

Rich Kabat (former *Scene* publisher)

A few incidents stand out when I think of the times we've had over the years. I'll never forget the day when Rodney Dangerfield came into the office for an interview. He took one look at Raj [Bahadur], who is Indian, and said, "Is this man going to interview me or sell me a rug?!!"

Then there was the time Xavier Cugat's wife, Charo, arrived for an interview wearing this tight, bright red jumpsuit—at 8:30 in the morning! She waltzed in saying things like "Oooh, baby" and immediately went into her "koochie-koochie" act. I'll tell you that woke the office up!

James "Lucky" Restina (a former proprietor of the Rare Cherry)

Duffy Gallagher was the manager at the Rare Cherry. While I was away in Europe, I sent Duffy to New York to find some hot acts. When I came back, I learned he had booked a bunch of acts, and one of them was the Village People [just after their *Macho Man* LP was released]. Well, I had seen what they looked like and wasn't impressed. So when I heard Duffy had booked them for the nightclub I went ballistic. I told him, "How could you do this, bringing these [expletive] into the club? You'll ruin me." I was furious.

I wasn't aware how big they were at the time, so I was shocked when 1,600 people showed up! You couldn't move in the place and we were turning people away at the door. They put on two shows, and at the end of the night I tried to get them to sign a contract to come back. That's when they told me they weren't going to play a "small club" again, and believe me, the Rare Cherry wasn't small. But they told me, "We'll be playing for 100,000 people and up from now on." I said, "Where're you guys comin' from?" They said, "Trust us, we have a new record coming out Tuesday, and soon as that song hits the airwaves, we're on our way to the top." They wouldn't tell me any more, not even the name of the song.

Sure enough, come Tuesday, out comes "YMCA," and of course, it took off like a rocket. And today, whenever you play that song, people can be crippled and they get up and dance. It's amazing. And here I had no clue.

Radio, Radio, Radio

Chuck Dunaway (WKYC deejay)

When my friend Ron Sunshine, who was working for a booking agency in St. Louis, called me about booking Hendrix in Cleveland, and the price was very low, I said, "Absolutely." Ron sent the contracts and I cleared the date at Public Hall. Then I asked my manager, Dino Iani, if I could buy commercial time to promote the show. When Iani went to clear it with NBC Legal, they said it was a "conflict of interest." That's when I called Mike Belkin and told him who I had a contract with. We tied the call

WKYC deejay Chuck Dunaway (*third from left*) with Jimi Hendrix (*third from right*) at Otto's Grotto, 1968. Joining the two were also Hendrix's bass player, Noel Redding (*second from left*), Leonard Nimoy, of *Star Trek* fame (*center*), as well as several unidentified friends. *Courtesy of Chuck Dunaway.*

letters to the concert and advertised the tickets to be sold in the station lobby on a Saturday morning. As long as I had no financial gain, there was no conflict of interest.

I got to the station an hour before tickets went on sale and found a line about a block and half down the street. The people in front had camped out over night, and in less than two hours the show was sold out! The Belkins set up a second show, and we were on the air announcing it that same day. I was emcee.

Now, the week before the show was jam-packed with events. I was scheduled to host a fashion show at Higbee's department store with Leonard Nimoy of *Star Trek* fame. Leonard came into Cleveland a day early, Thursday, to promote an LP of him singing, which was released on Dot Records. The record promoter, Jerry Hall, was a friend and invited me for dinner with him and Leonard. We met at Leonard's hotel thirty minutes after I got off the air. And the three of us sat around and began discussing the Vietnam War.

The next day, my friend Joe Eszterhas, who wrote for the *Cleveland Press,* called me and said he was doing a stringer article for *Time* on this hot new guitarist, Jimi Hendrix. He told me Hendrix was to show up at a club in downtown Cleveland. We couldn't announce it on the air, but I invited some people from the station and asked Nimoy to come, too. He'd heard about Hendrix and extended his Cleveland visit in order to meet him. About 7:00 that Friday night we walked into the club where a band was playing. Very few people were there. Sure enough, around 8:00 Jimi Hendrix, his road manager, bass player, Noel Redding and Eszterhas (notebook in hand) arrived. Jimi and Noel came over to our table, and we started talking. Once again, the conversation turned to antiwar. A little while later, Jimi went up on stage and played a right-handed guitar with his left hand. Later that night I asked him if he would be a guest on my program before the concert, and he agreed. I thought for sure he'd forget. At 3:00 P.M. this long black limousine pulls up in front of the station, and out steps Jimi Hendrix. And Jimi and Noel stayed the entire program! I remember giving him a love-bead necklace and an album Jimi liked, by the group Spirit. After the radio show we headed to Public Hall. The first show started at 7:00 P.M.

"Welcome, Cleveland, to the Jimi Hendrix Experience," was all I had to say to bring the sold-out house to its feet. And there they stayed.

After I left Cleveland, I never saw or talked to the Belkins again. But, oh, the memories they gave me and Cleveland!

Shauna Zurbrugg (first female FM disc jockey in Cleveland)

I think over the years Cleveland audiences have always been underrated as far as their extraordinary open-mindedness. I can recall one incident in particular. What was really great about working in radio there was our listeners welcomed any direction we decided to take as far as exposing different music. Thus, we were able to be as experimental as we wanted. That was the most exciting part of it. That extended to concerts, as well. One, in particular, I'll never forget was a Seals and Crofts concert we [WNCR] sponsored, in which Leon Redbone was also on the bill. Well, once Seals and Crofts' manager discovered he was on the bill and what he sounded like, she wanted to pull them off the ticket. Leon Redbone was basic heavy-footed rock and roll, whereas Seals and Crofts were more on the mellower side. So Billy [Bass], Martin [Perlich], and I had to try to convince her that wasn't going to be a problem. But she kept saying things like, "No audience that likes *that* will like them [Seals and Crofts]." We kept telling her Cleveland audiences were very open-minded and could appreciate both because this was how we programmed, so they were used to an eclectic variety in their music.

It took until twenty minutes before curtain time that she finally relented. And I think she was totally blown away when, after Redbone appeared and was well received, Seals and Crofts got a standing ovation when they walked on the stage. She realized what we were talking about.

That one incident reflects what was happening around the country in terms of how narrow things were and why Cleveland had more insight and appreciation of different forms of music. I don't know if it was in the air or water or what, but that whole area was just a lot more open to anything that was not the norm.

David Spero (former FM deejay)

I remember doing the Saturday morning show when I was a deejay at 'NCR. And believe me that was tough after Friday nights! This one particular morning at 6:00 A.M., I was really tired. So I put on side two of the second Poco album, which was about twenty-eight minutes long, figuring I'd wake up when the last song stopped. Well, I slept good, and finally at a quarter to ten I lifted my head to see the phone lines are flashin' like crazy, the hotlines are ringing, and immediately I'm trying to think up some excuse. Like the transmitter was down, the phone lines were down—anything to get me off the hook. It was pretty nuts. And yes, I got in trouble.

Another rough Saturday morning when I was at 'MMS, I put on a [reel-to-reel] tape from a Coffeebreak Concert I'd done with Loudon Wainwright III, who had the song "Dead Skunk in the Middle of the Road." That assured me a good hour or so. And I was starving. So I went down to Burger King. And here, they're playing 'MMS on their speakers. I thought, *well, this is pretty cool. Here I am standing in line for a burger, and everyone thinks I'm there in the studio.* So I'm listening to myself talking when all of a sudden I hear this [he makes a propeller noise], because somehow the tape slipped off the machine and was spiraling all the way through. I'm standing there—next in line, starving, and thinking, *oh, shit, I've gotta get back there!* So I rush back to the studio to find the tape flappin' away, and the phones are ringing and ringing . . . . Boy did I get in a lot of trouble for that one!

Then there was the time I had to "explain" about the song, "One Toke Over the Line." The FCC wanted to ban it, believing it was promoting marijuana use. This was during the time they were always trying to get those kinds of songs off the radio. I told them it was my understanding that the song was about bus tokens. Like when you pitched pennies, these guys were pitchin' bus tokens and that was the "toke over the line"—and they bought it!

There Are Places I Remember

Jimmy Ley, on Leo's Casino

Back then [early 1960s], white kids could go into a black club and it wasn't a big thing. At Leo's, if you didn't have an I.D. and looked fifteen, like I was when I started going there, they'd still let you in, long as you had the five bucks. One thing you couldn't do, though, was drink alcohol. They made sure of that by making you wear a Hawaiian lei so waitresses would know not to serve you. You wouldn't dare think about taking the thing off 'cause before you got past the door, this huge black guy would look at you and say, "You take that off, fellow, and I'll kill you." But really, you didn't care because you came for the music, not the booze.

Joe Vitale (Crosby, Stills and Nash drummer)

One story that truly reflects the generation gap, particularly in the '60s, involves one night at Kent's JB's. It actually began the night before at Public Hall, where Led Zeppelin was playing on the first leg of their American tour. Joe [Walsh] had gone backstage to see them because, of course, everyone knew the James Gang. So Joe told Jimmy Page and Robert Plant, "Hey, tomorrow's your day off. Why don't you guys come down to JB's? 'Cause we play there on Wednesday nights." Now, no one knew they were coming. But once they got there, they went up on stage and sat in on a couple of numbers. Well, Kent being this small college town, in a matter of a half an hour, the whole town knew two of the guys from Led Zeppelin were playing with the James Gang at JB's! And zoom, before we knew it, the place was wall-to-wall. I swear you couldn't get one more person in there. Now Joe Bujack, the owner of JB's, bless his heart, didn't know Led Zeppelin from Adam. All he knew was that he was selling more beer than he normally sold in a year! So after the gig, Bujack, who'd just lost his Thursday night house band, goes up to Robert Plant with that broken English of his and says, "Hey, you guys are pretty good. You busy on Thursday nights?" Well, we all just howled! We talk about that to this day and have a great laugh over it! Those who knew Joe Bujack can really appreciate that story the most.

We used to call him "Mr. Ninety Bucks A Band, That's It" because he would never offer a band any more than that. But you know, the thing was, we'd have done it for nine bucks. And he knew it.

Henry LoConti Jr. (son of Hank LoConti, Agora proprietor)

Growing up around the Agora environment, I thought every band was a local band! My first concert was the Buckinghams when I was about nine. But it was a Brownsville Station concert I remember most. They put on one hell of a show. I remember at one point the bass player ripped off all of his clothes and continued the show stark naked. My fourteen-year-old sister was there, too, and I can still see my mother putting her hand over her eyes!

In terms of impression, no one can match the Artist [formerly known as Prince]. It was 1983, and he brought Sheila E. to the Agora for her first live performance as Sheila E. Prior to that, she'd performed as a percussionist/backup singer, but had never done a live show on her own. When the time came, she refused to go on stage. She was just scared to death. She was so petrified she was sick. So I'm standing real close to her, watching Prince as he starts talking to her. It was almost magical to see. How he just mind-locked with her, calmed her down, controlled her, and gave her the confidence to go on. And then she went on and just blew everyone away. I happened to catch a glimpse of Prince then and watched his face watch her, then seeing the crowd reaction.

It was something I'll never forget, and that moment I gained a lot of respect for him. It was the most incredible thing I ever witnessed.

Jim Jones (Mirrors, Pere Ubu, Home and Garden)

I have only good memories of Cleveland in the '70s, oddly enough. Not to be overly sentimental, but downtown Cleveland back then, particularly the Flats area, was visually stunning. And perhaps most important of all, abandoned at night. At sunset, the city would virtually close up and workers would go home to the suburbs. That would leave the city to the few of us who appreciated the compelling beauty and mystery that existed there—as if it existed just for us. There was nothing to compare seeing the Terminal Tower at midnight, outlined by a luminescent orange sky, provided by LTV Steel blowing its stacks every few hours . . . . Or grabbing a thrilling free ride a hundred feet in the air on the Conrail Bridge at the mouth of the Cuyahoga . . . . Or playing on the slag heaps that dotted the river's edge and exploring the deserted power station on Old River Road.

The soundtrack of this time was equally brilliant and important as well. The Flats were alive with the unearthy [sic] music of shrieking steam valves, the rhythmic pounding of automated metal-stamping machines, the sirens and metallic clanking of the many moving bridges, the horn blasts of trains, tugboats and large cargo vessels winding their way down the river—an industrial symphony, played nightly for those with the ear for it.

Groups like Pere Ubu and the Dead Boys could have only come from Cleveland. Both groups have publicly acknowledged the rare and charged atmosphere of the time and place and circumstance that spawned them.

Mike Shea (publisher, *Alternative Press)*

The Pop Shop was one of my favorite places to go around '84, '85. It wasn't just the bands that played there, but I thought it had such a cool atmosphere. Like here I was at the time, this clean-cut jockey type from the 'burbs. Then I'd go downtown on the weekends and here were these guys walking around in Mohawks, and the girls in their fishnets. The place was the absolute antithesis of my weekday world. It was this dark, dank, smoky, smelly, noisy bar, and certainly shook up my Norman Rockwell suburban roots. I loved it!

The punk scene back then was pretty wild, decadent. I remember being at the Cleveland Underground, with kids throwing their beer bottles on the floor and jumpin' on 'em, then go across the street to the crematorium, break in and play in the coffins and stuff. And sure it [the scene] is kinda morbid, but when you're nineteen and you're into punk rock and into being rebellious, and you hate the world, and Reagan's president, you tend to do weird stuff for entertainment. Take Marilyn Manson, Nirvana, Nine

Inch Nails, or any other wave of music. I think they represent the times where kids can fulfill that rebel side of themselves through the music, which has always been the core of rock and roll. I'm not saying it's right or wrong, it's the way it is.

The trick for Manson is to see if he can adapt to the next sign of the times, to stay on top. But he will be an icon because he's got such a loyal, fanatical fan base.

Cameron Crowe (rock journalist and writer/director of film *Almost Famous*)

[Crowe recalled a visit to Cleveland in the early '70s.] We were in the restaurant at Swingos, and it was a booth and for some reason it ended up with the four members of Led Zeppelin in a row and then Neil [*sic*] Preston [*Rolling Stone* photographer] and me.

And this fan, like a true Cleveland rock fan, walked by. And he stopped and he looked at the table and he looked at all of them, and it's all Led Zeppelin sitting there and us, and he goes, "Are you Neil [*sic*] Preston?" And the guys in Led Zeppelin were so disappointed! It was hilarious.

But I never forgot that, that they were so rock knowledgeable in Cleveland that, OK, that's Led Zeppelin sitting there, but THAT's the famous rock photographer, Neal Preston! And that was the way Cleveland always felt. Beyond the cliché of Cleveland rocks and WMMS and all that stuff, was the fact that all those bands couldn't wait to get there. So they would count down the days to Cleveland. Seriously. Even then. [*Plain Dealer,* Sept. 17, 2000.]

Appendix

Cleveland-Area Clubs and Venues

The '50s and '60s

The Hullabaloos

Chesterland Hullabaloo (West Geauga Plaza, Rt. 306 and Mayfield Road)

Hullabaloo Scene (16110 Lorain Avenue)

Mentor Hullabaloo (7681 Mentor Avenue, Rt. 20); formerly the Torchlight Lounge

North Ridgeville Hullabaloo (38871 Center Ridge Road); later the Exit, Cyrus Erie West

The Armories

Akron Armory (161 S. High Street, Akron)

Chagrin Armory (Rt. 422, Chagrin Falls)

Grays Armory (1234 Bolivar Road)

Painesville Armory (housed in the YMCA, 933 Mentor Avenue)

And Others . . .

The Agora Ballroom (1730 E. 24th Street)

Breezewood Teen Club (1461 Lake Breeze Road, Sheffield)

Brick Cottage (11423 Euclid Avenue)

The Dome (121 W. College Street, Kent)

Donny's Place (690 Oberlin Road, Elyria)

D'Poo's Tool and Die Works (1700 Columbus Road); later Otto-Site

Eastlake Teen Center, or "Nike Sight" (33617 Curtis Boulevard)

English Grille (Euclid and E. 105th)

Euclid Roller Drome (22466 Shore Center Drive)

Fagan's (966 W. 11th Street, Flats)

Garfield Heights Canteen Club (12000 Maple Leaf Drive)

The In Spot (Eastgate Coliseum, Mayfield Road and SOM Center)

It's Boss Teen Club (16820 Brookpark, Parma); formerly the Rolling Stone

JB's (244 N. Water Street, Kent)

The Kent Kove, "Home of the Blues in Ohio" (256 N. Water Street, Kent)

Otto's Grotto (Hotel Statler-Hilton, 1127 Euclid Avenue)

The Plato (1748 E. 22nd Street)

The Stables (1535 Mentor Avenue, Painesville Shopping Center)

Tom Jones Backroom (1187 Old River Road)

The '70s

Cleveland Area

The Agora (1730 E. 24th Street)

Bobby McGee's (1612 Euclid Avenue)

Brick Cottage (11423 Euclid Avenue)

Clockwork Orange (1812 Payne Avenue); later changed to Loose Lounge

The Euclid Tavern (11629 Euclid Avenue).

Fat Glenn's (2506 Chester)

The Grapes of Wrath (2000 Chester); formerly the Oar House

The House of Bud (1910 Euclid Avenue)

The Mad Hatter (2150 E. 18th Street); formerly Socrates' Cave

Otto's Grotto (Statler-Hilton Hotel)

The Piccadilly Inn (E. 30th and Euclid); formerly the Versailles, later Jicky's English Disco

Pirate's Cove (1059 Old River Road)

The Plato (1720 E. 22nd Street)

The Round Table (242 Superior Avenue)

The Smiling Dog Saloon (3447 W. 25th Street)

The Viking Saloon (2005 Chester Avenue); formerly the Barracks

On the Outskirts of Town

Castaways (Route 534, Geneva)

The Corral (26910 Cook Road, Olmsted Township)

The Cove (Lake Road, Geneva)

Governor's Chateau (3456 W. 177th Street)

Hennessy's (11729 Detroit Avenue, Lakewood)

The House of Swing (4490 Mayfield Road)

Spanky's (38929 Center Ridge Road, North Ridgeville)

Fottenbotten's Inn (4110 Erie Road, Willoughby)

Disco Fever

Disco Den (34225 Vine Street, Eastlake)

Dixie Electric Company (5100 Pearl Road at Brookpark)

The Last Moving Picture Show (1375 Euclid Avenue, basement of the former Playhouse Square building)

Night Moves (1640 Euclid Avenue); formerly Alpine Village

Rare Cherry (35101 Euclid Avenue)

Wickliffe's Disco Queen (30322 Euclid Avenue)

What's in a Name?

Apparently not much. The following clubs were hits in the '70s, just as they'd been in the '60s, though under different names.

The Beachcomber (108 Henry St., Grand River)

The Cyrus Erie West (38871 Center Ridge Road, North Ridgeville); formerly the North Ridgeville Hullabaloo

The Draft House (12492 Prospect, Strongsville);
formerly the Skyline, later the Jail, now Flying
Machine

Insanity (22480 Shore Center Drive, Euclid);
formerly the Looking Glass, later Sensations

The '80s

Cleveland Area

Cleveland Agora (1730 E. 24th Street, closed due to
fire; reopened at 5000 Euclid Avenue)

The Pop Shop (1730 E. 24th Street)

The Cleveland Connection (10630 Berea Road)

Bobby McGee's (1612 Euclid Avenue, Downtown)

Elegant Hog Saloon (1254 Euclid Avenue, Downtown)

Phantasy Nite Club (11802 Detroit Avenue)

Cleveland Convocation Center (2000 Prospect
Avenue, Cleveland State University)

The Empire (Sumner Court)

Tommy's (19015 Lake Road, Rocky River)

Shadows (9125 Brookpark Road)

The Cleveland Underground (1700 Columbus Road,
Flats)

The Mining Company (5100 Pearl Road, Parma)

The Lakefront (1265 W. 9th Street)

Maxwell's (733 W. St. Clair)

Governor's Chateau (W. 117th Street)

The Library (3751 Prospect Avenue)

The Rascal House (2064 Euclid Avenue)

Flash Gordon's (17001 Lorain Road)

Spanky's West (38939 Center Ridge Road, North
Ridgeville)

Brother's Lounge (11609 Detroit)

Peabody's Cafe (2140 S. Taylor Road)

Flipside (3935 Mayfield, Cleveland Heights)

Rick's Cafe (86 N. Main Street, Chagrin Falls)

Sahara Club (34500 Chardon Road, Willoughby)

The Cosmopolitan (35101 Euclid Avenue,
Willoughby)

The Old Front Bar (34225 Vine Street)

Waylon Willie Walkers (7847 Lakeshore Boulevard.,
Mentor)

Jicky's after Dark (1700 Columbus); formerly
D'Poo's and Otto-Site; musician Jicky Zaar took
it over and made it a popular disco nightclub.

The Lower Level (22833 Euclid Avenue); formerly
Hires Lounge

Mr. Pete's (34441 Lakeshore Boulevard, Eastlake)

Mrs. Minniver's (1187 Old River Road); formerly
Tom Jones Backroom and Otto's Backroom,
later Fitzpatrick's

Painesville Agora (54 S. State Street); later the Urban
Cowboy

Peabody's Cafe (corner of Cedar and Taylor Roads,
Cleveland Heights); formerly the Alibi Room,
later the Cellar Door

The Stables (1541 Mentor Avenue, Painesville
Shopping Center)

Utopia (37415 Euclid Avenue, Willoughby)

Akron/Kent Clubs

Akron Civic Theater (182 S. Main Street)

The Bank (316 S. Main Street, Akron)

Filthy McNasty's (200 S. Depeyster Street, Kent)

JB's (244 N. Water Street, Kent)

Kaiser Bill's (259 E. Market, Akron)

Mother's Junction (135 Franklin Avenue, Kent)

The Odyssey (452 N. Arlington, Akron)

The Stone Jug (227 Franklin Avenue, Kent)

Utopia Light & Power (125 S. Main Street, Akron)

The '90s

Cleveland Area

Around the Corner (18616 Detroit Road, Lakewood)

Babylon A Go Go (2523 Market Street)

Barking Spider Tavern (11310 Juniper Road)

The Basement (1078 Old River Road)

Cebars Euclid Tavern (595 E. 185th Street)

Cleveland Cafe (11901 Berea Road)

Cosmopolitan (35101 Euclid Avenue, Willoughby)

Danny Boy Tavern (14529 Puritas Avenue)

Dick's Last Resort (1096 Old River Road)

Fagan's (996 Old River Road)

Fat Fish Blue (21 Prospect Avenue, Downtown)

Flash's (17001 Lorain Avenue)

The Flying Machine (3970 Josephine Street, Lorain)

Gatsby's (8455 Station Street, Mentor)

Goodfellows (1265 W. 9th Street)

Grog Shop (1765 Coventry Road, Cleveland Heights)

Horseshoe Bar (747 E. 185th Street)

House of Swing (4490 Mayfield Road)

Iggy's (13405 Madison Avenue, Lakewood)

Jimmy's in the Flats (1061 Old River Road)

Odeon (1295 Old River Road)

Pat's in the Flats (2233 W. 3rd Street)

Peabody's Down Under (1059 Old River Road)

Phantasy Theater and Niteclub (11802 Detroit Avenue, Lakewood)

Rhythm Room (2140 S. Taylor Road, Cleveland Heights)

Ryno's Sports Bar and Grille (35700 Lakeland Blvd, Eastlake)

Savannah Bar and Grille (30676 Detroit Road, Westlake)

Shooters on the Water (1148 Main Avenue)

Stamper's Grill Pub (21750 Lorain Road, Fairview Park)

Symposium (11794 Detroit Avenue, Lakewood)

Wilberts Bar and Grille (1360 W. 9th Street, Warehouse District)

Akron/Canton/Kent Clubs

Banana Joe's (271 S. Main Street, Akron)

Cheer's Tavern and Grille (4339 Dressler Road NW, Canton)

Cobalt Club (1730 Merriman Road, Akron)

Cosmic Cow (273 S. Main Street, Akron)

The Dusty Frog (1272 Weathervane Lane, Akron)

Pal Joey's (4717 Dressler Road, Canton)

The Robin Hood (503 E. Main Street, Kent)

Screwy Louie's (200 Depeyster Street, Kent)

Tangier (532 W. Market Street, Akron)

The Thunderdrome (370 Orleans, Akron)

Index

Smokey Robinson and the Miracles, 39, 47, 74
Snake Eyes, 416
Snake Rock, 423, 447–50
Snyder, Dave, 170
Sobol, Matt, 522
Sodja's Music, 151
Soeder, John, 200
Solomon, Roland, 55
Sonny and Cher, 96
Sons of Elvis, 503–4
Sopuch, George, 272
Sosinski, Eroc, 281
Sostaric, Rick, 289, *291*
Soul Asylum, 85, 585
Southside Johnny. *See* Lyon, "Southside"
   Johnny
Spahlinger, Laura (Pistillo), 596–97
Spanky's, 285, 409, 430, 512, 571
Speaker/Cranker, 502
Spero, David, 63–67, 100, 103, 104, 117, *122,*
   177, 263, 307, 310, 322, 324–26, *325,* 486,
   603
Spero, Herman, 63–67, 268
Spina, Rich, 59, 83, 283–85, 418, 472, 581
Springsteen, Bruce, 80, 85, 117, *125, 251,* 490,
   579, 585, *598, 599*
Spudmonsters, 504–7
Spy, 81
Stabb, Kenneth, 277
Stacey, Michael, 298, 300
Stagepass, 470
Stagg, Jim, 97, 108, 115
Stanley, Michael, 82, 85, 117, 261–68, *265, 268,*
   470, 557, 581
Stardust, Ziggy, 79. *See also,* Bowie, David
Starr, Frankie, 147–50, *149,* 535
Starr, Joni, 147–48
Starr, Ringo, 310
State of Being, 502
State Theater, the, 80, 552
Statesmen, the, 83
Stein, Burt, *122*
Stein, Dia, 117, 126, 338, 492–95, 499
Stein, Seymore, 566
Stephan, Andy, 532
Stephenson, Tom, 308, 311
Steve Miller Band, the, 80
Stevens, Dewey "the Dew-Master" (Dewey
   Roach), 550–53, 556, 557
Stevens, Eric, 97, 98, 99, 100, 347–48, 486
Stewart, Rod, 82
Stewart, Terry, 76
Stewart, Tim, 454
Stile, Shelley, 117, 126
Stineway, Bill, 434
Stoller, Mike, 33
Stone Poneys, 297
Strader, J. D., 48
Strain, Sammy, 39
Stratton, Robin, 414

Strawberry Alarm Clock, 157
Stray Cats, the, 427
Strazek, Brian "Zed," 510
Street Survivor, 470
Streisand, Barbra, 44
Stress Eliminators, 535
Strouhal, Alex, 505
Studniarz, Thomas J. (T.J. the Deejay) Sr., 95
Stutz Bearcat, Glen, 148, 418–19, 420, 534
Styrenes, 77
Substitute, 470
Sugar Magnolia, 470
Suicide Commandos, 366
Sullivan, Billy, 285, 418, 430, 471, 472
Summers, Brett, 552, 556
Summit Beach Ballroom, 8
Superkream, 522
Supreme Court, 473
Supremes, the, 39, 46, 66, 75
Swanson, Dave, 465, *466,* 468, 508
Swanson, Scott, 442
Swanson, Steve, 505
Sweat, Keith, 445
Sweet, Rachel, 397
Sweet City Records, 287
Swingo, Jim, 75
Symposium, 520, 523
System 56, 382

Tallon, Don, *599*
Tallus, 455
Tattoo, 259
Taylor, Brian, 542
Taylor, David, 363
Taylor, James, 78, 85
Taylor, Johnny, 271, *272*
Taylor, Ray, 51
Tea, 421
Teagle, John, 530
Television, 358, 369, 389
Temple, Michele, 366–67
Temptations, the, 34, 39, 74
Ten Years After, 552
Terdd, Kurtt, 44
Terrell, Michael, 383
Terrible Parade, 466
Terry Knight and the Pack, 64, 76, 114
Testa, Jim, 55, 56
Thaler, Les, 432
Theatrical Restaurant, 71, 432
Third Wish, 502
Thomas, David, 202, 301, 358, 359–61, 362–
   68. *See also* Behemoth, Crocus
Thompson, Donnie, 286
Thompson, Larry R., 575, 578
Thompson, Mayo, 366
3D, 422, 502
Thrills and Company, 314
Throckmorton, 522

Tiburski, Walt, 72, 96, 103, 117, 121, 122, 131,
   293, 309, 552
Tin Huey, 299–300, 362, 363, 388–90
Tiny Alice, 273–75
Tischler, Norman, 273, *274,* 286
Toby, Fred, 149
Tolliver, Lynn, 425, 438, 570
Tom Jones Backroom, 83, 168, 271
Tom King and the Starfires, 44, 53, 56, 72
Tomczak, Larry, 158
Tommy Edward's Record Haven, 25–26
Tommy James and the Shondells, 96
Tommy's, 471
Tomorrow Club, 369
Topinka, Karen, 42
Topper, Jack, 55
Torchlight, the, 72
Tower City Cools, 570
Town Tavern, the, 528
Townshend, Pete, 84, 157, *248,* 579
Trabuzzo, Fred, 300
Traffic, 80
Tramend Lounge, 48
Tranchito, Nick, 140
Traxx, 81
Treadwell, Faye, 32
Treadwell, George, 32
Trilogy in the Flats, 511
Triumphs, the, 38
Troiano, Dominic, 176
Tulu Babies, 55
Turner, Sid, 51, *52*
Twilighters, the, 50, 72, 230–31
Twist Offs, the, 501, 530–33
221 Club, 82

Ullman, Debbie, 126, 128
Uncle Vic, 485
Undercurrents, 528
Unknown Stranger, 285
United Artists, 35
Uptown Sinclair, 504
Uriah Heep, 452
Utopia, the, 72, 571
U2, 79

Valentine, Dave, *436,* 438
Valentine, Kevin, 449, 512
Valentinos, the, 35
Van der Kuil, Jan Eddy "Ed," 528
Van Natter, Rich, 286
Vanilla Fudge, 163
Varga, Ray, 471
Variety Theater, the, 452, 455
Vazzano, Frank, 508
Vecchio, Jay, 413
Vee, Bobby, 158
Vehr, Duane, 395
Velvet Underground, the, 76, 356
Verbick, Mike, 443